SNCC's Stories

SERIES EDITORS

Sarah E. Gardner, Mercer University

Jonathan Daniel Wells, University of Michigan

Print Culture in the South addresses the region's literary and historical past from the colonial era to the near present. Rooted in archival research, series monographs embrace a wide range of analyses that, at their core, address engagement and interaction with print. Topics center on format/genre—novels, pamphlets, periodicals, broadsides, and illustrations; institutions such as libraries, literary societies, small presses, and the book industry; and/or habits and practices of readership and writing.

SNCC's Stories

The African American Freedom Movement in the Civil Rights South

Sharon Monteith

The University of Georgia Press
Athens

© 2020 by the University of Georgia Press
Athens, Georgia 30602
www.ugapress.org
All rights reserved
Designed by Kaelin Chappell Broaddus
Set in 10.3/13 URW Century Old Style
by Manila Typesetting Company

Most University of Georgia Press titles are
available from popular e-book vendors.

Printed digitally

Library of Congress Number: 2020022349
ISBN: 9780820358031 (hardcover)
ISBN: 9780820358024 (paperback)
ISBN: 9780820358048 (ebook)

In memory of

My father (1925–2009)
My mother (1931–2013)
Lise Lavelle (1959–2013)
Craig Phillips (1987–2019)

Contents

List of Abbreviations xi
Acknowledgments xiii
Prologue xv

Introduction	"All of Us Are a Book" 1	
Chapter 1	"Troublemakers": From College Campuses to Freedom Houses 32	
Chapter 2	Supersnick and Junebug Jabbo Jones 57	
Chapter 3	Inside Stories: From Field Reports to Field Texts 75	
Chapter 4	Adjusting the Lens of Professional "Objectivity" 104	
Chapter 5	"Go to Writing and Write Up a New Day": Local People 132	
Chapter 6	Forging a Literary Culture beyond SNCC 155	
Chapter 7	"Words You Want?": Black Power, the Black Arts Movement, and the Worlding of SNCC 173	
Chapter 8	Battle Stories at the Grassroots and Beginnings of Bitter Ends 193	
Chapter 9	The Walking Wounded: "Who We Were and Where We Came From" 222	

Epilogue 241
Notes 253
Selected Bibliography 315
Index 343

Abbreviations

BAM	Black Arts Movement
COFO	Council of Federated Organizations
CORE	Congress of Racial Equality
DoJ	Department of Justice
FBI	Federal Bureau of Investigation
FST	Free Southern Theater
LCFO	Lowndes County Freedom Organization
MFDP	Mississippi Freedom Democratic Party
NAACP	National Association for the Advancement of Colored People
NSA	National Student Association
RCNL	Regional Council of Negro Leadership
SCEF	Southern Conference Educational Fund
SCLC	Southern Christian Leadership Conference
SDS	Students for a Democratic Society
SNCC	Student Nonviolent Coordinating Committee
SNYC	Southern Negro Youth Congress
SRC	Southern Regional Council
SSOC	Southern Student Organizing Committee

Acknowledgments

My critical archaeology of lost and forgotten texts has included considerable archival work. It may seem invidious to single out librarians and archivists when the professional expertise of so many underpins this book, but I would like to record special thanks to Christopher Harter at the Amistad Research Center, Loretta Deaver and Lewis Wyman at the manuscript division of the Library of Congress, Kathleen Shoemaker and Kira Jones at Emory University's Stuart A. Rose Manuscript, Archives, and Rare Book Library, Hal Hansen at Georgia State University Library's Special Collections, Deborah S. Davis of Valdosta State University Archives, and Brian Woodman at Washington University Libraries.

My thanks go to James Forman Jr. and Chaka Forman for making their father's unpublished novel available for study through the James Forman Papers and to Adrienne Cannon at the Library of Congress for discussing it with me. The warm welcome at the J. D. Williams Library at the University of Mississippi is always appreciated, and I thank Dorothy Atherton, Emma Duncan, Alice Griffin, John Harral, Claire Stickley, and Samuel Rowley, the excellent resource acquisition and supply team at Nottingham Trent University.

For support, I am very grateful to the Leverhulme Trust, the British Academy, the Arts and Humanities Research Council, Santander Universities UK, Nottingham Trent University, and the University of Nottingham. The British Academy funded and hosted a conference I organized with George Lewis, Helen Laville, and Nahem Yousaf that brought activists, filmmakers, and historians together with the subjects of their documentary films. John Akomfrah, Reece Auguiste, Clayborne Carson, Jon Else, Allison Graham, Judy Richardson, and each other participant made the event more enjoyable than any other I have experienced in an academic context. Julian Bond had agreed to take part, and, after his death, the symposium was dedicated to him. I am grateful to his widow Pamela Horowitz for participating and to Joan Trumpauer Mulholland for sharing ideas and contacts.

As *SNCC's Stories* evolved, I did not want to draw conclusions too soon but presented keynote lectures at Nottingham Trent University; the Scandinavian Association of American Studies in Karlstad and Orebro, Sweden; the Center for the Study of Southern Culture at the University of Mississippi; and the Oxford Conference for the Book. Richard H. King's thought-provoking work sparked my early interest in this subject, and many conversations have enriched my thinking, particularly with Allison Graham, Nahem Yousaf, and Peter Ling. Among many other colleagues and doctoral students with whom I have enjoyed talking about the project are Panya Banjoko, Clay Carson, Patcee Francis, Tony Hutchison, George Lewis, Rachel Sykes, Jimmy Thomas Jr., Scott Weightman, and Charles Reagon Wilson. Family and friends always inquire about my writing. Among them, Zaif kept me on the straight and narrow, and Neelo persuaded me to talk about it in detail during our beach walks and was more helpful than she knows in pushing me to the finish line.

Finally, I would like to acknowledge anonymous readers of the manuscript, notably one who later identified herself to me—Wesley Hogan, and, of course, Walter Biggins, Jon Davies, and Beth Snead at the University of Georgia Press. Over the years, my most positive experiences of working with a copy editor have been when publishing with the University of Georgia Press; a copy editor who engages the content of the work is invaluable, and Chris Dodge was invaluable.

Prologue

We have written tales about ourselves and told them everywhere.
—Jane Stembridge, 1966

The Student Nonviolent Coordinating Committee (SNCC) published widely. Jane Stembridge tucked the fact into a poem—"We have written tales about ourselves and told them everywhere"—but scholars have yet to trace the organization's print and publishing culture through SNCC's life and legacy. The prominent role of writers in the National Association for the Advancement of Colored People (NAACP) is acknowledged through study of W. E. B. Du Bois, James Weldon Johnson, Claude McKay, Walter White, and other activist-writers, but what SNCC wrote has been subject to literary and historical amnesia. Organizers created a cluster of narratives forged out of lived experience, an imaginative endeavor in which literature merged with politics. This writing was not a by-product of their civil rights work but entwined, comprising a rich cache of field reports, journalism, short stories and novels, poems and poetry collections, plays, and personal, lyrical, and aphoristic essays. SNCC's internal culture is visible in these works, dispelling the assumption that imaginative evocations of civil rights struggles in the 1960s were only published in the movement's aftermath. SNCC's historiography is broad and deep but its narrative culture and literary history neglected. Subjective and imaginative works are not sources that traditionally feature in histories, and memoir is assumed to be the written form in which activists elect to share their stories. SNCC's literary history has been overlooked because the view persists in literary criticism that observers rather than young grassroots organizers wrote imaginatively about civil rights. Additionally, literary and critical attention focused on the Black Arts Movement (BAM) has contributed to the occlusion of what SNCC published in the 1960s.

Inaugurated in April 1960, SNCC coordinated the different student groups that came together through sit-ins challenging racial segregation of public accommodations in the Upper South and border states. Julian Bond remembered, "The SCLC, the NAACP and CORE wanted us to become youth wings of their organizations." But the students were already bonded in friendships forged in activism, and fifty-seven-year-old Ella Baker, SNCC's generating force and first mentor, worried that young activists' creative agency might be stifled, though the Southern Christian Leadership Conference (SCLC) funded their first meeting at her request.[1] She had reason to worry. Student-led demonstrations not only challenged the conservative leadership of black colleges in the South but also the pace at which civil rights were being negotiated by organizations.[2] Gwendolyn Robinson (later Zoharah Simmons) recalled, in her 2008 essay "Living It Out": "The high visibility, dramatic events that brought the media and front-page headlines that were SCLC's stock [in] trade went against the grain of SNCC-style organizing.... We SNCC 'radicals' were... on a collision course with Dr. King, SCLC, the NAACP, white liberal allies, and the entire religious and strategic thought underpinning the movement."[3]

By 1961, SNCC's foundational cadre of field secretaries prioritized grassroots political action as community mobilization, supporting local activists and communities in the freedom struggle. Some twenty-five state and branch presidents of the NAACP worked with SNCC and were among its mentors—including Aaron Henry, C. C. Bryant, Medgar Evers, and Amzie Moore—but national movement leaders remained skeptical of young activists, and the relationship was uneasy, often spikey.[4] SNCC was supported by the Regional Council of Negro Leadership (RCNL), inaugurated in 1952 in Mound Bayou, Mississippi, by Dr. T. R. M. Howard. Its veterans would embrace the Mississippi Freedom Summer project, rolled out under the auspices of the Council of Federated Organizations (COFO) in 1964. Historian Howard Zinn, an advisor to SNCC, recognized: "[SNCC's strength lies] with the mass base... in [the] Negro community. We are at times closer to the rank and file of other civil rights groups in the principles and actions we support than are their leaders."[5] SNCC liaised with the SCLC and regularly with its leader Martin Luther King Jr., but their approaches often clashed. In penetrating the most violently recalcitrant southern places to support the empowerment of some of the poorest communities, SNCC stood out. Only CORE operated a similar model, with SNCC's Bob Moses and CORE's Dave Dennis COFO's representatives. The SCLC devoted fewer resources to organizing, and individuals employed as field-workers typically began that work in SNCC, as did Diane Nash, James Bevel, and Bernard Lafayette. Forging a narrative culture meant that SNCC's grassroots support of indigenous leadership could be understood more widely for its successes, missteps, and how it impacted individuals who gave their youth to the cause. Youth was also a factor in reviewers and critics bypassing SNCC activists' writing and looking to established authors instead for depictions of the movement.

SNCC's deep, prefigurative cultural roots are in the U.S. South, and the narratives I have uncovered are southern stories. They are anchored in projects that supported local people in Greenwood, Mississippi, and the Mississippi Delta; McComb, Natchez, and southwestern Mississippi more broadly; Danville, Virginia; and Lowndes County, Alabama. Although Shirley Sherrod contends that histories see SNCC's work in Southwest Georgia as auxiliary, SNCC's work in Albany and surrounding counties is depicted in detail in its literature.[6] Bob Moses has worried, "Kids today . . . do not know much of this story," saying that "[a] lot of this is the failure of those of us who were involved [because] we have not put down our stories."[7] My research reveals otherwise and that the problem lies in recovering what activists committed to print in the 1960s and thus seeing how SNCC's political-cultural imaginary evolved. Over the years, organizers have emphasized how they were transformed by the experience, and that the SNCC era remains a vital and enduring period in their lives, that making a difference by engaging in an epoch-defining cause lies at the core of their identities, and that their work was by turns defiant, dangerous, inspiring, and damaging. It is unsurprising, then, that organizers should have written so much about it. Studies extending the geographical and temporal reach of the civil rights movement are valuable for moving us beyond the 1960s and out of the South, but aspects of SNCC's story are yet to be analyzed.[8] This study contributes to that work and traces SNCC's literary history from the 1960s to the present.

Once I identified short stories and poems among SNCC's life-writing, the crucial question was whether these were sources through which a richer, emotionally articulate account of the organization's discourse, internal debates, and submerged tensions might be perceived. Was there an aesthetic, evidence of a SNCC cultural imaginary? Where did writers publish? Was what they published reviewed or even noticed by contemporary critics? Was the psychological toll of organizing explored? What could this research contribute to the historiography when SNCC is already the subject of substantial, interpretative histories and has one of "the best detailed records (for its short life) among its contemporary and often competing organizations."[9] Carolyn Steedman's observation that "the practice of history in its modern mode" can be "just one long exercise of the deep satisfaction of finding things" was both a touchstone and a warning as my analysis evolved.[10] Another issue to address was whether literature by young organizers would prove to be aspirant, neophyte at best. Would I discover only derivative, apprentice fictions, self-expressive but obsessive works "that only a coterie could love," as Mark McGurl wondered when he began to examine creative writing courses in "the program era" (post–World War II)? Would Flannery O'Connor's scathing response to the idea that universities stifled creativity—"my opinion is that they don't stifle enough of them"—turn out to be painfully true in the case of individuals who began publishing as students?[11] I needed to ascertain whether all SNCC's writers developed in a campus mold, and, of course, I found that in such a heterogeneous organization they did not. The more I retrieved, the more I began to see how what we know about SNCC could be made more nuanced, and augmented, if attention were paid to its narrative culture. SNCC stories constitute a commentary on the activists' work and the febrile atmosphere. I have selected texts that are revealing aesthetically and historically, less polished works when they exemplify the impetus behind creating a narrative culture and because the cathartic role of personal writing is made manifest in provisional, impressionistic sketches. My focus is thought-provoking investigations of what it felt like to live history and to make it.

Bringing together SNCC activists' imaginative writing was not easy because the pieces are scattered; putting them together felt like constructing a jigsaw puzzle from the edges for a clearer picture to emerge. What emerged quickly is how early in SNCC's history, even its prehistory, writers began exploring the campus mood propelling students into the movement and how definitively the SNCC Executive Committee promoted narrative as a vehicle for self-expression as well as a way to record and preserve organizational history. There is imaginative writing in the SNCC papers, but it is usually located in the personal papers of organizers, like James Forman's unpublished novel "Thin White Line" among his papers and a draft of Bill Mahoney's novel *Black Jacob* (1969) preserved by Doris Derby.[12] John O'Neal's papers are a treasure trove, and in them can be traced his conception of "story circles" within SNCC. Editors of anthologies usually neglected to signal when a writer was an activist. This too has led to the isolation of SNCC's body of writing; it is divorced from what is considered to be literature of "the civil rights movement," in which "civil rights" is a theme and organizations are barely referenced. A search of short story competitions found that Ekwueme Michael Thelwell won awards for stories published first in *Prize College Stories*, the offshoot of *Story* magazine that introduced to readers Richard Wright, Erskine Caldwell, Tennessee

Williams, and J. D. Salinger.[13] Reading SNCC's print culture for self-defining discourse, poetics of context, and self-consciously politicized commentary gives the lie to another of Flannery O'Connor's worries, one shared by the mainstream white literary establishment in the 1960s and by some African American critics: that empirical, political writing would be constituted as protest, treatise, and tract.

SNCC's narrative history is becoming more visible through the digitization of materials.[14] Veterans' website Crmvet.org collates poetry as well as personal essays, and the Digital Gateway spearheaded by the SNCC Legacy Project at the Duke Center for Documentary Studies curates stories under the guidance of veterans, notable among them Charles Cobb, Jennifer Lawson, Courtland Cox, Judy Richardson, and Karen (Edmonds) Spellman. The Legacy Project's "critical histories," under Wesley Hogan's directorship, represent a primary seam of resources through which to understand how former activists view their activism now.[15] Nevertheless, SNCC's writers rarely promote their creative work, even though it opens a window on how they felt and acted and is evidence of how skilled many were, and are, as writers. Organizers may be unaware that a coworker has written about campaigns and projects in which they were involved, and SNCC's publishing culture continues to evolve.

What do we discover that we do not already know from SNCC's histories? We learn more about the interior dynamics of a social movement through sustained attention to how it forged its narrative and consciously curated a range of storytelling practices. Such writings afford access to feelings inherent in organizing that are less discernible in other kinds of sources. We see how many organizers and volunteers self-identify as writers, that the majority are African American, and that, while men dominate most studies, women in SNCC are equally visible as literary practitioners—although not as protagonists. SNCC recorded activity in field reports, and they were foundational documents that acted as templates for poetry and novels where the visceral immediacy of organizing is elucidated in more detail as witness-participant texts. SNCC's narrative culture is richer than its voluminous papers make it appear. I hope the combination of period knowledge and aesthetically informed literary criticism will make this an engaging study of a neglected component of SNCC's culture for activists as well as historians, literary scholars, students, and interested readers. In 1998, O'Neal asserted that SNCC's culture represented a useable past because "[t]he aesthetic process and its products are inseparable from history, economics, and politics, politics being the process by which we make decisions about our collective life. Along with the greater consideration of the nature and challenges of our spiritual life, politics, history and economics provide the content that art celebrates or cautions us about."[16] As SNCC's literary history is uncovered, individuals involved in its construction are no longer occluded, and the importance SNCC placed on narrative, print, and publishing is acknowledged.

SNCC's Stories

Introduction

"All of Us Are a Book"

> All of us are a book.
> —James Forman, 1972
>
> SNCC's story could well have been a novel.
> —Julian Bond, 1983
>
> Our stories in our own words are largely absent from the historical canon.... We need to use them.
> —Bob Moses, 2001
>
> [T]he sensibility underlying the facts of what happened in the civil rights struggle is at risk of being lost... the canon defining what the movement was is [too] narrowly conceived.
> —Charles Cobb, 2008

As SNCC's executive director, James Forman committed to ensuring that organizers would tell its story from their multiple perspectives. "Who can write better than we how it feels," he wrote in advocating for a print culture: "We need young writers, storytellers, pamphleteers, our own Tom Paines, some more Richard Wrights.... We got to get the word out. Write our own history."[1] Julian Bond, a published poet before leading SNCC's communications team from 1962 to 1966, promoted the writing of others throughout his life. Neither Forman nor Bond held a positivist view of narrative; when a dispassionate and depersonalized language of facts was called for, then the communications team delivered just that in press releases and affidavits. Mark Joseph Walmsley argues, "SNCC felt it necessary to craft its public face to match the demands and needs of a white mainstream media," but there is more evidence of SNCC crafting stories to address what Charles Payne calls "the rough draft of history" produced by news media in the 1960s.[2] When grassroots mass action was ignored or ancillary to a concatenation of "big events," organizers wrote missing pieces of the story.[3] With hindsight, Bond observed, "SNCC's story could well have been a novel: romance, danger, death, personal tragedy, and federal indifference to gross civil rights violations and hostility toward SNCC's militance and political openness in the middle of a rapid transformation of relationships between southern blacks and whites."[4] In the narrative forms in which its story coalesces, organizers, local activists, and summer volunteers are all protagonists.

SNCC's richly recorded history was pioneered by Howard Zinn in the 1960s, sustained and extended by Clayborne Carson in the 1980s and Wesley Hogan in 2007, and is embedded in multiple studies of grassroots organizing, from Steven Lawson's *Black Ballots* (1976), John Dittmer's *Local People* (1994), and Charles Payne's *I've Got the Light of Freedom* (1995) through J. Todd Moye's *Let the People Decide* (2004), Emilye Crosby's *A Little Taste of Freedom* (2005), and Hasan Kwame Jeffries's *Bloody Lowndes* (2009). These and many other studies are conceptually important in framing SNCC scholarship, with Jeanne Theoharis and Komozi Woodard dedicating *Groundwork: Local Black Freedom Movements in America* (2005) to Dittmer, and Crosby acknowledging Dittmer and Payne in *Civil Rights History from the Ground Up: Local Struggles, a National Movement* (2011) for opening up the field. Historical delineation of the "organizing tradition" drew attention to what Jeffries calls "the special character of grassroots insurgency in the rural South" that underpins this cultural and literary study.[5] In previous decades, as Robin D. G. Kelley and other recovery researchers reveal, the National Negro Congress and youth affiliate Southern Negro Youth Congress (SNYC) mobilized antilynching protest and black labor unions, and their artists strove to make black culture "an integral part" of American culture.[6] Red-baiting was a major contributory factor to the demise of SNYC, and "the possibilities for open intergenerational dialogue were foreclosed," but former SNYC workers, including Esther Cooper Jackson in her role as editor of *Freedomways*, would support SNCC and ensure that this history was appreciated by organizers who dedicated themselves to the same causes.[7]

Carson writing out respect "as one of many black people SNCC influenced," leavened "early emotional attachment" with critical distance in his book *In Struggle: SNCC and the Black Awakening of the 1960s* (1981) to identify three phases that remain the prevailing architecture for understanding the shape of SNCC's life and times.[8] The first stage, between 1960 and the intervention of the Mississippi Freedom Democratic Party (MFDP) at the Democratic National Convention in August 1964, involved eclectic adoption of ideas around nonviolent direct action, including those promulgated by the Congress of Racial Equality (CORE) and the SCLC, and the evolution of a distinctive "secular, humanistic radicalism" influenced by wider reading but primarily by the experience of organizing in the form of community projects, especially in the Deep South.[9] Charles

Sherrod, black, southern born, and SNCC's first field secretary, championed an interracial project in Southwest Georgia, with Penny Patch being the first white woman to join full-time in June 1962.[10] He persisted with this model, as would Bill Hansen, the white volunteer who worked with Sherrod and then set up SNCC's Arkansas project. Sustaining interracial activist communities was a precarious enterprise, not only because of the affront it represented to white supremacists and the violence that ensued but also because of pressure to repel a racial history designed to separate black organizers from white. Freedom Summer expanded SNCC beyond its originators' recognition. As Jean Wheeler Smith expressed, suddenly there were "so many new people" not yet aware of the risks involved who "you couldn't know or depend on" when putting "life on the line."[11] From a tight cadre of sixteen organizers, SNCC became a group of many constellations, especially once pessimism deepened over the possibility of political realignment when the Democratic National Convention refused to seat representatives of the interracial MFDP, seating only the white segregationist bloc. The MFDP received the party establishment's offer of "two seats at large" as a betrayal of democratic principles. It convinced many of the logic of pursuing third party politics, espousing Black Power more decisively for majority-black populations, and, for some, taking a black separatist position.

Now historical studies emphasize how distinctive it was to create integrated Freedom Houses in racially segregated southern towns and hamlets, which activists achieved by working closely with African American communities at the grassroots. SNCC spoke truth to power, taking the federal government, including the FBI, to task for failing to ensure the constitutional rights of black southerners registering to vote, their safety, and that of civil rights workers battling racist intimidation ratified by a segregationist status quo. SNCC worked for African American political representation, managing congressional campaigns, mobilizing for local elections, and supporting the MFDP and FDP and local branches of the NAACP. What faith young activists had in party politics and, indeed, democratic processes, was tested sorely when massive resistance to racial change remained unremittingly violent and federal intervention frustratingly slow and its effects limited. Territorial disputes between more established organizations and groups also frustrated young people catalyzed by the freedom struggle at the grassroots.[12]

Carson focuses on inward-looking debate as the second stage in understanding SNCC's development. The Waveland, Mississippi, retreat in November 1964 where staff took stock was said to be characterized by "intense emotions ... daily—and nightly—discussions about democracy versus education and privilege as sources of power, white-black dynamics, grassroots leadership challenges, the stresses of growth, and the relationship between the Atlanta office and the field project." Nancy (Shaw) Stoller recorded, "Stress was high, and some people were at the breaking point emotionally."[13] Position papers shared at Waveland texture the literature. "We are," Moses wrote, "on a boat in the middle of the ocean": "It has to be rebuilt in order to stay afloat. It also has to stay afloat in order to be rebuilt. Our problem is like that. Since we are out on the ocean we have to do it ourselves."[14] Forman expressed his fear that, without clear direction, they would drift "on a river of no return," and Cleveland Sellers borrowed that image to title his memoir, in which being whipped up in "the strong current of a river of no return" is equated to loss: "My being is inseparable from the struggle. I have thought about this a great deal, who I am, where I've come from and where I'm going.... I am not unique. It's the same for almost everyone who *lived* the SNCC experience."[15] Tom Dent in 1967 and Sellers in 1970 assumed a communal understanding of the politics behind the poetics. Dent wrote, "We are in search of central rivers [as the] veins and arteries. The blood of experience our people know."[16] The role of whites was raised as an insurmountable problem at Waveland, despite programs and initiatives designed to address it, notably the Southern Student Organizing Committee (SSOC). Black Power politics prompted a surge of writing because the media made it a moral panic. Black organizers focalized Black Power as their logical response to white power structures at federal, state, and local levels, as Mitchell Zimmerman explained when refuting black journalist and federal official Carl Rowan's attack on SNCC's "black nationalism."[17] In this widening context, SNCC was the first civil rights group to openly and unequivocally protest the government's pursuit of war in Vietnam, throwing itself behind the National Black Anti-War Anti-Draft Union.[18]

Carson's third phase focuses on SNCC's sharpening of black political and cultural consciousness until weakened by internal divisions and external forces that presaged its disbanding. The Kingston Springs, Tennessee, retreat of May 1966 characterizes debates then cresting in the organization. The Lowndes County project involved white organizers, but all were aware of the additional danger of white supremacist reaction to interracial demonstrations. These concerns were not new and had been evident in the McComb, Mississippi, project in 1961 and Bob Zellner's experience as a white activist singled out by a white mob as "one evermore standout eyesore of a white man" in an otherwise all-black demonstration.[19]

When Atlanta organizers composed a position piece on Black Power, they addressed the role of whites directly. Black Mississippi activist Bill Ware suggested that it took honesty as well as commitment "to take painful experiences and formalize them into the kind of thinking you will find here," and he expressed his hope that the decision to be an all-black project could be respected.[20] When SNCC declared itself a black-only organization, many veterans fell away; most whites understood, even as they felt spurned, and many black staff regretted the decision's effects while upholding its premise. The projects in Arkansas and Albany, Georgia, remained interracial, but splits in SNCC became fissures. Projects closed or continued under other auspices, such as those of the MFDP or Lowndes County Freedom Organization (LCFO), or through individuals working independently. Ed Brown's formation of the Delta Foundation and Mississippi Action for Community Education, was such as case, as was Hollis Watkins's cofounding of Southern Echo as a leadership development, education, and training organization. In 2015, Watkins advised organizers through the Mary Reynolds Babcock Foundation on the importance of forging "generational transition."[21] The naming of Charles Sherrod Civil Rights Park in Albany in 2006 is also evidence of how SNCC and post-SNCC work in communities has forged a long legacy.

Some pioneering organizers had hoped that SNCC could work itself into redundancy by achieving its goals within five years, and in that sense it died on schedule, but factionalism accelerated its demise. In Forman's view, that its purpose could be realized within so tight a window was merely hopeful rhetoric.[22] SNCC was destroyed from the outside while imploding from the inside. Staff members were exhausted, and ideological division grew. Affiliation with the Black Panther Party in Oakland, California or to the Marxist-Leninist, and Maoist, ethos of the radical black nationalist Revolutionary Action Movement (RAM) marked some individuals out, and, like other antiestablishment groups of the time, SNCC was subjected to the machinations of the FBI's counterintelligence program (COINTELPRO). Charles Cobb observed, "By 1967, SNCC was history." It was the year Charles Sherrod resigned, afterward declaring, "I didn't leave the SNCC, the SNCC left me," but remained in Southwest Georgia, where he continued organizing in black communities.[23] Cleveland Sellers admitted, "The whole movement—life itself—seemed to have dissolved. The parts and elements were missing that I had come alive with—the people in Mississippi and Alabama."[24] Nevertheless, SNCC pursued consultative NGO status at the United Nations and in 1967 was the first civil rights group to receive it.[25]

The stages in SNCC's history are not discrete, and in 1966 activist journalist Jack Newfield assessed that there had already been four iterations of SNCC but noted, "Even these categories are outsiders' generalizations that ignore eddies and countertendencies that have always strained for expression just below the surface of this chaotic and decentralized organization."[26] SNCC affiliation is itself a subject of debate for a fluid group that did not conceive of itself as a membership organization, with "joining" described as being "too formal" an expression to describe involvement with the organization.[27] Peter Ling's examination of SNCC conferences from April 1960 through April 1963 identifies 891 delegates but "only a handful of perennial attendees."[28] SNCC cosponsored other conferences, and its organizers spoke at various non-SNCC events. Martha Prescod says she was "completely captured" when she attended a joint SNCC/SDS conference, when "SNCC folk told stories of struggle interspersed with freedom songs," and Forman liaised with the Pan African Students Organization in the Americas (PASOA), delivering a speech at its 1963 conference.[29] Maria Varela, Casey Hayden, Tom Hayden, Tim Jenkins, and Rob Burlage were among organizers working in both SNCC and SDS. SNCC history intersects with that of multiple groups, including the SCLC, the National Student Association (NSA), the SSOC, and the Black Panther Party, and Dorothy Dawson Burlage describes her peripatetic lifestyle creating networks between SNCC and SDS, NSA, SSOC, SCLC, and YWCA, "lugging around boxes of papers, notes, mailing lists, position papers, pamphlets, and leaflets."[30] What SNCC meant for journalists on the civil rights beat or means to historians now also depends on what they emphasize. While David Halberstam follows sit-in leaders from Nashville into SNCC, J. Todd Moye's grassroots history *Let the People Decide* opens with activist Charles McLaurin arriving to organize in Sunflower County in the Mississippi Delta in 1962 and closes with his work there over five decades, excepting a spell in Jackson in the 1980s. Richard H. King cites Julius Lester and Willie Ricks often in *Civil Rights and the Idea of Freedom* for how they registered the mood underpinning Black Power. Author and psychiatrist Robert Coles felt, "I would be doing them [SNCC] an injustice [by] not seeing the many truths of their many lives in the interests of my own tidy, categorical inclinations."[31] He suggested that SNCC resists synopsis: "We want the 'subject matter' we are studying to have coherence to it, an intactness, a consistency," but "that was not SNCC."[32] All of us who write about the organization address this problem. Wesley Hogan self-consciously allows that her four-hundred-page history, *Many Minds, One Heart*, has some twenty key people standing in for more than four hundred participants over SNCC's lifetime, saying, "I hope this work encourages others to tell the stories of those not present on these pages."[33]

Investigation of narrative culture brings familiar but also lesser-known figures into view—James Forman, Julian Bond, Jane Stembridge, Charles Cobb, Jean Wheeler Smith, Peter De Lissovoy, Julius Lester, Maria Varela, Gloria House, Gloria Wade Gayles, Kathleen Collins, Elayne DeLott, Sam Block, Michael Thelwell, Denise Nicholas, Worth Long, Richard Hall, Mitchell Zimmerman, and Bill Mahoney among them.[34] It is only through what Mahoney wrote that he is made visible, not only as SNCC's first published novelist but also in multiple roles he performed within the organization. That Julius Lester's novel *And All Our Wounds Forgiven* (1994) is rooted in the SNCC experience has been overlooked, and when Denise Nicholas's *Freshwater Road* was included in an "Essential Civil Rights Reading List" (2013) as "maybe the finest novel about the civil-rights era," the author failed to acknowledge that Nicholas was a member of the Free Southern Theater (FST) or in SNCC.[35] In printed collections that make a difference to the visibility of civil rights literature, only a biographical note occasionally indicates that an author was an activist. Most literary anthologies focused on the civil rights movement do not contain work by activists.[36] If it is difficult to discern when and where SNCC enters literary history, the problem is compounded when the activism underpinning a work is not addressed. Jerry Bryant notes that Mahoney was a Freedom Rider in 1961 but does not mention his sustained activism across a decade or what it contributes to his writing other than "sad" observation based on "hard-won knowledge."[37] *SNCC's Stories* unpacks what that knowledge portends at different moments in SNCC's life. Even African American poet and publisher Dudley Randall struck an awkward balance, seeking to legitimate House (Aneb Kgositsile) by comparing her poetry to Chaucer and Robert Burns and enumerating her academic credentials before alighting on the pertinent information: "She worked two and a half years in Alabama in the freedom struggle as a community organizer and a teacher, and is still active in community work. From this richness of experience and feeling we see the power of her present work."[38] Thelwell facilitated the "eye-witness history" of Stokely Carmichael (Kwame Ture) in *Ready for the Revolution*, published 2003, five years after his subject's death, describing Carmichael as composer and himself as arranger. But short stories Thelwell published in the 1960s drill down into a range of SNCC's concerns, and his political essays and literary criticism exemplify sustained engagement with the politics of culture and the culture of politics. Cobb, a prolific poet in the 1960s, journalist in the 1970s, and historian since, has published in a variety of genres but has yet to receive attention for the sustained, creative contribution he has made to SNCC's self-representation.

SNCC dissolved in stages, and completely by 1971, although the FBI kept individuals under surveillance at least until December 1973. Organizers have published in every decade since the 1960s, but when SNCC made the news in the 1970s and 1980s it was often for fallout that was misunderstood, as in 1980 when Dennis Sweeney murdered Democratic congressman Allard Lowenstein, who had marshaled student volunteers, including Sweeney, for COFO's Freedom Summer project in 1964. That the murder took place so many years later suggested a complex history involving brutal violence in McComb, where Sweeney had suffered a psychological breakdown. Three books about him were published in the 1980s, a disproportionate number about a single volunteer.[39] In 1987, television documentary series *Eyes on the Prize*, made by Henry Hampton's team at Blackside, Inc., turned the tide for how the public, scholars, and teachers understood the civil rights 1960s—and SNCC. Its archival footage fixed grassroots SNCC organizers (such as Bob Moses, John Lewis, Diane Nash, and Hollis Watkins) and community activists (such as Fannie Lou Hamer, Mississippi NAACP president Aaron Henry, and William G. Anderson in Albany, Georgia) in the public imagination, making them as visible as heralded leaders like Martin Luther King Jr. Each of the six episodes airing on PBS secured some twenty million viewers who listened to scores of participants recounting their experience of sit-ins, Freedom Rides, and mass meetings, alerting viewers to the activist agency of unsung people. *Eyes on the Prize* changed how SNCC could begin to be understood by a wider public, not least because the "shock troops" that Carson wrote about to preserve them from "the fate of obscurity" were contextualized, particularly in episodes "Mississippi: Is This America?" and "Bridge to Freedom." SNCC organizers were centrally involved in its making: Judy Richardson as researcher and interviewer, Julian Bond as narrator, and volunteer Jon Else as director of photography and series producer. Else describes its impact: "It chronicled that great expansion of American democracy through legal victories, direct action, voter registration, and legislation. Hampton was not afraid to show the movement's raw realities: conflicts between secular and religious leaders, the shift toward black power and armed black resistance in the face of savage white violence. Henry Hampton utterly changed the way social history is told in the media, taught, and remembered today."[40] In 1990, when funding was secured for a second series, *Eyes on the Prize II* ("America at the Racial Crossroads, 1965–1985"), the story continued.[41] Richardson pushed for more complex engagement with the grassroots but was forced to acknowledge, "Nowhere in the Lowndes County story in *Eyes II* do you hear that we were building an all-Black political party, but we were." Recognizing how works of history have opened up understanding since, she expressed the wish that in the 1990s "we had a book like Hasan Jeffries's *Bloody Lowndes*."[42]

Eyes on the Prize was personal for SNCC. It was the catalyst for a poetic elegy by Dorothy (Miller) Zellner. When Ruby Doris Smith Robinson appears on screen, she looks directly at the camera to be seen as unafraid when hauled away in a police wagon in 1961. Zellner's poem distilled the feeling of "then" in "now," a confusion "Of time / And space / And face / And age." Grief over Robinson's death of leukemia in 1967 is transfigured into an apostrophe to a dear friend: "Ruby Doris, I saw you on TV last night ... my youngest daughter was named for you Ruby."[43]

Literature as a Lacuna

In 1987, the year *Eyes on the Prize* was screened, Thelwell drew attention to how what was conveyed on the screen had already been explored in writing by organizers: "There was a moment in the South ... in which the very texture of reality intensified. A brief circumstance, which can never return or be repeated, in which major and disparate themes of American history—politics, culture, race, and sex—rang together in clamorous dissonance and creative tension." Like Bond, he concluded that texts into which "elements of character, culture, fear, courage, faith, doubt, love, and bigotry were woven" were "the very substance of great fiction," but he observed with regret, "We have let it pass insufficiently explored." Thelwell pointed toward what remains invisible: a print culture "called forth by the necessities of the Movement," where it is possible to discern "the sensibility underlying the facts of what happened" that Cobb worries may be lost.[44] For Cobb, "creativity defined the Movement as much as protest," yet the writing of civil rights movement historians "almost always ignores its creativity in the arts."[45] This is not the case with the NAACP. Sondra Kathryn Wilson pioneered the anthologizing of literature first published in organizational magazines such as the NAACP's *Crisis* and the Urban League's *Opportunity*, as well as the independent *Messenger* cofounded by A. Philip Randolph. The *Student Voice* and the *Movement*, both anthologized by Clayborne Carson, are a cultural store, but as Cobb assessed, SNCC's creativity had still been "missed by scholars."[46] In 2016, Cobb's self-description as "an African-American writer and a SNCC veteran who believes that our art has always been tied to our struggle" reinforced my belief that SNCC literary culture remained a lacuna in the record.⁴⁷ In 1965, Dona Richards (Marimba Ani) celebrated Cobb as "one of the finest creative writers in the movement" when compiling an indicative selection of writing for the African American literary periodical *Freedomways*. She explained that the writing by organizers was "very sharp and real to those of us who are immersed in 'the Movement'" and depicted "problems which are somehow seldom touched on by the Movement's many 'analyzers.'" Like Forman, she emphasized that "day to day realities of our existence, as only we can know it," were captured in writing. Cobb reiterates that "popular memory [focused] on iconic figures and moments [has been] at the expense of the thought and structures of day-to-day Freedom Movement actions at the grassroots level."⁴⁸

What "defines a people internally" is "not always clearly visible" and in SNCC's case was "constantly in flux."⁴⁹ It was clearest in 1961, when Diane Nash's privileged insider knowledge was inherent in her "personal interpretation" of the sit-ins, but by 1964, when Howard Zinn tried to capture SNCC's "temperament" through "conversation[s] which reflect not a precise doctrine but an emotion . . . not an ideology but a mood," it was "hard to define" but important to convey.⁵⁰ In 1967, when Cobb and Lester set up a Cultural Program Committee, they invited John O'Neal, although no longer in SNCC by then, because after cofounding the FST in 1963 with fellow field secretary Doris Derby and dramatist and journalist Gilbert Moses, O'Neal had laid out for SNCC's Executive Committee a plan for a broader cultural program. O'Neal wrote, "Our work as artists derives its significance from its relation to the process of history," and he conceptualized a problem I address in this present study: "We have clouded the real relationship between artist, artifact and audience. We have set the artist off in another realm."⁵¹ Thelwell echoed O'Neal, consciously or intuitively, when describing short stories published in the 1960s as "artefacts of history."⁵² As historian of emotions Peter Stearns argues, "intellectual artifacts— particularly in literature and art [are] outlets for emotions not normally freely permitted."⁵³ Through them, it is possible to glean more about how SNCC organizers managed dangerous situations and bitter aftershocks.

SNCC's self-created narratives are the cultural mooring for its infrapolitics, "offstage discourse," the "cultural and structural underpinning of the more visible political action on which our attention has generally been focused," in the words of political anthropologist James C. Scott. Scott focuses on disempowered, subordinate groups, not an articulate group that spoke truth to power, but his foregrounding of neglected substructures is pertinent, as is his dialogic explication of the "zone of constant struggle" between "hidden" and "public" transcripts.[54] SNCC felt responsibility to local people and knew that care and nuance were needed. As Forman wrote, "When one is locked, poised, and fighting the enemy one cannot reveal all for that is to give him strength and information that he can use."[55] Some stories had to be withheld from publication. While Louis Allen waited to testify against the murderer of McComb activist Herbert Lee in 1961, any publication depicting Allen's courage would only "place his life in further danger." In fact, Allen himself would be murdered in 1964, after which Julian Bond eulogized him in a series of articles.[56] In literature, dangers at the grassroots could be explored.

In the precise context of civil rights historiography, Richard H. King suggests that we might "establish a more immediate relation" to the feeling of the movement through fiction because "it is there that one gets something like a simulacrum of the experience." King sensed that literature sheds light on "certain dimensions of the experience of politics that otherwise might have remained hidden." His essays on the cognitive and historical value of fiction were an early inspiration for *SNCC's Stories*, as was his assertion that "historical understanding may be enhanced—though never automatically—by a fictional working-through of historical phenomena."[57] The caveat is important. I do not subscribe to a simplistic "literal pantextualism."[58] SNCC's history is synergistic with its literature, but I do not measure imaginative writing against historical works. Such yardsticks would be blunt and "historian cop" too brittle a role to play when writers create surrogates, avatars, composite characters, conflate events, and telescope different moments and locales to strategic effect.[59] King judged that "mainstream historiography/historians ... lack the language, or perhaps the will, to handle the agonizingly personal, racial and sexual confrontations that Alice Walker insists were at the heart of the movement."[60] He addressed literary critics too, wondering whether "political engagement in the civil rights movement may have given rise to a narrative pattern in black writing which would be an alternative to those of ascent or immersion—the narrative of political engagement."[61] Jennifer Jensen Wallach agrees that "subjectivity of historical agents is not something we should try to guard against but ... [instead] embrace as a vehicle for a richer understanding of the past." But she limits subjectivity to a single narrative mode in *Closer to the Truth than Any Fact: Memoir, Memory, Jim Crow* (2008): "[A] literary memoir is historically significant because, unlike the novel, it is based in fact and refers to a real past rather than a fictional world.... Memoirs, despite the myriad ways in which they might stretch, evade, or incorrectly portray the truth, are grounded in real people, places, and things and thus are better suited to tell us 'what really happened' than are fictional texts."[62] This epistemological distinction indicates how fiction is pushed away as if inherently dishonest, even though saying a memoir reads like a novel is considered high praise: "A novel is not rooted in real people, places, and events and these cannot make literal truth claims. Our historical insights are enriched by the efforts of realist novelists to capture aspects of a particular social reality artfully. However, despite the valuable insights provided by fiction writers, they do not write about the real world that exists outside the text."[63] Historical claims for memoir are blunt if the novel is merely a fallible yardstick.[64]

Facts may be as slippery as the sources in which they are contained, but there are fewer differences than suggested by an external reality check. Wallach and John Kirk suggest as much in *Arsnick* (2011), a rare work of eclectic primary documents for a case study of the Arkansas SNCC project. Although historical assessments are separated from "firsthand accounts" in the book, it includes interviews and fiction. When Wallach assumes that memoirs are more reliable sources than fiction, she neglects to address how an aura of reliability is rooted in subjectivity and how an impression of historical accuracy is produced through literary techniques, including amplification, allusion, and telescoping. Telescoping is a feature of life-writing in which separate events are collapsed into one, with telescoping, transposing, and refiguring all common facets of authorial selection. Nor are memoirs automatically or unequivocally sources where past feelings in the moment are conveyed. At the end of *Walking with the Wind: A Memoir of the Movement* (1998), John Lewis hesitates: "There is no way to describe how palpable the fear was among black people living in the South just thirty and forty years ago. I'm talking about raw fear... that James Meredith could be shot in broad daylight, that a boy like Emmett Till could be dragged from his home and beaten to death, that three young men such as Mickey Schwerner, James Chaney and Andrew Goodman could be murdered and buried with the complicity and cooperation of law enforcement officials."[65] A core feeling is closed off from Lewis's ability or willingness to excavate and express a feeling he points readers toward nevertheless. Cobb is revealing about what SNCC veterans withhold in memoirs when admitting that *On the Road to Freedom* is "a story as I might tell it to you in face-to-face conversation—not the whole story or even most of the story."[66]

Literature's roots in historical knowledge are tangled, as evidenced in Erich Auerbach's historicist theory of "mimesis," in New Journalism when lauded as fables of fact (as in John Hellmann's 1981 book by that title), and in Robert Penn Warren's description of poetry as "the deepest part of autobiography" and "a hazardous attempt at self-understanding."[67] Jacques Derrida encapsulated the problem: "Literature has the political right to say everything. It's there, it's published, but nobody can trust it, because it is fiction." He extrapolated that authors of fiction may have "lied, invented, deformed," but that is "the case in all so-called autobiographical texts." Derrida overstretched to argue that when "a truth" is "transformed," it is "in order to access an even more powerful, more 'true' truth."[68] What is expressed imaginatively is not more true, in my view, but it does drill down into phenomenological and psychological layers of experience. Literary critic Barbara Foley and historian and novelist Shelby Foote get to the nub of the matter. Foote observes through his own practice that writers of history and literature seek "the same truth—only they reach it, or try to reach it, by different routes. Whether the event took place in a world now gone to dust, preserved by documents and evaluated by scholarship, or in the imagination, preserved by memory and distilled by the creative process, they both want to know how it was."[69] Foley addresses the perceived difficulty of interpreting literary texts for "how it was" by proposing a "documentary mode" to anatomize "the different varieties of truth—whether private or public, generally representative or historically specific," conveyed in African American fiction. In her analysis, fictions "call to mind not so much 'reality' itself as a factual text that *could have been written*" and, revealingly, "what *was not written* about that 'reality'" (my emphases).[70] Through stories and poems, SNCC writers filtered compassion, empathy, guilt, helplessness, anger, repulsion, shock, madness, and loss, emotions characteristic of the "very dangerous, very intense, very heightened experience [that] left people profoundly emotionally exhausted."[71]

That poetry has a political function has been noted in histories, usually via the example of sixteen-year-old Joyce Brown reciting her poem "The House of Liberty" after the McComb Freedom House was bombed. The black community was fearful of further reprisals, but Brown's performance persuaded hesitant deacons to let COFO use their church, ensuring that the McComb Freedom School could continue.[72] But in 2004, Richard King reminded us again that we were yet to find analytical tools to "tap into the rich psychological explorations and historical textures offered in even early fictional treatments [of the civil rights movement in the 1960s] beginning with the work of [Alice] Walker (1976) and of Rosellen Brown (1984)."[73] SNCC narratives of political engagement were published in the 1960s, and veteran organizers have subsequently pointed us toward them. In a eulogy for Forman in 2005, Cobb reiterated,

One of his most significant lessons for SNCC and the broader movement itself was Forman's constant injunction to "Write! You've got to Write!"

Of all the organizations involved in the southern movement during the early 1960s, SNCC left the clearest written trail.[74]

Intimations of SNCC's Narrative Culture and Literary History

When Sterling Stuckey asserted that "civil rights leaders were not overly interested in matters of culture or heritage," he disaggregated this claim from information made ancillary in a footnote: "A number of leading figures in SNCC were interested in cultural questions. Mike Thelwell, Charlie Cobb, Stokely Carmichael, Bill Mahoney, and Courtland Cox—all students of [Sterling] Brown at Howard—possessed more than a little knowledge of the folk heritage of Afro-America, which was not altogether unrelated to that consciousness within SNCC which led to the call for black power."[75] Poet and professor Brown influenced writers in Howard University's SNCC affiliate Nonviolent Action Group and alluded to Thelwell, Cobb, and Mahoney as a "driving wedge," but he assumed that the "types of writing" that "freedom fighters" produced were "tracts, pamphlets... squibs, lampoons, parodies, burlesques," comparing them to "propagandists who functioned so ably a century ago."[76] Embedded with SNCC as a counselor, Robert Coles neither expected nor suspected that organizers were writing their own field texts while he wrote about them. At Spelman College, Vincent Harding recalled, "We were especially impressed by the itinerant band of radicalized poets, playwrights, historians, and musicians who joined the political organizers." The artists," he wrote, "moved among us... wherever we gathered to organize, confer, and celebrate."[77] In 2009, he reiterated that a rich artistic output "marked the movement years" but failed to note just how many of "us" were artists.[78] Jerry Ward intimated that writers were "caught up in very active way(s) with SNCC" but as associates. Individuals in SNCC are defined as artists only occasionally. For Nicholas Lemann, Thelwell is a "secret sharer" of life inside a radical student movement, revealing its "inner geography," and Houston Baker hails Bernice Johnson Reagon for transforming southern jails into "independent black studios for writing and singing the terrible workings of race in America."[79]

For Doris Derby, the Free Southern Theater was "a cultural, artistic tool" designed to "involve, inspire, enlighten, and galvanize black people to critically think and create for themselves, within the context of the Civil Rights Movement in the segregated and closed society of violent Mississippi."[80] The FST's creativity is usually the context for any artistic evaluation of SNCC. It is Joe Street's focus when addressing SNCC in *The Culture War in the Civil Rights Movement* (2007) and that of various articles, including Christina Larocco's analysis of its "usable aesthetic," but the FST was not SNCC's sole cultural arm, nor was theater its route to publishing.[81] Otherwise, SNCC is cited for how vocalizing Black Power in 1966 influenced the Black Arts Movement (BAM) or for how the FST evoked a new black aesthetic in its repertoire after the BAM took hold. FST-styled writing workshops in the 1970s, like BLKARTSOUTH, led by Tom Dent and Val Ferdinand (Kalamu ya Salaam), and its journal *Nkombo* are occasionally noted.[82] But the foci for SNCC's creativity before 1966, are consensually accepted as education and songwriting. Peter Ling examines the "social capital" of citizenship and Freedom School classes, and John N. Hale and William Sturkey examine Freedom School–based creativity that is recounted by those involved, including Sandra Adickes in *Legacy of a Freedom School* (2005), Liz Fusco in essays, and song-crafting as delineated and analyzed by Bernice Johnson Reagon. It was the topic of Reagon's PhD in 1968, and she traces SNCC's Freedom Singers through Sweet Honey in the Rock, the group she initiated post-SNCC, in essays and books. Other organizers, notably Si Kahn, take up similar work.[83]

The educational impetus and religious faith that animated Freedom Schools and freedom songs do not feature significantly in literary works. Christian beliefs undergirding the activism of Reagon, Sherrod, Lewis, and many southern organizers were not the inspiration for writers of fiction or poetry. When Forman explored the crisis of conscience of a white clergyman in "The Song Festival," his purpose was "to hit white Christian America in the face." In Gloria Wade Gayles's ode to Fannie Lou Hamer, renowned for faith-based activism, her refusal to be cowed by politicians is accentuated and the "husky / you-gotta-listen voice for freedom" with which she delivered speeches.[84] Thelwell and Mahoney's minister characters accommodate a segregated status quo, and only Denise Nicholas depicts a community rooted in a church. Some gaps in the critical assessment of SNCC's culture are being filled. Vanessa Murphree traces how it presented itself to the press and potential funders, and Leigh Raiford describes how photographers exemplify "the inherent diversity and internal differentiations that were prevalent and unavoidable, destabilizing and enriching to the organization."[85] As I argued in "'I Second That Emotion': A Case for Using Imaginative Sources in Writing Civil Rights History" (2015), myriad more cultural forms communicate activist sensibility.[86] Literature is key. Forman argued with feeling that, even internally, in other kinds of texts, "[S]o often . . . we just describe the facts. Someone is in jail. Others are beaten. One more killed here, two more there, three over yonder; but the Movement is more than a set of facts. It is not just... demonstrating. We have love lives. We have conflicts. We have vocations, aspirations, personal problems, dreams deferred."[87]

Historians have intimated that there is a wider narrative culture to explore. Carson's *In Struggle* is axiomatic because, as O'Neal recorded, when "somebody in SNCC started closing their letters with 'yours in struggle,'" the phrase became "the epistolary equivalent of a clenched fist raised high in defiance or pressed to the heart with reverence and resolution." It was, he mused, a good idea for a play.[88] When Cynthia Griggs Fleming framed her biography of Ruby Doris Smith Robinson with poems by Fay Bellamy (Powell) and Dorothy Zellner, SNCC's literary culture was implicit, but the poems stand without analysis as monuments of grief. Fleming assumed that Bellamy was "moved to write a poem" on Robinson's death, but what she wrote was an open letter when George Bess and Henry McFarland died in an "accident," drowning when their car left the road on a bridge in Clay County, Mississippi. Bellamy recorded shock and grief in subdued statements: "[Willie] Ricks left the house when I told him about it. Stanley [Wise] went to the office. Both cried." Her letter appeared in an internal newsletter and was rearranged into a lyric poem by an unnamed coworker. It struck a collective chord for "our utter frustration" when Robinson's death followed hard on Bess's and McFarland's and expresses the collaborative context in which literature must be understood. When structured poetically, the shift from first person to a reiterative "we" is accentuated:

> I want to cry but am not able to do so.
> With each death we cry a little less.
> Soon we will not cry at all.[89]

Bellamy was "trying to write about the pain I feel at this moment," asking openly of others, "Can one write about pain?"[90] Raw private feelings were also communal, and, when Forman dedicated "Liberation Will Come from a Black Thing" to Robinson, he performed his poem during a speech, making those feelings public.[91] Forman embodies the frenetic role of executive secretary as the first and longest serving person in the position, but Robinson symbolizes it in poetry. In an homage, Gloria House distinguished her for having

> the energy of a dozen organizers...
> calling you for a hundred reasons,
> to make a hundred complaints

> followed by a hundred requests,
> to say we need, need, need,
> can we have, have, have?
> And your voice, hoarse, disciplined, trying
> to say yes, to give
> everything.

For House, Robinson personifies holistic understanding of

> the hunger, the loneliness, the failure,
> the triumph and desperation
> of the field.

The elegy closed on a promise: "We hold you tenderly in our hearts and our history."[92]

Carson has suggested that organizers made "a profound, often ignored, contribution to political thinking," and in *Civil Rights and the Idea of Freedom* (1992), Richard H. King explored their political education as self-transformation.[93] Historians who work closely with former SNCC workers now suggest that they provide "a useful blueprint and way of rethinking the intersections between various movement approaches and philosophies (and the ways that people understood them on the ground)."[94] Nevertheless, as Emilye Crosby argues, "The insights of the field remain too peripheral to historiographical debates and essentially inviable or nonexistent in popular versions" when they "belong at the heart of our scholarship... and must be part of any attempt at synthesis."[95] Robyn C. Spencer and Wesley Hogan argue that they are underexplored because "scholars and activists largely disagree [over] how important this interior culture is, and how important it is for historians to record it." In a thought-provoking essay, they point out that individuals in SNCC and the Black Panther Party committed "their thoughts and reflections to paper" but that "very few scholars have figured out either how to get at such material, or, once they have it, how to piece it together with other kinds of sources."[96] Subjective sources are typically held at arm's length because when imagination and emotion texture writing, it is assumed that critical perspective is lost. Sociologists examine how participant narratives "open up a culture and reveal the operation of otherwise obscured transactions, social conventions, mythologies, meanings and motivations," but even the most open of scholars, like Wallach, are cautious about the imaginative qualities of sources, with Spencer and Hogan observing, "*Although* ... Dallas Panther Skip Shockley's self-published memoir freely blends fact and fiction, it raises interesting questions about the Panthers' health advocacy that scholars can pursue *in other mediums with more traditional sources*" (my emphases).⁹⁷ As Tim Tyson muses in *Blood Done Sign My Name* (2004), what is "personally meaningful" is expected to be subsumed in order to write "objective history."⁹⁸ *SNCC's Stories* engages the problem of "objectivity" while investigating how what organizers composed involved self-reflexive intellectual, political, and artistic negotiation of their activism. If "movement interiority matters and is key for the historical record," it is incumbent on us to discover where it has been expressed, to put texts under scrutiny and assess whether literature is inimical to the organization's history.⁹⁹

Hogan took her title metaphor *Many Minds, One Heart* (2007) from a phrase Chuck McDew coined and draws on it as a figurative thread positing that staff "created a language of words, gestures, jokes, and behavior so interior that it was only with other SNCC people that many felt truly comfortable."¹⁰⁰ Tracy Sugarman's diaries bear this out. Organizers orienting summer volunteers seemed like "tired old-young men [who] regarded us politely, nodded, and returned to the private society of those who knew because they had shared it together." Jesse Morris was "not much older" than Elayne DeLott (later Elaine DeLott Baker), but she perceived "a seriousness about him that placed him beyond time." CORE volunteer Debbie Louis decided it was difficult to know COFO organizers because their experience "made communication with those outside the struggle impossible."¹⁰¹ It is meaningful, therefore, that the first cadre of organizers are among individuals who elected to explore their experiences in literature.

Storytelling and Self-Defining Discourse

Organizers lauded for storytelling skills include Cobb, Reagon, McLaurin, Bob Mants, Charles Sherrod, Bertha Gober, Ed Brown, and Chuck ("Tell the Story") McDew in Bob Moses's poetic evocation of SNCC's second chairman as "a black by birth, a Jew by choice, and a revolutionary by necessity" who "dares to stand in a strong sun and cast a sharp shadow."¹⁰² McDew mesmerized audiences, as Dion Diamond did in "dramatic style" inviting students into his experience of the Freedom Rides: "Close your eyes and let me take you on the trip."¹⁰³ A single staff meeting in September 1963 demonstrates the imperative to narrate as an ongoing priority. The "need for more people to write about the movement" appears in minutes, and the communications team was "commended on press releases: SRC refer[red] to them, newspapers commented on them, and Margaret Long has given written praise of them." Organizers agreed to produce "more background and feature pieces" because "the College News Service and other sources [had] asked for them," and it was agreed that fora "to publish writings by people in the movement" needed to be found. The Stern Family Fund agreed to support articles through its charitable foundation and "through *Harper's* magazine."[104] SNCC's campus travelers would liaise with campus newspapers to "get them interested in SNCC and see if they will do a feature story."[105] Among new staff, Dona Richards and Mendy Samstein would write and promote writing, and, after working on a literacy project with organizer and poet Worth Long, Maria Varela launched Flute Publications with Jane Stembridge's poetry in 1966 and collections by Cobb and Lester in 1967.

As SNCC minutes indicate, campaign slogans were linguistic bedrock for writers. "Freedom Now" was the original title of SNCC's first major publication, the photo documentary *The Movement* (1964), on which Lorraine Hansberry collaborated.[106] Joanne Grant's articles tied demands for "freedom now" to young activists in SNCC. If, as Eric Foner claims, freedom is the most popular American master narrative, the "oldest of clichés and the most modern of aspirations," it gained new currency through a culture of Freedom Houses, Freedom Schools, freedom songs, freedom ballots supported by Freedom Days to promote voter registration, Freedom Primers, and newsletters titled *Freedom Flame, Freedom Train,* and *Freedom News*.[107] Grant judged that the radical ramifications of "freedom now" might not be appreciated until later but said: "There is nowhere in American life today that the cry for freedom exists, except in the Movement.[108] "Black Power for Black People" dates back to 1961. "One Man, One Vote," SNCC's slogan for the wider Voter Education Project, was similarly long-standing, endorsed at its April 1963 conference. Moses defined it as "identification of SNCC workers with poor and often uneducated blacks" to "vote out police brutality, to vote out officials that keep the Negro down."[109] Nicholas's fictionalization of SNCC as "One Man, One Vote" reasserted it for twenty-first-century readers. At the March on Washington in 1963, John Lewis lodged "One Man, One Vote" as "the African cry," declaring, "It is ours too." Borrowing the motto from the independence movement in Zambia, Forman "brought that knowledge into SNCC" as the result of graduate work in African studies at Boston University.[110] Tracing this discourse through the literature supports those histories that give the lie to a popular simplification that SNCC shifted suddenly from an "integrationist," reformist model to a black nationalist one.

Gently satirized internally, as in the menu for 1965's Thanksgiving dinner—"Nonviolent ... turkey" with "Freedom Fighting ... dressing," and

"One Man, One Vote... cranberry salad"—shared discourse also acted as a driver for, or brake on, difficult discussions.[111] In a position paper, for example, an organizer challenged a core tenet even while affirming it: "that every man, farmer, lawyer, illiterate, PhD, has a right to speak and to be heard. I believe that no [other] man, regardless of whether he calls himself SNCC, NAACP, or anybody, can speak for him. I believe that he has a right to speak, to vote, and to associate freely even if I do not agree with what he says or does. That is what ONE MAN–ONE VOTE means to me, what does it mean to you? What does it really, really, mean to you?"[112] Bob Moses observed, "The concept of 'one person, one vote'" provided "*a minimum of common conceptual cohesion.*"[113] It crystallized agreement to "let the people decide" and promote voices "in the fields, bayous and deltas of our deep South" because organizers worried that the national NAACP and SCLC bypassed the poorest, least visible constituencies.[114] It is unsurprising, then, that local people feature prominently in literary texts. Steadily a gateway imagery accrued for individuals inscribing organizers as protagonists in fiction and exploring group tenets in other narrative forms. In jail in Magnolia, Mississippi, "sitting with smuggled pen and paper, thinking a little, writing a little," Moses expressed community work as "a tremor in the middle of the iceberg—from a stone that the builders rejected."[115] His open letter, published in *Liberator* magazine and campus newspapers, became an iconic document, appearing in documentary books *The Movement* and Grant's *Black Protest* (1968). The ripples his words created may be understood, but the language was being examined in literature.[116] Martin Luther King Jr. is renowned for proverbial, literary language, telling the crowd at the March on Washington that "a stone of hope" would be hewn from "a mountain of despair."[117] SNCC's figurative language, wrought of ice, stone, brick, and steel, leitmotifs for political explication and mobilization, influenced people close to the organization, like SCLC field secretary Annell Ponder: "The people of the Delta have started from the inside to melt the iceberg, and I'm happy to share in the thawing process with them."[118] Aphorisms like "Crack Mississippi and you crack the South" built on "tremors" that local leaders, sharecroppers, and plantation, factory, and domestic workers made in a supposedly "solid" region. Black southern organizers, as well as NAACP and RCNL advisors, ensured that peers had a sense of the long history of fighting for democracy in the South, which Nan Woodruff uncovers in rich, meticulous detail in *American Congo: The African American Freedom Struggle in the Delta* (2003). It was SNCC's "mandate for history," Lewis declared in 1963.[119] Varela wrote a paean for "the night Willie Peacock preached us... a history lesson beginning at the ice age."[120] Images of massive resistance as a mastodon frozen in a glacier were refined as local mass movements penetrated "the seat of power in the iceberg of Mississippi politics."[121] Metaphors and similes served as shorthand when debating Mississippi's exceptionalism: "The civil rights organizations have argued that Mississippi is an iceberg that must be cracked from the outside. SNCC has operated on the premise that the state must be cracked from the inside.... Mississippi dramatizes the problem of the entire nation."[122] A SNCC project director in Mitchell Zimmerman's novel *Mississippi Reckoning* (2019) likens organizing to "snow piling up on the side of a mountain": "Someday, there's going to be a thaw, and when that day comes, a mighty river of power will come rushing down."[123]

A metaphorical language of climatology risked casting white supremacy as a natural phenomenon and massive resistance as a white monolith, though, and new imagery was introduced. In Moses's words: "Only when metal has been brought to white heat, can it be shaped and molded; this is the annealing process. This is what we intend to do to the South and the country, bring them to white heat and then remold them."[124] Stone walls "block[ing] expectant Negroes in every town and village of the hardcore South" and "stained with the blood of children" would "have to be crumbled by hammer blows."[125] Such language intensified sociological definitions of "the white power structure," a phrase associated with SDS and attributed to the New Left. Mary King credited Jack Minnis with single-handedly popularizing the term.[126] As director of research, he used it repeatedly, drawing on political scientists Floyd Hunter and C. Wright Mills, and his own statistical analysis, to create materials for organizers to use when guiding their projects. Judy Richardson reiterates that the pamphlets that Minnis produced were also "invaluable" for journalists seeking to understand "the extent of what we were up against." In such pamphlets as "The Care and Feeding of Power Structures" (1963), "Mississippi: A Chronicle of Violence and Intimidation since 1961" (1964), and "Genocide in Mississippi" (1964), Minnis probed direct action, refining the language through which SNCC's battles could be understood, whether opposing House Bill 180 when the Mississippi state legislature sought to imprison unmarried parents or expressing open resistance to the war in Vietnam and increasing support for international decolonization and struggles for self-determination.[127] In 1968, as SNCC's Atlanta project became all-black, Roland Snellings's poem "The Final Song (for White America)" drew on motifs that had infused SNCC discourse: his song was "granite strong," made of "stone and steel," and "bursting with anger."[128]

The phrase "circle of trust" resonates throughout *SNCC's Stories* for writerly responsibility to the group. At Waveland, Forman suggested that he needed time away but would be writing a "personal history of SNCC" titled "A Band of Brothers, a Circle of Trust," reminding coworkers, "All of us have our little histories within us and I would wish that all of us could set them down on paper."[129] Journalist Pat Watters observed SNCC being "endless[ly] introspective" when "toiling away at defining itself."[130] In that context, even a text ostensibly carried by a single voice had to contain multiple others—and a collectively constituted story would not necessarily equate to a consensual one. Vision and revision, grouping and regrouping, fragile consensus and flexibility, clear accord and vociferous dissent: all are characteristic, and it would be invidious to assume consonance between any single historical impression of SNCC and its creative output in manifold forms. Forman saved "little histories," like a ballad Dorie Ladner composed in Waveland. In rhymed quatrains of the form's folk tradition, it celebrated Moses, Peacock, and Sam Block among the "band of brothers... leading the Freedom Line."[131] The phrase became more inclusively "sisters and brothers," but the "circle of trust" has never changed.[132] It is freighted now by debate about how accurately or reliably SNCC has been recounted by organizers.

It is often assumed that organizers looking back will be self-affirming rather than analytical. In *A Circle of Trust: Remembering SNCC* (1998), Cheryl Lynn Greenberg's transcripts from a reunion organized by Jack Chatfield in 1987, David Garrow discerns nostalgic inflection. He cites another historian, Alan Matusow, for posing interventionist questions and declaring that, as "authentic heroes of the 1960s," organizers "deserve a full and complete history, not a history that's going to romanticize."[133] When Maurice Halbwachs expressed how memory troubles the writing of history, he distilled the problem: "The totality of past events can be put together in a single record only by separating them from the memory of the groups who preserved them, and by severing the bonds that held them close to the psychological life of the social milieus where they occurred, while retaining only the group's chronological and spatial outline of them... relocating them within the frameworks with which history organizes events. These frameworks are external to these groups and define them by mutual contrast."[134] Greenberg herself detected "a certain romanticization of the past" in *Hands on the Freedom Plow: Personal Accounts by Women in SNCC* (2010), observing, "In keeping with SNCC's commitment to unconditional support, the editors' historical commentaries are uncritically affirming, which makes them less analytically useful than historians might want." This view is complicated by "critical histories" that form part of SNCC's Legacy Project now. It was challenged in William R. Beardslee's study of common experiences, *The Way Out Must Lead In: Life Histories in the Civil Rights Movement* (1977), and it was complicated by activist and sociologist Wini Breines distinguishing "the loyalty of most female SNCC activists" to the organization and each other from "white women in the new left and antiwar movements," emphasizing internal division and "rupture."[135] If subjectivity has to be an acceptable feature of the historiography, it is because, as John Tisdale argues, attempting to confine oral history to "the box of objectivity" is spurious when it "reveals less about the event and more about what the event meant to the participants."[136] Subjectively nuanced sources are more revealing than self-imposed constraints imply.[137] These debates too texture *SNCC's Stories*.

"Tell It Like It Is"

"Telling it like it was" is the focalizing conception of the Crmvet.org website: "We tell it like it was, the way we lived it, the way we saw it, the way we *still* see it."[138] But, in a multifarious skein of texts, it is not as straightforward as this suggests. Pat Watters gauged: "Like the postwar German writers, they [SNCC activists] sought to bring language down to a level of concreteness that would impart to it once more a relationship with the real world. 'Tell it like it is,' they would say."[139] For Watters, SNCC organizers engaged "the perhaps fatal fault of much of our [society's] communication— from Congressional debate to news coverage" because "[t]hey live with the people they want to help... besides the hell of racist oppression, living in the culture of poverty with all the dislocations that implies.... What such youngsters know of racism and poverty is known in their guts."[140] He was a careful observer but assumed that SNCC instinctually had a stable, consistent voice. When Jean Wheeler Smith addressed liberalism's universalizing "we," she argued that it was a strategic fiction and was careful not to construe racism and poverty as instinctively understood but instead as witnessed and dissected in the precise context of organizing in communities.[141] Moses distilled in a field report that circulated as a letter to Friends of SNCC groups in 1963:

> [Y]ou dig into yourself and the community and prepare to wage psychological warfare; you combat your own fears about beatings, shootings, and possible mob violence; you stymie by your own physical presence the anxious fear of the Negro community, seeded across town and blown from paneled pine, and

white sunken sink to windy kitchen floors and rusty old stoves, that maybe you *did* come only to boil and bubble and then burst, out of sight and sound; you organize, pound by pound, small bands of people who gradually focus in the eyes of Negroes and whites as people "tied up in that mess"; you create a small striking force capable of moving out when the time comes, which it must, whether we help it or not.[142]

In a long, winding, Faulknerian sentence in which the richly ambiguous pronoun "you" extrapolates from his anxieties to those of coworkers, he wrote a literary précis of feelings the literature unpacks.[143] In his short story "The Organizer" (1966), Thelwell exposed how field secretaries managed the demands Moses summarized, and in Mahoney's *Black Jacob* (1969) civil rights workers move out, exhausted when a campaign fails. In Lester's *And All Our Wounds Forgiven*, an organizer quits after he breaks down in the field, while another stays past SNCC's demise, both suffering inexorably from psychological warfare waged in the 1960s. At the end of the decade, Hoyt Fuller identified "the angular, cold-eyed and emotionally wounded veteran of SNCC campaigns in Mississippi and Louisiana who soothes his wounds by 'telling it like it is.'"[144]

For Thelwell, the "texture" and "feel" of experience was a writer's "first and major responsibility," and he praised writers acting as "conduits through whom the collective force and experience of the people is reflected, shaped maybe, refined a little perhaps, and given back." He tucked into "The Organizer" an encomium for "shapers of horror, artists of grief, giving form and shape to emotion."[145] In "Tell It Like It Is" (1968), *The Movement*'s editor Terry Cannon rebuffed critics for whom movement writing equated to "propaganda, didacticism, and pamphleteering." "Whenever [these words] are used," he warned, "notice who uses them, and why. Maybe they're the ones who feel threatened."[146] If contemporary reviewers registered discomfort when trenchant social critique was empirical, delegitimizing literary works as propaganda or inferior history writing was a prevailing strategy. James McBride Dabbs paid cursory attention to Stembridge's *I Play Flute* (1966), and when Zinn published his on-the-ground study of SNCC it was reviewed as a treatise by a "partisan enthusiast."[147]

It may seem surprising that SNCC's output is rarely propagandist, but I am struck by how quietly contemplative it can be. In Casey Hayden's "On Organizing" (1965), writing evolves out of "a silence far inside / secured by suffering," equating to "revolt / without the god of should."[148] Stembridge's controlled, organic poetics is meditative and bleak, the organizer persona poised in metaphysical contemplation of what is materially present. She is shocked in "Autopsy" when viscous cotton dust chokes a child to death and in "Hunger" where the simple act of an organizer giving an orange to a child results in six starving children fighting for it (12, 14). In "Mississippi Street Song in Hinds County" (1961), by Abdul Aziz Khaalis (Jan Leighton Triggs), little Joe Abel Smith becomes similarly "hysterical at a penny tossed." In the penny he clutches are "futile dreams."[149] Stembridge's "Mississippi Field" is a place to pause where you "can sit down with your friend" as mockingbirds sing and butterflies cavort. A final line undercuts the bucolic scene with the knowledge that it was impossible to relax when "somebody can come and shoot you both."[150] Lyric utterance fused with flat, unelaborated diction construes an organizing sensibility in naturalistic detail, modernist contemplation, and simple statement of witness.

If a poem accrued meaning inside SNCC for "telling it like it is," it was re-invoked. Julian Bond's "I Too Hear America Singing," a dialogue with Langston Hughes's 1926 poem, appeared in the first issue of the *Student Voice* in 1960. For Carson, Bond's poem was "about the increasing race consciousness of many student protesters."[151] The quiet final lines evoke steadfastness and the self-containment it took to stand firm in the face of massive resistance: "Then I don't mind standing / a little longer."[152] In January 1966, the poem was positioned in the *Movement* newspaper beneath the headline "Vietnam Issue Used to Attack Civil Rights," illustrated by a photograph of Bond standing firm as representative elect to the Georgia statehouse, by 2,305 votes to 486. With Bond one of eight African Americans elected to state legislature in 1965, the first time African American candidates had been elected to the Georgia house since 1907, his poem was used to censure the refusal of his white peers to seat him as a member for Atlanta because of SNCC's stand against the war; it would also take the Supreme Court to get the decision reversed in recognition that his right to free speech had been violated.[153] Also in 1966, as the media blamed SNCC for sparking urban "riots," Lester asserted, "One needs a lyric poet in this now," making explicit poetry's relationship to the social, political, and historical. In "In the Time of Revolution (Atlanta, Georgia, November 20, 1966)," Lester suggested that without complementary voices situating Black Power politics in a subjective history, it could not be "reasoned" as more than reactionary.[154] Poetry circulated via organizational newspapers the *Student Voice* and the *Movement*, broadsides, and simple pamphlets distributed to Friends of SNCC and other groups but also appeared in political and literary journals and the foremost anthologies of the day. Writers published with Third World Press, founded by Don L. Lee (Haki Madhubuti), and Dudley Randall's Broadside Press. And what they published can be described by lines in Charlie Cobb's "In the Furrows of the World": "WE / can only be / do / from what we are."[155]

Writers grappled with how to communicate a collective subjectivity while telling it like it was. Forman declared, "I know a truth about SNCC that will never get written and yet I do not feel I can write that truth," bemoaning self-censorship if "problems of egoism, personalities, quirks, are never discussed."[156] The organization prompted organizers to be "honest," not to use the movement as "an abstract cause" or "a way to quick glory," or as "a dramatic device."[157] Individuals were never to seek publicity for themselves, as disagreement over statements to the press by Stokely "Starmichael" suggests, and John Dittmer examines tensions when volunteers privileged their skills over those of organizers and local people.[158] Writerly responsibility to experiential truths that were not solely one's own was difficult but crucial because SNCC was "such a cooperative venture." As Sheila Michaels discovered on beginning a memoir: "I exhausted myself calling and cross-questioning."[159]

Balancing Subjectivity and Collectivity

At the first meeting she attended in 1964, Jean Wiley heard "disagreement, debate . . . stomp-down, drag-out argument," and after another contentious meeting Muriel Tillinghast observed, "There are many inconsistencies in SNCC and what we say and stand for." Mike Miller suggested that "[n]o two SNCC workers will sound alike" but saw that there was "a core of shared values." Thirty years later, Joan Trumpauer (Mulholland) reiterated, "There is truth in what all of us are saying."[160] But, within SNCC, how to represent that was a loaded issue. Forman focused on individuals who were not the movement's media faces. After Sammy Younge Jr. was murdered, he interviewed Younge's family, fellow students at Tuskegee, and SNCC coworkers, threading the thoughts of thirty-eight people through an homage designed as interpretative history to "go beneath the surface" and "bring forth all the humanity of Sammy Younge." The murder touched him personally, and Forman wrote that he felt "somewhat responsible" for Younge's involvement in the movement.[161] The result is subjectively nuanced analysis and a eulogy that benefited hugely from Elizabeth Sutherland (Martínez) as interviewer, advisor, editor, and agent.[162] Conceptualizing a panoptic history of organizers, even collaboratively, was more difficult. An early template for *The Making of Black Revolutionaries* filtered SNCC through John Hardy, Fannie Lou Hamer, Ralph Allen, and Bill Hansen to convey intergenerational and interracial cooperation, but Forman found his own voice dominating. He confided his difficulties to Sutherland and Len Holt: "I can't extricate myself from the entire organization and only speak of my own role. That is too difficult and borders on egotism and sounds self-serving."[163] She advised that in fiction he might "go all the way, not having to hedge" concerns over personalities. Holt intoned: "Write as if you didn't have to choose between doing a documentary and a straight novel. Do them both.... Write everything as if you were trying to explain to Lumba or Dinky or some person that you love just what went on in SNCC and its significance to the struggle."[164] Their advice informed *The Making of Black Revolutionaries*. "There is a great[er] effort to give background material and focus to the work of my brothers and sisters in SNCC," Forman wrote of another draft.[165] He may have discovered his approach in William Kunstler's *Deep in My Heart* (1966), for which he wrote the preface: "Undoubtedly, Bill Kunstler's book was begun as the personal narrative of one of many who became deeply involved in the quickening tide. But *Deep In My Heart* has evolved as something very different . . . it is not a story of the law or lawyers alone. It is a saga of the Movement itself seen from one vantage point."[166]

Writing within SNCC and about it involves finding a vantage point. When Lester decided on "Four Faces from SNCC" for a photo-text in 2003, he rationalized his choice and ensured gender balance, with Forman "probably the most brilliant tactician the civil rights movement had," Hamer "the soul of the civil rights movement in Mississippi," Carmichael "the spokesman for Black Power that revolutionized racial consciousness," and Ruby Doris Smith Robinson, a Freedom Rider and SNCC cofounder. As its only female executive secretary, Robinson was exceptional but also representative of many other women in SNCC.[167] Cobb dedicated *On the Road to Freedom* to local leaders Hamer, who joined SNCC in 1962, Annie Devine, and Victoria Gray Adams, signaling the importance of women with whom entire communities crossed into the movement. That Charles Payne described *On the Road* as revealing of "how many different kinds of people it took to start a movement" and John Lewis called it "a rare opportunity to walk through the pages of history with a man who was there" indicates the balance Cobb achieved.[168] In *Radical Equations*, Moses and Cobb name themselves among the "core cadre" in COFO ("thirty of us") but call that core but "a fraction of the young people in this book": "[H]overing over every one of these pages were all the SNCCs."[169] Editors of *Hands on the Freedom Plow* speculate that its fifty-two first-person narratives by black and white women in SNCC may tell "one central story" from different perspectives, and Barbara Ransby writes in the preface to *Deep in Our Hearts: Nine White Women in the Freedom Movement* that the book is not a "simple one-dimensional profile of whites in the movement." In the collaborative introduction, contributors emphasize coresponsibility for communicating that they are "all very different: southern and northern; rural and urban; state university and Ivy League; middle class, and working class, and poor."[170] With SNCC being a complex and unwieldy group despite its short life, it is not surprising that there is not "one central story."[171] Lester declared, "I write because the lives of *all of us* are stories," and Peter De Lissovoy asserted that "movement stories do well to be told in a chorus," but SNCC's stories do not all strike the same note or follow a chronological narrative line.[172]

Writing was both an intensely private experience and a group activity. Elayne DeLott (Baker) recalls a poetry retreat for organizers at Highlander Folk School in Tennessee, publicized in May 1964 as "an invitation to the weary and sometimes shell-shocked civil rights veterans to spend a few days without struggle in a safe venue, outside of Mississippi." While "not so far that the darkness could not be felt," the ambience of workshops was "almost sanitarium-like." She described those attending with her as "soldiers, pausing in time of war, looking for ways to express themselves."[173] If those who came to writing within and because of SNCC wrestled with how to represent shared yet heterogeneous experiences, it involved the creation of texts that dissolve the border between self and others. Composite characters are a bonding device, since telling a collective story that is inherently multifarious and avoiding the generic conventions of memoir means that protagonists do not need to fit an individual's biography or dictate responsibility for "getting it right." Individuals are blurred, experiences pooled, shaped, made representative or rendered indicative, and imagistic bridges close gaps between politics and art, with the organizer embodying the dialectic.

Opening SNCC's Book

Chapter 1 examines campus-based politics as incipient activism. In his unpublished novel "Thin White Line" Forman fictionalized students at Chicago's Roosevelt University while studying public administration there in the late 1950s. Freelance reporting from Tennessee and Arkansas for the *Chicago Defender* heightened Forman's "consciousness for the need of a mass-based organization," and in the novel he sought to convey "the kind of organization needed."[174] As a manuscript it is an archive in itself; there are multiple versions, additional scenes, notes, fragments, diary entries, and correspondence around it. When pieced together, it comprises an imaginative exploration of how student politics moved off campus in the moment before the founding of SNCC and SDS. It should be read alongside antic stories of student leaders and volunteers: Thelwell's "Direct Action" (1963) and De Lissovoy's novel *Feelgood* (1970).

Ralph Ellison observed that in folklore may be discovered "the first drawings of any group's character" and "the values by which the group lives and dies."[175] In Supersnick and Junebug Jabbo Jones, the subjects of chapter 2, SNCC's first cadre of organizers imagined totemic characters. Supersnick evolved out of a cartoon to entertain field-workers, created by Claude Weaver. Junebug's monologues, delivered in the language of "the folk," were created out of conversations inside SNCC. Michael Thelwell communicated Junebug outward in essays, while John O'Neal performed Junebug on stage in the belief that artists who "work with and in the context of the struggle of the Black Nation are part of one of the major historical developments of our era ... grassroots community efforts all across the South."[176]

Charles Payne notes the "inventive syntax" of field reports.[177] In chapter 3, I explore them as foundational texts for writing in other genres when transmogrified into lyrical essays, poetry, and fiction. Here writers examine tricky, sometimes murky issues difficult to resolve internally, the kind of writing that Terry Cannon commended for leading readers "beyond the work itself."[178] When the organization began to feel rudderless "on a river of no return," Forman returned to field reports in an effort to induct recruits in 1967 into the grassroots ethos of SNCC's beginnings as the bedrock for understanding the organization.

Vincent Harding expressed concern that identification with the movement and "deep immersion in its flow" would result in *There Is a River: The Black Struggle for Freedom in America* (1981) being received as uncritical and partisan "by those who consider 'scholarly objectivity' the measure of all things."[179] Chapter 4 pays attention to professional writers David Halberstam, Pat Watters, Joanne Grant, Howard Zinn, Len Holt, and Robert Coles, who published field texts based on close association with SNCC and adjusted the professional expectations of the genres in which they were comfortable to do justice to their subjects. The incipient narrative culture around the organization chimes with what organizers were writing themselves: "the fine line between life and death in the back roads of the South."[180] For disenfranchised communities, organizers represented the outside world: "It was important to people... [to] say where you're from... they know that what they're doing is getting through to the outside."[181] Writers recounted and dramatized the courage of local people and the African American culture that sustained them. Chapter 5 focuses on how Dorie and Joyce Ladner, Tom Dent, Forman, Thelwell, and Denise Nicholas told community stories, stretching from the 1960s to the present. Payne argues that community stories "are not lacking in drama or human appeal" but that "the people involved were just not socially significant."[182] SNCC put them at the center.

Chapter 6 demonstrates how SNCC engaged the literary marketplace by liaising with writers at conferences and making inroads into periodicals. SNCC published widely, in *New South*, *Liberator*, *Redbook*, the *Nation*, and the *New York Times*; in coproduced and planned texts with renowned writers including Lorraine Hansberry, John O. Killens, and Sarah E. Wright; in defining texts of the Black Arts Movement (BAM), like *Black Fire* (1968); and with African American presses. This chapter pays particular attention to the key African American periodicals through which its writers told stories, with Jean Wheeler Smith's writing in *Negro Digest* representative. SNCC's writers did not expect to forge consensus, though, or to shape a literary canon in the way BAM practitioners set out to do; they rarely thought that words could be weapons in the way anti-apartheid activists would in South Africa. Nevertheless, O'Neal posed the question: "How long before we learn that art is to the struggle for understanding among the people as a weapon is to warfare?"[183] Precisely how writers in SNCC pursued ideas aesthetically in the evolving contexts of Black Power and pan-Africanism is examined in chapter 7 in relation to the BAM.

Subsequent chapters examine how writers used the novel to depict multiple organizers and projects over the organization's life and times. Chapter 8 focuses on African American veteran Mahoney's *Black Jacob* and a campaign to elect physician Jacob Blue of "Matchez," Mississippi, to serve as the state's first black congressman since 1872. The culmination of Mahoney's writing in the 1960s, it is paired with a novel written by African American Richard Hall, who described volunteering in 1965 as "on-the-job training" for writing *Long George Alley*.[184] He created a Faulknerian disquisition on two days in the Natchez project channeled through twenty-two different narrative viewpoints: tired, tense southern organizers, black and white northern volunteers, and local people who rally to SNCC or undermine its goals. Chapter 9 addresses what Pat Watters was beginning to apprehend in the 1960s: "We have avoided... truths about the southern Movement's most deeply involved workers, blaming them for the symptoms caused by the insanity they fight.... So we have been willing to accept the whole rationale of non-violence without daring to look behind it for what our knowledge of human beings will reveal."[185] In my analysis of *And All Our Wounds Forgiven*, Lester focused on difficult truths and made a case for the hidden, unsung "walking wounded" to be considered on equal memorial terms with charismatic, national leaders. The problem of burnout is at the heart of this novel. In a nonlinear and recursive sequence of character-driven, stream-of-consciousness narratives, and with third-person access to characters' thoughts, Lester explored what might otherwise be left unarticulated: the event after which nothing can be the same again, and about which it may not be possible for an organizer to speak openly but that must still somehow be represented. Published in 1994, the same year as Dittmer's *Local People*, it is an exploratory companion piece to the history Dittmer unpacked.

Chapter 1

"Troublemakers"

From College Campuses to Freedom Houses

Young writers, talented and unfettered, are bound to rise to the challenge.
—**L. D. Reddick, 1960**

To what books do you go? How do you account for Little Rock and the sit-ins? How do you account for the strength of those kids?
—**Ralph Ellison, 1961**

When you see something that is not right, not fair, not just, you have a moral obligation, a mission and a mandate, to stand up, to speak up and speak out, and get in the way, get in trouble, good trouble, necessary trouble.
—**John Lewis, 2016**

In 1969, Gareth Stedman Jones opined that while students were "formally trained to develop a creative and critical intelligence" and operate as "apprentice intellectual workers," they were expected to be "alert and intelligent within their narrowly defined discipline." Students were neither required nor expected to apply their intelligence "to the institutions where they [were] studying or to the society which produce[d] them."[1] When students transitioned into the civil rights movement, they broke this paradigm. For E. Franklin Frazier the sit-ins demonstrated how African American students were refusing to adhere to bourgeois values he analyzed in *The Black Bourgeoisie* (1957). Howard Juncker pronounced them mavericks.[2] In Lester's view, demonstrators "refused to learn the lessons of compromise and rationalization that define maturity in this society": "Like a fire leaping from one room to another until the entire house is consumed," the young "came out of their rooms and their parents did not recognize them." For McDew, sit-ins equated "student" to "activist."[3]

Students hurled themselves against racialized barriers to equality, risked future careers, amassed criminal records for their activism, and dropped out of college; some never returned to complete their degrees after devoting themselves to the freedom struggle. Observing the revolt from his "fascinating observation post" at Spelman College, Howard Zinn witnessed them questioning educational institutions, and, with hindsight in 1987, Tom Hayden explained: "You cannot underestimate how important it was that no black person in the South could vote, and no college student in America could vote."[4] When Mario Savio initiated the Free Speech Movement in the fall of 1964 after a summer in Mississippi, he framed it as "another phase of the same struggle... for the right to participate as citizens in democratic society." By the end of the 1960s, Jerry Farber argued that students were "politically disenfranchised... in an academic Lowndes County," referring to SNCC's project there. This channeling of the southern movement reduced it to metaphor, but it was the bridge from campus politics into social movements in the 1960s. In SDS's Port Huron Statement, drafted by Hayden, students were countering apathy and overcoming inner alienation, the "defining characteristics of American college life."[5] As Paul Potter told Jack Newfield when antiwar protestors descended on Washington, D.C., in 1965, "The reason there are 20,000 of us here today is that five years ago a social movement was begun by students in the South." Vincent Harding concluded, "[W]hite students who left Mississippi, Alabama, and Georgia... returned to the halls of Berkeley, Wisconsin, Harvard, and Chicago, carrying with them a new vision of the deep flaws in American higher education and in the Vietnam War."[6] All too quickly, students gained empirical understanding of how segregation was enforced through economics, discovering how the white South's power structures sustained corrupt racialization of crime through the courts.[7] The students operated at strategic levels for national and transnational concerns. Courtland Cox represented SNCC in planning the March on Washington and sat on the Bertrand Russell commission's evaluation of the Vietnam War. Cobb and Lester traveled to Vietnam with the same commission. Charles McLaurin's political apprenticeship was meetings with national strategists Joe Rauh and Walter Reuther during the MFDP challenge to the Democratic National Convention in 1964. Martha Prescod canvassed the Democratic Party for support of the MFDP. "There weren't any instructions... we had never done anything like this," she recalled, "Yet it made sense to us and we *did* it." When the MFDP refused the compromise of "two seats at large," McLaurin understood that "the movement was bigger than just getting some recognition.... I couldn't have gotten this lesson in school." In 1966, Jean Wiley worked with the United Nations to ensure that SNCC was granted NGO consultative status. Jack Chatfield, who enjoyed a long post-SNCC career as a history professor, cited voter registration as the catalyst for becoming "a true student of American history."[8]

Students debated federal support of civil rights and the efficacy of nonviolence, but, once in the field, the contrast with college was sharp, "For a young person going through the intense learning experience of a direct clash with the entrenched social structure, to sit in a classroom seems pallid and unrewarding," Howard Zinn wrote. Zinn judged that among political life lessons learned in SNCC were "public speaking from appearances at church rallies" and how to write "grammatical and pungent leaflets."[9] His emphasis on group-centered organizing did not address lonely, dangerous work undertaken by individuals, and sources explicating the reasons northern students joined the movement rarely focus on what being "on the ground" would entail, as typified in a graduate student's volunteer statement: "I want to understand from the inside, the dynamic of social action; after too many years in school, I want to participate in the society I have studied for ideals which are important to me." In her study of northern volunteers in 1964 and 1965, Mary Aickin Rothschild concluded, "Students from every field from sociology to philosophy uttered similar statements about their disciplines."[10] African American students in the South, though, were foundational for the inspiration that volunteers identified, wherever they lived before joining the struggle. In the second issue of the *Student Voice*, SNCC published a letter from African American historian L. D. Reddick that expressed his confidence in them as "troublemakers." He hoped they would write their story: "I shall expect it to be authentic, comprehensive, revealing, penetrating—and with a certain something of the college atmosphere. Perhaps not all this at once, now, in the beginning. But with a subject so worthy, young writers, talented and unfettered, are bound to rise to the challenge."[11] Reddick drew on the discourse of creative disruption—described in an aphorism by SNCC's imaginary Junebug Jabbo Jones: "People in trouble is the ones to make trouble."[12]

The college atmosphere Reddick expected to see evoked was expressly political. As Kenneth Rexroth observed as early as 1960, it equated to "the revolt of youth": "A head of steam was building up, the waters were rising behind the dam; the dam itself, the block to action, was the patent exhaustion of old forms. What was accumulating was not any kind of programmatic 'radicalization,' it was a moral demand."[13] In 1963, independent journalist I. F. Stone lent his voice to the burgeoning social commentary on youth-led activism: "There is nothing wrong with our younger generation when it can produce a movement like SNCC. Not since the great prerevolutionary generation in Russia, its assorted Narodniks, SRs, Marxists and Tolstoyans, has any great power produced as devoted a group of youngsters as the four hundred or so Negro and white young men and women of the Students [sic] Nonviolent Coordinating Committee."[14] Stone created space for SNCC in his publication, commissioning features by field-workers. John Perdew's disquisition on the difficulty of convincing a nervous black middle class to support sharecroppers, for example, was submitted from jail in Americus, Georgia. When he left Harvard, he believed the experience would prove "adventurous and different," but, charged with "sedition," Perdew was all too aware of how entrenched massive resistance was in the Deep South and how dangerous. In a note accompanying the article, Stone advocated "the widest possible public support... for these heroic young."[15] Zinn asserted, "For the first time in our history a major social movement, shaking the nation to its bones, is being led by youngsters," and Lillian Smith, having characterized racial segregation as "a strong wall behind which weak egos have hidden for a long time," claimed that students had created "an opening in a wall where there was no door."[16]

This politicized impulse to rebel could not be reduced to juvenile delinquency or a restless disdain for "phoniness" in the way it had been construed and contained in the 1950s; it was life-threatening work. When John Doar, "the face of the Justice Department in the South," answered Charlie Jones's call for support in McComb, they hid in a butcher's shop with blinds drawn while Jones detailed the mass arrests of local and SNCC activists. It was, he told Taylor Branch in 1980, "a significant moment in his political and racial education to realize that the [federal government's] boldest representative was almost as apprehensive about Klan surveillance as he was."[17] In 1961, Ralph Ellison wondered, "Now, when you try to trace American values as they find expression in the Negro community, where do you begin? To what books do you go? How do you account for Little Rock and the sit-ins? How do you account for the strength of those kids? You can find sociological descriptions of the conditions under which they live but few indications of their morale." Much later, Richard H. King posed similar questions: "[W]hat did it mean to become involved in the civil rights movement and to become political? And what was the new sense of self generated by participation in the movement?"[18] Charlie Cobb is typically searching about what is held back when admitting that *On the Road to Freedom* is "a story as I might tell it to you in face-to-face conversation—not the whole story or even most of the story."[19] In first-person writing, even protesting students could be reluctant; in an open letter Joan Browning described anonymity as "a protective cloak... shed reluctantly so that future activists might know more about the freedom struggle."[20] From the beginning of their writing lives, SNCC's writers experimented with forms that afforded more freedom.

Students contributed to a shift in the conventions of the college novel from the upper-middlebrow formula borne of academic frustration that emphasized faculty and administrators. In Leslie Fiedler's arch summary, in the 1940s and 1950s students figured only as erotic narrative relief from academic tussles, when seduced by faculty.[21] Whether in vicious satires or discursive contemplations of university life, faculty dominated. Elaine Showalter concludes that political protest was absent from the genre because "the novel is always a belated form of social commentary," but publishers often elected not to publish what was uncomfortably close to headlines.[22] Between 1957 and 1959, James Forman composed a campus novel that unpacked the political mood as a stepping-stone into the movement. He did not secure a publisher, nor did he pursue one after joining in SNCC, but the manuscript opens a window on the campus atmosphere. The same energy inspired Michael Thelwell's short story "Direct Action" (1962), set in "the summer when this sit-in thing broke out all over ... and everyone was going out to picket Woolworths every weekend."[23] Thelwell's troublemakers perform an anarchic sit-in as a loud example of "student exhibitionism," and other students take up their challenge to integrate public accommodations.[24] This story is another window on the moment because, as Francesca Polletta discovered, in many university publications "there was no mention of student demonstrations in 1960 or 1961" because coverage was prohibited by the administration, even in student newspapers.[25] In fiction, Thelwell illustrated the feeling Joseph McNeill claimed lay behind the Woolworths sit-in in Greensboro, North Carolina, that it would be "a badge of honor."[26]

If sit-ins fired the imaginations of students, so did SNCC. Its image was romantic, heroic, and seductive, especially for white students at a distance from the racial crucible in which black students negotiated college life in the South. Lerone Bennett compared SNCC's "mystique of total commitment" to a secular order: "leaders with contempt for leadership, organizers who despise imposed organization, heroes with contempt for heroism." Peter De Lissovoy drilled down into the mystique whereby organizers were rhapsodized, even fetishized as "coffee-soaked, smoke-stained, stretched like a guitar string and hopeful like a song." After dropping out of Harvard to join the Albany project, he told students how slow civil rights work could be and that organizers were skeptical of "cocky" and "naïve" college types with a yen to go to jail but "set to turn cynical" and retreat to the safety of academe.[27] The class privilege and racial privilege he exposed is submerged in most historical studies, although Dittmer raises its significance in *Local People*.[28] In *Feelgood: A Trip in Time and Out* (1970), De

Lissovoy took the college novel in a new direction, moving his protagonist into grassroots organizing and out the other side into the counterculture. His unnamed "everyman" embarks on a sixties trip stirred by dramatic derring-do but fizzles out and drifts, more enervated than energized, into a hedonistic search for selfhood. Kathleen Collins explored the seductiveness of the mystique in the 1960s, after volunteering with SNCC, although her stories were unpublished until 2016.

A Campus Novel in the Making

In 1940, Philip Rahv bemoaned that the intellectual was missing from the American novel. He failed to account for the radical writing of the Depression and the Progressive Era but made an intriguing statement for university-set fictions when he noted that while professors, artists, and scientists were featured, rarely did characters "transform ideas into actual dramatic motives."[29] Forman's novel was an extension of his political journalism, composed between covering the aftermath of the Little Rock school crisis for the *Chicago Defender* and the beginning of his career in SNCC. At Roosevelt, he read widely in philosophy, politics, and "the American color complex" (a phrase he uses throughout "Thin White Line").[30] He told Robert Penn Warren, "I worked more on a novel than [on] any other assignment, trying to learn to write for the forthcoming revolution and to get myself together mentally. From September, 1958 to June, 1959, I continued writing and finishing this novel about the life of a black college student raised in the South who returns to wage a mass struggle against segregation and discrimination and the system which produces these two monsters. It was evidently an extension of my innermost wishes."[31] In *The Making of Black Revolutionaries*, Forman linked his decision to join SNCC to his writerly ambition: "I knew I was definitely going South in the near future to build a revolutionary youth organization and to write about the struggle of black people as I participated in it."[32] After Warren published their conversation in *Who Speaks for the Negro?* (1965), Arthur C. Fields, fiction editor at Crown Publishers, wrote care of SNCC's Atlanta office, "I understand that once early in your career you tried your hand at a novel. Apparently, I gather, you met with the fate of many writers—a negative response—and withdrew it from circulation." He requested the manuscript and cited his editorial expertise as publisher of Langston Hughes's *An African Treasury: A Pictorial History of the Negro in America* (1956), a text used in SNCC's Freedom Schools, and South African Richard Rive's *Quartet* (1963). Like Forman in Korea, Fields was a war veteran, and he too was a novelist. In *World without Heroes* (1950), he mounted a scathing critique of World War II via a semiautobiographical protagonist who believes at first that he will find in the war "real drama, throbbing with intensity, waiting for expression" but experiences senseless violence and "rubbled hopes."[33] Fields believed that Forman could intervene in the battle for civil rights: "I have a special interest in this whole area and in you particularly."[34] There is no evidence that Forman shared his manuscript with Fields. Had he done so, he might have received editorial advice that could have resulted in publication in the moment in which it intervened.

Forman had tried to embark on a career as a writer of fiction. "I devote most of my time to writing," he told potential publishers in a litany of correspondence that stopped in 1959. Publishers did give him constructive criticism.[35] When declining the Forman story "Steal Away," for example, Merrill Pollack of the *Saturday Evening Post* commended "a stark and effective piece of writing" but made the incisive comment that, "in terms of short story construction, [it is] really more of a lengthy incident than a fully developed plot."[36] Sociologist St. Clair Drake, his tutor at Roosevelt and mentor thereafter, advised that Forman break with "sociological jargon." With Lorraine Hansberry, with whom he went to high school, he discussed literature but did not seek advice about his own work.[37] By the time Fields contacted him in 1965, Forman was immersed in SNCC and considered "Thin White Line" already dated: "History was enacting what I had advocated in the novel.... It was all down there on paper, the suffering, the hope, the plan. It was only left for me to write the ending with my own life in the South."[38]

Set over 1952–56, "Thin White Line" is peopled with characters from Forman's campus context for whom race, politics, and literature are "vital to existence": "Arabs, Jews, Greeks, Lithuanians, Africans, West Indians, Negro Americans, and Caucasian Americans. Some were sitting in segregated groups talking about desegregation, the Arab-Israeli fight, the Cypress Affair. Others were sitting in integrated groups talking about the lack of integration in American foreign policy."[39] Despite telling Warren that he had created a single protagonist in "Thin White Line," only in the shortest, incomplete version did he create an unequivocally autobiographical character, using a bricolage of racist incidents and encounters recalled over a drive from Chicago to Mississippi to visit his dying grandmother.[40] In the most complete manuscript he balances two focal characters: Ted Lynch and Paul Brown, both veterans of the war in Korea. Paul grows up in segregated Texas and is elected president of Roosevelt's student government, as Forman was between 1954 and 1956 (he would receive an alumnus award in 1963 for his work in SNCC).⁴¹ Ted grows up in Chicago, spending childhood summers in the South as Forman did. Paul even smokes a pipe like Forman. Forman conceived of them as doubles as well as surrogates: "the Ego-Alter-Ego Twins" (183). Paul plans to teach, as Forman did in Chicago, but believes he is prepared to die for "the Black Cause" (210).⁴² Overall, Forman values debate over characterization and structure. Students argue over how, as "Negro intellectuals," they might initiate a more militant organization than the NAACP or Urban League and whether it could be located in the American political tradition and democratic compact, modeling activism on their reading. Despite the political machinations of Mayor Daley's Chicago—and Forman maps the city with topographical precision—the issues that incense students force their attention south, presaging Forman's own activist trajectory. As student delegate to the Democratic National Convention held in Chicago in August 1956, Forman had listened as the son of segregationist Alabama governor John Patterson declared, "If we allow the Negras to crack our power in any way that is an invitation to further weaken it"; Forman observed, "I was learning."⁴³ His characters in "Thin White Line" are affected by the murder of Emmett Till in 1955, a catalyzing memory for many activists, and condemn the "Bilbo-Eastland-Talmadge crew" of segregationist southern politicians who epitomize the political iceberg that SNCC would seek to smash (194). In the unpublished novel, Roosevelt students agree that social justice must be realized first in the South, conceiving a three-step program: "the right to vote for Southern Negroes, a chance for Northern Negroes to move out of the black belt, a right to work for all Negroes," and a "unity of common interest" to combat "racism U.S.A" (155–56). A majority believe in forging common cause across racial and gender differences. Paul lodges with a coeducational, interracial group of eighteen students in a "Co-Operative House" that is a prototypical Freedom House, the nucleus of SNCC's internal culture and radical mission to make cross-racial cooperation visible: "By all standards of conventional dress and thought, these Negro and white students...breaking bread together were extremely unconventional" (165).⁴⁴

The politicized group Forman depicted at the end of the 1950s chimes with experience of others in SNCC. Casey Hayden joined the interracial Christian Faith and Life Community at the University of Texas; Bill Hansen cofounded the Interracial Council at Xavier University in Cincinnati. Awarded a Woodrow Wilson Scholarship at the University of Michigan, in Ann Arbor, Jean Wiley discovered an interracial "hotbed of activity" that propelled her south.⁴⁵ Forman explored how interracial cooperation evolved in three settings: the Co-Operative House, the student council, and the Cosmopolitan, a nightclub where "town and gown" mingle, prefiguring the dangerous activist "islands" on which SNCC constituted its projects in southern places. The concomitant challenge inside a Freedom House was, as Moses observed, whether SNCC could "integrate itself" and sustain "an island of integration in a sea of separation."[46] This imagistic component of SNCC's discourse may be traced back now through Forman's depiction of segregated housing holding out against racial change in Chicago's Hyde Park, "an oasis of segregation amidst an island of integration" (372).

"Thin White Line" is discursive in ways that resonate with SNCC's discourse, but characters function as talking heads. When Paul joins the movement, Peter and Ted argue over whether Ted as black or Peter as white would have more effect as demonstrators were they to follow him. Attempting to write fiction, with themselves and friends as material, they discuss its efficacy. Ted asserts, "One does not have to go to history to understand the plight of peasants in Russia" but cites *Anna Karenina* when challenged that "the printed word cannot convey, by any means, the intensity of a situation, the uneasiness in the guts, or the exact mental reaction" (114).

Forman kept faith with the idea that literature could get close to this intensity. It is threaded as a metacommentary throughout "Thin White Line" and influenced his approach in *The Making of Black Revolutionaries*, wherein putative distinctions between memoir, literature, subjective history, and verifiable facts are made superfluous in a hybrid text designed to refute them. A student suggests that Peter and Ted read Lillian Smith, as Forman did, because she exemplifies how characters gain "depth" when "grounded in reality," but Peter subscribes to "building a character to fit the idea," a conceptual weakness in "Thin White Line," where characters chide each other for perceived lack of political commitment. One suggests dropping a hydrogen bomb on the South to kill all whites after removing all blacks; a faculty member (a rare voice) believes "the white South" needs to be psychoanalyzed; other students are intensely hostile toward discussing or intellectualizing "race" at all (121, 134, 141). Ted dominates by asserting that "the acid test" is an individual's "stance on civil rights," expressing frustration that "we're always talking about race from an academic perspective" when told that "the exercise of the mind" is "value enough" (192, 395, 80, 198). With hindsight, these discussions foreshadow Kathleen Collins's "Whatever Happened to Interracial Love?" At the time, they were prescient of struggles about to take place in the New Left on campuses around the country, encapsulated by Mario Savio saying that "students are permitted to talk all they want as long as their speech has no consequence."[47] Occasionally, articulation of commitment has concrete results: a speech Paul makes carries the motion to raise funds for the Montgomery Bus Boycott despite an "element in the Student Government which believed student interest should not extend beyond the School corridors" (383). Students rally to Autherine Lucy when she speaks at Roosevelt—as she did while visiting Chicago on March 16, 1956, when Forman interviewed her—but the visit passes in a single paragraph. For the most part, characters make speeches that are finally too insubstantial to carry the weight of Forman's many ideas.

More interesting is how Forman self-consciously tested the role of storytelling in racial struggle. When a Chicago woman shares the story of her ancestor with a white student who is conducting a study of "the psychology of a Negro family" for her master's in sociology, the student's hypothesis is trite, and the story of Louisa is "stronger" and more affecting than the history she is studying.[48] Savannah-born, New Orleans–bred Fran Walker is painting a portrait of a dark-skinned girl evocative of her "militant" black consciousness, titled "In Our Time." Light enough to pass as white and disdainful of those who do, Fran is scornful of "moderation" in civil rights and of "policy drift" (272–73, 277–78). She lives the standpoint she explores in art by confronting racism at every turn, hitting a woman on a bus who declares that whites in the Trumbull Park neighborhood in Chicago "need to lynch those Negroes" who are "disturbing the peace" by buying homes there (279). Only Ted and Fran move "beyond the stage of student politics" to teach and demonstrate in the civil rights South, and she demands that they protect themselves with guns (302, 273, 347). Fran is important because Forman made his most militant character a woman. Never satisfied with how he ended the novel, though, Forman thought about Fran for forty years, finally adding "an addendum" where her father dreams that the KKK kills her.[49] In the versions he retained, the most telling line recurs: Ted assuring aspirant novelist Paul, "You will find all the dramatic material in the movement you need to become a good writer. And we need you here" (429). The implications of this line resonate with Forman's belief that SNCC needed "Richard Wrights" as well as "Thomas Paines," and the line reverberates in the writing of others, as in Doug Youngblood's desperate apostrophe to students on a Chicago campus in 1967 when the activist persona silently screams "mental messages":

> lay down your books and abandon this
> campus
> leave this factory that teaches obedience
> ...
> we need you now, not tomorrow...
> when we have won we can come back for the
> education we all desire.[50]

Forman published other books to acclaim but invested time reworking this manuscript, slicing it into sections, creating new scenes, and adjusting its structure. He parsed it as "novelette" and novel, separate short stories, and even a play, but he did not take the advice of his character that the movement would inspire stronger fiction.[51] He did not update the material gathered at Roosevelt and held fast to what he saw as the prestige of the novel as a form while finding it difficult to interpret editorial advice. It is like a house under construction for too long, with the builder moving from room to room, continually remodeling so that the house is never completed. It teems with ideas. If the heft and substance of its social critique is not sustained, it is because Forman shut the door too quickly on some ideas while leaving others piled up untidily, couching as dialogue what would be better plotted as story. The novel conveys the "freedom mood" on campuses and is prototypical movement fiction, but its aesthetic execution fell short of Forman's hopes.[52] To piece together its many ideas is to trace the thinking of an important activist whose dream it was to be a novelist but who instead molded "SNCC's near-anarchic personality" into "a functioning, if still chaotic organizational structure."[53] In my view, writing this novel was Forman's stepping-stone into the movement, in the way cultural sociologist Arjun Appadurai argues that "the imagination [can be] a staging ground for action." It consolidated his belief that to "describe the realities of black life ... would be a form of action" and explains why he actively advocated that organizers write and publish.[54] As Forman's papers reveal, he engaged compulsively in considering the role narrative could play in activism, and SNCC's literary history begins with this novel.

Thelwell's "Direct Action": Taking Action off Campus

As Forman despaired of his college novel, Thelwell was discovering a talent for short stories. James Baldwin described them as having "the intense precision of the listening ear."[55] The writing is confident, looser than Forman's but honed. In "Direct Action," narrator Mike is nonchalant: "The cats in our pad were kind of integrated, but we never thought of it that way. We really dug each other, so we hung around together." Mike and brother Dick are African American, Art is Jewish, Lee Italian American, and Doug of "sturdy Anglo-Saxon Protestant stock" and "the only cat who had adjustment problems" (216). Serious students all, they combine good grades with strenuous effort to appear cool, independent of mind and action, and they are seasoned pranksters. When Dick brings home an art professor to assess the homage to Jackson Pollock he has painted on the living room walls, he pleads for the white instructor to acknowledge "the faintest glimmer of merit" before "sobbing hysterically" (215). Loath to wound a black student's feelings, the professor departs—and has barely closed the door before laughter overtakes him. The housemates' pet hate is "crusading liberal types," particularly a white student organizing pickets of Woolworths in their midwestern college town, a student they call "The Crusader."

Thelwell drew on a host of actual protests. As Frances Beal summarized, "[T]here was this sense that Woolworth's was a national corporation, and that they had something to say about local policies... we were trying to show our solidarity with our brothers and sisters in the South."[56] The Southern Regional Council recorded 70,000 sit-in participants across twenty southern and border states—including Missouri, where the sit-in in "Direct Action" takes place—and at least 141 students and 58 faculty expelled and dismissed.[57] Trawling news media in 1968, though, a writer for SDS's journal *Radical America* identified the narrative gap Thelwell exploited by electing to set his story outside the South: "I have not come across anything except scattered allusions... to the impact the sit-ins had on northern campuses. Yet it appears that more than a hundred northern colleges had some kind of demonstration in support of the sit-ins. It seems safe to say that for most campuses, these were the first political demonstrations in years."[58] The Crusader's tight-lipped disapproval of a lack of engagement is misjudged: Mike's household is uninterested in picketing because at integrated stores protests are symbolic: "We'll go across the state line and in two weeks we'll integrate some institution! That'll show you what direct action means" (220). Such feelings were common and initiated Cobb's journey to Mississippi. In New York, he confided in "The Story of Charlie Cobb" (1963), "I felt *moved* by the sit-ins but I also felt *removed* because I was so many miles away." He picketed with CORE at Columbia University and while studying at Howard was arrested in Washington, D.C., but "school and sitting-in didn't go together."[59] Inspired by a frustrated comment Doug makes that sit-ins should disrupt human as well as social functions, Lee suggests desegregating department store restrooms in fictional Deershead, Missouri. Twenty students sit in the toilet stalls of "white" facilities after sprinkling laxative in old-fashioned "white" water coolers. As white men stand in line, Mike peeps through a crack in his cubicle to see one man "doubled up, holding his middle and grimacing." With mock concern, Lee advises another, whose red and sweaty face discloses his effort to contain himself:

> "Why don't you just go down to the other restroom?"
> "What?" someone shouted, "You mean the nigger john?"
> Then Lee said ever so sweetly, "Oh well... there's always the floor." And he started laughing softly. (222)

Students ridicule the exclusionary privilege of defecating in an area of white designation, forcing whites to use "the nigger john." A photographer for the campus newspaper takes their pictures as they exit. This story's pantomimic theatricality harmonizes with the same sort of antic humor of Supersnick, the character imagined by the first cadre of SNCC organizers (examined in the next chapter). The humor translates here as a short, sharp reckoning for whites sampling indignities that blacks constantly endured. Elizabeth Abel, one of few cultural historians to consider public bathrooms, elucidates how the "imaginary [white] purity they maintain by managing human waste behind closed doors" functions only if restrooms are "marked but kept unremarked" because "calling attention to them brings the processes they regulate into public view."[60] In "Direct Action," students create uproar by making this process not only visible but also painfully physical.

Thelwell drew on a social imaginary according to which restrooms were the last bastion of segregation in public accommodations. When Diane Nash first encountered segregated restrooms, "the experience was so transcending, her anger so immediate and so complete that she was effectively politicized from that moment." An incident in Nashville indicates how restrooms located close to lunch counters generated attempts to desegregate both. Nash wrote: "Two Negro students who had sat-in at the lunch counter, went into the ladies restroom which was marked 'white' and were there as a heavy-set, older white lady, who might have been seeking refuge from the scene taking place at the lunch counter, entered. Upon opening the door and finding the two Negro girls inside, the woman threw up her hands and, nearly in tears, exclaimed, 'Oh! Nigras everywhere!'"[61] Shocked that a store's most private places could be integrated, her "possessive investment in whiteness" was punctured.[62] Thelwell riffed on this knowledge, as when the segregationist *Jackson Daily News* warned that the "real goal" was for black men to stand "hip-to-hip" with whites in public restrooms. Dick Gregory joked repeatedly that white southerners were unable to function outside the architecture of segregation, his punch line: "When the white man is threatened with losing his toilet, he's ready to kill." In his 1964 autobiography *Nigger* ("if ever you hear the word 'Nigger' again, they are advertising my book"), Gregory celebrated "the beauty of those college kids from SNCC" making clear that the only difference between races was "a segregated toilet." Of segregationists he added, "No wonder so many of them have shithouse ways."[63]

In the *Student Voice*, Jim Laue identified "a wonderful byproduct of the movement," humor maintained during direct action protests: "The waitress told a pair of sit-inners, 'I'm sorry, but we don't serve Negroes here.' 'Oh, we don't eat them either,' came the reply. 'I just want a cup of coffee.' Or how about the flustered counter clerk who, when approached by an integrated group in Miami, blurted out, 'I'm sorry we don't serve, er... ah... people here.'"[64] Gregory reworked the first: "That's all right, I don't eat colored people. Bring me a whole fried chicken."[65] The second case exposes the deleterious fiction that white supremacists struggled to maintain to deny fundamental human equality to black citizens. Thelwell did not have to stretch to find the kernel of this story, and neither did readers to see its relevance to long-standing struggles for basic amenities and courtesy. The lack of respect accorded African American women was particularly galling. Cleveland Sellers confided, "I yearned to live in a world where I would never again be confronted with restroom signs saying WHITE LADIES TO THE RIGHT AND COLORED WOMEN TO THE REAR."[66] Joan Trumpauer called attention to the problem in March 1962, when she was arrested in Baton Rouge courthouse for using the "colored" restroom instead of "white" and was issued a $500 bond. In 1963, SNCC's lawyers used the government's amicus brief to argue that the trial of demonstrators in Danville, Virginia, should move to a federal court because segregated toilets in the state courtroom were an unequivocal manifestation of subscription to segregation.[67]

Thelwell's story may be read in the wider context of other altercations over segregated facilities. The only guaranteed pit stop in Mississippi for African Americans driving from Memphis to Jackson was veteran organizer Amzie Moore's gas station in Cleveland. Moore, Dr. T. R. M. Howard, Aaron Henry, and the Regional Council of Negro Leadership launched a boycott in 1953 with the slogan "We Don't Buy Gas Where We Can't Use the Washroom." Black motorists were not guaranteed service thereafter, hence the continued need for the frequently revised guide for African

American travelers, *The Negro Motorist Green Book*, commonly known as *The Green Book*, which had been published since 1936 and would continue to come out in new editions until the late 1960s.[68] Refused access to the "white" restroom at a gas station in Natchez, SNCC's Bill Ware demanded that the attendant stop fueling his tank. He was arrested and "blasted by a policeman across the mouth with a night stick, resulting in shattered front teeth, one of which was crushed to pieces." He required thirty stitches to suture his lips.[69] Bill Hansen recorded being chased out of a gas station in Brownsville, Tennessee, because he "goofed up their segregated lavatory system."[70] If "Direct Action" seems outlandish, the vehemence with which restrooms were policed and defended is evident in Ware's experience and offensively apparent in a photograph of a sign at a gas station in Sandy Run, South Carolina: "No Nigger or Negro Allowed Inside This Building; No Negro or Ape Allowed in Building."[71] Through its connections with Pan African Students Organization in the Americas, SNCC was aware of Ghanaian student Stephen E. Koli being kidnapped at gunpoint and beaten in Tuscaloosa after taking a photograph of signs on restrooms.[72] In 1965, a "Toilet Revolution" took place during a demonstration at Montgomery's State Capitol. If protestors needed a restroom, police prevented them from returning, so they were forced to relieve themselves while huddled between picket signs. The sight of urine in the street caused friction between SNCC and SCLC as well as demonstrating physical difficulties for demonstrators denied access to facilities—black-owned in this case.[73] After the Civil Rights Act supposedly made segregated facilities illegal, Sammy Younge Jr. was murdered in Tuskegee by filling station attendant Marvin Segrest, on approach to a bathroom designated "whites only."

"Direct Action" was hailed as demonstrating "an effort to take on society" when Thelwell was selected as a finalist by *Story* magazine out of more than five hundred entries from 150 colleges in forty-three states.[74] He submitted a mordant, demotic tale in which a sit-in is sharply comedic, deglamorizing the mystique Septima Clark worried was changing the SCLC's agenda and sustaining a droll, sardonic tone that entertained *Story* judges.[75] Langston Hughes selected it for *The Best Short Stories by Black Writers, 1899–1967*.[76] Why, then, has it received no critical attention? Literary critics may avoid fictions that seem to demolish the sanctity of the civil rights movement, but sit-in narratives "transformed a too-common story of humiliation into one of triumph," as Polletta asserts. They convey how "the adventure" could be funny and exciting rather than always and only frightening. Editors of one college newspaper wrote, "Here were two harmless young people sauntering through a store... stalking them in true dragnetness were no less than half a dozen police officers, while customers and managers hovered in corners as if the invasion from Mars had come!" In Polletta's sociological context, participants' stories capture "the action-compelling character" of sit-ins "better than... the concept of frames by virtue of narrative's combination of familiarity and undecidability, convention and novelty, and truth (representing reality) and fiction (constituting reality)."[77] In my reading, by making white supremacist ideology visible and risible, Thelwell's satire echoes the approach Harry Golden, intermittent advisor to SNCC, pursued over a long career. His "Golden Plans" included an "Out-of-Order Plan" for retail stores, as described in his newspaper the *Carolina Israelite*. In an equally anarchic "Vertical Plan," whereby black and white would stand together—students at desks in integrated schools, patrons at lunch counters side by side—Golden observed wryly, "It is only when the Negro 'sets' that the fur begins to fly."[78] In "Direct Action," Lee pilfers signs, "especially proud of the POSITIVELY NO STANDING sign he had in the john" (213). Satire in this context is grounded in specifics: Danville city fathers removed desks and chairs from the library, and Clarksdale, Mississippi, followed suit to ensure that sit-ins could not occur.[79] Thelwell provided ironic commentary on the social absurdity that necessitated direct action, but it is rare for cultural critics to examine the fiction of white racial purity shored up by segregated toilet facilities. Even in *The Jim Crow Routine* (2015), Stephen Berrey's study of the "everyday performances of race," restrooms are alluded to just once, even though they equated to quotidian indignities enforced by custom.[80]

Like many SNCC writers, Thelwell exposed a backstory. "Direct Action" leads readers to a place they do not expect to go, as Terry Cannon advocated activist writing should. The story closes on more students instituting new pickets with the slogan "Let Us Sit Down Together" and Mike and friends declining an offer from the local branch of the NAACP to erect a statue of them "sitting on the john" (223–24). It is a sly sideswipe at the conspicuous respectability of the model of nonviolent demonstration on which this audacious story also turns—and an echo of Howard Zinn's comment that student activists were "finishing school pickets."[81]

The SNCC "Mystique" and a Movement "Trip"

If Thelwell began "Direct Action" by setting up an autobiographical framework—"We were all sitting around the front room the night it started" (213)—De Lissovoy shaped a popular novel out of the period he spent in

Albany from 1963 through 1965, renaming the city "Meansville." Houghton Mifflin marketed *Feelgood* as "part of a new mythology... laying its roots among us," echoing Leslie Fiedler's assertion that a "mythologically representative minority" was coming to "stand for the times." Always controversial, Fiedler believed that fiction and verse joining the civil rights movement with Beat drug culture eschewed "the general piety of the press which has been unwilling to compromise 'good works' on behalf of the Negro by associating them with deep radicalism of a way of life based on the ritual consumption of 'pot.'"[82] *Feelgood*'s psychedelic cover was influenced by Milton Glaser's countercultural designs for LPs, and a Pocket Books edition in 1971 ensured a longer reading life. It would be easy to situate *Feelgood* among of the era's many freewheeling texts where "the sixties" figures as a Dionysian lack of restriction: "authority less respected, violence less tolerated, love less fettered, wealth less worshipped, power less coveted, guilt less shouldered."[83] Surprisingly, *Feelgood* has not received attention in this context, but in my reading it is a brave and anarchic example of a SNCC story with a troublemaking student at its center.

De Lissovoy has been telling stories about SNCC in print and publication since the 1960s, ranging from caustic imaginative exploration in *Feelgood* to nostalgic autobiographical reflection in *The Great Pool Jump and Other Stories from the Civil Rights Movement in Southwest Georgia* (2010). *Feelgood* was reviewed as an autobiography of "a freedom rider, confidence man and lover" but departs from the experience of its author who left Harvard with John Perdew and Claude Weaver to join SNCC.[84] De Lissovoy filters into the story arrests he described for the *Nation* but spins away, winking disingenuously, "I offer only my own story," and he notes that "the historian is also the diligent spinner of a tale."[85] In a metafictional twist, the protagonist makes notes toward a novel he hopes will be myth busting. De Lissovoy wrote to undercut stereotypes of worthy volunteer saints, as if only Abbie Hoffman, registering voters in 1964 and 1965, could make drugs a cause by pursuing a countercultural lifestyle in the "Pot Left."[86] He extrapolated to depict a "tenacious if sometimes comical minority" of white volunteers, the likes of whom Zinn admitted were "close to caricature [and] came and went." Zinn considered De Lissovoy their most "devastating" critic.[87] De Lissovoy provided a writing platform for dedicated organizers in Albany in *The Great Pool Jump* but here in *Feelgood* spotlighted one of "the drifters, the life-collectors," that he identified in his journalism among "varieties of white" who "checked out the rough black bars, picked up chicks, and... slipped off into an old Southern tradition."[88] For his hippie character seeking to push beyond social norms, the movement is "just" a way to "veer off at a new angle."[89] *Feelgood* is, then, an idiosyncratic take on youth culture, framed by a brook symbolizing the antihero's desire to tune in to a "mellow" existence in the middle of a war zone (3, 308). Like Heraclitus's river, when the antihero returns to the brook at the narrative's close, he is now different than before, less able to conceive of himself as a bystander in his own life because De Lissovoy has injected an older, evaluative voice into the narration: "I was so young and such a kid!" (267).

Feelgood begins at Harvard, but exactly what the protagonist is studying is unclear; as in Forman's and Thelwell's texts, the classroom is not as important as the campus mood. It does not proceed as a critique of the Ivy League but, instead, of the meaningless ennui he feels on finding himself there as merely "the next and easiest thing to do" (3). It explores a state of mind that equates school with drugs and that equates coming to political consciousness with drifting away from institutions. Disaffection, anomie, and anticonformism, reflected in different ways across postwar literature, are here explored in the movement context. The single subject that "turns on" this white student is the African American freedom struggle, in which, he imagines, he may discover something that matters more than academe, where argument is "the style of life" and "civil rights" merely a battle of words between the socialists (for whom he writes leaflets) and the Hasty Pudding member who taunts, "Hey, angryyoungman, where's the revolution?" (4–5). Harvard is just a repository where "all the books and stories, including mine someday," will be deposited—after being shaped somewhere else (21). In his desire to be part of "a fine struggle," De Lissovoy's protagonist is closer to Forman's characters than appears on first reading, but while in "Thin White Line" multiple viewpoints are weighed and measured, De Lissovoy follows a single motivation for a would-be-activist with "feet of clay," a motivation that is "not pure, only real" (14, 6). He is fascinated by a subculture of "troublemakers": "[T]ales told by the fieldworkers of pursuit by southern sheriffs, escape, jail, deeply stirred my imagination" (21). He marches for "an embattled people" and experiences an adrenaline rush, as if mescaline and morning glory seeds at Harvard have been supplanted by a more righteous high (20–21). Demonstrations, though, are a "pious gesture" and his declaration "I would starve myself to punish a sheriff" (357) expressive of what sociologist Daniel Bell suggested was "the modern hubris" of believing oneself to be autonomous.[90] He disparages other volunteers, like Sara (in one contemptuous profile), who "decided to forgo the pleasures of surf and sun in order to devote her summer to fighting [for] racial justice in the turbulent south" (80).[91] As

De Lissovoy was in 1963, his protagonist in *Feelgood* is assigned to CME, a neighborhood named for its church but known locally as "Crime, Murder, and the Electric chair."[92] There he encounters Knight Collins, former "warlord" of a disbanded "gang," with whom he feels triumphantly anarchic: "John Brown! You meant nothing to me back in school when I had to read about your body, man! But tonight I meet you in the air!" (134). He dashes through Albany's streets committing vandalism: "If I felt any danger, I know it only as excitement." Arson is "a fine moment" as he lobs a lighted match into gasoline at a bottling plant refusing to employ African Americans except in menial roles (42). He admires Knight's gang for kidnapping a brutal police officer, chaining him to a tree, and force-feeding him dog food (43).

Knight Collins is an avatar for James Daniel, highly exaggerated in *Feelgood* but also appearing in De Lissovoy's journalistic bulletins from the front lines cloaked by the same pseudonym. Daniel joined SNCC after integrating the Tift Park swimming pool with Randy Battle and was "applauded to the speaker's stand" at a subsequent mass meeting, as De Lissovoy reported in the *Harvard Crimson*:

> "Well, we had a fine little swim all right. Even got me a tan.... Only we had to jump the fence, and I want to see the day we can all go through the gate."
>
> ... A few days later, when we demonstrated against segregation in public accommodations, he [Daniel] went to jail with us.[93]

De Lissovoy's journalism is replete with stories of people the mass media ignored. Fifty years later he reflected: "Transcending moral spheres as [James Daniel] did, he was as mystifying to the local white law as he must be little countenanced by official Movement historians today if they ever heard of him. James Daniel is one for whom I would like to find a home in the history of the Movement. It took all kinds to make a Movement."[94] "Suitcase" was another African American who registered to vote in Albany. Writing in the *Nation*, De Lissovoy conveyed what he saw in this man: "a very fine feeling, a hard and deep pleasure, to stand in line at the courthouse and look the registrar in the eye."[95] Suitcase played poker and dice but was not a conman-gambler like the character who shares his name in *Feelgood*. In the novel De Lissovoy writes, "As soon as I got good enough, he wanted to drive to other towns in the state, pretending to be SNCC workers. He'd borrow some overalls for the trip, and I'd hesitantly walk into the hippest local pool parlor, pretending to be a 'movement sucker' and let myself get sucked into something. I would have no trouble playing the 'sucker,' but I'd have to be sure of playing the winner" (217). Despite reviewers assuming this felicity to represent fact, this imaginative work deploys facticity to create a "floor of understanding" to underpin the "creative rendering of the actual, the re-constructed, the twice-told life," as Elizabeth Hardwick, a novelist as well as a journalist, observed of fictions close to an author's experience.[96] It suggested a generation for whom dropping out was a social statement and a disavowal of social norms. Webster Schott judged, "American youth has become our conscience. That is what *Feelgood* is about.... Even De Lissovoy's misty, heady style rises from that inner source where the monologue never ceases: What to do with a life? How to use experience? Where to find and keep intimacy?"[97] After less than a year, the protagonist drifts away from the Albany project's strictures, like the director's rules that there be no alcohol in the Freedom House or fraternizing with locals that risks the project's image and loss of focus. He admires the director, modeled on Charles Sherrod and one of few characters not subjected even to gentle irony, recognizing that his own commitment is "shallow" in comparison, but is careless of how his relationship with a local woman, Cara Lee, will be viewed by the director's "judging eyes." Instead, he claims specious authenticity for having crossed the color line—until he moves on: "I was into something else, that's all" (114, 94, 160). When he jettisons the project and Cara Lee, he feels "kinda free," but "freedom" equates to lack of responsibility. Soon he is living off a criminal underworld in the shadow of the Freedom House, an "errand boy" for conman Jones: "I felt like I was something on the corner, Jones's partner, and I had to have a gold-green suit, and slacks and shirts, and some hip Italian boots. I felt like I was into something, like the best life I'd known" (169). He sells reefers for Jones, shares girlfriends with Jones, and helps him exploit people, black and white. After Jones lights out for new territory, the protagonist sells reefers for Suitcase. Edging further off the grid, he loses a foothold in the movement, reifying personal freedom over collective commitment.

When De Lissovoy was writing the notes for this novel, stereotypes of white volunteers were being stage-managed to create a new set of debased protagonists in what *Variety* called the "racism-sex-violence genre of civil-wrongs films" released in this febrile political moment. In these films, such as *Girl on a Chain Gang* (1966) and *Murder in Mississippi* (1965), lawmen are "obscene caricatures of humanity," like those who "made Philadelphia, Mississippi newsworthy," and organizers and volunteers shockingly naïve.[98] *Feelgood* intervenes in this exploitation of the minority edges of SNCC's volunteer force, the "beatnik" students and protohippies subjected to scathing commentary in the mainstream as well as segregationist press.[99] When Tracy Sugarman befriended a white family in Ruleville and was told, "I never saw such a filthy bunch of people! Where did they get these creeps?," he explained:

> At Harvard... And Swarthmore. And Stanford. And Reed. And Howard... these kids aren't creeps. For the most part they're middle-class kids from our best schools. They're the only ones who could steal a summer without working. These "filthy" kids you're talking about are just like all the kids who have been hanging around our house with my teen-age son for the past four years. This is not the sandal and beard contingent, the "Beats." These are idealistic youngsters who want to help right what they think is wrong.[100]

The mother of volunteer Ellen Lake wrote similarly to the editor of the *New York Times* after even civil rights journalist John Herbers described them as "unkempt revolutionary types."[101] As Robert Coles noted, "There are many ways to be defiant, adventurous or rebellious that are less idealistic and dangerous than civil rights work."[102] *Feelgood*'s satire may have masked how myth busting this novel was in 1970 by making a "beatnik" its primary subject.

De Lissovoy also gave the lie to the impression created by Police Chief Laurie Pritchett that demonstrators were not mistreated by police in Albany. In histories, Pritchett's behavior is often contrasted with police brutality elsewhere, but John Lewis recalls Pritchett as "cunning," and Stephen Tuck argues that he was "shrewd" and hardly an advocate of nonviolence.[103] In the novel, violence is pervasive on Pritchett's watch: "Three [officers] were carrying me and a fourth was smacking me with his club. In my memory is a photograph of fifty white chins, crossed by long sticks working like windshield wipers" (59). A police officer arresting small children tells them, "If I had my way, I'd see every one of you hangin from the highest limbs!" (60). Men with guns under legal authority threaten the protagonist's sense of adventure, and, on occasion, rhetorical second-person insertions are directed at De Lissovoy's peers: "[D]id this fear born of lost bearings take its cold grip on your throat as you got into the unknown automobile?" (62). When suddenly released from jail, the protagonist is terrified, even in daylight: "Why had they just let me go? I remembered what had happened in Mississippi.... They had arrested them and then suddenly, arbitrarily, let them go. Now I couldn't avoid the bitter remembrance, and it was blending with the memory of the cop trying to kick me minutes ago: and a chill of fear and a cold brittle hate were soon all I felt" (283). He is musing on Chaney, Schwerner, and Goodman when forced to dive into a ditch as "some honky" drives straight at him.

No matter how far beyond the Freedom House he travels, he is marked by association and drawn back to SNCC on hearing "a movement song." He slides into a church pew, and observes that the project director "[is] angry and more vocal than I had ever seen him." He picks up that "a gentle child ... as little deserving of being hurt as any man on this earth" has been shot in the back by a police officer (288–89). When condolences are extended to him personally, though, he comes to the hot, shocked realization that the murdered man is "Yellow," a gentle soul he neglected while running with Jones: "Tears full of hate like bullets sped down my face" (293).[104] He comes closest in this moment to understanding the pain and rage that his project director feels, begins to enact in public, but then reins in by striding out of the church.

Feelgood rejects a simplistic dichotomy whereby nonviolent direct action tactics and faith-based activism gave way to angry Black Power politics. The depiction of Knight Collins both prefaces and supports *This Nonviolent Stuff'll Get You Killed*, in which Charles Cobb revisits civil rights historiography from an insider's perspective to determine the role of guns and armed defense. Don Harris estimated that more than 50 percent of staff in Southwest Georgia opposed strict adherence to nonviolence in 1961–62, and Miriam Cohen told Emily Stoper "a story circulating" that organizers were "protected by an armed gang of black teenagers": "Whether or not the story was true, it seemed to appeal to SNCC people."[105] In *Feelgood*, the stories Knight tells of black defenders and avengers challenge the white protagonist's stereotypical assumptions. While the white men taunting him on the street are something he had "once read about in the newspapers," the protagonist admits: "The idea where I'd come from was that the negroes down here [were] in a more pitiful shape." Knight personifies a long "tradition of violence against the set-up in the South" to which the volunteer is oblivious (111, 99). Having originally conceived of himself in the role of a knight, he does not expect to find himself protected by one.

In 1962, Thelwell was already troubling "the comforting over-simplification of the sit-ins" that Pat Watters believed did not begin to be addressed until 1965.[106] His story challenges readerly and critical assumptions that civil rights fiction will be serious, moralizing—even sententious. Forman was SNCC's novelist manqué, intervening in the college novel genre in the late 1950s, through young protagonists, southern and northern, black and white, conveying the campus mood and temperament that contributed to SNCC's formation. It was an ambitious project to write a novel about the cross-hatching of political ideas in which "the acid test of evaluating a person is their stance on civil rights," but he elucidated the campus shift from "ghost-state of conformity" to dissent and action.[107] Reading the manuscript now alongside *Sammy Young Jr.* (1968), subtitled "The First Black College Student to Die in the Black Liberation Movement," is to acknowledge how Forman captured the mood that inaugurated SNCC and the mood that presaged its end. In "Thin White Line," students debate what the battle for civil rights will demand of proponents; his biography of Younge exemplifies their ideological break with strategic nonviolence. The Tuskegee student's murder on January 6, 1966, was too much to bear after "1,835 days of danger, discouragement, too little sleep and never enough money."[108] Forman's novel is a presentiment for issues Kathleen Collins explored through a similarly large cast in her short story "Whatever Happened to Interracial Love?," where socially privileged volunteers "go to jail for freedom (which in their parents' minds is no different from going to jail for armed robbery, heroin addiction, or pimping, and other assorted ethnic hustles)."[109] The Freedom House morphs into a bohemian commune of recuperating activists and aspirant artists in New York City, its backdrop the "hidden enclaves" of Frazier's *Black Bourgeoisie*.[110] Nina Lorez Collins grounds her mother's stories in "a watershed" moment in 1962 when Charles Jones, Charles Sherrod, and Margaret (Peggy) Dammond visited Skidmore College, where her mother was enrolled. She then followed Dammond, with whom she became close, to Georgia—and jail in Albany.[111] In Collins's stories, troublemakers are tempered by recursive irony; like De Lissovoy, she put under the microscope volunteers who "thought it was possible to rupture every membrane and begin at zero."[112] Cheryl's "dejected" white lover Alan "calls forth the most picturesque of metaphors": his "white face floats in a sea of black protest," and his Boston accent "flirts with the edges of a Southern drawl." Then he "come[s] up bleeding" against "the grainy sands of illusion" (38). He cannot convince Boston Brahmin parents why he should be "beaten to a pulp... [t]eeth mashed in, jaw dislocated, nose rearranged... for the 'negroes' of this land we call America," while Cheryl's father worries she is pursuing a "queer integrated life with some pasty Freedom Rider who liked to flagellate himself for 'negroes'" (37–38, 55). Alan believes he needs to "become Negro" for Cheryl, and Collins performs a satirical exegesis of John Updike's *The Centaur* (1963), a novel suffused by self-absorption, quoting its disturbing lines, "Listen to me, lady. I love you. I want to be a Negro for you" (38–39). The seeds of future despondency are inherent in Alan and Cheryl trying to convince themselves that "race" is "part of the past" and love "color-free" (34, 37). Collins fuses 1963 with the "year of the hippie," making it "the year of racial, religious, and ethnic mildew," and Forman's idea that interracial relationships are healing is rendered a sad cliché (34, 36, 38).[113]

The commitment and cost of volunteering infuses histories, but how some students used the movement to "find" themselves is difficult to exemplify through sources other than literature. Mario Savio confessed to feeling that a comfortable white, middle-class existence was a suffocating "death-in-life" that might be escaped in the movement: "I thought about... my own involvement when I went to Mississippi where I could be killed. My reasons were selfish. I wasn't really alive. My life, my middle-class life, had no place in society, nor it in me.... I needed some way to pinch myself to assure myself that I was alive."[114] However, Savio was a "standout" worker. Hollis Watkins recalled, "When there was any leisure time, he would ask me questions about organizing. He had a real interest and passion for the logistics (nuts and bolts) of organizing."[115] Although he begins in the same emotional territory, De Lissovoy's protagonist in *Feelgood* is very different. Likewise volunteers like Alan, who "come to the Negro and to the poor in search of meaning," are not discoverable in nonfiction sources.[116] The life of an organizer is "too serious, too somber, too real" for De Lissovoy's character, and, like Collins's Alan, he is seduced by an image, which Lawrence Swaim debunked as "exciting trips down to the settlement house in dirty jeans with a copy of James Baldwin in the back pocket."[117] Incorporated into ostensibly laid-back, droll fictions is an increasingly merciless, sometimes ribald, revealing critique. These pellucid dissections of "the lessons, logic, and liabilities of the white SNCC Southern summer vanguard" are among the most clear-eyed stories about the movement published at the time.[118] De Lissovoy lost, or destroyed, his original manuscript, just as his protagonist loses his notes when wanderlust takes him beyond the Freedom House and later burns what he retrieves. He fears he has stolen the story from those around him whose lives are "real and inimitable," a metafictional comment that suggests a dilemma with which other writers wrestled.[119]

De Lissovoy captured the moment when student troublemakers were associated with "the counterculture," riffing on this divisive term as it was understood in the popular imagination, as meaning a culture of self-gratification through drugs, sex, music, and sensual pleasures. In my reading, the texts that are the focus of this chapter are countercultural in more complex ways, with Forman's novel suggesting "non-hierarchical ways of relating [that] formed the initial 'counterculture,'" when Hogan reclaims the term for SNCC. Carson's observation that "the 'countercultural' values of the mid-1960s were extensions of the questioning of conventional middle-class values that had occurred in the Movement" resonates with Collins's stories.[120] Each narrative examined in this chapter is a rebel tale written in the spirit of the vanguard, with the sense of anarchism that was emblematic of the New Left. In 1969, David Llorens asserted that organizers in SNCC "put to death an America where 20-year-olds were seen but not heard" through their "unpredictable style of transforming ideas into action."[121] SNCC's literary history rests on more than these foundations, though. More comprehensively, it is rooted in its organizing and imagined through two black, southern, antic tricksters in the African American tradition of the tall tale. Supersnick and Junebug Jabbo Jones evoke the resilience of local people and the ebullience necessary to sustain SNCC field-workers in difficult and dangerous times. These invented characters are the focus of the following chapter.

Chapter 2

Supersnick and Junebug Jabbo Jones

> Each new "Supersnick" cartoon sped from hand to hand across the southland ... Eagerly anticipated, Claude's cartoons brought mirth and self-deprecating humor to every office.
> —Mary King, 1987

> The traditional art of tall-tale telling was raised to new heights [in the movement], which is one reason it's so hard for historians to get a clear idea of what the facts actually were.
> —John O'Neal, 1960s

> You see, that ain't my name, it's a *title* of a job I've got to do, like "King" or "Prince."
> —John O'Neal as Junebug Jabbo Jones, 1980

Two distinctive imaginary characters illustrate the internal culture that Wesley Hogan began to define when discerning that organizers "created a language of words, gestures, jokes, and behavior so interior that it was only with other SNCC people that many felt truly comfortable." In 2016, Judy Richardson put it another way: "Sometimes we're only talking to ourselves ... trying to get ourselves right. For me, SNCC was that."[1] It is possible to detect something of SNCC's inside culture in correspondence and in-house documents like newsletters, where nicknames are used, but in-jokes are difficult for external readers to comprehend.[2] Supersnick was called forth repeatedly after being brought to life in a series of cartoons by Claude Weaver, who joined from Harvard for the Mississippi Freedom Vote campaign in 1963 and stayed through 1964 in Batesville and Greenville.[3] In Weaver's cartoons, an African American janitor named Tom transforms, at SNCC's instigation, into a social justice superhero. "Each new 'Supersnick' cartoon sped from hand to hand across the southland," Mary King recalled, and "circulated with amazing speed throughout the SNCC network. ... Eagerly anticipated, Claude's cartoons brought mirth and self-deprecating humor to every office."[4] Weaver's drawings of an exuberant everyman-turned-hero were "plastered on the walls" of the Atlanta office.[5] Some organizers attributed the coining of his name to Ed Brown, others to Courtland Cox.[6] In John O'Neal's recollection, the character Junebug Jabbo Jones appeared in a conversation between Cox, Charles Cobb, and Julius Lester in the Freedom House in McComb, Mississippi, in 1962: "As questions came up in the argument they were having, they'd say 'as Junebug says...,' 'as Jabbo says...,' using aphorisms to support an argument.... The idea of Junebug Jabbo sorta stuck and became a phenomenon in SNCC conversations. And later on, Jones got added to the name and he stayed."[7]

Supersnick and Junebug are folk characters in the tradition of African American tall tales. Lester molded traditional tricksters in the form of a ballad, or "toast," to SNCC lore—for example, adapting mythical characters High John and Stagolee in a pamphlet published by Maria Varela's Flute Publications as *Our Folktales* in 1967. Grove Press reprinted it as *Black Folktales* in 1969. Gaining a wider audience, novelist John A. Williams assessed in the *New York Times*: "Although these tales have been told before... Lester brings a fresh, street-talk language to them and thus breathes new life into them. It is a tribute to the universality of these tales—and to Lester's ability to see it—that we are thus presented with old truths dressed for today."[8] Lester's plantation heroes live where SNCC organized in the Mississippi Delta and Southwest Georgia. His High John embodies the imprimatur of cool, with which SNCC was associated by student volunteers. His narrative model was communal: "Each person who tells a story molds the story to his tongue and to his mouth, and each listener molds the story to his ear. Thus, the same story told over and over is never quite the same.... Stories can be changed and should be, as the storyteller feels. The stories don't live otherwise... These stories are told here not as they were told a hundred years ago, but as I tell them now. And I tell them now only because they have meaning now."[9] Imbuing archetypes with signs of the times, Death is tired from making too many trips to Vietnam, and, when he catches up to Stagolee, the folk hero not only battles Death but also turns hell into a Black Power jamboree.[10] Lester dedicated these stories to Zora Neale Hurston, whose tales in *Mules and Men* (1935) were among those he retold, and H. Rap Brown (Jamil Abdullah Al-Amin), SNCC's chairman in May 1967, locating SNCC in an African American cultural continuum.

While Lester found ways to accommodate folk heroes, Supersnick and Junebug Jabbo Jones are components of a SNCC imaginary. In asserting them as signifiers of its internal culture, I draw on Slavoj Žižek's assertion that when examining the "social and ideological edifices" of a group, one should excavate vernacular traces of what it left behind.[11] Supersnick indicates that what may be peripheral historically can be symbolically central. In 1999, for example, Michael Thelwell shared with the *Boston Globe* an idea for a production company called Supersnick Inc. but did not explain the name. He was riffing on Cobb's idea for "a situational drama": "Think *M*A*S*H* or *Hill Street Blues*. We'd call it Freedom House ... with a Mrs. Hamer type, a Stokely Carmichael type, a couple of white volunteers. ... The moment I heard it, I said, 'Charlie, you got a partner, whether you like it or not.' We are going to set up a production house called Supersnick Inc., and we're going to interview all the SNCC people and get all these incredible stories that you couldn't possibly imagine or invent, that really happened."[12] Here the moniker "Supersnick" is shorthand for telling "incredible" stories that "really happened," filed as an in-joke. It was inflected in more morose terms in a poem where the collapse of the organization is a nightmare. In "There Was Horror," Stembridge fused "super snick" with "silver flute," the metaphor through which she symbolized Bob Moses in *I Play Flute*, and questioned whether either they or she as a poet could "tell the whole truth" of the "grieving in the leaving / in the heaving of the sea" as the SNCC "circle" fell away.[13]

While Supersnick faces inward, Junebug Jabbo Jones was pushed outward, elaborated in print and performance culture down the decades, refreshed and reinvigorated by Thelwell, quoting Junebug in essays, and by John O'Neal, for whom Junebug focalizes "storytelling theater" as a legacy character personified by O'Neal and later by his son William.[14] O'Neal blended what he heard and experienced as an organizer with invented stories and scenes. His performances as Junebug from 1980 through 2013 extended "story circles" designed by the FST to mobilize communities. As O'Neal noted, "[Actors] learn from our audience what theatrical forms may most aptly serve to carry the meanings most significant and useful to them."[15] O'Neal's story circles reflect debates ongoing in SNCC, as when Casey Hayden visualized its structure in circles: "Instead of lines and boxes and hierarchy in the diagrams of how to organize SNCC, I was drawing circles indicating people working together and the circles overlapping other circles as we all generated programs and things to do together."[16] SNCC conducted small-group facilitations as circles in meetings and conferences, and O'Neal explored the idea of a "story circle" when interviewing fellow organizers for a book project he called "Will the Circle Be Unbroken?"[17] He has defined story circles as a creative strategy designed to "get people thinking and talking about real stories, suspending argument for a time, and building relationships through sharing narratives." This has translated into community-focused performances combining verbatim theatre with an imagined life story and genealogy for Junebug Jabbo

Jones.[18] If storytelling generates "mutual respect and listening," O'Neal wrote, "people can then approach points of contention and issues of injustice productively and with fresh perspectives."[19] Junebug embodies SNCC's story circles, and Supersnick was a totemic champion for organizers in the field.

Supersnick and James Forman's Salutary Broom

An agent of racial justice and a social bandit, Supersnick is anarchic, like rebels Eric Hobsbawm identified when relying on what he called the "rather tricky historical resources" of poems and ballads in *Bandits* (1969).[20] A census of rebels would need to include both imaginary and historical figures. The egregious image of "Uncle Tom" was an archetype Weaver deployed to name his character, and the black janitor was another stereotype; both had cultural currency in the 1960s. For example, in September 1962, when the University of Mississippi student newspaper the *Mississippian* supported James Meredith's application to study at the school, segregationist rival *Rebel Underground* latched on to the janitor stereotype to rebut an attempt "to plant in the mind" of the white student body the idea "that Meredith is just a quiet, timid young Negro, similar to our janitors."[21] A comic foil in performances of blackface minstrelsy, the janitor character was popularized in *Amos 'n' Andy*—on the radio between 1927 and 1960, with a television spin-off in 1951–53, followed by reruns broadcast through 1966. A concerted NAACP campaign finally succeeded in getting the program off the air. In the television show, Lightnin' moved at a snail's pace to conform to the work-shy caricature, but if read against the stereotypical grain, Nick Stewart played him as a comedic troublemaker. Regardless, Stewart used what he earned to build a black theater and received an NAACP Lifetime Achievement Award in 1996. Like Stewart but more audaciously within in a close community, Weaver intervened in the stereotype.[22]

"Supersnick," like "Freedom Now," was one of the names demonstrators submitted to police when arrested. It was a SNCC alias, and, in June 1964, when the communications team issued new guidelines to enable accurate newsgathering through WATS (Wide Area Telephone Service) reports, a template for how a report should be structured was signed "Supersnick."[23] Drawing his character wearing work-a-day overalls, Weaver also created a comedic commentary on the tendency to romanticize SNCC's "uniform." Dressed down in denim coveralls to blend into rural communities, African Americans in SNCC, men especially, were fetishized by fascinated college students and other observers, including writer Norman Mailer. Mailer commented on the "tasty choice in what they wore, a long thin feather in the hat... or an old pair of boots with turned-up toes." He concluded, "They had flair." The idea that civil rights workers were black cavaliers exuding the kind of cool Mailer championed in essays about the hipster and "White Negro" didn't pass without comment. Lorraine Hansberry flatly called it "romantic racism."[24] Weaver may be seen as intervening in this image when he made Tom a proletarian superhero. When the janitor character bursts through his overalls, his costume as superhero is not much different: jeans and work shirt, the SNCC uniform.[25]

Supersnick was an in-joke. When volunteers arrived in the Atlanta office demanding that Forman immediately assign them to a project they considered dangerous enough to match their skills and commitment, Forman's usual response, Julian Bond later recalled, was that they sweep the office before reporting to him. "Some left before they finished," Bond wrote, but "those who completed the task were given a second look."[26] Bond noted that students who tried to self-select a project were usually white. The role reversal enacted when a white volunteer was being handed a broom by SNCC's black executive secretary quickly and economically served a purpose. If one accepted the need to clean and undertake "mundane work," Forman saw hope. It was, Fred Meely underlined in an organizer's handbook, "the first step towards becoming a relevant movement organizer" before embarking on what Cobb would later summarize as "barely visible work in southern backcountry, dangerous work punctuated by awful violence that included murder."[27]

Anyone could be tested. When Robert Coles approached SNCC to allow him to study the psychological effects of organizing on staff and volunteers, he was turned down after a difficult interview with Forman, Moses, and Bob Zellner. Smarting, he nonetheless offered to help in whatever way they saw fit. Forman suggested that he clean the office, and Coles set to work, assuring himself that he would be granted access for being persistent as well as "flexible." Days turned into weeks, and he was still sweeping the office: "I had an official position with SNCC: I was the janitor. I even bought us a vacuum cleaner." Finally, Forman asked Coles what he had learned from his "janitorial research." Installed as an unobtrusive and nonthreatening presence, Coles had listened carefully, observing organizers "as they went about their activist lives." He was recognized and trusted. With hindsight, Coles chose to classify the experience as a lesson in service in a somewhat disingenuous description of his fieldwork methodology in *The Call to Service* (1993)—but suggested that everybody involved laughed with him later about his induction.[28]

Weaver's cartoon is code for the importance that Forman placed on janitorial work, and failure to understand it is to misread SNCC's internal culture, as Robert Penn Warren did when assuming that the "brisk young woman" sweeping the Atlanta office when he arrived to interview Moses was a "charwoman-secretary."[29] Judy Richardson took the measure of the situation immediately after arriving in Atlanta in November 1963 with Reggie Robinson: "I saw this large man at the top of the stairs, dressed in overalls and sweeping the stairs. Reggie saw him too, then ran up the stairs and, with broad smiles and much hollering, they hugged each other like long-lost brothers. I thought, *Whoah, this is truly an egalitarian office*, since I assumed the man to be the janitor" (original emphasis). She realized why Forman swept whenever it was quiet, "not so much to clean the perpetually dirty office (which was good, since he wasn't all that good at it). Rather, he was showing us that, as he often said, no job was too lowly for anyone in SNCC to do."[30] In notes smuggled out of Leflore County Jail in spring 1963, Forman chose to record that the cell he shared with seven other organizers was cleaned regularly: "For the last two days Bob, [Lawrence] Guyot and I have swept the cell and scrubbed it on our hands and knees."[31] Elayne DeLott found herself cogitating on the emphasis placed on cleaning in a letter to her sister:

> in this movement the really top people sweep the floor. i think it might have something to do with not delegating menial tasks or the dignity of labor ... it turns out that bob moses and jim foreman [sic] are known for always sweeping the floor. jesse can also be seen on slow evenings cleaning the toilets or sweeping the floors or the sidewalk in front of the office. as a matter of fact, it's contagious: when there's no one around and i'm in charge of the office i take to sweeping up and cleaning too.[32]

Forman remained consistent in the belief that an organizer "must be willing to do the nitty gritty and shitty work that people are often not willing to do," because, in turn, it "develops an awareness in others that they too have a responsibility to do the so-called dirty work." In *The Political Thought of James Forman* (1970), he stressed the axiom: "If any cat tells you that he has nothing to do, that he is waiting direction while he sits in a pile of dirt or sees a dirt[y] floor, and does not get a broom right away, then that cat is not an organizer."[33] It is hard to imagine that the janitor-freedom fighter Weaver created did not play on these idiosyncrasies as a source of comedy. Supersnick also developed as a character according to where and how SNCC located him because, as Lester's narrative model makes clear, "stories don't live otherwise."

Supersnick in "Run'emout" Mississippi, Washington, and Atlanta

A Supersnick cartoon was displayed in panels on the walls throughout SNCC's annual conference in Washington, D.C., in December 1963. In his opening remarks to delegates, Moses emphasized that "the only hope for Negroes lay in creating a situation which would force a confrontation of federal and state authorities."[34] Supersnick commented on that goal. In the cartoon, Tom is working in the basement of the building that houses the citizens' council in fictional Run'emout, Mississippi. The Justice Department is aware of his secret identity and taking "careful notes on everything that happens to the hero." Weaver's satire was acidic. A DoJ official instructs Tom, "Tell me only what you know to be true" and then scribbles assiduously while "the hero is beaten by police [and] poked with cattle prods," all of which the official studiously ignores because he is "constitutionally bound" not to interrupt the fracas. SNCC staff was painfully aware of the many occasions when the FBI documented violence but failed to act. Jack Minnis enumerated instances in *A Chronology of Violence and Intimidation in Mississippi since 1961* (1964), and telegrams and press releases requesting or demanding federal intervention, signed by McDew, Moses, Forman, Bond, and John Lewis, were numerous.[35] As Weaver depicted, turning away and doing nothing when violations clearly occurred was galling.

In McComb in October 1961, when Bob Zellner was beaten bloody by a mob on the steps of city hall, the FBI told him, "We took real good notes": "I was so mad I didn't want to speak to them anymore. I never ever had any illusions about the FBI or the federal government from that point. That taught me more about politics in this country . . . than anything I ever learned after that. . . . The FBI refrain, 'We can't protect. We can only investigate' had become a grim joke with us in SNCC."[36] When Sam Block saw a white mob with chains, ropes, and shotguns approaching the Freedom House in Greenwood in the middle of the night, he called the DoJ and local FBI. Block, Guyot, and Luvaughn Brown leapt onto the roof and fled via an adjacent building, and Block called the FBI again. "Two weeks later a couple of those southern FBI men came around to interview me," Block later recalled with "faint sarcasm." Reporting in the *New York Post* under the headline "Combat Story," James Wechsler recounted: "Nothing the U.S. government has done in Mississippi has convinced Block and his 'freedom fighters' that they have any real personal protection against the lawless local structure.... Talking to him is like interviewing a fugitive who has momentarily slipped through the Iron Curtain to address the outside world."[37] Weaver's comic strip reflected deeply held convictions. Bill Mahoney staged a protest about federal government inaction in Attorney General Robert Kennedy's office in March 1962, and in 1964 Mario Savio wrote angrily, "The FBI establishes a new office in Jackson and then releases its figures... 'proving' that Mississippi has the lowest crime rate of any state. Murder of Negroes isn't a crime here. And what about crimes committed by the law itself?"[38] Another of Weaver's cartoons, "Scenes from the South," in the November 1964 *Student Voice*, distilled the issue in a single frame. A frowning "J. Edgar Standby" assesses that murder is "a local matter" and asks, "Would you like to contend that the sheriff denied this Negro some civil rights in killing him?" An editorial follows on "the Hoover version of the FBI" taking notes while murders, arson, bombings, and beatings proliferate.[39]

After SNCC's 1963 conference, socialist weekly the *Militant* applauded: "Sheriff McCruel has failed to reckon with SUPERSNICK's secret weapon 'soul force.' The last panel shows SUPERSNICK disintegrating McCruel with a stare marked 'ZAP.'"[40] Weaver punctured the principle of Satyagraha popularized through Gandhi's practice and reinforced by Martin Luther King: "We must not allow our creative protest to degenerate into physical violence... we must rise to the majestic heights of meeting physical force with soul force."[41] Most closely, though, the cartoon that the *Militant* commented on reflected debates inside SNCC and at the conference about the value of nonviolence if federal officers refused to intervene when federal laws were contravened and violent assailants found innocent in court. The cartoon echoed the evaluation of FBI reporting practice that assistant attorney general for civil rights John Doar was forced to make, as early as September 1961, when the fact that Moses had been severely wounded by Billy Jack Caston was omitted from the FBI report Doar received from McComb and no photographic evidence included.[42]

Life magazine's John Neary invokes Supersnick as "a mesomorphic caped black Galahad hustling off to the rescue" in his 1971 biography of Julian Bond. After the refrain "and then Bond came... and then Bond was heard" builds to an anaphoric chant, Neary spins into a fantastical disquisition on the need for a "Supernegro... riding hard against injustice and inequity." At the apex is an image of Bond as a "black rebel" politician and a potentially "real Supersnick." Neary certainly drew on Weaver's cartoon— and perhaps John O'Neal's depiction of Bond as a "black cavalier" where, following Hansberry, he turned Mailer's imagery on its head.[43] Another rare reference to Supersnick came in 2002, when Hunter Gray (formerly John Salter and a professor at Tougaloo College when he joined the Jackson sit-ins) published a blog post ("Where's the Humor in the American Radical Movement These Days?") that celebrated "the kind of stuff my old friend Claude Weaver, great SNCC cartoonist (as well as great activist) used to generate day and night."[44] Weaver drew from on-the-ground experience and insider knowledge when he imagined Supersnick.

The insider knowledge of Weaver's cartoons is evident in the work of other artists in SNCC, notably volunteer Tracy Sugarman, who sketched day-to-day activity and whose drawings appear in his books *Stranger at the Gates: A Summer in Mississippi* (1966) and *We Had Sneakers, They Had Guns: The Kids Who Fought for Civil Rights in Mississippi* (2009). For Sugarman, drawing was both a profession and reportorial. His drawings appeared in the *New York Times* and *Saturday Evening Post* and CBS television documentary *How Beautiful on the Mountains*, and the U.S. Information Agency used his words and art to tell the story of the southern freedom struggle overseas.[45] Weaver's cartoons, on the other hand, were more important in bolstering the spirit of organizers at the grassroots, though they did reach hundreds at the 1963 SNCC conference, which achieved the highest attendance of any conference in the organization's history.[46] With insider humor, Weaver presented SNCC activists with an entertaining hero who surmounted the pressures they constantly felt. SNCC's other cultural standard bearer, Junebug Jabbo Jones, has enjoyed a much longer narrative life in print and performance, drawing multiple, new audiences and readers to stories forged inside the group.

Junebug Jabbo Jones and Collective Heritage

The New Action Army (1967) was a satirical pamphlet in the form of a comic, with each panel representing President Lyndon B. Johnson's program for the war in Vietnam, with "maximum feasible participation" from all, black and white, "to show we are a freedom-loving people." It was attributed to Junebug Jabbo Jones.[47] Junebug is prolific in print culture, deployed for folk wisdom, political acumen, scathing social commentary, and even literary criticism, with his aphorisms quoted as epigraphs. For example, when Thelwell wrote about Jesse Jackson's first presidential campaign, in 1984, it was in response to an article in *Dissent* by Julius Lester. Thelwell disagreed with Lester, who thought that Jackson's declaration "Our time has come!" echoed the demand for "freedom now!" but that neither were "effective politics" in the 1980s.[48] Thelwell returned readers to the stand made by the Mississippi Freedom Democratic Party at the Democratic National Convention in Atlantic City in 1964, for which he secured U.S. representatives who would support the alternative delegation. For Thelwell, Jackson's candidacy was a deferred but sharp retort to the MFDP's betrayal by the Democratic Party. With his presidential campaign, the black vote could no longer be "maintained in obscurity as the Democratic Party's dirty little secret" or brokered into two seats "at large," Thelwell argued. With Jackson running for president, he said, "We shed our invisibility." Thelwell substantiated his assertion with a "curbside address" by Junebug: "'Member y'awl. When you gits to Atlantic City, grab them Democrats by they delegate count."[49] For readers with limited knowledge of SNCC, Junebug may appear to reference a real person. Thelwell alluded to speeches Junebug had delivered in pool halls, cotton fields, and even Ivy League schools. Junebug is said to have made a speech to Harvard students in May 1964 and been present at Cornell University to address demonstrators occupying the Willard Straight Hall in April 1969, with Thelwell channeling what he had witnessed as a research fellow at Cornell: black students arming themselves.[50] Thelwell interpolated Junebug's "cynical wisdom" into book reviews, making him a shrewd cultural commentator who tells it like it is. Of white publishers, Junebug observes roguishly, "Those honkies don't take us seriously; if they did we'd all be dead."[51] Junebug appears in *Ready for the Revolution* (2003), without explanation as to who he is, and elsewhere Thelwell refers to him as "the peripatetic black sage who is a legend in his own time."[52] It is as if he were a member of SNCC—which in a way he was. In *Ready for the Revolution* Carmichael follows mention of his name with the invocation "may his tribe increase," and in the 1980s O'Neal imagined an entire tribe of Junebugs in a cycle of plays.

Don't Start Me to Talking or I'll Tell Everything I Know: Sayings and Writings from the Life of Junebug Jabbo Jones (1980) was the final play the Free Southern Theater developed and the play O'Neal chose to inaugurate Junebug Productions. The company asserted this mission statement: "Through theater, we think to open a new area of protest. One that permits the development of playwrights and actors, one that permits the growth and self-knowledge of a Negro audience, one that supplements the present struggle for freedom."[53] This statement echoes goals of the FST, and *Don't Start Me to Talking* is a bridging text in SNCC writers' dramatization of the longer freedom struggle. Through this invocation of Junebug, SNCC's contribution to African American community-led theater from the

1960s to the present is also asserted. When O'Neal began performing as Junebug in the 1980s, Derek Walcott was worrying that "[the] narrator as performer does not exist anymore.... No one is told a story by a living voice." Walcott celebrated Caribbean "calypso tents" and some African theater practices but lamented that the griot was disappearing elsewhere. "The strongest theater," he asserted, "will always be the one that goes directly to the elementals of art... because the audience shares in, rather than being instructed by, the experience."[54] O'Neal underlined the griot's connection to listeners; the griot "mold[ed] the story to his tongue and to his mouth and each listener molds the story to his ear," in Lester's phrasing, when privileging Junebug's storytelling as dynamic performance. As elsewhere, in *Don't Start Me to Talking* Junebug is aphoristic, and in reading the play one can practically hear him—"You can't judge a book by looking at the cover"; "every shut-eye ain't sleep"—as he rolls out monologues, sings, raps, recounts, and tucks lessons into stories. In one scene, two slick politickers called One Stop and Handsome Bailey use voter registration as a sure start to lining their pockets, but when they attempt to trick brothers Ed and H. Rap Brown, their bluff is called, and Ed tells them, "You burning the bridge that brought you over."[55]

In the five-play cycle he calls "Junebug's Storytelling Plays," as well as tributary dramas such as *Junebug/Jack* (1990), O'Neal attributes the invention of his character to "young people from SNCC"—and notes that Junebug "knows the dignity of a well-mopped floor."[56] Junebug is reincarnated in different historical periods, with each performance a literary X-ray exposing a long, sustained folk memory plumbed for life lessons. The lessons Junebug imparts are based, O'Neal says, "in historical and social realities that he has witnessed."[57] O'Neal asserts that the "traditional art of tall-tale telling was raised to new heights" during the civil rights 1960s, and that is "one reason why it is hard for historians to get a clear idea of what the facts actually were." As Lester noted, "information is not the same as knowledge, because knowledge is more than, other than, facts."[58] Junebug is made to emphasize repeatedly that grassroots leaders were as important as national figureheads like Martin Luther King by foregrounding the wisdom of black rural southerners. Junebug disdains those who "try to hide from the light that shines through the tales I tell," stating emphatically, "I'm here to tell you I might look like a farmer but I ain't no fool!"[59] Embodied in Junebug, then, is SNCC's witness testimony that civil rights history was lived by local people on the front lines of the freedom struggle.

O'Neal imagined an ancestral line for Junebug, going back to a seven-year-old enslaved child whose "smarts" challenge a plantation overseer and so make him vulnerable. Rather than see him scapegoated and murdered to frighten other slaves to stay in line, the plantation community stages Junebug's death by drowning, followed by a mock funeral and an affecting performance of mourning. The burial serves to screen the boy being smuggled away to be raised in the local swamp by a runaway slave, Old Crazy Bill, whom whites avoid because he plays "crazy." The swamp is a powerful trope in African American oral and literary traditions. Its symbology is everywhere present, as in W. E. B. Du Bois's *The Souls of Black Folk* (1903) and his novel *The Quest of the Silver Fleece* (1911) and as the trope Zora Neale Hurston used when reviewing Wright's *Uncle Tom's Children* and noting its unrelenting grimness: "The Dismal Swamp of race hatred must be where [his characters] live."[60] Thelwell turned the trope against William Styron, seeing Styron's fictionalization of slave insurrectionist Nat Turner in *The Confessions of Nat Turner* (1967) as diminishing the historical figure who led a colony of free rebels in the Dismal Swamp in Southampton County, Virginia, in 1831.[61] O'Neal's character Old Crazy Bill evokes Turner and the enslaved Squier (aka Squire or "Bras Coupé"); the latter held out with a band of escaped slaves in cypress swamps close to New Orleans until murdered in 1837. Bill may be old but is neither crazy nor abject. He is given a backstory in O'Neal's notes. When the white preacher who owns him aims a rifle at Bill, Bill shouts in an African language to conjure a bolt of lightning. The lightning "struck the barrel of that gun, welded it shut, knocked the preacher down square on his butt, and turned every hair on his body from jet black to silver white right on the spot."[62]

The name O'Neal gave the folk hero who raises and educates Junebug riffs on the propensity to label black radicals "crazy," from Nat Turner through Stokely Carmichael and H. Rap Brown. In 1969, Don L. Lee asserted, "Crazy is crazy only when black people move... to confront the real craziness of the world," and, as historian Hasan Kwame Jeffries argues, mischaracterization of black activists as "crazy Negroes" ensured that pragmatic solutions to real problems could be rejected.[63] Such stories are legion inside SNCC. Cobb commemorates men and women deemed "crazy" by whites—like James Evers, father to Medgar and Charles, and Fannie Lou Hamer's mother Lou Ella Townsend—because they refused to cede their dignity, their intransigence as dangerous for them as it was ennobling for their communities.[64] O'Neal imbues Old Crazy Bill with elements from biographies of rebel slaves and courageous elders. When Jack O'Dell interviewed Fannie Lou Hamer, for example, she told him about tenant farmer Joe "Pulliam" (usually referred to as Pullum or Pullen in news and historical accounts) as one of the catalysts for her own activism. She told *Freedomways* readers why Pullum, the "Negro Murderer" of newspaper accounts in 1923, was her hero. Pullum exemplified a long battle against economic repression and violent intimidation in the Delta. When Pullum challenged a white family in Drew, Mississippi, who had "robbed him of what he earned," his employer shot him. After Pullum fired back, killing the white man, he hid in Powers Bayou. According to Hamer, he then killed thirteen men and wounded twenty-six others who converged on him. The exact numbers convey that Hamer knew what she was talking about, and she named assailants, including a Clarksdale man who turned a machine gun on Pullum, although other accounts tend to put the tally of white dead at nine. Finally, whites poured gallons of gas in the bayou and set it on fire. Catching Pullum, "they dragged him by his heels on the back of a car and they paraded about with that man and they cut off his ears and put them in a showcase and it stayed there a long, long time—in Drew, Mississippi. All of those things, when they would happen, would make me sick in the pit of my stomach and year after year, every time something would happen it would make me more and more aware of what would have to be done in the State of Mississippi."[65] Unlike Pullum, Old Crazy Bill survives—he is a wise elder, a "baaad man," and a canny mentor, but he survives because he is a trickster. He is formative in Junebug's story because he instructs Junebug to travel undercover around plantations to collect stories of slave resistance, secretly recruiting storytellers for the same purpose, to spin out new story circles.

In the Junebug plays, O'Neal transfigures Richard Wright's chronotopic description of the legacy of slavery as an "uneasily tied knot of pain and hope whose snarled strands converge from many points of time and space." Multiple iterations of Junebug converge as "the taproot of the modern freedom struggle," in the way Cobb traced back generations to his own great-grandfather founding an all-black community, New Africa, in the Reconstruction-era Delta, his uncle's union organizing, and his father's activism in Springfield, Massachusetts.[66] O'Neal attributes to SNCC's griot the role of keeping such stories alive: "You see, [Junebug] ain't my name, it's a title of a job I've got to do, like 'King' or 'Prince.'" Junebug stresses that orators performing this community role "don't just have to be colored. And they definitely ain't all men."[67] O'Neal's inclusive story cycle intervenes imaginatively in SNCC's self-conception as "a band of brothers and sisters"—and points toward a fact *SNCC's Stories* uncovers, that in SNCC's narrative culture women are as prevalent as men, but as organizer characters they are woefully absent.

Junebug's Inside Story of the 1960s

The 1960s iteration of Junebug hails from fictional "Four Corners," which O'Neal identifies as being close to McComb in Pike County, a foundational site of SNCC's organizing in southwestern Mississippi in the summer of 1961.[68] McComb was also the location of the "maiden performance" of the FST when O'Neal acted "under a carport in the backyard of the Freedom House... next to the room that had been damaged by the blast of some night riders' bomb a few days before."[69] Junebug begins organizing in McComb but is jailed first for integrating the waiting room at the bus station in New Orleans, the city where the FST based itself after transferring from Jackson, Mississippi, in 1965. In prison, Junebug learns how vital storytelling is from his cellmate, who directs him to African American cultural histories, books he studies on release. He campaigns for the Mississippi Freedom Democratic Party, exhibiting the homiletical power Willie Ricks and Carmichael demonstrated when declaiming "Black Power" in Greenwood, Mississippi, in 1966. And, like Joyce Ladner in "What 'Black Power' Means to Negroes in Mississippi" (1967), Junebug grounds that call in communities.[70] In this way, O'Neal designed a metaphorical and interpretive framework for an organizing fable, thereby realizing a writing ambition held since the 1960s, exemplified in unpublished works like "Going against the Tide," for which Bill Hansen had sent him suggestions.[71]

The Junebug plays are a self-referential exploration of SNCC's organizing. One of the locales in which O'Neal worked was Lee County, Georgia, where plantation workers "could be fired for simply leaning on the wrong tree" but attempted to register as voters.[72] In a 1963 field report, O'Neal recorded the tenacity of a Mr. C. as crucial to community endeavor; if Mr. C. were to be evicted or hurt, O'Neal feared, plantation workers could "quickly turn back to their shriveled existence."[73] He fused unsung local leaders like Mr. C. with SNCC's black southern organizers in the Junebug character. Hollis Watkins, who, like Marion Barry, John Lewis, Unita Blackwell, Fannie Lou Hamer, McKinley Mack, and Carver (Chico) Neblett, grew up in a sharecropping family, describes black southern field-workers as "young lions" intermingling with potential voters in cotton fields beneath the notice of overseers, escaping across the fields whenever a plantation owner marched into late-night meetings.[74] Junebug organizes a union on a plantation belonging to a Colonel Whitten to challenge the corrupt status quo wherein the planter rigs his scales so that sharecroppers remain perpetually in debt to plantation commissaries.[75] Whitten is clearly modeled on Democratic congressman Jamie L. Whitten, chairman of the Agricultural Subcommittee of the U.S. House of Representatives Appropriations Committee, who protected the subsidies of white farmers in the Mississippi Delta. He was elected on a segregationist platform in 1941, the same year Richard Wright described the "long shocks" of slavery that endured because politicians like Whitten sustained a plantation economy.[76] In O'Neal's play, Colonel Whitten personifies Old South patronage, offering a side of salted pork in lieu of fair pay for each man's labor. In response, pickers strew cotton sacks on the ground and walk off the job, but having catalyzed the strike, Junebug lets the people decide, as a SNCC motto advocated. When a family loses everything in a fire and insists on harvesting Whitten's crop to survive, Junebug says, "I told them, 'Well, all right.' And that's what they done."[77]

Behind such scenes are historical subtexts for readers familiar with SNCC. As J. Todd Moye encapsulated, Fannie Lou Hamer was "the absolute personification of 'let the people decide,' the archetype of SNCC's organizing strategy," and she defined the issues with which agricultural laborers contended "in their own vernacular." As timekeeper on the Marlow plantation near Ruleville, she found ways to ensure fairness.[78] After she was dismissed for civil rights activism in 1962, her family ousted after thirty-eight years on the plantation, she challenged Jamie Whitten for his seat in the U.S. House of Representatives in 1964, symbolizing a longer resistance to the "Mississippi Plan" initiated in 1875 by the Democratic Party to counteract black agency and political representation instituted in the Reconstruction era. In the 1960s, Mississippi counties like Sunflower and Panola still functioned as "one large plantation," and O'Neal conveys their material realities as SNCC apprehended them in his Junebug plays.[79] When McKinley Mack joined SNCC in Indianola, the fact that his sharecropper father had been cheated out of everything but "breaking even" was instrumental in his decision.[80] Jean Wheeler Smith exposed the plantation system in the short story "Frankie Mae" (1967), and Lester took up the story of a "young lion" in *And All Our Wounds Forgiven*. Lester's organizer character Bobby Card rises early every morning to drive "rutted, dusty plantation roads, stopping to talk to anyone he saw about starting a sharecroppers' union, or registering to vote, and almost daily there was a confrontation with some white man, a plantation overseer, the sheriff, or just a good ol' boy with a wad in his cheek and a rifle in his hand."[81] While working with SNCC, Lester discovered on the McIntyre plantation near Itta Bena "a leader if ever there was one" in Scott Harris, jailed for fifty-eight days in 1963 for leading a demonstration.[82] Harris taught Lester the communal language of the plantation. This language is a fulcrum of the

1960s iteration of Junebug, whose storytelling model is elucidated through his grandfather's principles:

> Number One—you got to tell them what you goin to tell them
> Number Two—you got to tell them
> Number Three—you got to back up and tell them what you told them.[83]

O'Neal echoed SNCC's "Organizer's Handbook": "A speaker should first tell the people what he is going to say; then he should say it; then he should tell the people what he has said. Be to the point—speaking should not be seen as an end."[84] These steps comprise Junebug's storytelling mantra, but in the play O'Neal leavens the didacticism with humor.

In *Don't Start Me to Talking*, a mule called Senator Bilbo—named because "the Bilbo in Washington didn't look no better and was about half as smart"—is the butt of the joke when Junebug's grandfather creates a new community tradition. Every Saturday he takes the mule to town and performs a symbolic beating of the errant animal while declaiming "You a no-good jackass Senator Bilbo, you ain't no good" for a laughing black crowd (24).[85] These antic tales contain what Ralph Ellison calls the "homeopathic" properties of black humor, parodying white segregationists and vanquishing them momentarily with what was, for whites, the "confounding, persistent, and embarrassing mystery of black laughter."[86] Tall tales were part of what John Dollard called "the arsenal of reprisal against white people" and contained a humor Sterling Brown asserted could elicit "a sort of laughter out of hell." In Brown's "Slim Greer" poems, for example, when Slim dies and discovers hell is "Dixie" and the devil a "cracker wid a sheriff's star," St. Peter sends him straight back to Earth in disgust because he really should have known that all along.[87] SNCC harnessed this humor. One of Sterling Brown's favorite aphorisms for the artfulness of African American speech was "hitting a straight lick with a crooked stick," and Ed Brown and Bob Mants were renowned for exhibiting this skill in their storytelling.[88] Thelwell commands it as a narrative strategy in "Direct Action," "Fish Are Jumping an' the Cotton Is High: Notes From the Mississippi Delta" (1966), and "The Organizer" (1966). Feistiness is a core component of SNCC's narrative culture and saturates the stories O'Neal wrote and performed in the persona of Junebug.

In Junebug Jabbo Jones, organizers invented a character that resonates with the long African American freedom struggle, his voice ingrained with the sophisticated folk wisdom they respected in the communities where they lived and worked. A story by Kathleen Collins contains a tongue-in-cheek allusion when Henry, a poet from the New York City writers' group Umbra, writes a poem titled "June Bug!" Henry's exclamation mark suggests that the verse is blanched of meaning because he is "not about to go south," is "uninterested" in voter registration, and his writing is "curiously apolitical."[89] Henry's poetry is anemic because he is oblivious to the meaning of the name. Junebug is rooted at the nexus of African American oral and literary traditions, a centuries-long history of spoken-word artists, from slave orators through works by Langston Hughes and Sterling Brown, recounting resistance stories. Underpinning all Junebug's stories is agency, and sometimes this comes with vengeance: "All the slaves built a huge fire. They put a heap of wood on it. And they took that old overseer and sent him right back to hell."[90] Junebug's saws have enriched Thelwell's essays, O'Neal's reports for the New Orleans *Data News Weekly* in the 1970s, and O'Neal's plays. O'Neal adapted the fourth in his cycle of five plays into a column in *Southern Exposure* ostensibly posted by Junebug. *Southern Exposure*, the journal of the Institute of Southern Studies in Durham, North Carolina, was founded in 1973 by SNCC and SSOC organizer Sue Thrasher and journalist Howard Romaine, with Julian Bond chairing its board. The journal took its name from Stetson Kennedy's satirical *Southern Exposure* (1946) to sustain a storytelling tradition that, like Kennedy's book, "links analysis to action . . . tells the truth and makes clear the imperative for change."[91] Junebug's column was featured in *Southern Exposure* from 1993 through 1999, and it relocated his Pike County, Mississippi, home to Louisiana, from where, it was said, "[he] travels the country collecting the wisdom of everyday people" and "sends along his stories . . . through his good friend John O'Neal."[92] O'Neal sent Junebug to Chicago, Peoria, Detroit, and even Hawaii, spinning homespun sagacity from the South and adapting it to other places. In the tagline that follows each column, readers are reminded how Junebug "came to life sometime during the turbulent '60s . . . in the civil rights movement."[93]

While Supersnick is a figure of SNCC lore contained within its circle, Junebug has a wider print history. Thelwell kept the character alive from the 1960s to the 1980s by quoting him in essays and including him as an organizer in Stokely Carmichael's "as told to" autobiography. "When SNCC began to lose its impact," O'Neal said, he determined that "Junebug would live to symbolize what the organization had fought for."[94] He grafted the character onto himself, became him, and sustained him. His son William O'Neal contributed to the writing of the play *Trying to Find My Way Back Home* in 2011, and thereafter another iteration of Junebug began when he took on the mantle after his father retired from the stage in 2013. Passing this story on by ensuring that it would be embodied by one of SNCC's children is fitting because Junebug emerged out of the cross-generational continuity of struggle. Now Junebug acts as a custodian of SNCC's legacy and has his own webpage on the activist site CRMvet.org. Now SNCC and Black Panther activist S. E. Anderson introduces readers to his website Black Education for Liberation by way of Junebug, through an imaginary statement and a photograph of John O'Neal on stage. While Frederick Douglass frames the site, Junebug is its herald.[95] In 2016, in his foreword to the Junebug plays, Cobb wrote, "by way of introducing John O'Neal and this book, I must introduce you to Black Art, particularly Black Art as part of Black Political Struggle."[96] Succinctly and firmly, Cobb situated O'Neal, Junebug, and SNCC in the wider literary history that *SNCC's Stories* uncovers and analyzes, turning now to field reports and creative responses they inspired.

Chapter 3

Inside Stories
From Field Reports to Field Texts

> The bare facts we can get from reading newspapers. What we want is the inside story, behind the scenes stuff that is so crucial to the final action taken.
> —Marion Barry and the *Student Voice* staff, 1960

> Does it become real in recognizing that those Negroes are down there, digging in, and in more danger than nearly any student in this American generation has faced? What does it take? When do we begin to see it all not as *remote* but as breathing urgency into our beings and meaning into our ideals?
> —Tom Hayden, 1962

> The southern civil rights movement is best understood as a movement of community organizing rather than one of protest.
> —Charles Cobb, 2003

There is a story according to which every document about SNCC was contained in a briefcase left in Bob Zellner's charge when he arrived at the Atlanta office on September 11, 1961. He was to safeguard it for Forman. In the briefcase were "letters, minutes of the meetings, all the files from a year and a half since the organization was founded on April 14, 1960." They had been preserved by Jane Stembridge, the organization's first secretary and Edward King Jr., the University of Kentucky student elected SNCC's "historian" at its founding, an early indication that its historical record was important to the fledgling organization. In Zellner's account, when Forman arrived to take up his post as executive secretary, he opened the briefcase and said, "This is SNCC. Probably everything about SNCC is right here."[1] When journalist Alice Gardner Murphy sent an article to the *Texas Observer* in 1964 she included SNCC brochures and wrote, "Here is Snick—in a bundle considerably larger than I imagine[d]." Brochures explaining the organization's work were titled "SNCC," "Freedom," "Now," and "This Is SNCC." Murphy seems to have thought they summed up the organization, though she limited SNCC purview to Bond and the Atlanta office.[2] The idea that SNCC could be synopsized in a capsule history has been disproved time and again. As Joan

Browning asserted, in SNCC's view, "the movement was not something imported in the briefcases of a few 'leaders' but... an ongoing, living process, involving thousands of people." Before the House Judiciary Committee in May 1963, members of the organization testified, "We in SNCC [include] thousands that make up its base."[3]

When Forman described his arrival in Atlanta, he focused on organizers "struggling in" from SNCC's projects to meet him, bringing "tales of violence and fierce civil strife" and a story that came together "in bits and pieces."[4] He would become renowned for reminding everybody to write it all down, saying that no individual could write the whole story. No individual has written the whole story, and I think that Forman, on opening that briefcase in September 1961, realized that organizers would all need to tell their inside stories. Field-workers fulfilling SNCC's mission to cooperate "closely with local groups in the intensification and extension of the movement" all needed to write down their stories if SNCC's distinctive organizing culture were to be understood. The tensions inherent in SNCC's original role as a channel of communication for the student movement were also apparent in the materials passed to Forman. In the briefcase were copies of the *Student Voice*. To "afford dynamic communication" required monthly reports from each campus group present at SNCC's founding, but securing them was a challenge.[5] Forman inherited a letter signed by Marion Barry as SNCC's first chairman, reminding student groups, "You are making the news, so send it in... and we will get it out!" Contributing writers were not to act as clerks of facts but instead to convey "the inside dope," and Barry advised that their style should not be pedestrian nor their content generic: "The bare facts we can get from reading newspapers. What we want is the inside story, behind the scenes stuff that is so crucial to the final action taken."[6]

The pressure SNCC felt to coordinate decreased once SNCC transformed itself from a facilitative organ for other groups into a small cadre of full-time organizers, with Forman the sixteenth organizer. In 1962, he consolidated communications under Julian Bond's directorship, and together they emphasized telling the inside story as a collective enterprise. Bond ensured that SNCC could act as "a press agent" for reporters "looking for ways to keep up with the unpredictable student demonstrations across the South."[7] Forman recruited Jack Minnis to set up a research department, with a multimedia library. His legal experience with the Southern Regional Council (SRC) meant that he could turn a proposal into a political program, as when he uncovered a Reconstruction statute allowing for the creation of a new political party in Alabama and SNCC-supported launch of the LCFO in 1965.⁸ While some organizers felt that submitting reports cramped their semiautonomy in the field and represented a "coercive structure," most did not.⁹ Bond never wavered in crediting Forman with "accounting for the large repository of field and other reports, giving SNCC the best-detailed records (for its short life) among its contemporary and often competing organizations." As "a devotee of W. E. B. Du Bois and a former high school teacher and newspaper reporter for the *Chicago Defender*," as Bond wrote of Forman, Forman certainly understood the importance of creating "a rich record of day-to-day doings not normally available to the public."¹⁰ The pace and intensity of organizing might have precluded time for examining it if Forman, Bond, Elizabeth Sutherland (Martínez), Cobb, and O'Neal had not underlined the importance of writing. Bernice Johnson Reagon would quote Forman: "We had to preserve what we were doing for our archives; no one else would do that for us."¹¹

Creating an archive is vital to any group's history. As Shawn Michelle Smith elucidates, "If one cannot or does not produce an archive, others will dictate the terms by which one will be represented and remembered; one will exist in the future in someone else's archive."¹² Marshall Ganz, who left Harvard for Freedom Summer and then remained in Amite County, Mississippi, was unequivocal: "If you don't interpret to others your calling and your reason for doing what you're doing ... other people will ... claim authorship of your story." In "Why Stories Matter" (2008), Ganz echoed Forman's metaphor that SNCC together comprised a book, saying, "All of us walk around with a text from which to teach, the text of our own lives."¹³ SNCC wrote on its own terms, using project and area reports to create press releases, fact sheets, descriptions of funding drives, and material for speeches.¹⁴ For example, when Dick Gregory delivered a powerful speech to a mass meeting in Selma on October 4, 1963, he was scathing about the clergy's failure to offer support. David Houck and David Dixon suggest that Forman had showed Gregory a field report by Bernard Lafayette listing attempts he and Colia Lafayette had made to convince ministers, black and white, to support the Selma project, most of which were rebuffed. Forman lauded this report as "one of the finest accounts of just what it meant to be a SNCC field worker."¹⁵

In Forman's conception, a report ought to contain an organizer's ideas and analyses as well as what might have been unsaid in a meeting or articulated incompletely. In 1965, for example, Chicago organizers expressed "notes for position papers never written" as a poem: "cause we as SNCC / are too clumsy with ourselves ... we have 'no time' to know / touch deeply... I guess we'll have to concern ourselves with running / organizing the 'revolution.'"[16] Forman emphasized that reports could contain "lyrical descriptions" of "exactly how an organizer goes about his or her work."[17] They strengthened communications then (and SNCC's legacy in print now) because, as Forman put it, "Nothing that might be written in retrospect could capture the full reality of our work so well as on-the-spot recording."[18] The weight placed on self-narration and group narration did not go unchallenged. Elaine DeLott admitted that she "scoffed" in 1964 when Forman told volunteers "he was keeping a record of our actions for history, and that when this was all over he would be the author of this history." She believed then, "To consider one's place in history was reactionary thinking. How could anyone act in the moment and think of history at the same time?"[19] However, DeLott's archive is among the most useful for researchers; the introductions she has written to each document conserved are self-aware and illuminating. If all organizers did not agree unhesitatingly, the most surprising dissenter was Stembridge because she facilitated the purchase of a printing press; her poetry is a valuable primary resource, but she was concerned with how penury was understood.[20] As a member of the communications team, Mary King was adamant. "How can we expect the rest of the country to understand the need for this struggle if they don't know how bad things are in Mississippi?" she told Stembridge, echoing an internal report that reminded organizers: "Ninety-five percent of the time our staff forms the primary link with 'the outside world.' Whenever there are atrocities committed against the local population, we must assume responsibility for communicating these to the news media and interested groups."[21] King elicited Stembridge's help with a publication, but she was concerned that they were "mechanistic": "'To make a flyer, it takes at least one gimmick,' Jane said cynically.... 'There's no gimmick; these people are starving and they're cold.'" In a letter in which Stembridge unpacked her view for King, she wrote, "If you want the record, it's inside of me and I can write it out again and can write through this night or any other night five thousand pages of people and faces and long lines stretching from Yazoo City to Greenville and backed up to Itta Bena, wrapping around Winona and ending up at my front door—cold and hungry and tired and waiting."[22] This long run-on sentence paragraph closes with a present participle that features often in SNCC's writing, "waiting": "To a person going through one of these towns, the dominant impression is of large numbers of people who are *waiting*. That is precisely their condition, they have been *kept* available in a kind of perpetual waiting for the times when their labor would be needed on the plantations."²³ Guyot and Thelwell's analysis suggests why the FST chose to perform Samuel Beckett's *Waiting for Godot* (1953) and Douglas Turner Ward's *Day of Absence* (1965) for audiences waiting to work, waiting in line to register to vote, "waiting for somebody to bring Freedom in," as Mrs. Hamer observed on seeing *Godot* performed.²⁴ In personal writing, Stembridge conveyed rural poverty as unremitting and urgent, but while campaign brochures were strategically adroit (and fund-raising kept in mind while creating them), she feared exploiting poor people as objects of pity. A Bob Moses letter to Martha Prescod encapsulates the moral dilemma in SNCC over the privacy of penury:

> Just this afternoon, I was sitting resting, having finished a bowl of stew, and a silent hand reached over from behind, mumbling some words of apology and permission, and stumbled up with a neckbone from the plate under the bowl, which I had discarded.... The hand was back again, five seconds later groping for the potatoes I had left in the bowl. I never saw the face, I didn't look. The hand was dark, dry and wind cracked, from cotton chopping and cotton picking. Lafayette and I got up and walked out. What the hell are you going to do when a man has to pick up a leftover potato from a bowl of stew?²⁵

The "cold and hungry and tired and waiting" are visceral. King saved Stembridge's letter, seeing in it the "radical moral vision of the early student movement" and sensing their conversation as being important to record.

In a 1963 pamphlet telling "the story of Danville," Dorothy Miller (Zellner) put a new spin on the words of a chamber of commerce publication that said "Danville, Virginia invites you to make our city your city—a fine place to live and work." Her prose was taut and irony sharp:

> A young Negro woman who will bear the scars of a police billy stick on her face for the rest of her life—she questions Danville as "a fine place to live and work." A Negro man who was beaten so savagely by police that he nearly lost an eye and was refused medical attention in jail for three days—he has questions also.
>
> This "fine place" erupted into racial turmoil in late May, 1963 and, for its size, is running a close race with Birmingham for top honors in police brutality.

She closed on a caveat as sensitive to the responsibility to record on behalf of others as Stembridge might have wished to see: "The end of this story cannot be written now, and will only be written by the Negro community in Danville, the heroes who were beaten but were not afraid to go back." Miller ventriloquized demonstrators as a chorus of voices challenging lies promulgated by civic leaders: "You can work with us to make this a truly 'fine place to live and work' or you can, as you have already done, try to thwart us in every way you devise. But no matter which way you choose, the outcome will eventually be the same. We will win."[26] SNCC told the Danville story in different narrative forms. Matthew Jones celebrated Reverend McGhee in "Move On: Legend of Danville" and commemorated Buford Holt as the "demonstrating G.I. from Fort Bragg" arrested in his hometown:

> The police said 'You ain't overseas,
> And don't forgit one simple fact:
> That your skin is still black.

The power of musical performance is lost on the page, but song composition was one of many ways individuals drew creatively on field reports.[27] When submission of field reports declined, people in the Atlanta office thought up and encouraged new methods of documentation that were instituted, to varying degrees of success. Without reports it was impossible to provide up-to-the-minute press releases.[28] Cobb celebrated field reports as a rich cultural store, judging in 2010 that "somebody in the year 2110 will find them useful in understanding the work." They are fundamental to SNCC's internal culture and, when reworked for external readers, a narrative tool explicating SNCC's organizing model because, as Cobb affirmed, "movement experience is an organizer's experience."[29]

Reports as "Vivid Little Stories"

SNCC was supported by the Southern Regional Council (and wrote for its newsletter *New South*) and by the Southern Conference Educational Fund (SCEF), publishing in its journal *Southern Patriot*, edited by Carl and Anne Braden.[30] SCEF also donated $5,000 annually to support a white southern SNCC organizer. In Bond's view, the Bradens identified SNCC as a "vanguard challenging not just the segregation system but older organizations too," and in the early years *Southern Patriot* was a rare outlet for news of southern battlefields.[31] It was a model for the *Student Voice*, and SCEF and SRC writers advised SNCC's communications team.[32] Anne Braden would remain a staunch advocate after Carl died in 1975, helping craft SNCC's legacy by situating it in relation to subsequent struggles in *Southern Patriot* (which would cease publication in 1976) and other publications, including *Southern Exposure*.[33] The Bradens' support is acknowledged in historical studies, but the SRC's Margaret Long is not. She was proactively involved in how SNCC composed its stories.

A progressive columnist for the *Atlanta Journal* and *New South* and a novelist whose daughter, Margaret "Sissy" Leonard, joined sit-ins and was jailed as a Freedom Rider, Long advised Bond's team how to write copy in imaginative ways—by building on field reports. In 1965, for example, she was the consultant for a brochure aimed at colleges. Long recommended that each abstract phrase and jargon term be reworked and deleted formulations that risked reducing SNCC's role to coordination rather than agitation or that made it seem reliant on external, "adult," resources—the "resource mobilization" Doug McAdam identified later for screening insurgent, indigenous politics.[34] She commended to Bond *Revolution in Mississippi* (1962) by Tom Hayden, a twenty-cent pamphlet and one of SDS's "Southern Reports," it circulated in SNCC and CORE, as a model because Hayden wrote vividly of the effects of violence and feelings of "outrage and suffering." Drawing on his experience in McComb, Hayden wrote a personally political evocation of the "southern struggle against racial bigotry," the first social movement flagged in SDS's Port Huron Statement (1962) because "it compelled most of us from silence to activism."[35] He asked: "How do we make the situation real to outsiders—those who know not the people involved, the state, the county, and, most of all, the social, political, economic, cultural, religious, historic pattern we have labelled 'segregation'?" His stated aim was "to make the facts real and evoke not reader interest but productive commitments" (1). Pausing to cogitate on the act of writing, Hayden worried, like Stembridge, that "perhaps this situation cannot be adequately conveyed":

> Does it become more real in noting that a white man connected with the broadcasting system *there* sees the solution to the problem in "throwing those little niggers in one bag, castrating them, and dropping the bag in the river?" Does it become more real in visualizing Herbert Lee lying on his face for two hours [dead]? Does it become real in recognizing that those Negroes are *down there*, digging in, and in more danger than nearly any student in this American generation has faced? What does it take? When do we begin to see it all *not as remote* but as breathing urgency into our beings and meaning into our ideals? (my emphases, 20–21).

To breathe urgency into participatory democracy, Hayden put flesh on the media's "human interest stories," from which he believed readers had not yet gleaned "even a skeleton of the truth of Mississippi." His objective was to rally students in the burgeoning New Left by showing them how "SNCC was instrumental in initiating the turmoil" in the civil rights South (1). In his foreword, Chuck McDew as SNCC chairman in 1962 underlined that it conveyed "more than an abstract reality [of what] 'colored people are doing down there'" and praised Hayden for imparting a "real picture."[36] The synergistic relationship between writers in SNCC and SDS is a feature of the New Left's print culture. Paul Lauter, volunteering with Florence Howe in 1965, recalled an MFDP leaflet, "No Vietnamese Ever Called Me Nigger," as inspiration for another SDS pamphlet and saw noncompliance with the military draft as "another fire which began there in Mississippi."[37] Jack Newfield, a charter member of SDS, located SNCC as the vanguard of the "prophetic minority" of student-led groups coalescing as a social movement. Carson and Hogan emphasize SNCC's importance in the conceptualization of the New Left, and Polletta notes how closely "SDS's fortunes were intertwined with SNCC's from its inception."[38] Nevertheless, in studies of print generated by the New Left, SNCC gets short shrift, occluded there as in most literary histories of the Black Arts Movement.[39]

Long extolled Hayden's style, advising SNCC to publicize its "vitality, effectiveness and even heroism" to indicate why "this SDS fellow goes to jail and gets beaten up in the street with you." Her letter was a master class for telling "vivid little stories" of projects, "vignettes" of operations "from McComb to Baton Rouge," and "exactly what a field secretary does when [he or she] goes into a place." This was the kind of information Forman and Bond expected to receive via field reports, and in Long's view it would enliven all communications if adapted to depict "vividly the aid, comfort, training and fellow-suffering and action you contribute to the local uprisings all over the South." That she conducted such a detailed review reflects how impassioned she was that SNCC write its own stories.

Long featured SNCC in her monthly column "Strictly Subjective" in *New South*. She castigated other news media for not covering what was related "ably and assiduously in the press releases of civil rights organizations" and evidenced in innumerable court affidavits SNCC collected in black southern communities harassed by white supremacists: "the sorry story of southern ... tyranny [otherwise] protected from public view." While "brutal abuse in jails of Negro demonstrators" was "carefully reported in SNCC releases," she saw it discarded by her white media colleagues "as so much more mimeograph."[40] She wrote a portrait of Ruby Doris Smith (Robinson) as "an indefatigable revolutionary" of "that incomprehensible band," interweaving Smith's account of being suspended from walls by "wrist breakers" and forcibly scrubbed in jail.[41] Long positioned herself on behalf of "humane southern newspaper readers" who deserved to know how their tax dollars were spent on a corrupt justice system: "I saw a picture of Worth Long, a North Carolinian with an Arkansas and Alabama police record in the Movement, after a stay in the county jail in Selma with his face so battered and swollen I hardly recognized him. I asked Sheriff Jim Clark about this appalling photograph and he said 'somebody might have slapped him.' I can't imagine why a deputy or jailor should slap Mr. Long, except out of distaste for his career in the Deep South liberation."[42] This was the subjective reporting she advocated, her use of the honorific "Mr." a rebuttal of newspaper editors who refused to use titles for African Americans or to report systematic abuse in jails and courtrooms.[43]

Long was not alone in recognizing that writing by organizers was a rich primary source. Pat Watters and Reese Cleghorn collated field reports from 1962 through 1964 in *Climbing Jacob's Ladder* (1967). They selected "dramatic" and "colorful" examples, asserting their "unique contribution to the literature of American history," but left them to stand without analysis beyond a single introductory paragraph.[44] Excerpts from field reports are scattered throughout civil rights histories, and some compilers of anthologies include selections, as John F. McClymer does in *Mississippi Freedom Summer* (2004) and Jennifer Jensen Wallach and John Kirk in *Arsnick* (2011). Reports themselves have not received focused attention except for Sarah Riva's study of Bill Hansen's.[45] They have yet to be read for how they may constitute "the literature of American history."

Windows on the Work

Inside SNCC, obsession with reporting could be the subject of wry humor. Mahoney was the butt of jokes when he bleached all feeling from a letter to his girlfriend, organizer Jeanie Bell. On paper embossed with SNCC's letterhead, it "read like a field report. 'Look at how he ends the letter,' she said, laughing almost tearfully. Her true love concluded after reporting matter-of-factly on movement events, 'Yours for freedom, William J. Mahoney.'"[46] Reports demanded a sense of readership, whether Atlanta office staff or the authorial self. De Lissovoy admitted to affecting "what I hoped was a sophisticated irony, in order to disguise from myself that I had already fallen in love with Albany, GA." Organizers took pains to demonstrate creative flair, and Bond confided in Moses how field-workers in Southwest Georgia wrote like "frustrated novelists" after Forman shared reports in which he discerned "a decided[ly] Proustian influence."[47] John O'Neal and Jack Chatfield conceived of an anthology of "notes from native sons and daughters," urging peers to mail a copy to the Albany project "if [their] participation in the movement [had] been set down on paper."[48] Reports were usually more modestly literary, of course, a memory aid for a project director who needed to summarize and distill the difficulties of grassroots organizing. They typically included requests for financial support, as epitomized by one Frank Smith submitted in 1962. After traveling 470 miles around the Mississippi Delta, speaking with some five hundred people over November and December, he expended more words diagnosing subsistence-level problems: "If we aren't trying to scrape a few nickels for gasoline, then we are trying to get money to pay bills for supplies, or to pay the garage man or the gas station bill. These are extra difficulties which add to the already existing difficulties and serve not to aid the projects at all."[49] Willie Ricks recounted similar problems in Lee County, Georgia, in March 1964, when sixty people came forward to register to vote in one week:

> On Monday we took 15 down, after getting the people to the courthouse, we had a blowout. NO TIRE, NO GAS, NO MONEY: . . .
> WE ARE BROKE AND HUNGRY, GOING DAY BY DAY WITH NO MORE THAN ONE MEAL, AND SOMETIMES NOTHING. I HAVE BEEN SPENDING MY SUBSISTENCE MONEY FOR THE LAST SEVEN WEEKS ON NOTHING BUT NEEDS IN THE FIELD.[50]

Reports contain astute analyses extrapolated from local situations. Charles Sherrod uncovered how white supremacists prevented cross-county cooperation by sheer force of rumor: "[T]he people in Albany have been afraid to go to Terrell County; the people in Terrell are afraid to go to Leesburg; the people in Sumter County feel that the people in Leesberg and Dawson are the victims of merciless situations . . . and the people are therefore afraid to associate freely at any time of day or night." A community enterprise, spearheaded by a local man in the form of a credit union, promised to strengthen cross-community links.[51] Concerned about gang culture in North Albany, and the problem of maintaining a professional image when sexual relationships were developing between white male civil rights workers and young black women in the city, Sherrod raised issues fictionalized by De Lissovoy in *Feelgood* in 1970. Three months into his post as director, Forman discerned that the Albany movement comprised a publishable case study. He wrote to Ballantine Books arguing that such a book could constitute "an answer" to John Bartlow Martin's *The Deep South Says Never*, published by Ballantine in 1957. Martin had argued that after the *Brown* decision, massive resistance to desegregation was implacable, impenetrable. Albany's mass protests represented the tremors reverberating through the supposedly "solid" South. Apart from Sherrod, Cordell Reagon, or Charlie Jones, who initiated the project in Southwest Georgia and did not consider themselves writers, it would be difficult to imagine anyone whose résumé fit the subject better than Forman: "As Executive Director of the Student Nonviolent Coordinating Committee and as one who took the original Freedom Ride to Albany and participated in the decision making of that week—as I shall continue to do—I feel I am very well qualified to write on this subject." Forman assured Ballantine that he was poised to begin, with access to evidence other potential authors could not amass, in the form of field reports, affidavits, and recordings.[52] A surge of mass protests in December 1961 saw 737 people jailed in a week, and Howard Zinn reported to the SRC, "Into that week of protest and excitement was compressed every major issue debated today in the changing South."[53] Even Albany police chief Laurie Pritchett admitted that the protest united African American communities.[54] Publisher Ian Ballantine responded to Forman:

> Although the efforts of the Freedom Riders are most important, it seems to me early for us to do a book on this subject. Newspaper and magazine coverage is intense. We are not commercially successful when we fail to offer either a unique subject or point of view.
>
> Sometime in the future we hope to find a history of the Non-Violent Resistance Movement.
>
> Thank you for writing.[55]

He misunderstood the difference between Freedom Rides and local organizing. Nor did Ballantine see Forman's insider perspective as unique, as Julius Lester would when describing Forman as "perhaps more qualified than any other individual" to write a biography of Sammy Younge Jr. in 1968.[56] In 1961, Forman was prescient. In *The Southern Mystique* (1964), "a speculative essay based on personal experience," Zinn found Martin's assessment in *The Deep South Says Never* suspect, and Albany bore out his speculation.[57] Forman's book would have been a precursor to studies published in the 1980s: William Chafe's tracing the movement in Greensboro, North Carolina in 1980, Aldon Morris's revisionist history *The Origins of the Civil Rights Movement: Black Communities Organizing for Change* in 1984, and Robert Norrell's examination of Tuskegee in 1985.

Forman conceived of his proposed book as weaving together "personal history stories of the people who make up this movement," as Anne Braden told radical lawyer Victor Rabinowitz, from whom Forman sought $1,500 for travel, tapes, and transcriptions. She believed Forman would bring "the *inner feeling of the movement that no outsider could have* . . . the human side of this great story in the South" when "[m]ost of what is being written is dry statistics or generalizations about what's going on—not the life-blood of the movement." Braden made an impassioned case, emphasizing, "[If] not done at the time it's going on, it gets lost and forgotten and never recorded."[58] In 1965, Robert Coles expressed similar urgency, admitting that "it is so easy to categorize and give names to experiences once we are done with them" but that "much of their original and spontaneous character" would be lost in retrospective interpretations.[59] SNCC communications condensed into flyers interviews like those Forman conducted. A New York magazine, the *New Freedom*, beseeched Forman for recordings made in McComb, and Staughton Lynd published a transcription of Moses describing working in Mississippi in 1962. The latter was a primary source for Zinn in *SNCC: The New Abolitionists* (1964), but Lynd admitted, "Neither Howard nor I know exactly when, under what circumstances, and by whom the tape was recorded."[60] It was probably Forman with a study like Zinn's in mind.

Most windows on the work were smaller but no less revealing. Reporting from Benton County, Mississippi, in the summer of 1964, Pete Cummings submitted character sketches of Sheriff Brookes Ward, his deputies, and the county attorney. His insights let incoming workers know who was "a snake in the grass," who might protect them against violent reprisals, and who "might end up hitting someone because he won't know what else to do." He named local whites who professed to support SNCC but were afraid "to stand up and do anything."[61] Such reports show how local politics worked in the segregated South. Jack Chatfield's detailed reports contained character studies and vignettes that were made resonant by his overarching personal narrative of coming to consciousness. One "ancient man" Chatfield met while canvassing was blind, and Chatfield expressed their conversation as an epiphany: "It was as though he had been waiting for us a very long time—and the wait was not for someone who could lift him out of the tragedy, but who could understand it." Chatfield located the power of understanding in the man before he found it in himself but made him symbolize his own evolving political convictions.[62] This report also epitomizes the tightrope literary writers would need to negotiate to portray local people sensitively but not sentimentally.

Field Texts

Julian Bond cofounded a student newspaper at Morehouse College and reported for the *Atlanta Inquirer*, an independent weekly founded in July 1960. He was media savvy as well as a talented poet.[63] The first issue of the *Student Voice*, produced by Jane Stembridge in June 1960, included a poem by Bond, but, once he became focused on media operations, Mary King credited him for "originating and developing the creativity" of SNCC's approach in wider efforts to change national opinion.[64] Bond reminded staff continually, as he did Cynthia Washington in the Washington, D.C., office, that they would need to push stories whenever journalists were "too lazy" to pursue them.[65] At any one time, there were five people on Bond's media team, including King, Dorothy Miller (Zellner), Betty Garman, Charles Cobb, and Bill Mahoney, but it was always broader than its small, changing staff. Casey Hayden did such work on SNCC's behalf, inviting rabbi and political activist Arthur Waskow to publish "the implications of the civil rights movement in the South," stressing, "First-hand accounts... need so much to be published in journals like *Saturday Review*. Think about it. I think you could be very valuable if you could get down even for a few weeks to travel and observe and then write about it."[66] Bond's team edited field reports into what he called "actualities," as Margaret Long advocated, increasing SNCC's print production and readership exponentially in August 1964 when biographies, "actualities," and photographs were mailed to television and radio stations in hometowns of Freedom Summer volunteers and the *Student Voice* reached forty thousand mailings per issue.[67]

Elizabeth Sutherland (Martínez) was writing all the time.[68] An editor at Simon and Schuster in New York, she edited *Letters from Mississippi* (1965) and plowed royalties into COFO. The American Library Association declared it one of five most notable books published that year.[69] She focused on SNCC in articles for the national press. "The Cat and Mouse Game" in the *Nation*, for example, examined SNCC's record across Hattiesburg, Indianola, Greenwood, Greenville, Natchez, Biloxi, Gulfport, Shaw, Itta Bena, Clarksdale, and Jackson, Mississippi. Building on field reports and her experience in SNCC, Sutherland gave readers a chilling picture: "My most frightening hour... was not on a dark road with a police spotlight suddenly turned on my car, or watching the pick-up truck in my rear view mirror. It was in the office of a county attorney who chatted politely about the lack of rain.... Then unexpectedly he stopped smiling and said, in a calm voice, 'You know, everything I have is in this town—my work, my family, my farm. *I intend to protect them.*' It was a simple little statement delivered with unmistakable portent and maximum hostility."[70] A project Sutherland and Forman conceived resulted in *The Movement: Documentary of a Struggle for Equality*. Mary King described it as Simon and Schuster's "contribution to the movement rather than a business venture."[71] When

Sutherland joined SNCC, Alan Rinzler inherited the responsibility of taking the book through production, and he later recounted how Lorraine Hansberry, having raised funds for SNCC, agreed to write the text even before she saw the photographs, most taken by Danny Lyon, that would provide context.[72] Hansberry completed her contribution between stints of hospitalization, recording in her journal, "I think when I get my health back I shall go into the South to find out what kind of revolutionary I am." But cancer killed her in 1965.[73]

The Movement is a capacious field report. In an allusive, speakerly text, Hansberry ventriloquized SNCC's organizers "working, talking, persuading: 'Come down and try to register. You may lose your job, you may even lose your house. You may be beaten ... but join us, come down and register to vote.'" The freedom struggle is "the bitter weariness of a Mississippi field hand; the dauntless good humor of a twelve-year-old girl in a Georgia jail; the rage and hatred of a Ku Klux Klansman; the troubled expression of a white Southerner forced to reconsider his way of living and thinking."[74] The book situates SNCC among other organizations, from the NAACP to the Nation of Islam. If the latter's mythologizing of black history seems to contradict that mapped in *The Movement*, John Lewis pointed out in 1964 that the Nation of Islam's *Muhammad Speaks* reported "more of SNCC activities and the entire freedom struggle than any other paper in the United States, black or white."[75] SNCC battlegrounds from Monroe, North Carolina, and Cambridge, Maryland, through Deep South states are represented, but Hansberry reminds readers that "the Movement is very old" and that African Americans are "old stock" Americans and *"certain of the rightness* [that] we ... borrow as freely from Patrick Henry as from contemporary slang" (38, 99). While working on this project, Hansberry told a forum on "The Black Revolution and the White Backlash" that "[since 1619] Negroes have tried every method of communication ... from petition to the vote—everything—we've tried it all ... and now the charge of impatience is simply unbearable."[76] Tracing revolutionary insurrectionists from Nat Turner through Robert F. Williams, *The Movement* emphasized that, inspired by forefathers, African Americans had "rekindled" their righteousness and were marching "across the southern landscape" (23, 42). The words of sharecroppers, demonstrators, and organizers are densely interwoven and humanize statistics: "This man earns about $2.50 a day" (22). An opening image shows U.S. 49, SNCC's main line from the Gulf Coast through Jackson, Yazoo City, Indianola, and Greenwood, Mississippi, into Arkansas. Documents include Moses's letter from the Magnolia jail,

Executive Committee minutes, a succinct retelling of the Danville story, and evidence of the privation of the Leesburg Stockade, where schoolgirls in Georgia were imprisoned for weeks and Danny Lyon snuck inside to photograph them staring through cell bars (79, 44, 125, 80–81). Sara Blair argues that Hansberry found in *The Movement* a means to "press beyond the expressive limits of conventional realist drama" and makes an intriguing case for it as an extended meditation, but she foregrounds Hansberry as the book's maker, assuming that she selected and arranged photographs "in the absence of commentary about the origins of the project."[77] My research reveals that for SNCC *The Movement* was "Danny Lyon's book"; in Rinzler's experience he acted as collaborating editor.[78] Lyon selected and captioned the book's photographs, and his commentary appears in an appendix (125–28). Forman signed off the project, including the title change from provisional *Freedom Now* to *The Movement*, with copyright held by SNCC.[79] Hansberry accepted the commission to collaborate. Lending her name promoted sales and indicated quality, but SNCC had final say on content.

The Movement inspired other publications, like one intended to teach children about the long African American freedom struggle. Frank Cieciorka's drawings and his wife Bobbi's text combined in *Negros in American History: A Freedom Primer* (1965), designed to rival the popular coloring book *Color Me Brown* produced by the Johnson Publishing Company. Cobb introduced it as "a history book about us ... us today, as well as about us yesterday," and this dual focus can be seen in the section on Reconstruction. Illustrated by a cartoon urging people to "Vote for Julian Bond" for the Georgia legislature, it compares Union Leagues in the 1880s to the MFDP in the 1960s and situates Bond's campaign in a continuum.[80] In an audit of its print culture in 1967, SNCC assessed, "The *Freedom Primer* read by 10 or 15 students in one rural community center does more to break down the myth surrounding Afro-Americans[,] i.e. 'niggers never did nothing anyway, so they ain't gonna do nothing good now,' than a dozen street demonstrations."[81]

In 1963, Bond opened an interpretative piece on nonviolence for *Freedomways* with an epigraph from a field secretary's report and then studded his article with quotations from SNCC's organizers, numbering forty-two at that point in the organization's history, including Ruby Doris Smith (Robinson) and William Porter.[82] Pioneering projects in McComb and Albany established the value of reports as analysis and illustration. In *The Making of Black Revolutionaries*, Forman transcribed a report Bob

Moses wrote on August 29, 1961, because it distilled "all the major elements of SNCC's struggle in Mississippi": flagrant denial of voting rights, violence and terrorism directed at all those challenging the status quo, and the conspiracy of police and courts to maintain a rigid, implacable, racialized system.[83] Affidavits and depositions were another source drawn upon by writers working in a wide variety of narrative modes. *The Making of Black Revolutionaries* is representative, as Forman substantiates his subjective-collective history by referencing field reports by Charles Sherrod, Bob Moses, Lawrence Guyot, Luvaughn Brown, Willie Peacock, and Ivanhoe Donaldson.

Field reports comprised the first form in which travesties of justice were recounted by organizers. Used in literary texts, they constitute signature scenes, as Denise Nicholas recognized when she suggested to John Lewis, SNCC's chairman in 1965, that field reports constituted the optimal source from which playwright George Tabori might produce original plays for the FST to perform.[84] Ivanhoe Donaldson transformed an incident from a 1963 field report in his "southern diaries" for *Freedomways* in 1964, and Charles Cobb returned to the same incident for new readers in poetic form. When Donaldson, Cobb, Frank Smith, and Jesse Harris were pulled over by four police officers, Donaldson came close to death when an officer turned a gun on him inside a police car before beating him with the butt. He demonstrated how ubiquitous such encounters were, concluding, "There was simply nothing to do except to chalk it up as something to be expected, especially when you're trying to bring the vote to the black man in Mississippi."[85] Incidents like this—a Landy McNair affidavit details a similar encounter with Al Lingo in Gadsden, Alabama, in the summer of 1963—were lenses through which analysis was filtered in other genres. Donaldson reported that organizers had been close to a gas station just inside Rankin County when pulled over, just outside of the officers' jurisdiction. The officer who abused Donaldson seethed: "'*Black son of a bitch, I'm gonna kill you, nigger. God damn it, I'm gonna kill you!*' he was almost hysterical as he lifted his gun and put it just inches from my face. He cocked the hammer and for a couple of seconds I felt it was just about all over. Just about the same time he was cocking the hammer, one of the other three policemen who were outside with the fellows, came in and told the other cop, '*You just can't kill that nigger heah!*'"[86] The poem Cobb wrote turns on the words the officer spat: "If I had your goddamn ass over in Brandon, I'd kill you." Cobb distilled the ritual wherein "four black boys with hands up at gunpoint on a / near deserted Mississippi highway" were "amusement."

Polemic was unnecessary. Rather than reproduce all of what Donaldson called the "routine Mississippi cop interrogation," Cobb isolated the precise phrase containing the reason Donaldson escaped death, compressing his fear at the time into two visceral lines:

> Shivers from cold and shivers from fear, blurred
> into an uncontrollable convulsion of the body.[87]

Cobb signed off on the poem as for a field report, "Brandon, Miss. Winter 1963."[88] This poem operates in the way T. S. Eliot posited an event may be concentrated in a poetic encounter with readers after the fact: "There is ... a moment that can never be forgotten, but which is never repeated integrally; and yet which would become destitute of significance if it did not survive in a larger whole of experience; which survives inside a deeper and calmer feeling."[89] The poem was published in Cobb's *In the Furrows of the World* and anthologized in Todd Gitlin's *Campfires of the Resistance* (1971). Gitlin included a number of SNCC writers—Cobb, Stembridge, Casey Hayden, Maria Varela, Terry Cannon, and Marilyn Lowen—as poets living "on the edge where public and private meet, within the events" and within "the history [that] they are trying to fill out and communicate by writing," by conveying "what lies beyond the slogans."[90]

The first of SNCC's poets to publish collections, Stembridge and Cobb were at the forefront of the endeavor to convey being "in the event" in poetry. They crystallized subjective history in poetry, but Stembridge questioned the role of politics in writing in a way Cobb did not. Lillian Smith impressed upon Stembridge that poetry and politics would not mix: "When I begin to be political, I begin certainly to lie because poetry is in opposition to ideology." Stembridge wrote to Mary King that she had been stunned by Smith: "[She] refused to talk to me when I became political." Her mentor's correspondence dwindled to silent disapproval that Stembridge felt as misunderstanding of her fieldwork. She wrote to Smith in frustration: "Mississippi is hell. My life here has been hell—goddamn fucking hell of a nowhere of death." In Pete Daniel's view, the tension lay in the "shifting of generational plates" and Smith's "disregard of Stembridge's risk and bravery."[91] It is ironic that in 1950 Smith had told a mostly black audience at Howard University, when awarded an honorary doctorate, that "moderation had never mastered an ideal or met a crisis successfully ... never invented anything, never dreamed a new dream." Smith was honored as a "revolutionist" with enough "dynamite" in her words "to blow up segregated civilization."[92] At SNCC's October 1960 conference,

Smith's stirring speech emphasized "self-sacrifice." She offered herself, and those of her generation whose support she was sure young activists would inspire, as "a sure strong bridge over which you can cross into the new unmade world." Her imagery resounded in SNCC, with Chatfield musing, "You cannot forget the force of two hundred years [when you attempt to] break a world in two." However, the bridge became a wedge, with the condescension Smith showed Stembridge implied even then: "We who are older can help you out of the quicksands and the worst whirlpools."[93] Smith failed to comprehend the young activists' independence and to predict how despondent they would feel, as Stembridge suggested in a field report from Greenwood: "The sky is very gray and soon it will be very dark and between now and then the revolution will not have been completed and I wonder if the sum total of field reports, clothes distribution, mass meetings, and voting will make us love each other more or if anything will or if it matters."[94] This splicing of the lyrical with the material informs Stembridge's poem "Field Report" (1966), wherein the political is fused with the metaphysical. The "five thousand pages" Stembridge told Mary King were inside her are compared to insubstantial cotton bolls

> caught in
> the weeds
> on
> the
> edge
> of
> the
> highway
> from
> Greenwood
> to Tchula.[95]

The highway was the north–south artery of SNCC's registration activity in Mississippi.

Poetic bulletins from the field were many, but Thelwell perceived synergies between the firsthand experiences described in field reports and the creative expression of personal essays and short stories. His sharp critical thinking was evident in staff meetings when his "hard-hitting" statements of purpose augured debate.[96] In a heterotopic, camera-eye depiction, he filtered field reports into a story of a tour he undertook with Stokely Carmichael.[97] In an intimate conversation with readers of "Fish Are Jumping an' the Cotton Is High: Notes from the Mississippi Delta" (1966), he delicately enabled an inclusive glimpse into SNCC. The use of second person creates a sense of active solidarity and resonates with Walter Benjamin's formulation: "The storyteller takes what he tells from experience—his own or that reported by others. And in turn makes it the experience of those who are listening to his tale."[98]

Thelwell locates readers on a porous border between his witness testimony and their visualization of the Delta. He discloses thoughts and feelings as he shapes readers'—as if talking to himself in their hearing: "[It] reminds you of a field report from Panola County" (40).[99] Author and reader are conflated when entering the black section of Indianola: "Although this is your first time there, you recognize when you have come home. When the pavement runs out—the street lights become fewer or nonexistent and the rows of weather-textured, gray-grained clapboard shacks begin—you experience feelings of relief, almost love. This chaotic, dilapidated shantytown represents community, safety in numbers, friendship, and some degree of security after the exposed vulnerability of the highway" (42–43). Thelwell would explore finding a "home" in the movement in "The Organizer" (1966), where a fictionalized Delta project director feels he has "returned to a home he had never known, but always missed" (8). In this essay, he puts readers inside a SNCC car, creating a bridge for readers to cross into an urgent, continuous present for organizers. He made them privy to the gallows humor necessary to tamp down fear: "'Man, watch for a '63 Chevy, light grey, no plate on front an' a long aerial. . . .' The tension in the car draws to a fine edge. The patrolman who polices the next fifty or so miles of highway is known: 'Once is enough. That man would rather whup your head than eat shrimp . . . and he's a sea-food lover'" (41). The seemingly endless cotton fields fray Thelwell's nerves as they drive. He confides that "one might be in another century," but an airplane reminds him that a civil rights rally in Indianola was bombed by a crop-spraying plane in the fall of 1964 (39).[100] A highway billboard advertising pesticide to keep down boll weevils takes on equally chilling significance—"KILLS 'EM FAST, KEEPS 'EM DYING." For Thelwell this recalls the distress evident in a field report describing children who are exposed to "pizen" that eats flesh like acid and who are "plagued by running chancre-like sores." The field-worker wrote helplessly, "What can we do? . . . Isn't there some law . . . ?" (40).[101]

Thelwell's "notes from the Delta" comprise an orientation, as if readers may be compelled to join SNCC after absorbing sensory prose. Thelwell interlaces the words of SNCC colleagues with those of local people: "Is yo' a freedom fighter? Yo' come for the Meeting?" (43). Facts and statistics like those Minnis unearthed for organizers texture his prose. But only after readers are made to visualize children with distended bellies, "emaciated limbs, big prominent joints, [and] narrow chests in which each rib stands out" does Thelwell reveal that 33 percent of black babies die in the first year of their lives in Tallahatchie County (49). SNCC organized food and clothing drives from its inception after witnessing hunger and starvation, like that Moses recorded in his letter to Prescod, and the SRC funded six distinguished physicians to make a similar tour. Their report was unambiguous: "We do not want to quibble over words, but malnutrition is not quite what we found.... They are suffering from hunger and disease and directly or indirectly they are dying from them—which is exactly what 'starvation' means."[102] Thelwell explored what was witnessed, analyzed in scientific and medical reports, and explicated in sociological and legal discourse. For a wider readership, he returned to college reading of Faulkner for "the physical impact" of the Delta, weaving in quotations from Faulkner's "Delta Autumn" (1942) when guiding readers through a landscape that was unchanged, its ruling forces still racism and cotton. But Thelwell drew them beyond what was familiar from Faulkner into what Terry Cannon called "unsafe territory": "This is ... the very center of the myth and image, but what is its reality? For you right now, its only reality is heat, and an almost unbearable cumulative discomfort, sweat burning your eyes ... For the SNCC workers who are your companions the reality seems to be a certain tense caution. They watch the background intently for the car that may be the sheriff, the Highway Patrol, or one of the new radio-equipped prowl cars of the Klan" (38–39, 44, 40). Thelwell attuned readers to what volunteers discovered. Tracy Sugarman confided that before arriving in Ruleville he had imagined "The South" as "an exotic mixture of William Faulkner's *Intruder in the Dust*, Billy [sic] Holiday's 'Strange Fruit,' BB King's Delta blues, and Howard Fast's *Freedom Road*." In her novel *Freshwater Road*, Nicholas has her African American volunteer character admit on arrival, "I couldn't have imagined this place. Nothing I read, nothing I heard from any speaker on campus, no Bob Dylan song, no blues song, no photograph tells the truth about Mississippi."[103]

Jail Texts

Writers, especially those who majored in literature (like O'Neal, Thelwell, Cobb, Bond, and Stembridge), philosophy and history (like Moses and Chatfield), or political science and sociology (like Forman, Wheeler Smith, Mahoney and Nicholas), explicated the workings of SNCC's base camps. But individuals who did not conceive of themselves as writers also dug into organizing culture. In a stream-of-conscious journal entry, Elayne DeLott wrote about her first experience of jail—on December 3, 1964, after she was arrested for fielding African American candidates for the Agricultural Stabilization and Conservation Service. For SNCC workers, jail was quotidian after a "jail no bail" policy was initiated that built on sit-ins and Freedom Rides. Martin Luther King Jr. admired Nashville students for changing arrests "from badges of dishonor to badges of honor," and in Rock Hill, South Carolina, a "jail-in" took place on the first anniversary of the February 1, 1960, Greensboro, North Carolina, sit-in, and SNCC "bent the leaden habits of jail to their own convictions." It was "an emotional breakthrough" publicizing the moral, ethical, and political message of the movement.[104] Jail writings comprise a veritable genre of SNCC expression. These included letters written and smuggled out of jail by Moses, Forman, Charles McLaurin, and Randy Battle. For Pat Watters, "[t]he jail experience was central to all the movement, the symbolic ordeal, the mark of the highest honor. It had special symbolic significance for Negro Southerners who had, all their lives, known the white-controlled laws, courts and jails as a threat hanging over them."[105] Bernard Lafayette described the honor as being euphoric, but that changed when abuse and torture were rife.[106] When Dick Gregory was released from custody in Pine Bluff, Arkansas, with Bill Hansen, he told the press that jails were "torture chambers."[107] Sexual assault was rife, as discussed in chapter 9, and some officers of the law turned jail cells into their private fiefdoms. Charles Ware was shot in the neck while in the custody of Sheriff Warren Johnson of Baker County, Georgia, and Lawrence Guyot was tortured for hours in Winona's jail when detained for trying to check the well-being of Mrs. Hamer, beaten while in custody there, in June 1963. Richard H. King has since argued that "even the wretched jails of small southern towns became public spaces, an irony in its own right, since of all public institutions, the place of incarceration is the quintessential private place of dishonor where rights are drastically curtailed and freedom suspended, where there are no citizens[,] only subjects."[108] DeLott elucidated her sensibility as it shifted from treating arrest as honorable to discovering precisely how white supremacy operated in a closed society's jail.

De Lott recorded her arrest as a euphoric rush, exhilarated: "i kind of lay back on my cot, smiling kind of to myself, digging the filth and horror as a kind of justification of why i was there." It is the feeling De Lissovoy satirized as a rite of passage, when a short jail stint is "hardly enough to get a taste of jail" and "romance . . . still strong on the tongue."[109] DeLott's account split in two, first before CORE's George Raymond—her COFO project director—was thrown in the same jail, and then afterward.[110] She confessed self-centered pride and neither hid nor diluted her naïveté: "nervous, body alive, mind jumping, taking in all of it." DeLott had devoured Rilke's poetry, and her style reads as an attempt to channel the modernist's self-searching existentialism: "I possess an inner self of which I was ignorant. Everything now passes in thither."[111] She plays a "game," imagining what it would be like to spend a month in jail, but "then george came in." When Raymond is punished severely as a black organizer, DeLott's prose changes, as the "particular horror" of incarceration for Raymond pushes her into self-evaluation: "i am ashamed now of the way i felt when i came in."[112] When Raymond screams, she writes, "the whole meaning of people in jail, cruelty, humanity, society . . . began crystallizing in my body and emotions (and the mind which abstracts nonverbally for the body and emotions). i was screaming back at him." Her initial feeling of adventure is shattered. Fear and empathy cut through smugness and the sense of induction as a badge of honor. The affidavit DeLott wrote confirms her journal and describes demanding, over the course of three hours, to make a telephone call: "One of the prisoners was looking over a partition into the anteroom . . . and told me he was handcuffed. George was saying his arm was broken and that he wanted to see his doctor and his lawyer."[113] The difference between the introspective journal entry and the letter DeLott wrote her parents is even more marked: "[A]nother girl came in the next hour from another community. then george came in. the three of us talked, and were pretty much okay, except for being bored and a little hungry. the next morning they released us on bail. that's about it." Fear is pushed behind phrases that render the experience typical, mundane: "[J]ail was in some ways just like it is supposed to be in the south, with people playing harmonicas and singing every once in a while." For her worried parents, she screened facts, and elsewhere she described letters home as "half-true."[114]

DeLott's journal entries refute what she told her parents and show what is lost if we do not look beyond published accounts and legal depositions. William McCord doubted that "the usual prose" could convey intimidation, harassment, and the terrorism of beatings, bombings, and murders, believing that "somehow these words lose their force when one has to repeat them so often." In his 1965 participant-observer account of Freedom Summer, he turned to field reports, hoping to find "simple, direct language" to convey "nightmarish reality."[115] Self-consciously literary writing can convey this without the need for self-censorship. In a short, expressionistic piece that differentiates her experience carefully from Raymond's, DeLott suggests that jail and confinement writings must be understood in the collective context of civil rights organizing in the South. Now they may also be understood in the wider national context explicated by Michelle Alexander in *The New Jim Crow* (2010), the activist landscapes Dan Berger set out to define in *Captive Nation* (2014), and the rise of the neoliberal carceral state that Jordan T. Camp defines in *Incarcerating the Crisis* (2016).

Violent jail-cell interrogations and kangaroo courts were part of SNCC's reality. Sam Block, a veteran organizer who evidently never thought of himself as writer of literature, wrote an unpublished play that in another context would be read as excessively sensational. In "A Day in a Mississippi Court," Block condensed a long, dangerous, troubling, activist experience.[116] He had acquired, Taylor Branch wrote, "a reputation as a stubborn, lonely figure among the strange new breed of devout daredevils."[117] He decanted into the play a letter to President Lyndon Johnson, like those SNCC sent to federal officials on multiple occasions, that is read in a kangaroo court. He included a statement of evidence derived from warrants made on June 8, 1964, when, with Frank Smith, Charles McLaurin, Willie Peacock, and James Jones, he was arrested in Columbus, Mississippi. Block was beaten badly, while outside the other organizers were tied to trees in hundred-degree heat.[118] His civil rights worker protagonist sings "Let The Circle Be Unbroken" and intones a section of Baldwin's "Down at the Cross" (1963) as a secular prayer.[119]

Jail and court are rendered indistinguishably corrupt via characters based on individuals Block encountered in Greenwood while initiating SNCC's project there single-handedly in the summer of 1962. His courage and tenacity are the stuff of accolades and recorded by the organization's historians. Block worked alone, sleeping in a car before securing an office. He wrote an open letter exposing police brutality that Joan Trumpauer circulated widely, including to DoJ's Burke Marshall, Carl and Anne Braden for the SRC, and *Jet* magazine, among other media.[120] Greenwood was an "occupied city," as Frank Smith conveyed when cataloging escalating reprisals to signs of African American agency.[121] In the play, Captain Ussar is based on a police officer with whom Block tangled and Deputy Smitty on Wilbur Wardine Smith, infamous as "Big Smitty," henchman of Sheriff John Ed Cothran and the movement's most visible adversary in Greenwood.[122] Block told Paul Hendrickson, "We called him Sheriff Smitty. I didn't know he was the deputy sheriff. That distinction didn't even matter to me." Smith dislodged one of Block's eyes with the butt of his pistol and spat in his face, telling him to get out of town, and Block retorted,

"I came here to do a job." With Smitty visible on the streets of Greenwood, Cothran succeeded in "staying out of the camera eye."[123] As a consequence, perhaps, Block names his fictional sheriff "Matthews," suggesting Z. T. Matthews, sheriff of Terrell County, Georgia, notorious for having told *New York Times* reporter Claude Sitton, "We want our colored people to go on living like they have for the last hundred years."[124] Block exposed the institutionalization of corrupt sheriffs like Matthews, who was in his fourth consecutive term in 1962 when talking to Sitton.

In the play, a newspaperman's quest to unearth how "a Negro hung himself in . . . jail" is pointless. No amount of guile will sway the sheriff: "Nothing strange to us, quite a few Nigras have killed *theirself* in our jail." The only thing the sheriff does not withhold from a northern reporter is the vehemence with which he defends what he calls "our way of living." Block's white characters are twisted symbols of the justice system that he parodies; their warped mentality is that which resulted in the murders of Chaney, Schwerner, and Goodman, to whom he alludes in prefatory notes to the play. The moment the reporter exits the jail, an organizer is brought on stage in handcuffs, blood streaming down his face. Block's script is unusual because he names his avatar "Frank Smith" after a co-organizer, a student at Morehouse College with whom he worked closely. Block's prefatory notes indicate that he sought to illustrate "how much the Southern white man fears today's Negro." While he makes this character Mississippi-born, as Block was (in Cleveland, Mississippi), he is "a very educated person," undertaking graduate study in law at Yale, so that he will be considered an "outside agitator." A veteran of twenty-six incarcerations, prepared and articulate, the fictional Frank Smith quotes the law during a farcical, secret "trial" when officers of the court converge on the jail and "try" him according to articles written by the segregationist press that brand him a communist funded by the Southern Conference Educational Fund. Smith is alone in jail, as is typically the case in literature, because, as Mitchell Zimmerman noted in his movement diary, "like most mass injustices, these incidents only become meaningful [to readers] on the individual scale."[125]

The heart of the play is the double murder, and the impression created is business as usual. "Mrs. Robinson," present as court clerk, rushes offstage when the judge is shot and killed for expressing hesitancy in supporting his peers, and then Smith is shot (35). The story contrived for the press is that Smith grabbed the sheriff's gun, killed the judge, and then shot himself. When the "attorney" charges the white trustee Reid to "git rid" of the activist's body, Reid nods "Yussa" but cradles Smith and sobs

(37). The image is that of a pietà, but here the play reads like a model of the "theatrical procedure" E. V. Walter conceptualized in a 1969 study of state power and political violence: "Stripped to its essentials, a dramaturgic model of the terror process would include three actors: a source of violence, a victim, and a target. The victim perishes, but the target reacts to the spectacle."[126] The timing was wrong for such a cross-racial epiphany, and the FST did not perform this novice melodrama. In very different ways, Block and DeLott conveyed how harrowing jails were for organizers considered "guerilla fighters in the field of social change."[127]

SNCC organizers were more creative in their narratives than even Forman or Bond might have imagined. Thelwell points to one reason why in a metafictional comment on his method in his short story "The Organizer." The protagonist is on the communications team in Atlanta before organizing in the field. His role involves compiling depositions and turning incidents from field reports into press releases and affidavits: "He had written hundreds of coldly factual reports of burnings, bombings, and murders. And the 'statements,' how many of these had he written, carefully worded, expressing rage, but disciplined controlled rage, phrases of grief balanced by grim determination, outrage balanced by dignity, moral indignation balanced by political demands. Every time it was the same, yet behind those phrases, the anger and the sorrow and the fear were real."[128] Literary writers reconfigured what a SNCC working paper defined as "interpretive pieces which tell our story to those outside the movement, which pinpoint the issues that our action is directed toward."[129] In literature, it was possible to shape the organizing experience, and Charles Sherrod allows, "A lot of stuff was not written in view of record keeping. It was written out of passion and intensity."[130] This is a central component of SNCC's culture.

At Rock Bottom

Despite Bond and Forman's consternation that too many journalists wrote lukewarm, equivocating stories, SNCC's narrative culture did influence sympathetic reporters. Jack Newfield opened a feature article by quoting from a poem Stembridge would publish in *I Play Flute*:

> The real and exact job of a cop: STOP
>   STOP
> that is also true
> of executive committees
> and every government and

> organization in the whole world
> except
> small quick ones
> and plain people
> who love.[131]

In 1965, this poem distilled debates cresting in SNCC as to the efficacy of making centralized structures more robust after eighty-five new recruits stayed on at the end of the Freedom Summer project. Consensus decisions could be managed within a small, dedicated group, but by 1965 there was pervasive concern that SNCC was hemorrhaging as core staff left. Organizers were undervaluing what they achieved day by day, so Dorothy Zellner condensed field reports into a newsletter, *News from the Field*, to bolster morale in 1966 because "they tend to think that routine work and activity isn't important. *It is*."[132] Forman ruminated on the problem, circulating a "condition report" titled "Rock Bottom," in which he wrote, "Definitions of our goals have varied and still do vary from individual to individual, from this group of people to that group, from one period to another. However, there has been an underlying thread... the people in and associated with SNCC agreed that racism and segregation in this country [are] degrading, unjust, and a denial of our dignity, and that massive action was necessary to change the blatant forms of racism operating in the South."[133] Forman decided not to stand for reelection at the Kingston Springs, Tennessee, meeting in May 1966, not only because Ruby Doris Smith Robinson was the popular choice for executive secretary—his too—but also to "analyze and reflect on our experiences," but then he accepted Carmichael's request at the December 1966 meeting to return as organizational secretary. An education program to induct new staff and "instill [in them] a sense of the history of the organization" had been advocated by Diane Nash, Bob Moses, Casey Hayden, Fay Bellamy, and Mike Miller, among others.[134] In September 1966, Robinson, Minnis, Lester, Cleveland Sellers, Jennifer Lawson, Johnny Wilson, and John P. Tillman met with novelist John O. Killens and political scientist Charles V. Hamilton to devise workshops for comparative analysis of black protest organizations since Reconstruction, a cultural festival, and series of primers.[135] In 1967, Forman tried to introduce a journal, also called *Rock Bottom*, slated to appear monthly, using his position piece as the template and urging others to reciprocate. It was a last-ditch attempt to save SNCC from descending into factionalism by channeling its history to refocus its goals because, as Lester would summarize in 1969, "The political perspective of someone who has been in 'the movement' since 1960 (and how many are left?) was, of necessity going to be different from that of one who entered in 1968. The viewpoint of the former was not necessarily superior to that of the latter, but the differences between the two had to be recognized and understood. The 'movement' veteran had a sense of 'movement' history, having lived it. The 'movement' neophyte did not. As far as he was concerned, 'the movement' began when he became aware of it."[136]

In my view, the single issue of *Rock Bottom* that exists equates to an internal audit of SNCC's culture. "Should we ... actively work to do something about inadequate housing, inferior education, the inequities of welfare, unemployment, insufficient medical attention?" Forman asked. How effectively did colleagues believe SNCC could intervene in "the malignant nature of America's racist foreign policy"? He bared his political soul:

> Six years after the student movement started in February 1960, we are at Rock Bottom. There is nowhere to go but up or under ... [W]e must quickly revamp our entire style of operation—or there is no other way for us to go but out, nothing to do but destroy our effectiveness through lack of direction, lack of confidence in the future, a sense of failure, fatigue, despair, frustration, and bad health. These conditions in turn lead to internal bickering, feuding, factional fighting, resignation ... walking-out, Fuck-it, it ain't worth it.[137]

Coworkers were to sharpen individual and shared terms of engagement by debating in print the difference between revolution and reform, human and civil rights, and efficacy or redundancy of slogans. "What is the relationship between program, work and words?" he catechized, entreating colleagues to reconsider foundational values evidenced in field reports. "We used to say that we live and work and eat with the people we organize. Is this true today or is it a myth?" He insinuated: "Could it be that one of the reasons we don't keep ongoing or viable projects [is] not rooting ourselves in the communities and living there and going to meet the man and working after hours in talking and organizing people with whom we live and work?"[138] Forman believed community-facing work still had currency, like that outlined by Mike Miller in an unpublished paper, "What Is an Organizer?": "To organize people who have been exploited all their lives is a tough job. It demands of an organizer that he bring out of people what they have within them but have been told isn't there—because they aren't 'educated' or because they are Negroes or because they are poor. It requires that the organizer know who he is and that he not confuse what he wants with what the people with whom he is working want."[139] In 1966,

Forman was aware that Charles and Shirley Sherrod, Hollis Watkins, Bob Mants, Worth Long, John Buffington, and Michael (Oshoosi) Wright continued to organize like this in locales where SNCC no longer operated.

Nearly concurrent with the appearance of *Rock Bottom*, Bob Lawson called in December 1966 for an "organizer's notebook," a forum for contributions to the *Movement* newspaper written in "honest appraisal." Under that rubric it built on previous articles, like Jimmy Garrett sharing lessons learned in Freedom Schools, emphasizing the need to "discuss in nightly meetings all your successes and failures, little or big. Always question, always evaluate your work." The "Organizer's Notebook" slot in the *Movement* was also a repository for ideas about creative organizing, exemplified by Melody James's entry on community drama.[140] Simultaneously, the *Student Voice* encouraged "staff expressions... poems, plays, essays and articles, and short stories" to "flow regularly among SNCC staff." Like *Rock Bottom*, it was an effort to have an open conversation as SNCC was fragmenting: "Fling words back at us.... Y-o-u! should contribute things for future booklets of this type."[141] Charles Cobb, Bill Mahoney, Len Holt, and Denise Nicholas contributed, alongside Bob Moore and George Curry.[142] These injunctions to write for each other suggest that SNCC lost sight of its core tenets, but they infuse its literature. The organizer became the archetypal character because, as Carson discovered while conducting interviews in the 1970s, "SNCC was most of all organizers... [that was] the story that I got."[143]

Extracts from field reports pepper Cobb's travelogue *On the Road to Freedom* (2008), and in Moses and Cobb's *Radical Equations* (2001) the organizing model is said to be the foundation on which the Algebra Project was built, "our version of the civil rights movement 1992," as Moses told Dittmer.[144] *Gonna Sit at the Welcome Table* (2002), coedited by Julian Bond and Andrew Lewis, reprints reports that Watters and Cleghorn featured in *Climbing Jacob's Ladder*. For Wesley Hogan, SNCC's willingness to share field reports is striking for its openness, with Casey Hayden "typing them on to stencils, mimeographing, and delivering them to other groups for use in their own "civic development." In the 1960s it was a way, Hogan assesses, "for SNCC's skill-based tactics and ideas to move to Ann Arbor, Philadelphia, and Berkeley—indeed, to many places throughout the North and West."[145] It was also a means of "exchanging ideas and experiences between community organizations" to help others avoid mistakes made by "older groups" like SNCC, as Lawson suggested.[146]

The instruction to "write it all down" in the throes of confrontation underpins SNCC's narrative culture. Field reports exemplify narration, not simply recording, and comprise a qualitative resource for understanding what Cobb asserted: "The southern civil rights movement is best understood as a movement of community organizing rather than one of protest."[147] Storytelling is integral to SNCC's culture of organizing; authors take meaning from it, appraise it, and explore it imaginatively. When stories move from one genre to another, in "modulations from one key to another," as Lester described, "the real world enters the work and its world as part of the process of its creation, as well as part of its subsequent life." Narrative was "spoken about, argued over, evaluated." In J. Peter Euben's assessment, that is "a way of talking about the politics of literature without endorsing either studied naïveté or socialist realism, without seeing political power in everything or not seeing it at all."[148] Taking notes at SNCC's founding conference, Charlie Jones recorded an overarching feeling that "our basis and methods of communication should work not for us but with us, for the principle of empathy."[149] The principle of empathy would be an issue considered by SNCC's early champions: professional writers, observers and evaluators conducting fieldwork with SNCC as their material in the 1960s. How they addressed empathy and objectivity is the subject of the next chapter.

Chapter 4

Adjusting the Lens of Professional "Objectivity"

> These reporters were right with us from the start ... Plenty of others followed them in later but the first ones in were with us when we were laying the foundation. They could see and understand what was really going on.
> —John Lewis, 1998

> I will tell their story so as to let them come to word.
> —Robert Coles, 1963

> Holt did a magnificent job in court. He took every possible opportunity to make the case political, speaking eloquently about race relations in this country and the need for the type of action in which we were engaged. Now he gave his summation, a brilliant one, but this was a kangaroo court and his words were like pearls thrown to swine.
> —James Forman, 1972

In the first half of the 1960s, a small, eclectic group—David Halberstam, Pat Watters, Joanne Grant, Howard Zinn, Len Holt, and Robert Coles—used skills honed in journalism, historical research, the law, counseling, and psychiatry to tell SNCC's stories. The emphasis on local people deciding the direction of local struggles set SNCC apart. David Garrow judged that, by November 1960, SNCC had taken the lead "in pursuing the true mass action that [Martin Luther] King had spoken of for over four years" and that SNCC's work in Albany in 1961 "led King forward to the first real mass direct action that the movement had seen."[1] The SCLC's strategy was summarized by Adam Fairclough as "'hit and run,' striking one target at a time," bringing the media with it to ensure national coverage.[2] SNCC focused its efforts in communities over months and years rather than days or weeks, negotiating organizational differences with local NAACP chapters before the SCLC or King arrived. When the media conceived of Albany as a failure, it focused on King's experience, neglecting to see what the community achieved, as Albany-born Bernice Johnson Reagon and Shirley Sherrod have reiterated, and as Forman knew when proposing a book on Albany to Ballantine, foregrounding local leadership over "any single image of a leader's personality." Forman wrote,

"Too often we have seen masses of people out in the streets, aroused and willing to stay there in the face of brutality, only to have some big leaders off in a cosy negotiating room making decisions which do not really represent the wishes of the people."[3] In Selma, SNCC organized for three years before the media descended on the Selma to Montgomery March in 1965 and focused the spotlight on King. Grassroots organizing demanded a different approach: writers who would follow where SNCC led.

As they turned off a highway north of Albany down a dirt path, Charles Sherrod observed to Jack Chatfield, "This is where CORE and SCLC stop."[4] Sherrod was initiating Chatfield into SNCC's effort to transform "a set of social arrangements whose roots rested in plantation slavery" by sticking "close to the soil of discontent."[5] Chatfield had been propelled south by a Claude Sitton report in the *New York Times* in June 1962. He would later say, "What had been unimaginable became ineluctable, and I was in southwest Georgia by early September."[6] Following SNCC into poor, disenfranchised, agricultural communities had to be a deliberate choice for a journalist too, and Sitton was one of few who moved off the beaten track. Martin Luther King Jr. served so effectively as "a convenient stand-in for the whole civil rights movement" that the press corps shadowed him. His marches commanded press attention. Jack Nelson admitted, "The truth is, it was a lot harder for us to cover other aspects of the movement, such as the fieldwork conducted by the Student Nonviolent Coordinating Committee, ... [which] sent hundreds of young field workers to live in some of the most dangerous places in the South."[7] The media was trying to shape the movement into "the first great national story," in Harry Ashmore's summary.[8] The responsible story that cohered in the sympathetic press was a narrative symbiosis of a century of tropes—"democratic freedom," the American "dilemma" of "race," and a propensity to emphasize individual "race men."[9] The independence SNCC sought from cross-organizational compromise, and the distance it traveled from established models of leadership, meant that the only way to apprehend its culture was by watching organizers work in rural hamlets, cotton and tobacco towns, the sites of the majority of its projects prior to 1966. Julian Bond explained in *Freedomways*, "SNCC does not speak for the movement, for no one does, and no one can. But SNCC is working in the South in areas no other civil rights group has ever been to, with farmers, domestics, laborers, and people who really want to be free." In 1961, its appeal for funds focused on twenty dedicated organizers working in "an untouched area of the struggle," but it also emphasized grassroots leadership thereafter.[10] Bond explained that one of his tasks was "to get reporters to differentiate between SNCC and the SCLC"—or "Snick and Slick, as we put it—and to make sure our story was told."[11] As a volunteer opined, "[E]ven if you read the *New York Times* you practically had to wait for a disaster—a shooting, a dynamiting, or a riot—for some of the background story, as the reporters called it, to come out." When local papers reported "the facts of life" in the grassroots struggle, the volunteer said, "We feel stronger."[12] Individual writers and editors, like the SRC's Margaret Long and SCEF's Anne Braden, told these stories but soon grappled with the feeling that, as Coles put it, "if the students were attacking conventions, they demanded similar of those who sought to keep up with them in print."[13]

The Journalists

On the civil rights beat, journalists were caught in a double bind, as Watters elucidated: "Within ourselves and pushed by compulsions from without, we resisted the movement and ignored its meaning (which was the very thing that drew us to it), writing of it in *conventional* terms, doing our part in pushing it toward the *conventional*, reshaping it, destroying its meaning" (my emphases).[14] The movement was not coherent, even as a moral imperative—and SNCC was unconventional. Field-workers made themselves dangerously visible going house to house, plantation to plantation, to gain the trust of potential registrants: "We would carry them to the store downtown, help pick cotton and cut wood." Carson emphasized this facet of organizing, and Wesley Hogan noted the time it took to get recruits familiar with quotidian expectations.[15] This forms part of the historiography now, but in the 1960s D. Gorton observed news crews paying "more attention to each other than to the subjects they were covering." This propensity "cut them off from intimate contact" with organizers and "serendipitous moments" on which community stories could be built.[16] Gorton recognized what Paul Good would analyze: that most of the press corps was "astigmatic." During the March Against Fear in 1966, for example, Good watched television and newspaper reporters in the media truck staring past—and not seeing—"the shacks where the essence of the march was being made flesh."[17]

It was difficult for reporters to function in rural locales without hotels or a media hub. Even fascinated freelancers were reluctant to embed themselves unless a newspaper commissioned them to research and write stories during a period of immersion. Albany was Karl Flemings's first foray into civil rights, and he stayed close to SNCC for sixteen hours a day. By the time Martin Luther King Jr. arrived on December 14, 1961, Fleming was attending every demonstration. He wrote a twelve-page report that took a different approach to "the 'Five W's—Who, What, When, Where, Why'— that guided news reports." When he submitted it to his editors at *Newsweek*, they informed him that the magazine would not be covering Albany after all. With hindsight, Fleming accepted that "there was a lot of competition for not much space in the magazine." He had already observed a *Time* correspondent reading poetry because "New York" would rewrite his story anyway, but resigning oneself to the status quo was not conducive to getting SNCC's stories out either.[18] In 1964, though, Nicholas Von Hoffman, a community organizer before he became a journalist, persuaded Chicago's *Daily News* that he could turn ten weeks of dedicated observation into *Mississippi Notebook*, its title a rejoinder to Tom Ethridge's acidic, race-baiting column by the same title carried by Jackson's *Clarion-Ledger* since 1951. Von Hoffman was in McComb when SNCC's Freedom House was bombed and distilled the frightening silence in the aftermath, the police reaction ("it looks like termites"), and how he felt about interviewing organizers in dire circumstances:

> They said they were going to try to have a mass meeting of the Negroes that evening, but they were doubtful about many people being brave enough to come. Then, for a time, we sat, three of us, in the living room with windows blown out and the curtains and glass all over the floor.
> "It's not the heat, it's the fear," a girl from Pittsburgh breathed.
> I was afraid for them. I wanted to tell them to pull themselves together. Instead, I interviewed them, and they recounted how they had been asleep and dreaming thoughts of death just before they awoke to see the bloody face of one of the youths who had been wounded by the bomb.[19]

Committing to sustained on-the-spot investigation demanded a different narrative form from the usual journalistic approach (who, what, where, when?). In *Mississippi Notebook*, Von Hoffman strung episodes along a road trip. Danish journalist Per Laursen contacted SNCC to commend the *Student Voice*, saying that he was negotiating a syndicated column on civil rights and found SNCC publications indispensable."[20] Laursen researched SNCC thereafter for a book provisionally titled *Grace and Grits*, contracted to Viking Press, but it was never published. Bob Zellner recounts how he traveled with organizers on the Atlanta to Albany Freedom Ride of December 10, 1961, interviewing them throughout the train journey. Arrested on arrival, Laursen remained locked up "long enough to see how it was so he could write about southern jails."[21] By March 1963, he informed SNCC that the book was "finished but for some sequences." His agent Lynn

Nesbit was convinced that it would be "the first book about civil rights—before any of us really knew what civil rights was."[22] It was never completed. Nesbit cited writer's block, but assembling and distilling the story was difficult; it would be left to others to write about "the leading edge of the movement in the Deep South," as Zinn described his approach, and the tone that SNCC was setting "for a new generation's approach to politics and social change," as Watters asserted.[23]

David Halberstam found himself in a position conducive to "working the story" at the *Nashville Tennessean* because most southern newspapers were "looking the other way on the issue of race, both on their editorial page and in their news columns." After the 1954 Supreme Court decision in *Brown v. Board or Education*, the *Tennessean* decided to cover African American challenges to the racial status quo "aggressively... if need be, combatively." Halberstam observed, "In the old and not very pleasant political vernacular of the era, we were the nigger-lover paper."[24] Robert Churchwell was the first African American reporter employed by the *Nashville Banner*, but publisher James G. Stahlman cleaved to states' rights, and he was forced to work from home rather than sit with white reporters in the newsroom.[25] Halberstam turned twenty-five in 1960 and conceived of himself as "a witness to history" with a propitious opportunity to capture in writing "the courage and nobility of ordinary people in times of stress."[26] John Lewis assessed that Halberstam was "like us in many ways—about the same age, young and idealistic... he sensed the historic importance of what he saw happening." "If he had any problem with being objective," Lewis concluded, "it might have been that he was sympathetic to us and it showed."[27] A component of SNCC's media strategy was to assess the personal goals and potential impact of white professionals who sought to get close to them. Halberstam espoused a journalism of attachment, observing that the story he told of student activists was "in no small degree my story." Lewis assessed that reporters "[who paid attention] when we were laying the foundation... were laying a foundation themselves."[28] It is intriguing, therefore, that, despite close relationships with student protestors, Halberstam decided that what he published in the 1960s was "quite clinical."[29] He experimented with different styles of political commentary once his career took off—popular history, investigative exposé, a crime novel—but believed he had something to rectify on behalf of Lewis and Lewis's peers. The reparations he made were in the form of an eight-hundred-page epic history: *The Children* (1998).[30] If he feared he had not conveyed the commitment or courage of the Nashville student movement in the 1960s, it was because he had not breached the media's modus operandi: "We did little to try to humanize the demonstrators.... there was a belief, editor down to working reporter, that the story told itself" (724–25).

In *The Children*, Halberstam adjusted his authorial lens to get closer to the feeling of the sit-ins and consequently their significance in SNCC's evolution, in a comprehensive study and permanent record. He combined witness narrative with participants' thoughts and feelings, dramatizing anxiety and anticipation, like that felt by twenty-one-year-old Diane Nash during Robert Hayden's literature classes at Fisk University. In the hour before she set off downtown to participate in a sit-in, "both her hands were soaked with sweat by the end of the class and left the clear handprint of her fear on the wooden desk" (6). Halberstam created an impression of omniscience through the novelistic technique of free indirect discourse, conveying subjectivity without syntactical markers as if speaking the minds of individuals in a collective biography. In an apparently seamless narrative, with barely noticeable shifts from third-person account to first-person testimony, he suggested the interiority of his subjects. He retold the sit-in story through its protagonists but, in my view, withheld them at the same time, as the result of exerting such tight narratorial control over portraying their mental landscapes. Halberstam purports to communicate their "secret selves," information they did not share in the 1960s, based on interviews undertaken a quarter of a century later. Rather than quote demonstrators, Halberstam folds their words into his narration so that it is impossible to see where their words segue into his interpretation. Lewis is "a shy, awkward young man who felt so graceless," and Nash, elected a leader by her peers, suffers "pure terror in her heart" and, "if there had been any way she could disappear from the movement, without causing great shame to herself and letting down those others, she would have done it" (70, 4, 73). Until Halberstam accesses them, he construes such feelings as hidden.

To dramatize urgency, excitement, and trepidation, he adopted a different approach to the role of a reporter, a method and style through which he might "validate a lifetime in this profession" (726). Despite Halberstam's having received a Pulitzer Prize in 1964 for reporting on the Vietnam War, one reviewer judged *The Children* to be Halberstam's "greatest story" because he opened "a new window" through which readers could view intimate portraits and access a story "largely untold." The combination of drama, reach, and scope achieved by weaving subjects in and out of a history he extended into the 1990s suggests the heterogeneity of activist experience. The *Chicago Sun-Times* found *The Children* "magisterial, a book one can get lost in, like a Dickensian novel." This astute assessment may be why David Oshinsky valued Halberstam's "dramatic" story but expressed his frustration that "people drop from sight and reappear a few hundred pages later."[31]

Halberstam's story appears to be determinedly of the teller's making, but, in my reading, he found a template in the "sit-in clinics" conducted to prepare young activists for resistance and violence at store and restaurant counters.[32] In workshops, they were encouraged to "unburden themselves of their inner thoughts and pain on the subjects of race." Halberstam uncovered how important these fora had been in bonding young people in racial trust across class and geographical differences. In Nashville, Reverends James Lawson and Kelly Miller Smith forged cross-denomination and cross-college alliances between students at Tennessee State's American Theological Baptist School and Fisk University in their workshops at First Baptist Church and Clark Memorial Methodist Church. In their sit-in clinics, Halberstam found the roots of "the stories they had never told to friends" and a guiding structure (75, 74). Hogan judges that workshops in Nashville "signaled the future of the civil rights movement in the South: discussions routinely grew heated and ranged over many subjects."[33] They informed SNCC's culture because they were a form of "socio-drama," in Lawson's conception, "a laboratory" that tested and sustained protestors through the creation of story circles, like those O'Neal describes as a component of SNCC meetings. Chude Pamela Allen and Kathie Amatniek (Sarachild) examine their legacy in the context of consciousness raising in *Free Space: A Perspective on the Small Group in Women's Liberation* (1970) and *Outline for Consciousness Raising* (1970) respectively. In addition to imparting a galvanizing version of liberation theology, the exchange, debate, and role-playing created by Lawson and Smith anchored participants in each other. Halberstam drew on this interaction when bringing his subjects together in a narrative reconstruction, tracing emotions that were surfaced in political action through students' afterlives—in a morality drama that was indeed of Dickensian scale.

Decades earlier—in 1961, in Albany—Pat Watters was already interrogating the writing method that worked quickly and effectively for news journalism. In *Down to Now* he writes that in an effort to let organizers speak for themselves about what they saw as vital, rather than what he perceived in observing them, he tried not to "intrude" with questions, "reporter questions, skilled processing questions, that would draw out details of headcracking and heroism." He abandoned the pattern of "orderly note-taking" that he had established to write his column for the *Atlanta Journal*.

Instead, he "filled page after page with impressionistic, descriptive jottings full of discovery, the awe I felt, trying to capture all that was happening" (86). Watters felt that what he was witnessing was "too important, too big to be confined to a column" and adopted literary strategies: "My idea for the column was to have a news peg, but I would try to write it like a novel" (163). Watters would write an unpublished novel in the 1990s, a more cynical and unhappy time for him, but he used his impressionistic notes in *Down to Now: Reflections on the Southern Civil Rights Movement* (1971), part history and part meditation, and in *Climbing Jacob's Ladder* (1967), coauthored by Reese Cleghorn. Robert Coles reviewed the latter as indispensable to historians and political scientists but "even more valuable" for communicating the "'feel' for what makes social change." In his estimation, it was "a beautiful book in its blend of documentation and passion."[34] It is just this blend, and the narrative techniques harnessed to achieve it, that characterizes the writing of SNCC's earliest champions.

In *Down to Now*, Watters set out to filter ("through my own consciousness") what he had reported in order to "find again in detail and exactitude all there was back then" (xviii, 3). Figuratively, he returned to Albany where "there was no time and no room in my emotions for such introspection" (7). This self-conscious quest extended beyond "the limitations of newspapering." There was "so much" back then, he mused, but "sitting at a portable typewriter in the motel room's air-conditioned cigarette smoke, [he] couldn't begin to convey it." A narrative return to the early 1960s involved thinking about whether "historical event" could express "the individual's personal, inner experience, as the movement did for so many southerners" (9). He saw this experience as extraordinary and unarticulated in news reports, and he excavated his own feelings before trying to discern them in organizers.

Fred Hobson discusses *Down To Now* in *But Now I See: The White Southern Racial Conversion Narrative* (1999) and sees Watters as more "emotionally moved by what he sees and hears" than other writers he studies. He detects in Watters the same fundamental shift toward redemptive racial liberalism that he uncovers in his other subjects: Lillian Smith, James McBride Dabbs, Katharine Du Pre Lumpkin, Sarah Patton Boyle, Will Campbell, Larry L. King, and Willie Morris. Watters was inducted into the movement as he traveled around SNCC's trouble spots, finding meaning in local struggles before following Martin Luther King Jr. to Birmingham, Alabama, and St. Augustine, Florida. Only later did Watters realize he had "missed the meaning" of the Montgomery Bus Boycott (50). Hobson mentions SNCC in relation to the SCLC, for what he sees as Watters's despair over their split ideologies, while tracing his racial "conversion." He does not mention Barbara Foley's work, but as Foley pointed out, the convention of a "conversion plot" is that it is expected to "embody the broad contradictions of a history in a single concrete instance."[35] This was not the case for Watters, even in Albany. After he resigned from the *Atlanta Journal* in 1963 and joined the Southern Regional Council as information officer, he had space to write and time to consider "how much of a reporter's emotional reaction and response are tied into an event" or a particular "instance." Such an event would include, I would argue, conversion from a segregationist worldview to support for racial change (xii–xiii). Watters thought about his "deeply personal reaction to the movement" as he sat in the back pew of Shiloh Baptist Church in Albany but acknowledged that no single instance, not even one as emotionally powerful as a mass meeting, could communicate what was "beyond the normal limits of American culture" (11). "Extra-cultural" was the term he used to describe both SNCC and his own feelings; they spilled beyond southern cultural norms—including the white southern racial conversion "plot."

In 1993, in a new preface to *Down to Now*, Watters assessed that "SNCC was in a hurry, and I guess so was I." He castigated himself for what he had not written in the 1960s: "Why didn't I just say, 'The media missed the damn point?' And they are still missing it" (xii). With hindsight extended by another twenty-two years, he told a journalism student that his "every instinct" had been to "get a story."[36] Nevertheless, he was concerned that he had not apprehended the essential point of the stories he heard or wrote. Like Halberstam, then, Watters was self-critical, even though he tunneled behind SNCC in thought-provoking articles, from *Encounter with the Future* (1965), in which he described SNCC as "rich with infinite creative possibilities, potent—and dangerous," through "The South and the Nation" (1969), an elegy to the organization.[37] In 1969, on leave of absence from the SRC while pursuing a creative writing fellowship awarded by the Rockefeller Foundation, Watters argued that, at its best, SNCC was "the most visionary group of the young ever organized in America" because it operated outside cultural norms. He asserted, "Most of SNCC's impact on the revolutionary young people of the world (and it was vast) was out of a Southern feel for the particular, a grasp of *the field's reality* that overrode the cautions and equivocations of headquarters. They knew that in the matter of a child's starving, a man's being beaten to death in a Black Belt jail, for example, a situation existed which was not susceptible to the processes or compromise and conciliation ordinary to American self-government" (my emphasis). It is "the field's reality" that SNCC's writers elucidated, from Stembridge's poetic telegrams from the front lines and Thelwell's personalized bulletins through Jean Wheeler Smith's open letters and Charles Cobb's poetic crystallizations of black consciousness as "Black Power for Black People." In a long passage in "The South and the Nation," with the refrain "They knew... They knew," Watters sensed something of SNCC's internal culture that others missed in the moment, a narrative approach and refrain: "They knew that in America language had become in many ways as corrupted as it had been in Nazi Germany... so unrelated to truth that it had more often than not ceased to reflect reality. Like the postwar German writers, they sought to bring language down to a level of concreteness that would impart to it once more a relationship with the real world. 'Tell it like it is,' they would say."[38]

More than Halberstam, Watters intuited that SNCC had a narrative culture but assumed that it was left to outside writers to share it because SNCC "had a disdain for the efficacy of words spoken to an audience outside its own circle." Like volunteers who joined organizers, Watters believed "the context in the circle [was] so terribly different from that of any audience outside of it."[39] He addressed the professional brakes he was expected to put on his journalism, but, despite conflicted feelings about what he wrote and published in the 1960s, Watters endeavored to explore SNCC's culture. He attempted to convey "the field's reality" of local entrenchment and sustained community-focused work and how different the approach was to initiating demonstrations and then quickly moving on. He hazarded a guess at what SNCC might have meant by "telling it like it is," while acknowledging that his proximity was a privileged position. He knew that professional skepticism, instilled in journalists in particular, was tested in rural locales which the national media considered distant outposts. He did not name the "tough, sardonic, case-hardened" reporter who departs from a mass meeting in tears, saying, "These are great people, great people." "That was the reality," concluded Watters, but he harbored doubts about how to convey it without seeming to romanticize. For Richard Lischer, Watters, "more than any other professional observer, ... recognized the genius of the mass meetings, [and he] expressed his frustration at their elusiveness to historians." He certainly recognized how observational "objectivity" separates fact and "event" from value, in the way Christopher R. Martin does in his book *Framed! Labor and the Corporate Media* (2004). Martin asserts that "the goal of objective news is to separate fact from value or emotion, reduce (or inflate) events into a story with two 'sides,' and use quotes as pure 'data' without any reporter interpretation." Objectivity is thus a veil that the "real" news may hide behind.[40]

"The field's reality" that fascinated Watters captured Joanne Grant. Her political background was very different from Watters's insofar as she followed her politics into the movement, where she continued writing for the left-wing *National Guardian*, for which she became associate editor. An African American journalist of mixed racial heritage, Grant attended SNCC's conference in 1960, cofounded the New York Friends of SNCC group, raised funds for the COFO project in 1964, and involved herself fully by joining SNCC. She did not step outside journalistic objectivity immediately and described for Margaret Long the trepidation she felt on her first trip South. But after she was arrested for taking part in an "illegal" sit-in in Talladega in 1962, Grant balanced operating as a field-worker with reporting what was happening in the field.[41] She built media platforms for SNCC, including a syndicate distributing articles for the *Nation*, and publicized individual organizers and high school students inspired by SNCC, like Brenda Travis, as "heroes of the South who have gained life and given life through the movement." She challenged readers: "Who knows the name of Dion Diamond? Who has heard of Charles McDew? . . . Are there many in this land above the Mason-Dixon line who know of Brenda Travis, of Bob Zellner?" In *Revolution in Mississippi*, Tom Hayden cited Brenda Travis for a commitment that resulted in expulsion from school in McComb and remand to a detention center in Jackson, adding, "Maybe, just maybe, [the nation knows] that a student organization, SNCC, was instrumental in initiating the turmoil there." Grant was unequivocal, telling readers that they were "in the debt of these young people" (as she wrote, "for the challenge they represent, for the people they are"), and she assiduously conveyed the day-to-day grind and gains, from a position of involvement and understanding.[42]

Grant was a SNCC organizer for six years, her commitment to SNCC contiguous with her politics. She was already inured to the ways in which writing could be spun as partisan and propagandist: she had acted as research assistant for W. E. B. Du Bois, and she was named before the House Un-American Activities Committee in 1960.[43] If Grant did not perceive a need to adjust her writing style like others in the group of writers examined in this chapter, she sought alternative forms in which to explore what she was forced to condense as news. In *Black Protest* (1968), she compiled an anthology of primary documents of protest and resistance, paying attention to SNCC's participation in the most recent iteration of a much longer African American freedom struggle. *Black Protest* shared SNCC's statement of purpose, statement on Vietnam, open letters, field reports, Moses's "Letter to Northern Supporters," a report from Danville by Avon Rollins, Forman's "random notes" from the Leflore County jail, an extract from Sally Belfrage's memoir *Freedom Summer* (1965), and a disquisition on Black Power written by Carmichael. She excerpted writing by SNCC's early champions—Hayden's *Revolution in Mississippi*, Len Holt on demonstrations in Birmingham in 1963, Zinn on the limits of nonviolence in 1964—and anthologized John Lewis's speech at the March on Washington, the original version for the first time, not the one he actually delivered, changed out of respect for veteran organizer A. Philip Randolph.[44] Grant kept grassroots struggles in view in *Black Protest* via Cobb and McLaurin's essay on Ruleville's economy, and she closed with a press statement by the Mississippi Freedom Labor Union, "We Have No Government" (February 1966), to ensure that local leaders were on record. Her documentary history was the first in a series of SNCC-inflected histories that include Bond and Lewis's *Gonna Sit at the Welcome Table*, Cobb's *This Nonviolent Stuff'll Get You Killed*, and Sue (Lorenzi) Sojourner's *Thunder of Freedom: Black Leadership and the Transformation of 1960s Mississippi* (2013).

In 1987, Grant told a SNCC reunion, "I'm terribly impressed by the changes that we all helped to bring about and I don't want any of us or any of them to forget it."[45] She dedicated herself to promulgating the legacy of Ella Baker in a film, *Fundi: The Story of Ella Baker* (1981), conveying Baker's salience in SNCC, the NAACP, and SCLC, and her book *Ella Baker: Freedom Bound* (1998) memorialized Baker as the foundational lifelong activist she came to know well as a mentor. Grant evolved into a historian who emphasized what Staughton Lynd would describe as SNCC's "organizing in a spirit of accompaniment." In the 1990s, Julian Bond located Grant's 1998 book about Ella Baker as part "a welcome new trend in civil rights historiography... that bring[s] its personalities and events into sharper focus."[46] Today Connie Curry embodies the role of movement biographer for SNCC, Regional Council of Negro Leadership activists, and the unsung in communities, facilitating memoirs and grassroots studies by Bob Zellner, Winson Hudson, and Aaron Henry, and writing about Mae Bertha Carter's fight to desegregate schools in Drew, Mississippi. In the 1960s, though, acting as a historian of SNCC involved some difficult choices, not least about taking the advocacy role Grant espoused, knowing how this could be perceived unfavorably in academic circles.

The Historians

Beacon Press approached Howard Zinn in 1963 to write about the NAACP, but he declined, saying, "The real story in the South today is SNCC." Instead, he mapped a proposal for the book he wanted to write, with royalties to be transferred to SNCC because he was uncomfortable about accepting payment. "Youngsters risk their lives for ten dollars a week," he told Beacon.[47] Chair of the History Department at Spelman College since 1956, Zinn acted as a mentor to SNCC from 1960, when he was appointed to its Executive Committee with Ella Baker and Connie Curry. He observed community relationships being forged in project locations between 1961 and 1964 and wrote, "I had begun to understand, back in Albany and Selma, how much of what is called history omits the reality of ordinary people—their struggles, their hidden power."[48] Throughout his career, Zinn focused on the lives and rebellions of ordinary people who otherwise might not have appeared in histories, and he analyzed grassroots racial and labor struggles across multiple movements for social change. His study of SNCC was the catalyst for all his later work. When Lynd joined Spelman "with a head full of conventional ideas about doing history," he realized through Zinn that "suddenly it seemed possible to do oral history oneself" and that a historian could write field texts.[49]

Zinn's *SNCC: The New Abolitionists* is the first sustained study of the organization, a 1964 field text grounded in interviews and direct observation. On that basis, Zinn asserted, SNCC was challenging "the *entire* value system of the nation" (emphasis in original).[50] While he was careful not to deny the ongoing impact of the NAACP and SCLC or veteran activists including A. Philip Randolph and Bayard Rustin, what fascinated Zinn was the spirited commitment of "young rebels" (1). When he called SNCC "the new abolitionists," he asserted that it was "not fanciful to invest them with a name that has the ring of history." He wrote, "We are always shy about recognizing the historic worth of events when they take place before our eyes, about recognizing heroes when they are still flesh and blood and not yet transfixed in marble" (4). He eschewed customary academic caution around revealing anything other than the dispassionate objectivity of his professional training. With SNCC as his prism, he declared, "There is no doubt about it, we have in this country today a movement which will take its place alongside that of the abolitionists, the Populists, the Progressives— and may outdo them all" (4). Zinn made large, hopeful claims but balanced them with studied observation, not only in Albany and Selma but also in Hattiesburg, Greenwood, and Greenville. In my view, Zinn's study was radical because of his approach and not because he endowed organizers with the mantle of the abolitionists—a label that risked locking them into a reformist tradition. His study was controversial because he took the federal government to task for failing to take responsibility for the constitutional rights of black southerners and the safety of civil rights workers.

He made the case that this failure amounted to collaboration with white supremacist guardians holding fast to the way of life the wider movement was overturning. He undergirded assertions with SNCC's telegrams and letters to President John Kennedy, Attorney General Robert Kennedy, the Department of Justice, and the FBI, and provided specific examples like the federal government's indictment of the Albany movement for picketing a segregated store peacefully in 1963.

Zinn had been making this case incrementally since November 1962 and his report for the SRC on Albany. He made it in letters to national newspapers and magazine, such as the *New York Times* and *New Republic*, and in feature articles. In "Kennedy: The Reluctant Emancipator" in the *Nation* in December 1962, he argued that by dispatching federal troops to Oxford to ensure James Meredith's enrollment as the first black student at the University of Mississippi (founded in 1848), President Kennedy created the impression that he was less cautious than his record on civil rights revealed. In Zinn's view, Kennedy had diverted media attention from mass action in Albany. He detailed a beating in jail during which Bill Hansen had his jaw broken, an attack on Hansen's African American attorney C. B. King by county sheriff Cull Campbell, and the devastating assault by police on Mrs. Marion King, the pregnant wife of C. B. King's brother, Slater, that resulted in the loss of her baby. Zinn put on record that federal officers took no action: despite affidavits submitted to the FBI office "in a steady stream, attesting to violations by local officials of the constitutional rights of Negroes ... nothing was done."[51] In "SNCC: The Battle-Scarred Youngsters" (1963) he also took a sideswipe at the "grandiose speeches" and "air of unreality" of the March on Washington. The event's rhetorical triumphalism contrasted markedly with what he observed in Greenwood as SNCC activists left jail on the day of the march. The Freedom House had, he wrote, the "eerie quality of a field hospital after a battle." The risk, he warned, was that monumental rallies would obscure what he saw: that the government remained disappointingly "circumspect" in its dedication to racial equality.[52]

By publishing frequent accounts of entrenched battles against the forces of massive resistance to desegregation, Zinn located SNCC and its sustained grassroots activism as "a power beyond orthodox politics" (13). In 1965, Jack Newfield echoed him, observing that a "battered brotherhood of organizers, poets, hipsters and visionaries" was democracy at work "in its purest and rawest form." Harnessing language similar to Zinn's in his journalism, Newfield asserted that SNCC was at "the cutting edge of history" because its "prophets and pioneers ... give the whole movement the urgency that William James once called 'the moral equivalent of war.'"[53] When Lynd pursued a similar argument in *The Intellectual Origins of American Radicalism* (1968), he was criticized as "an ideologue of the New Left." Eugene Genovese took Lynd and other "recent scholars, most of them under forty" (presumably including Zinn) to task for "a glorification of the lower classes, and the self-defeating tendency to read the past according to the political demands of the moment." Entangled within the impassioned debate that ensued between Lynd and Genovese was the expectation that professional histories of American radicalism would be dispassionate and retrospective.[54] When COFO volunteer William McCord published *Mississippi: The Long, Hot Summer* in 1965, for example, he saw fit to write in his introduction that, as "a minor participant," he felt "compelled to tell some of the stories of suffering and heroism which, for various reasons have not always received proper attention in the national press."[55] McCord recorded this as "a scholarly lapse" but also defended himself, saying, "The human meaning of the Mississippi revolt cannot be adequately conveyed in textbook manner." He had not designed his social history, he reiterated, to treat activists as "sociological data."[56] If his language was brittle, it indicated caveats that professional historians felt bound to provide. When they wrote about organizing up and down the backroads of the Black Belt, they were conscious that their peers could judge their work as insufficiently objective, an unreliable offshoot of advocacy journalism.

When *SNCC: The New Abolitionists* was reissued in 2002, Zinn added a caveat, despite being renowned for championing people's histories "from the bottom up." It would have been impossible to write such a study without participant-observation, but he declared that it was not "a comprehensive scholarly book on SNCC, but a work of on-the-spot reportage."[57] In this context, "reportage" took on connotations of thin rather than thick scholarly analysis. Carol Polsgrove assessed, "So quietly did he play his role that later historians would miss it all together." Moye called it a "tentative history," in tacit acknowledgment of Zinn's equivocation.[58] It was received differently inside SNCC. In 2010, when Zinn was posthumously awarded the Ridenhour Courage Prize, Bernice Johnson Reagon explained what it meant to organizers: "I knew about it as it happened because with the Albany Movement I joined SNCC. But when I read *SNCC The New Abolitionists*, the organizing, the cost, the determined people—it was there. That was a surprise to me for a history book. I was absolutely amazed to have in my hand accountable stories where not only did I recognize the struggle, I could feel it."[59] Zinn's study preceded Geoffrey Elton's summation of how professional historians preclude "bias and personal character" from entering their work, remaining mutely impersonal behind their sources.⁶⁰ Nor did Zinn strive for "that noble dream" of professional objectivity Peter Novick delineated in the 1980s. In the 1960s, he was disparaged for writing an unbalanced account with "wild claims" unworthy of a historian, claims one reviewer asserted snippily "could be asserted only by a partisan enthusiast or a sociologist."⁶¹ Even in Ralph McGill's measured assessment, Zinn was "a passionate idealist and partisan," his approach equated to "sentimentalizing and romanticizing," despite McGill's admiration: "Let no one minimize the grit required to go into the Southern towns where there was (and is) so much hate and venomous resistance."⁶² The issue for the Pulitzer Prize–winning publisher of the *Atlanta Constitution* was not whether SNCC merited such a work, at least so early in its history: "The smell of jails and injustice, of brutality and ignorance, is in Mr. Zinn's chapters on Mississippi, Alabama and southwest Georgia." It was criticism of the federal government that disturbed McGill. Nor could he countenance other civil rights organizations as secondary: "Because of the work of SNCC and the superb support of Dr. Martin Luther King, the NAACP and others, a beginning has been made in school desegregation in Mississippi." When McGill pulled back to the *Brown* decision, though, he reverted to strategies associated with the national NAACP, deemphasizing the community-led activist model foregrounded by Zinn in 1964.⁶³

Zinn put organizers at the center and inspired Reagon's own post-SNCC career as a cultural historian as well as acclaimed freedom singer, defining her method as "different from the way I was trying to write as a historian." In short, she says, "I wrote myself in." In her speech on the occasion of Zinn's being awarded the Ridenour Courage Prize, she said, "Howard Zinn dared to suggest that right along with any documentary evidence, you must hear from most of the people who are impacted by the subject you are studying.... They must share the pages."⁶⁴ Worth Long argues similarly that, in writing recent history, the problem is that "even the scholars ... separate the person from the genre."⁶⁵ SNCC stood out in the 1960s for the myriad different voices and views that combined within a single organization. Emily Stoper's 1968 PhD dissertation involved an attempt to afford SNCC staff space to speak—of fifty-one interviews undertaken, those transcribed in her appendix take up as many pages as her analysis—but it was not published until the end of the 1980s.

The Lawyer

Zinn's book was followed swiftly by Len Holt's *The Summer That Didn't End: The Story of the Mississippi Civil Rights Project of 1964* (1965) and *An*

Act of Conscience (1965). Holt worked closely with SNCC as one of its lawyers, and *The Summer That Didn't End* drew on affidavits he received over the summer of 1964 and COFO's running record of incidents of racial terrorism, both included as appendices. He was ironic about his new métier as a lawyer writing history, recounting a conversation where Lynd suggested he consider acting "as a 'wastepaper basket,' i.e. historian," of Freedom Summer. Holt accepted "the *ordination*" (his emphasis) as a thoroughgoing advocate for COFO.[66]

SNCC nicknamed Holt "Snake Doctor" because he would "slither into towns wearing patched jeans" and was "proud, abrasive, and uncompromising toward expressions of racism from officers of the 'courts.'" He pioneered "omnibus" desegregation suits, rolling up multiple protests into an interlocking series that sent a fusillade of shots through southern courts that attacked segregation throughout a community—"the cemetery, swimming pool, public hospital, dog pound, parks, auditoriums, buses, public housing and you-name-it... simultaneously," with one lawsuit. In *An Act of Conscience*, he confessed to feeling bone tired as the result of "long drives, alone down country roads in Georgia, Virginia, Alabama, North Carolina—even Mississippi, if the phone calls came asking for the 'Snake Doctor.'... I could have slept for a year."[67] For Thelwell, Holt was "fearless," "legendary," and for Carmichael he was "an unsung hero." Bond declared in 1962, "We need 300 Len Holts," and in 1991 he described *The Summer That Didn't End* as "a forgotten and ignored classic," saying, "This personal and candid account... met the fate of many books written about civil rights in the middle sixties—events moved quickly then, and were presented to the public as brief flashes in headlines and television bites, so that Holt's book was doomed to be overlooked as history—and the movement—rolled quickly on."[68] *The Summer That Didn't End* is referenced in some subsequent histories, Holt's correspondence with members of SNCC is cited on occasion, and Carson notes how Holt contributed to SNCC conferences, like one in 1962 where he presented on the legal implications of activist work. Dittmer notes that, having worked with the Mississippi movement since 1960, Holt and Ben Smith "pioneered the innovative legal maneuver of using a Reconstruction statute to remove civil rights cases from local to federal jurisdiction, thereby improving the chances of favorable verdicts." Holt, on the other hand, nicknamed this maneuver "the Kunstler Statute" because William Kunstler had invoked it while defending Freedom Riders, saying the strategy had been brought to *his* attention by Mississippi lawyer William Higgs (137, 226). Deciphering the individual contributions movement lawyers made is not easy since their work was collective, designed to coalesce as a protective legal mesh around activists. Holt is quoted once in Hogan's study of SNCC but goes unmentioned in most and is mistaken for a reporter by Wayne Greenhaw when quoting an article Holt wrote for the *National Guardian*.[69] In his memoir *Unrepentant Leftist* (1996), Victor Rabinowitz, whose daughter Joni joined SNCC in Albany in 1963 and whose son Peter joined in 1964, memorialized Holt's "vivid and effective description of the work he was doing" for how it galvanized others in their profession. When Holt delivered a speech in Detroit in 1962, for "the first time in years" the National Lawyers Guild was "moved to cheers."[70] Holt led peers in the movement anthem "We Shall Overcome," and his stories stirred them to action, with around 150 members of the guild heading south to aid in the struggle.[71] Holt's legal prowess is acclaimed by Babson, Riddle, and Elsila in *The Color of Law* (2010), and Tomiko Brown-Nagin's *Courage to Dissent* (2011), a magisterial legal history of the civil rights movement, emphasizes Holt's "bottom-up approach to lawyering."[72] Like Zinn's approach to writing its history, it fit SNCC's ethos exactly.

What is clear from my research is that Holt wrote widely in different genres throughout the 1960s, publishing two books in 1965, acting as a member of the *Liberator*'s advisory board, cowriting with Mahoney, and supporting Forman's writing. This was remarkable for a full-time lawyer, and the depth and breadth of this contribution beyond his professional activity are important to record. He was an advocate of SNCC writing its own narrative and supported the FST and John O'Neal, advising him to "put your heart and soul into an article telling the folks why the rocks are crying out for a theater of the people and by the people and for the people."[73] He wrote a Black Power short story for the *Student Voice* that circulated inside SNCC in 1967.

After graduating from Howard University's School of Law in 1956, Holt had hoped to join the NAACP's legal team but discovered "a closed society."[74] Instead, he joined Norfolk, Virginia, lawyers Joseph A. Jordan Jr. and Edward A. Dawley and found in his partners the incorrigibly tenacious spirit he himself would embody for organizers. In 1990, Edward A. Dawley— whose poems Holt interwove in *An Act of Conscience*—told the story of "the three blind black lawyers." It is an ironic parable of legal sharpshooting: "These three lawyers were not only blind but they were also young, foolish, reckless, irresponsible, and impractical. Because they did not listen to the advice of the wise leaders they were thought to be deaf; some of the most intelligent people in the community called them dumb. These qualities made them excellent warriors and were the qualities needed to do foolish, reckless, and irresponsible things, such as declaring war on Dixie."[75] Jordan, Dawley, and Holt suffered a white backlash to their activist-based legal counsel; their office was raided by the Committee on Offenses Against the Administration of Justice, a joint committee of the Virginia house and senate designed to hamper the work of civil rights lawyers and litigants, and they were forced to suspend their joint practice.[76] Holt wrote and published in this climate and wrote *An Act of Conscience* in the midst of a trial during which he was turned into one of those accused of inciting violence, facing five to ten years in prison. *An Act of Conscience* delineates two months during the summer of 1963 in Danville, Virginia, centering on a particular "Night of Infamy." Holt feared that the events of this night might be lost unless he wrote about it, because "[t]he Danville city government had decided to crush the movement, and everyone connected with it, into a fine powder to be scattered by the wind; and then to do more, to destroy even the memory of such protest" (126). Danville would not become infamous like Little Rock, Oxford, or Birmingham. When forty-seven demonstrators on the courthouse steps were severely injured by a police attack with clubs and flesh-tearing fire hoses on June 10, 1963, the press arrived belatedly, with little left to photograph, because attention had been focused on events in Birmingham.[77] After demonstrators were beaten and tortured, they were indicted, under what was still termed "the John Brown statute," for "inciting the colored population to acts of violence and war against the white population" (4). Holt wrote to ensure that this would be recorded, building on Dorothy Miller (Zellner)'s account.[78] Among those charged with her were Forman, Avon Rollins, Bob Zellner, and Daniel Foss of SNCC. Some fifteen organizers who supported the Danville protestors—including Matthew Jones, Ivanhoe Donaldson (working nearby in Prince Edward County), and Annie Pearl Avery—were also arrested and charged subsequently. Fourteen people were still awaiting trial when Holt's book went to press.

In *An Act of Conscience*, Holt confirmed Miller's account, but where she followed SNCC's decision not to denounce other civil rights groups, he situated himself as a radical outlier by performing a dissection of the extent to which civil rights organizations supported African American citizens in Danville. He acknowledged local NAACP leader Reverend Lendell Chase but was disappointed by the national NAACP. He called out the SCLC for preventing Martin Luther King Jr. from being present at the trial as a media draw and protection for the community, despite the fact that SCLC field-workers were among those charged.[79] King had visited the city in March 1963 before protests began and had promised to return. At first,

King declined to return to Danville. Holt quoted a note King sent while visiting Suffolk, some 170 miles away: "Tell the people that I shall, regrettably, not be able to come to Danville at this time because of pressing business involving SCLC in Atlanta" (199, 53). For Holt, King was "the unseen guest in every conference... the giver of all solutions" but was "neither omnipotent nor omnipresent" (52, 117–18).[80] He was equally disdainful of the SCLC's claim to be broke: "Every week *Jet* magazine was showing pictures of [King] getting checks for $75,000 from mammoth rallies which eventually fattened the coffers of SCLC to over $800,000 in 1963" (43–44, 192). King eventually did come back to Danville that summer, on July 11, and thousands cheered, but when he visited again on November 15, Holt writes that fewer than five hundred turned out: "For some reason, Danville's Negroes honored King's presence with their absence" (222). He deprecated King almost as keenly as he censured Danville city councilman John Carter and U.S. district judge Thomas Mitchie, the latter alluded to in a couplet that Mary King had stuck to the wall over the desk where she worked on the Danville movement's communications:

> Some men ride through the night and wear white robes
> Others sit on high benches and wear black ones (210).[81]

In Holt's assessment, "nitty gritty field secretaries" who backed protestors unflinchingly proved their commitment to civil rights in Danville, with Forman trusted "as few persons would ever be trusted by them" (121).

Like W. E. B. Du Bois after the lynching and mutilation of Sam Hose in 1899, a "red ray" of rage broke Holt's faith in "careful and reasoned statements concerning the evident facts."[82] In *An Act of Conscience*, he retained the unequivocal discourse for which he was renowned in court. His excoriation of the guilty verdict handed down on July 2 is indicative: "The depth of disappointment... rolled like a wave of human excrement being spewed forth from a volcano-like septic-tank throughout Danville's Negro community" (52). Holt inserted an epigraph he attributed to Thelwell for the chapter titled "Bitterness": "Justice and peace are complementary terms; they can only exist together. This is why the *white man's peace* is for us a *slave's peace*. We can never again accept or keep such a peace" (original emphases, 58). These are the angriest words that Thelwell, an elegant and measured writer, has had committed to print and are more evocative of Holt's passionate politics than his own. Holt wrote with force that Zinn judged was vital, inevitable if one were to accurately convey the movement in the moment. He opened each churning chapter with an epigraph, using poetry by Claude McKay, Sterling Brown, Langston Hughes, LeRoi

Jones (Amiri Baraka), and Julian Bond. Lines by Bond—"Watch that gal / Shake that thing, / Everybody can't be / a Martin Luther King"—prefaces the chapter in which King arrives in Danville and match his critique (193). Ed Dawley's poems threaded throughout are bitter pills labeled "The Wisdom of Dawley" (181). Lines from "Asininity 1/10" introduce a chapter titled "Bitter Laughs," its sardonic doggerel echoing McKay's "If We Must Die" (1919) and Sterling Brown's assertion that African Americans have the resilience to produce laughter in dire moments:

> No screams, stifle lacrimal flow
> Though dying
> Mock!
> Laugh like hell! (181)

One historian commended Holt's "candid description" of events in Danville as a "picture of Southern justice" and declared it a work of "national history."[83] Holt used literary works as a means to draw readers toward a responsive understanding of the militant context in which he lambasted the criminalization of protestors. When civil rights activist Luther P. Jackson Jr. reviewed *An Act of Conscience*, he judged that Holt's "refreshing candor" was rare and said that "from such a book ... material for the definitive history of the Negro Revolution will be drawn."[84] Holt himself pointed out that he was "the *only* Negro author of a book about Mississippi in the summer of '64 and *that* should make a difference" (original emphases). This prompted *Negro Digest* to add, "Knowing what happens when the 'sociologists' and 'authorities' and 'analysts' get through with 'civil rights,' Mr. Holt must be said to have something there."[85] But Holt was barely remembered until Brown-Nagin's book focused on protests in Atlanta and his role there.

SNCC's activism was central to both books Holt published in the 1960s, in which he expressed "the struggles within the guts of the protest movement which sap more energy, corrode more spirits, and immobilize more 'soldiers'" than cataclysmic events like assassinations, presaging the critique that Lester would fold into *And All Our Wounds Forgiven* in 1994. Holt's resoundingly personal prose contrasted markedly with other writers in his profession. In *Deep in My Heart* (1966), for example, Kunstler confessed that over the course of representing Freedom Riders, SNCC, and COFO, and despite admiring Holt's fire and brio, he concerned himself with projecting a patina of professionalism that he associated with creating impersonal distance. He unpacked how debilitating the professional norm could be for demonstrators: "I can still recall with shame my earnest recommendation to a brother attorney during the Freedom Rider trials that he not address our clients at a mass meeting." After three years working with the movement, Kunstler realized he had been "playing a fool's game.... No member of a great social movement can remain untouched by the forces that drive it."[86] The nineteen lawyers who contributed to *Southern Justice* (1965), compiling examples of how justice was being administered, attempted to maintain a tone of detachment while enumerating legislation passed to block civil rights initiatives and cataloging how the legal infrastructure—judges, lawyers, mayors, sheriffs, and registrars—punished those who challenged it. Its essays are short, factual, and unemotional and, as George Feifer was honest enough to write, it disturbed him that he could read them calmly; he worried that readers' responses to outrageous miscarriages of justice would be equally flat. Therefore, he closed his review by detailing a kangaroo court conducted in a gas station in Oktibbeha County, Mississippi, where an eighteen-year-old African American organizer forced off the road by a white truck driver was prosecuted for reckless driving and the presiding "judge" invited a "jury" of thugs to play a game with the defendant called "Dropkick the Nigger."[87]

What was parenthetical in *Southern Justice* was front and center for Holt, and, as Robert Coles learned while "caught up in what was happening day to day," observing from a distance put one at risk of seeming "fake" or "disloyal."[88] The expectation to emphasize the "larger perspective" concerned Coles, but so did the idea that other professional writers would be taken to have more credence, a better purchase on the situation for not having been part of it and for not having broken the analytical frame. Like Zinn, Coles was subjected to some withering critique, this time as a "prototypical liberal" and "'soft' authority." "I am no historian or political scientist," he wrote apologetically. Coles's most open advocate was another psychologist, Kenneth Clark, who worked with the NAACP's Legal Defense Fund and testified in *Brown v. Board of Education*. "Who cares if he's not classifiable," Clark said of Coles; "[l]ike any original thinker, he's broken down the artificial academic barriers."[89]

The Counselor

More than other writers discussed in this chapter, Coles had to convince organizers of his right to study them, even though the SRC sponsored his work. The particular stories he would elicit were intensely personal, involving fatigue, depression, and withdrawal, battle neuroses that the organization tried to manage internally. In 1964, Coles was interviewed, as examined in chapter 2, to be sure he could recognize the responsibility he would carry on SNCC's behalf: "They gave me clear notice that they had no immediate reason to trust me."[90] Once he was granted access to undertake individual and group-focused "documentary work," organizers emphasized that he should "'tell their stories,' not try to 'shrink' them." Coles concluded that he needed to find a way to "walk the tightrope of being both observer and involved."[91]

In 1961, Coles began to challenge the "institutional rigidity" of psychiatric discourse, believing that it was apt to "slip into wordy and doctrinaire caricatures of life ... cluttered with jargon" and hollow words that risked becoming shibboleths. The consequence, he worried, was an "icy reasoning": "As the words grow longer and the concepts more intricate and tedious, human sorrows and temptations disappear."[92] He had begun practicing in a neuropsychiatric ward at the Keesler Air Force Base hospital in Biloxi, Mississippi, before graduating from Harvard as a specialist in child psychiatry, then supported black children—most famously Ruby Bridges—who were integrating schools—interviewing their families, white classmates, and teachers. The case histories he produced precipitated a shift in his thinking that was further catalyzed by his work with SNCC.[93] To begin with, though, he relied on tried and tested psychiatric tools to drive therapeutic conversations with organizers and summer volunteers worn down by the white supremacist status quo, depressed by difficult and dangerous fieldwork, and traumatized by racial violence. He was uncomfortable when mentors suggested that as a doctor he could "construct" stories and urged him to listen to his subjects in "the special way a story requires." But he began to note "the manner of presentation; the development of plot, character; the addition of new dramatic sequences; the emphasis accorded to one figure or another in the recital; and the degree of enthusiasm, of coherence, the narrator gives to his or her account."[94] When he first wrote about SNCC, in the essays "Serpents and Doves" and "Separate but Equal Lives" (both in 1962), he described what he was producing as "nonprofessional" writing.[95] The tension between his professional insistence on producing clinical assessment and what he was hearing and witnessing would be worked out over many more essays, the first volume of his five-volume Children in Crisis series, *Children of Crisis: A Study of Courage and Fear* (1967), and over the decades when revisiting this period in his writing life. If Coles was initially cautious in reconciling his method and the task, he found a way. Counseling psychiatric patients in a clinical setting was different from supporting organizers coping with sadistic sheriffs and brutal jailers. The symptoms the latter exhibited were neither based in neuroses nor captured adequately by psychiatric labels. Coles transformed a combination of clinical notes and personal observations into a body of work that pivots on the discovery that "the vicissitudes of the strong and willful are not adequately described by a language that hopes to document the pains of the ill."[96]

Coles was in Oxford, Ohio, when COFO oriented student volunteers for Mississippi Freedom Summer, and he stayed in Freedom Houses from June through September. His interviews with staff and volunteers consolidated what he began to conceive as a narrative methodology at the nexus of medicine, psychology, history, and political science. When poet and general practitioner William Carlos Williams commented on drafts of Coles's reports, he was clear in his criticism: "For God's sake, try to find a cure for that passive voice you use, for the third person, for all that highfalutin technical language—it's a syndrome.... Take your readers in hand, take them where you've been, tell them what you've seen, give them some stories you've heard. Most of all, write for them, the ordinary folks out there, not for yourself and your buddies in the profession of psychiatry."[97] Coles discarded the language of diagnosis for a more subjective literary style. Reconceptualizing therapy as conversations and seeing diagnosis in cultural terms was a switch. However, the love of literature that had compelled Coles to pursue his first degree—in English and history—imbued *Children of Crisis* with the "character" of those he interviewed and their "habit of being." The latter phrase was borrowed from Flannery O'Connor, whose writing he admired, as he did that of William Faulkner, Richard Wright, Eudora Welty, and Shirley Ann Grau.[98] Reporters on the civil rights beat, including Margaret Long and Pat Watters, were among those Coles credited for inspiring him in finding a narrative strategy through which to convey "special, often dangerous, even fatally dangerous lives of constant protest."[99] The result did not "shrink" the stories activists shared, and they established a wider readership beyond peers in psychology and medicine.

In my assessment, Coles opened himself to a permeable, dialogic, conceptual framing of his subjects, harnessing the feeling of being a trespasser that had colored his induction into SNCC. He dropped tautological discourse that identifies only with itself. When he crossed putative divisions between disciplinary norms, he began to answer a question Spencer and Hogan pose now, in the twenty-first century, because "we [still] need to ask": "Why is the personal clearly justified in personal histories... but not as easily justified in collective biographies of groups?"[100] In Coles's case, the answer was a more-than-clinical narrative of the adjustment young activists were making to "a grim, hard-won awareness of the world": "I want to make sure that I am not read as an observer of 'the' civil rights movement, as an expert on the *general* subject of activist youths, or as a psychiatrist who knows about a new—the political—dimension to what textbooks in adolescent psychiatry call 'activity-passivity'.... I have used their words and mine, their observations and mine."[101] Coles ensured that organizers would "share the pages," as Bernice Johnson Reagon suggests they should. He committed himself to what he has described as "the call of stories," thinking of how Jean-Paul Sartre wrote "freely and profoundly about psychiatry," and how one might "blend poetic insight[,] ... unite intimately the rational and the intuitive," and, while protecting his subjects by not naming them, eschew the version of anonymity enshrined in neutrality and objectivity.[102]

Coles became progressively more skeptical of social science methodologies and spoke against issuing questionnaires to field-workers when researchers at the University of Wisconsin elicited information in that format.[103] Like Zinn and McCord, his idea of data collection was personal: "I went to study them and I came to respect them and so I will tell their story so as to let them come to word, and through them, their tasks and fate."[104] The phrase "come to word" is strikingly literary, as is the symbolism of "Serpents and Doves" that marks this particular essay as transitional. Coles dispensed with footnotes and pointed to a self-conscious revision of his practice and honed this approach for *Children of Crisis*: "I had to weave together fragments and cut away at long monologues or dialogues. In each case, I had in mind conveying to the reader what about that person, that life, that situation or problem, that series of interviews, sheds light upon the central (and vexing) issue this book aims to examine: the relationship between individual lives and the life of a nation—where a crisis has come upon them both."[105] In the final section of *Children of Crisis: A Study of Courage and Fear*, he shifts into a series of disquisitions—"The Meaning of Race," "The Meaning of Prejudice," and "The Place of Crisis"— to argue that to understand behaviors in cultural context "nonpsychiatric influences must be summoned." Coles draws on writers who refused to "confine themselves" to a monologic framework or set of generic conventions, closing on James Agee's unconventional *Let Us Now Praise Famous Men* (1941), reprinted to acclaim in 1960. It is a self-reflexive work and, for Coles, "alive with Agee's sense of the difficulty, and maybe the impossibility, of his project." In a self-aware, often frustrated, examination of a group of pseudonymous subjects, Agee problematized the ethics not only of readers seeing them, via Walker Evans's photographs, but also of hearing their voices. Coles concluded, "I am glad that, finally, I could begin to learn what Agee knew."[106]

By 1970, Coles was vehemently protecting civil rights activists against what he called a "fashionable kind of slander" written in the prolix language of his peers. He mounted defenses against what he regarded as partial studies, even spurious and sensationalist ones, in which clinical terms reduced activism to "protest psychosis."[107] In 1980, he was as clear as he had ever been that his method had evolved by paying attention to how novelists, poets, and intellectual historians perform cultural work, and how doctors and psychiatrists might learn from literature, reiterating his sense of personal responsibility to organizers: "The hope is, if you're caught up in the civil rights movement... that the writing and the testimony and some of the medical work at least pay back some of the debts that you've rung up from going place to place and asking people to tell you things which you then write up and tell to the world at large."[108] *Children of Crisis*'s subtitle—*A Study of Courage and Fear*—signals that emotions and trust were as crucial as psychology and facticity in building a culturally thick and self-reflexive account of what Coles discovered in the civil rights South with SNCC. If that was "hard enough to encompass," when he revisited his memories in poetry he ventriloquized many voices, including sharecroppers with whom COFO worked closely, in poems that he described as "fragments of ideas and feelings."[109] However, he did not speak in the voices of organizers, in the hope, I would judge, that they had "come to word" already in what he published in the 1960s.

While examining what she calls a "crippling sanitized version from afar," Wesley Hogan observes that "journalists, academics, and politicians recorded the civil rights movement for posterity" but says that "almost all of them got it wrong because they had not experienced a transforming moment when they discovered that their prior understanding of race in America had been fundamentally skewered by white supremacy." Hogan posits that, as whites, what they wrote was hampered by the fact they belonged to "the very part of society the movement was trying to change, a society replete with hierarchy and unearned condescension."[110] In the 1960s, though, a small group of white professionals pursued fieldwork that challenged their own conventions and were willing to adjust the discourse in which they operated. Some, like Watters and Karl Fleming, may have also experienced a "transforming moment" or epiphany in the form of racial conversion, but the majority of SNCC's early chroniclers were already convinced by the demand for racial change. Zinn was a mentor of long standing, and the African American writers examined here were unequivocal advocates and activists; both Grant and Holt joined SNCC. But they were all troubled by how to label their work for skeptical readers so that it could not be dismissed as partial or "the reality of the field" dismissed. Nor did they romanticize their roles; even Holt's allusion to his nickname is shaded with exhaustion from driving hundreds of miles to represent jailed protestors. That is not insignificant when a smattering of self-regard is evident even in the writing of acclaimed journalists, like *Nation* editor Andrew Kopkind when recalling a trip in 1965 to observe the Selma project for the *New Republic*: "I just thought these people were real heroes. The SNCC workers and the black workers from the counties; we would just go and hang out in the sharecroppers' houses and in the little chapels, and this was so beautiful. I thought I was part of this tremendously exciting historic, romantic movement. And . . . I was. So I came back, and I wrote the first piece sort of discovering SNCC for a national left-liberal audience."[111] From Halberstam to Coles, they reassessed their prose in order to communicate more attentively and intimately the import, meaning, and feeling of what was happening at the grassroots in the 1960s.

As academic writers, we are wary of failing to take a sufficiently "detached" or "objective" approach, of becoming imbalanced, and, despite my democratic openness to sources in this study, checks and balances remain. SNCC's writers have punctured this caution. For Thelwell, "scholarly objectivity" is a privilege of distantiation, the creation of mental or emotional distance, "a delusion that liberals (of both races) may subscribe to" when "black people and perceptive whites know better." When he made a case for interdisciplinary black studies in 1969, Thelwell advocated a "radical stance" for "reevaluation of the treatment of the black experience in disciplines," which could be enacted by "active black intellectuals with experience in the political and cultural battlefronts of this country and the Third World."[112] In this formulation, neutrality denotes not only a lack of political involvement but also a lack of writerly agency. When Joyce Ladner edited *The Death of White Sociology* (1973), she selected essays that contend with the idea that writing can be value free and, when the collection was reissued in 1998, parse the channels into which the study of black lives have typically been forced as "deviant" from social "norms." Ladner cast back to the movement when she asserted that sociologists should not be wary or afraid of being read as "advocates for the black masses" or refrain from rejecting the white universalizing "norms" that underpin the illusion of value neutrality.[113]

SNCC's early chroniclers sought ways to liberate their prose when the schemata according to which they traditionally made sense of "subjects" or "clients" seemed insufficiently perceptive. They wrote as close to the inside of the organizing experience as they could, as close as they dared. The result is rich. These texts—evocative, empirical primary sources, not idiosyncratic on-the-spot reportage or history in a hurry—are foundational for apprehending the character, mood, spirit, and emotion in SNCC. This incipient narrative culture around the organization helps to locate those stories that only organizers could write. These derive from "cotton fields, prison cells, and the minds of young people reflecting on what they see and feel," as Zinn recognized.[114] Nell Salm was struck by the quotations from field reports, diaries, and letters he included in *SNCC: The New Abolitionists*. "These remarkable young people have talent as well as courage and conviction," she wrote, "and one has reason to hope that out of their experience will come a rich literature."[115] Salm was prescient. Organizers were exploring what remained elusive, imperceptible even to those writers who followed them closely, not least their passionate identification with local leaders, bridge leaders, sharecroppers, and myriad other individuals in communities in which they were embedded, as the next chapter explores.

Chapter 5

"Go to Writing and Write Up a New Day"
Local People

> One day somebody will do as Mama Dollie said one day in Lee County: "Now boy, you go to writing and write up a new day."
> —**Charles Sherrod, 1962**
>
> The people are our teachers.... There is a fantastic poetry in the lives of people who have survived with strength and nobility.
> —**Prathia Hall, 1968**
>
> What we cannot do is tell or understand this history without recognizing that southern black folk played an activist role in initiating and carrying out the civil rights struggle.
> —**Martha Prescod, 1988**

Today, in the twenty-first century, studies of grassroots organizing, since William Chafe on Greensboro, North Carolina, Emilye Crosby on Claiborne County, Mississippi, and Hasan Jeffries on Lowndes County, Alabama, put local people front and center, but in the 1960s local people at the heart of the movement were largely hidden from public view.[1] If writers in SNCC feared that the communities in which they worked would not find a place in civil rights histories, journalism of the day was certainly not a safe forum for communicating the courage of local people. In a 1964 article for *Redbook*, Alice Lake hid the names of those hosting her daughter and other volunteers in Greenville: "The Negro families who offered hospitality to the three girls still live in Madison County. For their own protection, their names have been altered." In *Mississippi: The Long, Hot Summer* (1965), William McCord acknowledged "those who must remain anonymous," hiding their identities by truncating names: "the McLs and all of the others who keep watch" and "Rev. W. who had the courage to talk and Mr. H. who had the courage to act."[2] Coles worried about publishing "'too much' of what local people told him because "that 'war' was still actively going on."[3]

In such a febrile atmosphere, literature offered a safer space than journalism, a place where writers could do justice to local people, dramatize the courage that made their lives more than ordinary, and contemplate organizers' responsibility to communities endangered further by their presence. Admiring the creative resilience of black communities, they sought ways to represent it. Whether the SNCC writers were raised in the South and in African American culture, like Gloria Bishop (now Gloria Wade Gayles) in Memphis and Dorie and Joyce Ladner in Hattiesburg, in the North (like Cobb in Philadelphia and Denise Nicholas in Detroit), or outside the United States, like Thelwell in Jamaica, similar concerns are evident in their writing about disenfranchised communities. Gloria Wade Gayles was hosted by Reverend and Mrs. McKinney in Valley View, a few miles north of Canton, and commemorated them later because "people like [the McKinneys] never made the national headlines," especially during Freedom Summer, when "cameras focused on activists, mostly on white activists, whom evening news anchors considered the real heroes of the movement. The McKinneys were the real heroes. And like real heroes, they expected no praise for their courage."[4] Carmichael was still frustrated by the occlusion of local people and black southern organizers when talking to Thelwell near the end of his life: "Why on earth would some nineteen-year-old suburban freshman be a more interesting subject than a Mrs. Hamer, a Jesse Harris, or a Mr. Steptoe either in political terms or even for simple human interest?"[5] If the fact of their invisibility was galling, so was media publicity when individuals did make the news, as Annie Lee Cooper did on January 25, 1965, when prodded with a billy club by Sheriff Jim Clark while waiting to register to vote in Selma. She retaliated with a punch that sent Clark sprawling, and then his deputies held her down so he could beat her. He protested to the *New York Times* that fifty-four-year-old Cooper had "stolen" his club and started the brawl, castigating any "damn newspaper fellows" who might make it "look like I was beating her." Local leaders and SNCC told a different story than the one appearing in newspapers. Mrs. Cooper murmured that neither she nor any other registrant would be intimidated; that was why Clark had struck her in anger.[6]

Hidden Lives and Tragic Deaths

The media overlooked indigenous activists, and it completely ignored the "bottom rail," the sharecroppers, factory and domestic laborers, and the children who were instrumental in making civil rights gains that the sympathetic press did report, as Bond reiterated.[7] When he returned north to Morehouse College from Southwest Georgia, Bob Mants attended a class where peers made speeches lauding Martin Luther King, Benjamin Mays, and other renowned leaders, while he honored a twelve-year-old, Sandra Gail Russell. As he left Americus for Atlanta, he had noticed her standing in line with another child, quietly intent on integrating the Martin Theater.[8] Maria Varela threaded hidden lives and deaths through her poetry in the 1960s and reasserts local people in life writing published in 2008 and 2011 and a photography exhibition catalog. Her overarching metaphor is cotton:

> two were found
> dead
> in a bed where damp,
> 50-year-old cotton quilts
> refused to get warm
> and instead became
> a frozen-cotton death sheet.
> born in a cotton field,
> worked 70 years in cotton fields,
> and, finally,
> to die under cotton.[9]

In concrete diction, Varela exposes the fact that in January 1963, when temperatures dropped to record-shattering lows, sharecroppers froze to death in Leflore County, Mississippi. When she exhibited photographs to "serve as counterpoint to pictures of the defeated, starving, and ragged," she suggested the hidden dead in an image she titled "Plantation Road (Rosedale, Mississippi)," a muddy, rutted, dirt track and bare cabin surrounded by bleak, leafless trees. The shot is empty of people, and the road tapers to the horizon, but her caption creates a temporal arc yoking the fate of those who froze to death in 1963 to the political loss and despondency of the following year with the Mississippi Freedom Democratic Party's failed challenge to the Democratic Party. "It was the winter of evictions of striking cottonpickers ... old people freezing to death under damp flour-sack sheets. . . . And we came back from Atlantic City, crowned in powerlessness, to start all over again on lonely plantation roads."[10] In the 1960s, Varela answered a question Judith Butler poses that transcends time and location: "Who counts as human? Whose lives count as lives? And finally, *what makes for a grievable life*?" (original emphases).[11] Stembridge wrote an epitaph for "those / who froze / Friday night," filtering fact as affect, feelings a veteran organizer cannot hold back:

> I have walked ragged
> on American roads

>   and it wasn't enough
>   that I smiled. I
>   knew a
>   lady
>   who froze[12]

Hopelessness is immediately evident in this memento mori, with an organizer's walking "ragged" juxtaposed with real poverty and death, the effects of a sharecropping system that seemed indomitable and immutable. The polite term "lady" jars with the anonymity of a woman who is invisible before being literally frozen out of society. Neither Varela nor Stembridge attribute names to those they mourn, respecting the privacy of pitiful deaths. In media reports, the weather constituted the news, and such deaths were evidence of an unusually harsh winter.[13] Black deaths were whited out, and Stembridge concluded acidly, "[I]n my / country ... everything's / proper and white."

Local leaders who organizers admired, some associated with the NAACP or the Regional Council of Negro Leadership, included Amzie Moore, Herbert Lee, Aaron Henry, Fannie Lou Hamer, C. B. King, Slater King, Unita Blackwell, Hartman Turnbow, Annie Devine, C. C. Bryant, Victoria Gray, Alyene Quinn, Ora Bryant, E. W. Steptoe, Carolyn Daniels, and Annie "Mama Dollie" Raines. Moses wrote that in Amzie Moore he found a father in the movement who reminded him of his own, and, for Martha Prescod, Moore was "at the heart of SNCC": "our spirit and our substance."[14] In a Freedom School workshop at the Waveland Work-Study Institute in 1965, Carmichael foregrounded Hartman Turnbow as representative of community leaders in Holmes County, Mississippi, who were asserting black participation in "every scintilla of what was political and what was economic."[15] He emphasized Turnbow's leadership in the context that Jimmy Garrett summarized: "We are taught that it takes qualifications like college education, or 'proper English' or 'proper dress' to lead people."[16] Stembridge reported that Carmichael's class was "the most successful" one in the Waveland program.[17] It modeled participatory democracy by teaching that spurious voting "standards" for "qualification" were calculated attempts to eliminate African Americans from voting. Rob Wood distilled the issue in a manifesto poem, wherein "Fredm" is chalked on a brick wall:

>   FREDM
>   And no literacy tests
>   Can disqualify him
>   'Cause he knew

It's FREDM
And the knowing
And the telling
Not the spelling.[18]

When Robert Moses looked back, he acknowledged Ella Baker by citing a Swahili term, *fundi*, to describe her. Hogan, in turn, calls Moses a *fundi*, saying that a *fundi* is a person from the community who has achieved mastery and now helps and teaches others outside of any institutional bounds. Hogan uses this term in her account of Moses's speech at the Democratic National Convention on June 18, 2016, when he mapped a long activist history rooted in communities.[19]

SNCC's creation of a civil rights imaginary was a way to address the neglect of local people. Pat Watters described SNCC as "a metaphor speaking the greatest strength and beauties of the Negro people of the South, the people of the movement," but most SNCC writers were not so romantic.[20] That was because of what was defined internally as "local-people-itis."[21] A soft sentimentalization of "the folk" was noted in position papers, as when Thelwell presented "SNCC's Goals and Bourgeois Sentimentality." Thelwell described how important it was not to succumb to a "fuzzyminded" sense of "redemptive compassion": "Our orientation must always be towards eliminating causes rather than trying to make their effects more bearable for a few."[22] SNCC workers became conscious of the plight of the day laborer, "the forgotten man in southern agriculture," working from "can see to can't see," to borrow an image Thelwell employed in a short story, "Bright an' Mownin' Star" (1966).[23] Organizers wrote imaginatively about local leaders and their hosts in black communities, finding affidavits, press releases, and even field reports to be cramped containers. Thelwell explored this pointedly in "The Organizer" (1966), set in "the day-day grittiness of the movement" on the night a beloved local leader is murdered because he is a catalyst for change. Thelwell conveyed how profoundly murders were felt, and his protagonist hesitates to express "the burden of his feelings" to the man's widow: "Unless he could find new words that would come fresh and living from his heart that had never been said before, he could not say anything." The protagonist concludes: if the sole vehicle for telling activist stories is strategically unimpassioned reportage, "there is nothing left of that emotion" (22). The narratives explored in this chapter emerged out of "Mama Dollie" Raines's expectation that organizers would "go to writing and write up a new day" by drawing on "what they see and feel."[24]

Clyde Kennard's Story

While high school students in Hattiesburg, Joyce and Dorie Ladner were members of an NAACP youth chapter, and Clyde Kennard was their chapter advisor. In 1960, he was imprisoned in the Mississippi State Penitentiary in Parchman after being convicted on a spurious charge of stealing $25 worth of chicken feed. He had been targeted because he'd had the temerity to try to enroll at Mississippi Southern College (now University of Southern Mississippi). In 1962, SNCC was acutely aware that his continuing plight was hidden behind James Meredith's success in enrolling at the University of Mississippi, some 250 miles away. McDew wrote in a SNCC press release, "America must not forget Clyde Kennard, like Meredith a veteran, whose reward for trying to enjoy an education in his home state is a seven-year prison sentence on a trumped-up charge."[25] SNCC's mobilization in support of the NAACP's campaign, led by Medgar Evers and involving Thurgood Marshall petitioning the U.S. Supreme Court, was an extension of the Ladner sisters' unceasing support of Kennard. The mobilization was deeply personal, especially once Kennard was diagnosed with cancer, still forced to work on the prison plantation, and denied treatment by prison warden C. E. Breazeale.[26] The effort the Ladners made to keep this honest and honored member of their community in the public eye would continue long after his death in 1963.

Ron Hollander broke the story in 1962, locally in *Mississippi Free Press* and nationally in the *Reporter* (a biweekly news magazine based in New York), where he wrote: "In a year and a half Meredith is scheduled to earn his degree. Clyde Kennard, however, faces five more years at Parchman Penitentiary."[27] Hollander credited Bob Moses for handing him a five-page summary of Kennard's situation on a street in Jackson while they canvassed for voter registration in July.[28] Hollander followed up and produced a report of twenty-one typed pages, provisionally titled "How Mississippi Southern Stayed White: The Story of Clyde Kennard," then sent this to Dorie Ladner to check. This was a clear case of SNCC feeding a story to a sympathetic journalist, as Bond advocated organizers should. Hollander had investigated by visiting Kennard in jail.[29] Over four decades later, when Timothy J. Minchin and John A. Salmond published an article tracing Kennard's story from 1955 to 2006, they asserted that "Clyde Kennard Day," instituted in 2006, "helped bring the case to the attention of national figures such as NAACP leader Julian Bond and Pulitzer Prize–winning author Taylor Branch."[30] However, Bond had been close to the case in 1962 through SNCC's drive to "Free Kennard," when "freedom-loving

Americans" were urged to send telegrams to their members of Congress and President Kennedy. Dorothy Zellner mimeographed hundreds of copies of the NAACP's clemency petition, leading to the collection of thousands of names, and in Freedom Schools Kennard was a special subject.[31] In January 1963, when Governor Ross Barnett finally agreed to release Kennard to avoid more adverse publicity, Tom Dent went with Medgar Evers to collect him from Jackson, and Dick Gregory paid for Kennard's flight to Chicago and hospitalization.[32] The Ladners visited, and on July 4, 1963, Kennard told novelist and journalist John Howard Griffin, at his bedside the night he died,

> I would be glad that this happened if it would only show people in this land where racism finally leads. But they're not going to know, are they? . . .
>
> [B]e sure and tell them that what happened to me is less terrible than what the system has done to that warden, because it has turned him into a beast and it will turn his children into beasts.[33]

Kennard had attempted to tell his own story in "Double Jeopardy," a novel, and "Death Angel," a poem, but it was left to others—the Ladners, Griffin, Larry Still in *Jet*, and Tom Dent in *Freedomways*—to get out the word.[34] In "Portrait of Three Heroes" (1965), Dent folded Kennard's story into Evers's and Meredith's, describing him as "a soldier who had been captured at the front." Meredith was his original focus, but Evers's murder in June and Kennard's death in July ensured that they shared the pages. Having judged that journalist Walter Lord could not hope to tell Meredith's story after a single conversation, Dent was conscious that he himself had spent only a few hours with Kennard. He was tentative in expressing to Kennard that "in a way" Kennard "had laid the groundwork for Meredith," to which Kennard had "replied sadly": "Maybe . . . but we look in life for success most of the time." More evocative is the story-within-the-story that Dent tells, presented in Kennard's voice: "The night I left to come to the hospital, they held a prayer meeting in our barracks. I told them not to do it because it's against the rules and I didn't want them to get whipped because of me. But they sang and sang and the guards took names and names. . . . I know they were all whipped the next day."[35] If Dent provided a glimpse of the man, Hollander exposed his betrayal by William D. McCain, president of Mississippi Southern, whom Kennard trusted as a "liberal." McCain led Kennard through three years of interviews that Kennard assumed would result in his being able to complete the degree he had begun at the University of Chicago. (He had moved back to Hattiesburg to be close to his ailing mother.) After McCain conspired with Governor J. P. Coleman, the prosegregation Mississippi Sovereignty Commission, and local citizens' councils, Kennard was doomed. McCain asserted his position only after Kennard was imprisoned. "I've got 270 years behind my feelings," he told Hollander. The "integrity" of a racially segregated university was paramount, and he refused to commit "silly martyrdom for one Negro" (5, 9).[36]

The Ladner sisters ensured that the activism Kennard embodied would be understood, mobilizing with others to finally achieve Kennard's full posthumous exoneration in 2006.[37] Joyce Ladner has commemorated Kennard as one of three mentors, with Vernon Dahmer and Evers, who "had a profound influence" on her life and who "died for their beliefs," situating Kennard among other unsung men and women who "pried the state open."[38] In 2016, she posted a forceful indictment of the University of Southern Mississippi claiming Kennard posthumously:

> His actions of speaking out and attempting to enroll in an all-white college should not have caused his death. He lived his own truths and for that he was killed at the hands of a system ruled by hatred and fear. His powerful words in his letters to the *Hattiesburg American* newspaper frightened white racists to the point that he became a marked man. It is insidious that those who created and enforced the system of racism that caused his death would turn around and name a building for him on the campus of the University of Southern Mississippi that denied him entry. May we never forget this great man.[39]

It makes for an ironic ending to what John Dittmer observed is "arguably the saddest story of the whole movement" and demonstrates that individuals who inspired organizers remain their concern.[40]

"After Joe Holmes" and "Somewhere in Glory"

Another unsung individual was Joe Pullum, Fannie Lou Hamer's inspiration, as she told Jack O'Dell of *Freedomways*. Bernice Johnson Reagon recounted Hamer's respect for him in "Songs My Mother Wrote Me," and Worth Long recalled that Hamer would say in times of trouble, "We may need us a Joe Pullum."[41] Still another was Mr. Joe Holmes of Reform, Alabama, the inspiration for a local organizer who had joined SNCC in 1961 when just fifteen years old. Coles recounted that organizer's words in *Children of Crisis*. When Holmes asked his church's congregation "Are you ready for the Day?," declaring that they could "rewrite the history books in our lifetime," the organizer's father advocated forgetting "that kind of talk" because Mr. Holmes was "funny in the head"—one of the "crazy Negroes" O'Neal celebrates as rebel leaders in his Junebug plays. The teenager's mother counseled, "Don't forget [Holmes's words], but don't let them fasten on your tongue, or they'll be no end for you but the chain gang." After hosting civil rights workers, Holmes was ambushed by police, beaten, and died within a week, but SNCC "didn't up and leave us the way we thought": "That's how I became one of the leaders here in Reform, and how I got to go to Selma, and up to Washington. It was Joe Holmes who did it, and the students who came here and stood by him at the graveyard and stayed with us."[42] Whether a volunteer's advocacy journalism with details provided by SNCC or a foundational tale that inspired an organizer, the storytelling authority is distributed in these examples. Hollander saved the notes Moses gave him in 1962, acknowledging SNCC in 2010.[43] Joyce and Dorie Ladner were, and remain, instrumental in ensuring that Kennard is remembered as a courageous individual whose imprisonment was a travesty, a conspiracy between white supremacist guardians of Mississippi society in government, education, the law, and the prison system.

James Forman celebrated another inspiring individual, Georgia Mae Turner, in an unpublished three-act play he titled "Somewhere in Glory." In 1960, as a member of an emergency relief committee sending supplies from Chicago to Fayette County, Tennessee, Forman taught in "Freedom Village," a tent city there, while reporting the situation for the *Chicago Defender*.[44] Mrs. Turner had been turned off the McNamee plantation after thirty-eight years of service, and Forman's oral-history-derived play memorializes an individual of more historical significance than she or others realized. "On the paved road running along the embankment where the tents stood, an occasional car passed by. I wondered how many of the people in those cars knew anything about the life of a Georgia Mae Turner." Forman used Mrs. Turner's words as transcribed from his recordings, following her life from childhood but focusing on the tent city in the play, incorporating other residents while ensuring that hers is the focal voice. This principle of expressing "the meaning of struggle" in the words of local people is evident across SNCC's writing, and Worth Long encapsulated the issue in the voice of a black southern woman: "Where am I / in our history books?"[45] Forman's play is an intriguing precursor to Ernest Gaines's *The Autobiography of Miss Jane Pittman* (1971), in which a fictional editor records interviews over nine months in 1962, until, aged 108, Miss Jane walks off a Louisiana plantation to lead a civil rights demonstration. When the editor is asked, "What's wrong with them books you already got?," he answers, "Miss Jane is not in them." Gaines's explanation of his practice mirrors that of writers in SNCC: "I go to other sources, the newspapers, magazines, the books in the libraries, but I also go back and listen to what Miss Jane and folks like her have to say": "Truth to me is what people like Miss Jane remember."[46]

Through Georgia Mae Turner, Forman criticized religion as a shield for corruption. In the play, Mrs. Turner discerns "no religion in [the] heart [of the white Christian plantation owner]," and a black minister runs her out of church at gunpoint because he is frightened of the movement. Turner's daughter is "put in the field" at four years old—"you know that girl picked 30lbs of cotton one day"—and her hope that her grandchildren will "see a new day" is undercut when they are forced to miss school to help pay spurious "debts." The toll that agricultural labor was taking on generations is tied to racist economic practices, and Forman depicts farmworkers' tent cities as comprising a resistance movement in their own right. A "black underground" steals a list of residents targeted for reprisal from a citizens' council and discovers that the council has raised $2,000 to pay for the murder of John Hope, a character Forman modeled on John McFerrin in Fayette County.[47] Whites shoot into the tent city, and, after a resident is hit, no local doctor will treat him—the nearest who will is fifty miles away. Scenes like these recur across SNCC's literary texts, but Forman never returned to this manuscript. While he vacillated over the most effective form in which to write this story, he may have felt that journalist Fred Travis had beaten him to it, opening an article in the *Progressive* with Mrs. Turner saying: "Last summer I wen' down to Somerville an' register to vote and she say she seen my pi'ture in th' paper... Then she tell me las' fall I got to get offn her farm. She say she don' want me there no mo."[48] Travis couched Turner's testimony in the vernacular, while Forman emphasized her articulateness, eschewing picturesque eye-dialect.[49] When he published what he witnessed at the tent city, it was not a play but "an account," in *The Making of Black Revolutionaries* (1972) and *High Tide of Black Resistance* (1994). But Forman encouraged others, and Si Kahn described a 106-year-old woman in Forrest City, Arkansas, who wanted to register to vote but explained, "[I] don't ever leave my rocking chair." Born a slave, she was the oldest member of her community, and organizers carried up the courthouse steps as if on a throne.[50]

Community Focus through the Organizer Archetype

Initially Thelwell and Carmichael considered Mississippi and "folks like Fannie Lou Hamer, Hartman Turnbow, E. W. Steptoe, [and] Miz Susie

Ruffin" as "Sterling Brown territory." In "The Professor and the Activists: A Memoir of Sterling Brown," Thelwell writes that at Howard University Brown had prepared them "culturally and psychologically for the people most of us would be working with in the Mississippi Delta." Thelwell believed, "Because of him, we later met them with the recognition of family members you'd never seen but had grown up hearing about." In "Fish Are Jumping an' the Cotton Is High," Thelwell conveyed the feeling of "return[ing] to a home he had never known but always missed." For Carmichael, Brown helped him to understand "the beauty of our people's language and the power of that extraordinary culture that sustained them."[51]

In 1966, as SNCC was fragmenting, Thelwell focused on that culture and SNCC's community role in a story that could have underpinned the educational program Forman conceived when he believed SNCC had hit "rock bottom," as discussed in chapter 3. "The Organizer" was first published in Whit and Hallie Burnett's *Story: The Yearbook of Discovery 1968*, and it was reprinted by Chinua Achebe in Nigerian journal *Okike* in 1974. It is among Thelwell's "essays in struggle" collected as *Duties, Pleasures, and Conflicts* and introduced by James Baldwin in 1987. Marge Franz, an activist from the 1930s through the 1950s, declared it "a classic" and "the finest epitaph I know for SNCC," but it has received no critical attention aside from my introductory remarks on the story in "SNCC's Stories at the Barricades" in 2012.[52]

Grassroots leaders and families hosting field-workers had their homes bombed, torched, and targeted for drive-by shootings. Telephone calls threatening violence were quotidian, especially through the night; Natchez project director Dorie Ladner admitted to enduring sleepless nights and a habit of vomiting after supper in anticipation.[53] A pervasive sense of what it was like to live under siege underpins "The Organizer," set during a single night, partly in a Freedom House but mainly in a community. It is rooted in a spate of bombings in McComb in 1964, including the bombing of Society Hill Missionary Baptist Church and the home of Mrs. Alyene ("Mama") Quinn. Active in McComb's Citizens' League, Quinn was one of the women sociologist Belinda Robnett identifies as "bridge leaders" (and Karen Sacks as "centerwomen"), who were "key actors in network formation and consciousness-shaping" in their communities.[54] Quinn's South of the Border café was a movement place, raided regularly by police. When her white landlord ordered her to close so he could "tell the sheriff and the police chief and you won't be bombed," she refused, and soon a bomb exploded on her porch, close to the bedroom where her children, aged five and nine, were sleeping.[55] They were injured in the fourteenth bombing in

McComb that summer, and Quinn was accused of bombing her own home to stir up trouble.[56] To extrapolate imaginatively from this situation, Thelwell revisited SNCC's journalism—specifically its "Response to the 13th and 14th Bombings" report and Mendy Samstein's article "The Murder of a Community."[57] In the 1960s, presumably to protect the identity of Quinn, Thelwell set "The Organizer" in Bogue Chitto, Mississippi. It was nuanced with foreboding resonance for readers because, after the COFO project opened and CORE workers Chaney and Schwerner and COFO volunteer Andrew Goodman were murdered by a conspiratorial mob of Klan and police, Bogue Chitto was where their station wagon was buried in a swamp. Their bodies would be discovered in an earthen dam on a farm in Neshoba County.[58]

As Julian Bond encapsulated, field-workers offered themselves "as a protective barrier between private and state-sponsored terror and the local communities."[59] Whatever internal disagreements there were, the agreement not to impose views on local communities was among the most enduring, despite some chafing that community-led organizing was interminably slow. In "The Organizer," Thelwell elucidates Ella Baker's thesis that an organizer begins where the people are, but he unpacks how difficult that could be when affected emotionally and transformed personally by people who feel like family. Travis Peacock embodies this feeling when a firebomb kills local leader Jesse Lee Hightower and he struggles to manage the aftermath for the community and himself. The kinship Peacock feels with Mr. Hightower's family is stronger than that binding him to his own relatives, who now seem "shadowy figures leading barren and futile lives in their northern suburb."[60] Twisted by grief and guilt, Peacock is expected to use Mr. Hightower's death "against the people that killed him," as underlined by Truman, the organization's "true man," modeled on Forman. Truman is big, "shaggy, imperturbable, bearlike . . . always scrambling to keep the organization afloat, to keep the cars running, the rent paid" (24).[61] Before the murder, Peacock bristles when Truman suggests that he take a sabbatical because "we owe it to the movement to take care of our health," retorting, "Look, if you don't like the way I'm running the project come out and say so, man" (4). After the murder, Truman is the calm, firm voice on the phone from Atlanta, reminding the exhausted organizer why he must work with the media. This story conveys the difficulty of balancing immediate and personal responsibility to the community with the movement's far-reaching goals, and the sacrifices entailed in each.

The definite article in "The Organizer" denotes an archetype deriving from the original cadre of field secretaries. By name, Travis Peacock is a fictional conflation of two real people—Jimmie Travis, beaten unconscious in McComb in 1961 and narrowly surviving after being shot in the neck in Greenwood in 1963, and Willie (Wazir) Peacock, who Moses says "had come through the fires of Greenwood annealed like steel."[62] To create his composite, Thelwell summons up a larger group of African American organizers, southern and northern, including Moses, Sam Block, Frank Smith, and Lawrence Guyot in Greenwood; Charles Sherrod, Cordell Reagon, and Charlie Jones in Southwest Georgia; and Jesse Harris, project director in McComb in 1964. When Peacock clashes with Sheriff John Sydney ("Bo") Hollowell, Thelwell draws on Charles McLaurin's encounters with Sheriff William I. Hollowell in Indianola.[63] A composite character obscures differences between locales, city and hamlet, and the specificity of organizing in each, and the archetype is indubitably male, even though the first cadre included Diane Nash, Ruby Doris Smith (Robinson), Jane Stembridge, and Angeline Butler, and, by 1962, women were organizing in all project locations. By 1966, when Thelwell was writing, women were legion in SNCC. However, this is a community story and an object lesson: the test for all field-workers was how to uphold SNCC's "first rules" and to manage the "secret fear of every organizer" that someone close to them will be murdered (24). As enumerated here, the first and "maybe the hardest" rule is "never to let the community know you are afraid" and the second that "the organizer is always responsible." Thelwell stays close to the role as understood internally; like Fred Meely's "Organizer's Handbook," his story serves "to inspire those who read it to see beyond the mysticism that shrouds the movement's work."[64]

Samstein wrote, in his report on McComb, a "city of terror": "It is hard for someone who has not lived in... the Negro community in McComb... to understand the reality behind the two bombings of September 20." He deployed literary and rhetorical strategies to ventriloquize community anguish: "[W]hose house, who is dead? It's not mine. Then who? My neighbor, my friend—my mother, my brother, my son, or maybe SNCC again. Who?"[65] In Thelwell's story, when Peacock hears the firebomb explode, he freezes in the same way: "*Oh God. Oh God. Let it be the church, not anyone's house*... he retched and puked... Somebody's dead. They killed someone. Mama Jean. I don't want to know. I can't go" (original emphasis, 9). When he must calm an enraged community, Peacock vomits again, this time fearing he will be judged as "the stranger who brought death among them" (10). It is Mama Jean, the surrogate Thelwell creates for Alyene Quinn, to whom Peacock clings. Without her, he worries, "the community would crumble overnight" (7). She echoes

Fannie Lou Hamer's famous lines to call out a minister retreating from the scene: "Ah'm sick an tard of bein' sick an' tard of yo' selling the folks out" (16).[66] She galvanizes Peacock to "adopt the accent of the folk" to commune with the crowd, and he echoes her: "Yeah, mah brothahs an' sistuhs, that cracker know we sick an' tard, thet we sick an' tired o' *bein' sick an' tard*" (19). As his incantation builds to an "ecstatic sermon," the crowd responds: "Tell it, Tell it" (19). To tell it like it is, Thelwell balances Peacock with Mama Jean, and both of them with the crowd. Her leadership, and his willingness to heed her, ensure that an embattled community caught in the crosshairs of racial terrorists and complicit lawmen sees no more killings over the long night. A bridge leader, an organizer, and local people are equally emblematic of courage and resilience.

Before the bomb goes off, Peacock steels himself to withstand late-night calls telling him, "Nigger, yo' subjeck to bein blowed up" (6). This taunt echoes Sheriff Hollowell's words when he learns that new volunteers from the "Nonviolent Council" have arrived in town: "Ain't nothing but trash nohow, an' mighty subjeck to needin' buryin'" (3). Peacock is forced to signify on the same sheriff, turning his ability to "play the dozens" into a strategy to maneuver people to disperse without they or him losing face—or their lives. United in rage and militancy, he hopes they will be pragmatic while the sheriff's gun points at his back. Peacock tells the crowd, "Why bad ass Bo Hollowell's standin there shakin jes lak a dawg trying to shit a peach stone," and he is relieved when he hears "real laughter, vindictive and punitive to the lawman, but full, deep and therapeutic to the crowd" (18). "The arsenal of reprisal against white people" that Dollard defined is captured in the "folk expression" Thelwell studied with Sterling Brown but only came to understand in Deep South communities. Thelwell also learned this rich, carnivalesque language from southern organizer Ed Brown, who performed a seemingly "inexhaustible repertoire" of parable, proverb, poetry, and blues.[67] Each time someone tries to register to vote, for example, they are informed that the office must close, but Mama Jean calls out the registrar sweetly, "Why, thass all right, honey. Usses done waited a hunnerd yeahs, be plumb easy to wait till fo' o'clock" (7). When churches are burned—as thirty-eight were during the summer of 1964—barbed humor rallies congregants who joke that, based on Hollowell's redundant reports, the culprit must be "a mysterious and very active arsonist called Faulty Wiring."[68] As the sheriff levels his gun, then, Peacock puts himself in the line of fire to exorcise the crowd's escalating anger: "He scared jes' lak them peckerwoods whut blowed up this house ... You watch 'at ol' big belly Bo. He scared right enough to kill me right heah."

He is hot with fear: "I have to do it just right, one word too much and he' goin' break, he warned himself" (18). Only afterward, in the Freedom House, alone because the other field-workers have not yet returned from a meeting in Atlanta, does Peacock allow fear to wash over him. CORE and COFO's Jerome Smith described that feeling as the "jump-off point": "All the fear was never in the moment itself. It was always after, when you'd think about what you'd done, what you'd been through, and tremble."[69]

By having Peacock load a shotgun and carry it through the streets, even though he worries "it'd be in every lousy newspaper... that the local representative of the organization had arrived on the scene carrying a weapon" (10), Thelwell conveyed how armed defense was inextricably bound into strategic nonviolence. Peacock fantasizes a violent, pitched battle, "the swift liberating relief of wild, mindless, purging violence, ending maybe in death" (14). But he enacts in practice what he has accepted in principle, that the murder of a man he loves must be exploited and pain packaged, acknowledging that the widow Mrs. Hightower has "a great face... great on a poster or TV" (27). Peacock fortifies himself with moonshine, frets, vomits, and exhibits similar symptoms to those of a shell-shocked veteran of war, but he personifies what Moses identified as "SNCC people" who "move within the boundaries of fear... even though afraid."[70] He stands with the community, and the story closes with him planning a mass meeting to follow hard on this sleepless night.

Mendy Samstein closed his report in the *Student Voice* with an exposé of the cover-up of "the real story" of McComb. Police told the press that three thousand black people took to the streets even though the population of McComb barely touched three thousand in total, and broadcaster Mike Wallace authenticated this on CBS's *Morning News*. "And so," Samstein opined, "the story of the murder of a community goes untold."[71] Thelwell dramatized "the real story" and captured the resilience of communities. A similar impetus lies behind *Freshwater Road*, the novel Denise Nicholas would publish forty years later.

Freshwater Road and "Souls of Great Price"

In *Freshwater Road*, Denise Nicholas follows African American college sophomore Celeste from Detroit to Mississippi for Freedom Summer in 1964. The book's epigraph discloses it as a story she felt compelled to tell: "History claims everybody, whether they know it or not, and whether they like it or not."[72] Nicholas burned the journals she kept while acting in the Free Southern Theater from 1964 through 1966. After "dragging this stuff around for years," she says, her memories were "distilled down to impressions," and these, with subjective knowledge based on her experiences as a volunteer, comprise rich sediment in this novel.[73] Freed from the generic expectations of memoir, she privileged imagination, though she consulted civil rights histories to ground her fiction.[74] Celeste studies at the University of Michigan in Ann Arbor, as Nicholas did before following roommate Martha Prescod into SNCC in May 1964. While Prescod pursued fieldwork, Nicholas wanted to contribute through the arts.[75] In the FST, she could have found the drama to drive a novel; performances in Louisiana and Mississippi attracted police and were attended by citizens' council members, with the Deacons for Defense and Justice and local people acting as armed guards on occasion.[76] The FST lodged in Jackson and then New Orleans, and while only John O'Neal and Doris Derby lived for sustained periods in project locations as field secretaries, Fannie Lou Hamer hosted Nicholas in Ruleville when the FST toured.[77] Spinning away from the FST in *Freshwater Road* to focus on the "typical" involvement of a Freedom Summer volunteer, Nicholas illustrates what Vincent Harding pressed upon students during orientation, that their hosts "could not be having you in their homes unless they were freed, unless they had somehow been able to transcend their history... they are souls of great price."[78] After a long post-SNCC career as an Emmy Award–winning television and film actress, Nicholas won the Hurston/Wright Legacy Award for debut fiction and the First Novelist Award of the American Library Association's Black Caucus, and *Freshwater Road* was adapted for the stage in 2008. Nicholas has described imaginative writing as a "second act" to her career.[79] In my reading, the novel is a reclamation, a return to SNCC's principles of community-facing organizing. For nineteen-year-old Celeste, "Mississippi gave her life a higher meaning, shoved it to a different plane, separated her from the past like a soldier who goes to war and always has that as his marker." When Nicholas adds, "It would be the same for everyone who'd been there," she intimates that her tale has wider significance for those who shared the experience (404).

Freshwater Road is a coming-of-age novel, its narrative arc a difficult learning curve for a volunteer who imagines herself "a cross between Joan of Arc and Harriet Tubman, the fires of righteousness flaming in her heart stoked by news reports that had been coming out of the South for the last three years" (28). The symbolic importance of Freedom Summer outweighs the number of participants—some seven hundred students buttressed by lawyers, ministers, and doctors—and white volunteers have been projected into popular culture as its main historical actors ever since. Freedom Summer fascinates writers, but the brutality and tragedy of the murders of Chaney, Schwerner, and Goodman that were its inauguration made it difficult for writers inside the movement to consider as a dramatic trigger for literary works.[80] For performances of Martin Duberman's *In White America* (1963), the FST added scenes cowritten by O'Neal and Gilbert Moses to address the "Freedom Summer murders," and student volunteers have published memoirs, but Nicholas is the first insider to explore Freedom Summer in fiction.[81] Mitchell Zimmerman would be the first volunteer to write a novel about the murders, in 2019, but Nicholas's unwavering focus is on the community that hosts Celeste.

From the opening pages, Nicholas indicates that Celeste needs to listen to local people.[82] She is a bag of nerves when alighting from the train in Jackson, suffering a culture shock that Peter Jan Honigsberg encapsulated when admitting that Jackson had seemed to him "as far from New York as the moon from the earth."[83] Celeste tentatively follows an African American woman into a restroom: "They were *in* the *Whites Only* bathroom, had already *used* it." She feels proud already: "She had a story to tell, and she hadn't even gotten to the One Man, One Vote office" (original emphasis, 4). Only by pausing to listen does she learn that these facilities have been desegregated and the signs resurrected only to make Freedom Summer volunteers feel unwelcome; locals carry on regardless. When the woman warns, "*Mississippi ain't nothing to play with, girl*," her words signal the shift Celeste must make toward responsible accountability (38, 332). Nicholas makes her naïve, engaging protagonist "a straggler" assigned alone to a Pearl River County hamlet a few miles from the Louisiana border to initiate one of the thirty-seven Freedom Schools that Charles Cobb envisioned and run voter registration classes (31). By isolating Celeste, Nicholas focuses on the relationships her hosts build with her as she gains a more assured sense of purpose over the two months she spends with them. Nicholas demonstrates scant interest in the interracialism that made Freedom Summer newsworthy. Celeste has split from her white college boyfriend: "[O]ne of the reasons she'd come South was to get J. D.'s white world out of her system" (186). Chapters set in Detroit emphasize the privileged lifestyle enabled by her father, Shuck, a "race man" who builds a loving home for Celeste and her brother in the city. New Mexico, where her mother, Wilamena, has remarried, represents an alien outpost for Celeste. She finds Wilamena "prickly" and disdains her pride in being light skinned and her enjoyment of a bourgeois lifestyle "less anchored in things Negro." In rejecting them and heading instead to Mississippi, she sets out to prove "how Negro she [is]," to "shore up her own Negro-ness," feeling guilty—"she'd thought she was above it" (27, 10, 85, 42).

SNCC was torn over the extent to which an influx of white volunteers would "trample the very fragile grassroots" by undermining local leaders and black southern staff helming projects.[84] Nicholas includes a single white volunteer, Margo, a New Yorker with six months of experience, who inducts Celeste in Jackson: "The last thing she'd expected in this office was a white girl telling *her* what to do, even if it was only signing some form. Mississippi *and* the civil rights movement meant pushing two years of Ann Arbor's surrounds of white people to the rear" (original emphases, 26–27). Desiring immersion in African American southern culture, she is resentful of instructions on how to behave from a "white-girl boss":

> "If you're with a white person and you get stopped by the police, let the white person do the talking.... Act like you're the maid getting a ride home from work."
>
> "Are you *serious*? ... So what do I do if I get stopped with all Negro people in the car? Jump out and start tap dancing?" (23–24)

This culture shock is evoked as a racial tension that Robert Coles believed was "toned down" and rarely examined self-consciously. For Coles culture shock was "structural," part of "the carriage of an entire life" for privileged northeastern whites.[85] Paul Cowan's *The Making of an Un-American* (1970) is an exception, but Cowan approached the issue of privilege from the opposite direction. He criticized the "modern version of *noblesse oblige* tied to a radical definition of the interests of my class" and the volunteer type that Dittmer calls "the Ugly American."[86] Nicholas notes complaints from local people that some volunteers were "condescending" and others "aggressive" but remains focused on how Celeste adapts to her hosts in the rural South and what she learns (81).

Celeste learns that the movement exists because of her hosts and that she is expected to support their activism. With a master's in divinity from the University of Chicago and an offer to minister a church in Seattle, Reverend Singleton has returned to the South as "a civil rights minister" (366). Churches are significant in the topography of SNCC's stories as places that are attacked by segregationists; but the church in *Freshwater Road*, St. James A.M.E., in fictional Pineyville, Mississippi, is a place in which the movement coheres. Mrs. Geneva Owens is a sure-footed community touchstone, representing the myriad bridge leaders on whom volunteers relied. Through her, Celeste finds courage, in the way McLaurin and Lewis celebrated women who showed them "the way to mobilize in the towns and communities."[87] There is a moment when Celeste hesitates over whether to remain after the summer ends because, she thinks, "if someone like me is here, some things will go a lot faster" (386). In the heavy silence that follows, she realizes she has revealed a mistaken sense of prerogative and checks herself when told that locals "need to do it on their own so they know they done it on their own" (386–87).

It takes time to modify her behavior, during which Nicholas digs gently but resolutely at Celeste's "siddity" ways (124). She annoys Mrs. Owens with her "petulant need for things to be the way they were at home— exactly what the office in Jackson had warned them against" (81). When Matt Higgens, an African American "seasoned volunteer" from Kansas City, drives her from Jackson to Pineyville, they are pulled over by state troopers on Route 49 to Rankin, the same road on which Ivanhoe Donaldson was almost killed by police (111). Matt's advice is shaded differently from Margo's: "No strong black woman smart talk cause they'll kick my black ass" (51). She then feels "pitiful and weak" while he is beaten, a gun is leveled at his head, and troopers fire into the car. The other advice Matt imparts is saved for when they reach Mrs. Owens's house in Freshwater Road: "Don't go bringing that siddity Detroit shit down here. I know you got it in you" (70). He alights on an element of culture shock that tests Celeste almost as much as hiding her fear when shots are fired into the house and she wets herself. Nicholas writes, "If the One Man, One Vote office told the truth about the living circumstances, some of those volunteers would have taken a pass and stayed in the cities to do their volunteering. She checked herself. She of all people needed to do the harder thing, and this was going to be it" (72). Plumbing is a quotidian test for Celeste, as it was for many volunteers—90 percent of black homes in Mississippi had outhouses in back and water spigots in front.[88] When Celeste washes her hair at the spigot, Mrs. Owens is "sharp and clear in her disapproval." Celeste is reminded curtly, "People clean themselves down here. I got a tub for that. No need to be washing your hair out in the front yard." She feels "like Shuck's little girl again, scolded for stepping out of line"; in offending her host she has lapsed in the courtesy her father taught her to exercise with elders (123).

Nicholas does not suggest that a black volunteer will automatically empathize with her hosts because they are black. Celeste seems at first like an awkward student of anthropology: "They told me in Jackson—there was a lynching here in '58. She blurted it out, fear like a river undertow right beneath her words. She hoped she sounded like a researcher" (98). Mrs. Owens closes her down, "They do that all over Mississippi. Always have," leaving Reverend Singleton to respond to her anxiety: "Don't fret. We'll be all right" (99). She is recognized for what she is: a panicky visitor whose pervasive fear encompasses not only people and place but also her own abilities. She tells regional director Ed Jolivette, with whom she enjoys a romantic tryst, that she is sharing Bible study with Mrs. Owens because "she knew that kind of thing would impress . . . valuing the gifts of the local people was part of the mission" (206). Celeste comes to rely on Mrs. Owens's sagacity, though, and loves being "grabbed up in [her] 'us'" until she feels, "for a feather of a moment, like her dutiful daughter" (369, 383). She learns that Mrs. Owens and Reverend Singleton exhibit "a courage she'd never find in herself," especially as members of "the Pineyville Six," the most overtly activist locals, three of whom are registered to vote by the summer's end (358).

What Celeste achieves is limited. "Pineyville's so bad," Jolivette tells her, that "black people better not laugh even in the street" (226). Few children attend her Freedom School, and the close affinity she feels with one leads to her hardest lesson. When Sissy dies in mysterious circumstances, Celeste is forced to accept that not every violent act is part of the battle the movement is fighting. Sissy's story echoes a half-told tale that De Lissovoy tucked into *Feelgood* when a little girl wanders into the Freedom House enquiring, "Is this the movement?" The girl has run away from home but trembles when organizers try to talk with her. Instead, she quietly washes dishes and sweeps the floor before disappearing, then returning to sleep fitfully, nightmares etched on her face.[89] Celeste's suspicions that Sissy is the victim of abuse from her father express that the small community is more complex than Celeste imagined, as is her discovery that the community endures partly due to an anonymous benefactor. Nicholas patterns the church's financial supporter, opera singer Sophie Lewis, on Leontyne Price, world-acclaimed soprano born and raised in Laurel, who performed for an integrated audience in her hometown in 1963, having refused to perform otherwise, and who sang a spiritual at the memorial service for James Chaney in 1964.[90] Celeste begins to understand that Miss Lewis is "both in touch and out of touch" because her profession affords her a cultural life beyond the South (113). Consequently she understands the quotidian heroism of Dolly Johnson, a voter registrant and the first to send her children to Celeste's Freedom School, even though their father is white and married and she is the subject of scandal. She admires Mr. Landau, an armed member of the Deacons for Defense and Justice who guards the rebuilding of Pineyville's church after it is burned to the ground. Nicholas limns out these characters, leaving whites peripheral. Sheriff Trotter Rock is described succinctly as "hard and full of hate" because his father has been run through with a pitchfork by a worker he never paid a decent wage or called by name; he "blames the entire Negro race, never having given so much as a mumbling thought to how mean-spirited his daddy was" (101). The registrar personifies the courthouse, a "future-denying fortress" and "museum of oppression," his eyes "bloodshot hatred" (30, 303). They represent the status quo and figure only when the Pineyville Six challenge them. When Celeste drinks at a "Whites Only" water fountain in the courthouse, for example, the sheriff bashes her face into its chrome, breaks her teeth, arrests all six, and charges Celeste with "endangering the lives of others" (334).

What Nicholas privileges is still partially submerged in histories: the bravery of black hosts unafraid "to sit on their front porch in the evening and talk to the blond girl from Iowa while the traffic goes by." Lester speculated that their courage might not seem "dramatic" and was not "easily observed." He concluded, "The real stories are of the Mississippi Negroes who walk to the courthouse to register to vote, knowing that loss of job or loss of life may be the consequence."[91] Carson judged that there was "no way of accurately assessing how most black Mississippians felt about the volunteers."[92] In the 1960s, Sally Belfrage's self-consciously searching memoir delves into how supportive the "Amos" family was but how her relationship with Mr. Amos developed with difficulty: "We were so scared of offending each other, with our roles so undefined, that each kept bowing to the other in an utterly foolish sort of dance. He had never sat at a table with a white woman, and since that situation is within the heart of the mess of the South, it was not something done easily." This remains a rare example of a volunteer's depiction of a host (one, Belfrage writes, who "otherwise accepted me from the first moment"), although in 1992, in a somewhat autobiographical novel, Sandra Adickes reflected briefly on her host in Hattiesburg, Addie Mae Jackson.[93] Gloria Wade Gayles's *Pushed Back to Strength* (1983) stands out in this context because local heroes include her uncle, "in my mind and my heart in every demonstration and in every cell block," and her elders in Memphis, "powerful beings, forces that belonged, I thought, to another world but chose to live in this one because we needed them." Her decision to join the movement is located in family, community, and anger: "There is more to black rage ... than the stories which are currently considered to be the only good copy on the subject."[94] Wade Gayles was among the 10 percent of volunteers Dittmer identified as African American, of which Nicholas makes Celeste representative of those who were also northerners.[95]

In an increasingly self-conscious metacommentary, Celeste equivocates about what she should reveal to others about her experience: "Of how Matt was beaten at the hands of state troopers on the way down from Jackson? Or of humidity so thick her body felt clumsy when she stood perfectly still, heat so ferocious her internal organs struggled to function? . . . She had the distinct feeling that she was knocking them dead all over the place. She'd won Matt over, Mrs. Owens had softened" (84). When she finally writes, it is to acknowledge that she learns far more than she teaches. Later, when she is back in Detroit, she imagines Jolivette telling her to "spread those stones," his phrase for letting go feelings that weigh one down, but for Celeste, the "stones" are her stories. "She did not know if she could spread them": "Mississippi summer. That was all hers" (401, 205, 403). Nicholas suggests a reason that individuals may have resisted sharing community stories, and in *Freshwater Road*, forty years later, she begins to fill a lacuna in the literature of Freedom Summer.

Literature is a space for thought, not simply a place of refuge, and SNCC literature is a place where local leaders and communities are re-invoked. In "The Organizer," Thelwell investigates an organizer's guilty fear that he has brought murder and violence to one of the "base communities" of the southern movement.[96] This feeling was real and raw inside SNCC, as when Herbert Lee's widow turned grief into anger on the occasion of Lee's 1962 funeral, telling Moses and McDew: "You killed my husband." She would later thank them for returning to McComb in 1964, but, as Charles Payne points out, Lee's murder was "pivotal in shaping the world view of Mississippi-SNCC."[97] Thelwell's community story "reek[s] of the stench of the struggle."[98] Organizers embedded in communities had to find ways to manage fear, and, without recourse to literature, the knot of fear is rarely discernible. In one oral history interview, Lawrence Guyot slips between tenses, as if locked in a continuous present, but then closes down discussion: "It was just part of the fabric. In order to do anything in Mississippi, you must first deal with the question of fear. You either transcend it or move beyond it. And that's what you did."[99] For Pat Watters, some of the decisions project directors were expected to make went "beyond ordinary limits . . . in that lonely place," and Francesca Polletta posits an attendant difficulty: how to explain experiences that "defy conventional rationales for action."[100] It was difficult because, as Bob Moses told Robert Penn Warren in 1965 and reinforced in 2001, SNCC was "anchored" in communities.[101] That involved respecting their privacy as well as celebrating them, respecting the privacy even of "outspoken" individuals, fictionalized here as "Mama" Quinn and Geneva Owens, renowned for being "willing to catch hell," as Charles Sherrod described.[102]

In *Freshwater Road*, Nicholas examines what is "hard to summarize": "There were so many stories, burned-down churches and houses shot into and injuries and incarcerations." She accepts the need for a media-ready "shorthand" and "statistical version" of Freedom Summer but opens up to exploration the reasons why Celeste feels that her "truest life" has been her time spent on Freshwater Road (394). Nicholas explains why she deferred telling this story for so long: "I didn't really know the full value of everything that was going on then. I know it now."[103] In 2011, John O'Neal celebrated unsung local people who "never ever had no fame" with hindsight of how figureheads came to be celebrated:

> They had the ocean-deep commitment where Medgar got his flow.
> They had the deep-burning fire within where Myrlie got her glow.
> They had the rat-a-ta-ta-ta-ta power that helped Malcolm rock and roll.
> They had that clear, still water deepness that rested Betty's soul.
> They had the soaring wings of faith that raised Martin mountain high.
> They had the stainless-steel commitment that raised Coretta to the sky.
> They had all that and then some.[104]

Worried that "ordinary people[–]without whom there would have been no movement–have barely been acknowledged," O'Neal recognized them for qualities honored in the movement's named representatives. Martha Prescod reiterates how "southern black folk played an activist role in initiating and carrying out the civil rights struggle."[105] This mode of "telling it like it is" contains an imperative, a moral force to make visible communities where organizers discovered their *fundis*, their bridge leaders. These stories are companion pieces to grassroots histories, the literary equivalent of handheld cameras pointed at communities, and the next chapter explores what the organization did to try to ensure that they would be read.

Chapter 6

Forging a Literary Culture beyond SNCC

> You may remember me as the girl in the neighborhood who went off to join the civil rights movement. . . . I'm sure you knew me once.
> —Jean Wheeler Smith, 1967
>
> Some of us think that the Movement is suffering from an overdose of 'college-trained,' middle-class oriented control . . . This set of problems is . . . discussed and argued about in our work in the Deep South.
> —Charles Cobb, 1965
>
> As we engaged . . . each evolving issue in the struggle toward political liberation, organic and fundamental questions concerning the politics of culture and the role of literature— and the literary establishment—therein, took their effect.
> —Michael Thelwell, 1987

In May 1966, at the first black writers' conference at Fisk University, Forman asked delegates to consider their responsibility to the freedom struggle, concerned they had published too little and were "out of touch." He treated the conference as a platform for promoting "fruitful dialogue between the artists and the activists." Dudley Randall was inspired to write a short story, "Shoe Shine Boy" (1966), and Sarah Webster Fabio a paean to SNCC and CORE souls "seared / by unrelenting tormenters."[1] Inside SNCC, the roles of writer and activist were not as separate as the conference made them seem, but grassroots organizing was intensely empirical, as assistant editor of *Negro Digest* David Llorens learned when volunteering for a summer in Columbus, Mississippi, and then initiating the column "On the Civil Rights Front" in 1965. Covering the Fisk conference for *Negro Digest*, he disseminated Forman's call.[2] Cleveland Sellers, SNCC program director by 1966, had attended with Forman. Playwright Loften Mitchell recalled that they sought collaboration with writers, arranging a meeting in New York to continue the conversation. On August 27, Forman, Ivanhoe Donaldson, and CORE's new director, Floyd McKissick, met with Mitchell, Hoyt Fuller, John O. Killens, William Branch, and James Woodruff, and Sarah E. Wright, Alice Childress, John Henrik Clarke, and Sylvester Leaks agreed to commission poems, plays, essays, and fiction for an "anthology for SNCC." As Black Power was spun negatively in the press, Forman, Carmichael, and McKissick lobbied publishers, television stations, and film studios to try to ensure that African Americans would "participate in the handling of things written about the Freedom Movement."[3] For Sarah E. Wright, it was personal. Her son Mike (Michael Oshoosi Wright) had joined SNCC at Tuskegee and was jailed in Atlanta on a "frame-up charge of inciting to riot." Wright judged, "Just about all our 'Establishment' leaders have come out against the SNCC youth," and she decried "the ferocity of the attack." "[They] need their writers *now*," she wrote. "They need us to help articulate their cry." Even early champions like Lillian Smith and Pat Watters fell away as SNCC began to call for Black Power in May 1966. Watters soured because of what he believed was "black-power venom against blameless whites" and a "betrayal" of tenets exemplified in the Albany movement in the early 1960s.[4] Wright's poem "A Message to My Son, Mike" was written "for love of you, / for love of all the courageous yous."[5] Randall, Fabio, Ted Joans, Margaret Danner, and Calvin Hernton were among poets who rallied to the project, and SNCC took responsibility to publish a collection but declared itself broke by December 1966. Instead, Fuller published a number of the pieces in *Negro Digest*.

SNCC's interventions in conferences continued, however. In 1967, George Ware contributed to the Student Press Association's panel on artists and activists, and H. Rap Brown opened the second Black Arts Convention in Detroit in 1967. Nikki Giovanni later dedicated a poem, "Detroit Conference of Unity and Art," to Brown. The poem opens:

> We went there to confer
> On the possibility of
> Blackness
> And the inevitability of
> Revolution.[6]

Brown, SNCC's new chairman, was coming to symbolize the politics underpinning the Black Arts Movement in the way that Carmichael was being seen as "Black Power's glamorous *enfant terrible*." Brown was even the subject of a poem that the FBI wrote when duplicitously ventriloquizing "blackness," as William J. Maxwell has uncovered in an illuminating literary history.[7] In Keorapetse Kgositsile's "When Brown Was Black" (1969), SNCC is emblematic of the collective insight underpinning a black aesthetic, with Brown personifying a raised black fist:

> Are you not the fist
> which articulates the passion
> of the collective power of our rebirth
> ....
> blowing up white myths
> which built up layers of mist[8]

The black clenched fist featured in Frank Cieciorka's woodcut among four other hands reaching skyward on the cover of *Negroes in American History: A Freedom Primer* (1965). Renowned since then as the "Black Power salute," it would appear repeatedly in the *Movement*, among illustrations Cieciorka contributed to the newspaper published by the California branch of SNCC.[9] When Carmichael spoke at the 1967 Congress on the Dialectics of Liberation in London, the culmination of his presentation on Black Power was a poem by Worth Long, published in the *Movement* (and again in *New South*, in 1966), "Arson and Cold Grace, or How I Yearn to Burn Baby, Burn":

> We have found you out, four faced Americans, we have found you out.
> ....
> ... the fires are burning
> ....
> And preachers can't pray with hopes for deceiving
> Nor leaders deliver a lecture on losing
> ....
> For now is the fire and fires won't answer
> To logical reason.[10]

The ballad crystallized deeply held feelings in a richly aural incantation of relentless couplets with accented present participles that pound out Long's compulsive reasoning. Following Carmichael's performance, delegates debated who held the power of language.[11] While Carmichael was in London, Brown, Phil Hutchings, Ralph Featherstone, and Charles Cobb were among organizers attending the first Black Power conference in Newark, New Jersey, where Brown shared the platform with Amiri Baraka and Ron Karenga, leading figures in the Black Arts Movement. Forman and Carmichael were among those attending the Congress of Black Writers in Montreal in 1968, and Cobb, Courtland Cox, and Jimmy Garrett joined them at the Pan-African Cultural Festival (PACF) in Algiers in 1969.

Attempts to influence cultural production and literary debate were various and strategic. Outside of conferences, cultivating relationships with magazines was also strategic—and eclectic, with SNCC's contributions visible from *American Dialog* through *Youth: A Bi-Weekly Pocket Magazine for High School Youth*.[12] Lester noted how much "significant writing on race and culture" appeared in the *Massachusetts Review*. In 1970, Thelwell served as a contributing editor, after founding the Department of Afro-American Studies at the University of Massachusetts, and Lester was appointed the first African American contributing editor at *Evergreen Review*.[13] However, the foremost periodicals supporting and indeed developing writers in SNCC were African American: *Freedomways* and *Negro Digest*.

Freedomways and Negro Digest

The first issue of *Freedomways*, a leftist, activist-edited journal rooted in communist and pan-Africanist thinking, coincided with the Freedom Rides. Its masthead announced: "A Quarterly Review of the Negro Freedom Movement." *Freedomways* quickly secured a circulation of ten thousand, with managing editor Esther Cooper Jackson recalling that an initial press run of two thousand copies increased quickly to fifteen thousand, "particularly for special issues, which were read by many thousands more."[14] SNCC is barely mentioned in studies of the periodical, but *The Freedomways Reader* (2000), compiled by one the founding editors, Jackson, evidences how the journal supported the organization.[15] Julian Bond commemorated its advocacy of "[t]ruths that seldom found an outlet elsewhere and arguments that suffered suppression more often than refutation," celebrating its "proud roster of aggressive participants, not just observers or recorders, of the movement for human rights." Bond painted a vivid picture of "writers with picket signs as well as pens in hand, scholars whose classrooms were the union halls, students who took instruction in the cotton fields or lunch counters, artists who brushed conscience as well as canvasses."[16] It was an outlet for writing by and about the BAM, but in forging a devoted readership in the early 1960s it was also a route to publication for civil rights activists. SNCC maintained close ties with its editors, especially Jackson and former SCLC member Jack O'Dell.

Bond wrote to the journal first, a letter published in its "Readers' Forum" (Summer 1962), politely but firmly registering surprise that SNCC had not been mentioned in a previous "Readers' Forum" piece, "Negro Leaders and Organizations," and thereafter he contributed regularly.[17] A staff-written editorial in the Spring 1962 issue, "Culture in the Cause of

Negro Freedom," highlighted "the new creative activity" inspired by the movement as "the threshold of a new cultural renaissance" because "*now* the Negro cultural worker . . . has a great function of the utmost social significance to perform" (original emphasis). *Freedomways* berated "most big publishing houses," saying that they failed to harness this energy or to publish books on such themes as "the Negro as 'hero,'" and Joanne Grant hailed SNCC organizers among "heroes of the South" who had "gained life and given life through the movement."[18] A 1963 survey of "literature of the Negro revolt" cited the *Student Voice* among "books, articles, and record albums of value."[19] In 1964, SNCC dominated a special issue on "The Southern Movement," an unprecedented first in magazine coverage of the movement because it showcased "writing from the battlefronts": "Seldom has the story of these activists been told by the persons themselves."[20] The Rabinowitz Foundation sponsored another special issue, "Mississippi: Opening up a Closed Society" (Summer 1965), that included Dona Richards's compilation of SNCC's creative writing, Grant on "Mississippi and the Establishment," Lynd on SNCC's Freedom Schools, Minnis on the Mississippi Freedom Democratic Party, Eric Morton (a member of SNCC's communications team) on Freedom Summer, and an interview with Fannie Lou Hamer conducted by O'Dell. In 1966, when Guyot and Thelwell published a considered two-part evaluation of the MFDP's parallel party structure, they contextualized campaigns for five congressional seats.[21] SNCC communicated the life of the organization outward through *Freedomways*. Its other major publishing channel was the Johnson conglomerate based on the influential triptych of *Ebony, Jet,* and *Negro Digest*.

Jet and *Ebony* tracked the progress of all civil rights organizations, and, among articles focusing on SNCC, Lerone Bennett's 1965 assessment "Rebels with a Cause" stands out. SCLC field secretary and COFO organizer Annell Ponder said of it: "This is the most perceptively written account of SNCC's philosophy which I have read."[22] *Jet* and *Ebony* typically promoted civil rights through personalities, as Bennett had in "The King Plan" in 1956, but *Negro Digest* was the main publication channel for SNCC.[23] Among reasons John H. Johnson had listed for reviving it in 1961 after a ten-year gap in production was that "the talented young Negro writer does not always find a ready outlet for his creative efforts," and editor Hoyt Fuller was instrumental in this regard.[24] Its circulation was smaller than *Jet* and *Ebony*, but the activist stance was clearer. John A. Williams said that it was considered a "guidepost" for "militant intellectuals" under Fuller.[25] When Bennett was appointed an associate editor and in-house historian, he had already written a "Black Power" series for

Ebony beginning in its twentieth-anniversary issue in October 1965, and his credentials were authenticated by a "battle-weary" SNCC organizer visiting the journal's Chicago office "fresh from the Mississippi front." A compliment paid Bennett and Fuller—"those cats were real"—was underscored: "Our knowledge of SNCC people has taught us that they—and the very nature of their involvement makes this understandable—are inclined to think of most of us as unreal. We shall not attempt to improve upon the tribute rendered by the SNCC worker."[26] When Llorens channeled its editorial voice, he revealed the extent to which *Negro Digest* sought endorsement by young activists and would, in turn, nurture their writing.

In a 1966 symposium, "The Meaning and Measure of Black Power," Bond highlighted Carmichael as the voice of Black Power and reaction against it as melodramatic "white fright" or the failure of an older generation of civil rights leaders to acknowledge the direction the movement was going.[27] Black Power was folded into a longer history via SNCC and communities it served. Cobb sent Llorens a written sketch of Carmichael to continue the conversation, reiterating, "Black people's power—lies in their sense of themselves, and control of themselves and their circumstances."[28] Outside of demonstrations and off the podium, *Negro Digest* situated Black Power as the extension of "let the people decide," rather than an interregnum between the "end" of an "integrationist" movement and the "beginning" of a call for black separatism. Like *Freedomways*, *Negro Digest* is acknowledged for promulgating the Black Arts Movement, but it has been underread, as if mooted by black cultural nationalism when it did not change dramatically (and did not change its name to *Black World* until 1970).[29] Memorializing Fuller in 2008, Cobb celebrated his helming of a literary magazine that "opened up its pages to young voices."[30] The clearest example of one of those voices is Jean Wheeler Smith, who *Negro Digest* described in 1967 as "one of the new crop of writers brightening the literary scene."[31] Fuller maintained a regular column called "Perspectives," and its November 1963 focus was Jean Wheeler and Prathia Hall: "Every self-satisfied American Negro, North or South, should be made to listen to [their] stories—and dozens of young people like them." Fuller explained that they had put college on hold to dedicate themselves to activism and that "the sheer horror and indignity of what they go through" needed to be understood. "They have been jailed more often than many hardened criminals and treated worse," he declared, chiding readers "get up and go out and *do something to help them*" (original emphases).[32] Fuller made himself an emblem of the privileged black middle class, creating a bridge for Wheeler to cross in her inaugural essay for *Negro Digest*.

"Let Us All Be Black Together"

Fuller commissioned Jean Wheeler's "Let Us All Be Black Together: A College Coed's Plea to the Middle Class" when she and Hall visited Chicago a second time from projects in Mississippi and Georgia.[33] Wheeler situated her essay as a personal appeal to "comfortable, educated Negroes, uninvolved in movements... [who] made me comfortable, well-groomed, soon-to-graduate-from-college."[34] It was "a cry of alienation": "I am your child and yet I am alienated from you" (19). She hoped readers could understand what she had learned on "dirt roads... [and in] jail, demonstrations,... and mass meetings": "I am black while you in your minds, are white" (20). In an analytical framing of self and subject, a heartfelt confession by one of their own, Wheeler criticized liberal individualism and her own espousal of middle-class ambitions and attempted to mobilize an action-oriented response. Her method exemplifies what movement sociologists and psychologists have since conceptualized as the main components of their "frames" of analysis: diagnosis, prognosis, and a consequent call to action.[35] Wheeler diagnosed seductive myths associated with middle-class mores, called for intraracial and cross-class solidarity, and told readers "you must become black" (21).

In 1967, as Jean Wheeler Smith, having married fellow SNCC worker Frank Smith, she developed "Let Us All Be Black Together" into "I Learned to Feel Black," a disquisition on "the road to black consciousness," published in *Redbook* magazine in 1967. Fuller directed readers of *Negro Digest* to that essay, convinced that Smith spoke for "a large and growing segment of the Black community" in a style that appealed to intellectuals as much as to "boys on the corner."[36] *Redbook*'s circulation was around ten million and expanded its coverage of sociocultural issues in op-ed commentaries in the mid-1960s, exemplified by "Margaret Mead Answers," where topics included "How would you advise a son or daughter who wanted to work for civil rights in Mississippi?"[37] Despite *Redbook*'s predominantly white female readership, Smith retained the same intimate, second-person address, as if to continue the conversation initiated in *Negro Digest*, couching this essay as an urgent reminder:

> I think that once you knew me. It was a time not long past, about four years ago. I was the bright, well-mannered girl who lived down the street from you.... Or you may remember me as the girl in the neighborhood who went off to join the civil rights movement.... I'm sure you knew me once. At least you knew something in me, something that continued to grasp at the reality

of the American image of the full person, blessed by our society with the resources and opportunities to be whatever [one] wants to be.[38]

Smith was creating a collage of personal essays. With Cobb, Carmichael, and Casey Hayden, for example, she contributed to a forum in the *New Republic*. In "How to Help the Ones at the Bottom" (1966), she described "our American ideals and upward mobility" as pernicious myths. She had come to denounce them after witnessing the grinding poverty of dispossessed sharecroppers and mismanagement of federal funds. Corrupt oligarchs kept the rural poor dependent on a plantation economy, even as agricultural labor mechanized them out of full employment.[39] Urban, middle-class assumptions about the indolence of a rural poor risked creating a barrier to empathy and action, for which Smith deployed a strategic analogy: "People at the bottom. Facing them is like being on your way to a terribly important meeting on which your future hangs, seeing a kid get hit by a car, and realizing that no one will help him. You can't keep driving" (57). In plain language that reduced the risk that she might be perceived as naïve, sensationalist, or preaching from a moral high ground, Smith wrote, "We saw the kid on the highway and this is what we thought we could do" (62). She outlined skills support in literacy, math, voter registration, and vocational training, including Freedom Now Brick Company, instigated by Frank Smith, with directors drawn from a Poor People's Corporation, and enterprising cooperatives like those initiated by Jesse Morris.[40] From the platform provided by Fuller, she demanded—and counted on—support. Now, Smith explained, being "consciously black" was the "next logical step" toward Black Power politics (56). Her essay was selected by Floyd B. Barbour for *The Black Power Revolt* (1968), which traced Black Power back through David Walker, Nat Turner, Frederick Douglass, and W. E. B. Du Bois, and forward through Robert Williams, Malcolm X, Carmichael, Vincent Harding, Alvin Poussaint, and Smith. With a sense of sad irony, I discovered that this collection mirrors another of Forman's unrealized projects: a "Black Power Book" that would span 1619 to 1954 and incorporate SNCC's experience thereafter.[41]

Smith's essays are quietly insistent, evaluative, and explicative. In campaign after campaign, activists banged their heads against walls that "according to our society did not exist." Efforts to loosen the white power structure, from the first "stone that the builder rejected," saw more battlements erected to keep African Americans out.[42] She developed her writing further in literary genres.

Smith's Literary Field Texts

Fuller located Jean Wheeler Smith and Jane Stembridge with Alice Walker, Carolyn Rodgers, and Nikki Giovanni as the most talented writers "spawned by the Black Revolution."[43] When she turned her attention to fiction, Smith did not pursue her relationship with *Redbook*, even though it published fiction and was the first periodical to win the National Magazine Award for fiction twice, but returned to Fuller.[44] In short stories for *Negro Digest*, she crystallized being "black together" as urgent work, refusing to separate fidelity to facts from how her imagination extrapolated from them. In "That She Would Dance No More" (1967), Smith enters a sharecropper's consciousness to uncover the humiliating "lesson" he is taught at eight years old, with fourteen-year-old Emmett Till's abduction from his uncle's home in 1955 a silent subtext. In a flashback, Ossie Lee is forced into a cotton sack and abducted while his father shields the rest of the family, powerless to prevent the abuse of his son who is punished for having failed to prevent a chicken being killed by a car. A chicken is worth more to a plantation owner than the black child on whom he will inflict lasting psychological damage. The boy screams "No!" when forced to take down his pants to be whipped, "the last willful act that Ossie Lee was to perform in his lifetime."[45]

The tragedy Smith uncoils takes place in Miss Lula's café in the Mississippi Delta thirty years later, but it stems from that incident at age eight: "The remainder of Ossie Lee's life followed the order established that night. He did carefully what he was told, never more, never less" (63). He finds solace, even joy for a while, in Minnie Pearl, whose dancing relaxes him: "He pulled her still closer, drinking in the ease with which she lived and moved" (65). Despite her mother and Miss Lula warning Minnie Pearl that this taciturn man will crush her spirit, she marries Ossie Lee. "Slapped" repeatedly by the agricultural system, he finds it impossible to countenance the simple joy his wife takes in shaking herself free from the quotidian: "He could no longer lose himself in her dancing. He was held too tightly... too closely to all the meaningless ditches he had dug" (67). "Able neither to accept nor to reject his life," Ossie Lee "had constantly to buffer himself against it" (64). One night, drinking moonshine outside the café with other men, he "sat down on the steps, rested his head on the wall, and looked out into the darkness" (67). When he reenters the café, he hits Minnie Pearl with the force of all that is wearing him down; the walls imprisoning him should contain her too. Only Miss Lula's shotgun calms the situation.

Ossie Lee is a literary precursor of Alice Walker's Grange Copeland, who, beaten down by sharecropping and cowed by the ever-present threat of racist violence underscored by rural penury, turns "unnaturally bland" like a stone, "an object, a cipher."[46] Walker affords Grange the opportunity to redeem himself by protecting his civil rights worker granddaughter in his "third life," but Smith closes her story with Ossie Lee trying to make Minnie Pearl pregnant, hoping a baby "would weigh her down and destroy her balance so she would dance no more" (68). The long-term consequences of his abduction as a child are also visited on his first wife, absent from the story because she has taken herself and their children to Memphis to escape him, and the implication is that, like Grange Copeland in his first two lives, Ossie Lee is unable to break the cycle. Minnie Pearl will live accordingly, leave or, ground down by him, die, as Copeland's wife Margaret does when she kills herself and their baby son at the edge of Grange's smallholding.

Fuller discerned the "soul" in the story but said it had "nothing at all to do with The Movement."[47] However, in this instance, as she would in others, Smith was transfiguring what she witnessed as an organizer into literary field texts. In Smith's "Frankie Mae," published in *Negro Digest* (June 1968), the "thin white line," Forman's metaphor for the imprisonment of black lives by white power structures, strangles the ambitions of a bright girl and shortens her life in Leflore County, Mississippi. Frankie Mae Brown is smart, sensitive, and sealed hermetically into the system of agricultural labor. The tenor of her life is dependent on her father's continued employment. His memories of her childhood and life (and eventually her death) are the warp and weft of Smith's story and filtered through an omniscient narrator. Her proud father wants Frankie Mae to pursue her education, but when Mr. White, the plantation owner, demands she pick cotton, her family's subsistence depends on it: "Don't nobody stay in my house and don't work."[48] It is a wrenching twist on the white line tethering her life to the cotton field, but she is resilient: "The child's eyes lost their brilliance. Her shoulders slumped, and she began to cry, softly.... The next morning Frankie was up first. She woke up her daddy and the others, scolding them for being so slow.—They had to get that cotton chopped" (89). Despite losing months of schooling, at thirteen she is the family bookkeeper, assuring her father a return of $180 when Mr. White calculates year-end costs. She stands in line awaiting confirmation, her father seduced by her energy: "He felt like something was wrong when each year he came out owing money. But he didn't know how to do anything about it" (43). When Mr. White announces that they are in debt,

Frankie Mae challenges him in disbelief. Astounded at her agency, he is tempted to gun her down on the spot, and her father knows it is "as it had always been" (45). This tightening of the white line constricts her life irrevocably: "Frankie stumbled out to the car and crawled onto the back seat. She cried all the way home." A night passes, and Frankie has to be awakened. "This time Frankie had not bounced back to her old bright-eyed self. The line that held her to this self had been stretched too taut. It had lost its tension and had fallen, slack, at her side" (45–46). Frankie Mae gives birth to her first child at fifteen and by nineteen is mother to four. She dies giving birth to her fifth. When Mr. White refuses her father $40 to let him achieve the $100 required for Frankie to give birth in the county hospital, she bleeds to death on the hundred-mile journey to the nearest charity clinic, in Vicksburg.

The inclusion of "Frankie Mae" in Woodie King Jr.'s *Black Short Story Anthology* in 1972 and Mary Helen Washington's *Black-Eyed Susans* in 1975, and Washington's decision to retain the story in *Black-Eyed Susans/Midnight Birds* (1989), ensured it a longer life than it would have had if only published in *Negro Digest*. The legacy of slavery haunts the freedom struggle so indelibly that some student responses to "Frankie Mae" assume the story is set during slavery, or shortly afterward, when its plantation setting was contemporaneous with what Smith witnessed in the Deep South in the 1960s.[49] Smith alludes to this in her opening: "Soon one morning, the wheels of 400 years of slavery ceased to turn. I don't know the precise way in which it happened, but I can sketch the events for you" (84). In my view, excising these lines in subsequently published versions of the story was a narrative decision to minimize the risk of seeming didactic or creating the impression that a single strike, even one supported by civil rights workers, could impact decisively a plantation economy that was so entrenched. The result is a more controlled story that is still framed by the strike in which Frankie Mae's father will participate. Her premature death is the spur for the action he will take, risking home and livelihood in an effort to force change. Smith's story, like her essays, is a provocation. She poses a picture of neoslavery for the same readers, steering them to read between her lines to apprehend what Tillie Olsen calls "the silence for centuries as to how life was, is," and notice people who "never came to writing."[50] It is an exposé of a historical impasse. Frankie Mae's life and death rely on a premodern plantation existence persisting into the 1960s, as Stembridge and Varela depict in poetry. The continuation of this kind of life could pass beneath notice if movement successes were judged at the level of national events like the March on Washington. SNCC participated in that march but decried it as a political waste, as Thelwell wrote: "a subtle and terrible betrayal" that "drained the anger of our people into irrelevant channels."[51] In *Jet*, with Prathia Hall, Smith drew attention to "the ones at the bottom," the "thousands of poor, jobless, [and] hungry" excluded from participation in "the social processes of the country in which they were born," consigned to live as if in another century.[52] "Frankie Mae" was another bulletin from the South in which Smith served notice of "an American failure" to end peonage and reminded readers of locales beyond media spotlights.[53]

Mary Helen Washington is Smith's most important critic, foregrounding Smith's SNCC experience in "forging an understanding of the black experience as it has been menaced by this society" and reading her story through Joyce Ladner's sociological study of poor black girls: "It is startling to see in Frankie Mae such a perfect example of Ladner's observations."[54] The realities of the field were the fulcrum of analyses in SNCC's interlocking texts. For Ladner in *Tomorrow's Tomorrow: The Black Woman* (1971), "How I Learned to Feel Black" was a model for refuting a "value-free" position of "objectivity." Countering Daniel P. Moynihan's report "The Negro Family: The Case for National Action" (1965), Ladner situated poor black communities as "a product of American social policy, not the cause of it." Institutionally racist policies were "designed," she argued, "to create the alleged 'pathology' of the community, to perpetuate the 'social disorganization' model of Black life."[55] Smith fictionalized the effects of pathologizing poor black people, pulling readers across the thin white line into the life and death of a child-mother. It is surprising, then, that Washington revised her 1975 reading of "Frankie Mae" in 1988 after attending a talk by Smith, by then a respected child psychologist, in which Smith shared her thoughts on women in SNCC, bridge leaders, and spoke of a teenage girl politicized by the movement. Washington interpreted Smith's presentation as being feminist but also revisionist, arguing in her 1989 *Black-Eyed Susans/Midnight Birds*, that "Frankie Mae" proceeds as it does because it was first published "years before a new feminist discourse made us aware of the gender-based ideologies that connect female sexuality with death ... and trap female characters in passivity in silence." For Washington, Smith's narrator remained "superior ... outside the tale and distant from the community she is observing."[56] Washington found Smith guilty of observing from the remote middle-class distance she exposed; her proximity to the material conditions she dramatized was lost. In my reading, by electing to write in the third person, Smith ensured that authorial anger was held back. Emotion then develops in readers forced to examine the straitened circumstances that produce the girl's situation and their own response to reading about them. A more complete authorial identification with Frankie Mae would have closed the distance rather than enabling readers to traverse it. She is a "death-bound subject" because she is bound by indenture before her life is determined by a "female script."[57] She challenges Mr. White in a way that her illiterate father cannot, risking her life and his. He knows that if his daughter is attacked or killed, he will die defending or avenging her. For the first time, "he drew a line for himself" (45). Frankie Mae's pregnancies are dangerous because circumscribed by poverty, as in other brave fictions where the death of mothers or children is the direct result of poverty.[58]

"Frankie Mae" is a field text in which Smith exposed the debt peonage that sharecroppers were challenging with SNCC's support, and "those who attempted to crush peonage in the South were surrounded by almost as many circles of futility as the peons." Pete Daniel uses this metaphor, and the simile "the dark side of the moon," to explain its occlusion: "It remained largely unexplored, charted only in law books and statutes which remained regrettably removed from the reality, from the vertiginous and stagnant world of peonage."[59] Smith found novel ways to make visible what she was witnessing, realities that informed the feminism evolving through women in SNCC—Joyce Ladner, Margaret Dammond, Gwen Patton, and Frances Beal among them—with Patton chairing SNCC's Black Women's Liberation Committee in 1968.[60] Smith reinforced how the women's movement was modeled in and through the organization, telling Cynthia Griggs Fleming that they felt neither patronized nor impeded as black women but that "an inappropriate application of current feminist theory" had led to their experience being reinterpreted antithetically and anachronistically, emphasizing this again in her essay for *Hands on the Freedom Plow*.[61] Literary texts in which women are beaten down by circumstances beyond their control risk being underread if not appreciated as a narrative mode through which politically active authors drew attention to what was hidden from the majority of Americans in the 1960s. Historians may avoid revealing "the unavoidable obstacles of their passion," but in literary criticism that seeks out characters "with options," as W. Lawrence Hogue and Trudier Harris do in the context of "Frankie Mae," the same "obstacles" pass as the basis for critical judgment.[62] "Frankie Mae" was an unwavering close-up on the southern rural poor in the moment that the Black Arts Movement was focusing attention on urban settings and the North. Smith was quietly insistent in locating the girl at the center and dramatizing how she was withheld from public view. The FST saved "Frankie Mae" among stories that might be adapted, and later *Southern Exposure* solicited similar stories about racism, poverty, and community because "few kids... have oral historians standing at their elbows with tape recorders and eager questions."[63]

In another field text, Smith intervened creatively in a different space of containment that organizers knew intimately.[64] "The Machine" (1967) opens in the Mississippi State Penitentiary as Jason barely controls his violent reaction to a prison officer who extinguishes a cigar on his hand and who almost crushes his hand in a steel door: "Jason was so angry, he could hardly see. He could focus only on the guard's huge neck, bulging from a grey collar... he longed to grab the red splotched neck, to squeeze it until the network of blue veins stood out like railroad tracks. But he was out of reach.... realizing the futility of his anger, he turned away from the guard, to face the other fellows who had been packed into the tiny cell with him" (60). A group of African American organizers is jailed at Parchman, with bail set at $45,000, indicative of specious sums instituted because legal statutes were designed to stymie civil rights initiatives.[65] Smith unravels a knot of tensions, not only between guards and prisoners but also between nonviolence as a strategy and the natural desire to retaliate when violently provoked, and between northern graduates (preconceived as leaders) and less formally educated locals, and between veteran activists and new recruits. Willie C. surfaces as the sad, reluctant source of consternation for Chenault, the only veteran in a cell of locals, with commentary on the fallout provided by a local organizer, Ben, and filtered through the consciousness of Jason, Chenault's former college roommate: "What Willie C. had to teach them was a lesson that would guide them all their lives" (60).

At first glance, bespectacled, soft-spoken Chenault seems to be modeled on Bob Moses: "It was Chenault's practice to encourage everyone to speak... and then come up with a plan which reflected the feelings of everyone" (61–62). He keeps the group aligned in its decision to give up clothes when requested but to refuse to work the prison plantation. Smith confirms the character is otherwise fictional when the others square up to Chenault. Ben speaks the chorus: "Ain't no more than anyone else in here. Just 'cause he talk 'bout 'concepts' and such ["theoretical crap"] don't mean he know better than me or you 'bout these crackers." Ben advocates that Jason be ignored, saying "He just got to Mississippi a month ago. Ain't been in jail a time in his life before now. And he gonna tell us how to act" (62, 69). Ben's commentary puts Jason's narration in doubt. This confined space is a laboratory where Smith takes the measure of internal pressure points, cracks and fissures, in a less-than-solid cohort of organizers.

On the eighth day, seventeen-year-old Willie emerges as the weak link guards exploit by installing him in the cell opposite, with food, tobacco, and a mattress, none of which the others have. He signs a statement that he has been corrupted as a minor, making Chenault liable for a five-year sentence.[66] Willie holds a grudge. As a cellmate reminds Chenault, after being slated for project directorship, "You found you couldn't give Willie eight years of education in two months. He couldn't do 'research' on the 'power structure'... And you cut his ass loose" (72). Chenault has made Willie "the director of the mimeograph machine" and, Ben says, "made it worse by telling him that running that silly machine all day was very important for the Movement." Self-belief, dignity, and manhood, twisted and warped by whites in Smith's other stories, are filtered through Chenault's stupefaction that the need for effective organization has made Willie feel less than he is or could be. He blames himself and withdraws into guilt-ridden silence, but the local organizers believe that, regardless of Willie's chagrin, he is accountable for his behavior toward Chenault in jail. Late at night, though, Willie is crying, and local organizers cajole him: "Make that fat guard so mad he throw you back in here with us 'bad niggers.' Nothing to worry about" (74). Literally, "the machine" is the mimeograph back at SNCC's office; figuratively, it is a metaphor for the white power structure, explored aesthetically, as Lester did too when turning a speech Mario Savio made in December 1964 into a poem:

> And you've got to put your bodies
> upon the gears
> and upon the wheels,
> upon the levers,
> upon all the apparatus,
> and you've got to make it
> stop.[67]

Smith turns the machine metaphor inward to expose the power structure inherent even in a leaderless, or leaderful, organization. This is the lesson Willie imparts. Supporting leaders in the community was the crux of grassroots organizing but threw up difficulties internally. Smith depicts middle-class educational values as a residual force that risks undermining local leadership. Organizers castigated others, like the SCLC, when they deemed someone like Willie "unqualified" for decision making or leadership.[68] White volunteer Paul Cowan criticized himself and Al Lowenstein for devaluing indigenous styles of leadership, seeing in hindsight that they "did not believe that Southern black people, and the young, militant staff members who advised them, could make wise decisions about tactics for defeating the system."[69] This "ugly tendency" has been evoked as recently as 2019, in Zimmerman's *Mississippi Reckoning*, in which a white volunteer with merely three weeks of experience instructs a black southern organizer to create a chart of local harassment. He is informed by the project director, "You're here to help, not take over... to listen and learn from him, not expect him to learn from you" (154–55). Zimmerman makes clear how local organizers draw on a long history of struggle to which his white volunteer Gideon is oblivious, including the work of the Southern Tenant Farmers' Union in the 1930s and local NAACP branches across many decades (155). Moses declared in 1965, "The people on the bottom don't need leaders at all. What they need is the confidence in their own worth and identity to make decisions about their own lives." In SNCC's *Movement* newspaper, Jimmy Garrett asked, "If we destroy people for an objective what good is the objective?," and Cobb shared the concern with readers of *Freedomways*: "[S]ome of us think that the Movement is suffering from an overdose of 'college-trained,' middle-class oriented control, by a leadership which too often borrows forms and structures from the institutions it organizes demonstrations against. This set of problems is... discussed and argued about in our work in the Deep South."[70] Black organizers fell less heavily into this trap, but Smith indicates how it was set, conjuring a sad scenario to expose not only how fragile the confidence of potential local leaders could be but also how a supportive relationship could be undermined from within when class and education trump activist solidarity. Embarrassed by his lack of education and seeking endorsement as a youth yet unable to vote, the only lever Willie can pull is the one on the mimeograph machine. Feeling disempowered, he is at the mercy of jailers, but the underlying problem is that he is boxed into a corner at the rear of the movement. "The Machine" is one of the most revealing of SNCC's stories because it evokes issues that were debated internally but otherwise largely submerged.

Intertextually, writers were shaping an aesthetic path "close to the soil of discontent" in "the fields of wrath."[71] A short poem by Worth Long helps explain. In "Dealer" (1964), he demands of readers, "Come with me... trek with me... follow me [into the Mississippi Delta]":

> SIGN IN A
> MISSISSIPPI
> JUNKYARD
> WE BUY

BURNT
BODIES.[72]

It takes a moment's pause before the implication that these could be human bodies dissipates in relief that they are car chassis, with moral shock expressive of how thoroughly violence textured the 1960s South.[73] "Dealer" suggests the burned-out car driven by James Chaney when, with Schwerner and Goodman, he could not escape the conspiratorial mob of Klan and police who murdered them and then hid their bodies and the car. The poetic technique of defamiliarization ensures that readers are pulled up sharply in recognition of how racist violence equates to domestic terrorism. When reworked as "Safari" (1969), Long imbued this poem with pan-Africanist imagery: "a black soul searching," on a deeply ironic "safari," into the "vast congos" of Arkansas, Alabama, and Mississippi—but paused in the same Mississippi junkyard, invoking a catalog of violence in a syntagmatic chain of repetitively compulsive images.[74] Together, Smith's essays and stories suggest how field-workers came to understand the agricultural system through the individuals it was designed to constrain in servitude, and across these texts their material conditions dominate. Wesley Hogan gauges that "SNCC workers never discovered an effective tactic to dramatize the economic inequities of the region," adding that "no one else has either."[75] SNCC's literature contributes to that attempt because it demands politicized understanding of local people, grassroots priorities in the field, the need for organizers to be "guerrilla fighters in the field of social change," and activism as inseparable from thought, emotion, and analysis.[76]

Harold Cruse's *The Crisis of the Negro Intellectual* (1967) was a tour de force for activist writing, but he dismissed "civil writism" as intellectually weak, a "cult of belles-lettres fortified with the current phraseology of the protest movement." He left the writing unspecified but concluded that it connoted a "superficial literary mode of involvement when pitted against the ideas of the ranking exponents of social reform, liberal, radical or otherwise" (99, 181, 475, 549). Cruse did not conceive of activists as writers. The political contours that SNCC explored intertextually barely figured in 1960s criticism, in part because while Black Power was a conceptual fulcrum for the Black Arts Movement, SNCC never delivered a cultural manifesto.[77] When Thelwell looked back, he assessed that "each evolving issue... in the struggle toward political liberation" exposed "organic and fundamental questions concerning the politics of culture and the role of literature—and the literary establishment," but he added that "cultural and literary patrimony" was left "untended."[78] Francesca Polletta argues that movement narratives "retain continuity in change" and "preserve the self or collectivity through change," but writers addressed and expressed change, embracing it rather than rolling with it. Fuller advanced a "Black literary community," turning away from "white editors anthologizing, interpreting, and organizing their material," or "entrepreneuring Black literary work."[79] Jean Wheeler Smith explicated SNCC's evolving black consciousness throughout the 1960s in bulletins from the South. In 1969, she and Jimmy Garrett presented at the Pan-African Cultural Festival in Algiers with Ted Joans, Don L. Lee, Ed Bullins, and Maya Angelou. In "Let Us All Be Black Together" and literary field texts, she distilled what would become a credo for the BAM, condensed by Lee in *Black Pride* (1969) as "I seek integration of Negroes with black people," and by Baraka in "S.O.S" (1969) as *"calling all black people, come in, black / people, come / on in."*[80] "Power for black people" was a constitutive component of SNCC's literary culture.[81] If the May 1966 black writers' conference at Fisk University involved an attempt to steer writers toward SNCC, at subsequent conferences organizers inserted themselves into myriad conversations around Black Power and international liberation struggles. In black periodicals, most notably *Negro Digest*, they evinced and evaluated grassroots concerns. Smith shared a belief with others, including Cobb, Thelwell, Lester, House, Garrett, and Forman, that political analysis would not move readers to believe in ideas they could not imagine. The next chapter examines this through different strategies and literary genres in which Black Power is explicated and writers explore where responsibility lay for the burgeoning despondency in SNCC. For Vincent Harding, witnessing "the agonizing steps" of "young and tender warriors," that feeling equated to a "revolutionary parable" and "the beginning of our age of blackness."[82]

Chapter 7

"Words You Want?"

Black Power, the Black Arts Movement, and the Worlding of SNCC

> maybe
> if i give america a chance
> I'll be able to
> wear the uniform
> and have the gun
> of the cop
> that shot
> Jimmy Lee Jackson
> —**Charles Cobb, 1965**

> Black Power and Black Arts came as the same ball of wax . . . [T]he Arts were artistic expression of the same determination, or the same new vision or the same new sense of identity of who we were, who we are as a people . . . the same spirit of redefining ourselves. . . . establishing ourselves in opposition to the mainstream, and for many of us identifying with Africa, and identifying with our origins, and attempting to understand that connection in a new way, and articulate it.
> —**Aneb Kgositsile (Gloria House), 2015**

Black Power inspired the Black Arts Movement, with SNCC understood as the tinder for the fire, but studies "rarely give much consideration to black cultural activity in the South," as James Smethurst asserts while recovering Atlanta's significance as a cultural hub. Smethurst, following David Lionel Smith in this instance, points to the importance of "local responses" to black cultural nationalism in the 1960s, noting that artists were involved in SNCC, CORE, and other civil rights groups.[1] Once black cultural nationalism took hold, SNCC's literary interventions were overtaken by more polemical definitions of a black aesthetic. Even though Ron Karenga's credo that literature should "expose the enemy, praise the people, and support the revolution" may be seen to underpin writing in SNCC, such precepts were divorced from civil rights, and, for many, SNCC was rolled into the integrationist ethos maintained by more moderate organizations.[2] That SNCC was interracial until 1966 contributed to its sidelining by those defining a black aesthetic. Even Llorens celebrated Baraka as the "newest cultural hero in the black community" because he had not published in "a white journal of any genre."³ As David Lionel Smith observes, proponents of the Black Arts Movement often stated that they had "few if any antecedents."⁴ Despite ample evidence to the contrary, equating a black cultural consciousness with the BAM made both seem new. Larry Neal wrote in the 1970s, "Black writers of the midsixties . . . were not concerned with linking hands with their 'white brothers.'"⁵ SNCC may be the subtext here because of a button that organizers wore, which had the image of black and white hands clasped in solidarity. The Free Southern Theater subsequently adapted the motif into a new logo depicting two black hands breaking a shackle.⁶ For Harold Cruse, the civil rights South had receded by 1967.⁷ What Tom Dent called "the very blood cells of the South as we knew it," and what Aldon Morris referred to as the movement's "indigenous base," were "hinterlands" for Cruse when he suggested that the "race question" would be settled in the North.⁸ Cruse and Neal were champions of writing about the freedom struggle, but, when surveying "the writer as activist," Neal neglected civil rights organizations. This was the case despite his having been on a panel with Denise Nicholas at the Black Arts Convention in Detroit in June 1966, shared a platform with Jean Wheeler Smith for "Black Writers' Views on Literary Lions and Values" for *Negro Digest* in 1968, and coedited field-defining *Black Fire*, which anthologized stories and plays by SNCC's Cobb, Mahoney, Lester, Smith, Garrett, and S. E. Anderson. In 1972, Neal created a graphic distinction between "protest art" (that "screams and masturbates before white audiences") and "Black Art." The former, he asserted, had taken "the path of Negro literature and civil rights literature."⁹

In a capsule history of SNCC, "What We Want" (1966), Carmichael focused on the language of Black Power: "Black people are going to use the words they want to use, not just the words whites want to hear."¹⁰ Cobb mapped this as an activist black aesthetic. His "Words You Want?" (1966), read here as a companion poem to Carmichael's polemic, confronts the redundancy of classically poetic diction when it asserts: "We / I / turn toward / today."

> Speak,
>   how!
> with all the shit
> shoveled
> into my mouth
> . . . .
> Words, in rational rhymes

> constructed imagery
> cannot come
> with my mouth
> ....
> raging
> rampant
> on fire
> ON FIRE![11]

By 1968, Cobb's rage resonated with Forman's declaration, "If we can't sit at the table of democracy, we'll knock the fucking legs off." Although he regretted the language, as Carson records, Forman said that it was "difficult not to speak out in anger."[12] Outrage and invective are associated with the Black Arts Movement's militant poetics but, as Barbara Christian spelled out, its "emphasis on one way to be black resulted in the works of Southern writers being seen as non-black since the black of Georgia does not sound like the black talk of Philadelphia. Because the ideologues, like Baraka, come from urban centers they tended to privilege their way of speaking, thinking, writing, and to condemn other kinds of writing as not being black enough."[13]

Among writers associated with the BAM, Askia Touré (Roland Snellings) served on the Atlanta SNCC project, contributing to its position paper on Black Power in 1966, and was contributing editor of *Liberator* with Len Holt and Bill Mahoney. Haki Madhubuti (Don L. Lee) attended SNCC meetings with Llorens, and Nikki Giovanni reinvigorated a quiet, almost moribund SNCC chapter at Fisk in 1965. South African poet Keorapetse Kgositsile, in exile in the United States from 1962 to 1975, stayed close to the organization, with House and Dent both celebrating him as a mentor.[14] Poet Jayne Cortez visited Mississippi in 1963 at Forman's request, spent two summers registering voters, and set up a Friends of SNCC group in Los Angeles before founding Studio Watts and the Watts Repertory Theater Company in 1964 and 1967.[15] In 1979, she wrote an elegy for the "big, fine woman from Ruleville"—Fannie Lou Hamer—considering "how to weave your web of medicinal flesh into words," and asserting that Hamer's strength lives on: "I will push forward your precious gift of revolutionary courage."[16] A. B. Spellman married Karen Edmonds and celebrated SNCC in "The First Seventy":

> my choice of commitment was karen &
> the southern struggle. her tribe was sncc
> & if they owned fear they burned it for fuel

> alabama, mississippi—
> hear the cadence
> of those names.[17]

It is impossible to understand how heavily the Black Arts Movement leaned on Black Power without acknowledging, as House summarizes, that "it came as the same ball of wax. . . . the same new vision or the same new sense of identity."[18] Black Power was neither new nor sudden—its 1960s incarnation was rooted in SNCC. Nor, once it intersected with the BAM, was it an exclusively urban literary phenomenon.[19] Similarly, as Fanon Che Wilkins unpacks, SNCC's internationalist agenda was not the result of its call for Black Power. The "worlding" of its activism was inherent: "Longstanding material, psychic, and existential concerns with freedom, dignity, and political powerlessness enabled many in SNCC to recognize—as previous generations of black freedom activists had—that the problems that black folk faced in the United States extended far beyond the borders of Mississippi and Alabama."[20]

SNCC's Black Arts Movement Texts

Among SNCC writers, Jimmy Garrett and occasionally S. E. Anderson are considered as part of the Black Arts Movement, although more activist writers might be added, like Mae Jackson in *Can I Poet with You* (1969). Daniel Matlin points toward one reason why organizers have been overlooked in this context when observing how rebellions in cities outside the South "disrupted" civil rights activists' ability to make inroads into the culture industry: "Publishers, editors, theater producers and gallery curators looked to black intellectuals to act as indigenous interpreters of black *urban* life to the white American public: to combine their intimate, experiential knowledge as racial 'insiders' with the rigor of academic analysis, the crackle of polemic *or* the poignancy of art" (my emphases).[21] Kenneth B. Clark, Baraka, and Romare Bearden, Matlin's Harlem-based subjects, were expected to confine themselves to interpreting urban crises, with the South tacitly understood as less urban or less "ghettoized."[22] Holt and Mahoney used "Harlem" as a more complex nodal point for rebellion:

> Harlem-Philadelphia!
> Harlem-Detroit!
> Harlem-Los Angeles!
> Harlem-Birmingham![23]

Rebellions occurring across the South, in Atlanta, Houston, and Jackson, made the news, but, as Dent summarized in 1967, "The South's not where it is now. America does not care about Luling or Sunflower or Jackson."[24] Garrett's cultural nationalism did not begin at San Francisco State, where he founded the Black Student Union and a Black Arts and Culture series that brought Baraka and Sonia Sanchez to campus in 1967. His apprenticeship was SNCC, setting up a student-focused black studies program at the Center for Black Education in Washington, D.C., and SNCC's *Movement*, for which he wrote regularly. Positioned as a revolutionary playwright in the company of Baraka, Bullins, and Neal, his literary credo echoed Forman's that writing was action: "A Black writer has the responsibility of collecting, distilling, clarifying and directing the energies of black people leading toward purposeful, meaningful action. Black action that is the black writer's individualism and his life."[25] Garrett's city-set *We Own the Night: A Play of Blackness* (1968), its title echoing a poem by Baraka, opens three days into a "riot" as young black revolutionaries battle police: "This is judgment day, and we're the judges" (530).[26] A white officer lies dead on stage killed by Lil'T for wounding his friend Johnny. Against Johnny's wishes, his mother is sent for because he is bleeding heavily, and Lil'T struggles against her ideologically when she dismisses them as angry teenagers who should be "actin' like the white man 'stead of tryin' to kill him" (540). In this short, sharp shock of a parable, as Johnny lies dying, he shoots her as she walks away reiterating that "white people would never do these things" and that he should "trust in them" (540). Garrett's play typifies how the Black Arts Movement made this generation gap grotesque, in Baraka's *Great Goodness of Life: A Coon Show* (1966) and Ben Caldwell's *Family Portrait, or My Son the Black Nationalist* (1967), for further example, but civil rights workers were not expected to espouse blatantly violent paradigms. When they did, their organizing history was occluded: they were perceived part of "the new breed" with "dynamite growing out of their skulls."[27] Glenda Dicker/sun asked in 2008: "Could a Freedom Rider in 1961, singing, 'If my mother don't go, I'll go anyhow, I'm on my way to freedomland,' have imagined that Jimmy Garrett would interpret the notion of freedom in such violent terms?"[28] However, Garrett knew precisely what it was to occupy both positions, having been a Freedom Rider with CORE before joining SNCC in 1965.

Cultural preoccupations widely accepted as characteristic of the Black Arts Movement are evident across SNCC's writing. Thelwell's "Community of Victims," written in 1963 and published in 1964, for example, foreshadows Baraka's *Dutchman* (1964) and Bullins's *The Electronic Nigger*

(1968), but it was inspired by a touchstone for civil rights workers debating the ethics of organizing, Camus's thesis that "the community of victims is the same as that which binds victim and executioner."[29] In the rush hour of Washington, D.C., an African American student intellectual confronts his responsibility to the "ones at the bottom" and the "black masses."[30] Mitch has just been awarded a year's study in Europe: "The 'spook' halfback isn't doing so bad! All you had to do was to learn to maneuver in their world, speak their language" (205). His thoughts are peppered with sociological sound bites—"the affluent society," "the community of the city," allusions to Jean Genet's *The Blacks* (1959), enjoying a successful run in New York in the moment the story is set—and disdain for author of the book he is reading, a white psychologist surprised by the hatred for whites that his black African subject discloses. At a bus stop, an older black man, drunk and staggering, propositions a young white woman. Mitch reflects smugly, ventriloquizing Hamlet, "*tis a consummation devoutly to be wished*," but Thelwell writes, "Mental wisecracks did not relieve the embarrassment he felt growing and his anger at himself for feeling vulnerable and compromised by the actions of some drunken Negro" (209). The burden of representation falls heavily on Mitch's shoulders, and he is unable to skirt his responsibility for ensuring that the man leaves the encounter with a vestige of dignity. The composure of "Miss Ann" enrages Mitch as whites nearby snicker or fidget, readying themselves to intervene. He fails to shake an "engulfing sense of personal loss, and of being somehow diminished himself," but when he tries to deflect the black man's attention from the white woman, Mitch is rebuffed (214). When he and "Miss Ann" board the bus and the drunken man recedes into the distance, the woman thanks Mitch and tells him, "I—I think I understand. I don't blame him." He is curt with her and incensed: "What the hell does she understand? A generous, compassionate, tolerant white woman. Well, she's either too late or too early. Who in the hell needs her compassion or understanding? Hope she chokes on it" (215). The crux of the story is Mitch's reaction to the sting of superiority he chooses to interpret in her comment. The intriguing phrase "too late or too early" suggests that while "Miss Ann" rarely acts on her conscience when harnessed as "the South's palladium," at a bus stop in the nation's capital, in a moment of heightened black consciousness, racial liberalism has no place in the intersectional critique stewing inside Mitch.[31]

Black Arts Movement tenets are explored before the movement really existed, with *Dutchman* being a violent and more disturbing evocation. In the play, Clay Williams's Ivy League pretensions are undone stealthily and cruelly when the psychotic rage of a white woman, Lula, is turned on him on the New York subway. She taunts Clay into revealing the racial antagonism behind his façade, "I sit here in this buttoned-up suit to keep myself from cutting all your throats," forcing him to see himself through her eyes, sneering "You're an escaped nigger. . . . You crawled through the wire and made tracks to my side."[32] The taunt echoes Thelwell's Mitch and his acerbic evaluation of his academic success. When Lula murders Clay, he is dispatched from the train with the complicity of white passengers, while she proceeds like a serial killer to prey on her next target. Mitch, on the other hand, controls his thinking on the bus by dismissing the white woman as irrelevant while scrutinizing what assimilating to the white academy will mean personally and politically. Thelwell's "Community of Victims" is a caustic commentary on the white woman character as a dramatic device. As Thulani Davis writes, "Once you put her in there it's no longer about the Negro, it's about the race question, the ways of white folks and all that."[33] Thelwell refused to make his story about her, focusing instead on how an individualistic, educated middle class disconnected itself from a black underclass it would leave in the same dire straits, as Smith reiterates across her essays and stories. Thelwell was one of ten black writers who together, in print, in 1968, excoriated William Styron's Pulitzer Prize–winning *The Confessions of Nat Turner* (1967) for playing fast and loose with the real rebel leader's biography and reducing him to a pale cipher of what he represents in African American culture. Turner was hanged in August 1831 in Southampton County, Virginia, after his army of twenty-eight slaves killed fifty-seven whites. Styron inserted a white woman character into the life of the insurrectionist, omitting the real Turner's marriage to a black woman, recorded by Thomas Gray in his 1831 pamphlet—the ur-text. Styron's character is sexually obsessed with the white woman he kills. In 1965, in "This Quiet Dust," Styron had taken for granted that the problem of race had "long since resolved itself into an aesthetic one." In 1967, he defended himself in a long letter to the *Nation* responding to Herbert Aptheker's critical review of *Confessions*.[34] For Thelwell, like Aptheker, historical record mattered, as did the problem he reiterated across his literary criticism: that in the "literary circles" of the 1960s, even "the best intentioned and most enlightened" white writers demonstrated "largely uncritical acceptance" of racial stereotypes and myths.[35]

When Eugene Genovese assessed the controversy over Styron's novel raised by *William Styron's Nat Turner: Ten Black Writers Respond* (1968), he focused on Thelwell's and Vincent Harding's essays: "Virtually all the serious points made in the book may be found, skillfully presented, in

Thelwell's essay, but for some suggestive material on slave religion we must turn to Harding's."[36] Responding to Genovese, Thelwell refused to stay within the critical parameters set by Genovese, Styron, or, indeed, his own essay. He took the opportunity to criticize the "limited intellectual structures" in which the debate was conducted, and advocated telling it like it is:

> It is the responsibility of the black scholar of this generation to pull out, articulate, and define the form and meaning of that past in ways that have never been done. This is our particular responsibility since we appear to have the freedom to do this and have it recognized—which was denied to other generations.... [M]any of the most cherished shibboleths of white scholarship will have to be reexamined.... Black people have nothing to lose or fear from a hard unsentimental reexamination of the American past and a loosening of the cramped and limited intellectual structures into which all history and reality have been stifled.[37]

Houston Baker cites Carmichael, H. Rap Brown, Malcolm X, and Huey P. Newton as "men of words" who could "hold the stage verbally."[38] Thelwell held his own in writing, his politicized credo expressed in response to Genovese presaging "neo-slave narratives" or "liberatory narratives," from Barbara Woods's "The Final Supper" (1970) and Ishmael Reed's *Flight to Canada* (1976) through Sherley Ann Williams's direct response to Gray's and Styron's framing of Turner, *Dessa Rose* (1986).[39] When he published *The Harder They Come* (1980), a Jamaica-set novel based loosely on the 1972 film, Thelwell argued, "One has to write a realistic political novel in the language, the idiom of the people." This echoed SNCC's ethos of responsibility to promulgate community voices while simultaneously refuting the idea that "artist" and "cultural nationalist" are incompatible.[40] It is impossible to read the ironically titled "Community of Victims," his intervention in *Ten Black Writers Respond*, or the debate with Genovese without recognizing how each text engages struggles for cultural authority, prefiguring and complementing writing in the Black Arts Movement.

SNCC debated its responsibility for promulgating a national and international black cultural consciousness too. Gwen Robinson (Zoharah Simmons) shared experience of organizing in Paterson, New Jersey, with SNCC's Executive Committee, suggesting that its "cultural arm" ensure that "people in the South know about the North—including Black Nationalism." Tina Harris suggested that SNCC "teach blackness" to make visible "connections that already exist."[41] In fiction, Len Holt imagined militant Black Power activists in SNCC in "Defendant or Decedent?," published by the *Student Voice* to encourage "staff expressions" in the way that O'Neal advocated story circles to "get people thinking and talking."[42] In the story, Ricks is modeled on Willie Ricks (Mukasa Dada), and Regina, a recruit from Detroit, suggests the more military Revolutionary Action Movement and its Black Guards.[43] They are armed when arriving at night at Mt. Moriah Church in fictional Gruva, Mississippi, to register a Lowndes County Black Panther candidate for an upcoming election. African Americans in the county have "the strength of numbers [to] allow them to invoke Black Power," but running for office, for a black candidate, is "rumored to be a last will and testament" (15, 13). They wait in the empty church with nomination forms, Freedom Primers, Black Power anthologies, and a growing feeling that it is a trap. Holt describes "circles of frustration" and "widening circles of anxiety" as the "circle of trust" dissipates in gendered tension (13, 17, 14). Ricks entertains himself with sexist taunts, holding his veteran status over Regina: "Wish to hell that damned state coordinator would stop trying to force shit-ass women in the field when, like here, a man is needed.... Hit ain't been three months yet, since you told your mammy to go to hell and joined SNICK" (12). She is unfazed—"I'll die as dead as you if this is a trap.... You're just scared.... You think you're hell on wheels"—secure in her ability to make a shotgun cause someone to "do the Watusi at 65 yards" (13–14).

As they prepare to defend themselves against the armed posse, they are convinced is on its way, they resolve their differences: "he wanted to be at peace with somebody he had razzed for weeks," and she confirms her suspicion that behind chauvinistic bluster he is a "lovable cat" (17). When police attack, Regina kills the sheriff and blasts his deputies, "ripping off the front half of one man's head and splattering the face and bodies of four others." As she reloads, an explosion in the center of town signals relief: "Some helpless, unarmed cullud folks done found a weapon, the match" (18). As police rush away to the fire that follows, Regina and Ricks escape past burning buildings, and a sign falls at their feet: "JESUS SAVES" (19). For readers in SNCC, Mt. Moriah was recognizably the Hayneville, Alabama, church where the Lowndes County Freedom Organization met. As Randy Battle recounted about the real event that Holt's fiction is based on, "The crackers pulled up on both roads that went up to that church and they parked there in dozens of cars ... you know it was do or die." Alerted to the raid, congregants took out guns to deter attackers, turning the headlights of their cars back on those trained on the church, until the white mob backed down.[44] Battle ensured it would be understood that congregants had acted in their own defense.

Holt's is the most overtly violent fantasy in the literature I have uncovered. Black revolutionaries battle the same representatives of the white power structure as in Garrett's play but without a sense of tragic waste or irreconcilable differences. Holt tucked in a lesson for Ricks, and readers, making sexist assumptions when Ricks swallows his taunts and says: "Baby you can always work with me cause you is the best man with that thunder stick." Without missing a beat, Regina retorts, "Ya moma is the best man," besting Ricks in skill and banter (18). Holt issues a warning to men not to devalue women in behavior, language, or according to the "fallacious reasoning" that Frances Beal identified: "[F]or a Black man to be strong, the Black woman has to be weak."[45] He imagined his aptly named Regina as a sure-shot "sistuh" in the mold of Annie Pearl Avery, Mabel Williams, Assata Shakur, and Elaine Brown, the only woman to lead the Black Panther Party. Avery's pragmatic adherence to self-defense, from the moment she joined SNCC in Birmingham, guarding Freedom Houses with her .22, gets respectful nods in *Hands on the Freedom Plow* and *This Nonviolent Stuff'll Get You Killed*.[46] In Holt's "Defendant or Decedent?," the gun is a symbolic equalizer for a woman who is cool under pressure and tips the scales. Holt depicts militancy usually associated with the Black Panther Party and Revolutionary Action Movement and aesthetically with the BAM, but foregrounding an African American woman organizer is rare in fiction. Forman made his character Fran Walker "militant" in his unpublished "Thin White Line." In 1962, he wrote a story in which organizer Jesse flirts with Faye Jones in the Atlanta SNCC office and is told firmly, "I don't fool with Snick men." Faye has a date with a man outside the movement, but when a crisis in Greenville, Mississippi, demands that she break it, he cannot accept what she tells him—"The movement comes first! You can wait"—and is jettisoned.[47] Women organizers are a lacuna in the published work.

"Everywhere Is Here"

What Peniel Joseph has referred to as "the SNCC diaspora" widens if its writers are acknowledged for their influence in exploring the thinking behind Black Power and SNCC's critique of U.S foreign policy.[48] In "What's Wrong with the War in Vietnam?" (1965), SNCC compared the use of cattle prods on civil rights workers with the torture—"or 'frying' as one U.S. advisor called it"—of Viet Cong prisoners. President Diem's erosion of free elections, endorsed by his American advisors, was likened to the unconstitutional prevention of African Americans from voting in the U.S. South. In the same moment, Courtland Cox made a public statement: "We have to convince the country that civil rights workers get killed in the South because the government has a certain attitude toward killing in Vietnam. The concept that it is all right to kill an 'enemy' affects the morality in the country so that people can be murdered here."[49] In "Charlie's Poem," published in June 1965 in the *Student Voice*, the U.S. South and Vietnam are parallel war zones:

> the cop
> in Selma
> pulls the trigger
> that
> kills for alabama
> for god and alabama
> as he's been taught
>
> just like his brother
> who fought
>   or bombed
>   or gassed
> in south vietnam last week.

Anger burns and sarcasm whips through ten jagged verses until democratic notions of equality are conflated with federally sanctioned violence:

> someday
> maybe
> if i give america a chance
> I'll be able to
> wear the uniform
> and have the gun
> of the cop
> that shot
> Jimmy Lee Jackson
>
> Or be the commander
> of the army...
>
> that's what will happen to me
> when I'm given
> equality.[50]

When an excerpt from Charles Cobb's long, bitter poem appeared in the *Movement*, its title was changed to an emphatic "I Want to Say."[51] Cobb echoed Malcolm X, influential in SNCC, when satirizing integration into a "burning house" but also crystallized feelings held by many in SNCC across the 1960s.[52] California-based Doug Youngblood's "Tales of the Ghetto" (1968), for example, evokes an equally sardonic persona:

> I've
> been given
> the
> freedom
> to die
> for
> my country
> in Vietnam
> and protest
> the owners of this ghetto.[53]

S. E. Anderson, cited often as a founder of the Black Panther Party in Harlem in 1966 but rarely as a SNCC organizer, intoned in "Junglegrave" (1973) a dying black soldier's wish: "Send the President my flowers cremated and / scented with the odors / Of my brothers' napalmed flesh and my / sisters' bombed-out skulls."[54] In January 1966, when SNCC was the first civil rights organization to speak unequivocally against the war and the draft, its collaboratively written statement, to which Cobb contributed with Cox, House, Gwen Patton, Forman, and others, included a correlative:

> The murder of Samuel Young [sic] in Tuskegee, Alabama, is no different than the murder of peasants in Vietnam, for both Young and the Vietnamese sought, and are seeking, to secure the rights guaranteed them by law . . .
>
> Young was murdered because United States law is not being enforced. Vietnamese are murdered because the United States is pursuing an aggressive policy in violation of international law.[55]

SNCC issued its condemnation three days after Younge's murder. That it exposed the relationship between foreign policy and domestic terrorism distinguished the organization from others. Only days before Cox's statement, the NAACP's Roy Wilkins asserted that war was "not a proper sphere for public analysis or criticism" and that civil rights groups did not have sufficient information "to make it their cause." Wilkins would openly disagree with Martin Luther King Jr. when King took a public stand against the war in April 1967.[56] SNCC persisted, with Forman equating Black Power to a refusal to be "fooled" by politicians, saying "Fighting your wars [is] killing my people." Margaret Long and maverick newsman I. F. Stone were supportive: "Before condemning SNCC for its opposition to the war," Stone wrote, "every white American ought to ask . . .: If we were a minority in a black Republic, if we and our friends were murdered with impunity, if we were underpaid and overworked by Negroes, if we were the last to be hired but the first to be drafted, how would we feel if we were sent to fight another white people on some distant Continent?"[57]

Diane Nash traveled to Hanoi with an antiwar coalition of women in December 1966, and Cobb and Lester went there at the instigation of Bertrand Russell's International War Crimes Tribunal in 1967. Cobb wrote an ode to Hanoi because there he "stood free." "[The wind sang a] song / of nation on my black face."[58] Cobb performed a personalized exegesis in "Letters from Hanoi" (1967): "I knew that I had traveled the roads and paths and fields I saw. The houses and shacks were differently styled but still sharecropper shacks in the Mekong Delta." This evokes Cobb's thesis on Freedom Schools, "where creativity must be molded from the rhythm of a muttered 'white son of a bitch'" and "the roar of a hunger-bloated belly," as students learn "the link between a rotting shack and a rotting America."[59]

Cobb's poetry expressed SNCC's thinking as it consolidated what Black Power could mean internationally, resonated for antiwar activists, and presaged concerns associated with the Black Arts Movement, but it is rooted in organizing. His haiku for Sammy Younge Jr. is illustrated in *In the Furrows of the World* by a haunting photograph of Younge in a pool of blood behind the Tuskegee gas station where he was murdered. Still, it succeeds in avoiding voyeurism and instrumentalism because in *In the Furrows of the World* the haiku rests on an architecture for mourning. Cobb peels back to the "dangerroad" where organizers took "gas pedal flight," suggesting other deaths.[60] Impressionistic, spectral haiku may seem a surprising choice of form for activists at this difficult juncture in SNCC's life, but its writers had a particular affinity for the Japanese form, with Robert Hayden publishing six of Lester's haiku in 1967.[61] Whether following the precision of haiku's seventeen syllables extended across only three lines, or adjusting the form as Cobb did, SNCC's poetic telegrams "burst from silence and peel back the layers of perception." Lester wrote, "I come to books for this experience of confession and recognition . . . information is not the same as knowledge . . . knowledge is more than, other than, facts."[62] Vietnam catalyzed Lester's understanding of how not to become an "executioner" (in Camus's terms): "Revolution changes whole patterns of living and thinking . . . most people just throw that word around without letting it get into their lives, without letting it transform them.... In Vietnam I learned that the revolutionary is he who cries for those he has killed."[63] War was a heavily politicized prism through which to expose twisted relationships between patriotic protestations and corrupted visions of democracy. Black Power was SNCC's focal lens, as Gwen Patton defined in "Black People and War" (1967) and Lester did in *Revolutionary Notes* (1969). As Lester wrote: "For so long / We sang My Country 'Tis of Thee / For so long / We died in wars not our own. But / We are reclaiming ourselves."[64] Cobb enumerated the terms "qualifying" African Americans to fight but not to vote: "'patriotism,' 'our way of life,' 'the American way of life,' 'nigger' [and] a thousand other [terms], infinitely more subtle and complex."[65]

While historians delineate the trajectory by which SNCC's endorsement of black cultural nationalism and its official statement against the war could be understood, Cobb eschewed chronology when arranging poems for Maria Varela to publish. *In The Furrows of the World* is a nonlinear collage, in which SNCC's black cultural taproot is anchored in its genesis but shoots out lateral roots in colonial critique. In "Mekonsippi," the Mississippi runs into the Mekong delta via the flows of "whitey's wars" (50).[66] Transnational comparison of global souths was more than intertextual, and the title poem "In the Furrows of the World" was retitled "Nation" when selected by Walter Lowenfels for *In a Time of Revolution: Poems from Our Third World* (1969). In poems centered on specific protests, like "Birmingham 1963," written in the winter of 1966, horrific "pools of red" and "pieces of black" in Sixteenth Street Baptist Church are compared to "fiery blasting bombs" in Vietnam—"Beneath the burning / a mother / sifts / and finds / a piece of arm / and wisps of hair" in the poem that follows, "11pm News Nightmare" (25–26). Cobb's poetry rages "around the world":

> our cries have crashed
> through
> terror torn nights
> our bodies burnt
> the earth
> a bitter black
> to rise in anger (2).

The cumulative effect is illustrated in a photograph of a young person wearing a T-shirt that has been marked on the back with "FREE" and further hand-lettered BLACK POWER below it in darker print (59). A transitional image conflating "Freedom Now" and "Black Power," this conflation would be reprised in Wade Gayle's "The Pilgrimage" (1991) when she walks "to the rhythm of memories":

>holding a picket sign
>FREEDOM
>in my left hand
>and a tight fist
>BLACK POWER
>in my right.[67]

Organizers in SNCC were continually exploring a black cultural consciousness aesthetically. In Cobb's "First Views of the Going," black consciousness is traced back to elementary school and the back of the school bus: "How far back / was the discovery of black?" (27).

Cobb's prose poem "Ain't That a Groove" gained traction in SNCC, like Bond's "I Too, Hear America Singing." When first presented, then titled "Toward a Theory of Communication," Cobb's piece suggested internal communication and hybrid forms others might explore.[68] After publication in *In The Furrows of the World*, in a SNCC pamphlet, and in Baraka and Neal's anthology *Black Fire* (1968), it epitomized Black Power: "Let every black, packed, on every block; bent in every field... make it against the man." Cobb harnesses the image of being on the ocean in a rudderless boat debated at the Waveland retreat when ventriloquizing an Atlanta deejay: "It ain't the size of the ship / that makes the wave" but the "motion of the ocean" and "where we at" (53). Cobb also returns to core tenets via the Black Panther motif of the Lowndes campaign: "Our work and responsibility is meeting the needs of our people. Black people. Know, that in this white man's country, talking as a black, and gearing yourself to meeting the needs of black people, is revolutionary in itself" (53). "Ain't That a Groove" is also a creative look at the nitty-gritty street-level work of the project operating in Atlanta's Vine City neighborhood in 1966.[69] An organizer chalking "Freedom Now" and "Black Power" on a child's hopscotch squares ponders, "Are our words legitimate enough for folks to keep the words in sight?" (55–56). When the scene shifts from a Vine City street to Atlanta Stadium on July 4, black kids spill in to hear James Brown, and white police scramble after them. "Ain't that a groove," Cobb writes, as the kids elude the cops, but when the scene switches to teenagers harassed by police in Harlem, it anticipates the anger of Garrett's *We Own the Night* (56–57). Cobb is the more inventive. In "LA—the order of things" (11–15), for example, an angry persona turns himself into a Molotov cocktail as Cobb expounds on SNCC's identification with rebellion. In jail in Lowndes

County when Watts ignited in August 1965, Gloria House wrote, "Those brothers and sisters, in venting their resentment against oppressive conditions, somehow acted as our very own champions as we sat behind bars."[70] Cobb locates Watts, rage, and police brutality in a longer history:

> You
>
> gave me the bottle
> and taught me
> to
>
> empty
>
> its burning inside my body.
>
> I
>
> gave it back
> Stuffed
>
> with the rags you made me wear
>
> Kerosened
> with my sweat
>
> Lit
>
> with the match
> of your oppression
>
> Burning baby
> burning. (14–15)

The grim, precise voice is diffused, echoed, and made female by House, as Aneb Kgositsile, in *Blood River* (1983), when in "Sister Love" an organizer becomes a "walking bomb":

> Future, children, community, new world—
> blown daily from her innards
> like scorched seeds,
> shrapnel, scattered and lost (13).

Another commits suicide after "scaling those treacherous crags of pain" (17). Kgositsile shares her doubts that words will "carry us through this flood to Dawn" or "make the way / bearable" (15). In "Incantation," the voice is forlorn: "Will they soar, lift us out / of this red sea?" (13). She is bereft in "Woman": "Where is the revolution to be seen / Through all those tears?" (15, 16). Casting back, Kgositsile's overarching metaphor is a "deep groan... pouring out of the heart, / flowing like a blood river" (11). In the 1980s, she finds "strength in music," a "survival lesson" in "the tradition of our elders' faith," but the elders offer fragile hope against the backlash of the so-called War on Drugs and the "racial caste system" of mass incarceration (30).[71] Blood seeps from prison cells, and the "spaces between us become hazardously slick / with our own blood":

> We must stop this.
> See through those lies called "criminal,"
> called "pathological," called "recidivistic."
> Call our men by their true names:
> Father, Brother, Son, prisoners of war—
> and bring them home. (14)

The tributaries of Kgositsile's "blood river" are various, but like Cobb she eschews chronology, and toward the end of the collection are revenants such as "Meridian, Miss., August 1964," in which Chaney, Schwerner, and Goodman leave "us now bereaved" (32). "Ghosts of civil rights marchers" in Selma and the elegy "To Ruby Doris" are quietly commemorative, but grief is boundless, timeless. An "Alabama Farmer's Dialectic" is even quieter, a paean to people with whom Kgositsile worked closely in Lowndes County. "Now I see it like dis," the farmer explains: a shade tree for whites "makin' it cool an' easy for dem" over many years; the tree has "got to come down" (35). Kgositsile catches up manifold feelings in intimate, geospatial symbolism: "courage in devastation" and "shards of hope" are stimulated by Cuban and Vietnamese activists in *Como en Vietnam,* and in Bermuda the persona feels for a moment that "we were one people" (24, 38).

Gloria House (Aneb Kgositsile) assessed, "We were seeing ourselves on the world stage, in the larger light of internationalism, not simply within the boundaries and political context of the United States."[72] The worlding of SNCC that Clayborne Carson and Peniel Joseph emphasize was being explored by organizers themselves and gave rise to myriad literary activities. Aimé Césaire's poem "Mississippi" (1961) receiving its first English translation in the *Movement* in 1967 is one example.[73] In 1964, Howard Zinn described "the present movement" as "planted firmly in the deepest furrows of the Deep South." Cobb's poetry is rooted in the soil of the

Black Belt but also, Cobb writes, "in the furrows of the world" because with "long, strong roots . . . we grew into the world." John Lewis has noted that SNCC's 1964 tour of Africa at the same time that Malcolm X was in Nairobi consolidated the organization's approach to internationalism.[74] For Cobb, though, SNCC's internationalism was inspired by Forman and linked, much earlier, to "the southern African liberation movements."[75] House was influenced by South African poet Keorapetse Kgositsile, from whom she took her pen name. Simultaneously she was rooted in Detroit, which was affirmed when she succeeded Dudley Randall in 1977 as editor of Broadside Press, now the oldest African American publisher of poetry (as Broadside Lotus Press, having merged in 2015 with Lotus Press). Cobb cofounded the Drum and Spear Bookstore and Center for Black Education in Washington, D.C., with Cox and Judy Richardson in 1968. A founding committee for both also included Karen Spellman, Ralph Featherstone, Ivanhoe Donaldson, and Curtis Hayes (Muhammad), and a related community program in which Jimmy Garrett was involved was supported by pan-Africanist writers and intellectuals, notably Hoyt Fuller and C. L. R. James. Cobb and Cox were inspired by Présence Africaine, the Parisian bookshop founded by Senegalese Alioune Diop and named after the periodical he edited, which they visited en route to Africa in 1967. By 1969, Drum and Spear had launched a publishing arm, with offices in Washington and Dar es Salaam.[76] Cobb moved to Tanzania for a couple of years, and the poetry collection he compiled while living there, *Everywhere Is Yours* (1971), exudes a pan-Africanist sensibility:

> From sahara to Bantu lands
> savannah plains
> rain forest greens
> . . . 14th street 6000 miles across the water
> ....
> my people, Nation
> black, black my
> people black nation
> Now![77]

Looking back from Tanzania, where he and Moses were part of "a small circle" of African American expatriates, Cobb reasserted,

> Must not a tree sink its roots into soil?
> ....

> And who will sow the seeds?
> forge the metals?
> ....
> If not you blackman
> who?"[78]

A founding member of the National Association of Black Journalists in 1975, and the *National Geographic*'s first African American staff writer, Cobb expanded his oeuvre into revisionist works of SNCC's history. In whichever genre he writes, Cobb emphasizes, the autobiographical is "more than a personal narration of my experiences." His model for storytelling is Ella Baker's paradigm: "[W]e not only must *remember* where we have been, but we must *understand* where we have been" (original emphases).[79] Forman vocalized such understanding on November 3, 1967, in Los Angeles, when performing his poem "Liberation Will Come from a Black Thing." He dedicated it to Ruby Doris Smith Robinson's sustained "resistance spirit" and SNCC's black consciousness pursued in "a spirit of internationalism." As SNCC was vilified for being too militant, Forman ventriloquized what "they" were thinking about "us": "They used to be wonderful.... They have just gone too far... They do not understand it takes time. / They are hurting their cause."[80] In "Mother Africa" (1969), he explained,

> We have a responsibility to the future of all mankind
> but especially black people, our people.
> We know this.
> We have known it.[81]

As the Black Arts Movement tenets took hold, Forman wrote a Black Power cry for freedom framed by an incantation:

> And if Africa is lost
> We are all lost.

Across six stanzas, Forman underscored Africa as "our home," its diaspora

> towns, cities, states / and nations... Alabama, Mississippi, and Georgia / Nassau, Cuba, Bolivia, and Jamaica... Snow Hill and Atlanta and New York / San Francisco, and Chicago and Mississippi and Alabama.

Claiming states where SNCC struggled at the beginning and end of its organizing in the Deep South, in draft it is a raw, wrenching panegyric:

> Blacks in America scream
> Across four centuries of oppression
> And across bottomless oceans of death
> Through the corridors of time filled
> With fights and flights and
> Black Struggles to
> Be Free.[82]

If Forman's "Mother Africa" echoes Baraka's "black scream and chant" in "Black Dada Nihilismus" (1964), it does not suggest its ferocious nihilism or murderous political rhetoric.[83] As SNCC's stories reiterate, Black Power derived from a "much older tradition of Black resistance."[84] And it was the impetus for Forman's "1967: The High Tide of Black Resistance" and "Black Manifesto" (1969), together comprising "the first systematic, fully elaborated plan for reparations to emerge from the black freedom movement."[85]

The following chapter examines how Bill Mahoney and Richard Hall used the novel form to assess the effects of activism on organizers and communities. In Mahoney's *Black Jacob*, the eponymous character is a tragic representative of many SNCC-backed electoral candidates whose campaigns to represent their communities in civic and political roles galvanized southern towns and endangered the populations who supported them. Hall's *Long George Alley* is a modernist, polyphonic evocation of SNCC's Natchez project in the summer of 1965, when Hall was a volunteer. Both novels were published after SNCC had begun to fragment, quickly and irrevocably, with Hall composing his right after SNCC's demise.

Chapter 8

Battle Stories at the Grassroots and Beginnings of Bitter Ends

> Revolutionary writing is usually alienating to those not involved in understanding the bases for revolution.
> —Mari Evans, 1970
>
> Natchez was to be the last mobilizing campaign of the Mississippi movement.
> —John Dittmer, 1994
>
> "Black Power, Nitty-gritty. Freedom. Sheeeit."
> —Bill Mahoney, *Black Jacob*, 1969

In 1967, Hoyt Fuller expressed his discontent over a conceptual blind spot that he identified in book reviewers: "The critics keep crying for good novels, and then they keep ignoring them when they appear—if the novels do not say what critics want to hear in the way the critics want it said."[1] In 1969, Macmillan promoted *Black Jacob* as "the first major novel to come out of the Movement" and Mahoney as intimately familiar with the recent history out of which this fiction was shaped.[2] Nevertheless, it did not receive critical attention as immersive writing of the times. While Fuller was a major proponent of a new black aesthetic, especially as the driving force and mainstay of the Organization of Black American Culture, criteria for "revolutionary art" were underscored more audaciously by 1969 by Baraka, Neal, Karenga, graphic artist Emory Douglas, and pugnacious position pieces like Julius Lester's *Look Out, Whitey! Black Power's Gon' Get Your Mama* (1968) and H. Rap Brown's *Die, Nigger, Die* (1968).[3] Works of reflection in literary genres failed to gain as much attention, although in 1969 Dorothy Sterling recommended that teachers select Thelwell's "Direct Action," and Lester's *To Be a Slave* alongside *Look Out, Whitey!* and Forman's biography of Sammy Younge Jr. for students seeking to understand the movement.[4] *Ebony* described *Look Out, Whitey!* as "perhaps the best report of the actual Movement of the past decade written by one who has lived it and who is without the need to apologize for a point of view as black as his prose style." The *New York Times* called it "a magnificent example of the new black revolutionary writing that could generate the tidal force to sweep aside all the tired and dead matter on our literary shores."[5] *Black Jacob* may not have seemed "black" or "revolutionary" in precisely the right way at the time, when Lester, Brown, and Carmichael were being read along with Eldridge Cleaver and Huey Newton.

As Mari Evans observed, "revolutionary" writing could seem "alienating to those not involved in understanding the bases for revolution," and *Black Jacob*'s setting in one of SNCC's southern bases may also have consigned it to oblivion. As Harold Cruse wrote influentially in *The Crisis of the Negro Intellectual*, "True revolutions are never settled in the hinterlands, or . . . the more backward regions of any nation."[6] Black writing was "instructional, directional, informational" in the taxonomy that Evans advanced to distinguish it from "Negro" writing, although she wondered whether some key texts would survive "only as historical record of the ritual role of the writer in stimulating and maintaining the fervor of revolutionary intent and purpose at its apogee."[7] Mahoney's novel does not focus on fervor; it weaves together revolutionary threads that date from the movement's beginnings but also suggest its end. It was composed over a number of years and its writing interrupted "to give hours of help" to Holt in his writing of *An Act of Conscience*, for example.[8] For Toni Cade Bambara, *Black Jacob* was redolent of the "explosive move from the Civil Rights Movement to the Black Liberation Struggle," but inside SNCC the movement was incremental rather than explosive.[9] SNCC had been struggling for black liberation for almost a decade when *Black Jacob* textured how that felt for organizers and communities.

When *Black Jacob* received thoughtful reviews, they were in publications where the bases for revolution were understood. The NAACP's *Crisis* described it as "an apocalyptic story of the terrifying conflicts that rage throughout the South" and judged that "this novel on the Movement offers something unique in current fiction—a cool, unsparing, yet wholly sympathetic portrait." In the *Liberator*, launched in 1960 as the organ of the Liberation Committee for Africa, Bambara introduced "a vital book" by a participant, not a "two-minute tripper" parachuting into a battle zone to extrapolate on what is glimpsed "with only a murky perception of what these risky summers in the Deep South were all about in the first damn place." While the novel's structure could have been tighter in her view, the drama was "searing."[10] Mahoney was unsparing when delineating how a campaign fails because it lacks what Moses reiterated is essential: the "minimum of common conceptual cohesion" between activists and communities.[11] Only two literary critics discussed *Black Jacob* in any detail, in 1973 and 1997, and neither read the novel as experiential, losing sight of what was distinctive about Mahoney's creative intervention in the moment and what "hard-won knowledge" of the movement brought to readers.[12] Mahoney and Richard Hall (in *Long George Alley*) focus on veterans who are exhausted, depleted, as the organization is beginning to dissolve. Hall also explores the feeling that it was "too damn bad about the good ones" but "time to move [whites] out" (44, 17, 134). He atomizes characters, enclosing voices in recursive, looping monologues. Different perspectives are cut and spliced, and they coalesce in a long tracking shot searching out each character's interconnectedness with events unfolding in Natchez. The critical blind spot that Fuller identified left this novel underread and underappreciated. *Long George Alley* faded "off the radar screen" between 1972 and 2004, when it was republished.[13] Despite Thelwell's support, James Baldwin's endorsement of "a very beautiful book, painful and true," and Jan Carew, author of *Cry Black Power* (1970), discerning "a kind of painful enlightenment that perhaps brings one as close to objective truth as possible," it received no critical attention. After the ubiquitous nod to "objectivity," Carew compared Hall's style to Jean Toomer's modernist collage in *Cane* (1922).[14]

When Jerry H. Bryant assessed *Black Jacob* in *Victims and Heroes: Racial Violence in the African American Novel* (1997), he rolled Mahoney into a group of writers responding to "the kind of revolutionary activity propagated by Malcolm X." Sandwiched between Du Bois's *The Ordeal of Mansart* (1957) and Sarah E. Wright's *This Child's Gonna Live* (1969), he placed Mahoney among writers depicting "the African American experience as a continual drain upon the strength of those who would do good" and "how extremes of poverty in the midst of systemic racism can promote resignation rather than revolution."[15] The black middle class is the scourge of Mahoney's critique because comfort and apathy equate to disinclination to build cohesive support for a black congressional candidate. There is anger in these texts, not solely resignation.[16] Bryant acknowledged that *Black Jacob* was "an unusual act of self-scrutiny in those revolutionary times" when summarizing its subject as "politics, election campaigns, and the reality of the perversity of the ignorant, the educated, the well-meaning."[17] He assumed, though, that Medgar Evers or Martin Luther King were inspirations for Jacob Blue though neither Evers nor King ran for political office. Jacob is a tragic representative of SNCC-backed candidates who ran for Congress in Mississippi, Georgia, Alabama, North Carolina, and Virginia and stood for election under the aegis of the MFDP and for civic posts via the LCFO. The wider context is the Freedom Vote in Mississippi in 1963, the MFDP in 1964, and political campaigns in Natchez, Mississippi, and Lowndes County, Alabama, after SNCC had spent five years in the field.

Bryant echoed Noel Schraufnagel. In *From Apology to Protest* (1973), Schraufnagel created attitudinal categories—labeling fiction protest, propagandist, apologetic, accommodationist, or militant—to rank works even when they did not fit this schema and was hamstrung by the redundant term "objective" that proliferates in reviews of political fiction.[18] He twisted the novel to fit sociological precepts, calling it "a relatively thorough and objective study of the racial scene in the South," and placed Mahoney "in the second rank of protest novelists," based on what he interpreted as melodrama and polemic.[19] In fact, *Black Jacob* is the first sustained, fictional evocation of the tortuous twists and turns of a SNCC-supported campaign, saturated with politicized rage, as the *Crisis* reviewer recognized. As Jon Else felt it necessary to remind readers in 2017, "Encounters between individuals—sharecroppers, volunteers, CORE and SNCC workers, sheriffs, farmhands, lawyers, ministers, judges—were the core fabric of the Mississippi movement but they were outside the frame, neither filmed nor photographed." This may seem ironic when voiced by the series producer of *Eyes on the Prize*. However, as a volunteer in 1964 and 1965, Else was empirically aware of what did not make the news and admitted that Blackside Inc., the series production company, struggled initially to find film footage beyond Birmingham and Selma.[20]

Natchez has been described by historians as "the single greatest community victory for the civil rights movement in Mississippi" and "the last mobilizing campaign of the Mississippi movement."[21] Mahoney and Hall challenge the idea that what happened there was exceptional: Hall in *Long George Alley* fuses Natchez with McComb, and Mahoney links it to Lowndes County.[22] Mahoney avoided locating *Black Jacob* definitively so that it would conflate multiple campaigns, like attorney C. B. King's in Albany in September 1964 as the first African American to run for a congressional seat in Georgia since Reconstruction. Jesse Harris's management of James M. Houston's campaign in Vicksburg, north of Natchez, may also have been a source, but the seventy-four-year-old veteran of civil rights struggles was not reluctant to make campaign speeches, as the thirty-five-year-old doctor is in *Black Jacob*. Natchez was the center of the tourist industry in a state otherwise infamous for holding out as the last bastion of segregation. As a setting for fiction, it was firmly associated with nostalgia for the "Old South," epitomized by Stark Young's *So Red the Rose* (1934) selling four hundred thousand copies within a month of publication.[23] SNCC's writers eschewed Confederate nostalgia, of course, emphasizing "innumerable" forms of intimidation and "many other killings and maimings... kept quiet by those whose mouths have been sealed by fear," as Minnis summarized when juxtaposing them with the city's heritage claims.[24] In immersive witness-participant fiction, this tense climate could be exposed. Into a letter that a white volunteer, Parnell, sends to her parents, Hall tucks the incident when undertaker Archie Curtis, president of the Natchez Business and Civic League, was lured to a deserted location where he and his assistant were "beaten with bull whips until they were almost unconscious."[25] It is one of three incidents Parnell shares, the other two being a violent jailing ("they beat one of the black guys so bad he had to have his eyes pushed back in") and being shot at on the Freedom House porch: "We scattered and ran for cover. Nobody was hit. The whites drove away. Some of us ran back outside and began throwing rocks at their car." The laconic way she signs off, "That is how it goes here," indicates how quotidian such incidents were.[26] By *Long George Alley*'s culminating scene, when state-sanctioned violence quells demonstrators and a black child is killed, the battleground is contextualized beyond Parnell's limited summer experience.

Natchez was the locus of four factions of the Ku Klux Klan in the 1960s. For Dick Gregory, it was "moderate [as] a white man who hangs a nigger from a low tree."[27] When Hall was there in 1965, Stephen Bingham's field reports reflected on its infamy as a weapons distribution center "receiving automatic rifles, submachine guns, and hand grenades" for Klan use. "We were not afraid to go into the most dangerous territory," Bingham confided, but he added, "[We] begin to see ourselves as possible sacrifices, horrible but perhaps necessary when a country refuses to recognize such basic wrongs within its borders."[28] In harangues against civil rights workers, the *Natchez Democrat* called them "disreputable.... disgusting... anti-American." Three weeks after President Johnson signed the Voting Rights Act, there were bombings in Natchez that Jack E. Davis asserts launched the city into "a belated era of collective black activism."[29] Mahoney and Hall puncture the notion of belatedness and the idea that a heterogeneous African American populace could be cohesive, seeing the tension of contrasting views as systemic. For the NAACP, fictionalized as the National Negro Advancement League in *Long George Alley*, young organizers are "renegades" and "Freedom House freaks": "I've witnessed them tramping up and down these hills, coercing black folks, trucking them off like cattle to register to vote... we don't push too hard... Our organization has history and tradition behind it. Over fifty years" (27–28). When the league deems the project director irresponsible, Cal stands firm, telling his elders, "Let the people decide" (29).

The Making of Activist Writers

Hall drew on his own experience as a volunteer for the character Tom Rice. Educated and successful, Rice leaves a Madison Avenue career, as Hall left a lucrative post and "enviable life" in selecting SNCC as "the most militant organization at that time."[30] The call to action in Chicago that Forman depicted in "Thin White Line" echoes in New York in Hall's characterization. Rice feels remote from forces of history "unfurling out of the South." The movement is his angel of history "hurling high-winded out of the bastions of slavery," shocking him into sensibility: "there was nothing left to do but to act" (57–58). At novel's close, "somehow he felt reborn"; he is considering staying on (213). Hall worked in a single locale but makes Cal and Cates veterans of the McComb project, situating Natchez in a continuum. The same experiences pertained across the region as Hall suggests—and as Mahoney knew intimately.

Mahoney is left in the background in SNCC histories but is brought into the foreground when the focus turns to narrative culture. He joined SNCC from Howard University, abandoning his studies like others, such as Jan Leighton Triggs. At nineteen, Mahoney was considered "one of the driving forces" behind Howard students continuing the Freedom Rides after their bus was burned in Anniston, Alabama, on May 14, 1961, with Carmichael stating, "Bill Mahoney decided we should all go South." Zinn assessed that he was the person "to whom the others looked for leadership," and Forman described him as leading the Nonviolent Action Group.[31] Mahoney was self-deprecating. Like Charles McLaurin, who inspired a mass meeting in Ruleville by confessing that he'd had to screw up his courage more than a few times before following Jim Jones on the Freedom Rides, Mahoney did not alienate readers of "Risking Life and Liberty: In Pursuit of Freedom" (1961) by presenting commitment as impossibly heroic.[32] His on-the-spot analysis of protestors distinguished motivations as political, emotional, and moral and was taught as a model in Freedom School classrooms.[33] Mahoney was jailed in Mississippi, Georgia, Alabama, and Maryland while in SNCC. He was designated Executive Committee member "at large" when helping set up the New York office in 1962 and the Washington, D.C., office in 1963 with Cynthia Washington, Cox, and Thelwell. He launched strikes and was instrumental in developing a conference on jobs and food in 1963, working closely with Cox in this and other endeavors. Their emphasis on workers' rights recalls Southern Negro Youth Congress–style organizing in previous decades, exemplified in a retreat co-organized with Cox that brought trade unionists and labor organizers into conversation with the organization, and Mahoney ensured that field secretaries were in touch with local unions.[34] In Washington, he was among organizers harnessing "the challenging proximity of the White House and Capitol Hill." Howard's location presented the Nonviolent Action Group and its members who joined SNCC with "a clear duty: to carry the southern student uprising to the very seat of national government," echoing National Negro Congress lobbying throughout the 1930s and 1940s.[35] In January 1964, Mahoney organized a rent strike, with children picketing the White House carrying placards demanding an end to "rats, roaches and rent-robbers," insisting on a community-facing agenda for change: "You talk about us—talk *with* us."[36] The importance Mahoney placed on challenging the economic impact of racism is evident from the first pages of *Black Jacob*, where bleak and unremitting poverty is depicted through a tent city of evictees, in unequal employment practices in a tobacco warehouse, and by the chronically ill poor people who Jacob Blue treats in his medical practice.

While writing *Black Jacob*, Mahoney was a member of SNCC's communications team with Cobb and Lester, and he was appointed national press relations officer when Carmichael became chairman. In 2002, Carmichael described him as "one of our casualties, having been severely damaged psychologically" and admitting that a number of other SNCC veterans were contending with similar issues.[37] That he went no further in elucidating the post-SNCC life of this activist-writer is testament to the respect and protection organizers accord one another. It is also one reason why it is essential to recover SNCC's writers. Mahoney is not spotlighted in histories and is mentioned less often as decades pass; only Doris Derby keeps him in view.[38] His activism is visible through what he published in the 1960s, culminating in this novel in 1969 that undermined the popular impression that Mississippi had a singular status as a bastion of white supremacy. He mirrored the approach SNCC took in press releases, like those urging "responsible members" of news media to "throw a spotlight" on the LCFO when it ran as a third party in 1966.[39] In order to situate Lowndes within the wider struggle, Julian Bond expressed SNCC's "fervent hope" that there would not be repetition of "Birmingham's firehoses, Selma's tear gas and mounted club-swinging policemen, Camden's electric cattle-prods, or Haynesville's shotgun blasts in the night."[40] The tent city in *Black Jacob* is representative of makeshift encampments proliferating wherever voter registrants were evicted. Sheltering the poorest of the disenfranchised, they were microcosms of community activism. A tent city struggled into view on Markham Street in Atlanta in 1966. Another, on the highway out of Greenwood, Mississippi, announced itself with a massive sign of a black fist breaking a chain shackle.[41] The "rag-tag community of canvas and tarpaper shacks" on the outskirts of Somerville in Fayette County, Tennessee, erected in 1960, was still there when Mahoney published the only civil rights novel to focus on a tent city. Therefore, this is the only novel that depicts a version of what was by 1969 "the longest sustained civil rights protest in the nation."[42] A tent city Mahoney knew well was "Freedom City" on black-owned land off Route 80 in Lowndes County. Fay Bellamy and Stokely Carmichael erected the first tents there on December 30, 1965.[43] In "Travels in the South: A Cold Night in Alabama" (1966), Mahoney recounted a trip to the site. It is a foundational text for understanding how *Black Jacob* drew on his activist experience.

SNCC's "Fire Talk"

"Travels in the South" is where Mahoney first afforded readers a glimpse into SNCC's world.[44] It begins in medias res with organizers driving at high speed from Phenix City, Alabama, to the tent city in Lowndes County to reach Selma before nightfall because snow is beginning to settle. As they travel, Mahoney muses on the "Faulknerian South" as "a façade which hides a sinister intelligence" that organizers expose as "misfits" who "live in a constant danger." He thinks about the "bravery" of black communities, their "genius" for managing and resisting segregation, about individuals like Carmichael who "personally embody the movement," and he suggests the credo propelling this group-centered essay: "[A] people's character is laid bare by the stories they tell" (145–47). Like Thelwell in "The Organizer," Mahoney distills a longer history into a single night. In the depths of winter, he shares a memory of a summer day when, in blistering heat, voter registrants wait in line outside a courthouse barred against them, surrounded by police but unprotected. Suddenly, from the white mob encircling them, a man thrusts a writhing snake into their faces. A young girl faints, and a boy grits his teeth against the attempt to force it into his mouth. When a black man knocks the angry snake to the ground, he is arrested, not his white assailant.[45] Mahoney does not inform readers that the altercation occurred in Selma in 1963 but describes it as "years past" (146). The temporal slippage suggests a year in the field equated to an age for those embedded in a war zone, fighting age-old wrongs, devoting youth to the struggle.

Among SNCC workers accompanying Mahoney are Erich (probably Eric Farnum, a white student at the University of North Carolina attached to the Alabama project in Wilcox County), Gloria Larry (House) (who joined SNCC in 1965 and initiated funding for the tent city), Carmichael, and Willie Ricks.[46] They wait on the edge of Selma before resuming in the relative safety of daylight. Their hosts are not Mahoney's focus, but their hospitality is suggested by how little they have yet how much they are willing to share. Winter cold penetrates thin walls as organizers engage in a typical conversation, in this case "fire-talk" while gathered around the sole source of heat (148). Gloria has just visited with the family of "an organizer who was killed at Tuskegee" (Sammy Younge on January 3, 1966). Erich is investigating "the murder of Daniel Colson [sic]" outside a mass meeting at Antioch Church in Wilcox County, Alabama. (David Colston Sr., thirty-two, was shot in the head by white farmer Jim Reeves on January 23, 1966. Reeves was later acquitted despite witnesses).[47] Mahoney confides that, despite their proximity to murders, "most of us refused to confront the reality of death" (147). Willie circles them distractedly, and Erich leaves the circle by exiting the room. "For some of us," Mahoney explains, "talk of those who were dead was sacrilegious" (147). Rumination on racist murder is rooted deeper in SNCC's culture when Mahoney shares another recollection. He describes an organizer criticized for admitting fear before a project director "drew a ring around death and examined it"—so that all present were "brought to the same level of understanding" of feelings that their coworker had brought to the surface (147). "Travels in the South" is an inside story, with death the subject and talk of death difficult to manage, even when feelings are shared. As soon as day breaks, the group sets off "to work with evicted sharecroppers camping just down the road" (148). When this essay was selected for *Black Fire*, the contributor bio Mahoney submitted to Neal and Baraka stated that he was completing a novel wherein his activist philosophy might be revealed may be revealed ("to myself and friends who are kindly probing me to finish the thing").[48] This indicates the belief that an organizer's sensibility could be conveyed analytically in fiction. "Travels in the South" closes where *Black Jacob* begins.

Jacob Blue for Congress

At "first dark" on Thursday evening prior to polls opening on Monday, two civil rights workers, Jesse and Curt, speed at eighty miles per hour in a truck loaded with stoves and tents.[49] Curt deems it unlikely that their candidate will show up to meet his potential voters: "That nigger's got too much to lose" he charges, "a BIG doctor like him to risk his GOOD name handing out pills in Tent City" (6). But Jesse is sure that Jacob will come. On the edge of town, having slowed down, they see flashlights shining at the truck, and Curt reaches for a pistol until he discerns that faces behind the flashlights are black. They stop and learn that more tenants have been evicted from the Nicholson plantation for trying to "regish." When an elderly lady jokes, "Dey can't put us no further than out," Jesse laughs with her, but Curt retorts, "They can put you under," turning her resilient maxim into wounding cynicism (8). Curt is loath to carry passengers since the truck is nearly full, and Jesse is forced to take him aside before he agrees. By the end of the first chapter, it is clear that friction between project director Jesse and Curt, visiting to monitor the election, is neither new nor unexpected:

> "Look, I appreciate it whenever you folks from the central committee come into town. But here, I'm running things. Anything to do with the movement, I okay. Got it?"
> "All right bro'," Curt said without the least conviction. (8-9)

The history Cobb recounts in *This Nonviolent Stuff'll Get You Killed* mirrors SNCC's fictions, where firearms offer a measure of protection and tensions exist between representatives of centralized structures and those doing fieldwork (who demand less stricture and more decision-making power). Internal disagreement, explored with economy in "The Organizer" and exposed by Smith in the excruciating circumstances of "The Machine," intensifies when a febrile political situation is sustained over a four-hundred-page novel. Curt continues to exhibit tired cynicism, and, as Jacob drives alone to tent city, Mahoney affords access to Jacob's worries: "He'd wanted to visit the colony of farmers who were being evicted because of their involvement in his campaign for some time.... [T]hey knew there would be attacks and repressions, but they hadn't planned for anything like hundreds of people losing their homes" (22). By the time the doctor leaves late that night, Curt witnesses Jacob examining each temporary resident and discovers that Jacob was born on the Nicholson plantation. In a subplot, Jacob will discover a family history that proves that he is closer to this underclass than his middle-class status and candidacy for Congress suggest.[50]

Through his doctor character, Mahoney exposes cold and unsanitary conditions in the tent city that exacerbate frostbite and impetigo. A suspected case of hepatitis drives home how vulnerable tent dwellers are to a disease that could wipe out the camp. Jacob's professional care is encapsulated in a single morning in his clinic, where he moves between treatment rooms, assessing each impoverished individual respectfully, achingly aware that his medical ministrations—even when he overlooks payment, accepts apple butter in lieu of payment, or donates one patient's payment to another less fortunate—cannot address the underlying problem of indigent health. Well-being is impossible when food and rent are the bare minimum people can afford as indentured farm laborers, exploited factory workers, or domestic workers; evictees are losing even minimal subsistence. The black doctor is represented rarely in fiction of the 1950s and 1960s South, as Forman intuited when imagining, in an unpublished short story, a young woman who resolves to become "a good Negro doctor" as her contribution to the movement.[51] The few appearances of black doctors in literature focused on the South from the Reconstruction era to the 1960s express the danger and vulnerability of their position, and in *The Fire in the Flint* (1924) NAACP's Walter White depicted a black physician and World War I veteran returning to practice in Georgia. He is lynched by the Klan. In Ralph Ellison's *Invisible Man* (1952), the man who diagnoses Mr. Norton's condition in the Golden Day Inn is a former surgeon whose license is revoked when he challenges segregation on return from World War I: "Ten men in masks drove me out from the city at midnight and beat me with whips for saving a human life."[52] Carson McCullers's Dr. Benedict Mady Copeland in *The Heart Is a Lonely Hunter* (1940) practices in a southern town and has neither recourse nor right to a specialist's treatment for the pulmonary tuberculosis that is killing him. In William Demby's *The Catacombs* (1965), the writer-protagonist is aware that the life of a friend, the single black doctor "for over ten thousand Negroes" in Alabama, constitutes a hidden story.[53] Mahoney's protagonist is equally unsung when read in historical context. John Dittmer uncovered only fifty-five doctors in Mississippi in 1960, and fifty-two of the state's eighty-two counties had no black doctor at all, the consequent ratio calculated as a single black physician for every seventeen thousand African American residents. Jacob treats organizers when "[f]ewer than a dozen local black doctors would even treat civil rights workers during the early sixties." Playwright Endesha Ida Mae Holland, a former SNCC worker, commemorated Greenwood's Dr. Aaron G. Jackson for ignoring warning shots fired into his office and continuing to treat civil rights workers.[54] Mahoney makes the role and responsibility visible but does not make Jacob a paragon of virtue. While wife Leah longs for a child, he has an affair with organizer Rachel and has a secret son. His professional care never wavers, though, and, when the city becomes a battleground, he treats the gunshot wounds of all comers. He is a more confident doctor than he is a prospective politician, and various incidents foreshadow how massive resistance to his campaign will detonate his hopes and those of the community he seeks to represent as a congressman.

While hosting a dinner at his home for friends and potential voters, Jacob is called by the sheriff "full of satanic, ironic humor" because he has arrested "one of them Communist agitators," and Jacob is expected to assess the injuries the "agitator" has sustained (63). When Jacob arrives, an obese, red-faced deputy is "giggling girlishly" while picking out letters on a typewriter—as Sam Block dramatized with equal scorn in "A Day in a Mississippi Court."[55] Jacob's queries are stonewalled as the officers laugh over spurious charges:

> "What should I put down as reason for arrest on dis warrant?" . . .
> "Trespassin', armed insurrection, indecent exposure, bigamy and resisting arrest ought to do it." (66–67)

When finally led to a too brightly lit, ice-cold cell, Jesse is curled in a corner. They have clamped him in wrist breakers and administered electric shocks to his genitals. Such violations were not the stuff of melodrama, Noel Schraufnagel's rationale for demoting *Black Jacob* to the "second rank" of "protest fictions." The melodramatic mode involves ritual dramatization of pressing of social concerns; for Robert Heilman, it "seizes upon the topics that spring up with the turns of history and consciousness," its salient discovery "the local habitation of evil."[56] Those who commit evil deeds are representative of the time, rather than universal or elemental villains, as Block conveyed even in draft because, like Mahoney, he had numerous incidents of this kind of torture on which to draw.[57] Jacob Blue believes that Jesse's "total physiognomy" has been "revolutionized in the few hours since they'd parted," but burnout underpins the question Jesse whispers in rhetorical despair:

> "Do you know what will happen if we win?"
> "What?" Jacob asked.
> "Nothing. And do you know what'll happen in this state if we lose? . . . Nothing." (68)

Jesse is tortured as a proxy for Jacob: "They both understood that he'd been spared and why" (68). Jesse's arrest is designed to teach Jacob that he is as impotent in this situation as he would be as a congressional candidate. As he rushes away, putting distance between what he has witnessed and his conscience, "[f]rom the darkening sky, the swamp, the shadows of the courthouse, the hundreds of shot, lynched, mangled, consumptive, worn-out, deceased, pickled bodies he'd examined and written 'heart attack' on the death certificate screamed at his back" (70).

Running for Congress is an effort to combat the institutional corruption that interferes with Jacob's professional ethics, but whites wield power in each facet of the city's social schemata. The local media casts doubt on his qualifications and spews propaganda that "a subversive element," Jesse and Curt, controls his campaign (143). Like actual congressman Jamie L. Whitten, Jacob's opponent John Whiteman controls spending to funnel federal funds away from African Americans, and the plantation-owning Nicholsons control the city. Mahoney depicts a single, uncharacteristic moment of doubt when corrupt judge Marshall Clayton gazes at a mural of plantation owners and slaves, and an ethical question drifts through his mind: "Were we wrong?" With a resounding "Hell no!," he shouts down his conscience (49–50). His character is comparable to federal judge Claude F. Clayton, who presided at the trial acquitting officers charged with beating Hamer, Guyot, fifteen-year-old June Johnson, Annell Ponder, Euvester Simpson, Rosemary Freeman, and James West in Winona, Mississippi, in 1963, and whose record on civil rights was comparable with hard-line segregationist judge Harold Cox.[58]

In this way, Mahoney foregrounds the intrigues and setbacks that typically accompanied political campaigns. In 1961–62, when Bob Moses ran Reverend R. L. T. Smith's campaign in Mississippi's Fourth Congressional District, Smith told *Jet*, "Even if the campaign only serves to stimulate our people to try to register and vote, we will win." Although C. B. King finished fourth in his own race, he attained nine thousand votes in a Georgia primary and even secured almost three thousand votes in all-white Dougherty County. As Julian Bond summarized, "Each electoral challenge—from local races to the MFDP challenge—served as an object lesson for strengthening black political independence."[59] Fannie Lou Hamer's symbolic attempt to make visible the extent of a possible challenge to Whitten is a subtext, and Mahoney dedicates the novel to her. But, as the white power structure wised to the strategy, there were cunning and brutal reprisals. Clifton R. Whitley Jr. and Dock Drummond, attempting to unseat Mississippi's U.S. senator James Eastland and congressman Thomas Abernethy, were overwhelmed by the vehemence of the white voting bloc, and Reverend Theodore Trammell was arrested during a boycott of white stores conspiring to withhold trade and sentenced to six months in jail, in a move to disqualify him as a candidate for Congress.[60] Charles Evers's run for Mississippi's Third Congressional District, including Natchez, was ongoing when Mahoney completed *Black Jacob* and evidence of how difficult it could be to build bridges between civil rights organizations and local leaders, with Lawrence Guyot hoping to mend Evers's rift with the MFDP by acting as campaign manager.[61] The dangers for locals who stood against the political machine were a subject of self-scrutiny in SNCC. In the aftermath of Lowndes County elections, for example, Gwen Patton's ironic line was that there was "no cloud in the sky": "Mr. Charlie" voted for "all the Black folks on his plantation... determined the clouds, the lightning, the thundering... and the victims."[62] This was the dispiriting "hard-won knowledge" of corruption witnessed firsthand that Mahoney indicted in *Black Jacob*.

As a candidate to represent his community, Jacob is concerned by its lack of cohesion, illustrated in the middle-class nostrums of so-called friends Strop, Grace, and Frailty, whose civic roles are self-protectively individualistic. Mahoney is barbed when conveying how entrepreneurial ambition could be neutralized quickly. John Frailty courts white patronage, and as he prepares for induction into a secret society, aptly named the "Liars' Club," he washes in odorless soap, selects a suit that whites will not consider "adventuresome," and shaves off a neat moustache in case it offends. The members, for whom he is a token, revile his acceptance speech as exemplary of a "pork-chop preacher or Negro college president," and he leaves the Nicholson plantation in "tears of rage" (54–55, 84–85). For Bernard Nicholson, Frailty is "the Republican nigger who swung with any white who'd pay the bill" (53, 29). He is made deputy sheriff as a sinecure and ridiculed publicly by the sheriff, and even Frailty admits, "It don't mean much" (125, 184). Journalists on the civil rights beat stifle laughter when his role is announced, and Bernard watches Frailty sweat as he tricks him out of $10,000 of community funds that he is too eager to believe will grease the palms of an unspecified "government [official]" (185, 202–3). The white power structure ensures that "the proper precautions" are taken to prevent Jacob's election (44). This violence and corruption cuts across the class division that Frailty clings to with pathetic, farcical expectancy, not least when Bernard engineers a "riot" to scare black voters by shooting at Fats, a supporter of Jacob. As Fats runs and bystanders try to protect themselves, Bernard's henchmen, Art and Al, Mahoney writes, "leveled their weapons at the huddled forms and blasted them" (199).

Jacob is not unaware of personal risk, knowing that six successive presidents of local chapters of the NAACP have been murdered (143). Even his wife will not campaign beside him. Leah is scathing: "Only psychotics worry about the welfare of the whole world like you do. You ought to worry about your own business." When Jacob counters—"Why should we be rich when everyone around us is poor?"—she calls him "crazy" (140). Among his poorest potential voters, support is precarious, at the level of individuals rather than class or mass. One man blames the movement for his eviction. Even as he literally eats from Jacob's table, he taunts organizers: "Where the hell do you get the money to run around the country causing trouble and beating the court cases against you? Bull. Black Power, Nitty-gritty. Freedom. Sheeit" (131). The man's viewpoint may not be so far removed from Jacob's own because he "would have preferred not to have worked with the strange-looking, weird-acting movement people," but they are "the only ones with useful ideas about campaign strategy" and, unlike friends and family, support him openly (93). Late in SNCC's history, the hopes that infuse Jacob's campaign are the same hopes that always underpinned SNCC's work in communities, but organizers are volatile after battling the "reign of lawlessness" over years. As Moses reminded Robert Kennedy, successive federal governments had allowed antiblack violence to continue unchecked since the 1880s, after the collapse of Reconstruction.[63]

In Mahoney's novel, Jesse invests in Jacob's campaign and fights his own despair, explaining that "serious crimes, killings and robbings have almost stopped in the ghetto ... in Belzoni and even Jackson when the movement was organized there" (129). However, as Jesse rallies people to a mass meeting, a man who cheats while shooting craps has his throat slit in a bar ("no-one seemed excited or seemed to care much"), and another is killed in Fats's pool hall, despite it being a movement place (171–72, 198–99). In a chapter titled "Piss in the Cotton," foreshadowing failure, Jesse picks cotton in an effort to persuade plantation workers to attend mass meetings, and pickers mumble apologetic aphorisms like "votin's white folk's business" (175). When whites limit voter registration to a day a month, Jesse sues the registrar; when evictions begin, he brings the FBI and nationally known leaders to the city; when they change the locations of polling stations, Jesse finds them. But armed defense is increasingly necessary, symbolized by a local man who joins the organizers, changes his name to Raz X, carries a rifle openly, and uses it. Even Jesse pulls a .38 (27, 236, 221). Energy is running low, and cynicism is building. When Jacob warns coworkers that Jesse fears he will be killed in jail, they retort,

"He has a vivid imagination. He knew what he was getting into before he got in there, anyway."
"It's that cold."
"That cold." (95)

A mass meeting Mahoney depicts in detail bitterly parodies those that ignited southern communities in the early 1960s. As civil rights workers wait in a church, one hangs his vest over a plaster saint and another flicks cigarette ash in the collection plate (214). They drape a "Freedom Now" banner over an icon of Christ. Jesse is "filled with gladness" that the church is full, but the people are "taut as piano wire," strained by the fact that "the town was burning" (214). The violence Bernard Nicholson contrives to ruin Jacob's campaign delays Jacob, and the speech Jesse makes in his stead turns on frustration, similar to that which Carver "Chico" Neblett recorded in a field report: "Natchez.... Here God is used as a gimmick to keep the black man in his place. You know 'Accept the hell that we give you here so that yours may be the kingdom of heaven'.... This is the sermon by the jack-leg preacher who is rewarded by the 'good white folks' for keeping his flock in place."[64] Ministers, including Jacob's friend Reverend Grace, who is hosting the meeting, opposed the movement until it provided a mass audience for sermons about "children wandering in the wilderness" (216). The congregation urges Jesse to "make it plain," but, as news cameras roll, journalists in the front pew are no longer transfixed, as Watters recorded in Albany in 1962, but merely "placid" (217–18). Jesse points to a figure of the crucifixion, taunting, "What's that man done for you? Has that graven image put food on your table? Given you seeds to sow? Harvested your crops?" (219). When minister and deacons rush to silence him, Jesse instructs the congregation to "come out from under this cross" and follow him outside. When he speaks again, it is in the graveyard with an armed Raz X by his side: "That Son of God hanging on the cross in that church ... has given you nothing. He's promised you everything, just as the schools and the welfare people have promised you everything.... Follow me and I promise you nothing but struggle and hate and death, a significant death. You're going to die of consumption and anemia and lynching anyway. I know what forces my speech will set in motion. But we'll not be the losers" (220). When police turn dogs, tear gas, and shotguns on the congregation, Jesse escapes through a junkyard filled with "skeletons of cars," the image that Worth Long also used as an eerie portent (221).[65] As the weekend in which the story is contained accelerates toward the polls, Jacob appears in a public service broadcast with the sheriff and Deputy Frailty that spins the violence as if instigated by the black supporters of "the radical congressional contender." He is coerced into appealing to them to cooperate with the sheriff and "good white citizens" to end violence, even though his voters are its target (223). That Jacob gains as many votes as he does is testament to the desperate need for change, especially after puzzled constituents are forced to ask: "What we goin' ta do now... [o]ur big leader gone over to the white folks' side?" (224). The original manuscript Doris Derby saved ends with Jacob losing the election and Leah telling him that she is pregnant.[66] However, in the published novel, Mahoney wove the threads of this campaign story into secular symbolism in an epilogue.

Jacob and the Angel of History

As Scott Saul points out, the story of Jacob and the angel was a "favorite movement parable" associated with biblical symbolism of a promised land and with the writings of Martin Luther King Jr.[67] Having been forced to wrestle with an unknown assailant over a long night, Jacob's opponent reveals that he is an angel, and for refusing to abandon the struggle, Jacob secures a blessing, saying, "I have seen God face to face, and my life is preserved."[68] The secular supersedes the religious symbolism for Mahoney, as it did for many other organizers, including Carmichael, Forman, and Bond.[69] In an anonymous poem that Richard H. King unearthed in the SNCC papers, Jacob is cast as a civil rights worker, and, as King reads it, God is "associated with or at least inclusive of the negative forces to be overcome." This Jacob wrestles an organizer's doubts and fears:

> And we like Jacob
> have to find ways to say to the problem
> to say to our fear
> I will not let you go.

King writes, "The poem can be read as saying that God blesses those who struggle with the obstacles or that because we struggle with all the obstacles, including God, we are blessed—not by God but by the struggle." This ambiguity, King says, emerges in lines in which Jacob is renamed "Israel,"

> which means wrestler with God,
> wrestler with life,
> wrestler with evil,
> wrestler with segregation,
> wrestler with the problem.[70]

Mahoney may not be the author, but this long poem anticipates the epilogue he added to *Black Jacob*, and his evocation of an angel of history echoes Walter Benjamin's. Benjamin wrote: "His face is turned toward the past. Where we perceive a chain of events, he sees one catastrophe, which keeps piling wreckage upon wreckage hurling it before his feet."[71] Personally, the discovery of his father's lynching by Bernard Nicholson's father stuns Jacob, but Mahoney writes, "There was no way he [Jacob] could punish him [Nicholson]. There was no way he could outrage people about the outrage" (243). Politically, he has lost the election by fewer than a thousand votes, brought down, in Jesse's scathing assessment, after the television broadcast confused black voters by suggesting that white supremacists had Jacob "in their hip pocket" (231). He cannot "make whole what has been smashed" to wrestle as a congressman with "evil... segregation... the problem," nor has his campaign been an "object lesson for strengthening black political independence."[72]

The code name given Jacob by Jesse may be "Snake Doctor," but Jacob exhibits none of Len Holt's passion, brio, or communication skills: "Within Jacob there had always been a problem of how much of himself to reveal to others, how much to make vulnerable. How much of his training could he display in an impoverished community and how much of his folksiness could he display when in the presence of entrenched white power.... When pressed to the wall, he'd changed personalities like overcoats" (115). He feels "deep humility" that people are evicted because they want to vote for him but barely talks to them about his campaign (25). When boys surround him in the tent city, offer to distribute his leaflets, and beg him to make a speech, asking "You come to make us free?," Jacob laughs but does not answer (24). He does not articulate his hopes, even to Rachel, the organizer with whom he is having an affair: "Jacob knew that there was something that he, a respected community leader, and she, a member of a revolutionary movement, had to say to one another that would be different than anything two people who had created a black child had said before; something like our child will have a history and a land to call his own; but he was silent" (111). Jacob does not communicate a vision of political power for black people. Rachel spits at his feet after he addresses constituents with the sheriff at his back and leaves town as segregationist media broadcast the "scandal" of "Jacob Blue's most unusual personal life" (242). When Leah discovers she is pregnant the day after the election, in the manuscript version he kisses her and tells her he will join her in bed, but in the novel he feels only a "sad kind of happiness" (244). In SNCC's fictions, children are rarely symbols as they so often are in literature by writers outside the movement; the urgency of "Freedom Now" and "Black Power" was not a bequest for subsequent generations to realize. Each campaign was intended to build carefully toward the next, but this one lays no groundwork for "next steps" let alone future challenges.[73]

In the epilogue, Jacob ruminates on the "evil system" in which black people are caught and held, describing the freedom struggle as "a hundred years of toughening," as "thoughts, visions, dreams and the thousands of faces he'd come to know in the town" parade through his mind. But he can imagine "no place... in life as a Black American." Now, he fears, he may be "forced to choose martyrdom," but, in "the confusion of distorted reports in the press, his choice might never be known" (242, 244–45, 235). "Surprised that the night of wrestling had not exhausted him," he feels freed from responsibility (245). When the sun rises on a new day, he leaves the house for a walk but is shot dead on his porch, "the mark of an assassin on his neck" (246). The sniper is one of Bernard Nicholson's henchmen, Art. The act is of his own volition; committed without Nicholson's knowledge, it makes Art a liability and his own death imminent. But, when Mahoney chose martyrdom for his protagonist, he suggested diminishing hope in "old movement parables."

What hope there may be is instead textured faintly in figurative lines, in two abstract paintings in Jacob's study. The first is a watercolor, "an experiment with materials," in "toned down blue and red forming simple lines that suggested a crowd of people who seemed to be hailing a leader." It is "almost representational." The second burns with red: "Concentric ellipses filled the background (or foreground depending on the interpretation) and enveloped the huddled red figure of a shawled woman" (243). Jacob gazes on both paintings, as if fused with them, immediately before he is killed on his porch. Mahoney may have read "Theses on the Philosophy of History" in Benjamin's *Illuminations* in 1968 and Benjamin's interpretation of Paul Klee's "Angelus Novus" wherein the viewer is "about to move away from something he is fixedly contemplating."[74] In my reading, in his allusions to abstract art in the epilogue, Mahoney was beginning to explore improvisatory connections between power and its symbolic representation. Here he was approaching what he anticipated in his bio note for Baraka and Neal's *Black Fire*, where he expressed his belief that his movement philosophy could be expressed in the form of a novel. The abstract expressionism suggests Norman Lewis's most delicate works. A member of SNCC's Artists' Committee, he sponsored an exhibition to raise funds for SNCC in 1963, cofounded Spiral, the group of painters who came together to commit their art to the movement, and was a labor activist and union supporter, like Mahoney. In oil paintings and sketches, Lewis depicted the freedom struggle in tiny figures congregating in meetings, marches, and processionals, suggesting mass action in *Post Mortem* (1964) and *Journey to an End* (1964), titles evoking Jacob's contemplation.[75]

Jacob's paintings are juxtaposed with the stylized mural of slaves and plantation owners on which Judge Clayton gazes with mythologized nostalgia. It recalls the massive mural installed in 1938 in Hinds County courthouse in Jackson. For Thelwell, the mural in Jackson was "so inept in technique and execution that at first flush one [was] inclined to mistake it for parody."[76] The paintings Jacob owns are speculative, presaged in the novel by a sketch he admires in Rachel's room. In the Cubist sketch, a black crowd is listening to one person who rises above them (110). Both the fictional mural and the Jackson mural sentimentalize what the freedom struggle battled to overturn, and the abstracts mount a counter-aesthetic, a political avant-garde in which the onus is on mobilizing to forge a collective consciousness for what Jacques Rancière calls "the community to come."[77]

There is doubt, pain, anger, remorse, and uncertainty over the long night that Jacob wrestles "the problem." The paintings arrest him because they are tentative, fragile. They help to strike the hesitant note on which the novel ends. The next phase of the struggle is indeterminate, imagined figuratively as figures with blurred outlines. Mahoney left a speculative aesthetic trace for readers' contemplation but returned to concrete aims once the novel was published. He traveled the country and reported to Jesse Morris and Doris Derby his progress in work "to bring about a [black] movement publishing house of the type you and I had dreamed about earlier in this decade."[78] In *Black Jacob*, Mahoney took readers back to Southwest Mississippi, where SNCC's organizing began, but it resonates as a lament for what was happening in communities there and more widely by the end of the 1960s. Readers are left in no doubt: Jacob's murder will be misrepresented in the press, and, despite how close he has come to election, he has failed to unify the black community or leave a political legacy. In Jacob, the community's only willing representative is defeated. After wrestling the angel, he is depleted, murdered, and no other character has been prefigured as a possible successor. The organizers—even Jesse—have moved on. What remains is difficult to discern, and Mahoney eschewed representing it as other than indistinct and uncertain.

Return to Natchez

In 1972, when Richard Hall turned attention back to SNCC's combative campaign in 1965, he called Natchez by name. Like Forman's "Thin White Line," *Long George Alley* balances many voices, but here twenty-two individuals are atomized, alienated from one another, contained in vignettes, 111 in total, some only a single line and others running to six pages. Only

Lester, much later, would deploy similar stream-of-consciousness techniques in *And All Our Wounds Forgiven*, with far fewer characters. Among Hall's ensemble are two bone-tired southern veterans: Cal, black, overworked and irascible, as project director; and Cates, white, broken, and estranged from his family. Volunteers, notably Parnell, white, and Rice, black, are out of step with Cal, and Solly represents how difficult it is for a veteran organizer to witness Cal's diminished trust in Cates. Locals are as eclectic as the views they hold, including representatives of the African American Business and Civic League, denizens who celebrate organizers, and others who rue their presence. Representatives of the white power structure are few but include shopkeepers as well as the sheriff, with one, George, the only sustained depiction of a white liberal across SNCC's fictions that I have discovered. Hall avoids big media events in *Long George Alley*, such as Governor Paul Johnson Jr. deploying 650 National Guardsmen to Natchez at the end of August 1965, in order to focus on two events in 1964 and 1965 that he telescopes into a single story. On August 14, 1964, the tavern next to SNCC's Freedom House in Natchez was destroyed by a bomb. As police circulated through "several hundred spectators," organizers overheard mutterings that "the wrong place" had been bombed. Project director Dorie Ladner reported hearing, "Those outside agitators are in that house. The bomb was set for that house."[79] The second historic incident was a freedom rally on August 5, 1965, to desegregate Duncan Park, the site of a Klan rally in 1964. It involved some two hundred protestors and is called Liberty Park in the novel.[80] No one died in the bombing or demonstration, but the possibility of death in such incidents was real and stark. Hall imagines what might have happened if the bomb had been set in the Freedom House, if the demonstration had resulted in death, and if a local black activist had been murdered in jail.

In 1964, Nicholas Von Hoffman tried to imagine the bomber "crawling up the hill in the rear from the railroad tracks," mistaking the bar for SNCC's headquarters.[81] Neblett suggested in a field report that the bar was bombed to intimidate an interracial couple: "Our office directed attention to the area where a white man had been living with a Negro woman for thirty years... his tavern behind was bombed."[82] The *Natchez Democrat* dismissed the bombing as a ruse to create publicity for COFO. Hall intervened by humanizing what was hidden behind headlines denying attacks like this happened.[83] The bombing of the McComb Freedom House on July 8, 1964, is folded into the story through Cal and Cates as veterans of that project: "[it] put two of our best people in the hospital. Cates was one" (80).[84] In Cates, Hall creates a composite of white organizers who lived the cause, basing him, in part, on Dennis Sweeney, who was injured in the McComb bombing alongside project director Curtis Hayes, with Sweeney receiving psychological support from Robert Coles in the aftermath.[85] A year later Cates is suffering from posttraumatic stress disorder, his breakdown scored as the escalating beat of an incessant metronome in his mind, "Like something in me walking slow. Or something slow-walking in me. I was just a beat somewhere—a simple rhythm among so many" (80). His relentless organizing, posttraumatic stress, and estrangement from his segregationist father provoke a creeping psychosis that manifests as intrusive voices, obsessive thoughts about his dead mother, and prescient images of his own death. He exhibits the hallucinatory qualities of Darl's mental collapse following his mother's death in *As I Lay Dying*: "*Canvas and rope to lower us, Mother. Case us in wood and soft grey velvet, Mother. Clothe us, cushion us, then send us back forever to the unremitting Mother*" (90). Hall's character resonates in the way peers described what happened to Dennis Sweeney. Solly observes that Cates "didn't know where he was; or part of his mind knew and the other part didn't," chiming with Sweeney "running films in his head" and "struggling with things he could not articulate." Mendy Samstein sensed that while coworkers could support Sweeney's "externalization of inner difficulty" in the moment, afterward "there was only the inner difficulty." Mary King, married to Sweeney for a while, emphasized the privacy that remains intact when casualties are explored in fiction: "Everywhere you turned in SNCC meetings, you would see bottles of Maalox... the emotional concert of that time is a private thing."[86]

Dorie Ladner, Carver Neblett, and George Greene established the Natchez Freedom House in the spring of 1963. Ladner helmed the project when Hall was one of fifteen workers in 1965, but in fiction project directors are normatively male. As I have revealed incrementally in this book, the absence of women organizers was a significant lacuna. Hall patterned elements of Cal after Greene, a native of Greenwood recruited by Sam Block when Greene was twenty years old. Greene returned to Natchez in 1965 after working in Greenwood, Ruleville, and around Southwest Mississippi. Renowned for his driving prowess, he taught staff "high-speed turns and 'fishtails' and generally how to take evasive action at high speeds."[87] Cal drives like Greene and, as "the bullet dodger," withstands danger by not talking about it. Von Hoffman observed, "[Greene] knows about Mississippi, but he can't tell about it so that it is believable to nice kids from Columbia," and Coles wrote, "I well remember what historic, scenic Natchez did to the spirit of George Greene."[88] Cal is "soul weary" and "shell-shocked," ebullient in the style of Greene but enraged by Cates and contemptuous of summer volunteers, like Rice, whom he derides as "a house niggah full of Up North airs, high talk and bullshit" (4). Across their "pigeonholes" of difference, Rice exhibits the "intellectual crap" that Cal rejects: "I know Cal's had a tough life. And I know he thinks I've had all the breaks. In some ways I have. But in other ways he has more. I've had accessories, appurtenances. I've grown like a rock grows, by accretion; he by intussusception. But there is no explaining this to him" (155). Even while reflecting on the roots of their discord, Rice uses a medical metaphor to diagnose Cal as emotionally blocked, and a natural, geological image for himself. It indicates a failure of empathy, and this is what Hall exposes and explores closely throughout the novel.

After four years in the field, continually telling himself that he is working his "last summer in the Movement," Cal seethes (5, 44). His anger wrecks relationships, most tragically with Cates, presented as Cal's mirror. Cates's thoughts echo Cal's: "I've been three summers and three winters. Beat up bad. Blowed up. Shot at. Pissed on. Spit on. Stepped on" (149). But Cal's vignettes are the only ones presented in third person, to underline the distance he maintains from others and his unwillingness to share feelings, which he suppresses to be autocratic, like his musings on his father and grandfather—"men of splendid strength" who are "muzzled" by fear for their families. A Faulknerian refrain bubbles up through his unconscious: *"The gun and rope; a razor blade and poured turpentine. Hound dogs howling in the last black woods."* This imagery also echoes for George, haunted by a lynching he witnessed as a child: "I would never be a part of that... something profound wrong with... the ways of this whole land" (17, 18, 142–3, 190, 211). Hall reminds readers that some southerners pit themselves against this history—for Cal the movement is "all he possessed," and George is tired of violence: "If there was a way to give in and still save face, I believe us whites would do it. But the civil righters keep folks pushed right up against the wall" (157). The wall presses on all characters, but some northern volunteers are naïve risk-takers (5). As Rice and Parnell rally people to demonstrate in Liberty Park, Cal watches Rice raise a middle finger when a white man points his camera. Out of Cal's sight, they veer into a field and have reckless sex, despite the danger their interracial visibility poses when "somebody can come and shoot you both."[89] Oblivious, "they collect the scattered mimeograph sheets and continue on the trail" (65).

In the 1970s, Hall did not romanticize organizers, volunteers, or the local community. For the bomber of the tavern next to the Freedom House, he conjures up a broken, mentally disturbed black trusty, Zenola, coerced by the sheriff: "Don't forget long fuse you simple sonofabitch... and run for your life" (185). After planting "boomsticks," Zenola fails to escape the blast in an intertextual echo of Stevie, the man with the mental age of a child, used to plant a terrorist bomb in Joseph Conrad's *The Secret Agent* (1907). In my view, though, Hall drew on experiential knowledge more than literary allusion. He borrows from Ed Pincus's film *Panola* (1970), a cinéma vérité portrait of a black man called Panola who has grown up in Natchez, created out of excess rushes from his and David Neuman's filming of the documentary *Black Natchez* over ten weeks in 1965. Hall patterns Zenola after Panola, who in the eponymous film is seen to be worn down; "kill or be killed" is a phrase used repeatedly in his moving, tortured soliloquy. Panola reveals that, as well as being a father to a big and growing family, he is an alcoholic and, he implies, a police informant, confiding on camera, "The only way to be free in Natchez is to make people think you are crazy." The overwhelming impression is that artifice was becoming his reality, and Pincus withdrew from circulation this cinematic exposé of the effects of racial terrorism on an individual whose private feelings had exposed him.[90] When Zenola's bomb detonates in *Long George Alley*, it destroys not only the tavern next to the Freedom House but also neighboring houses, including Zenola's own, leaving his wife Clarice and their children homeless.

Hall mapped the novel closely to the St. Catherine Street area of Natchez in which Neblett bought a house (at 119 East Franklin Street) and then fought to keep it when unable to secure an insurance policy "for obvious reasons." It was, Neblett wrote to Forman when requesting financial support, "a place for local Negro adults to express their grievances about the existing structures, a place where the local kids can write their newspaper... a place where the entire Black community can come to when they need food, and clothing."[91] Hall also depicted a brothel nearby through the tender, awkward relationship burgeoning between Cates and Aurabelle, not yet seventeen but forced to follow her mother into prostitution. She is already cynical, jaded, but is entranced by the hope Cates represents. "Just pack up and we'll leave," he tells her. "I want you for my wife" (183). While Zenola begs Cates to leave the Freedom House, he is intent on meaningful conversation, unaware there is a bomb and that Zenola has set the charge. "I'm quitting," he tells Zenola. "I'm through. Don't cry, Zenola.... You and me, brothers in blood... we ain't never before sat down and had a real talk, Zenola. This is the freedom house. A place where all people can meet and talk.... You know, I done a lot for this Movement. Suffered so's your people and mine would all have it better"

(186–87). After the bomb goes off, killing them both, two characters damaged psychologically by racism are aligned, their bodies placed side by side, and Aurabelle can only gaze on Cates and mourn lost hopes. That he dies in the midst of a one-sided conversation shows one of many fault lines in the novel's bitter commentary.

The ill treatment of Zenola by the sheriff, for whom he acts as factotum, is not as melodramatic or unrealistic as may be assumed by readers unfamiliar with civil rights history. It echoes multiple attempts to recruit black informants to act as pawns of white supremacy and task them with making violent reprisals on communities and activists. In 1963, Roosevelt Knox admitted to a federal jury how, while in prison for passing a bad check, he was coerced to beat Fannie Lou Hamer. In 1964, in Shaw, Mississippi, a young man thwarted a bombing by informing SNCC that he had been offered "$40, for pointing out the office and another of $400 for blowing it up."[92] In Hall's novel, Zenola is cleaning the jail when the sheriff fatally beats Aurabelle's cousin, Josh Thomas. The brutality is conveyed not through Zenola, who knows Josh but disassociates, "poke, poke.... slap, slap, slap... Sweep, sweep, sweep," but by the response of a black police officer, Peters, who vomits—despite two years of hardening on the force (39–40, 169). Peters is an amalgam of the four black police officers and six black auxiliaries employed following mass action in Natchez, and his is one of multiple perspectives of this text, representing feelings otherwise unexpressed.[93] Peters is alienated: "They don't know how bad *I* feel.... I wish I could tell them how it makes *me* feel. But they wouldn't understand. All they know is how *they* feel (original emphases, 155). Readers spend as much time with characters who accommodate the status quo or thwart the movement as those who support it. Clarice is contrasted with Zenola because she respects organizers—"[they] come to save us... treating us poor folk like we were important"—like B. Jacks, tough as blackjack oak and loosely based on barber and "militant" James Jackson (62).[94] They march on Duncan Park the day after the bombing, Clarice clutching a Bible and B. Jacks a gun in his pocket, both striding "proudly and resolutely" (206). Any demonstration of mass protest cannot be apprehended, Hall suggests, without examining the contradictory forces and feelings that bring demonstrators together.

The deaths of Cates, Zenola, and Josh are followed by the culminating tragedy: a police horse trampling a black child. Benjie is another Faulknerian character: his interior monologues echo Vardaman's in *As I Lay Dying*, and, like Benjy in *The Sound and Fury* (1929), his comprehension is sensory, a synesthesia in which tears are colors running like rainbows whenever his mother leaves his side (19, 22, 53, 97–98). He dies amid clamor he does not understand and is a reminder of how many children were on the front lines. Five-year-old Anthony Quinn comes to mind. The son of McComb activist Alyene Quinn had a U.S. flag wrestled from him by a highway patrolman during a demonstration on June 14, 1965.[95] SNCC's literature is haunted, not least by unsung individuals brutalized by police, usually "beyond camera range."[96] Hall captures the sort of battle that sometimes took place. Police sit poised on horses whose nervous eyes flare—"huge, dark-rimmed, excited," mirroring the "permanent passions" of glowering whites descending on demonstrators (204). When Benjie falls beneath a charging horse, he reaches for his mother, but she is "out cold": *"Where Momma in the cold ground?* The horse came back" (210). Parnell is paralyzed, frozen, in a reprise of a demonstration in Atlanta where an elderly African American man was trampled to death under horses' hooves (205). Frantic, she echoes the witness-persona in Maria Varela's poem "Crumpled Notes (Found in a Raincoat) in Selma" (1965): "What happened... to children... under hooves... that lady in the panic of hooves, bull whips and gas?"[97] Barber Peavine spends the novel worrying about violent reprisals, risk to business, a bank loan, and his home, but after telling everyone he will *not* be marching, he cannot stay away (6, 94, 101, 145). He stands on the sidelines but is mistaken for a "civilrighter" and arrested. By Hall's epilogue, no character has avoided the racial standoff in the city.[98]

If Hall's evocation of turmoil was influenced aesthetically by Faulkner for kaleidoscopic structure and constellation of characters, the language is embedded in SNCC. Volunteer Jim Kates would become a poet, literary translator, and the publisher who reissued Elizabeth Sutherland's *Letters from Mississippi* in 2000. His field report from Natchez on July 29, 1965, displays the modernist imagery Hall deploys, and a sentence in it is suggestive of the structure of Hall's novel: "So many things are beginning to move together and intertwine like paramecia under a microscope."[99] There were some 200 full-time staff and 250 volunteers by 1965, "inside the eye of an American dilemma," with SNCC like "an amoeba with pseudopods reaching out in many directions."[100] For Sutherland, by 1965, Mississippi seemed "less a battleground between good and evil" and more like "a labyrinth where none of the possible paths is a sure way out." "Amid great confusion" that summer, she discerned "an atmosphere of fragmented reality" in the vacuum created by the demise of COFO, with SNCC searching for "a grip on the future."[101] Even as it pushed in new directions, forging more urban campaigns in North and South alike, visiting Vietnam, Africa, Latin

America, and backing Julian Bond's candidacy as a Democrat in the Georgia statehouse, it was breaking down. In an impressionistic mesh of images evident in field reports and other writings, participants expressed the fear that the center could not hold.[102] Hogan muses, "For the most compelling of reasons—survival itself—the entire history of SNCC was one of doubt."[103] Hall's novel suggests how that felt in an understaffed project and a city in turmoil: clashing consciousnesses, myriad personal pressures, and near delirium propelled by exhaustion, impotence, jealousy, violence, madness, and loss. When demonstrators gather in the "incandescent broil of sun," the "milling crowd" swirls, a child dies, and Cal, unable to quit no matter how enraged and dejected he feels, begins planning the next demonstration (203).

Bill Mahoney and Richard Hall commanded large casts in wide-angled, polyphonic fictions where communities are in flux.[104] Mahoney depicted vicissitudes, fractures, and fragile hopes specific to the situation he knew in the 1960s, but the *New York Times* likened *Black Jacob* to "agit-prop books written for writer-believers in the 1930s." When political commitment is equated to agitprop, remanded to past forms even as "a new example," an activist's purchase on the experiential is diluted.[105] Only Bambara and novelist Claude Brown acknowledged the experiential in "the cautious sophisticated world of Jesse the professional organizer."[106] Brown had studied alongside Mahoney and discerned that *Black Jacob* was reality driven: "Bill Mahoney has had his body and soul in the movement for the last ten years. Now he's put it all down in the first novel I know of by a young black man who's been there and knows. It's tough, true, powerful, and furious. Which is like it is."[107] If Mahoney was entrenched in the moment, Hall's perspective is a fish-eye lens on "the sixties scudding out of slumber and spilling over the lip of its decade into all those sequestered lives," as he writes in his novel (58). He dramatizes the racial split in SNCC as "messy" and "divisive." As Sutherland explained to Forman, "We accept withdrawal rationally but not emotionally," and she worried about the distance growing between "guilty masochistic whites" and "guilt-avoiding SNCC-ers."[108] Hall's narrators are compelling, and if the sheer number leaves insufficient room for some to emerge fully as characters, what is conveyed powerfully is that none may be understood in isolation. Mahoney and Hall became writers in SNCC and because of it. It was the Rubicon they crossed and chose to fathom aesthetically. As Aldon Morris observed, the role culture plays in collective action is largely "untapped."[109] Morris made his case briefly via the narrative model produced by sociologists studying the "framing" of social movements. Represented by Francesca Polletta, Charles Marsh, and James M. Jasper, that model foregrounds subjectivity, but imagination is only implied. Polletta champions origin stories because they "shed better light on the dialogue and activities that precede the establishment of formal movement organizations."[110] Forman's "Thin White Line" and Thelwell's "Direct Action" may be understood in this light, but most of SNCC's fictions cannot. The frame needs to be widened to encompass tense campaigns, frenzied demonstrations, and the swirl of emotions in the "maniacal world" of politicking that SNCC's writers reimagine.[111]

In the final chapter, I enter an emotional environment that is more difficult to navigate or to frame as story because it involves what is purposefully hidden in a "circle of trust." It drills down into how imaginative work exhibits tender awareness of organizers damaged by the experience, like Cates. It posits an answer to the question Fay Bellamy asked, "Can one write about pain?," and another that Rice poses for Cal in Hall's *Long George Alley*: "What would he do when the war was over? What happened to people like him?" (213). It was not in the interest of the communities they served for organizers to communicate doubt, despair, or fear, but each is explored in the literature. Thelwell foreshadows battle fatigue when Peacock drinks "fiery stump likker" in an effort to calm his nerves. When a bomb explodes, he shakes violently, vomits, fights the urge "to run somewhere and hide," suffers survivor's guilt, and has a premonition: "It was a nightmare that had hovered in the back of his consciousness ever since he had joined the movement—yet he saw himself limping away from the burning town, away from the dead and maimed, people to whom he had come singing songs of freedom and rewarded with death and ashes. The organizer is always responsible."[112] Mahoney titles the chapter in which Jesse doubts despondently that the movement will make a lasting difference, "Eating at the Table in Despair." Jesse battles enervation, resumes work, then finally he limps away from a town that is burning, and Mahoney brings Peacock's nightmare to life.[113] In *Long George Alley*, Cal tries to manage his burnout with disdain: "Dumb shits, he thought. Tit-sucking summer wonders.... He remembered his old comrades and their campaigns." After four years, he feels "too tired now not to fight back... Spent. Weary. Soul weary, and barely twenty-two... four years now felt like ten, and he felt old" (3–5). While Cal and Peacock find ways to endure, Hall deploys the metaphors of a truck that no longer runs and a short-wave radio that no longer works to suggest that what was mended in the past can no longer be fixed.[114] Although Cal knows "something's wrong with him . . . something serious," he passes Cates in silence, and his diminished racial trust overwhelms Cates until he feels "wore out, finished. Like everything else round here" (35, 177). He fixates on Cal's statement: *"We hereby proclaim this a black movement. 'Anytime you want to, Pete. Just pack up and leave'"* (186). In Nicholas's *Freshwater Road*, whenever Ed Jolivette suffers a similar "curvature of the soul," he asks a question that Julius Lester endeavors to answer: "We supposed to just wake up one morning like it didn't happen?"[115] The fallout is addressed via the characters of Bobby Card and George Stone in the convulsive context of grassroots organizing in Lester's *And All Our Wounds Forgiven*. The novel gives up progressively more on each reading, about Lester's perspective on the movement by the 1990s, and more when understood as textured by his experience with SNCC.

Chapter 9

The Walking Wounded
"Who We Were and Where We Came From"

> It may be that we have done all that it was possible to do at this point in history, given who we were and where we came from.
> —Julius Lester, 1969
>
> Myth plays the same role with respect to culture as history does for intellectual life . . . culture ultimately is the medium that carries on as the basis of any struggle. . . . [The] King myth is only an aspect of a story and SNCC is another aspect of that story.
> —Clayborne Carson, 1988
>
> [W]e were so young to have been exposed to so much death and so much violence and some people . . . we call our walking wounded, they didn't survive it intact . . . they were the casualties of the movement, and we don't talk about them enough.
> —Joyce Ladner, 2011

In the visual arts, a "reserve" is a space on a canvas an artist leaves empty because what it should contain has "not yet come fully into being."[1] It is a gesture toward something speculative or deferred, not because it lacks aesthetic or dramatic value but because it is difficult to manage or may never be realized as Mahoney suggests in *Black Jacob*'s epilogue. Burnout, or battle fatigue, is one such subject and indicates the limits of an external observer's ability to understand or interpret. If the naming of casualties risks breaching the privacy of peers by subjecting them to forensic personal intrusion, emphasizing psychological damage also risks detracting from facets of SNCC's history that comprise a useable past for new generations of activists. Nevertheless, on SNCC's fiftieth anniversary, Chuck McDew acknowledged "the high price paid by individuals" and "the effects of post-traumatic syndrome that developed while fighting the terrorism visited upon the African American community in these United States."[2] Dittmer devotes a chapter of *Local People* to interpreting burnout and trauma, and Payne traces "the demoralization of the movement," but the sources where it is mined by organizers are primarily literary.[3]

An exception is Charles Sherrod's moving disquisition on "hard-won survival" requiring continual management:

We are messed up. All of us. I can't forget all the things that have happened to me. I forgive. I can forgive. I can say I'm not holding this in my heart against anybody. I wouldn't hurt anybody because of the wrong that they've done me all my life. But, I've got to accept that there's something wrong inside me that hurts—that's suffering, that begs for release. But I'm not going to have it released in front of you to hurt you.

Some of these things I've got to deal with for the rest of my life. Things that white people have done to me. Things that they've said to me face to face, the beatings that I've taken, the jailings I've taken in five states. All of this is inside me. I can't just put it aside but I can decide who I want to be. Despite all the hurt I have, I'm not going to hurt another brother.[4]

In the safer space of fiction, Julius Lester mined what Sherrod could not put aside, discloses but does not pursue. Into a novel dedicated to diagnosis and triage, he decanted the emotional overload Robert Coles cataloged as exhaustion, anger, depression, despair, grief, and guilt—and guilt's psychological counterpart, blame. Lester's *And All Our Wounds Forgiven* is a story that is difficult to tell but necessary to impart. It opens with an admission that the real story is not necessarily "the one we recall," and "rarely is it the one we tell" (1). This inside story is an intimate elegy haunted by suffering, with grassroots organizers distinguished painfully from a national personality whose commitment is lived differently in the media's spotlight.

Lester graduated from Fisk University in 1960 and was close to the organization as a musicologist and singer of freedom songs, participant in Freedom Summer, and roving photographer before heading SNCC Photo— the organization's photography department—in 1966. In the 1960s, in Lester's *And All Our Wounds Forgiven*, his characters belong to the Southern Committee for Racial Justice (SCRJ), a fictionalization of SNCC, but the moment of authorial contemplation is 1993, the time of writing. Andrea Marshall, widow of the assassinated head of SCRJ, is hospitalized in Nashville. As she lies dying, she is visited by veteran black southern organizer Robert (Bobby) Card, who drops out of Fisk University in 1961 to follow John Calvin "Cal" Marshall into the movement as his acolyte. Andrea's other visitor is white, Lisa (Phelps) Adams, an exchange student at Fisk and Marshall's secretarial assistant, with whom he pursues a seven-year affair and in whose arms he dies in Atlanta in 1969. Lisa has failed to pass on Marshall's dying words, "Tell Andrea that I always loved her," because when he makes Andrea part of his final moment her heart freezes (211– 12). A cerebral hemorrhage that renders Andrea unable to speak is a cruel plot device through which Lester ensures that Lisa and Bobby feel safe to expiate fierce, congealed emotions, using Andrea as her husband's proxy in the days before she dies.[5]

Marshall is afforded monologic control over a posthumous narration, suggesting that "the movement" may be comfortably encased in the past lives of charismatic personalities if theirs is the prevailing story (2). His narration's lowercasing suggests that his version of events is ancillary in this novel: "although i am integral to it, i am not sure i know even what the story is as neither my life nor my death constitutes *the* story" (1, original emphasis). Marshall is Lester's vehicle for a literary-philosophical exegesis of the public role of leader and the private man behind the role, but Bobby Card's and George Stone's stories lie behind Marshall's, and fictional Shiloh, Mississippi, is the fulcrum of their stories, representing one of the movement's base camps. Bobby is a veteran of "the genesis," Sam Block's term for SNCC's creation story when fewer than twenty organizers established bulwarks in Black Belt counties, sometimes alone, as Bobby is in Shiloh before George Stone joins him. An act of torture in a jail cell, designed to inflict psychological damage, circumscribes his life, and it follows hard on the heels of the murder of a local leader to whom he is as close as family. Bobby anticipates that he may finally repair himself, with Andrea the channel through which to resolve unspoken anger and the guilt he feels over the suicide of George, in Shiloh, in 1974. Nashville is the setting but Shiloh the symbolic center, and disentangling what matters in the 1990s from what mattered in the 1960s is the problem this fiction addresses.

"History" may have "attached its strings" to Marshall, but, as Martin Luther King Jr. acknowledged repeatedly, behind him are the hidden and unsung (107).[6] On an initial reading of the novel, grassroots organizing appears to be in the background, but that is precisely how Lester appraises what is lost when field-workers are made auxiliary and become ciphers for a "movement" they embodied.[7] This is particularly true of the walking wounded.

The Walking Wounded

Organizers and those close to them are carefully generic when alluding to postmovement trauma, as when Thelwell allows that the "rollercoaster ride of political activity, a very dangerous, very intense, very heightened experience in the South, left people profoundly emotionally exhausted" and when Vincent Harding notes that "bleeding ulcers, nervous breakdowns, [and] mysterious ailments took their toll on young lives."[8] In 1964, Robert Coles was surprised to hear Martin Luther King Jr. describe burnout as "surrender." For Coles it was a "startling choice of words": "We surrender to self-pity and to spite and to morose self-preoccupation. If you want to call it depression or burnout, well, all right. If you want to call it the triumph of sin—when our goodness has been knocked out from under us, well, all right. Whatever we say or think, this is arduous duty, doing this kind of work; to live out one's idealism brings with it hazards."[9] King undertook a punishing schedule throughout 1964, culminating in his Nobel Peace Prize, while Coles remained close to the grassroots, masking the identities of the civil rights workers he counseled when anxiety, fear, and anger were no longer manageable. Coles focused on emotional truths, like one suggested by a "black civil rights worker": "It's hard to know who is really a survivor, and who is all washed up—ruined by the hate and bitterness and cynicism and plain old foolishness you run the risk of succumbing to if you work against the courthouse gang, the status quo."[10] In 1986, Sam Block recalled how he had "almost been killed by a speeding truck" in Greenwood and "beaten . . . real bad, been pushed under a car and left for dead." He paused before distilling for Joseph Sinsheimer how it felt to be marked for death. After the assassination of Medgar Evers and the first trial of Greenwood's Byron De La Beckwith for his murder, Block recalled: "The same people who were so happy to have me there and were begging [me] not to leave, were telling me that for the best of myself I should leave to protect my own life. . . . And that began to frighten me and I didn't want to die. I didn't want to die." Over the course of the Freedom Summer project, Sally Belfrage began to suffer "a constant agitation, unrest" and witnessed alarming physical manifestations of burnout in organizers. "They sometimes walked around like zombies," she writes, "never ate or slept, and fell off into some great depth in the middle of a sentence, so that you'd have to wait for them to come back from hell or the middle distance. . . . There are incipient nervous breakdowns walking all over Greenwood. One of the best left yesterday. He'd been wandering round in a trance, deteriorating every day."[11] She may have been referring to Block, and he closed on a painful summation: "It takes its toll, it destroys you." In prison in California, he described himself as "still paying" for this experience in the movement. With unusual candor, Sinsheimer considered the researcher's responsibility to individuals relied on for first-person accounts: "There are moments when I feel I am being deceitful . . . you talk about heroic acts [when] maybe you aren't telling people about all of the consequences."[12] The shift from confessional first person to an inclusive channeling of interviewers and interviewees suggests how this subject cuts across popular mythologizing.

In 2000, Mike Miller focused the issue, establishing the Walking Wounded network, writing, "We feel a debt to those of us who have specific problems that can be addressed by an effective support community." Miller was determinedly inclusive, seeking to "reach out to those who are isolated and bring them into the community we once knew. Some of us are the walking wounded, suffering the most dramatic effects of post-traumatic stress syndrome. This is manifested in addictions of various kinds, homelessness, mental illness and other problems. But all of us are wounded in one way or another from that experience."[13] Gut-twisting anguish is described synoptically in some of the letters Elizabeth Sutherland anthologized and in interviews with volunteers that Mary Rothschild threaded through *A Case of Black and White* (1982), but Rothschild admitted that what was impossible for her to convey was "the throbbing pain" she detected in many interviewees.[14] Volunteers who spent a finite period attached to a project might be able to draw boundaries around feelings concentrated in a single summer and locale, as Celeste does in *Freshwater Road*, and Parnell in *Long George Alley* when "the whole summer of frustrations and disappointments" converges in the final demonstration.[15] But the inner torment organizers could suffer—over years rather than weeks—was pervasive, diffuse. Hall layers it into stream-of-consciousness vignettes; Lester renders it a threnody for lost youth and idealism, exploring the difficulty of withstanding mind-breaking experiences. Lester's Bobby Card is rudderless, alone "on a river of no return," eschewing home and family as if impositions. After Bobby stops being an organizer, he perches precariously in his life, and George too is unable to surmount a defining moment of personal history despite anchoring himself in marriage and community.

In Shiloh

In the novel, Lester unearths a harrowing irony: "I cannot think of anyone in this country who lived in constant relationship to death like those of us who sought to make America whole and broke ourselves into pieces instead" (190). That he puts these words into Lisa's mouth reinforces the critique he folds into *And All Our Wounds Forgiven* because Lisa equates the movement to Marshall, distinguishing him from "the average civil rights worker, someone working in a small town in Alabama or Mississippi" (190). She satisfies herself that the "average" civil rights worker—which Lester ensures is obviously an oxymoron—retains the capacity to enjoy life, but she opines, "Imagine that you are John Calvin Marshall. Where do you go when you want to be reminded of joy?" (191). Lisa believes that Marshall suffers exceptionally. If, as readers, we give precedence to Marshall's story and rely on Lisa who privileges him over others, we miss how Lester renders it a metanarrative and clouds it in doubt. To the extent that Marshall takes a moral inventory of his life, he pays attention to his relationships with Andrea and Lisa, but Bobby barely figures, despite Andrea describing him as "the son she and John Calvin had not had," and he overlooks George entirely (133). In such an intimate novel with so few characters, all of whom are interlinked, sins of omission are conspicuous.

As fictionalized, Shiloh echoes Liberty in Amite County and the brutal, tragic repercussions of voter registration activity that led to the murders there of Herbert Lee and Louis Allen in September 1961 and January 1964.[16] In Lester's novel, Charlie Montgomery's murder is carried out by Jeb Lincoln, in precisely the way E. H. Hurst shot his childhood friend Lee. For Emilye Crosby, it was "the deadliest attack in southwest Mississippi," openly carried out by a state legislator. The movement "stopped... cold" for a while, as Moses recalled, because it revealed to organizers "the base of the iceberg most submerged beneath the ocean of terror."[17] In Lester's novel, Marshall's conception is very different. When Bobby tries to tell him what it feels like "to see the brains of someone you love spilling from the skull and into the dust," Lester makes Marshall's response so emotionally limited as to be offensive, and, "for the first time, Bobby wondered what he was doing and why" (111). Mr. Montgomery has been Bobby's "home in Shiloh," but Bobby is told, "He's not going to be the last one to die.... You have to get used to it." The clipped statement is followed by lofty rhetoric: "The price of freedom is death." Bobby is stunned by the realization that Marshall is "deaf to his pain" because "the cry of a people was easier to respond to than the tears from one pair of eyes" (104, 111). Of all the wounds that may be forgiven, this laceration is deep. It echoes Jerome Smith's failed attempt to explain to Attorney General Robert Kennedy what civil rights workers in CORE and SNCC and black communities in places like Shiloh were enduring. Kennedy dismissed him with an axiom, "We've all had hard times."[18]

And All Our Wounds Forgiven is attuned to organizers, what they lived and what they know. After driving from Shiloh to Nashville, some seven hours on the road, Bobby has to prise Marshall away from new acolytes who dismiss Bobby "as someone to be tolerated but only because he did the work necessary so that more important work could take place, like getting [Marshall's] picture on the cover of *Time* and having him interviewed by Mike Wallace" (109–10). Lester differentiates Bobby from these "intelligences" who feed on the movement (111). On previous visits Bobby makes, Marshall "was not so famous yet that he did not have time to sit around the kitchen table late at night... and in the talking, learn" (106). Now the sphere Bobby occupies is a satellite to the real work, and he is one of the "tired old-young men" Tracy Sugarman watched orienting volunteers, and that Mahoney and Hall depict in Jesse, Cal, and Cates.[19] Andrea opens her arms to Bobby as he sobs, but it is Charlie Montgomery's widow who warns him that survivor's guilt will be the death of him in Shiloh if he cannot absolve himself of blame.

When Ezekiel Whitson comes forward, he is modeled on the real Louis Allen, who was forced to lie that Hurst had killed Lee in self-defense but was subsequently prepared to testify to the murder. Like Allen, Whitson is left unprotected by the FBI, and in dramatizing his death via a firebombing rather than a shooting, Lester referenced a warning issued when the home of one of Allen's employees, Leo McKnight, was bombed on February 21, 1963. (McKnight's wife, pregnant daughter, and son-in-law all perished.) After Whitson's home is firebombed, Bobby can only stare at Whitson's body, "black as charred wood" (114). His reaction to the murders of brave men is to lose himself in drink and recklessly seek his own death: "He did everything he knew to force somebody to use one of those bullets" (111). In 1961, SNCC workers were beaten in Liberty for taking registrants to the courthouse. In the novel, Bobby is knocked unconscious, and at night, warning shots fired through windows interrupt his sleep. That Bobby persists, with the resilience Block demonstrated in Greenwood, is the tipping point for Sheriff Jebediah Simpson, who tricks Bobby into a position where, believing himself brave, he is demeaned, despises himself, and loses respect for himself and others.

Inviting Bobby to join him in the jail to discuss the situation in Shiloh, Simpson maneuvers him into a cell, where he is tortured. Sex between Marshall and Lisa is depicted graphically, but Bobby's rape by the sheriff and two African American prisoners is described sensitively. The sheriff runs a knife up and down Bobby's penis until he is aroused against his will and forces the men to perform oral sex. Bobby conceives of his body as a vehicle for protest and resists, so when his body reacts despite this, his faith in himself, the movement, and the survival of both is shaken to the core. Lester avoids abstracting "the black body."[20] In 1989, he philosophized, "The body is an organism with an intense awareness of itself. It knows when its existence is being threatened, even when the mind claims there is nothing to worry about." His context was precise, Mississippi in 1964: "At night my mind would tell me that the house I was sleeping in might be bombed... but it would add blithely, 'Everybody has to die sometime.' My body, trembling with incredulity, would... refuse to fall asleep."[21] The inability to sleep and the need to function while sleep deprived was a persistent problem for organizers. In 2013, Bernard Lafayette admitted, "Even to this day I sleep lightly after years of deliberate practice. It's a stress that has never left."[22] In Lester's *And All Our Wounds Forgiven*, Bobby is tortured in February 1962 and afterward barely sleeps, unless alcohol renders him unconscious, but he stands his ground alone. Marshall does not send George to Shiloh until the spring of 1963.

It is Christmas Eve in 1965 when Bobby conspires with George to murder Sheriff Simpson and Jeb Lincoln. The last straw is the murder of Mr. Howard on the courthouse steps. In Bobby's words,

> He was a tiny old man, wearing the overalls of a sharecropper, overalls that had been washed so often in lye soap, they were blotchy with white spots. I saw the single bullet hole in his head, the blood congealing around it, and the flies settling. . . .
>
> Mr. Howard probably saved our lives by getting killed first. Take that thought to bed with you at night.
>
> I willed myself not to think, not to feel. I looked at Sheriff Simpson and didn't nod or speak... I stooped down and lifted the body in my arms (146).

Bobby's rage breaks through the funeral. He derides the Twenty-third Psalm, yelling, "Bullshit! Wasn't nobody on them steps with Mr. Howard.... The Lord was a shepherd all right, driving his sheep to the slaughter," echoing Jesse's frustrated denunciation of religion in Mahoney's *Black Jacob* (147). The killing mission is couched as a necessary evil for overcoming Bobby's wish for death, an inverted morality linked to sanity and survival: "How could Negroes be free until we made white people as afraid of us as we were of them?" (151). Lester scrutinized Camus's existential and ethical conundrum according to which victims must ensure they do not become executioners. When he is unable to kill the perpetrators of heinous crimes, Bobby breaks down. Marshall acts by dispatching Lisa to drive him to a psychiatric hospital in New York but abstractedly makes him symbolic of "the madness white America will not take responsibility for" (194). "I've always known that to awaken the Negro to take action against the evil stifling him would also mean rousing the Negro's own evil," Marshall intones, restating not only Nietzsche and Camus but also King's explanation of burnout to Coles—in one iteration as "the triumph of sin" (193).

Lester makes clear that, in having to initiate a SNCC base camp without a sustaining culture, Bobby has borne more than should have been expected of him. In this Lester individuates a question SNCC asked of itself more broadly: "Once you got a beachhead ... could you actually survive?"[23] The eighth of thirteen children in a sharecropping family, Bobby survives poverty and is accepted into Fisk despite his earlier schooling being interrupted by the timetable of the cotton field. The decision to leave after one year to follow Marshall and "face down death" leaves him dependent on his own resources (151). When Bobby asks Marshall how to organize, Marshall replies ruefully, "We're all new at this civil rights stuff." The only advice he imparts institutes SNCC's community-facing model, but to a worried freshman without mentor or coworkers, it is merely a platitude: "You talk to people and you listen. When it comes time to do, either they or you will know what" (100). Not to know or not to act is to fail Marshall.

"Shiloh" may be the prophetic name for the Messiah, and Marshall is described as a messiah and "The Savior" hopefully and derisively in turn, but "the one sent out" to the novel's Golgotha is Bobby (55, 68). The novel is devoid of further biblical reference except for a mention of "the valley of the shadow of death."[24] Marshall does not visit Shiloh until Bobby is hospitalized in New York. He goes to apologize to Sheriff Simpson and Jeb Lincoln "that two people who work for me had wanted to kill them" as if he will be exculpated and "free to grieve without guilt" (209). Whether grieving for Bobby or "a subterranean stream of racial chauvinism" he believes is seeping into the movement is left unclear, but Marshall diagnoses Bobby's trauma as a flow in a "subterranean stream" that "once there ... would drown us all" (161, 193). Marshall's visit is aborted. When he knocks at the door of Lincoln's farmhouse, Lincoln's wife hurries Marshall back to his car, frightened that her husband will kill him, and he allows her. He visits neither the sheriff nor George, on whose behalf he would have apologized to the sheriff, but turns back to the highway and drives away. That this scene takes place on New Year's Day suggests a resolution recanted. Marshall endangers himself but takes no account of the repercussions for George.

It is Bobby who enfolds George's story into his own, taking responsibility for his death when, a decade after their botched assassination attempt, George shoots himself in the head, having parked his car where he and Bobby waited to ambush the two men forming the power axis in Shiloh. George is a victim of his hatred of whites if read according to Lisa's account: "I never liked George. He was the first black I ever met who didn't distinguish between those who were on his side and those who weren't. He hated white people and he hated me" (192). Lisa reduces George's feelings to racial chauvinism, as Marshall abstracts individuals no longer able to subscribe to nonviolence as "anger extravasated" (193). If read according to Bobby, who loves him, George is caught and held in the moment when he proves himself willing to kill and learns that Bobby is not. Despite a loving marriage and significant community role, he cannot get past it. The trauma at the novel's heart is hidden at the grassroots and so remains a mystery to Lisa. Having been sent to "get Bobby out of the South as quickly as possible," she asks George why. His reply epitomizes the circle of trust, "If [Bobby] wants you to know, he'll tell you." Failing to respect that, when George asks whether Marshall has sent her, she is hurt and shoots back, "If I want you to know, I'll tell you" (191-92). Her role sets her apart from organizers, like Kathy who she only pretends to recognize in 1993 and wonders, even then, if because Kathy is black she resents her for being white. Kathy loves Bobby, and they have a daughter, Adisa, but she is an "average" civil rights worker, and Lisa underlines her distance by displaying the specialness that she judges Kathy will resent her for as "Cal's girl Friday" (168).

Throughout the journey to "deposit" Bobby in New York, he is silent; it seems to Lisa he "never even blink[s] his eyes" (193). The novel turns on understanding that "who is seeing determines what is seen" (1). In an essay in *Falling Pieces of a Broken Sky*, Lester describes witnessing as imposing "the responsibility to know that we are seeing all that is there ... that what we are seeing is true."[25] Only George and Bobby are able to tell this story "like it is," but they are "imprisoned in the silence of knowledge unspoken" (114). What is subsumed prefigures Bobby's breakdown and George's suicide. When Marshall observes, "The measure of our lives is found in how we live with history behind the doors and walls of our homes," he speaks as a public figure contemplating a private life (123). In my reading, the measure Lester takes of his characters is not the same as Marshall's: he locates rank-and-file organizers as equal to the most visible leaders, as Zinn did borrowing a metaphor from Moses, who described the movement as an ocean and Martin Luther King Jr. as one of many waves.[26]

What Cannot Be Known

Lester posits that movement protagonists may never be fully understood because what they know may never be divulged. Lisa owns a recording of the final speech Marshall makes before he is murdered, a speech that is rumored to have been "strange" and "incoherent" (199). She withholds material evidence that would end speculation, just as she withholds from Andrea her husband's dying words for a quarter of a century. When historians and journalists seek Lisa out "with their tape recorders and notepads and smiles," she gives nothing away. "Do they think I will tell them the truth simply because they want to know?" she asks rhetorically. "And what makes them think they would recognize truth? What makes them think they have the capacity to understand and describe Cal?" (180). Lisa is disdainful of her "obligation to history": "I read their books and I underline this and that and write angry rebuttals in the margins but I will not talk to them and I will not write my own book" (180). The only thing she is certain of is that Marshall would never leave Andrea, and when Bobby shares Andrea's diaries before publication, Lisa discovers that Marshall confided his thoughts and feelings to his wife, while she cannot recollect similar conversations in which Marshall confided to her. Sex dominates her recollections, as it does Marshall's. She may be shoring up a fantasy: "I am not sure that any of what I've written about me and Cal is true... shared experience or imagined" (183). Marshall is "the central experience" of her life, yet she cannot know whether their affair has been purely physical: "I have wondered if the real work of the civil rights movement was not interracial sex" (73, 71). Lisa finally allows herself to contemplate, "Maybe that is why I am silent with his biographers. I have nothing to say" (185). In a letter she writes ostensibly to her husband but really to herself, she wraps her individual responsibility to the truth in generic pronouns: "Those of us who remember 'then' have an obligation to it. It isn't right that white people in the South walk around as if segregation never happened. How dare they act as if they don't need to remember what southern blacks can never forget. That is the sin—to live as if you have no responsibility for the pain of others" (166). She separates Andrea from her responsibility to remember "the pain of others" because "then" and "now" correlate superficially to the past and present moments of atonement.

Andrea is the repository for what is difficult for Marshall to manage long before she becomes the vehicle for Bobby and Lisa. When the 1964 Civil Rights Act is signed, Marshall attends the event at the White House, as King did. In Montgomery, where SNCC was demonstrating, Lyndon Johnson's words felt like "tinkling, empty symbols."[27] Lester has Marshall ruminate on the deaths that preceded its signing, but this is in private, to Andrea. Only to her does he acknowledge the movement's casualties: "i asked her to remember, and i started to list the names of all those who had been murdered. i listed the names of those civil rights workers we knew who had spent one day too many in a mississippi, alabama, louisiana or georgia small town who were now becoming alcoholics, who abused women, who burst into tears for no apparent reason. death had claimed their souls but, as a cruel joke, decided to leave their bodies behind" (102). In different ways, Lisa and Bobby cleave to the ressentiment they feel toward Marshall and hurt others: Andrea, Lisa's husband, Bobby's partners Amy (white) and Kathy (black), his daughter Adisa, and countless young white women Bobby uses when pursuing redundant, angry sex while bloated on drugs to numb his pain. Ressentiment is neither anger nor hostility, although Bobby exercises both, but "a long-term, seething deep-rooted negative feeling toward those whom one feels unjustly have power or an advantage over one's life."[28] Their refusal over many years to assign any blame to Marshall for exerting power over them contributes to their leading lackluster lives: Bobby slumps, and Lisa skis.

The possibility of forgiveness lies within each of the characters, but Lisa's refusal to grant her lover's dying wish betrays them both. Lisa visits Andrea often over the ten days she lies in the hospital, but she talks of her affair with Marshall and continues to withhold his message until the day Andrea dies. Andrea is used as the ultimate silent confessional, and Bobby tells Lisa, "I talked to her too, after you gave me the idea. I told her things I had never said aloud to anyone. I don't think I could've done it if I had really believed she was listening" (226). Lester makes it clear that Andrea hears every word but that not everything is worth hearing. Bobby rubs salt in Andrea's wounds when he relays Lisa's words about where the colored waiting room used to be in Nashville's Union Station, telling Andrea melodramatically, "The massive granite stones of that building are awash with shame but only she and I knew." Older than either of them and a Nashville resident as neither of them are, Andrea does not need to be told about segregation. She stops listening: "After all these years, she didn't want to hear, yet again, about Lisa's ability to feel the pain of black people" (136–37). Not all stories are necessary to tell, and some carry more important meanings than others. This is an important lesson that Lester tucks into *And All Our Wounds Forgiven* too.

In 1994, Lester published a sharper critique in this self-consciously subjective historical novel than has been acknowledged. Its title determined the emphasis that critical readings gave to forgiveness.[29] In my analysis now, the title holds as much irony as readers are willing to let it bear. In 1999, I read *And All Our Wounds Forgiven* alongside Charles Johnson's *Dreamer* (1998) for complementary representations of a Martin Luther

King Jr. type of character, emphasizing "the brief, turbulent, charismatic life" of Marshall, whose proximity to King has been the primary interest of literary critics since. I saw the dominant metaphor as doubling, through the distinction that Lester strikes between Cal, the private man, and Marshall, the icon. This is configured in late-night telephone calls aligning Marshall with Lyndon B. Johnson in a secret relationship and shared ethic until the war in Vietnam divides them (215). The doubling metaphor is most pronounced when Bobby refuses to answer to anything other than "Card" once his youthful idealism is destroyed; Card is the damaged, angry cipher that comes into being in the jail after Bobby's body is wrested from his control and abused, a carapace to protect himself from coming undone. I failed to see in my first reading how thoroughly informed by SNCC Lester's organizer characters are, with George's behavior mirroring Bobby's to a degree: while George stays in place, facing daily what Bobby runs so far to escape, neither can manage the past after they part ways.

Paul Tewkesbury, in the most perceptive essay about the novel to date, asserts, "Lester refuses to portray Marshall as a martyr."[30] As a professor of philosophy, Marshall is disassociated from religion, and Tewkesbury sheds new light when positing that in replacing King with a secular character, "the movement in the novel becomes secular" when Lester "reframes" King's religious arguments to reveal "their inherent weaknesses."[31] Now, having dug deeply into SNCC's cultural production, it is clear to me that Marshall is the subject of criticism as much as he is the subject of forgiveness, not only because he epitomizes the image of charismatic leadership with which SNCC wrestled but also because, by abstracting grassroots organizing from the movement's primary concerns, he fails Bobby and George, "the two people who worked for me" (209). Marshall may be a "philosopher-savior" (25), but he resonates with the "paradoxes of King historiography" that Carson has identified, and more astringently in the version of King that Taylor Branch has described as "blithely philosophical." Branch wrote of King, "He had traveled halfway around the world to wrestle with obscure Gandhian conundrums, and declared countless times that he was prepared to die for his beliefs, but he had never been quite willing to follow his thoughts outside the relative safety of oratory." When pressed by Diane Nash, Paul Brooks, and other students to join the Freedom Rides, the SCLC believed King too valuable to risk, and he reportedly told students, "I think I should choose the time and place of my Golgotha." It was an identification with Christ against which most recoiled and, for some, an early betrayal made acute at a subsequent press conference where King stated, "Freedom Riders must develop the quiet courage of dying for a cause."[32] In Marshall, Lester dramatized a concern that Jimmy Garrett summarized in 1965: "Leaders can go before the press and project a 'good image' to the nation and to the world. But after a while the leaders can only talk to the press and not with the people. They can only talk about problems as they see them—not as the people see them. And they can't see the problems anymore because they are always in news conferences, 'high level' meetings or negotiations. So leaders speak on issues many times which do not relate to the needs of the people."[33] King admitted how difficult it was to accept "the role of symbolism" even as he pursued to his death what it could garner for the movement, and Lester was sympathetic to the responsibility of the role: "He is free now and I'm glad. He suffered long enough."[34] Lester was at Fisk when he first heard King deliver a speech.[35] In 1970, he asserted that he had slept through the address from "the end of the first melodious paragraph," tuning back in "to hear him talking about three kinds of love," only to slumber again. He observed wryly, "He and I were on totally different wavelengths of love." When I first examined *And All Our Wounds Forgiven*, I went straight to Lester's most polemical work, *Look Out Whitey! Black Power's Gon' Get Your Mama!*, recalling the biting rhetorical question through which he signaled the failure of nonviolence as a strategy: "What is love supposed to do? Wrap the bullet in a warm embrace? Caress the cattle prod?"[36] I held that Lester turned *agape* into *ethos*, and his portrayal of interracial sex was striking because held back in other works, with Marshall a rare representation of emotional vulnerability.[37] I noted how Lester "plumbs the depths of civil rights pain" in Bobby but not in his quiet, contemplative essay "The Martin Luther King I Remember" (1970), which reads like prefatory notes toward the characterization of Marshall, nor in the "purgation" he performed of King's final speech by transforming it into a poem.[38] Cumulatively, Lester composed an extended lament while taking stock of SNCC's "ebb-tide." In 1966, he wrote:

> They still get headaches from the beatings they took while love, love, loving... they died on those highways and in those jail cells, died from trying to change the hearts of men who had none. They know, the ones who have bleeding ulcers when they're twenty-three and the ones who have to have the eye operations. They know that nothing kills a nigger like too much love.
>
> At one time black people desperately wanted to be American, to communicate with whites, to live in the Beloved Community. Now that is irrelevant. They know that it can't be until whites want it to be and it is obvious now that whites don't want it.[39]

The critique Lester mounted, here and in this novel, is rooted in Black Power principles and feelings he expiated in *Look Out, Whitey*. Alvin Poussaint judged that organizers promulgating Black Power were often "those with the oldest battle scars from the terror, demoralization, and castration which they experienced through continual direct confrontation with southern white racists."[40] SNCC's historians demonstrate how Black Power was more consistently strategic than this implies, but Lester channeled those field-workers with the oldest scars in this novel. In 1988, he felt the need to explain: "Because I can express Black anger does not mean that I am angry, and it certainly does not mean I hate white people. Because I articulate the experience of many blacks does not mean I am writing autobiographically. I have never been in jail, lived on a Mississippi plantation, picked a boll of cotton, been beaten by a policeman."[41] Nevertheless, in the same year, Lester surprised himself when overwhelmed by tears while describing to a class of 175 students the beating of Fannie Lou Hamer in the Montgomery County jail in Winona on June 9, 1963. Afterward, he wrote that the ubiquity of fear and death "lacerated the soul in ways one dared not stop to know, in ways that one could not know until a decade or two had passed."[42] In this poetic yet formal third-person phrasing of so intense a feeling, Lester pushed it away in memoir, as if less personally generated than a symptom he diagnosed in "the story of a wound that cries out," to borrow trauma theorist Cathy Caruth's parable of the wound and the voice.[43] With Maria Varela, Lester listened to Mrs. Hamer talk for hours while they recorded and edited her autobiography *To Praise Our Bridges* (1967):

> The State Highway patrolmen came and carried me out of the cell into another cell where there were two Negro prisoners. The patrolman gave the first Negro a long blackjack that was heavy. It was loaded with something and they had me to lay down on the bunk with my face down, and I was beat. I was beat by the first Negro til he gave out. Then the patrolman ordered the other man to take the blackjack and he began to beat. That's when I started screaming and working my feet 'cause I couldn't help it. The patrolman told the first Negro that had beat me to sit on my feet. I had to hug around the mattress to keep the sound from coming out. Finally they carried me back to my cell.[44]

She may have revealed more than they recorded on her behalf because emotions are drained from this account.[45] Lester knew that each instance of torture contains far more than is recounted in oral histories and interviews or, of course, classroom-based appraisals like his own for his students. The emotions that debilitated him in the classroom also suggest what is not examined, even in memoirs, but must be acknowledged.

As critics privileging Marshall's story, we failed to see that Lester's novel is a paean to organizers because we focused on how renowned leaders are depicted before looking to Bobby and, behind him, George. They are wounded and more easily discounted than Marshall, despite how often Marshall dismisses the messianic praise he receives or how often Lester points to his flawed humanity. In the spring of 1966, at a meeting of the SCRJ, Marshall's leadership is challenged when people rally to Bobby, the motion that whites leave the organization is carried, and it is renamed Black Revolutionary Liberators (194). Lester imbues this scene with hot feelings that characterized the difficult meeting where Carmichael was elected chairman over John Lewis. At every turn, emotions distilled from SNCC's experience penetrate the novel.

Bobby is its emotional nucleus because his story and the story he tells on George's behalf are otherwise submerged. When he finally speaks his feelings to Andrea, Bobby states, with a reasonableness controlled by irony, "Cal knew it was getting too much for me down there by myself" (144). He confesses, "I never told anyone why I cracked. Not Cal. Not even the psychiatrists. George was the only one who ever knew" (149). Despite their differences, Lester conveys that what they share as organizers includes unspoken understanding of how far beyond themselves their experience has pushed them. These are aspects of the novel that are withheld if our readings privilege the other characters. When Bobby opens up to Andrea, he addresses her as if she were Marshall: "I was too young[,] Cal. You took my love for you, my eagerness, my naïveté, my idealism. You took everything about me that I loved and I'm sorry, Cal, but youth and love and eagerness and idealism are no match for evil and hatred and violence" (151). This is the emotional center, not Lisa's confession to Andrea or the words she withholds for so long, and not Marshall's assassination or posthumous story. When Andrea decides to signal to Lisa, by opening her eyes, that she has heard Lisa deliver her husband's final words, there may be a modicum of atonement for Lisa, but there is only death for Andrea. Lisa and Bobby feel lightness, admitting to feeling "happy" because Andrea's death signifies the passing of an era and potential closure on their debilitating allegiance to Marshall (227). Lester leaves Bobby more in command of himself than Lisa is self-assured; while the novel begins with Marshall, it closes as Bobby walks away from Marshall's grave while Lisa lies "atop the grave like an unanswered prayer" (228).

Pat Watters suggested that SNCC was broken by its "personal approach to hard-core white southern racists," echoing Zinn's assessment that when white supremacist ideology hit SNCC full force, it produced "that terrible and special anguish with which youth discovers evil in the world."[46] In *And*

All Our Wounds Forgiven, Lester imaginatively reentered the emotional fallout from chronic day-to-day violence: "One would've thought he'd get used to it eventually. Not only had he not but the fear intensified, weaving itself into the fabric of the ordinary and there, like larvae, [it] ate away the innards of dignity, feeding until neither sunlight nor shade existed, feeding in tiny bites on the already fragile trust that he mattered in the scheme of things" (100–101).[47] The subject here is Bobby, but the sentiment also applies to George. That his story stands alongside Bobby's but also behind it suggests that there will always be tragedies that remain submerged in SNCC's history. A defining feature of trauma narratives, according to Cathy Caruth, is "the oscillation between a *crisis of death* and the correlative *crisis of life*: between the story of the unbearable nature of an event and the story of the unbearable nature of its survival" (original emphases). In Caruth's formulation, these stories constitute "an impossible and necessary double telling" and the "possibility of history."[48] In the 1990s, Lester's novel was a reminder that grassroots organizers were not being considered on equal memorial terms with leaders. This is clearest statement that Bobby makes, addressed to Marshall through his dying wife: "Yes, we won. Would you believe that the sheriff in Shiloh is a black man now? But, dammit, I think Mr. Montgomery and Mr. Whitson and Mr. Howard and me and George were too high a price" (152). Lester does not include Marshall in this litany. The challenge is to acknowledge the unsung others. As King wrote in "Letter from Birmingham Jail" (1963), if one day all the movement's heroes were to be recognized, awareness would follow of "the agonizing loneliness that characterizes the life of a pioneer." As Gloria House opined, "We will never know the total number of casualties in this domestic war on African Americans." She worried in 1998, "Historians continue to disregard the staggering burden these forms of violence imposed upon black communities."[49] Historians do not ignore violence, but the challenge is to find where and how casualties are acknowledged. The most powerful story in *And All Our Wounds Forgiven* is the one we failed to deduce was as important as Marshall's story in initial readings of the novel.

Julius Lester integrated the emotional toll of organizing into *And All Our Wounds Forgiven*. Through Bobby he fictionalized survivor's guilt, breakdown, suicidal thoughts, and other self-destructive feelings—including *ressentiment* of the public faces of the movement. It is not easy to discuss this, as Joyce Ladner allows: "We were so young to have been exposed to so much death and so much violence and some people[,] what we call our walking wounded, they didn't survive it intact... they were the casualties of the movement, and we don't talk about them enough."[50] Nor is it easy to find sources for what Thelwell and Moses emphasize is important: *"[T]he excavation, articulation, and legitimization of what has been ignored or misrepresented in our history."*[51] Literature is a space for this because imagination affords freedom to interpret as well as dramatize. In fiction, casualties may receive the thoughtful consideration that is their due. Without these sources, or reading them for what they reveal, the walking wounded remain screened. They have almost disappeared from view. They are not present in popular cultural representations on film or television and are obscured in commemorations of the movement's successes. What Hogan calls "the piled-up memories of white brutality [that] became unbearable" would need to be the subject of questions that are difficult for interviewers to pose and equally difficult to assess or take writerly responsibility for if they do.[52] Such questions are painful for activists to pose to themselves, let alone to field them when they are posed by others.

Occasionally there is a moment in an oral history that suggests what fiction contributes to a seam of historiography that is not easy to mine. In 2013, Thelwell volunteered to Emilye Crosby a story about Jesse Harris, a veteran of the sit-ins, Freedom Rides, and projects in Laurel, Greenwood, and McComb, who for Mary King personified the "flinty resourcefulness" of veteran organizers and "the guts of the civil rights movement." King wrote, "When I think back quietly, with my own wounds healed and with the benefit of twenty years perspective... [I wonder,] how did local staff like Jesse Harris feel?" She posed a question she did not attempt to answer, except to observe that "Jesse and the others bore the physical and psychological scars of the conflict but had no place to flee."[53] Harris dropped out, burned out, with Charles Cobb searching for him in vain. When Harris reappeared years later at a reading in Jackson, Mississippi, where Thelwell was promoting Carmichael's autobiography, Thelwell was overjoyed to see him. In response to Harris's admission that he had remained silent when people talked about the movement, Thelwell pointed him to passages where he was featured in *Ready for the Revolution*. He told Crosby that to his way of thinking the book included a "tribute to the disappeared Jesse," saying that Harris had to "leave some record in the world."[54] Resettled in Jackson, Harris became a board member of the Veterans of the Mississippi Civil Rights Movement and worked as a community activist till his death in 2015. More usually, burnout, disappearing, and finally abreaction are facts of SNCC's history that are almost completely occluded from the methods imputed to study them. Lester's novel goes some way toward ensuring that organizers damaged by the experience may be considered by readers. As Gloria House distilled, "The menace of unmitigated violence hung in the air like a heavy, suffocating humidity, but those outside the movement did not perceive it, understand it, or give it serious consideration as a crucial factor impacting every Black person's daily existence."[55]

"Memory is my subject," Lester wrote, and literature "the faithful psychic record of who and what was."[56] The inspiration for his writing life crystallized in 1964 when he paused during Freedom Summer: "It is a hot day in mid-July and, in a small town called Laurel, I stand at the edge of a vast field. A feeling comes over me and forms itself into a question: What was it like to be a slave and stand where I am standing now? What did that slave feel who stood here one hundred fifty years ago?"[57] Thirty years later, Lester returned to the same place to ask what it felt like to be a civil rights worker in the 1960s, because in the classroom he had discovered that movement history needed to include feelings he had buried. Such feelings get buried, Hogan writes, because "the stress of living in an environment of terror" remains difficult for others to grasp.[58] Lester conveyed it as an "experience of politics that would otherwise remain hidden" by conjuring feelings of profound loss. *And All Our Wounds Forgiven* is "a vast field" in which he planted those feelings firmly, dissolved "then" and "now," and suggested "a way of telling" that defies the passing of time because some moments are imperviousness to time.[59] In my reading of the novel now, SNCC's archetypal organizer character carries the weight of the most enduring parts of the story. Lester pointed readers to what lies behind "the story"—to the "circle of trust" where the walking wounded and casualties of the movement are protected. Fiction can contain the possibility of history. Here it constitutes a demand for their inclusion, recognition, and restitution.

Epilogue

SNCC was an extraordinary coalition of mostly young individuals whose alternative education in the civil rights movement South produced a body of work that contains thick descriptions of activist concerns, thought-provoking literary excavations of the practicalities and ethical quandaries of organizing, and creative evaluation of the organization's rise and fall. SNCC writers wrapped an arm around readers to draw them into communities and challenged them to see and understand why local people were their *fundis*—their true leaders. Charles Payne sensed that organizers sifted experience into an "institutionalized self-consciousness," and there is much evidence of that, but, as Chuck McDew reiterated in 2012, "We didn't want to institutionalize SNCC like the NAACP, CORE, and so on."[1] Writers share anarchic, community stories and self-consciously extemporize about emotions that were hard to manage. They intervene in debates between professional historians, overtly and presciently, by refusing to separate what happened as history from how it was experienced. Through their stories, we begin to understand more about SNCC's internal culture.

SNCC wrote so much, when even its closest observers assumed that organizers were not writers. While Watters and Cleghorn assessed that field reports "hinted truths and nuances of meaning," they concluded that SNCC "never communicated at large much of the depth of their unique experience." Carson observed that "preserving a record of their thoughts" was very much a secondary concern but that position papers and meeting minutes might enable readers "to experience political issues as SNCC workers once did."[2] He saw *The Making of Black Revolutionaries* as "the most ambitious, politically astute, and emotionally engrossing memoir to emerge from the 1960s" and an "outstanding example of engaged historical analysis."[3] The book was also Forman's attempt to channel frustrated literary ambitions and evidence that writing was a form of activism, whether couched as journalism, interpretative political history, biography, novels, plays, poetry, or short stories. "If I could describe the realities of black life," Forman wrote, "that would be a form of action. I talked with people always keeping in mind their potential story value."[4] Creative storytelling was intrinsic to the organization's cultural enterprise, and the volume and heterogeneity of narratives bears out how intricately, assiduously, and inclusively writers endeavored to communicate life in SNCC. These texts comprise its literary history.

The line separating civil rights protest from Black Power politics is fictitious, underpinned by misconceptions about the freedom struggle, as if black "radicalism" erupted suddenly in 1966. Drawing such a line, Hasan Kwame Jeffries argues, "at best minimizes and at worst overlooks important linkages between the two, making it nearly impossible to see the ways in which civil rights breathed life into Black Power."[5] The same problem is apparent if a hard distinction is made between the civil rights movement and the Black Arts Movement, especially when a consciously black activist sensibility is neither time bound nor limited to place, but diffuse, pervasive, and deeply felt. The need to represent SNCC's different significations is evident in blended "autobiographical" and "literary" modes of analysis that mine individual experience but suggest that only a polyphony of voices, beliefs, philosophies, and feelings could begin to represent such a heterogeneous organization, its shifting population, and different allegiances. As SNCC's writing developed, pseudonyms were used, composite characters became a trope, and creating large casts of characters representing many perspectives ensured that local leaders in communities were afforded the same attention as organizers supporting them.

That literature has been auxiliary to our understanding of SNCC and overlooked is not surprising. Iain Chambers identifies an "institutional fear" that leads the academy to separate "analytical discourses," including history writing, from "poetic languages," because it is tacitly agreed that historical discourse "can reside only in the restricted protocols of the former rather than also in the risks and revealing gestures of the latter."[6] This is ingrained and persistent. When David Nasaw introduced a roundtable on the role of biography, for example, he distinguished historians from other kinds of writers "differently bound by their evidence and more comfortable with random, untethered psychologizing, interior monologues, and imagined dialogues."[7] The use of "random" and "untethered"—let alone "imagined"— reflects the problem Peter Novick identified as "the substitution of neutral for evocative language" to approximate historical truths.[8] Literature offers readers nuanced understanding of political endeavor and deliberation and a richer account of it, but as Rita Felski demonstrates effectively in *The Limits of Critique* (2015), literary critics too are "ordained to read suspiciously," as if yielding to a text will betray "affective inhibition" if not wedded to a "hermeneutics of suspicion."[9] Bernice Johnson Reagon unlocked the dangers of delimitation, whether ideological, cultural, or tied to an academic discipline, with her guiding metaphor the "little barred room." Her imagery—checking everyone who enters the room and what they carry inside before barring the door—resonates for SNCC, especially once attempts to merge with the Black Panthers and forge alliances with the radical Black Liberators group in St. Louis left the few remaining veterans feeling they no longer recognized the organization.[10] Reagon's imagery is also analogous to what is lost when narrative modes are judged for utility, ranked, spliced, or negated. If imaginative sources are kept outside historiography, what they convey about dimensions of the political experience that otherwise remain hidden will continue to be overlooked.[11] J. Peter Euben comes to the same conclusion as intellectual historian Richard H. King when asserting that "literature gives voice to what the dominant forms of speech cannot, will not, or do only in antiseptic ways." He echoes Reagon when professing that literary texts "take us into rooms with psychic and political no-trespassing signs on their doors, into a real world that is both shadow and ground for the real world of political scientists."[12] SNCC writers dissolve boundaries that divorce one branch of knowledge from another at the expense of both. For SNCC's writers, the stories they tell dictate the genre in which they tell them, crafting details from experience, as recorded in field reports and communicated through journalism, and transforming both into literary texts where SNCC's history is explored subjectively in ways they could not be explored in other kinds of writing.

Some of what is left out of SNCC histories is present in its literary works, but there are still significant lacunae in the literature. For Lynne Olson unsung women were "the movement's engine," but there are no imaginative representations of African American women leading SNCC's projects, central office, or statewide operations, except where Ruby Doris Smith Robinson is commemorated in poetic elegies.[13] "The organizer" archetype is feminine only in *Blood River*, by Aneb Kgositsile (Gloria House), before Wade Gayles's *Anointed to Fly*. Peggy Dammond is textured biographically but obliquely into Kathleen Collins's "Whatever Happened to Interracial Love?" insofar as "Dolly" Raines hosted them both in 1964, but in Collins's fiction their shared experience is a launching pad for an anarchic sketch in which an imaginary summer volunteer reduces the movement to an "overwhelming realization: that she could marry *anyone*." "This," she believes, is "the ripest fruit from a summer spent picking cotton and cucumbers and taking sunbaths in Momma Dolly's chicken yard"—until "they shot holes in Momma Dolly's farm and she came home." This acerbic fiction contrasts with field reports, including a twelve-page delineation of Collins's sense of responsibility to the community.[14] Instead, in "Whatever Happened to Interracial Love?," ironies glitter, critique falls as shadow, and characters are danced quickly, sometimes cruelly, through scenarios spun beyond Collins's and Dammond's experience. Of women in SNCC, Annie Pearl Avery is "one of SNCC's legendary figures," but that is suggested only in Len Holt's Black Power story in which a feisty African American activist is a sharpshooter.[15] In 2015, Natchez began celebrating Dorie Ladner Day to honor her direction of SNCC's project there. In 2016, students at Tougaloo College made a documentary film *Well-Behaved Women Don't Make "Her-Story": The Dorie Ladner Story*.[16] In SNCC's literature, though, women organizers are an absent presence, even though their biographies contain all the drama an imaginative writer could need: Mary Lane in Greenwood, Muriel Tillinghast in Greenville and Jackson, Cynthia Washington in Bolivar County, and Joyce Barrett working closely with Charles Sherrod in Albany. However, just as there is no surrogate for Ladner in Natchez-set fictions, there is no character like Barrett in *Feelgood*. Gwen Robinson (Zoharah Simmons) codirected the Jones County project throughout Lester McKinney's time in jail, directed the Laurel project, and was instrumental in setting the direction of the Atlanta project, but she has no fictional surrogates. Jean Wiley took over from Julian Bond as head of communications when he campaigned for the Georgia legislature, Prathia Hall chaired the Finance Committee, and Fay Bellamy was a member of the Executive Committee in SNCC's final years. Peripatetic fieldworkers—Jean Wheeler Smith, Martha Prescod, Gloria Larry (House), Judy Richardson, Joyce Ladner, and many, many more organizers—have yet to find a place in imaginative literature. Despite women in SNCC publishing widely, they have not foregrounded versions of themselves as protagonists, beyond Nicholas's autobiographically inflected Celeste, who perceives herself "on the low rung" as a summer volunteer.[17] In 2017, Sonia Sanchez wrote a poem for Gloria House in which she pictured House "walking on freedom's legs" and pictured "us listening to her words ... calling all people / towards new lives," and in 2019, House was honored by a Kresge Eminent Artist Award in Detroit.[18]

In my view, SNCC's writers are self-effacing, rarely promoting their literary work or alluding to it. Bellamy edited and wrote for an internal magazine, *Aframerican News for You*, but in 1975, when she published a poem, "Being Me Is a Gas," in *Southern Exposure*, she described it as her "first crack at writing." When Cobb presented at a conference focused on art activism and social justice in 2008, he did not read his poetry or reference his writing in other genres, preferring to memorialize Hoyt Fuller and Gwendolyn Brooks. When he read aloud, he chose Reagon's words instead of his own, suggesting one of many ways in which women created an artistic culture in SNCC. When Thelwell spoke on a different panel at the same conference, he waived the moderator's introduction and made no mention of his substantial oeuvre.[19] Even in such fora, activists are rarely asked about their own writing. The "Meet the Authors" promotion at the fiftieth anniversary of SNCC's founding neglected to mention the emphasis SNCC placed on publication in the 1960s or its imaginative writing. In this sense, Bob Moses was right insofar as SNCC has written stories but not made enough of them. The organization's relationship to an African American cultural aesthetic was surfaced during its anniversary conference in the panel "SNCC and the Black Arts Movement: We Had to Change the Conversation," with A. B. Spellman, Amiri Baraka, and John O'Neal. Discussion focused on the Black Arts Movement but did not consider how organizers contributed to forging a black cultural consciousness. O'Neal shared how surprised he was by how many organizers were artists, but the observation was left hanging, except for his calling Cobb "a fine poet" and referring to Gilbert Moses as "the man in theater."[20] The conversation might have changed had the bridge between SNCC's creative output and the BAM been explored.

For some individuals, imaginative writing may have been therapeutic, cathartic for mitigating fear and frustration otherwise held in and suppressed, and thereby served its purpose in the 1960s. Casey Hayden intimates that the burden of representation on activists should not be onerous now: "We all remember the discrepancy between reality as we experienced it in the movement and what we read about that reality in print... We know that publication does not validate experience, nor do we need it for our experience to be valid."[21] This book privileges what organizers committed to print and published. It avoids the risk of privileging those writing now over others who wrote only as students and young activists. Students who began writing about activism on campus pursued it further in SNCC, while for others writing emerged in the field while working with "a dignified, proud, principled, decent people."[22] Stories may yet be written. Jim Kates, for example, returns regularly to the South seeking "backstories" because his experience in the 1960s represents "something he could never exhaust but also never quite grasp."[23] Other stories were designed for audiences, not readers, like Angeline Butler's "Voices of a Sit-in," performed in 1986 and 1987, and Endesha Mae Holland's "From the Mississippi Delta," which ran for more than two hundred performances off Broadway in 1991 and was nominated for a Pulitzer Prize.[24] John Perdew joked with Clayborne Carson about writing a book and decades later performed Curtis L. Williams's one-act play *Education of a Harvard Guy* (2006) as if his jailing in Americus in 1963 were "seconds ago." He spoke from a simple stage set of cell bars and a picket sign, while Rutha Harris punctuated his story with freedom songs. The play then inspired the memoir Perdew would publish in 2010.[25] Attorney Mitchell Zimmerman was inspired to write by his experience of defending a client on California's death row and securing a reprieve after twenty-two years. He folded into his legal thriller *Mississippi Reckoning* (2019) a story of SNCC, describing it as "a mixed work of imagination, truth, and fact" (391). He is bolder than he could have been in the 1960s in imagining a tale of vengeance, wherein a summer volunteer tasked with calling the FBI and DoJ to secure help for Chaney, Schwerner, and Goodman is racked with guilt thirty-three years later, despite having done all he could possibly have done in the moment. As a lawyer, Zimmerman's protagonist Gideon is aware of the risks he takes on setting out to become the executioner of Cecil Price, the deputy sheriff who was at center of the conspiracy to murder the three civil rights workers. Emotionally tied to SNCC, Gideon becomes equally aware, as he travels "South toward the source," that the tragedy has "too many roots," the movement a legacy, and that he risks rewriting "our history" with a "degrading" act for which a black person connected to the movement could find themselves accused (330, 324). In Price, he discovers a man who is "too hollow to stand for all the things I wanted to kill with [him]" and realizes that former comrades and the local people with whom they organized are far more freighted with meaning than his target could ever be (377). At the close, he is exploring instead how he might work with the Southern Poverty Law Center, for which Julian Bond was the first president.

When writing from the 1960s is read with texts published decades later, SNCC's corpus begins to be understood as a conceptual Freedom House, a "contact zone in which there are points of tension as well as shared understandings and trust."[26] There is evidence of a shared imaginary, with Supersnick invented out of camaraderie and Junebug Jabbo Jones rooted in collective understanding that he is "a symbol for the wisdom of common people." As O'Neal explained: "Whenever someone summed up experience in some unique way or when it was used to prevail over power, the event was cited as an example of how Junebug gets things done."[27] Writing could also be the means to explore private feelings, as it was for

Stembridge, in the way Audre Lorde described poetry as a "safe house," a "spawning ground for the most radical and daring of ideas," and a space in which to conceptualize "meaningful action," as it was for Cobb."[28] While Akinyele Umoja argued convincingly in 2003 that "scholarly and popular literature and media *re-creations* of the movement rarely emphasize the significance of armed resistance" (my emphasis), SNCC's writing in the 1960s was replete with depictions of organizers being protected by local people, armed for their defense as well as their own, and of organizers arming themselves, as Peacock does in Thelwell's "The Organizer" and Ricks and Regina do in Holt's "Defendant or Decedent."[29] Attacked, bombed, and burned, Freedom Houses were precarious but each was a "safe house for difference" within the organization, as a number of writers explore.[30] Lorde's spatial metaphor is suggestive; it resonates with the conversation Cates attempts with Zenola in *Long George Alley* and the intimate "fire-talk" Mahoney described in "Travels in the South."

In his assessment of social movements as "bundles of narratives," Gary Alan Fine suggests that civil rights groups typically "recount [the] 'adventures' of the collective," and Polletta and Murphree describe how narratives were strategic for recruitment and funding appeals, although Polletta does allow that some activists "may see personal storytelling *as* activism (original emphasis)."[31] SNCC's stories do not only fall into this pattern or conform to a logic of sociological frames or "plots." Literary activism was a core component of SNCC's culture. Storytelling afforded opportunities to explore multiple facets of grassroots organizing while avoiding the labeling intrinsic to psychological and sociological discourse, individuated self-disclosure, the generic constraints of memoir, and theoretical and solipsistic abstraction. SNCC's history was volatile, its rise and fall dramatic. Inherent in its history are various and compelling stories. In 1994, Chude Pam Allen crystallized a feeling that is fundamental to assessing what SNCC writers have contributed to civil rights movement literature:

> I lived so intensely,
> believed so absolutely,
> felt so acutely.[32]

She echoed Lester's "revolutionary notes" of 1967 and 1969, dedicated to organizers who

> care so much, so intensely, so deeply ...
> that every second of every day is
> filled with the pain of seeing what is

with the pain of knowing
what isn't.³³

We needed to recover this literature because, as Ellen Willis judged, what was missing from accounts of the 1960s was "emotional experience: the desire to live intensely... it turned our guts inside out and left us with a bone-deep sense of loss."³⁴ Literary genres bring narrative depth and dimension to the activist spirit Zinn captured in *SNCC: The New Abolitionists* rather than confirm the worries expressed after the reunion in 1987 that SNCC was romanticizing its past by affirming it. Literature is rarely sentimental or nostalgic in any wistful sense, and protectiveness is apparent only in narratives focusing on communities or on peers damaged by experiences in the 1960s.

If organizers were and are "heroes and heroines to each other," hero worship is rare.³⁵ In Kathleen Collins's short story "Conference: Parts I and II," in *Whatever Happened to Interracial Love?*, hero worship equates to a student's superficial adulation for the SNCC mystique. Collins does not hide Charlie Jones in a fictional composite. Like the real Charlie Jones, her character is a former student of Johnson C. Smith University, leads sit-ins in North Carolina, and serves thirty days on a chain gang in Rock Hill, South Carolina. When Mildred meets Jones at a National Student Association conference, he fulfills her desire to lose her virginity with "the right man," a "Freedom Rider" and "real-life Negro"; Mildred worries that her own racial identity is diminished in the "rarefied atmosphere" of her exclusive, white school. Visiting Skidmore, Jones is fêted by her white friends because "he's so good-looking, he doesn't even look like a Negro!" (62). Collins skewers all fetishization:

"It won't go in..."
"No, ma'am..."
"Not even with your green eyes..."
"No, ma'am."
"And your extra-light skin..."
"No, ma'am...:
"And your freedom riding..."
"No, ma'am..."
"I guess you're not the right person." (64)

With an economy of style and humor more sure-fire than sex, Collins conveys epigrammatically what "Gertrude Wilson" discovered on interviewing Ivanhoe Donaldson: that "one could make of him a romantic character but he will not permit it."[36] As Jones tries stoically to comply with Mildred's romantic demands, the story descends into absurdist, Cinderella-style burlesque, and its residue is that the organizer confounds the student.

There is respect for peers, of course. Collins tucked into another story a character based on Carmichael who is worrying away at the "romance" of integration, cogitating on its insidious subterfuge for the maintenance of white supremacy as "just another form of impersonation... just another form of stultification" (49). Another "quiet, diligent soul," modeled on Moses, envisions voter registration as "the politics of arithmetic"; it is, the narrator attests, "a stunningly correct analysis that will go down in defeat at the Democratic Convention in 1964, when that illustrious body turns its back on the New Math." This characterization of Moses turns on "our prophet" removing himself to Tanzania to escape the image accruing of charismatic leadership (50). Collins was prescient. On returning to the United States in 1980, Moses initiated the Algebra Project and, in 2001, explicated "New Math" for its "radical equations" to organizing in SNCC.[37] In poetry, volunteer Tim Hall celebrates project director John Love for imparting wisdom beyond that discovered through his college education while "driving through central Alabama / in the terrifying night."[38] In a community forever linked by organizing, colleagues act as muses but not in the way Collins satirized. Cobb's "Lowndes County Staff Sketches, May 31, 1966" is a poetic condensation of what an internal education project could have achieved. Courtland Cox is a "black Zapata... racing on the train tracks of his thinking / deep / beyond / what is said," and Carmichael a "hipster hero" defined by his axiom "if we come back alive / tomorrow / my day / baby." Bob Mants builds on communities, "on what they see in him and what he sees in them," teaching

> being country black
> is
> a
> proud
> thing.[39]

That Mants remained in Lowndes County from 1965 to his death in 2011, serving as county commissioner and chair of nonprofit Lowndes County Friends of the Historic Trail, confirms this early assessment. In another poem, "Most People" (1965), in which Cobb asserts that "we are gladiators all," the imagery is sharper. Peers cut each other; knowing the pain they inflict and suffer, they "fence" and "duel," but the narrator hopes that one day "there will be a time... to explain / and be understood."[40] Two decades after SNCC's demise, Wade Gayles confided,

> I had expected a well-posted sign
>
> HERE THEY ONCE WORKED
> TO CHANGE THE SOUTH
>
> or something that proved
> it was real
> we were real
> the pain was real
> the deaths were real
> and had meaning.[41]

Her poem suggests what is lost "if you forget to remember / that we have been with you."[42]

What SNCC wrote sets it apart even from writers considered the voices of the movement. In 1986, James Baldwin acknowledged that reading Thelwell's stories felt like "facing someone who has, in his hands, some crucial sections of the jigsaw puzzle of which you have in your hands some other sections."[43] If we overlook these pieces, we miss what participants add to the picture that emerges. Forman's idea that "we are all a book" speaks to collective creative endeavor, but, as he knew, there were many SNCCs, and forging a synoptic, synthetic, or panoptic history involves dexterity when some pieces will not fit together easily. For Stembridge, histories cohere "one corner at a time," and her aphorism provoked the metaphor I kept in mind while writing this book.[44] If SNCC is "a book," it coheres "in bits and pieces" and through emotional investment, as Nicholas signaled: "All These Little Pieces of Our Souls in This Thing." Into *And All Our Wounds Forgiven*, Lester tucked a salutary remark: "[Of] those us who sought to make America whole, [some of us] broke ourselves into pieces instead."[45] The pages that tell this particular story are few. Other pages may be missing and still others left uncut; the book has to remain unbound because it continues to be written retrospectively. But the rich weave of ways through which goals, campaigns, successes, and struggles are conveyed in literature is as novelistic as Julian Bond surmised, full of "romance, danger, death, personal tragedy, and federal indifference to gross civil rights violations and hostility toward SNCC's militance and political openness in the middle of a rapid transformation of relationships between southern blacks and whites."[46] His description equates to "the emotional concert of that time," and far from being irrelevant in the New Critical sense, "the life" of authors in the movement "is their voice."[47] I hope SNCC's writers will enjoy more readers now.

Notes

See bibliography for abbreviations of archival sources.

Prologue

1. Bond quoted in Paula Giddings, "Julian Bond: From Candidate to Commentator," *Encore American and Worldwide News*, January 16, 1978, 11.
2. In Baker's speech, she declared, "Negro and white students, North and South, are seeking to rid America of the scourge of racial segregation and discrimination—not only at lunch counters, but in every aspect of life." "Bigger Than a Hamburger," *Southern Patriot*, May 1960, 2.
3. Simmons, "Martin Luther King Jr. Revisited," 191–92.
4. Skepticism about SNCC is documented throughout the NAACP Papers, and in a letter to Benjamin Mays, May 19, 1960, Roy Wilkins summarized the extent of misunderstanding when writing of Bernard Lee, alleging that he made derogatory comments about the NAACP in April 1960: "He was a little boy when the NAACP was battling tooth and toenail before and during World War II to knock out Jim Crow in the armed forces and to knock out segregation in education. The irritating aspect to us [is] that these youngsters and many adults who don't know the facts assume that the NAACP has done nothing all these years and that now they come along with the fresh new and only effective method of attacking the problem." Bond and Lewis, *Gonna Sit at the Welcome Table*, 422–23.
5. Zinn in Executive Committee Minutes, April 18–19, 1964, Atlanta, 4, SNCC Papers, Library of Congress, Washington, D.C., available on microfiche: *Student Nonviolent Coordinating Committee Papers, 1959–1972* (Sanford, N.C.: Microfilming Corporation of America, 1982), hereafter SNCC. Byrum complicates the picture in *NAACP Youth and the Fight*, building on de Schweinitz's *If We Could Change the World* to unpack youth activism.
6. Shirley Sherrod makes this point in "The Emergence of Black Power," SNCC Oral Histories Conference transcript, July 9–10, 2016, 15, SNCC Critical and Oral Histories, Center for Documentary Studies, Duke (CDSD), David M. Rubenstein Library, Duke University Libraries, North Carolina.
7. Moses and Cobb, *Radical Equations*, 83. Connie Curry discovered that today's students did not know as much as she assumed about "a movement that young black people started and led ... [and] that lasted a short time but changed the country forever." Zellner and Curry, *Wrong Side of Murder Creek*, 13.
8. Steven Lawson is at the center of the debate described in his "Long Origins of the Short Civil Rights Movement."
9. Bond, foreword to Forman, *Making of Black Revolutionaries*, xi.
10. Steedman, "Something She Called a Fever," 1164.
11. Mark McGurl, *Program Era*, xi; O'Connor quoted in Margaret Turner, "Visit to Flannery O'Connor Proves a Novel Experience," *Atlanta Journal Constitution*, May 29, 1960.

12. Mahoney's untitled manuscript is not labeled. Box 4, Doris Derby Papers (DD), Manuscript, Archives, and Rare Books Library, Emory University, Atlanta.

13. "Ekwueme" means "he says, he does" in Igbo, and the name was given to Thelwell by Chinua Achebe.

14. For example, Cobb's poetry collection *In the Furrows of the World* (1967) is held at the Beinecke Rare Book and Manuscript Library at Yale University and other libraries but is also now accessible at http://www.crmvet.org/poetry/pcobb_furrows-r5.pdf.

15. The website created by Veterans of the Southern Freedom Movement (1951–1968) is at http://www.crmvet.org. SNCC's Legacy Project (http://www.sncclegacyproject.org) includes in its mission statement "the archiving of SNCC documents digitally to make them easily available for use; encouraging and assisting in the development of books and other media by SNCC's veterans with the idea of having the stories and interpretation of SNCC's work told by its veterans."

16. O'Neal, "Road through the Wilderness," 100.

Introduction. "All of Us Are a Book"

Epigraphs are from Forman, *Making of Black Revolutionaries*, 102; Bond, "Review of Clayborne Carson, *In Struggle: The Black Awakening of the 1960s*," *Journal of Higher Education* 54, no. 4 (July–August 1983): 471; Moses and Cobb, *Radical Equations*, 84; and Cobb, *On the Road to Freedom*, xv.

1. Forman, *Making of Black Revolutionaries*, 109–10. Peter de Lissovoy signals the difference between what can be measured externally and participant experience when sharing that, for him, "above all," the movement "was an inner experience." De Lissovoy, *Great Pool Jump*, 7, 129–30.

2. Walmsley, "Tell It Like It Isn't," 292; Payne, "The Rough Draft of History," in *I've Got the Light of Freedom*, 391–405.

3. Joyce Ladner described this process in "The Sociology of the Civil Rights Movement: An Insider's Perspective," a paper delivered in 1988 at the American Sociological Association. Payne, *I've Got the Light of Freedom*, 393, 481.

4. Bond, "Review of Carson, *In Struggle*," *Journal of Higher Education* 54, no. 4 (July–August 1983): 471.

5. Jeffries, *Bloody Lowndes*, 4.

6. "Integral part": Gellman, *Death Blow to Jim Crow*, 176. Kelley pays attention to SNYC's literary expression in *Hammer and Hoe*, 204–12.

7. Robert Rodgers Korstad, *Civil Rights Unionism* (Chapel Hill: University of North Carolina Press, 2003), 417. It continues to be noted that SNCC has a "more than passing resemblance" to the SNYC. Lynda Morgan, review of Gellman, *Death Blow to Jim Crow*, *Labor/Le Travail* 72 (2013): 379.

8. Carson, "Scholar in Struggle." Carson's study prompted other historians to suggest that "more effort" was needed "to keep the memory, spirit, and ideals of this group alive." Charles T. Hayley, "Review of *In Struggle*," *Journal of Negro History* 67, no. 1 (1982): 64.

9. Carson, *In Struggle*, 2–5.

10. Patch recalls that "other SNCC folk thought Sherrod was mad" but that in the early years "consensus" meant "if you wanted to do it, you could." Curry et al., *Deep in Our Hearts*, 140.

11. Jean Wheeler Smith quoted in Robnett, "Women in SNCC," 157.

12. Dittmer, *Local People*, 178; Byrum, *NAACP Youth and the Fight*, 53, 132–46.

13. Nancy (Shaw) Stoller, "Lessons from SNCC–Arkansas 1965," 137.

14. Moses, "Position Paper 33," Waveland, Mississippi, November 6–12, 1964, Document 37A, Elaine DeLott Baker Papers, Schlesinger Library, Radcliffe Institute, Harvard University.

15. Sellers with Terrell, *River of No Return*, 266–67, 114–15. O'Neal explored Forman's imagery in various drafts of "Motion in the Ocean," box 34, folder 4, O'Neal Papers (JO'N), Amistad Research Center, Tulane University, New Orleans. He published a version in 1968, O'Neal, "Motion in the Ocean," 70–77.

16. Dent, diary entry, July 10, 1967, Tuskegee, Alabama, in Dent, Schechner, and Moses, *Free Southern Theater*, 163.

17. Zimmerman, "SNCC's New Program for the Negro," June 5, 1966, box 4, folder 13, Margaret Long Papers, Valdosta State University Archives, Valdosta, Georgia.

18. On July 4, 1964, the anti-imperialist Revolutionary Action Movement congratulated the Vietnamese National Liberation Front in *Black America*, its literary magazine, and stated, "We . . . declare our independence from the policies of the U.S. government abroad and at home." "Greetings to Our Militant Vietnamese Brothers," *Black America*, Fall 1964, 21.

19. Zellner and Curry, *Wrong Side of Murder Creek*, 157.

20. *Black Power: A Reprint of a Position Paper for the* SNCC *Vine City Project*, United States National Student Association, http://freedomarchives.org/Documents/Finder/DOC513_scans/SNCC/513.SNCC.black.power.summer.1966.pdf.

21. Susanna Hegner, "Hollis Watkins: Advice to Young Organizers, Generation Transition," Mary Reynolds Babcock Foundation, November 3, 2015, https://www.mrbf.org/archive/hollis-watkins-advice-young-organizers-generational-transition.

22. Mary King, *Freedom Song*, 533; Forman letter to [Elizabeth] Sutherland, March 13, 1969, and Forman letter to Len Holt, Faye Holt, and [Elizabeth] Sutherland, March 4, 1969, box 1, folder 10, Elizabeth Sutherland-Martínez Papers, Manuscript, Archives, and Rare Books Library, Emory University, Atlanta (ESM). See also Carson, *In Struggle*, 215–303.

23. Sherrod quoted in Sherrod and Whitney, *Courage to Hope*, 74–77.

24. Cobb quoted in Sugarman, *We Had Sneakers, They Had Guns*, 189; Sellers quoted in Marsh, *God's Long Summer*, 200.

25. "James Forman of SNCC Addresses United Nations," *Liberator*, December 1967: 8–10.

26. Newfield, *Prophetic Minority*, 71.

27. Zinn, *SNCC*, 37; Browning in Curry et al., *Deep in Our Hearts*, 66; De Schweinitz, *If We Could Change the World*, 223.

28. Ling, "SNCC: Not One Committee, but Several," 87.

29. Martha Prescod Norman Noonan, "Captured by the Movement," in Holsaert et al., *Hands on the Freedom Plow*, 484, 486.

30. Burlage in Curry et al., *Deep in Our Hearts*, 103.

31. R. H. King, *Civil Rights and the Idea of Freedom*, 155–56, 151–52; Coles, *Farewell to the South*, 256.

32. Coles, *Farewell to the South*, 329–30. An unnamed African American organizer working in Yazoo City, Greenwood, and Jackson since 1963 thought that veteran organizers were likely to say "let the people decide," but this organizer thought that those who joined later, especially from the North, lacked patience. Jacobs and Landau, *New Radicals*, 146–47.

33. Hogan, *Many Minds, One Heart*, 296n1.

34. Jacobs and Landau described Stembridge as "one of the poets of the South whose talent might have remained hidden if not for SNCC" when gathering some of the "rich

literature" of the movement, dividing the chapter on SNCC between poems, documents, and interviews. Jacobs and Landau, *New Radicals*, 115. While Stembridge, Bond, and Cobb may be recognized as SNCC poets, there are no critical responses to the work of SNCC's poets except Roy Neil Graves's exegesis of Bond's "Habana" in 2008 and one eulogy to Bond focusing on his poetry: Paul Kuttner, "I Don't Mind Standing a Little Longer: Remembering Julian Bond through Poetry," Cultural Organizing, August 16, 2015, http://culturalorganizing.org/tag/langston-hughes.

35. Samuel G. Freedman, "The Essential Civil Rights Reading List," *Daily Beast*, August 27, 2013, https://www.thedailybeast.com/the-essential-civil-rights-reading-list.

36. Whitt selected twenty-two illuminating stories for "the first anthology dedicated to stories inspired by events of the civil rights movement" but with the briefest of introductions; there is no exploration of historical context or activist affiliations. Whitt, *Short Stories of the Civil Rights Movement*. Suzanne Jones included Thelwell's "Community of Victims" in her collection of short fiction about race relations, *Crossing the Color Line*. Another useful collection is Armstrong and Schmidt, *Civil Rights Reader*. It includes Nikki Giovanni and Connie Curry but nothing by writers featured in *SNCC's Stories*. Jeffrey Lamar Coleman's *Words of Protest, Words of Freedom* includes poems by activists and makes good use of the Civil Rights Movement Archive of Bay Area Veterans of the Civil Rights Movement, Crmvet.org.

37. J. H. Bryant, *Victims and Heroes*, 190.

38. Dudley Randall in introduction to House, *Blood River*, 8.

39. SNCC's first chairman Marion Barry's political success in Washington, D.C., was marred by accusations of corruption and rumors of drug use (he would be arrested in 1990 and jailed for his first drug offense, possession of crack cocaine). He served three terms of mayor and published his autobiography *Mayor for Life* in the year of his death, 2014.

40. Jon Else, emails to the author; Sharon Monteith, "Storytelling and the Evolving Historiography of the Civil Rights Movement," British Academy, May 11, 2016, https://www.thebritishacademy.ac.uk/blog/storytelling-and-evolving-historiography-civil-rights-movement.

41. Constance L. Hays, "Overcoming Obstacles to a Civil-Rights Chronicle," *New York Times*, January 14, 1990.

42. Richardson, "Womanpower and SNCC," 188.

43. Zellner wrote "A Poem for Ruby Doris Robinson" after seeing Robinson in the PBS series *Eyes on the Prize*: "You looked directly at the camera / Completely unafraid / And you nearly smiled." Zellner closes with: "It was even cold in the hospital room at Beth Israel [where she lay dying,] "At age 26 / Filling the bedpans full of blood." Quoted in C. G. Fleming, *Soon We Will Not Cry*, 192.

44. Thelwell, *Duties, Pleasures, and Conflicts*, xiii, xi; Cobb, *On the Road to Freedom*, xv.

45. Cobb, "Over My Head I See Freedom in the Air," xi, xiii.

46. Cobb, "Over My Head I See Freedom in the Air," xiii.

47. Cobb, "Over My Head I See Freedom in the Air," xi.

48. Richards, "With Our Minds Set on Freedom," 326, 342, 340; Cobb, *This Nonviolent Stuff'll Get You Killed*, 247.

49. Cobb and Lester letter to O'Neal, January 26, 1967, box 14, folder 19, JO'N.

50. Nash, "Inside the Sit-Ins and Freedom Rides," 43–62; Zinn, *SNCC*, 273–74. Carson suggested the value of immersion when admitting, "When I went to school and became a historian, it would never have occurred to me to make a distinction between being an activist and being a historian. My activism was writing *In Struggle*." Carson, *Circle of Trust*, 197.

51. Cobb and Lester, letter to O'Neal; O'Neal, "Theater: Debut in Mississippi" (1964), excerpt from an unpublished project "Let the Circle Be Unbroken," box 34, folder 9, Free Southern Theater Papers (FST), Amistad Research Center, Tulane University, New Orleans; O'Neal memo to Executive Committee: "A Program of Educational and Cultural Activities," January 1964, box 41, folder 12, James Forman Papers (JF), Library of Congress, Washington, D.C.; O'Neal's draft, "Some Current Trends among Afro-American Writers in the South," box 34, folder 38, 1, and "The Artist: A Social Development," box 34, folder 19, 2, JO'N.

52. Thelwell, *Duties, Pleasures, and Conflicts*, xi.

53. Stearns, "Historical Analysis in the Study of Emotion," 190.

54. Scott, *Domination and the Arts of Resistance*, 199, 184, xiii, 14.

55. Forman letter to Sutherland, March 9, 1969, box 1, folder 10, ESM.

56. See, for example, Bond, "Activism of the Late Mr. Allen," *New South*, March 1964, 14; "Death of a Quiet Man," *Rights and Reviews*, Winter 1965; "The Story of Louis. Allen," *Ramparts*, January 1967, 15–21.

57. R. H. King, "Politics and Fictional Representation," 163.

58. LaCapra disdains "literal pantextualism" that sees all texts as equally fictive when coining the term in *History and Its Limits*, 193–94. In the 1990s, debate centered in disagreement over poststructuralist meanings of history as pursued by Hayden White. See, for example, R. H. King, "The Discipline of Fact," and Munslow, "Reply to Richard King."

59. Robert Sklar coined the term "historian cop" in "Historical Films, Scofflaws and the Historian Cop," *Reviews in American History* 25 (1997): 346–50.

60. R. H. King, "Politics and Fictional Representation," 172.

61. R. H. King, *Civil Rights and the Idea of Freedom*, 76.

62. Wallach, *Closer to the Truth*, 50, 57–59.

63. Wallach, *Closer to the Truth*, 55, 154.

64. The writers Wallach selects to analyze—Richard Wright, Zora Neale Hurston, William Alexander Percy, Lillian Smith, Willie Morris, and Henry Louis Gates Jr.—are subjects of a substantial body of literary and cultural criticism. Aside from Gates, and to a lesser extent Morris (since 2007, an award for southern fiction has been sponsored by the Reba and Dave Williams Foundation for Literature and the Arts in his name), they wrote fiction as well as memoirs that operate in conversation in a synergistic network of texts.

65. Lewis and D'Orso, *Walking with the Wind*, 463.

66. Cobb, *On the Road to Freedom*, xiii.

67. Robert Penn Warren, "Poetry Is a Kind of Unconscious Autobiography," *New York Times Book Review*, May 12, 1985, 10. In Joe David Bellamy's assessment, New Journalism's facility for capturing experience and feeling as expressively "true to social reality" was the crux of the endeavor. Bellamy, "Tom Wolfe," *Conversations with Tom Wolfe*, ed. Dorothy M. Scura (Jackson: University Press of Mississippi, 1990), 44.

68. Derrida and Cixous, "From the Word to Life," 12.

69. Foote, *Civil War*, vol. 1, *Fort Sumter to Perryville* (1958; repr., New York: Random House, 1988), 815.

70. Foley, "History, Fiction, and the Ground Between," 397.

71. Thelwell in Greenberg, *Circle of Trust*, 202.

72. See, for example, Dittmer, *Local People*, 268; McCord, *Mississippi*, 88, Hale, *Freedom Schools*, 135. A section of Joyce Brown's poem was reproduced in the *Student Voice*, where Ralph Featherstone observed how the courage demonstrated by the young was affecting elders. "Freedom Schools in Mississippi," *Student Voice*, August 5, 1964, 2.

73. R. H. King, "Civil Rights Debate," 233. King is referring to Alice Walker, *Meridian* (New York: Harcourt Brace Jovanovich, 1976), and Rosellen Brown, *Civil Wars* (New York: Knopf, 1984).

74. Cobb, "Civil Rights' Tower of Strength," *Washington Post*, January 12, 2005.

75. Sterling Stuckey, introduction to Sterling Brown, *Southern Road* (1974), in *Collected Poems of Sterling Brown*, 4, 13.

76. Brown, "Century of Negro Portraiture," 355–56.

77. Harding, *There Is a River*, xvi.

78. Harding, *Hope and History*, 95.

79. Ward quoted in Cobb, "Over My Head: I See Freedom in the Air," xiii; Nicholas Lemann, "The Long March: What the Civil Rights Movement Looked Like When It Was Still Happening," *New Yorker*, February 10, 2003; H. A. Baker, *Betrayal*, 25.

80. Derby quoted in Michael "Quess?" Moore, "Talkin' Revolution with Dr. Doris Derby," Alternate Roots, 2007, http://alternateroots.org/talkin-revolution-with-dr-doris-derby.

81. Street, *Culture War in the Civil Rights Movement*, 8, 167–68, 172–73; Fabre, "Free Southern Theatre," 59; Larocco, "COFO Is Not Godot." Street begins by claiming that activists made "an explicit attempt to use cultural forms or expressions as an integral, perhaps even dominant, part of the political struggle," but closes more equivocally after a wide-ranging discussion.

82. Breaux, "Tom Dent's Role in the Organizational Mentoring of African American Southern Writers," 339–44; Dent, Schechner, and Moses, *Free Southern Theater*, 232; Crawford, *Black Post-Blackness*, 107–36. These developments are receiving attention now, in Margo Natalie Crawford's *Black Post-Blackness*, for example.

83. Ling, "Social Capital, Resource Mobilization," 211. Examples abound, like Deborah Flynn's *Seeds of Freedom* (1964), co-created with students in Holly Springs, Mississippi, who performed the play with the FST. Flynn's field report references a Freedom School Theatre Guild, English Class Club, and newspaper. Flynn, series 4, reel 7, 241, SNCC. Freedom songs are examined for their role in literacy activism in Lathan's *Freedom Writing*. For their reach across the wider movement, see Brian Ward's rich cultural history *Just My Soul Responding*. Guy and Candie Carawan's *Sing for Freedom*, bringing together volumes published in 1963 and 1968, focuses on adaptation of spirituals into freedom songs and the Freedom Singers as the public face of SNCC. See also Annette Jones White, "Finding Form for the Expression of My Discontent," in Holsaert et al., *Hands on the Freedom Plow*, 100–119. See also Kerran L. Sangor, *When The Spirit Says Sing! The Role of Freedom Songs in the Civil Rights Movement* (New York: Garland, 1995); Serge Denisoff, *A Song of Social Significance* (Bowling Green, Ky.: Bowling Green University Popular Press, 1995); Reiland Rabaka, *Civil Rights Music: The Soundtracks of the Civil Rights Movement* (Langham, Md.: Lexington Books, 2016).

84. Forman, *Making of Black Revolutionaries*, 113; Wade Gayles, *Anointed to Fly*, 10–12. SNCC lost much of its original religious character, as Carson unpacks in *In Struggle*, 29, 95, 199–204. See also Simmons, "Martin Luther King Jr. Revisited."

85. Raiford, *Imprisoned in a Luminous Glare*, 128.

86. Monteith, "I Second That Emotion," 440–65.

87. Forman, *Sammy Younge Jr.*, 27.

88. O'Neal, "Road through the Wilderness," 101. In 1999, O'Neal returned to this idea and the importance of writing about the movement for his children. See O'Neal, "Yours in Struggle," 31–32.

89. C. G. Fleming, *Soon We Will Not Cry*, 1.

90. The letter Bellamy wrote is quoted by Sellers, *River of No Return*, 204–5.

91. Forman, "Liberation Will Come from a Black Thing," *Making of Black Revolutionaries*, 510–12.
92. House, *Blood River*, 34.
93. Carson wrote later, "[Moses was] the most influential role model of my college years." "Charismatic Leadership in the Mass Struggle," 448–54. See also R. H., King, "Role of Intellectual History in the Histories of the Civil Rights Movement," 159–80.
94. Crosby, introduction to *Civil Rights History from the Ground Up*, 23.
95. Crosby, introduction to *Civil Rights History from the Ground Up*, 6.
96. Spencer and Hogan, "Telling Freedom Stories," 331, 361n1, 336.
97. Maynes, Pierce, and Laslett, *Telling Stories*, 129–30; Spencer and Hogan, "Telling Freedom Stories," 360, 359.
98. Spencer and Hogan, "Telling Freedom Stories," 336, 359; Tyson, *Blood Done Sign My Name*, 324–25.
99. Spencer and Hogan, "Telling Freedom Stories," 359.
100. Hogan, *Many Minds, One Heart*, 227.
101. Sugarman, *Strangers at the Gates*, 9; Elaine DeLott Baker in Curry et al., *Deep in Our Hearts*, 268; Louis, *We Are Not Saved*, 70.
102. Moses, "Letter from Magnolia Jail."
103. Dorothy Dawson Burlage, "Truths of the Heart," 100–101. Moye refers to McLaurin's storytelling skills in *Let the People Decide*, 215. Moses uses the nickname "Tell the Story" in "Letter from Magnolia Jail," his open letter smuggled out of the county jail in Magnolia on November 1, 1961.
104. For example, John Fischer, *Harper's* editor, wrote "A Small Band of Practical Heroes," *Harpers*, October 1963, 5–6.
105. Minutes of SNCC Executive Committee Meeting, September 6–9, 1963, Atlanta, 7, 11–12, 18, https://www.crmvet.org/docs/6309_sncc_excom.pdf.
106. *The Movement* was published in the UK as *A Matter of Colour: Documentary of the Struggle for Racial Equality in the USA* (London: Penguin, 1965).
107. Foner, *Story of American Freedom*, xiv, xvi. Among many newsletters, *Freedom News* originated in Holly Springs, Mississippi. A copy dated October 1, 1965, is in box 1, folder 10, Kathleen Dahl Freedom Summer Collection, University of Southern Mississippi.
108. Grant, "The Time Is Always Now"; "there is nowhere": Grant, "Negro Movement—New Heights," 168.
109. Forman, *High Tide of Black Resistance*, 129; Carson, *In Struggle*, 82, 89, 94; Hogan, *Many Minds, One Heart*, 91–92.
110. Cobb, "Civil Rights' Tower of Strength," *Washington Post*, January 12, 2005.
111. William Porter, "SNCC Tentative Agenda, 3rd Staff Meeting for 1965, November 24–28th with 29th Open," Southern Conference Educational Fund Records, box 3389, folder 1, Georgia State University, Special Collections, Atlanta.
112. "Position Paper #1," Waveland, Mississippi, retreat, November 1964, probably written by Frank Smith, http://www.crmvet.org/docs/6411w_us_org-dec.pdf.
113. Moses and Cobb, *Radical Equations*, 91–93. Emphasis in original.
114. SNCC" pamphlet, August 1963, 1, box 14, folder 114, JO'N. It drew on Ella Baker's advocacy of groundwork, exemplified in workshops she facilitated for the NAACP from 1944 through 1946 under the rubric "Give Light and People Will Find the Way." Grant, *Ella Baker*, 73. The ethos behind the motto is explained by Jimmy Garrett in "Who Decides?," *Movement*, April 1965, 1–2. The thirty-five-minute SNCC film *We'll Never Turn Back* (1963) is indicative, located in the Southern Media Archive, J. D. Williams Library, University of Mississippi. Fannie Lou Hamer reported that NAACP leader Roy Wilkins

called her "ignorant" and told her "you don't know anything about politics." Polletta, "The Structural Context of Civil Rights Claims," 395.

115. Moses, "Letter from Magnolia Jail."

116. Laura Visser-Maessen notes the religious imagery, from Psalm 118:22, whereby the rejected stone becomes a cornerstone, asserting that Moses knew this "would strike a chord with locals and with religiously-inclined SNCC workers." *Robert Parris Moses*, 86–87.

117. Keith D. Miller's *Voice of Deliverance* (New York: Free Press, 1992) remains the most concerted study of King's language, and Wolfgang Mieder unpacks the nested proverbs in his biblical language in *Making a Way Out of No Way* (New York: Peter Lang, 2010).

118. Annell Ponder's report for Mississippi Council on Human Relations, n.d., box 1, folder 8, Womanpower Unlimited Collection, Margaret Walker Center Archives, Jackson State University. For a history of the organization founded in 1961, see T. M. Morris, *Womanpower Unlimited*.

119. O'Neal, "Shaw, Mississippi: New Sounds in the Delta," box 12, folder 34, 2, 6, JO'N; background to the Mississippi Freedom Labor Union for Friends of SNCC available at http://www.crmvet.org/docs/sncc50_flu.pdf; Lewis quoted in Sutherland, "SNCC Takes Stock," 31.

120. Varela, "Night Willie Peacock Preached Us."

121. Zinn, *SNCC*, 89; Grant, *Black Protest*, 301; Carson, *In Struggle*, 80. Lester unpacked the idea of a white racial monolith more personally when recollecting the moment he apprehended that "white people were not an undifferentiated mass." As a twenty-one-year-old at Fisk University in 1960, they constituted for him "an implacable force as massive and undifferentiated as an iceberg" and engendered the feeling that "somehow I would have to find the way to steer the fragile craft of my life around it or be thrown into the icy waters, another victim of that hard and blinding whiteness." When he read telegrams tacked to a bulletin board supporting the Nashville sit-ins, he realized that some whites "did not think of segregation as a Negro problem, but ... knew it for what it was—an American problem." Lester, "Beyond Ideology," 93.

122. This debate is recorded in SNCC's Executive Committee Minutes, September 6–9, 1963, Georgia, 3, https://www.crmvet.org/docs/6309_sncc_excom.pdf.

123. Zimmerman, *Mississippi Reckoning*, 168.

124. Moses quoted in I. F. Stone, "SNCC's Devoted Handful, Determined to Change the World, Recalls Earlier Martyrs: Where Caesar's Lions Failed, Can the South's Cattle Prods Win?" *I. F. Stone's Bi-Weekly*, December 9, 1963, 7.

125. Moses letter to Jane Stembridge, undated [August 1960], series A, reel 17, SNCC, and discussed in Burner, *And Gently He Shall Lead Them*, 28; Zinn, "Limits of Nonviolence," 144.

126. Mary King, *Freedom Song*, 490.

127. Minnis, "Care and Feeding of the Power Structures Revisited."

Judy Richardson credited Minnis for the research model she adapted while researching for *Eyes on the Prize* and compiling press information supporting demonstrations post-SNCC. Richardson conversation with the author during the British Academy conference "Civil Rights Documentary Cinema and the U.S. 1960s: Transatlantic Conversations on U.S. History, Race and Rights," London, May 2016. Wally Roberts, Freedom Summer volunteer and later an investigative journalist nominated for a Pulitzer Prize, salutes Minnis's research methods as an influence at "Jack Minnis (SNCC)," http://www.crmvet.org/mem/minnis.htm.

128. Roland Snellings, "The Final Song (for White America)," *Freedomways* 8, no. 1 (1968): 48.

129. Forman's speech at Waveland reproduced as appendix E in Hogan, *Many Minds, One Heart*, 275–76.

130. SNCC pamphlet, "The Story of SNCC" (1966), 11, box 14, folder 114, JO'N; Watters, *Encounter with the Future*, 7.

131. Dorie Ladner, "Band of Brothers," December 22, 1964, in Forman's collection of poetry and song, box 44, folder 15, JF.

132. Forman would change the phrase to "sisters and brothers" in "Letter to My Sisters and Brothers," his preface to *Making of Black Revolutionaries*, xxi–xxiii.

133. David J. Garrow, "Review of *A Circle of Trust: Remembering SNCC* by Cheryl Lynn Greenberg," *Journal of American History*, 85, no. 4 (March 1999): 1672–73.

134. Halbwachs, *On Collective Memory*, 84.

135. Greenberg, introduction to *Circle of Trust*, 13; Cheryl Lynn Greenberg, "Review of *Hands on the Freedom Plow*, *Register of the Kentucky Historical Society* 108 (Summer 2010): 138–41; Beardslee, *The Way Out Must Lead In*, 161; Wini Breines, "Review of *Deep in Our Hearts*," *Signs* 30, no. 2 (Winter 2005): 1670–73. Tensions revealed by writers include Sutherland's feeling that she was respected while working in publishing but patronized by Forman and Moses when they intervened in her management of the New York office. Sutherland's letter attempting to explain this to her "most special friends" in March 1965 is in box 1, folder 3, ESM.

136. Tisdale, "Different Assignments, Different Perspectives," 41.

137. Charles Eagles allows that "personal reminiscences of people in the movement [have] added unusual intimacy and drama to the story of the civil rights struggle" but points out that, while writing about Meredith's integration of the University of Mississippi, he consulted oral histories "only when they provide[d] vital information unavailable from other sources." "Toward New Histories," 819; Eagles, *The Price of Defiance: James Meredith and the Integration of Ole Miss* (Chapel Hill, University of North Carolina Press, 2009), 545.

138. "About the Civil Rights Movement Archive," http://www.crmvet.org/about1.htm.

139. Watters, "South and the Nation," 19.

140. Watters, *Encounter with the Future*.

141. Smith, "Let Us All Be Black Together," 19.

142. Moses Voter Education Project report, February 1963, in Watters and Cleghorn, *Climbing Jacob's Ladder*, 159; Moses and Cobb, *Radical Equations*, 59.

143. Moses would parse passages in Sally Belfrage's memoir *Freedom Summer* (1965) into poetry in 1990. Monteith, "I Second That Emotion," 454–55.

144. Fuller's notes for a piece on expatriate African American writers, box 8, folder 4, Hoyt W. Fuller Papers, Robert W. Woodruff Library, Archives Research Center, Atlanta University Center, Atlanta.

145. Thelwell, "*Another Country*: Baldwin's New York Novel," 195, 198; Thelwell, *Duties, Pleasures, and Conflicts*, 230, 22.

146. Cannon, "Literature of Protest."

147. Monteith, "I Second That Emotion," 450–51; Paul R. Carlsten, "Bittersweet Truth," review of Howard Zinn, *SNCC: The New Abolitionists*, *North American Review*, 249, no. 4 (Winter 1964): 91.

148. Casey Hayden quoted in Newfield, *Prophetic Minority*, 104.

149. Abdul Aziz Khaalis (Jan Leighton Triggs), "Mississippi Street Song in Hinds County" (1961), http://www.crmvet.org/poetry/ptriggs.htm.

150. Stembridge quoted in Gitlin, *Campfires of the Resistance*, 32. David Gelfand told Benjamin Hedin at the fiftieth anniversary reunion of Freedom Summer volunteers that

Klansmen had stepped out of the woods when he was picnicking by a pond with coworkers. Gelfand had dived for safety but been hit by a bullet as he swam toward the far shore. He emerged to find shelter at a farmhouse. As shots battered the house, he had called the FBI and "heard the agent say he was unauthorized to offer protection." He then fell unconscious, the local ambulance service refused to come, and he was carried to the Laurel, Mississippi, hospital by a black mortician. Benjamin Hedin, "Do The Right Thing," *Oxford American* 86 (Fall 2014), Oxfordamerican.org/.

151. Carson, *In Struggle*, 25. Andrew B. Lewis reads the poem as a paean to 1950s youth culture, *Shadows of Youth*, 57–59. Little Richard and Fats Domino, to whom the narrator listens, may be celebrated but Bond creates an avatar of Ray Charles "drowning in his own tears."

152. Bond, "I Too Hear America Singing," *Student Voice*, June 1960, 4.

153. Bond, "I Too Hear America Singing," *Movement* (SNCC of California), January 1966, 2; Anne P. Buxton, "Julian Bond: Silhouette," *Harvard Crimson*, January 20, 1966; "Julian Bond Winner in Georgia Primary," *New York Times*, September 16, 1966; Roy Reed, "Negro Ousted by Georgia House Supported by 23 Congressmen," *New York Times*, January 13, 1966; "Vietnam War Spurs Peace Movement in United States," *Congressional Quarterly*, July 1, 1966, 1398–1400.

154. Mayor Ivan Allen blamed SNCC for rioting that erupted in Atlanta's Summerhill neighborhood on September 6, 1966 (WSB-TV news clip, October 1966), and Senator Herman Talmadge called civil rights leaders "outside agitators" creating strife in Atlanta (WSB-TV news clip, December 1966), Civil Rights Digital Library, University of Georgia, http://crdl.usg.edu/export/html/ugabma/wsbn/crdl_ugabma_wsbn_50503.html?Welcome; Julius Lester, "In the Time of Revolution (Atlanta, Georgia, November 20, 1966)," in Lowenfels, *In a Time of Revolution*, 77, 76.

155. Cobb, *In the Furrows of the World*, 1.

156. Forman letter to Len Holt, Faye Holt, and Elizabeth Sutherland ("Reflections on my current work"), March 4, 1969, and Forman letter to Sutherland, March 9, 1969, box 1, folder 10, ESM.

157. SNCC "Nonviolence and the Achievement of Desegregation," box 2, MSS818, Constance Curry Papers, David M. Rubenstein Library, Duke University Libraries, North Carolina.

158. On the nickname "Stokely Starmichael," see Forman, *Making of Black Revolutionaries*, 519–21; Mary King and Joyce Ladner in Greenberg, *Circle of Trust*, 129, 139; Zellner and Curry, *Wrong Side of Murder Creek*, 191; Murphree, *Selling of Civil Rights*, 110. Dittmer, *Local People*, especially chaps. 14–15, "Battle Fatigue" and "The Collapse of the COFO Coalition."

159. Michaels would turn instead to collecting oral histories. In "Telling Our Stories: A Discussion, February 2005" (http://www.crmvet.org/disc/histor.htm) Chude Pam Parker Allen said, "I thought I could mention on *one page* that I'd been in the Civil Rights Movement, and then move on." Others laughed knowingly.

160. Jean Wiley, "Letter to My Adolescent Son," in Holsaert et al., *Hands on the Freedom Plow*, 517, 522; Muriel Tillinghast in SNCC Executive Committee Meeting, April 12–14, 1965, Holly Springs, Mississippi, 23, https://www.crmvet.org/docs/6504_sncc_excom_min.pdf; Mike Miller, "2 Years Ago: A White SNCC Worker Talks about Black Power," *Movement* (SNCC of California), August 1966, 7; Mulholland quoted in Tisdale, "Different Assignments, Different Perspectives," 40. Si Kahn underlined: "One thing I've learned by studying history is how rare it is to find agreement even on what happened, let alone what whatever happened actually means." Kahn, *Creative Community Organizing*, 45.

161. Forman, *Sammy Younge Jr.*, 19, 27.

162. Correspondence over June 1967 includes reference to Sutherland taking the manuscript to Farrar Strauss and her frustrations: "It is possible that you feel uneasy about 'using' me on your books in the wake of the great White sweep-out," box 1, folder 5, ESM.

163. History of SNCC," March 12, 1969, box 128, folder 2, p. 2, JF.

164. Forman letter to Len Holt, Faye Holt, and Elizabeth Sutherland, March 4, 1969, box 1, folder 10, and Sutherland's advice to Forman, box 1, folder 9, ESM. The reply, probably from Len rather than Faye Holt, is a fragment headed "History of SNCC," unsigned to Forman, March 12, 1969, box 128, folder 2, p. 2, JF. "Dinky" and "Lumba" refer to Forman's partner Constancia (Dinky) Romilly and their first child, James (Lumumba) Forman Jr.

165. Forman, "A Black Revolutionary: The Autobiography of James Forman," 1, box 135, folder 1, JF.

166. Forman, foreword to Kunstler, *Deep in My Heart*, xx. Bond thought similarly, recording oral histories (with Phyllis Leffler), ensuring that activists' thoughts would be preserved through conversation with one who was there. Leffler, *Black Leaders on Leadership*. The selection of some fifty interviewees includes Lewis, Moses, Eleanor Holmes Norton, Bond himself, and BAM practitioners Nikki Giovanni and Amiri Baraka but none of the writers examined in this study.

167. Lester, "Four Faces from SNCC."

168. Lewis's and Payne's blurbs are among many on the jacket of Cobb, *On the Road to Freedom*.

169. Moses and Cobb, *Radical Equations*, 86, 222, 223.

170. Introduction to Holsaert et al., *Hands on the Freedom Plow*, 5–6; Barbara Ransby, foreword to Curry et al., *Deep in Our Hearts*, vii; Curry et al., *Deep in Our Hearts*, xiv.

171. Joan C. Browning, for example, has challenged the record of the Atlanta-to-Albany Freedom Ride of December 10, 1961, from the "Fact Sheet on Freedom Ride to Albany, Georgia" and news release issued by the Albany Movement on the day through the various histories that fail to record her as present. Browning, "Invisible Revolutionaries."

172. Lester quoted in Tim Tooher's liner notes for Julius Lester, *Dressed Like Freedom*, BGP, 2006, compact disc; De Lissovoy, *Great Pool Jump*, 9. The lyrics to "Dressed Like Freedom" (1967) capture one of the harshest lessons learned about the ontology of the white world in a SNCC-inflected transfiguration of the blues:

> Lord, if I get killed down South,
> I want a white boy by my side,
> 'Cos I don't want nobody saying,
> "Just another nigger," when I die.

173. DeLott, introduction to untitled poem (May 1965) celebrating Janet Jemmott (Janet Moses), document 85A, Elaine DeLott Baker Papers. Sugarman recalled in Ruleville, Mississippi, in 1964, "Page after page in my tattered notebooks would spill over with the excitement and emotion of what I was observing. And in my sketchbooks I was recording the images I was determined never to lose." Sugarman, *We Had Sneakers, They Had Guns*, 86.

174. Forman, *Making of Black Revolutionaries*, 113. It is really two separate stories. The first, a novella called "The Song Festival," worked through to find his way into the novel, has limited bearing on SNCC. That Forman intended to divide the manuscript is stated in a letter to Kenneth McCormick, November 3, 1958, box 44, folder 8, JF. When "Thin White Line" was almost finished, he "outlined the structure again." letter to Pat,

May 1958, a fragment of correspondence between Patricia Anna Johnson and Forman (1958–60), box 133, folder 3, JF.

175. Ellison, *Shadow and Act*, 167, 171, 183.
176. O'Neal, "As a Weapon Is to Warfare," box 34, folder 2, p. 9, JO'N. A later and slightly different version was published in *Callaloo* in 1981.
177. Payne, *I've Got the Light of Freedom*, 252.
178. Cannon, "Literature of Protest," 7.
179. Harding, *There Is a River*, xix.
180. Forman, *Making of Black Revolutionaries*, 289.
181. Lyon quoted in Val Willmer, "Early Days of Rage," *Independent* (London), November 22, 1992.
182. Payne, *I've Got the Light of Freedom*, 398.
183. O'Neal, "As a Weapon Is to Warfare," 9.
184. Hall, *Long George Alley*, 218.
185. Watters, *Encounter with the Future*, 103.

Chapter 1. "Troublemakers"

Epigraphs are from L. D. Reddick, "Letter of Congratulations," *Student Voice* 1 (August 1960), 3; Ellison, *Shadow and Act*, 17; Lewis quoted in Tony Gonzales, "In Nashville, Rep. John Lewis Gets Surprise from His Civil Rights Past," NPR, November 21, 2016.

1. G. S. Jones, "Meaning of the Student Revolt," 33.
2. Frazier, *Black Bourgeoisie*, 14; Howard Juncker, "Free University: Academy for Mavericks," *Nation*, August 16, 1965, 78. Halberstam marked "these young people, in so quiescent an age, as being dramatically different from the black college norm." Halberstam, *Children*, 73.
3. Lester, *Search for the New Land*, 4, 46; McDew, "Spiritual and Moral Aspects of the Student Nonviolent Struggle in the South."
4. Zinn, "Changing People," 60; Tom Hayden in Greenberg, *Circle of Trust*, 33.
5. Savio, "End to History"; Farber, *Student as Nigger*, 114; "The Port Huron Statement (1962)," in Bloom and Breines, *Takin' It to the Streets*, 61–74. Cohen discusses the racial sensationalism of the "student as nigger" controversy in *Freedom's Orator*, 287–88.
6. Potter quoted in Newfield, "Student Left," 492; Harding, "Black Students and the Impossible Revolution," 88.
7. Zinn, "Changing People," 65.
8. Prescod in Greenberg, *Circle of Trust*, 183; McLaurin quoted in Moye, *Let the People Decide*, 140–41; Jean Wiley, "Letter to My Adolescent Son," in Holsaert et al., *Hands on the Freedom Plow*, 521–22; Chatfield quoted in "Remembering Jack Chatfield," Cong. Rec. 160, pt. 11 (November 17, 2014).
9. Zinn, *SNCC*, 233.
10. Rothschild, *Case of Black and White*, 40.
11. L. D. Reddick, "Letter of Congratulations," *Student Voice* 1 (August 1960), 3.
12. O'Neal, "Don't Start Me to Talkin'," 36. In 1963, Bayard Rustin advocated making "a mountain of creative social confusion until the power structure is altered. We need in every community a group of loving troublemakers, who will disrupt the ability of the government to operate until it finally turns its back on the Dixiecrats and embraces progress." Rustin, "Meaning of the March on Washington," *Liberation*, October 1963, 12.
13. Kenneth Rexroth, "The Students Take Over," *Nation*, July 2, 1960, 4–9.

14. I. F. Stone, "SNCC's Devoted Handful, Determined to Change the World, Recalls Earlier Martyrs: Where Caesar's Lions Failed, Can the South's Cattle Prods Win?" *I. F. Stone's Bi-Weekly*, December 9, 1963, 7.

15. Perdew ("adventurous and different") quoted in Carson, *In Struggle*, 72. John Perdew, "Difficult to Organize the Poorest and the Wealthiest among Negroes," *I. F. Stone's Bi-Weekly*, December 9, 1963, 3, 6.

16. Zinn, *SNCC*, 4; L. Smith, "Ten Years From Today," commencement address Kentucky State College, June 5, 1951, in *Winner Names the Age*, 62; L. Smith, "The Moral and Political Significance of the Students' Non-Violent Protests," April 21, 1960, in *Winner Names the Age*, 92.

17. Obama quoted in Roy Reed, "John Doar, Federal Lawyer on Front Lines against Segregation, Dies at 92," *New York Times*, November 11, 2014; Branch, *Parting the Waters*, 513.

18. Ellison, *Shadow and Act*, 17; R. H. King, "Citizenship and Self-Respect," 8.

19. Cobb, *On the Road to Freedom*, xiii.

20. Browning in Curry et al., *Deep in Our Hearts*, 81.

21. Fiedler, "War against the Academy," 6.

22. Showalter, *Faculty Towers*, 34; Jeff Shaara, forward to Michael Shaara, *The Rebel in Autumn* (Brooklyn: Antenna, 2013), xiv, written in the 1960s but not published then. Paul Cowan began a novel, its protagonist a graduate of New England prep school [Choate 1958] and Harvard [1963] who falls in love during a civil rights demonstration in Cambridge, Maryland, "where I had spent several weeks after I graduated from college." Cowan, *Making of an Un-American*, 27.

23. Thelwell, "Direct Action," 217.

24. "Student exhibitionism": Carmichael, in Carmichael and Thelwell, *Ready for the Revolution*, 140.

25. Polletta, "'It Was Like a Fever," 139n1.

26. McNeill in *SNCC 50th Anniversary Conference*, vol. 2, *Early Student Movement Philosophy and Activism* (San Francisco: California Newsreel, 2011).

27. Lerone Bennett, "SNCC: Rebels with a Cause," *Ebony*, July 1965, 146; De Lissovoy, "Failure in Albany II." For a wide-ranging assessment, see G. Hale, *Nation of Outsiders*.

28. Joseph Sinsheimer, interview with Robert Coles, November 19, 1983, 12–15, Joseph A. Sinsheimer Papers (JAS), Robert W. Woodruff Library, Archives Research Center, Atlanta University Center, Atlanta, includes discussion of the types of student who could afford to spend a summer volunteering and Coles's irritation at the mass media emphasis placed on (white) northeastern, privileged, rich, connected volunteers.

29. Rahv, "Cult of Experience."

30. James Forman, "Pupils, White, Negro Tell of Experiences at Central," *Chicago Daily Defender* September 18, 1958. He was reporting while supporting Robert F. Williams's work in Monroe, North Carolina. Forman, "Riders Carry on Civil Rights Battle in N. Car.," *Chicago Daily Defender*, August 24, 1961.

31. Autobiographical fragment, box 141, folder 8, 8–9, JF. Forman tells Warren about his novel in Warren, *Who Speaks for the Negro?*, 173.

32. Forman, *Making of Black Revolutionaries*, 113–14.

33. Fields, *War without Heroes*, 8, 5. Fields died in 1974. "Arthur C. Fields: A Book Publisher," *New York Times*, May 11, 1974. He was a paraplegic as the result of being shot in World War II.

34. Arthur C. Fields letter to Forman, June 10, 1965, box 144, folder 9, JF.

35. Forman wrote to Kenneth McCormick of Doubleday, "I am an unpublished author who plans to live as a writer" (November 3, 1958) and similarly to all those to whom he submitted stories—for example, the editor of *Atlantic Monthly* (October 31, 1958) and Russell Lynes, managing editor of *Harper's Magazine* (November 5, 1958), all in box 144, folder 8, JF.

36. Merrill Pollack to Forman, November 10, 1958, box 144, folder 8, JF.

37. Forman, *Making of Black Revolutionaries*, 102. He read *Grapes of Wrath*, *In Dubious Battle*, *The Short Reign of Pippin IV*, *Native Son*, *Crime and Punishment*, *The Idiot*, *Killers of the Dream*, *Strange Fruit*, *Lady Chatterley's Lover*, *Bread and Wine*, and *Anna Karenina*, among many works. Box 1, folder 1, and box 133, folder 3, JF.

38. Autobiographical fragment, box 141, folders 8–9, JF; Forman, *Making of Black Revolutionaries*, 116. The novel has to be pieced together across incomplete drafts: Forman, "The Thin White Line," Box 142, Draft A (5 folders): folder 1: 1–65; folder 2: 66–171; folder 3: 172–297; folder 4: 298–377; folder 5: 378–446; Draft B: folder 1: 1–118; folder 2: 137–237; box 143, Draft B: folder 3: 238–335; folder 4: 336–446; Draft C (1992 revision published as "The Song Festival"), 3 folders: folder 1: 1–158; folder 2: 160–330; folder 3: 331–446; Draft D (possibly the oldest and certainly the least complete draft), 5 folders: folder 1: 32–46; folder 2: 47–118; box 144, folder 3: 120–46; folder 4: 147–64, notes from 1992; folder 5: 165–84 originals; folder 6, partial drafts of chapters 1–3; JF.

39. Forman, "The Thin White Line," Draft A, box 142, 404, 130 (subsequent references in this paragraph are in parentheses); Forman, *Making of Black Revolutionaries*, 113–14.

40. Autobiographical fragment, box 141, folder 8, 8–9; "Thin White Line" Draft D, 62–78, box 143, folder 7, JF.

41. "James Forman to Get Roosevelt U. Award," *Chicago Daily Defender*, November 6, 1963. Mills and Weiner, in *Roosevelt University*, trace some of the ways in which Roosevelt was "a crucible for leadership" in campus history (43).

42. Carson sees the connection as definite: "Paul Brooks described SNCC to Forman as the same kind of nonviolent activist group that Forman had earlier portrayed in his novel." Carson, *In Struggle*, 43.

43. Forman, "'Corrupt Black Preachers' and 'God Is Dead,'" 285; Forman, *Making of Black Revolutionaries*, 92.

44. Forman situates Co-Operative House on the corner of East Sixty-Second Street and Woodlawn in Chicago's Southside, close to a jazz club, presumably on Sixty-Third Street, that he calls Circular Lounge (a name and setting used in his short stories). He stresses this neighborhood's changing demographics as students mix with "the masses."

45. Jean Wiley interview with Bruce Hartford, October 26, 2001, http://www.crmvet.org/nars/wiley1.htm. For Casey Hayden's experience, see Olson, *Freedom's Daughters*, 168–69. Riffel argues that Hansen played down the significance of the council that he founded as "a venue for getting to know people," but it was instrumental for him setting up a branch of CORE in Cincinnati before dropping out to join SNCC. Riffel, "In the Storm," 24–25.

46. Moses in Hampton and Fayer, *Voices of Freedom*, 183.

47. Savio, "End to History," 24. In 1969, Staughton Lynd explored ideas that Forman's characters debate in a SNCC-specific context: "Surely 'the movement' is already magnificently articulate? Its leaders are themselves scholars-in-action. James Forman left graduate work in African Studies . . . Robert Moses, before he went to Mississippi, had majored in philosophy and mathematics at Haverford and Harvard. The young man at the Jackson COFO office who, late on June 21, received the telephone report that Michael Schwerner,

James Chaney and Andrew Goodman were missing, is a specialist in Japanese culture. The young woman who took my place at the end of the summer as director of the Mississippi Freedom Schools had been an English instructor at the University of Washington." "Freedom South. SNCC: The Beginning of an Ideology," 11–12, http://www.crmvet.org/docs/6501_zinn_ideology.pdf.

48. Forman, "Thin White Line," Draft A, 403–4, box 142, JF.

49. Notes scribbled on the back of paper headed "Friends of James Forman Campaign Committee, 1650 Harvard Street, NW Washington DC," box 170, folder 11, JF.

50. Forman, *Making of Black Revolutionaries*, 109–10; Doug Youngblood, "Poem in the Grass," in Gitlin, *Campfires of the Resistance*, 291–92.

51. "Sometimes I think the play would be a good form for expressing what I have to say about the people," Forman wrote in 1957. "Most of the time is spent loafing and thinking about my writing." Forman, letter to Gerry, 1957, box 170, folder 10. Of a short story, "All Too Soon," he wrote: "I'm thinking of changing this story a little to make it more actual and less fictionalized." Letter to Anna Johnson, editor, June 4, 1958, box 170, folder 6, JF.

52. Forman uses "freedom mood" in "Some Random Notes from the Leflore County Jail," 334.

53. As I pored over letters Forman wrote to publishers, I was close to tears seeing the many efforts he made to get this novel published, especially the letters in box 144, folder 5, JF. He never really gave up. In 2004, the year before his death, he explored joining the Writers Guild of America, affiliated with the AFL-CIO. Box 144, folder 12, JF.

54. Appadurai, *Modernity at Large*, 7, 31; Forman, *Making of Black Revolutionaries*, 102.

55. Baldwin, Introduction to Thelwell, *Duties, Pleasures, and Conflicts*, xx.

56. Beal and Ross, "Excerpts from the Voices of Feminism," 142.

57. *New South*, October 1963, in Bond and Lewis, *Gonna Sit at the Welcome Table*, 389.

58. O'Brien, "New Left's Early Years," 5.

59. Cobb, "The Story of Charlie Cobb," based on a talk delivered to the National Youth Forum, Atlanta, June 1963, box 27, folder 13, 1, JF.

60. Abel, *Signs of the Times*, 132.

61. Halberstam, *Children*, 5; Nash, "Inside the Sit-Ins and Freedom Rides," 47–48.

62. The phrase is George Lipsitz's. Lipsitz examines how white people profit from identity politics in his *Possessive Investment in Whiteness*.

63. Jimmy Ward, quoted by Tom Hayden, *Revolution in Mississippi*, 26 (from *Jackson Clarion-Ledger*, November 30, 1961). Dick Gregory in Zinn, *SNCC*, 15; Gregory, *Nigger*, 170.

64. Walzer, "Cup of Coffee and a Seat"; Claude Sitton, "Negro Sitdowns Stir Fear of Wider Unrest," *New York Times*, February 14, 1960; Jim Laue, "And Smiles," *Student Voice*, October 1960, 4.

65. Gregory, *Nigger*, 144; Gregory and Moses, *Callus on My Soul*, 57.

66. Sellers and Terrell, *River of No Return*, 16. Harvey Molotch and Laura Noren, eds., *Toilet: Public Restrooms and the Politics of Sharing* (New York: New York University Press, 2010) focuses on gender, with limited attention to racial segregation.

67. Joan Trumpauer's arrest, "Fact Sheet: Baton Rouge" (1962), 2, box 48, folder 7, SNCC; Holt, *Act of Conscience*, 48–49.

68. "The Green Book," New York Public Library Digital Collections at https://digitalcollections.nypl.org/collections/the-green-book.

69. The incident took place August 20, 1963. "Background Report on Natchez (October 1963–August 1965)," n.d., 1, box 38, folder 9, JF.

70. Henry and Curry, *Aaron Henry*, 81; Hansen, field report, November 26, 1962, 1, box 8, folder 2, SNCC Arkansas Project Records, MS 00488, Wisconsin Historical Society, Madison.

71. The image by NAACP photographer Cecil J. Williams appears in a North Carolina television documentary by Steve Crump, *Exposures of a Movement* (Charlotte, N.C.: WTVI, 1996).

72. "University Student from Ghana Gives Account of Gang Beating," *Cornell Daily Sun*, reel 7, 468, SNCC. Wilkins, "Making of Black Internationalists," 476–77, points out Forman's involvement with the Pan African Students Organization in the Americas through this and another incident.

73. Forman, *Sammy Younge Jr.*, 73–116. The closest bathrooms, at Dexter Avenue Church, were closed while clergy debated whether to support demonstrators. Forman clashed with a former SNCC staffer, SCLC's James Bevel, over the impression created by urine in the street. When the church opened, the water supply was off. Forman was forced to ask Martin Luther King, as former pastor of the church, for marchers to be afforded use of functioning bathrooms, *Sammy Younge Jr.*, 95.

74. Whit and Hallie Burnett, "Introduction: Behind the Ivy Wall," *Prize College Stories 1963: The Story Magazine Contest* (New York: Random House, 1963), viii; Tom Brien, "Previews and Reviews: *Prize College Stories*," *Michigan Daily*, September 12, 1963.

75. In a memo to Martin Luther King Jr., December 12, 1963, Septima Clark worried that her Citizens Education Project was being neglected by colleagues in SCLC: "Direct action is so glamorous and packed with emotion that most young people prefer demonstrations over genuine education." Document 16C, Septima Clark Papers, box 8, folder 2, Avery Research Center for African American History and Culture, College of Charleston, Charleston, South Carolina.

76. Thelwell's "Direct Action" was also selected for Bruce Glasrud and Laurie Champion, ed., *The African American West: A Century of Short Stories* (Boulder: University Press of Colorado, 2000).

77. "Column from Cambridge Correspondent," reel 62, 130, SNCC; Polletta, "It Was Like a Fever,'" 147–48.

78. In an inflammatory proposition, Golden suggested that out-of-order signs be posted on "white" drinking fountains, which would mean everybody drinking "colored" water, "without any bad effects, physical or emotional." "The Golden Out-of-Order Plan," *Carolina Israelite*, February 1957, 1; "Golden Plan Works and New One Proposed," *New South*, July–August, 1958, 14.

79. Harry Golden, "How to Solve the Segregation Problem," *Carolina Israelite*, May–June 1956, 1; Holt, *Act of Conscience*, 58–59. See also Wiegand and Wiegand, *Desegregation of Public Libraries in the Jim Crow South*.

80. Berrey, *Jim Crow Routine*, 144–45.

81. Zinn, in "Finishing School for Pickets," wrote, "Respectability is no longer respectable among young Negro women attending college today." On respectability, see Chappell, Hutchinson, and Ward, "Dress Modestly, Neatly."

82. Fiedler, "New Mutants," 505, 511, 515, 523. Fiedler (522) cites De Lissovoy and Susan Ryerson's arrest for possession of marijuana as evidence that drugs were "inextricably involved with the civil rights movement": "The mother who has sent her son to private schools and on to Harvard, to keep him out of classrooms overcrowded with poor Negroes, rejoices when he sets off for Mississippi with his comrades in SNCC, but shudders when he turns on with LSD; just as the ex-Marxist father, who has earlier proved radicalism impossible, rejoices to see his son stand up piously and pompously for CORE and SDS, but

trembles to hear him quote Alpert and Leary or praise Burroughs... LSD is the radicalism of the young."

83. Robbins, *Wild Ducks Flying Backwards*, 93.

84. Webster Schott, "The Rage of Being Young and Lost," *Life*, September 4, 1970, 13. Perdew describes their journey in *Education of a Harvard Guy*, 26. He describes being jailed together (De Lissovoy's character suffers jailing alone) and records De Lissovoy making notes because he wanted to be a writer (37–40).

85. De Lissovoy, "Moments in a Southern Town."

86. Newfield, "Student Left."

87. De Lissovoy criticized the "tenacious if sometimes comical minority" in "Failure in Albany II: The White Minority." Zinn counts him among whites who surmounted it. Zinn, *SNCC*, 81–82.

88. De Lissovoy, "Failure in Albany, Georgia."

89. De Lissovoy, *Feelgood*, 179.

90. Bell, *Cultural Contradictions of Capitalism*, 88.

91. This description mirrors one in "The Failure in Albany."

92. De Lissovoy, "Failure in Albany"; 1963 field report quoted in De Lissovoy, "Integrating Tift Park Pool Jump with James Daniel [sic]," in *Great Pool Jump*, 95.

93. De Lissovoy, "Failure in Albany."

94. De Lissovoy, "'Outside Agitator and Other Terms of the Times: Remembering James Daniels" (written sometime between 2003 and 2006), http://www.crmvet.org/nars/peter1.htm.

95. De Lissovoy, "Gambler's Choice in Georgia: C. B. King for Congress, June 1964," *Nation*, June 22, 1964.

96. Elizabeth Hardwick, "Reflections on Fiction," *New York Review of Books*, February 13, 1969, 4.

97. Schott, "Rage of Being Young and Lost," 13.

98. One of the first things the sheriff in *Girl on a Chain Gang* says to northern students is, "We don't cotton to no feds in local matters." In *Murder in Mississippi*, a psychotic sheriff's refrain is, "We ain't gonna let communist Yankees run our town for us." Monteith, "Exploiting Civil Rights"; Warren, *Who Speaks for the Negro?* 428.

99. The Memphis *Commercial Appeal* published a satirical cartoon of a COFO worker as a beatnik with sandals and unkempt clothes. In Clarksdale, white townsfolk were warned by the local paper that they were "infiltrated by juvenile delinquents, beatniks, and prostitutes" and should take a stand. "Warning—Citizens of Clarksdale," *Clarksdale Press-Register*, August 20, 1964. The *New York Herald Tribune* blasted SNCC for being "infiltrated by beatnik left-wing revolutionaries" and communists. Rowland Evans and Robert Novak, "Inside Report: Freedom Party Postscript," *New York Herald Tribune*, September 1, 1964.

100. Sugarman, *Stranger at the Gates*, 139.

101. Alice Lake letter to editor of *New York Times Magazine*, November 8, 1964, in response to Herbers's "Communique from the Mississippi Front," published that day, SC 3057, folder 1, Ellen Lake Papers, Freedom Summer Collection, Wisconsin Historical Society, Madison.

102. Coles, *Farewell to the South*, 248.

103. J. Lewis and D'Orso, *Walking with the Wind*, 185; Tuck, *Beyond Atlanta*, 151–52.

104. Yellow's murder echoes many others but most closely the police shooting of Isiah Taylor in Doddsville, Sunflower County, Mississippi, in 1964. Sugarman, *Stranger at the Gates*, 99–105.

105. Stoper, *Student Nonviolent Coordinating Committee*, 28.

106. Watters, *Encounter with the Future*, 1.

107. Forman, "Thin White Line," 395. Stanley Cavell unpacked the disavowal of "ghost-state of conformity" articulated by Ralph Waldo Emerson: "Unless you find some way to show that this society is not yours, it is; your being compromised by its actions expresses the necessity of your being implicated in them . . . fleeing before a revolution." Ralph Waldo Emerson, *Emerson's Transcendental Etudes*, ed. David Justin Hodge (Stanford, Calif.: Stanford University Press, 2003), 190.

108. "A Message from Harry Belafonte," open letter distributed by SNCC, commemorating Sammy Young Jr. (1943–66), and requesting funds to sustain "vital work for justice." Box 14, folder 14, JO'N.

109. Collins, *Whatever Happened to Interracial Love?*, 34–35. Collins skewered the black middle class in her plays *In the Midnight Hour* (1981), *The Brothers* (1982), and *Only the Sky Is Free* (1985).

110. Forman, "Thin White Line," 34.

111. Nina Lorez Collins, "Kathleen Collins," http://kathleencollins.org/about. *Ms.* magazine rejected a cache of Collins's stories in 1975. So far there is no evidence that she sent them elsewhere. Collins's papers are held by the New York Public Library: archives.nypl.org/scm/24264.

112. Collins, *Whatever Happened to Interracial Love?*, 56. Timothy Miller says the same thing about hippies: "The hippies saw themselves as the people of zero, the vanguard who would build a new society on the ruins of the old, corrupt one." Miller, *Hippies and American Values*, 3.

113. Monteith, *American Culture in the 1960s*, 173–75.

114. Savio quoted in Feuer, *Conflict of Generations*, 504.

115. Watkins and McInnis, *Brother Hollis*, 207.

116. Rustin, "New Radicalism," 528.

117. Swaim, "Hippies," 18.

118. De Lissovoy, "Failure in Albany II."

119. De Lissovoy, *Feelgood*, 137, 234–35.

120. Hogan, *Many Minds, One Heart*, 116; Carson, *Martin's Dream*, 39.

121. Llorens, "Julian Bond," 62.

Chapter 2. Supersnick and Junebug Jabbo Jones

Epigraphs are from Mary King, *Freedom Song*, 372; O'Neal, "As a Weapon Is to Warfare," box 34, folder 2, O'Neal Papers; O'Neal, *Don't Start Me to Talking*, 12.

1. Hogan, *Many Minds, One Heart*, 227; Judy Richardson, SNCC Oral Histories Conference transcript, 61, CDSD. Weaver is typically introduced with reference to Supersnick, but the character is never examined in histories or memoirs. For example, Watson mentions Supersnick quickly in parentheses when Weaver is noted in *Freedom Summer*, 118.

2. Charles Payne cites an example of teasing insider jokes where nicknames remain puzzles: "Dorie (Elephant) Ladner had 'tea' with Tom Gaither [of CORE]. So now we know why Dorie went to Atlanta." Payne, *I've Got the Light of Freedom*, 244.

3. Mississippi Freedom Summer application lists, box 41, folder 4, JF.

4. King, *Freedom Song*, 372.

5. Ivanhoe Donaldson mentioned Weaver during the panel "Living History: Activists on Art and Social Justice," April 17, 2008, Lannan Center for Poetics and Social Practice, Georgetown University, Washington, D.C.

6. See, for example, "Junebug Jabbo Jones," http://www.crmvet.org/vet/junebugj.htm.

7. O'Neal quoted in Paula Crouch, "Legend of Junebug Jabbo Jones," *Atlanta Journal*, January 16, 1985.

8. John A. Williams, "Black Folktales," *New York Times*, November 9, 1969.

9. Lester, "Our Folk Tales," box 5, folder 14, Sellers Papers, David M. Rubenstein Library, Duke University Libraries, North Carolina; Lester, *Black Folktales*, viii.

10. Lester, *Black Folktales*, 94, 114, 123, 133–34.

11. Žižek, *Fragile Absolute*, 3.

12. Mary Ann French's "The People's Professor," *Boston Globe Magazine*, September 12, 1999, is the most thorough biographical overview of Thelwell's long and creative career.

13. Stembridge, *I Play Flute* (1966), 90.

14. O'Neal observes that a "Dr Junebug" was a fictional professor invented by students at Howard University in the 1950s but, a self-serving stuffed shirt, he bears little relation to Junebug Jabbo Jones. O'Neal, *Don't Start Me to Talking*, xxv. Cohen-Cruz traces the theatrical life of Junebug through O'Neal's thesis of community-led theater and examines theatrical collaboration in *Local Acts* (60–64, 67–68). She mentions SNCC once as the originator of the character but does not say more. O'Neal died in February 2019. "John O'Neal, 78, Champion of Theater in the Deep South, Dies," *New York Times*, February 28, 2019.

15. John O'Neal to Tom Dent, June 18, 1967, box 69, folder 8, FST.

16. Casey Hayden, "Movement," 246. SNCC activists are sometimes described standing in a circle to sing at the end of meetings—or on leaving jail, as Mahoney described in "Risking Life and Liberty." O'Neal built on the model of the "story circle" for a play cycle.

17. O'Neal, "Let the Circle Be Unbroken," drafts, box 34, folders 7–13, JO'N.

18. Verbatim theatre draws on the playwright or performer's collation of oral history interviews. It dramatizes events and moments in history for how they were felt and experienced by those involved and how they are remembered in the present. Anna Deavere Smith is representative, with "On the Road: A Search for American Character," a series of plays she has been crafting and performing since the 1980s. She encapsulates how I think about O'Neal's process when she says, "Central to my creative process is active listening. My goal is to pay careful attention to the people I interview and then to reflect back what I have learned in the hope of sparking a conversation, of making change possible." Smith, *Notes from the Field* (New York: Anchor, 2019), xv.

19. O'Neal quoted in Michna, "Performance and Cross-Racial Storytelling," 51–52; O'Neal in John O'Neal, Cynthia Cohen, Polly Walker, Roberto Gutiérrez Varea, and Lesley Yalen, "Do You Smell Something Stinky? Notes from Conversations about Making Art while Working for Peace in Racist, Imperial America in the 21st Century," http://www.brandeis.edu/ethics/peacebuildingarts/actingtogether/casestudies/oneal/index.html. When Tavis Smiley references Junebug Productions, he praises O'Neal's story circle model. Smiley, *Covenant in Action*, 76–77.

20. Hobsbawm, *Bandits*, 26–27, 10.

21. Barratt, *Integration at Ole Miss*, 72.

22. An equally anarchic reworking of the janitor is Richard Wright's "The Man of All Work" in his short story collection *Eight Men* (Cleveland: World Publishing, 1961). For an analysis of African American comic superheroes, see Watkins, *On The Real Side*.

23. On SNCC using the names "Supersnick" and "Freedom Now" when reporting to police after being arrested, see "SNCC Meets Klan: Seventy-Three Arrested, Brutality Protested," *Student Voice*, January 20, 1964, 3; Forman, *Making of Black Revolutionaries*, 361. Spelman College students registered with police as "Freedom Quick" and "Freedom

Now." See Lefever, *Undaunted by the Fight*, 174. For a flat monthly fee, SNCC avoided telephone exchanges and operators listening in and made and received unlimited long-distance calls. WATS was a safety mechanism, and the Atlanta office staffed lines and logged calls twenty-four hours a day. "Gathering News Information (WATS)," Atlanta SNCC, June 24, 1964, 1, http://www.crmvet.org/docs/wats/64_wats_instructions.pdf.

24. Norman Mailer, *The Spooky Art: Some Thoughts on Writing* (New York: Random House, 2003), 99; Hansberry, "Genet, Mailer, and the New Paternalism."

25. Mary King, *Freedom Song*, 372.

26. Bond, Foreword to Forman, *Making of Black Revolutionaries*, xiii.

27. Fred Meely, "Organizer's Handbook," box 14, folder 36, 1, JO'N; Cobb, *This Nonviolent Stuff'll Get You Killed*, 246.

28. Coles, *Call of Service*, 10–13.

29. Warren, *Who Speaks for the Negro?*, 88.

30. Richardson, "My Enduring 'Circle of Trust,'" in Holsaert et al., *Hands on the Freedom Plow*, 348. Carson notes Forman's habit of cleaning at night in *In Struggle*, 69.

31. Forman, *Making of Black Revolutionaries*, 300.

32. Elayne DeLott letter to Renee De Lott, Jackson, Mississippi, December 27, 1964, document 75, Elaine DeLott Baker Papers.

33. Forman, *Political Thought of James Forman*, 154, 157.

34. "Over 300 Attend SNCC Conference," *Student Voice*, December 9, 1963, 2.

35. Murphree, *Selling of Civil Rights*, 31–35.

36. Zellner and Curry, *Wrong Side of Murder Creek*, 167–68.

37. James A. Wechsler, "Combat Story," *New York Post*, March 19, 1963.

38. Minnis, "Chronology of Violence," 5; *Student Voice*, November 24, 1964, 2; Savio quoted in Cohen, *Freedom's Orator*, 67. The sit-in Mahoney organized is described in "Sit-in Held at RFK Office, Faster Action Wanted in Rights Cases," *Times-Picayune* (New Orleans), March 14, 1962. In November 1961, when CORE's Jerome Smith, Alice Thomas, and Thomas Valentine were attacked by a mob of thirty white men in McComb, the FBI took notes until African American taxi drivers intervened. Jerome Smith, "Eyewitness Report Exposes Miss. Mob Action," *Jet*, December 14, 1961, 4–7. The FBI was present when South Carolina state patrolmen opened fire on student demonstrators on February 8, 1968, killing three and wounding twenty-seven African American students. Bass and Nelson, *Orangeburg Massacre*; Bestor Cram and Judy Richardson, *Scarred Justice: The Orangeburg Massacre 1968* (San Francisco: California Newsreel, 2009).

39. Weaver, "Scenes from the South," *Student Voice*, November 24, 1964, 2.

40. "Highlights and Sidelights of SNCC Conference," *Militant*, December 9, 1963, 3.

41. Martin Luther King Jr., "I Have a Dream" speech, August 28, 1963, Martin Luther King, Jr. Research and Education Institute, https://kinginstitute.stanford.edu/king-papers/documents/i-have-dream-address-delivered-march-washington-jobs-and-freedom.

42. Branch, *Parting the Waters*, 508–9.

43. Neary, *Julian Bond*, 18–21; O'Neal, "Cavalier of the Month Julian Bond: More Than a Hamburger," *Cavalier*, July 1969, box 7, folder 1, JO'N. Neary may be channeling the anaphora that Julian Mayfield used in "And Then Came Baldwin," *Freedomways*, Spring 1963, 143–55. See Neary, "Hero at Large."

44. Hunter Gray, "And a Note on 'Where's the Humour in the American Radical Movement These Days?'" May 16, 2002, http://www.hunterbear.org/organizer_12.htm.

45. Sugarman donated his drawings to Tougaloo College and his photographs to Jackson State University in 1966, "believing the history should be enshrined in Mississippi." Sugarman, *Drawing Conclusions*, 53.

46. "Over 300 Attend SNCC Conference," *Student Voice*, December 9, 1963. The article estimates five hundred participants.

47. SNCC, *The New Action Army*, Winter 1967, box 3, folder 6, Ed King Papers (EK), J. D. Williams Library, Archives and Special Collections, University of Mississippi, Oxford.

48. Lester, "You Can't Go Home Again."

49. Thelwell, *Duties, Pleasures, and Conflicts*, 248–49, 235. A number of former SNCC staff supported Jackson's 1984 and 1988 campaigns. Hollis Watkins and Curtis Hayes mobilized the black southern vote, with Watkins acting as Mississippi state campaign manager for Jackson's 1984 presidential campaign and state coordinator in 1988.

50. Thelwell imagines a Junebug address at Harvard on May 1, 1964, and a "Pool Hall address" on October 2, 1964, in Jackson, Mississippi, and Junebug addressing demonstrators at Cornell University, in *Duties, Pleasures, and Conflicts*, 119, 130.

51. Thelwell, "Publishing the Black Experience," 60.

52. Carmichael and Thelwell, *Ready for the Revolution*, 103, 113, 149, 815. Thelwell describes Junebug as "the peripatetic black sage who is a legend in his own time" in *Duties, Pleasures, and Conflicts*, 123.

53. Jason Foster and Kiyoko McCrae, "From Script to Screen: Documenting the Free Southern Theater," Alternate Roots, February 2, 2016, https://alternateroots.org/from-script-to-screen-documenting-the-free-southern-theater, quoting Dent, Schechner, and Moses, *Free Southern Theater by the Free Southern Theater*.

54. Sharon L. Ciccarelli, "Reflections before and after Carnival: Interview with Derek Walcott, in Harper and Stepto, *Chant of Saints*, 298.

55. O'Neal, *Don't Start Me to Talking*, 168.

56. O'Neal, *Don't Start Me to Talking*, 162. In the play *Junebug/Jack*, O'Neal uses Junebug to represent "the collective wisdom of struggling black people," pairing him with Jack, a similar persona for "mountain people" created by the Roadside Theater founded in Appalachia. *Don't Start Me to Talking*, 314.

57. M. M. Bakhtin, *Dialogic Imagination*, 84–258. Peter Hitchcock makes a similar point about community memory in *Dialogics of the Oppressed*, 55.

58. O'Neal, *Don't Start Me to Talking*, xxv; O'Neal, "As a Weapon Is to Warfare," 2; Lester, *Falling Pieces of the Broken Sky*, 67.

59. O'Neal, *Don't Start Me to Talking*, 65.

60. Zora Neale Hurston, "Stories of Conflict," review of Richard Wright, *Uncle Tom's Children* (Harper, 1938), *Saturday Review of Literature*, April 2, 1938, 32–33.

61. Thelwell, "Back with the Wind."

62. O'Neal, "I'm the One Who It Is Talking to You," box 36, folder 8, p. 2, JO'N.

63. Lee, "What Lies Ahead for Black Americans," *Negro Digest*, November 1969, 12; Jeffries, "Remaking History," 269–71.

64. Cobb, *This Nonviolent Stuff'll Get You Killed*, 93–99.

65. O'Dell, "Life in Mississippi: An Interview with Mrs. Fannie Lou Hamer," *Freedomways* 5, no. 2 (Spring 1965), 231–42; "Machine Gun Used in Hunting Down Negro Murderer," *Evening Tribune* (Providence, R.I.) December 15, 1932; "Negro Murderer Was Killed," *Daily Mail* (Nevada, Mo.), December 15, 1923; Woodruff, *American Congo*, 138–39. Kim Lacy Rogers calls the Pullum story "the stuff of legend" in *Life and Death in the Delta*, 35.

66. Wright, *12 Million Black Voices*, 11; Cobb's family history in Moye, *Let the People Decide*, 92; Cobb, *This Nonviolent Stuff'll Get You Killed*, 37, 27–54.

67. O'Neal, *Don't Start Me to Talking*, 12.

68. In the 1990s when the Junebug columns ran in *Southern Exposure*, Four Corners, Mississippi, was still referred to as his childhood home." Jones, "Preacher in the Cornfield," 52.

69. O'Neal, "As a Weapon Is to Warfare," 2; O'Neal, "Free Southern Theater," 11–13.

70. Ladner, "What 'Black Power' Means to Negroes in Mississippi."

71. O'Neal draft fragment "Going against the Tide," box 36, folder 11, JO'N; Bill Hansen's handwritten memo is in box 36, folder 12, JO'N.

72. For analysis of rural organizing in Lee County, see Tuck, *Beyond Atlanta*, 165–76, 214.

73. O'Neal, "Field Report, March 1963, Lee County, Georgia," box 14, folder 24, JO'N; field reports, July 25, 1962–March 15, 1964, series 3, reel 7, 214, SNCC.

74. Watkins and McInnis, *Brother Hollis*, 158–60.

75. Colonel Whitten reappears as the owner of the bank in McComb, a different kind of monopoly and the first statewide bank in Mississippi, in Jones, "Brass Balls of Handsome Bailey."

76. Wright, *12 Million Black Voices*, 31. Whitten's politics changed in the 1980s when they threatened his chances of reelection. For a history of the long struggle of black farmers, see Pete Daniel's *Shadow of Slavery* and *Dispossession*, and David Shulman's documentary film *Dirt and Deeds in Mississippi* (San Francisco: California Newsreel, 2015).

77. O'Neal, *Don't Start Me to Talking*, 17.

78. Moye writes that Mrs. Hamer "reputedly used a weighted 'pea' to skew the weight of cotton that the worker had picked, revising the workers' pay upward. Hamer saw to it that her employers credited an honest day's work with something closer to an honest day's pay, but for obvious reasons could not afford to use the 'pea' indiscriminately." Moye, *Let the People Decide*, 99, xxxvi.

79. Carmichael says that Panola County "was really just one large plantation." *Ready for the Revolution*, 281. SNCC organizers supported local activism and became aware of its longer history. The Mississippi Freedom Labor Union was inaugurated in 1965, and the LCFO's calls for strikes to fight starvation wages echo those of the Southern Tenant Farmers' Union, founded in 1934.

80. Rogers, *Life and Death in the Delta*, 36.

81. Lester, *And All Our Wounds Forgiven*, 104.

82. Lester, *All Is Well*, 121–22.

83. "Junebug Jabbo Jones" typescript, box 36, file 2, p. 1, JO'N.

84. Fred Meely, "Organizer's Handbook," box 14, folder 36, 2, JO'N. This advice matches the plain speech that Watkins celebrates as community "truth-telling." Watkins, *Brother Hollis*, 8.

85. O'Neal, "I'm The One Who It is Talking to You," box 36, folder 8, p. 6, JO'N.

86. Ellison, *Going to the Territory*, 190.

87. Dollard, *Caste and Class in a Southern Town*, 309; Brown, "Negro Folk Expression"; "Slim Greer in Hell," *Collected Poems of Sterling Brown*, 89–92.

88. Carmichael with Thelwell, *Ready for the Revolution*, 291–2. Brown's students in the Nonviolent Action Group and SNCC who were writing in the 1960s are missing from Joanne V. Gabbin, "The Howard Years: The Intellectual Milieu and Brown's Legacy," *Sterling A. Brown: Building The Black Aesthetic Tradition* (1985; Charlottesville: University Press of Virginia, 1994), 49–66.

89. Collins, "Whatever Happened to Interracial Love?," in *Whatever Happened to Interracial Love?*, 47.

90. O'Neal, "A Personal Invitation: With My Mind Stayed on Freedom!," introduction to *Don't Start Me to Talking*, xxv; O'Neal cited by Richard Christiansen, "Shallow 'Sayings' from Junebug Jabbo Jones's Life," *Chicago Tribune*, June 29, 1985, 12; O'Neal, "Don't Get Me to Talking," 13.

91. Bob Hall, cofounder in 1973 and managing editor of the magazine *Southern Exposure*, quoted in Monteith, "Stetson Kennedy," *The New Encyclopedia of Southern Culture: Media*, 289-91.

92. Jones, "Elmer Fudge's Fingers," 57; Jones, "Preacher in the Cornfield," 53; Jones, "So That's Where Junebug Came From," 54-55.

93. For example Jones, "Mama Dolly's Tale," 58.

94. O'Neal quoted in Paula Crouch, "Legend of Junebug Jabbo Jones," *Atlanta Journal*, January 16, 1985.

95. S. E. Anderson, Black Education for Liberation, http://www.blackeducator.org.

96. Cobb, "Over My Head: I See Freedom in the Air," xi.

Chapter 3. Inside Stories

Epigraphs are from Marion S. Barry and the *Student Voice* staff at SNCC, "Memo on 'The Student Voice," Fall 1960 [stamped November 3, 1960], http://www.crmvet.org/docs/60_sncc_sv-memo.pdf; Tom Hayden, "Revolution in Mississippi," 21; Charles Cobb, "Empowering Communities," 146.

1. Zellner and Curry, *Wrong Side of Murder Creek*, 138; Carson, *In Struggle*, 27.

2. Alice Gardner Murphy, letter to Ronnie [Dugger], cc. Julian Bond, series 4, reel 7, 221, SNCC. A selection of brochures is in box 14, folders 13-14, JO'N.

3. Browning in Curry et al., *Deep in Our Hearts*, 83; SNCC pamphlet, 1963, box 14, folder 14, JO'N.

4. Forman, *Making of Black Revolutionaries*, 223. In 1972, Forman did not recall his arrival in Atlanta in the same way as Zellner would in 2008. He wrote that he had to jimmy the lock to enter the office to answer a ringing telephone and did not yet have the information that the caller from *Newsweek* was seeking.

5. *Student Voice* 1 (June 1960), 3.

6. "Memo on 'The Student Voice," http://www.crmvet.org/docs/60_sncc_sv-memo.pdf.

7. Branch, *Parting the Waters*, 533.

8. Minnis left the SRC because he testified in the case of SNCC volunteer Joni Rabinowitz that the jury's prejudice placed her in "serious jeopardy of a miscarriage of justice." "Minnis, Biographical Sketch," series 4, reel 7, 221, SNCC.

9. MFDP's Al Johnson confided in Steve Weissman, Freedom Summer volunteer, that he felt this way. Renata Adler, "The Price of Peace Is Confusion," *New Yorker*, December 11, 1965, 195-202. Joe Street asserted that a "new obligation of staff members to submit regular reports on their work—in effect having to justify their existence—furthered [sic] fractured SNCC's community" after SNCC expanded its staff at the end of the Mississippi Freedom Summer project. Street, "From Beloved Community to Imagined Community," 124.

10. Bond, foreword to Forman, *Making of Black Revolutionaries* xi; Bond, foreword to *This Little Light of Ours*, 15.

11. Reagon, introduction to *We'll Never Turn Back*, 9. In 1966, students from the University of Wisconsin were prescient in collecting and archiving CORE and COFO records for the Wisconsin Historical Society. The work of Mimi Feingold (Real), Bob and Vicki

Gabriner, Leah Johnson, and Gwen Gillon, SNCC's youngest staff member, is celebrated by Michael Edmonds in the afterword ("Freedom Summer Documents") to his *Risking Everything: A Freedom Summer Reader* (209–23). They were aided by contacts made through Hollis Watkins and contributions of papers by Charles Sherrod, Lawrence Guyot, Sam Shirah, and others.

12. M. S. Smith, *Photography on the Color Line*, 9.

13. Marshall Ganz, "Why Stories Matter: The Art and Craft of Social Change," *Sojourners*, March 2009, 4. This essay originated in a presentation at a *Sojourners* Training for Change conference in June 2008, in which his three-part story model begins with the individual, shares the values of the group, and is understood as an activist strategy that Ganz grounded in his experience with SNCC.

14. Murphree details how Friends of SNCC groups were charged with writing letters to the editor when SNCC submitted press releases that wire services failed to use.

15. Dick Gregory, "Speech at Brown Chapel A.M.E. Church," in David W. Houck and David E. Dixon, eds. *Rhetoric, Religion and the Civil Rights Movement 1954–1965* (Waco, Tex.: Baylor University Press, 2006), 597. Houck and Dixon imply that Bernard Lafayette's field report was written in June 1965, but it was the June 1963 report that Forman reproduced in full and credited in *Making of Black Revolutionaries*, 317–26. Charles Payne describes a similar speech Gregory made in Greenwood, Mississippi, in April 1963 in which he denounced ministers by name, which led to thirty-one local ministers signing a statement of support and urging parishioners to register to vote. Payne, *I've Got the Light of Freedom*, 197–99.

16. SNCC Freedom Center, Chicago, box 3389, folder 1, Southern Conference Educational Fund Papers, Georgia State University Library, Special Collections, Atlanta.

17. Bond, foreword to Forman, *Making of Black Revolutionaries*, xi.

18. Forman, *Making of Black Revolutionaries*, 317.

19. DeLott, "A Reconsideration of the 'Freedom High' and 'Hardliner' Factions of SNCC," August 2, 1994 (revised September 15, 1994, and November 1994), document 93, 2, Elaine DeLott Baker Papers.

20. SNCC used Connie Curry's mimeograph machine, supplied by the SRC and located at her National Student Association office in Atlanta until Stembridge made the case for an offset printer. Curry in Curry et al., *Deep in Our Hearts*, 14.

21. "Explanation of Current Needs," July 15, 1963, series 2, reel 24, 642, SNCC.

22. Mary King records Stembridge's letter as written on November 15, 1963. M. King, *Freedom Song*, 122–23. In May 1966, Cobb proved the value of making and keeping copies in a different context when he was able to submit an article on SNCC's conceptualization of Black Power to *Negro Digest* despite having mislaid the original. Charles Cobb, letter to David Llorens at *Negro Digest*, May 31, 1966, box 138, folder 2, JF.

23. Guyot and Thelwell, "Politics of Survival and Necessity in Mississippi," 102 (emphasis in original). See also Grant, "Mississippi and 'The Establishment'"; Morton, "Tremor in the Iceberg,"; Richards, "With Our Minds Set on Freedom."

24. Hamer quoted in in Dent, Schechner, and Moses, *Free Southern Theater*, 178. See also W. F. Minor, "They Are Waiting for Godot in Mississippi Too," *New York Times*, January 31, 1965.

25. Bob Moses letter to Martha Prescod, December 11, 1962, Greenville, Mississippi, https://www.crmvet.org/lets/6212_moses-prescod-letter.pdf.

26. Miller, *Danville, Virginia*, 3, 15; "Demonstrations Begin: Five Arrested in Danville," *Student Voice*, December 16, 1963, 1, 4.

27. Matthew Jones's freedom songs, box 44, folder 15, JF.

28. SNCC Executive Committee minutes, April 12-14, 1965, Holly Springs, Mississippi, 26, 30, SNCC.

29. Cobb, "Depictions of the Movement in Popular Culture," in *SNCC 50th Anniversary Conference*, vol. 19, produced by Natalie Bullock Brown (San Francisco: California Newsreel, 2011); Cobb, *On the Road to Freedom*, xxiii; Forman, *Making of Black Revolutionaries*, 317.

30. Established in 1944, the SRC was a liberal biracial coalition that emerged out of the Atlanta-based Commission on Interracial Cooperation that was founded in 1919. The coalition sought ways to reform the segregated South by focusing on poverty and racial injustice and facilitated the funding for the regional voter education project in which SNCC participated. The more left-wing biracial SCEF was established in 1946 as the educational wing of the Southern Conference for Human Welfare. It pursued a more radical agenda and was persistently red-baited. In the context of SNCC, and by the 1960s, the SRC's think tank produced research that underpinned SNCC organizers' understanding of a longer history of activism in the South, and the SCEF worked closely with SNCC and is often seen as synonymous with the Bradens in the 1960s. "Southern Conference Educational Fund," https://snccdigital.org/inside-sncc/alliances-relationships/scef.

31. Bond, foreword to Zellner and Curry *Wrong Side of Murder Creek*, 10; Bond quoted in Tom Gardner and Catherine A. Fosi, *"The Southern Patriot, 1942-1973,"* in *The Encyclopedia of Social Movement Media*, ed. John H. Dowling (London: Sage, 2011), 502.

32. A finance report for January 1 through April 19, 1961, submitted April 21, includes $84.38 expense for *"New South* writer's services for work on *The Student Voice*. Series 3, reel 3, frame 78, SNCC.

33. Carson, *In Struggle*, 51-53; Dittmer, *Local People*, 230-31. See also Anne Braden articles: "What Is a White Person's Place in the Struggle?" *Southern Patriot*, September 1960, 4; "Student Protest Taking Permanent Form," *Southern Patriot*, October 1960, 4; "Student Movement: New Phase," *Southern Patriot*, November 1960, 4; "The Images Are Broken: Students Challenge Rural Georgia," *Southern Patriot*, December 1962, 1-3; "The Cry Was Unity," *Southern Exposure*, Fall 1999, 27-32; "A New Crusade for Racial Justice," *Southern Exposure*, 25th Anniversary Edition, 1999, 18-19.

34. Margaret Long's letter to Julian Bond (undated, but sometime in 1965), series 3, reel 4, frame 210, SNCC. Despite "Coordinating" being part of the organization's name, coordination was a structural problem for SNCC's self-conception as history-making rather than merely a "coordinating agency" for other student-led groups. Long advocated "a more vigorous and accurate and less wornout synonym," but as group identifier and branding it was too late to act on that suggestion.

35. Hayden was with Paul Potter (vice president of the NSA and later an SDS president), driving alongside marching demonstrators in McComb on October 11, 1961, when segregationists dragged both men from the car and beat them. "The Port Huron Statement," in Albert and Albert, *Sixties Papers*, 181, 187.

36. McDew, foreword to Hayden, *Revolution in Mississippi*, n.p.

37. Lauter quoted in Greenberg, *Circle of Trust*, 83.

38. Newfield, *Prophetic Minority*; Carson, *In Struggle*, 175-190; Hogan, *Many Minds, One Heart*, 133-140; Polletta, "Strategy and Democracy in the New Left," 163.

39. *A History of the Book in America*, vol. 5, segues from the black press in the 1950s and mid-1960s to entries on black cultural nationalism. SNCC is mentioned once: "[the Black Arts Movement] shared the categories of 'blackness' and 'black power' with radical civil rights groups such as SNCC." David Paul Nord, Joan Shelley Rubin, and Michael Schudson, eds., *A History of the Book in America*, vol. 5, *Print Culture in Postwar America*

(Chapel Hill: University of North Carolina Press, 2014), 232. John D. H. Dowling, *Encyclopedia of Social Movement Media* (Thousand Oaks, Calif.: Sage, 2011), 502, 504, mentions SNCC only in the context of the *Southern Patriot*'s impact in communicating SNCC's ideas. In his groundbreaking study of the underground press and alternative activist media, John McMillian acknowledges, "Participatory democracy did not originate in the New Left; many whites gleaned the concept from the civil rights movement, particularly the Student Nonviolent Coordinating Committee's emphasis on consensus building and 'group-centered leadership.'" But he leaves it there. McMillian, *Smoking Typewriters*, 9. SDS-centric personal and collective histories, exemplified by Todd Gitlin's *The Sixties: Years of Hope, Days of Rage* (New York: Bantam, 1987) and James Miller's *"Democracy in the Streets": From Port Huron to the Siege of Chicago* (New York: Simon and Schuster, 1987), rolled back from early recognition that SNCC was instrumental for understanding the New Left. Eric Conyers Jr. doesn't see white radical student initiatives dovetailing with SNCC until 1966. Conyers, *Afrocentric Traditions* (2005; repr., New York: Routledge, 2017), 178.

40. Margaret Long, "Strictly Subjective," *New South* 19, no. 3 (March 1964), 2, 5.

41. Long, "All God's Chillun," 12.

42. Long, "Strictly Subjective," *New South* 19, no. 3 (March 1964), 11, 14. Worth Long was subjected to beatings, including one logged in a field report in September 1963. Arrested for "parading without a permit," he was beaten by Mr. W. T. Marvell in the Selma, Alabama, jail. "When asked a question not related to the usual questions asked, and when [he] did not answer quickly, [he] was smacked against a wall four times, hit in the area of eyes and jaw, judo chopped across the neck 20 times—all this before 20 witnesses. Getting up affidavit now. Has pix of face when released from jail." Selma Report, September 17, 1963, 2, series 4, reel 210, SNCC.

43. When Margaret Long's editorial is read alongside Bond's eulogy for Louis Allen in the same issue of *New South*, how dangerous "telling it like it is" could be is achingly clear. Julian Bond, "Activism of the Late Mr. Allen," *New South*, 19, no. 3 (March 1964), 12. See also Hodding Carter, *Where Main Street Meets the River*, 253, where he describes denying honorifics to African Americans as "one of the longest-lasting of deep Southern taboos."

44. Watters and Cleghorn, *Climbing Jacob's Ladder*, 171.

45. Riva, "Desegregating Downtown Little Rock." Bill Hansen initiated SNCC's projects in Arkansas on October 24, 1962.

46. Carmichael and Thelwell, *Ready for the Revolution*, 160.

47. Bond letter to Moses, December 6, 1962, box 2, folder 9, Howard Zinn Papers, Wisconsin Historical Society, Madison. Denise Nicholas prefaced a field report with a poem to the Atlanta office: "I Guess / You Know Already/ How Hot It Is Here ... All These Little Pieces Of Our Souls In This Thing ... Here Are Letters For / Your Files ... Denise." Nicholas to "Joy," front matter epigraph to Dent, Schechner, and Moses, *Free Southern Theater*, n.p.

48. De Lissovoy, *Great Pool Jump*, 95; SNCC, Inter-Staff Newsletter, December 2, 1962, 2, reel 15, SNCC.

49. Frank Smith letter, December 8, 1962, http://www.crmvet.org/lets/621208_franksmith-let.pdf.

50. Willie Ricks, Lee County Field Report, March 15, 1964, series 4, reel 7, p. 230, SNCC.

51. Charles Sherrod, Albany Field Report, March 10, 1963, box 15, folder 23, JO'N.

52. Forman letter to Ian Ballantine, December 30, 1961, box 144, folder 9, JF.

53. An excerpt from Zinn's report is reproduced on the sleeve of *Freedom in the Air: A Documentary on Albany, Georgia*, the LP produced by Alan Lomax and Guy Carawan and released and distributed by SNCC, with a statement by Lewis W. Jones: "Saying and singing as they do on this record, the people of Albany strengthen their morale while telling their story to all who would hear." Author's copy, with thanks to Shaun Belcher for the gift.

54. Bond and Lewis, *Gonna Sit at the Welcome Table*, 526–27.
55. Ian Ballantine letter to Forman, January 3, 1962, box 144, folder 9, JF.
56. Julius Lester, "Review of *Sammy Young Jr.*," *New York Times*, April 13, 1969.
57. Zinn, *Southern Mystique*, 265, 6–7.
58. Anne Braden letter to Victor Rabinowitz, January 2, 1961, box 141, folder 8, JF; Forman, "Black Oral Documentary Project," box 128, file 1 (no date, but the project was still being envisaged in the early 1970s), JF. Rabinowitz was a white SNCC funder who joined the Freedom Summer project in 1964 when he met and married second wife Joanne Grant. He was legal counsel for Bond when Bond was denied his seat in the Georgia statehouse in 1966. Braden circulated interviews that Forman conducted in Little Rock in 1958.
59. Coles, "South That Is Man's Destiny," 257.
60. Lewis Perry, co-editor of the *New Freedom*, letter to James Forman, October 21, 1961, series 4, reel 7, 249, SNCC; "Facts ... McComb, Mississippi," and "Freedom Songbook," box 14, folder 114, JO'N; Moses, "Mississippi," 7.
61. Pete Cummings, "Benton Co. Report," August 15, 1964, series 4, reel 7, 239, 3–4, SNCC.
62. Chatfield, field report, in Watters and Cleghorn, *Climbing Jacob's Ladder*, 178–79.
63. Joan Browning's first impression of Bond was as a writer, and she thought of writers as "mysterious, creative, magical people." Browning, "Shiloh Witness," 67. Bond shared his poetry with Zinn whenever he visited his home on the Spelman College campus. Zinn, *You Can't Be Neutral on a Moving Train*, 192.
64. Mary King, *Freedom Song*, 233.
65. Bond, Letter to Cynthia Washington, December 14, 1963, series 7, reel 5, 256, SNCC.
66. Casey Hayden letter to Arthur Waskow, September 4, 1963, Arthur Ocean Waskow Papers, 1943–1977, Wisconsin Historical Society Digital Collections, http://content.wisconsinhistory.org/digital/collection/p15932coll2/id/29715; original correspondence and mailings, 1963–64, box 15, folder 11, SNCC.
67. Bond, "Media and the Movement," 33; Bond letter to Julie Prettyman, September 12, 1963, series 7, reel 3, 97–99, SNCC. Carson cites forty thousand subscriptions in *Student Voice, 1960–1965*, vii.
68. Sutherland's letters to Marion Barry, Betty Garman, and Forman in 1964 close, "[Getting] back to my book." Box 1, folder 1, ESM.
69. Jacqueline Bernard letter to parents of volunteers in New York; Frank E. Taylor, editor McGraw-Hill Books, to Sutherland, March 3, 1966, reel 1, 790, SNCC.
70. SNCC circulated Sutherland's *Nation* article as a driver for funding: "Over 200 Mississippi Summer Volunteers Have Chosen to Remain in the State. They Need You Help. Support SNCC Now." Box 2, folder 6, EK.
71. Mary King in Executive Committee minutes, April 18–19, Atlanta, 1964, 8, SNCC.
72. Rinzler interviewed by Julian Cox, in Cox, *Danny Lyon: Message to the Future*, 73.
73. Hansberry, *To Be Young Gifted and Black*, xx.
74. Hansberry, *Movement*, 116; publicity for *The Movement*, *Student Voice*, July 1965, 4.

75. "Exclusive Interview: John Lewis of SNCC," *Liberator*, July 1964, 15. In De Lissovoy's fictionalization of the Albany movement, *Muhammad Speaks* is the only newspaper to report the rape of a black girl that incenses organizers in Southwest Georgia. De Lissovoy, *Feelgood*, 89.

76. Hansberry, *To Be Young Gifted and Black*, 246. She wrote a letter to the *New York Times* to this effect, but it declined to print it, as "too personal," she told the forum.

77. Blair, *Harlem Crossroads*, 206, 203, 207–8.

78. Lewis in Executive Committee minutes, April 18–19, 1964, 8. SNCC; Mary King, *Freedom Song*, 232; Rinzler interviewed by Julian Cox, in Cox, *Danny Lyon: Message to the Future*, 76.

79. "Photographers with prints at S and S," January 17, 1964, reel A, 11, 36, SNCC. Ten thousand paperbound copies were priced to sell at $1.95, with a smaller cloth edition encouraging further sales. On rights to *The Movement*, see Simon and Schuster's letter to Forman, box 144, folder 11, JF.

80. Cobb, introduction to Cieciorka and Cieciorka, *Negroes in American History*, n.p.

81. "Student Voice Prospectus," 3, 115, SNCC.

82. Bond, "Nonviolence."

83. Forman, *Making of Black Revolutionaries*, 223–24.

84. Denise Moses, letter to John Lewis, January 6, 1965, box 101, folder 1, FST. Nicholas was married to Gilbert Moses at time of writing.

85. Donaldson, "Notes from Southern Diaries"; Donaldson, "Greenville, MS Field Report 30 October–5 November, 1963," 2a–2d, series 4, box 17, folder 1, SNCC. The article follows the field report almost verbatim. In 1979, Donaldson explained the fear this way: "I mean I think I cranked it up and for one of the few times for me you know I mean I think I felt really shaken by the experience and I put my hand on the driver's—I mean I couldn't do anything. I mean I was shaking; I just kind of sat there." Interview with Donaldson, conducted by Blackside, *Eyes on the Prize: America's Civil Rights Years (1954–1965)*, Henry Hampton Collection, Special Collections, Washington University Libraries, St. Louis. Statement by Landy McNair: SNCC Field Secretary," July 15, 1963, Gadsden, Alabama, series 4, reel 7, 227, SNCC.

86. Donaldson, "Notes from Southern Diaries," 141.

87. The first version of the poem is published as "BOY, if you feel sorry for these black sons of bitches, why don't you take them all up north you ... nigger." Cobb, *In the Furrows of the World*, 31. It is reprinted as "Poem #1," in Gitlin, *Campfires of the Resistance*, 11.

88. Cobb has four men present, while Donaldson records that they were three after having left Bob Moses at the Jackson airport.

89. T. S. Eliot, *Selected Essays* (London: Faber and Faber, 1958), 250–51.

90. Gitlin, *Campfires of the Resistance*, xiv.

91. Mary King, *Freedom Song*, 124; Daniel, *Lost Revolutions*, 289–302; Stembridge letter to Lillian Smith, August 3, 1964, Series A1283, box 4, Lillian Smith Papers, Hargrett Rare Book and Manuscript Library, University of Georgia Libraries, Athens. Much of Smith and Stembridge's correspondence of 1960–64 is available in boxes 24, 25, 88, Smith Papers. On Stembridge making visits to Smith's home, alone or with other civil rights workers, see Curry et al., *Deep in Our Hearts*, 22. Between them, Anne C. Loveland and Pete Daniel have unpacked the context in which support of SNCC by this courageous writer gave way to approbation. Loveland, *Lillian Smith: A Southerner Confronting the South* (Baton Rouge: Louisiana State University Press, 1986); Daniel, *Lost Revolutions*, 201–2.

92. Jo Ann Robinson, "Lillian Smith: Reflections on Race and Sex," *Southern Exposure* 4, no. 4 (1977), 43–48.

93. Lillian Smith, "Are We Still Buying a New World with Old Confederate Bills?," box 59, folder 40, Smith Papers; Chatfield quoted in Watters and Cleghorn, *Climbing Jacob's Ladder*, 154.

94. Stembridge, "Field Report, Greenwood, Mississippi," October 20, 1963, series 7, reel 17, 0123, SNCC.

95. Stembridge, *I Play Flute* (1966), 6.

96. Forman, *Making of Black Revolutionaries*, 449.

97. An extract from "Fish Are Jumping an' the Cotton Is High" appears in Carmichael and Thelwell, *Ready for the Revolution*, where Carmichael describes the Delta landscape as "my first experience in *unlearning*" because it was unlike anything he had encountered, and "a friend from Howard [Thelwell] I took on a tour of the Delta wrote about the experience" (280).

98. Benjamin, *Illuminations*, 87.

99. Thelwell's essay was used as a model through which college students could develop critical reading skills in Spears, *Modern College Reading*, in 1971.

100. "The plane dropped a flare, circled, and released a small explosive, which went off near the building without doing damage. Then it roared off into the darkness, leaving the meeting in a state of fear and confusion." John Herbers, "Communiqué from the Mississippi Front," *New York Times Magazine*, November 8, 1964.

101. There are many accounts of seeing children in this state, as summarized by McAdam, *Freedom Summer*, 87, and Watson, *Freedom Summer*, 61.

102. *Hungry Children* (Atlanta: Southern Regional Council, 1967). Physicians from Harvard, Yale, and MIT worked with private practitioners from Yazoo City, Mississippi, and Charlotte, North Carolina. Robert Coles represented Harvard. This is discussed in Watters, "South and the Nation," 9–10, and Dittmer, *Good Doctors*, 233–34.

103. Sugarman, *We Had Sneakers, They Had Guns*, 87–88; Nicholas, *Freshwater Road*, 119.

104. Garry Fullerton, "King Delayed by Bomb Scare," *Nashville Tennessean*, April 21, 1960; Houston, *Nashville Way*, 116–17; Branch, *Parting the Waters*, 392–93, 391.

105. Watters, *Down to Now*, 113, quoting from his 1965 journal.

106. Lafayette, "Freedom Rider," 11.

107. "Gregory, Hansen, Sentenced, Fined," *Student Voice*, March 3, 1964, 4.

108. R. H. King, "Citizenship and Self-Respect," 12. Colley begins to examine the history of the idea in *Ain't Scared of Your Jail*.

109. De Lissovoy, *Feelgood*, 23.

110. George Raymond died of congestive heart failure at age thirty in 1973. His legacy of sustained work, especially in Canton, Mississippi, is recorded in M. J. O'Brien, *We Shall Not be Moved: The Jackson Woolworth's Sit-In and the Movement It Inspired* (Jackson: University Press of Mississippi, 2013), 262–66.

111. Rainer Maria Rilke, *The Notebook of Malte Laurids Brigge*, translated by J. Linton (Oxford: Oxford University Press, 1984), 5.

112. DeLott, "the jail," document 66, Elaine DeLott Baker Papers.

113. De Lott, affidavit, December 15, 1964, document 68, 2, Elaine DeLott Baker Papers.

114. De Lott letter to Benjamin and Rosa De Lott, December 1964, document 67, 1–2; archival note that introduces her letter to Benjamin and Rosa De Lott, April 2, 1965, document 80, Elaine DeLott Baker Papers.

115. McCord, *Mississippi*, 189–90.
116. Samuel Block, "A Day in a Mississippi Court," box 67, folder 3, FST.
117. Branch, *Parting the Waters*, 715.
118. Zinn, *SNCC*, 211; Block interviewed by Joseph Sinsheimer, December 12, 1986, 68–70, JAS. Traveling from Greenwood to Starksville, they were arrested and jailed in Columbus on the eve of the Mississippi Freedom Summer project.
119. Samuel Block, "A Day in a Mississippi Court," box 67, folder 3, FST, 17–18, 30–32, 20. The section Block includes from "Down at the Cross" is Baldwin's depiction of the "pathos" that caused churches to "rock." Baldwin, *Fire Next Time*, 36.
120. Trumpauer letter to Anne and Carl Braden, July 28, 1962, series 4, reel 7, 242, SNCC. On March 14, 1963, *Jet* published "Burnings, Jailings, Shooting Reported in Greenwood, MS."
121. Frank Smith interviewed by Sinsheimer, May 23, 1986, 8–9, JAS.
122. Payne describes a "Captain Ussery" kicking Forman (basing this on "Harassment and Violence: Greenwood Mississippi," a written account by Stembridge). Payne, *I've Got the Light of Freedom*, 296–97, 473n15.
123. Hendrickson, *Sons of Mississippi*, 104–5, 323.
124. Block interviewed by Sinsheimer, 28, 58, JAS; Claude Sitton, "Sheriff Harasses Negroes at Voting Rally in Georgia," *New York Times*, July 27, 1962.
125. Samuel Block, "A Day in a Mississippi Court," box 67, folder 3, FST, 1, 4, 6, 8, prefatory notes, 12, 32; Mitchell Zimmerman, "Journal Entry, 6 December 1965," 231.
126. Walter, *Terror and Resistance*, 81.
127. Zinn in Carson, *In Struggle*, 142.
128. Thelwell, "Organizer," 22.
129. Mary King, *Freedom Song*, 562.
130. "Interview with Charles Sherrod, October 30, 1970, Albany Georgia," 22, box 40, folder 16, JO'N.
131. Newfield, "The Question of SNCC," *Nation*, July 19, 1965, 38.
132. *News from the Field* (SNCC Atlanta Office) 3 (March 9, 1966), 2.
133. Forman, *Rock Bottom* (1967), box 128, folder 1, JF.
134. Miller, "An Internal Education for SNCC," n.d., box 7, folder 1, Ella Baker Papers.
135. Moses advocated an internal educational program in 1963 because "three or four years from now people will step into office ... who have not been in any way identified with the movement." Visser-Maessen, *Robert Parris Moses*, 148. The program devised in 1966 was described in SNCC's *Aframerican News for You*, October 12, 1966. Nash assessed in 1988, "We did not devote enough time and energy into the education of the people coming in." Nash, in Greenberg, *Circle of Trust*, 22.
136. Lester, "To Recapture the Dream," 28.
137. Forman, *Rock Bottom* (1967), 3–4, box 128, folder 1, JF.
138. Forman, *Rock Bottom* (1967), 12, 17, box 128, folder 1, JF.
139. Miller, "What Is an Organizer?," n.d., box 34, folder 9, JO'N. The *Movement* solicited answers to the question "What is an organizer?" *Movement* (SNCC of California), June 1965, 1.
140. Lawson, "Organizer's Notebook," *Movement* (SNCC of California), December 1966, 2; Garrett, "How an Organizer Works: Some Rambling Guidelines for Freedom School Organizers," *Movement* (SNCC of California), August 1965, 7; James, "Organizer's Notebook: Theater That Does Something," *Movement* (SNCC of California), April 1967, 11.
141. Editor's preface to untitled pamphlet ("There is no title. The words will speak to what this booklet is.... The words you give other booklets will make them what they are"), *Student Voice* Inc., box 14, folder 114, JO'N.

142. Moore would become a significant labor leader. In 2009 he was writing "a history of my fifty years in the struggle to give voice to the powerless." "Bob Moore (Robert Moore)," http://www.crmvet.org/vet/moorebob.htm. George Curry was one of the most influential African American journalists of the twentieth century, with a long career from *Sports Illustrated* to editor-in-chief for the National Newspaper Publishers Association News Service. "George Curry," HistoryMakers, http://www.thehistorymakers.org/biography/george-curry-40.

143. Carson in Greenberg, *A Circle of Trust*, 198.

144. Dittmer, *Local People*, 432. A math literacy initiative, the Algebra Project, of which Moses is founder and president, builds on his experience of "bottom-up" organizing in the 1960s and his training in mathematics. Since 1982 it has supported young people, particularly in the bottom economic quartile, and changed the culture of the classroom. Algebra Project Inc., https://algebra.org/wp/.

145. Hogan, *Many Minds, One Heart*, 115–16.

146. Lawson, letter to the editor, *Movement* (SNCC of California), December 1966, 2.

147. Cobb, "Empowering Communities," 155; Michael Harrington, "Mystical Militants; Tom Hayden, *Thoughts of the Young Radicals*, 67.

148. Lester, *Search for the New Land*, 69; Bakhtin, *Dialogic Imagination*, 421, 254; Hirschkop, "Is Dialogism for Real?" 108–9, 113; Euben, "Politics of Literature," 327–28.

149. Charlie Jones in Bond and Lewis, *Gonna Sit at the Welcome Table*, 410–11.

Chapter 4. Adjusting the Lens of Professional "Objectivity"

Epigraphs are from J. Lewis and D'Orso, *Walking with the Wind*, 275; Coles, "Serpents and Doves," 188; Forman, *Making of Black Revolutionaries*, 209; Grant in Greenberg, *A Circle of Trust*, 70.

1. Garrow, *Bearing the Cross*, 172.

2. Fairclough, *To Redeem the Soul of America*, 143.

3. Forman, *Making of Black Revolutionaries*, 245. Journalist A. C. Searles, who founded and edited the African American newspaper *Southwest Georgian* in Albany, claimed that the movement changed attitudes. "What did we win? We won self-respect.... This movement made me demand a semblance of first-class citizenship." Quoted in Watters, *Down to Now*, 158. Shirley Sherrod made the point forcibly again in 2016: "It goes back to historians saying that Albany was a failure. And I run into that all the time and I say, 'Was Dr. King the movement?' Because the movement was going on before he came and it continued after he left. So we've had to battle that." "The Emergence of Black Power," SNCC Oral Histories Conference transcript, July 9–10, 2016, 15, CDSD.

4. Chatfield quotes Sherrod in his foreword to Greenberg, *Circle of Trust*, xiii.

5. "Soil of discontent" is one of many metaphors Zinn used to describe the mood. Zinn, *SNCC*, 269.

6. Chatfield, foreword to Greenberg, *Circle of Trust*, xii, xiii. The article was Claude Sitton, "Sheriff Harasses Negroes at Voting Rally in Georgia," *New York Times*, July 27, 1962.

7. Nelson, *Scoop*, 138.

8. Ashmore, awarded a Pulitzer Prize for editorials in the *Arkansas Gazette*, was speaking at "Covering the South: A National Symposium on the Media and the Civil Rights Movement," April 3–5, 1987, University of Mississippi.

9. Hazel V. Carby subjects the term "race men" to trenchant critique in *Race Men* (Cambridge, Mass.: Harvard University Press, 1998), as does Steve Estes in *I Am a Man! Race, Manhood and the Civil Rights Movement* (Chapel Hill: University of North Carolina Press, 2006).

10. Bond, "The Southern Youth Movement," *Freedomways* 2, no. 3 (Summer 1962), 309; SNCC Funding Appeal, "The Right to Vote... 100 Years Later," in Bond and Lewis, *Gonna Sit at the Welcome Table*, 430–33.

11. Bond quoted in Murphree, *Selling of Civil Rights*, 28. Brackets in original.

12. Anonymous volunteer in Coles, *Children of Crisis*, 228–29.

13. Coles, "Serpents and Doves," 188. Coles admitted, "Until I listened to those civil rights workers talk about their humble origins or the restrictions and confinement they had experienced while they worked in the movement, I was not able to comprehend their passionate outcries, their fierce insistence that their cause must prevail." Coles, *Call of Service*, 27.

14. Watters, *Down to Now*, 146.

15. "Registration Efforts in Mississippi Continue Despite Violence and Terror," *Student Voice*, October 1962, 2; Carson, *In Struggle*, 79 (citing McLaurin); Hogan, *Many Minds, One Heart*, 176 (cites Sherrod admitting he needed to supervise new recruits twenty-four hours a day).

16. D. Gorton quoted in Raiford, *Imprisoned in a Luminous Glare*, 78.

17. Good, *Trouble I've Seen*, 256–57.

18. Fleming, *Son of the Rough South*, 260, 255.

19. Von Hoffman, *Mississippi Notebook*, 35.

20. Per Laursen, letter to James Forman, June 10, 1961, series 4, reel 7, 212, SNCC.

21. Zellner and Curry, *Wrong Side of Murder Creek*, 182.

22. Per Laursen, letter to James Forman, March 16, 1963, series 4, reel 7, 212, SNCC; Lynn Nesbit quoted in Tracy Daugherty, *Hiding Man: A Biography of Donald Bartheleme* (New York: St Martin's Press, 2009), 253. Nesbit alleges that Laursen suffered "a terrible writer's block" but provides no details.

23. Zinn, preface to *SNCC*, ix; Watters, *Down to Now*, 127.

24. Halberstam, "Education of a Journalist." Halberstam felt that the *Tennessean* created the environment in which he could learn "how to work a story" and that its newsroom was a "joyous, combative, aggressive, and wildly independent place, staffed by a rare assortment of talented people who probably would not have been hired by any other respectable place. It was a rare paper in the sense that it had an institutional value system all its own." Halberstam, "The Education of a Journalist."

25. Robert Churchwell interviewed by Jerrad Davis, in Cosby and Poussaint, *Wealth of Wisdom*, 75–78; Fred Cloud, "Pioneer in the Newsroom," *Nashville*, September 1969, box 4, folder 1, Robert Churchwell Papers, Manuscript, Archives, and Rare Books Library, Emory University, Atlanta.

26. Halberstam, *Children*, 724, 721.

27. J. Lewis and D'Orso, *Walking with the Wind*, 105, 275.

28. Halberstam, *Children*, 726; J. Lewis and D'Orso, *Walking with the Wind*, 105.

29. Halberstam, "Education of a Journalist." Halberstam thought his sixties pieces had been "quite clinical" despite articles like "Kids Take Over."

30. Halberstam's *The Noblest Roman* (Boston: Houghton Mifflin, 1961) is a southern crime fiction based in bootlegging and local politics. In 2001 he described it as an apprenticeship that taught him that he was not a novelist. "In Depth with David Halberstam," November 4, 2001, C-SPAN, https://www.c-span.org/.

31. Ralph Wiley, "Young Heroes: An Epic Tale, Flaws and All," *Chicago Sun-Times*, March 15, 1998; David Oshinsky, "Freedom Riders," *New York Times*, March 15, 1998.

32. The "sit-in clinics" focused on stopping what James Lawson called "the clock of fear" that allowed segregation to tick on. Sanders, *Intelligent and Effective Direction*, 107.

33. Hogan, *Many Minds, One Heart*, 17–25.
34. Coles, "More on Southern Politics: *Climbing Jacob's Ladder*," *New Republic*, December 16, 1967, 20.
35. Hobson, *But Now I See*, 106–19; Foley, "Generic and Doctrinal Politics in the Proletarian Bildungsroman," 43.
36. Watters quoted in Sarah Spell-Johnson, "Beloved Journalist, Teacher Dies in Abbeville [Louisiana]," *Abbeville (La.) Meridional*, August 8, 1999.
37. Watters, *Encounter with the Future*. An important addendum missed when focusing on Watters's "conversion" is his later role of "angry middle-aged man" after being "laid off" by the SRC and finding no employment in the press or the movement, *The Angry Middle-Aged Man* (New York: Grossman, 1976), 28.
38. Watters, "South and the Nation," 18, 19.
39. Watters, *Encounter with the Future*, 2.
40. Watters, *Down to Now*, 185; Lischer, *Preacher King*, 246 (Lischer also references Birmingham Police department records of mass meetings); Martin, *Framed!*, 70.
41. Joanne Grant, letter to Margaret Long, October 23, 1960, box 2, Margaret Long Papers, Odum Library, Archives and Special Collections, Valdosta State University, Valdosta, Georgia.
42. Grant, "Time Is Always Now"; Tom Hayden, *Revolution in Mississippi*, 1; Grant "Way of Life in Mississippi."
43. *Communist Training Operations, Part 2, Communist Activities and Propaganda among Youth Groups, Hearing before the Committee on Un-American Activities, February 26, 1960*, 1471–76; Gosse, *Where the Boys Are*, 145.
44. Carson, *In Struggle*, 93–95.
45. Grant in Greenberg, *Circle of Trust*, 70.
46. Lynd, *Accompanying*, 54 (here Lynd built on his essay "Remembering SNCC"); Bond, foreword to *Ella Baker: Freedom Bound*, xv–xvi.
47. Zinn letter to Louie (no surname) at Beacon Press, September 17, 1963; the proposal was submitted to Arnold Trowell. Box 1, folder 15, Zinn Papers.
48. Zinn, *You Can't Be Neutral on a Moving Train*, 69.
49. A. Lynd and S. Lynd, *Stepping Stones*, 99.
50. Zinn, *SNCC*, 4.
51. Zinn, "Kennedy."
52. Zinn, "SNCC: The Battle-Scarred Youngsters," *Nation*, October 5, 1963, http://howardzinn.org/sncc-the-battle-scarred-youngsters.
53. Newfield, "Question of SNCC," 38, 39, 40.
54. Eugene G. Genovese, "Abolitionist," review of Lynd's *Class Conflict, Slavery, and the United States Constitution* and *Intellectual Origins of American Radicalism*, was published together with Lynd's rebuttal "Self-Evident Truths?, "*New York Review of Books*, September 26, 1968; Genovese's response to the rebuttal appeared in *New York Review of Books*, December 19, 1968. The tangled debate continued in letters published in *New York Review of Books*, February 27, 1969.
55. Bedford and Snow, "Framing Processes and Social Movements," 626.
56. McCord, *Mississippi*, 11–12.
57. Zinn, preface to *SNCC*, ix.
58. Polsgrove, *Divided Minds*, 225; Moye, "Focusing Our Eyes on the Prize," 158.
59. Reagon speech, "The Ridenhour Courage Prize," 2010, http://www.ridenhour.org/prizes_courage_2010.html.
60. Elton, *Practice of History*, 87–91.

61. Paul R. Carlsten, "Bittersweet Truth," *North American Review* (Winter 1964): 91. Donald E. Graham described Zinn's book as "glorification" of SNCC but "valuable as a history of the first three years of intensive, 'direct action' civil rights work in the deep South for its presentation of "the unusual philosophy that has been born out of SNCC work." Donald E. Graham, "SNCC: The New Abolitionists," *Harvard Crimson*, October 22, 1964.

62. Ralph McGill, "Race: Results Instead of Reasons," *Saturday Review*, January 9, 1965, 52.

63. Robert Penn Warren Warren quoted McGill in 1964, "The Civil Rights Bill is no panacea but by spelling certain things out it will give a basis for several kinds of operations—legal action instead of demonstration, an orderly attack on de facto segregation in housing, and a consolidation of responsible Negro leadership." Warren, *Who Speaks for the Negro?*, 234.

64. Reagon in Fred Bouchard, "Bernice Johnson on Freedom Fighting," April 10, 2009, *Berklee Now*, https://www.berklee.edu/news/634/bernice-johnson-reagon-on-freedom-fighting; Reagon speech, "The Ridenhour Courage Prize," 2010, http://www.ridenhour.org/prizes_courage_2010.html.

65. Worth Long in McGehee, "You Do Not Own What You Cannot Control," 19–20. In 1963, Worth Long co-organized a Freedom Festival with Sam Block. Long spent his career as a folklorist preserving the heritage of the blues, retrieving oral histories from around the South, and collating and showcasing SNCC's photographic record. He is celebrated by Roland Freeman in *A Tribute to Worth Long*. Kodish augments this assessment in "Imagining Public Folklore."

66. Holt, introduction to *Summer That Didn't End*, 12. Holt attended SNCC's inaugural conference, joined SNCC, and was a member of CORE.

67. Thelwell, "Fish Are Jumping," 75; Holt quoted in Brown-Nagin, *Courage to Dissent*, 190; Holt, *Act of Conscience*, 64–65. Brown-Nagin, *Courage to Dissent*, 194–200, discusses omnibus lawsuits in Atlanta.

68. Carmichael and Thelwell, *Ready for the Revolution*, 142; Julian Bond letter to Ernest Goodman (National Lawyers Guild), May 4, 1962, series 4, reel 8, 267, SNCC; Bond, preface to Holt, *Summer That Didn't End*, 3.

69. Carson, *In Struggle*, 67; Dittmer, *Local People*, 230; Hogan, *Many Minds, One Heart*, 160; Wayne Greenhaw, *Fighting the Devil in Dixie: How Civil Rights Activists Took on the Ku Klux Klan in Alabama* (Chicago: Lawrence Hill Books, 2011), 130.

70. Rabinowitz, *Unrepentant Leftist*, 175, 178. Corroborative accounts of the effect of Holt's speech include Babson, Riddle, and Elsila, *Color of Law*, 287–88.

71. The National Lawyers Guild commemorates Holt now as "a remarkable civil rights lawyer" whose organizing helped energize and strengthen the Detroit chapter of the guild in 1961. "Who We Are," National Lawyers Guild, Detroit and Michigan Chapter, https://www.michigannlg.org/aboutus.

72. Brown-Nagin, *Courage to Dissent*, 188. Holt is discussed in Brown-Nagin, *Courage to Dissent*, 187–200, and his books referenced, but his role as writer is not explored.

73. Len Holt letter to John O'Neal, in Dent, Schechner, and Moses, *Free Southern Theater*, 9.

74. Brown-Nagin, *Courage to Dissent*, 189.

75. Edward A. Dawley, "Kinoy contra Dixie," *Guild Practitioner* (National Lawyers Guild) 47 (1990), 42, about a banquet honoring Arthur Kinoy, who worked with Kunstler and Holt on the defense of Danville demonstrators.

76. For a history of the law firm, see Jeffrey L. Littlejohn and Charles H. Ford, *Elusive Equality: Desegregation and Resegregation in Norfolk's Public Schools* (Charlottesville:

University of Virginia Press, 2012), particularly 126–50. Former governor of Virginia L. Douglas Wilder, the first African American to be elected governor of the state, in 1989, commemorated Jordan, Dawley and Holt in 2016 as "the roots of the plants we don't see . . . we only got a see the 'fruit' of their works." Leonard E. Colvin, "Former Gov. Wilder Brings Message to Area," *New Journal and Guide* ("Virginia's Best Source of Black Community News"), April 21, 2016, http://thenewjournalandguide.com/.

77. For example, see "Bearing Witness to the Danville Civil Rights Protests of 1963," https://www.virginiahumanities.org/2016/04/bearing-witness.

78. Miller, *Danville, Virginia*. Birmingham protests ended in the middle of May and Danville protests began May 31. Danny Lyon observed, "They were always gathering evidence. . . . Forman, I think, was trying to do the whole civil rights movement by himself." "Segment 14: Danny Lyon, Civil Rights Photographer," NPR Weekend Edition, February 20, 1993, 28, box 44, folder 3, JF.

79. SCLC workers arrested in Danville were Lendell W. Chase, Milton A. Reid, Curtis W. Harris, and Hildreth McGhee.

80. Simmons, "Martin Luther King Jr. Revisited."

81. A Kennedy appointee, Mitchie supported Danville segregationists over severely injured African American protestors by abstaining when presented with a petition filed by Kunstler seeking an injunction against criminal prosecution of demonstrators for "race riot."

82. W. E. B. Du Bois, *Dusk of Dawn*, 602–3.

83. Roy P. Fairfield, "The Danville Story," *Humanist*, November/December 1965, 279.

84. Luther P. Jackson Jr., "Story of Danville," 432.

85. Holt quoted in "Notes on Writers and Writing," *Negro Digest*, April 1965, 90.

86. Lester, *And All Our Wounds Forgiven*, xi; Kunstler, *Deep in My Heart*, 38.

87. George Feifer, "Underlaw: Review of *Southern Justice*, ed. Leon Friedman (New York: Pantheon Books, 1965)," *Nation*, November 15, 1965, 366–67.

88. Coles, *Children of Crisis*, 173.

89. Joseph Epstein criticized Coles in a review of *Children of Crisis* in *Commentary* in 1967 and expanded his criticisms in interview afterward. When Paul Wilkes returned to those criticisms in 1978 it was to locate Epstein's comments alongside Kenneth Clark's assessment: "'He's criticized,' Kenneth Clark responds, 'for not being 'scientific,' which means he doesn't treat people like objects, as we were trained to do as so-called professionals. Listen, anybody who can make me understand—and like—some white racist, as Coles did in *The Middle Americans*, is doing something very right. Paul Wilkes, "Robert Coles: Doctor of Crisis," *New York Times Magazine*, March 26, 1978, https://www.nytimes.com/.

90. Coles, *Children of Crisis*, 27–28.

91. Coles, *Doing Documentary Work*, 97, 98; Coles, *Children of Crisis*, 29.

92. Coles, "Young Psychiatrist Looks at His Profession," 108–9.

93. Among Coles's many essays and feature articles, those most pertinent to his work with SNCC also include "Social Struggle Weariness" and Coles and Brenner, "American Youth in a Social Struggle."

94. Coles, *Call of Stories*, 23.

95. "Serpents and Doves" was based on his early work supported by the SRC and on work by a mentor, Erik H. Erikson, in 1963 (*Youth: Change and Challenge*); Robert Coles, "Separate but Equal Lives," *New South*, September 1962, 3–8.

96. Coles, *Children of Crisis*, 234.

97. As an undergraduate at Harvard, Coles wrote a thesis on William Carlos Williams under the direction of Perry Miller, sent it to Williams, and struck up a relationship. Coles,

Doing Documentary Work, 45, 95–97. Coles turned this thesis into a critical-creative appreciation of Williams's poetry and the story of their acquaintance in Coles, *William Carlos Williams: The Knack of Survival in America* (New Brunswick, N.J.: Rutgers University Press, 1975).

98. Coles, *Children of Crisis*, 388n5.
99. Coles, *Doing Documentary Work*, 77, 98.
100. Spencer and Hogan, "Telling Freedom Stories from the Inside Out," 331.
101. Coles, *Children of Crisis*, 230–31, 224.
102. Coles, "Young Psychiatrist Looks at His Profession," 110, 112.
103. Coles interviewed by Joseph Sinsheimer, November 18, 1983, 5, JAS.
104. Coles, "Serpents and Doves," 188.
105. Coles quoted in Tom Fricke, "Mystery and Manners: A Conversation with Robert Coles," *Michigan Quarterly Review* 45, no. 1 (Winter 2006), http://hdl.handle.net/2027/spo.act2080.0045.102. The interview is peppered with literary allusions that Coles makes to define his documentary work.
106. Coles, *Children of Crisis*, 364, 366, 381.
107. Robert Coles, "A Fashionable Type of Slander," *Atlantic Monthly*, November 1970, 53–55. In Feuer's *The Conflict of Generations*, "pathology" arises from unresolved Oedipal struggles. Walter Bromberg and Franck Simon coined the phrase "protest psychosis" in "The 'Protest' Psychosis" in 1968. See also Jonathan M. Metzl, *The Protest Psychosis: How Schizophrenia Became a Black Disease* (Boston: Beacon, 2010), in which Carmichael's definition of institutional racism is the opening salvo against which post–World War II psychiatric practice and doctor-patient encounters are measured. Coles's intervention is not noted.
108. Hellerstein and Coles, "On Medicine and Literature, 12, 14.
109. Coles, *Children of Crisis*, 210; Coles, *Festering of Sweetness*, xi, back cover; Coles, *Rumors of Separate Worlds*.
110. Hogan, *Many Minds, One Heart*, 237.
111. Kopkind, prologue to *The Thirty Years' Wars*, xxvi.
112. Thelwell, "Black Studies."
113. Joyce Ladner, *Death of White Sociology*, xxiv, xxvi.
114. Zinn, *SNCC*, 273.
115. Nell Salm, "The New Abolitionists," *Monthly Review* 16, no. 8 (January 1965): 563–64.

Chapter 5. "Go to Writing and Write Up a New Day"

Epigraphs are from Sherrod, "The New Barbarians" (1962–63), box 4a, 1, Southwest Georgia Registration Project, Faith Holsaert Papers, David M. Rubenstein Library, Duke University Libraries, North Carolina; Hall quoted in Carawan and Carwan, *Freedom Is a Constant Struggle*, 109; Prescod in Greenberg, *Circle of Trust*, 184.

1. For a sophisticated and thoughtful explanation of what "local" means in this context, see Theoharis and Woodard, *Groundwork*, 2–3.
2. Lake, "Last Summer in Mississippi," 114; McCord, *Mississippi*, 8.
3. Coles, *Call of Service*, 117.
4. Wade Gayles, *Pushed Back to Strength*, 150.
5. Carmichael with Thelwell, *Ready for the Revolution*, 133; Thelwell, "Professor and the Activists," 632; Thelwell in Tidwell and Tracy, *After Winter*, 416; Carmichael and Thelwell, *Ready for Revolution*, 281.

6. For example, Rev. Harry H. Hoehler's sermon to First Parish, Weston, Massachusetts, on return from Selma on March 21, 1965: "Selma Part II," box 139, folder 1, 7, "Writings by Others," Martin Luther King Collection, Mugar Memorial Library, Howard Gotlieb Archival Research Center, Boston University; SNCC incidents, 1963–1966, 6, microfilm 44, reel 3, segment 48, Lucile Montgomery Papers, Wisconsin Historical Society, Madison.

7. The phrase "the bottom rail" is that of Ned Cobb, the Alabama sharecropper whose as-told-to autobiography of 1969 was published under a pseudonym: Nate Shaw, *All God's Dangers: The Life of Nate Shaw*, by Nate Shaw and Theodore Rosengarten (New York: Random House, 1974), 7. Bond was "patiently explaining to newspaper reporters the historic events that were occurring scarcely noticed under their noses . . . the real story of the unsung heroes of the South." "Georgia's New Era: The Young Politicians," *Southern Patriot*, September 1965, 478–80.

8. Mants in Greenberg, *Circle of Trust*, 56–57. In early July, the theater was subject to bomb threats and mob violence. SNCC staff newsletter, July 7, 1964, 3, series 4, reel 15, p. 2, SNCC.

9. Varela, "Time to Get Ready," 2008), 14–15, https://web.stanford.edu/group/peacejustice/SNCC-Varela%20Edits-Final-1-2007.pdf; Maria Varela, "Time to Get Ready," in Holsaert et al., *Hands on the Freedom Plow*, 565. The poem in its entirety was published as "Mississippi Winter" in Gitlin, *Campfires of the Resistance*, 40–43.

10. "Maria Varela," in Worth Long, *We'll Never Turn Back*, 17.

11. Butler, *Precarious Life*, 20.

12. Stembridge in Gitlin, *Campfires of the Resistance*, 28–29.

13. The deaths in Mississippi were reported without names in the *Greenwood Commonwealth* on February 4, 1963, and "Snow Starts to Blanket Washington," *Washington Post*, January 27, 1963. On the unusually harsh winter, see also "150 Die in North and South," *New York Times*, January 25, 1963; and C. Payne, *I've Got the Light of Freedom*, 159.

14. Branch, *Parting the Waters*, 342; Moses and Cobb, *Radical Equations*, 40; Prescod in Greenberg, *Circle of Trust*, 178. Marshall Ganz described Steptoe as "an old hand" who harnessed the distribution of clothes for use in SNCC's organizing: "If you tell 'em clothes, they come running; if you tell 'em vote, they run the other way." Ganz requested a car for Steptoe so he could perform this "vital work." Ganz, field report, "Amite County, November 1964," document 56, 1–2, Elaine DeLott Baker Papers.

15. Guyot, "Foreword: Reflections on the Local Movement," xv–xvi.

16. Cobb in Richards, "With Our Minds Set on Freedom," 42; Jimmy Garrett, "Marching through Selma," *Movement* (SNCC of California), April 1965, 6.

17. Jane Stembridge transcript of Stokely Carmichael's Speech Class, February–March 1965, published as "Notes about a Class" in Carmichael, *Stokely Speaks*, 21–28.

18. Rob Wood, "Fredm," *Movement* (SNCC of California), November 1965, 3. The question of "qualification" for voting was a primary theme in SNCC's essays in *New Republic* in 1966, collected and published as Hayden, *Thoughts of the Young Radicals*. In a similar context, Dick Gregory was struck by a four-year-old boy he met in a Birmingham jail cell in May, 1963. When he asked why he was there: "'Teedom' he said. Couldn't even say Freedom but he was in jail for it." Gregory, *Nigger*, 178.

19. Hogan, "A Walk with Bob Moses," *First of the Month*, July 4, 2016, http://www.firstofthemonth.org/a-walk-with-bob-moses-2/#more-4010.

20. Watters, *Down to Now*, 137–38.

21. SNCC's historians note use of "local-people-itis" (e.g., Carson, *In Struggle*, 156; R. H. King, *Civil Rights*, 151) and usually cite as the source Forman, *Making of Black Revolutionaries*, 422.

22. Thelwell, Position Paper 4, "SNCC's Goals and Bourgeois Sentimentality," Waveland, Mississippi, November 6–12, 1964, document 42, Elaine DeLott Baker Papers.
23. Thelwell, *Duties, Pleasures and Conflicts*, 30.
24. Zinn, *SNCC*, 273.
25. McDew quoted in "SNCC Begins Drive to Free Clyde Kennard from Mississippi Jail," *Young Socialist* 6, no. 3 (February 1963), 1.
26. "Campaign to Free a Forgotten Hero," *Southern Patriot*, January 1963, 2; "Victory by Protest," *Southern Patriot*, February 1963, 1.
27. Ronald A. Hollander, "One Mississippi Negro Who Didn't Go to College," *Reporter* (New York), November 8, 1962, 30–34.
28. Ron Hollander, "Clyde Kennard," speech, Mississippi Southern University, Hattiesburg, Mississippi, October 23, 2010, http://www.crmvet.org/comm/kennard.htm.
29. Hollander's report is headed with his home address in New York and has Dorie Ladner's name scribbled at the top and underlined. "How Mississippi Southern Stayed White: The Story of Clyde Kennard," 1, series 4, reel 3, SNCC.
30. Minchin and Salmond, "Saddest Story of the Whole Movement," 191–234.
31. Dorothy Zellner, "My Real Vocation," in Holsaert et al., *Hands on the Freedom Plow*, 317. Derek R. King alludes to SNCC's campaign in his biography of Kennard but only via an article in *Southern Patriot*. Derek R. King, *The Life and Times of Clyde Kennard* (N.p.: Lulu Publishing Services, 2018), 269.
32. "SNCC Confab Launches 'Free Kennard' Drive," *Student Voice*, December 1962, 1, 4; "News in Brief," *Student Voice*, April 1963, 3.
33. John Howard Griffin, "Requiem for a Martyr," in *Prison of Culture: Beyond 'Black Like Me'* (San Antonio, Tex.: Wings Press, 2011), 16–21. Griffin's quotation of Kennard appears also in "Pardon Docket No. 06-0005, Before The Hon. Hayley Barbour, Governor of Mississippi, In the Matter of Clyde Kennard, Memorandum in Support for Application for Clemency of Clyde Kennard," 13, https://www.law.northwestern.edu/legalclinic/wrongful convictions/exonerations/documents/msKennardPetition.pdf.
34. Larry Still, "Negro Sent to Prison Instead of College," *Jet* January 24, 1963, 20–24; Clyde Kennard Leaves Final Message to All Mankind," *Jet*, July 25, 1963, 14–16.
35. Dent, "Portrait of Three Heroes," 256, 258.
36. Hollander, "How Mississippi Southern Stayed White: The Story of Clyde Kennard," 5, 9.
37. "Clyde Kennard," http://www.fannielouhamer.info/c_kennard.html; Jerry Mitchell, "Kennard Pardon Request Rejected," *Jackson Clarion-Ledger*, May 11, 2006. When Hayley Barbour refused a pardon, a way was found to hear the case again, which Barbour supported. William Winter and law students from Northwestern University were among those who worked for a pardon. Judge Bob Helfrich heard the case in 2006 and exonerated Kennard, and Barbour declared March 30 to be Clyde Kennard Day.
38. Joyce Ladner, "Standing Up for Our Beliefs," in Holsaert et al., *Hands on the Freedom Plow*, 219–20, 222.
39. Joyce Ladner, "The South: Old-New Land," *New York Times*, May 17, 1979; some of his letters and a comment by Joyce Ladner are posted on the Zinn Education Project website: https://www.zinnedproject.org/materials/kennard-clyde.
40. Dittmer, *Local People*, 79–83; "University of Southern Mississippi to Award Posthumous Degree to Clyde Kennard," *Hattiesburg American*, May 7, 2018; "Civil Rights Pioneer Clyde Kennard Honored by Southern Miss," *Jackson Clarion-Ledger*, May 4, 2018.
41. Long and Johnson cited in "Cultural and Educational," July 10, 2016, SNCC Critical Oral Histories Conference transcript, 119, CDSD.

42. Coles, *Children of Crisis*, 203-9.
43. Tearanny Street, "Conference Spotlights Civil Rights Movement in Hattiesburg, Southern Miss," *Southern Miss Now*, October 12, 2010.
44. Kenwood-Hyde Park Committee to Aid Fayette County flyer, box 171, folder 2, undated but around end of 1960, JF. The flyer urges that letters be sent to President Kennedy to remedy the plight of several hundred sharecroppers in Tennessee. Forman's notes for fictional pieces were often scribbled on documents of committees he joined.
45. McGehee, "You Do Not Own What You Cannot Control," 16; Worth Long, "Question," *Movement* (SNCC of California), April 1965, 3.
46. Forman, notes for "Georgia Mae: Hard Times" and the three-act handwritten play script titled "Somewhere in Glory," box 171, folders 1-3, JF. Gaines, *The Autobiography of Miss Jane Pittman* (London: Michael Joseph, 1971), 7; Gaines, "Miss Jane and I," *Callaloo* 1, no. 3 (1978), 37-38.
47. Forman, "Somewhere in Glory," box 171, folders 1-3, pp. 2, 17-18, 3, 9, 36-38, 70-71, 21-22, JF.
48. Fred Travis, "The Evicted," *Progressive*, February 10, 1961, 10-12.
49. Robert Hamburger would tell the stories of tent city dwellers in Fayette County as a collective oral history, *Our Portion of Hell: Fayette County, Tennessee: An Oral History of the Struggle for Civil Rights* (New York: Links Books, 1973).
50. Kahn, *Creative Community Organizing*, 22-24.
51. Thelwell, *Duties, Pleasures and Conflicts*, xiii; Carmichael and Thelwell, *Ready for the Revolution*, 133, 281; Thelwell, "Professor and the Activists, 632; Thelwell in in Tidwell and Tracy, *After Winter*, 416; "Fish Are Jumping an' the Cotton Is High," 42-43.
52. Marge Franz, "We'll Never Turn Back," review of Mary King's *Freedom Song* and Thelwell's *Duties, Pleasures and Conflicts*," *Mother Jones*, August-September 1987, 52; Monteith, "SNCC's Stories at the Barricades."
53. Dorie Ladner in John Biewen, "Oh Freedom over Me," American Public Media, February 2001, http://americanradioworks.publicradio.org/features/oh_freedom. Belfrage detailed the seemingly endless calls to the COFO office in Greenwood, usually delivering foul abuse, in her *Freedom Summer*, 114-18.
54. Robnett, "African-American Women in the Civil Rights Movement, 1954-1965"; Robnett, *How Long? How Long?*; Robnett, "Women in SNCC"; Sacks, *Caring by the Hour*, 121.
55. The landlord of Quinn's café is quoted in McCord, *Mississippi*, 123.
56. Dittmer, *Local People*, 307; Cobb, *This Nonviolent Stuff'll Get You Killed*, 289.
57. SNCC, "Response to the 13th and 14th Bombings in McComb," September 21, 1964, Social Action Vertical File, circa 1960-1980, Mss 577, box 47, folder 12, Freedom Summer Collection, Wisconsin Historical Society, Madison; SNCC, "Bombings and Burnings," SC 3045, folder 1, WIHVC1480B700-A, includes Mrs. Quinn's affidavit, Candy Brown Papers, Freedom Summer Collection, Wisconsin Historical Society, Madison; Samstein, "Murder of a Community." Dittmer describes the repressive situation in *Local People*, 99-115, 265-71, 303-14.
58. Thelwell, "Organizer," 3; Claude Sitton, "Graves at a Dam: Discovery Is Made in New Earth Mound in Mississippi," *New York Times*, August 5, 1964.
59. Julian Bond, "SNCC."
60. Thelwell, "Organizer," 8.
61. Descriptions of Forman as a reassuring presence abound. For example, Sellers calls him "a large man with the stature and disposition of a bear." Sellers, *River of No Return*, 47.

62. Moses and Cobb, *Radical Equations*, 66.
63. Sugarman details these encounters in *Stranger at the Gates*, 78–82.
64. Fred Meely, "Organizer's Handbook," box 14, folder 36, 1, JO'N.
65. Samstein, "Murder of a Community," 2.
66. Fannie Lou Hamer's grave in Ruleville, Mississippi, is situated on cooperatively held African American–owned land. The stone reads: FANNIE LOU HAMER / OCTOBER 6, 1917 / MARCH 14 1977 / I AM SICK AND TIRED / OF BEING / SICK AND TIRED."
67. Dollard, *Caste and Class in a Southern Town*, 309; Thelwell, *Duties, Pleasures, and Conflicts*, xiv. The language recalls Dick Gregory's performances in the South while speaking in support of SNCC and the movement more widely.
68. This is the grim humor one finds in Thelwell's essays, as when a Natchez judge is known as "Necessity" because of Horace's observation: "Necessity knows no law." Thelwell, "Fish Are Jumping An' the Cotton Is High," 81.
69. Jerome Smith in Williams, *My Soul Looks Back in Wonder*, 63.
70. "Questions Raised by Bob Moses," *Movement* (SNCC of California), April 1965, 1.
71. Samstein, "Murder of a Community," 3. James P. Marshall cites two thousand gathering on September 22, 1964, based on U.S. Commission on Civil Rights hearings in Jackson, February 1965. Marshall, *Student Activism*, 163, 252n136.
72. The quotation is Philip Roth, "The Story behind *The Plot against America*," *New York Times*, September 19, 2004.
73. Teresa Wiltz, "A Conversation with Denise Nicholas," appendix to Nicholas, *Freshwater Road*, n.p.
74. Nicholas, acknowledgments in *Freshwater Road*, 409. She names Carson's *In Struggle*, Fred Powledge's *Free at Last? The Civil Rights Movement and the People Who Made It* (New York: Little, Brown, 1991), Aldon Morris's *Origins of the Civil Rights Movement*, and John Lewis's *Walking in the Wind*.
75. Nicholas, "A Grand Romantic Notion," in Holsaert et al., *Hands on the Freedom Plow*, 257–69; Richard Schechner interview with Denise Nicholas, January 13, 1968, 3, box 69, folder 8, FST.
76. In 2016, with Ricardo Khan of Crossroads Theater and South African Sibusiso Mamba, she created the play *Letters from Freedom Summer*, performed in 2018.
77. "Outline for COFO Program—1964," box 41, folder 10, JF.
78. Vincent Harding speaking in archive film footage in the documentary film *Freedom on My Mind*, directed by Connie Fields and Marilyn Mulford (San Francisco: California Newsreel, 1994), and in "Freedom on My Mind" script, 38, box 3, folder 14, Inventory of Race Relations Collection, J. D. Williams Library, University of Mississippi, Archives and Special Collections, Oxford.
79. Teresa Wiltz, "Denise Nicholas, Mind, Body and Soul," *Washington Post*, October 25, 2005.
80. Cobb expressed ambivalence over a "county-produced 'Neshoba County African American Heritage Driving Tour' brochure," saying, "I know I am supposed to applaud this, but in all honesty, I still have unresolved emotions lodged in anger here, even though the brochure is useful and sends visitors where I would send them." Having known Chaney and Schwerner, returning to Philadelphia left Cobb "wrestling with my feelings again." Cobb, *On the Road to Freedom*, 279.
81. Fragments of scenes in the voices of a narrator, Rita Schwerner, and journalist James Wechsler are in box 69, folder 8, FST.
82. Moses, *Radical Equations*, 68.

83. Honigsberg, *Crossing Border Street*, 8.

84. Hogan, *Many Minds, One Heart*, 153.

85. Sinsheimer, interview with Robert Coles, Boston, Massachusetts, November 19, 1983, 15, JAS.

86. Cowan, *Making of an Un-American*, 24, 34, 44; Dittmer, *Local People*, 262.

87. McLaurin's field report from Ruleville in August 1963 celebrates the "six brave ladies." Series 4, reel 7, 238, SNCC. Lewis wrote: "Over and over again we found that it was these women—wives and mothers in their forties and fifties, hardworking, humorous, no-nonsense, incredibly resilient women who had carried such an unimaginable weight throughout their own lives and had been through so much unspeakable hell that there was nothing left on this earth for them to be afraid of." Lewis and D'Orso, *Walking with the Wind*, 188.

88. Stephen Bingham, "Mississippi Letter," February 15, 1965, 14, series 4, reel 7, 110, SNCC. Bingham reported, "Each morning I would wake up near dawn and wash in the cold water of the pump out back."

89. De Lissovoy, *Feelgood*, 99–102, 122–23.

90. Jean (Wheeler) Smith Young, "Do Whatever You Are Big Enough To Do," in Holsaert et al., *Hands on the Freedom Plow*, 248. Regarding Leontyne Price, Reynolds Price summarized: "[The] scope of her accomplishment has almost never been acknowledged frankly in her home country [nor has what she has achieved] in the teeth of the deadening realities of segregation that prevailed... through the nation." Reynolds Price, "Bouquet for Leontyne," *Opera News*, April 1, 1995. For Price's career, see Samuel Chotzinoff, *A Little Nightmusic* (New York: Curtis Publishing, 1964), 79–80; Elizabeth Amelia Hadley, "Leontyne Price: Prima Donna Assoluta," in *Black Women and Music: More Than the Blues*, eds. Eileen M Hayes and Linda Williams (Chicago: University of Illinois Press, 2007), 197–209.

91. Lester, *Search for the New Land*, 70–71; Lester, *All Is Well*, 112.

92. Carson, *In Struggle*, 116; Sinsheimer, interview with Robert Coles, Boston, Massachusetts, November 19, 1983, 21–23, JAS.

93. Belfrage, *Freedom Summer*, 75, 37; Adickes, *Legends of Good Women*, 14–15, 75–6.

94. Wade Gayles, *Pushed Back to Strength*, 181, 180, 51, 248.

95. The FST incorporated the words Rita Schwerner spoke to President Lyndon B. Johnson demanding he prioritize finding her husband. See Lynd, "Freedom Schools," 307; Dittmer, *Local People*, 244–45.

96. The phrase "base communities" is Aldon Morris's in *Origins of the Civil Rights Movement*.

97. Payne, *I've Got the Light of Freedom*, 396; emotional reaction of Herbert Lee's widow: Dittmer, *Local People*, 124; and Carson, *In Struggle*, 143.

98. Thelwell, preface to *Duties, Pleasures, and Conflicts*, xi.

99. Guyot quoted in Blake, *Children of the Movement*, 80.

100. Watters, *Down to Now*, 402–3; Polletta, "Contending Stories," 423–24.

101. Warren, "Two for SNCC," 42; Warren, *Who Speaks for the Negro?* 98; Moses, *Radical Equations*, 56.

102. Sherrod quoted in Forman, *Making of Black Revolutionaries*, 276

103. Nicholas interviewed by Farai Chideya, NPR, October 11, 2005.

104. O'Neal, "Trying to Find My Way Back Home," *Don't Start Me to Talking*, 198.

105. O'Neal, Yuen, and Holden, "Junebug Productions Color Line Project," 2; Prescod in Greenberg, *Circle of Trust*, 184.

Chapter 6. Forging a Literary Culture beyond SNCC

Epigraphs are from Smith, "I Learned to Feel Black"; Cobb quoted in Richards, "With Our Minds Set on Freedom," 339; Thelwell, *Duties, Pleasures, and Conflicts*, xv.

1. Dudley Randall, "Shoe Shine Boy," *Negro Digest*, September 1966, 53–55; Sarah Webster Fabio, "At Cross Purposes," *Negro Digest*, September 1966, 76.

2. Llorens, "Writers Converge at Fisk University," 65. James C. Hall describes the conference but focuses on debates with Robert Hayden in *Mercy, Mercy Me*, 107–18. Llorens named on Mississippi Summer application list, box 41, folder 4, JF.

3. Mitchell, *Black Drama*, 219–20.

4. "Work Meeting" minutes, Hollis (neighborhood in Queens), New York, August 27, 1966, box 19, folder 19, Sarah E. Wright Papers, Manuscript, Archives, and Rare Books Library, Emory University, Atlanta, and Wright's letter to poets, dated September 16, 1966, is in folder 19; "Synopsis of *ad obits*," box 1, Pat Watters Papers, Georgia State University Library, Atlanta.

5. Wright, "A Message to My Son, Mike," box 19, folder 34, Sarah E. Wright Papers.

6. Syble Avery, "Staff Members Attend College Editors Conference in Washington," *Wolverine Observer* (Morris Brown College) 36, no. 3 (March 1967), 1; Giovanni, *Black Feeling, Black Talk*, 3

7. Joseph, *Stokely*, ix; Maxwell, *F. B. Eyes*, 114.

8. Keorapetse Kgositsile, "When Brown Is Black (for Rap Brown)," *Black Dialogue*, 4, no. 1 (1969), 31–32.

9. Cieciorka and Cieciorka, *Negroes in American History*; Steven Heller, "Frank Cieciorka, Designer for the Left, Dead at 69," *New York Times*, November 27, 2008.

10. Carmichael, "Black Power," 174.

11. Cooper, *To Free a Generation*, 200.

12. In the summer of 1965, *American Dialogue* published poetry about the movement, "Four Poets Looking South," and hoped SNCC would contribute in a similar way. Jacqueline Frieder, *American Dialogue*, New York, to SNCC's Atlanta office, June 25, 1965, box 27, folder 3, JF. In 1963, *Youth* prepared a 64-page special issue, "Racial Justice Now," which included "The Story of Charlie Cobb." Herman C. Ahrens, editor, letter to SNCC, October 11, 1963, box 27, folder 6, JF.

13. In 1967, *Massachusetts Review* editor Jules Chametzky borrowed the word "Coordinating" from SNCC in naming the new Coordinating Council of Literary Magazines." Julius Lester, "For America on the Eve of the Second Civil War: Review of *Black and White in American Culture*," *New York Times*, March 29, 1970; Glass, *Rebel Publisher*, 156.

14. Jack O'Dell and Esther Cooper Jackson in Jackson and Pohl, *Freedomways Reader*, 47, xxii.

15. SNCC does not figure in David Levering Lewis, Michael H. Nash, and Daniel J. Leab, eds., *Red Activists and Black Freedom: James and Esther Jackson and the Long Civil Rights Revolution* (New York: Routledge, 2010); Dayo F. Gore, "From Freedom to *Freedomways*: Black Women Radicals and the Black Freedom Movement in the 1960s and 1970s," in *Radicalism at the Crossroads: African American Activists in the Cold War* (New York: New York University Press, 2011), 130–60; or Sara Rzeszutek Haviland, "*Freedomways*, the Communist Party USA, and Black Freedom in the Post–Civil Rights Years," *James and Esther Cooper Jackson: Love and Courage in the Black Freedom Movement* (Lexington: University Press of Kentucky, 2015), 229–72. Only Gore states that "numerous members" of SNCC published in *Freedomways* (136), but she does not name any, and Erik S. McDuffie's

essay in Theoharis and Woodard, *Want to Start a Revolution?*, 39, includes Bond and Carmichael in a list of those publishing in *Freedomways*.

16. Bond, foreword to Jackson and Pohl, *Freedomways Reader*, xvii–xviii.

17. Bond, "Southern Youth Movement" and "Nonviolence; Wilfred Callender "Negro Leaders and Organizations," *Freedomways* 2, no. 2 (Spring 1962): 197–205.

18. "Culture in the Cause of Negro Freedom," *Freedomways* 2, no. 2 (Spring 1962): 117–18; Grant, "Time Is Always Now."

19. Ernest Kaiser, "The Literature of Negro Revolt," *Freedomways* 3, no. 1 (Winter 1963): 37.

20. "The Southern Movement," *Freedomways* 4, no. 1 (Winter 1964): 5.

21. Guyot and Thelwell, "Politics of Survival and Necessity in Mississippi," 102.

22. Annell Ponder, "Rebels with a Cause," *Ebony*, September 1965, 18. Ponder was close to SNCC and embodied its organizing ethos. CORE and SCLC activist Bruce Hartford described her as "SNCC in essence except for the actual fact she worked for SCLC." Quoted in "Annell Ponder," https://snccdigital.org/people/annell-ponder.

23. Bennett, "King Plan."

24. John H. Johnson, publisher's note, *Negro Digest*, June 1961, 3. For his publishing empire, see J. H. Johnson and Bennett, *Succeeding against the Odds*; J. C. Hall, "On Sale at Your Favorite Newsstand."

25. *Negro Digest* described in Williams, *The King God Didn't Save: Reflections on the Life and Death of Martin Luther King Jr.* (London: Eyre and Spottiswoode, 1971), 91.

26. David Llorens, "Perspectives: To Busy Writers Who Are Also 'Real,'" *Negro Digest*, December 1965, 49–50.

27. "Black Power: Its Measure and Meaning: A Symposium," *Negro Digest*, November 1966, 20–21, 81.

28. Charlie Cobb letter to David Llorens, July 16, 1967, series 4, reel 3, 7, SNCC.

29. A. Johnson and R. Johnson, *Propaganda and Aesthetics*, 167, 162. There is a predilection for calling the publication *Black World* instead of *Negro Digest* in its pre-1970 incarnation. The name is not helpful in gauging its content. One example of assuming wrongly that the latter title was more radical: "Of almost incalculable significance was the magazine *Black World* which under the editorship of Hoyt Fuller had evolved from the bland *Negro Digest*." Hudson, "Activism and Criticism," 92. In another example, Charles Johnson calls *Negro Digest* "that old standby" in *Being and Race*, 22. There is, when read in entirety, as much continuity as contrast. Fenderson has now situated Fuller in "his proper place" at the center of the Black Arts Movement. Fenderson, *Building the Black Arts Movement*, 3.

30. Cobb, "Living History: Activists on Art and Social Justice," conference panel, April 17, 2008, Lannan Center for Poetics and Social Practice, Georgetown University, Washington, D.C.

31. Jean (Wheeler) Smith capsule biography, *Negro Digest*, November 1967, 74.

32. Fuller, "The Undefeated," *Negro Digest*, November 1963, 49–50.

33. Jean Wheeler capsule biography at bottom of page in Jean Wheeler, "Let Us All Be Black Together: A College Coed's Please to the Middle Class," *Negro Digest*, January 1964, 21.

34. Jean Wheeler, "Let Us All Be Black Together: A College Coed's Please to the Middle Class," *Negro Digest*, January 1964, 19–21.

35. Polletta, "Plotting Protest"; G. A. Fine, "Storied Group."

36. Jean (Wheeler) Smith, "I Learned to Feel Black," *Redbook* 129, no. 4 (August 1967), 15–18 (reprinted in Barbour, *The Black Power Revolt*, 247–48); Fuller, "The Road to Black Consciousness," *Negro Digest*, November 1967, 50, 78.

37. Margaret Mead Answers," *Redbook* 12, no. 4 (December 1964): 6–8.
38. Smith, "I Learned to Feel Black."
39. Jean (Wheeler) Smith, "How to Help the Ones at the Bottom." The essays were published in the *New Republic*, with Smith's appearing in February 1966 (13–15), then anthologized in Tom Hayden, *Thoughts of the Young Radicals* (57–62). Subsequent references in parentheses are to the latter.
40. Projects are enumerated by Sutherland, "Mississippi: Summer of Discontent," 214.
41. Forman (n.d. but 1960s), "Ideas for Black Power Book," box 135, folder 1, JF.
42. The "stone that the builder rejected" is the phrase Moses used in "Letter from Magnolia Jail."
43. Fuller's survey of African American writing, n.d, box 48, folder 24, 26–27, Hoyt W. Fuller Papers. Fenderson contextualizes Fuller's support of black women writers but makes no mention of Smith in *Building the Black Arts Movement*, his study of Fuller and the cultural politics of the 1960s.
44. On *Redbook*, see Kathleen Endres and Therese Lueck, *Women's Periodicals in the United States: Consumer Magazines* (Westport, Conn.: Greenwood Press, 1995), 304.
45. Jean Wheeler Smith, "That She Would Dance No More," 63. Subsequent references in parentheses. The story is collected in Baraka and Neal, *Black Fire*, 486–99, and Susan Koppelman, ed., *Women in the Trees: U.S. Women's Short Stories About Battering and Resistance, 1839–2000* (New York: Feminist Press, 2004), 137–46.
46. Alice Walker, *The Third Life of Grange Copeland* (London: Women's Press, 1984), 9.
47. Editor's notes, Hoyt W. Fuller, *Negro Digest*, January 1967, 4.
48. Jean Wheeler Smith, "Frankie Mae," *Negro Digest*, June 1968, 88. Subsequent references in parentheses.
49. For misassumptions that the story is set during slavery, see "Jean Wheeler-Smith, 'Frankie Mae,'" https://media180sec101.wordpress.com/2011/09/16/jean-wheeler-smith-frankie-mae.
50. Tillie Olsen, "Silences" (1962), *Silences* (New York: Delacorte Press, 1978), 10.
51. Thelwell, "August 28th March on Washington."
52. Wheeler and Hall quoted in, "Revolt Leaders Warn," *Jet*, September 19, 1963, 4.
53. The phrase "American failure" is Daniel's, *Shadow of Slavery*, xi.
54. Washington, introduction to *Black-Eyed Susans*, xiv.
55. Ladner, *Tomorrow's Tomorrow*, xv–xvi, 76–77.
56. Washington, "Jean Wheeler Smith." Smith's talk was "The Liberation of a People Happens One by One," University of Massachusetts, October 15, 1987.
57. JanMohamed, *Death-Bound Subject*, 2.
58. This literary genealogy would include Georgia Douglas Johnson's play *Plumes* (1927) and Sarah E. Wright's *This Child's Gonna Live* (1969) on through Jesmyn Ward's National Book Award–winning *Salvage the Bones* (2011). Monteith, "Never-ending Cycle of Poverty." Among discussions of how African American feminists, including women in SNCC, debunked the pathologizing of the black family, see Franklin, "Hidden in Plain View"; S. M. Ward, "Third World Women's Alliance"; and Geary, "Feminism and the Nuclear Family Norm."
59. Daniel, *Shadow of Slavery*, 191. In a cleverly modulated letter to Senator James Eastland, Cobb lodged his uncertainty over whether he understood what was happening on his own 6,000-acre plantation, calling out Eastland for the poverty in Sunflower County, Mississippi. Charles Cobb, letter to Senator James Eastland, August 14, 1963, 1–4, micro 599, reel 1, segment 5, Sally Belfrage Papers, Wisconsin Historical Society, Madison.

60. Patton, "Black People and the Victorian Ethos"; Beal, "Double Jeopardy"; Beal, "Slave of a Slave No More." On Beal, Patton, and the Black Women's Liberation Committee, see S. M. Ward, "Third World Women's Alliance"; and Lehman, *Power, Politics and the Decline of the Civil Rights Movement*, 173.

61. Hayden et al., "Old Hands, Young Blood," 47; Smith in Greenberg, *Circle of Trust*, 136–37, 149; Fleming, *Soon We Will Not Cry*, 156. Judy Richardson observed, "What's now called sexism *could* rear its head in SNCC. But it was usually possible to struggle against it—and even win." Richardson, "My Enduring 'Circle of Trust,'" in Holsaert et al., *Hands on the Freedom Plow*, 363.

62. Foucault, "Nietzsche, Genealogy, History," 156–57. Despite its power and longevity, this story has been subject to reductive readings when measured against a recuperative feminist paradigm. W. Lawrence Hogue used it as the control against which to herald writing in the 1970s when African American women characters were "allowed to become figures with options" unlike "the stunted and stifled stereotypes" of Smith's story. W. Lawrence Hogue, *Discourse and the Other: The Production of the Afro-American Text* (Durham, N.C.: Duke University Press, 1986), 55–56. Trudier Harris asserted that "strong African American women characters even with their limitations . . . are preferable to characters beaten down by the circumstances of their lives. Trudier Harris, *Saints, Sinners, Saviors: Strong Black Women in African American Literature* (New York: Palgrave, 2001), 179. Neither analyzes "Frankie Mae." It is the yardstick with which the fiction they *do* read is measured.

63. "Frankie Mae by Jean Smith," box 69, folder 4, FST; Chris Mayfield, introduction to *Growing Up Southern: Southern Exposure Looks at Childhood, Then and Now* (New York: Pantheon, 1981), x.

64. Moye assesses, "The image of Parchman [Mississippi State Penitentiary] was never far from any civil rights worker's mind." Moye, *Let the People Decide*, 28.

65. COFO, "The Mississippi Legislature—1964," http://www.crmvet.org/docs/6406 _cofo_ms_leg-rpt.pdf, details anti-leafleting laws, anti–Freedom School bills, an anti–Freedom Summer project bill, and a law allowing unlimited deputy sheriffs "to cope with emergencies" among thirty-seven anti-civil rights bills passed in the 1964 legislative session in June.

66. House Bill 786, Mississippi, "an act to prohibit 'enticement' of a child to violate the laws and ordinances of the state," was meant to keep those under the age of eighteen from participating in civil rights activities by making parents, teachers, and organizers liable. COFO, "The Mississippi Legislature—1964," 21, http://www.crmvet.org/docs/6406_cofo _ms_leg-rpt.pdf

67. Lester, *Search for the New Land*, 8–9.

68. Carmichael," Who Is Qualified?" For example, SNCC was angered by Ralph Abernathy making a statement to the press that the SCLC was leading the Albany movement. D. L. Lewis, *King: A Biography*, 152–67.

69. Cowan, *Making of an Un-American*, 75.

70. Moses and Garrett quoted in Jack Newfield, "The Student Left: Revolt Without Dogma," *Nation*, May 10, 1965, 491–95; Jimmy Garrett, "Marching through Selma," *Movement* (SNCC of California), April 1965, 6; Cobb in Richards, "With Our Minds Set on Freedom," 339.

71. Stembridge in Gitlin, *Campfires of the Resistance*, 30–31, an extended version of "In Our Steinbeck Yard," in Stembridge, *I Play Flute* (1966), 84; Zinn, *SNCC*, 269.

72. Worth Long, "Dealer," *Movement* (SNCC of California), July 1965, 1; "Summer School Poetry Laurels Won by Plumer," *Harvard Crimson*, August 7, 1964. The *Harvard*

Crimson states, "Third prize went to Worth Long, a 28-year-old SNCC worker enrolled in the Summer School."

73. On September 15, 1963, en route to Selma with Julian Bond, Long drove to Sixteenth Street Baptist Church, out of which the charred bodies of murdered little girls were retrieved. He told Cynthia Greggs Fleming how profoundly distressed he was; in her interpretation, he was "hit by an overpowering feeling of disgust." Fleming, *In the Shadow of Selma*, 151–54.

74. Worth Long, "Safari," in Lowenfels, *Writing on the Wall*, 131.

75. Hogan, *Many Minds, One Heart*, 249.

76. Carson, *In Struggle*, 142, quoting Zinn's memo to SNCC on their role as "guerrilla fighters."

77. Writers disagreed in print but also recorded admiration for each other's work. When Lester reviewed Chametzky and Kaplan's *Black and White in American Culture* (1968), he observed: "The strength of this collection lies in the strength of its material, not its name writers.... Only one writer is represented more than once, and that is Mike Thelwell... one of the finest young black writers now working, a writer who not only has a lot to say, but says it well. His short story and two articles are three of the strongest pieces in the book, particularly his analysis of William Styron's novel on Nat Turner, which details the racist character of the book with gentlemanly elegance." Julius Lester, "For America on the Eve of the Second Civil War," *New York Times*, March 29, 1970.

78. Thelwell, *Duties, Pleasures, and Conflicts*, xv.

79. Polletta, "It Was Like a Fever," 141; Hoyt Fuller, "The Black American Writer," *Negro Digest*, April 1970, 96.

80. Hoyt Fuller, "Pan-Africa Festival Draws Third World Unity Figures, "*Jet*, August 14, 1969: 54–7; Lee, "The New Integrationist," in *Black Pride*, 11. Baraka's "S.O.S" was written in 1965 or 1966 and published in *Black Magic: Collected Poetry, 1961–1967* (Indianapolis: Bobbs-Merrill, 1969).

81. Forman, "High Tide of Black Resistance: 1967," 129. Carson and Van Deburg date the slogan back to SNCC's Alabama campaign in 1966. Carson, *In Struggle*, 2019; Van Deburg, *New Day in Babylon*, 34.

82. Harding, "Black Students and the Impossible Revolution," *Journal of Black Studies* 1:1 (September, 1970), 95, 75.

Chapter 7. "Words You Want?"

Epigraphs are from Charles Cobb, "Charlie's Poem," *Student Voice*, June 6, 1965, 3–4; Casey Rocheteau, "Interview with Dr Aneb Kgositsile, February 6, 2015," accessed September 9, 2019, http://www.writeahouse.com/blog/an-interview-with-dr-aneb-kgositsile (site discontinued).

1. Smethurst, "Black Arts Movement and Historically Black Colleges," 77, 75, 76, 80–81, 84; D. L. Smith, "Chicago Poets, OBAC, and the Black Arts Movement," Smethurst, *Black Arts Movement*, 320, 343.

2. Karenga, "Black Cultural Nationalism," in Gayle, *Black Aesthetic*, 32.

3. Llorens, "Ameer (LeRoi Jones) Baraka," 82, 75. By 1970, Llorens was leading the Black Studies Department at University of Washington in Seattle when he died, aged thirty-four, in a car accident.

4. D. L. Smith, "Black Arts Movement and its Critics," 96.

5. Neal, "The Black Contribution to American Letters," 773–74.

6. "FST–Strong Black hands... to break the shackles of the mind," anonymously written fragment, box 65, folder 8, FST.

7. Thelwell, "What Is to Be Done?"

8. Dent, *Southern Journey*, 289; A. D. Morris, *Origins of the Civil Rights Movement*, xii; Cruse, *Crisis of the Negro Intellectual*, 383.

9. Neal, "Any Day Now," 154.

10. Stokely Carmichael, "What We Want," *New York Review of Books*, September 22, 1966.

11. Cobb, *In the Furrows of the World*, 3–4.

12. "Charlie Cobb's Rage," *Southern Patriot* 26, no. 3 (March 1968): 2; Forman quoted in Carson, *In Struggle*, 160.

13. Sterling Brown, in *Chant of Saints*, 17–18; Christian, "Race for Theory," 44.

14. Dent, "For Kgositsile in Tanzania," box 30, folder 3, Tom Dent Papers, Amistad Research Center, Tulane University, New Orleans; Rowell, "With Bloodstains to Testify," 23–42; Hooper, *Art of Work*, 102.

15. Kelley, *Freedom Dreams*, 187.

16. Cortez, "Big, Fine Women from Ruleville," *Black Collegian* 9, no. 5 (1979): 90.

17. Spellman, *Things I Must Have Known*, 128. Spellman spent thirty years as director of the National Endowment for the Arts and deferred collecting his poems until 2008.

18. Casey Rocheteau, "Interview with Dr Aneb Kgositsile, February 6, 2015," accessed September 9, 2019, http://www.writeahouse.com/blog/an-interview-with-dr-aneb-kgositsile (site discontinued).

19. Richard Wright published *Black Power* in 1954 and *White Man, Listen!* in 1957, and leaders and writers used the term "Black Power" in different contexts, from Frederick Douglass through Adam Clayton Powell and the Revolutionary Action Movement.

20. Wilkins, "Making of Black Internationalists," 469.

21. Matlin, *On the Corner*, 4–5.

22. For the South's image, see K. Cox, *Dreaming of Dixie*; and Graham, "South in Popular Culture."

23. Holt and Mahoney, "Make Harlem Black—Therefore Beautiful," *Liberator*, September 1964, 10–11.

24. Dent, Schechner, and Moses, *Free Southern Theater*, 152.

25. Garrett, in Baraka and Neal, *Black Fire*, 662.

26. Baraka, *We Own the Night*, in Baraka and Neal, *Black Fire*, 527.

27. Peter Labrie, "The New Breed", in Baraka and Neal, *Black Fire*, 64–77; Calvin Hernton, "Dynamite Growing out of Their Skulls," in Baraka and Neal, *Black Fire*, 78–103.

28. Dicker/sun, *African American Theater*, 145.

29. Camus, *Neither Victims nor Executioners*; Maurine Hoffman, "Student Wins Mention with Short Story," *Washington Post* March 1, 1964. Visser-Maessen argues that the fact that Moses "even posed his and African Americans' struggles into such frames [as Camus's philosophy] set him apart from most in the movement." Visser-Maessen, *Robert Parris Moses*, 3. Moses read Camus throughout his time in Mississippi, *The Rebel* (1951) while incarcerated in Pike County jail in 1961, and *The Plague* (1947) in Parchman, but Thelwell, Cobb, Lester, and Zimmerman are among organizers who were also examining the ethical questions inherent in Camus's disquisition.

30. Commended by *Story* as a finalist in its *Reader's Digest*–sponsored competition, it was published in *Story*'s anthology, *The Stone Soldier* (1964) and *Negro Digest* in January 1964. It is included in S. Jones, *Crossing the Color Line*, 39–45.

31. "The South's palladium" is W. J. Cash's phrase. Cash, *The Mind of the South*, 86.

32. L. Jones, *Dutchman*, 34, 19, 20, 29.

33. Thulani Davis, *1959* (London: Hamish Hamilton, 1992), 79. For critical discussion of white women as literary devices, see S. Williams, *Give Birth to Brightness*, 218–34.

Monteith, *Advancing Sisterhood?*, examines how white southern women writers occlude the voices of African American women characters by containing them within a friendship paradigm.

34. Styron, "This Quiet Dust," 138; "Truth and Nat Turner: An Exchange," *Nation*, October 16, 1967, 543. When Styron reviewed white Marxist historian Herbert Aptheker's *American Negro Slave Revolts* in 1963, which detailed some 250 revolts, he criticized Aptheker's thesis that slave insurrection was a prevalent form of resistance. Styron leaned on Stanley Elkins's *Slavery: A Problem in American Institutional and Intellectual Life* (Chicago: University of Chicago Press, 1959) to argue that slaves were infantilized. Thelwell returned to the fact that slaves rebelled "with a frequency that caused the masters to live in state of constant apprehension" in "Back with the Wind." His essay is anthologized in John B. Duff and Peter M. Mitchell, eds., *The Nat Turner Rebellion: The Historical Event and the Modern Controversy* (New York: Harper and Row, 1971) 181–90.

35. Thelwell, "Mr. Styron and the Reverend Turner," 29.

36. Eugene Genovese, "The Nat Turner Case," *New York Review of Books*, September 12, 1968; "An Exchange on Nat Turner: Anna Mary Wells, Vincent Harding, and Mike Thelwell, reply by Eugene D. Genovese," *New York Review of Books*, November 7, 1968.

37. Thelwell in "An Exchange on Nat Turner," *New York Review of Books*, November 7, 1968.

38. Baker, *Long Black Song*, 112.

39. "Liberatory narratives": Angelyn Mitchell, *The Freedom to Remember: Narrative, Slavery, and Gender in Contemporary Black Women's Fiction* (Brunswick, N.J.: Rutgers University Press, 2002), 4–6. For a summary reading of "The Final Supper," see Monteith, *Advancing Sisterhood?*, 103–4, 194.

40. Thelwell quoted in W. J. Weatherby, "When Literary Worlds Collide," *Guardian* (London), May 28, 1980; Thelwell, *Duties, Pleasures and Conflicts*, 229; Thelwell, "Harder They Come."

41. O'Neal, "The Artist: A Social Development," box 34, folder 19, 2, JO'N; Executive Committee minutes, November 24–29, 1965, 18, SNCC.

42. Preface, untitled pamphlet ("There is no title. The words will speak to what this booklet is . . . The words you give other booklets will make them what they are") produced by the *Student Voice*, box 14, folder 114, JO'N; O'Neal in Michna, "Performance and Cross-Racial Storytelling," 51–52.

43. In the story, Willie is identified via the surname Ricks. Holt, "Defendant or Decedent," untitled pamphlet, 18, box 14, folder 114, JO'N. Subsequent references in parentheses.

44. Randy Battle, "Charles Sherrod and Stokely Carmichael," in Lissovoy, *The Great Pool Jump*, 30–32.

45. Beal, "Double Jeopardy," 386. Nikki Giovanni expresses the same message in *Gemini*, 96, and in Baldwin and Giovanni, *Dialogue*, 47. For detailed study in this context, see Clarke, *After Mecca*.

46. Janet Jemott Moses, "If We Must Die," in Holsaert et al., *Hands on the Freedom Plow*, 266–67, 269; Judy Richardson, "My Enduring Circle of Trust," in Holsaert et al., *Hands on the Freedom Plow*, 353–54; Gwen Patton, "Born Freedom Fighter," in Holsaert et al., *Hands on the Freedom Plow*, 582–83; Cobb, *This Nonviolent Stuff'll Get You Killed*, 161. Fleming, *Soon We Will Not Cry*, 125–26, 136, discusses Avery in the context of stories of other powerful women in SNCC.

47. Forman, "Two Potatoes and One Onion," circa 1962, box 171, folder 7, JF. Another example is an unpublished short story by Forman about a social worker who attends

protest meetings and whose husband is an activist in Levittown: "A Sad Day for Eliza," box 171, folder 1, JF.

48. Joseph, *Waiting 'til the Midnight Hour*, 260. Elizabeth Sutherland (reclaiming her birth name Betita Martínez) edited newspaper *El Grito del Norte* in New Mexico after leaving SNCC, and Varela was fusing Spanish with English in the context of Mexican and Latino civil rights by 1969: "Lamento / quando usen la palabra / Revolución." Maria Varela, "Revolution," in Gitlin, *Campfires of Resistance*, 43.

49. Courtland Cox quoted in *Nation*, July 19, 1965, reproduced in "What's Wrong with the War in Vietnam?," a SNCC pamphlet prepared by Donna Allen and Al Vhrie, 1, box 15, folder 5, JO'N. The comparison was a surprise to Robert Penn Warren, who cites a visit David Halberstam made to the Greenwood COFO office, where he was told, "I've enjoyed reading your coverage of our other colonial war." For Warren it was an example of SNCC not screening recruits for opinions. Warren, *Who Speaks for the Negro?*, 177.

50. Cobb, "Charlie's Poem," *Student Voice*, June 6, 1965, 3–4. A veteran activist in Marion, Alabama, and a deacon of his church, Jackson was fatally shot by an Alabama state trooper on February 26, 1965, a catalyst for the Selma to Montgomery March.

51. Cobb, "I Want to Say," *Movement* (SNCC of California), June 1965, 2.

52. Michael Bibby cites poetry and essays by S. E. Anderson and Gwen Patton in the context of the black aesthetic's revolutionary underpinnings around the war but does not say that the writers were active in SNCC. Bibby, *Hearts and Minds: Bodies, Poetry, and Resistance in the Vietnam Era* (New Brunswick, N.J.: Rutgers University Press, 1996), 54–56.

53. Doug Youngblood, "Tales of the Ghetto," *Movement* (SNCC of California), February 1968, 8.

54. Anderson, "Junglegrave," in Taylor, *Vietnam and Black America*, 139. Anderson is rarely acknowledged until after his work in SNCC. For example, see Glass, *Rebel Publisher*, 148.

55. SNCC's Statement on Vietnam, January 6, 1966, in Grant, *Black Protest*, 416–18.

56. Roy Wilkins quoted in "Confusing the Cause," *Time*, July 16, 1965, 20; Robert S. Browne, "The Freedom Movement and the War in Vietnam," *Freedomways* 5, no. 4 (Fall 1965): 472; Martin Luther King, "A Time to Break Silence," *Freedomways* 7, no. 2 (Spring 1967): 103–17. Simon Hall delineates the evolving stand of King versus that of Wilkins in "The Response of the Moderate Wing of the Civil Rights Movement" and *Peace and Freedom*.

57. Forman, "Liberation Will Come from a Black Thing," November 3, 1967, box 1, folder 17, ESM; Forman, *Making of Black Revolutionaries*, 510–12; I. F. Stone, "What SNCC Said about the War and Why Negroes Feel the Way They Do," *I. F. Stone's Weekly*, January 17, 1966, 3.

58. Cobb, "To Vietnam," in Gitlin, *Campfires of Resistance*, 19. Diane Nash traveled with Barbara Deming, Patricia Griffith and Grace Mara Newman. See Herschberger, *Traveling to Vietnam*, 2–6.

59. Lester and Cobb, "SNCC Workers on War Crimes Mission: Letters from Hanoi," *Movement* (SNCC of California), May 1967, 5; Cobb, "Notes on Teaching in Mississippi," quoted in Holt, *Summer That Didn't End*, 106.

60. Cobb, *In the Furrows of the World*, 35–36.

61. Robert Hayden, *Kaleidoscope*, 224–25.

62. Lester, *Falling Pieces of the Broken Sky*, 60, 75.

63. Lester, *Search for the New Land*, 129–30.

64. Lester, "The Duty of a Revolutionary Is...," *Movement* (SNCC of California), December 1967; Lester, *Revolutionary Notes*, 23–24; Lester, "Us," (1968), in Lowenfels, *Writing on the Wall*, 110–11.

65. Cobb in Richards, "With Our Minds Set on Freedom," 340.

66. In Cobb's original conception, there was "no title / for this book." Publicity flyer tucked in my copy of Stembridge's *I Play Flute*. Promoted as "the Second Flute Publication," it included a poem to that effect: "It is not finished . . . / When Black America's struggle is finished . . . / Then / this book will / be finished. "The Second Flute Publication," *Movement* (SNCC of California), May 1967, 4.

67. Wade Gayles, *Anointed to Fly*, 129.

68. Cobb, "Aint That a Groove," typed manuscript, box 27, folder 6, JF.

69. Vine City was in the Georgia statehouse district in which Julian Bond was elected but denied his seat in January 1966. Stephen Tuck examines the SNCC project in *Beyond Atlanta*, 228–38. *Nitty Gritty* was the title of a newsletter written by the exclusively black project to "tell it like it is." From November 1966, "Nitty Gritty" was the title Chester Wright chose for a column in the *Movement* that focused on SNCC in Los Angeles. For more on "nitty gritty," see Grady-Willis, *Challenging U.S. Apartheid*, 86–93.

70. House, foreword to *Negroes with Guns*, vii.

71. Michelle Alexander describes the "racial caste system" maintained in subsequent decades in *New Jim Crow*.

72. House, "Road to Internationalism," 16.

73. Gregson Davis, "Aimé Césaire's 'Mississippi,'" *Movement* (SNCC of California), May 1967, 10.

74. Zinn, *SNCC*, 7; Cobb, "Nation No. 3," *Everywhere Is Yours*, 7.

75. After Lewis met Malcolm X in Nairobi in October 1964 Malcolm was invited to Selma in 1965. Cobb, "Civil Rights Tower of Strength," *Washington Post*, January 12, 2005.

76. Joshua Clark Davis, "Black-Owned Bookstores: Anchors of the Black Power Movement," *Black Perspectives*, January 28, 2017, AAIHS, https://www.aaihs.org/black-owned-bookstores-anchors-of-the-black-power-movement.

77. Cobb, "Nation," in Lowenfels, *Writing on the Wall*, 17–20; Cobb, "Nation No. 3," in *Everywhere Is Yours*, 5–7.

78. Cobb, "The Truth," in *Everywhere Is Yours*, 11. Angela Jackson wrongly assumed that Cobb's second poetry collection was his first, overlooking *In the Furrows of the World* (1967), as so much of SNCC's writing was overlooked. Angela Jackson, "Review of *Everywhere Is Yours*," *Black World*, February 1972, 91.

79. Moses and Cobb, *Radical Equations*, 193, 224; Cobb, "Afterword: Understanding History," in *This Nonviolent Stuff'll Get You Killed*, 246.

80. Forman, "Liberation Will Come from a Black Thing," November 3, 1967, box 1, folder 17, ESM; Forman, *Making of Black Revolutionaries*, 510–12.

81. Forman, "Liberation Will Come from a Black Thing."

82. Forman, "Mother Africa," an uncataloged poem tucked into the "Free Huey Newton" issue of *Black Dialogue* (1969) that I discovered in Forman's papers and submitted to archivists.

83. LeRoi Jones, *Dead Lecturer*, 61–64.

84. Cobb, "The Emergence of Black Power," SNCC Oral Histories Conference transcript, 17, CDSD.

85. Forman's "1967: The High Tide of Black Resistance" was distributed by SNCC's International Affairs Commission in New York for a dollar a copy. He demanded $500 million from white churches and synagogues that failed to address racial oppression or what he conceived as colonial capitalism. He delivered the manifesto as director of the National Black Economic and Development Conference, in Detroit in April 1969, and taped demands to church doors. "Reparations Demand Is Taped To N.Y. Church," *Chicago Daily*

Defender, May 8, 1969. Robin Kelley declares it the first systematic plan for reparations in *Freedom Dreams*, 120.

Chapter 8. Battle Stories at the Grassroots and Beginnings of Bitter Ends

Epigraphs are from Mari Evans, "Contemporary Black Literature: A Statement," *Black World*, June 1970, 93; Dittmer, *Local People*, 361; Mahoney, *Black Jacob*, 131.

1. Fuller, "Books Noted," *Negro Digest*, November 1967, 85. He was writing about critical responses to Ernest Gaines's *Of Love and Dust* (1967), set in rural Louisiana in 1948.
2. Mahoney, *Black Jacob*, dustjacket.
3. Fenderson, *Building the Black Arts Movement*, 65–90. See Joe Street's evocation of this period and Black Panther philosophy, *Culture War in the Civil Rights Movement*, 148–60.
4. Sterling, "What's Black and White and Read All Over?," 821, 823, 826.
5. "Ebony Book Shelf," *Ebony*, August 1969, 24; Truman Nelson, "Guerrilla of the Mind," *New York Times*, October 13, 1968.
6. Cruse, *Crisis of the Negro Intellectual*, 383.
7. Evans, "Contemporary Black Literature," 93
8. Evans, "Contemporary Black Literature," 94; Holt, *Act of Conscience*, v.
9. Toni Cade Bambara, review of *Black Jacob*, *Liberator* 10 (1970): 20.
10. "Books received," *Crisis*, December 1969, 438; Bambara, review of *Black Jacob*; Frank Cunningham, "Maimed Life-Style," *Saturday Review* 52 (1969), 39, 61. It was among books noted in *Nation*, April 14, 1969, 475.
11. Moses and Cobb, *Radical Equations*, 91–93.
12. J. Bryant, *Victims and Heroes*, 191.
13. R. Hall, *Long George Alley*, 218.
14. Baldwin, blurb on the cover of R. Hall, *Long George Alley*; Jan Carew, "Fiction: Irony, Elitism, Babbitt Updated, Africa, Civil Rights," *New York Times*, September 10, 1972. Carew commended "an impressive literary debut" but was equivocal when assessing technique "at the same time sharper and shallower" than Toomer's, as if literary portraits need "the extra dimension of a film" to do the novel "justice." It is Hall's only published novel although he submitted proposals for John O. Killens's consideration for a novel called "Bessie" based on his mother, and another with the working title *Going Home* about an African American child in Poland who returns to the United States in 1969. Box 68, folders 3–4, John O. Killens papers, Manuscript, Archives, and Rare Books Library, Emory University, Atlanta.
15. J. Bryant, *Victims and Heroes*, 191.
16. The seething undercurrent of *This Child's Gonna Live* stems from Wright's early life in its Depression-era setting, the death of siblings because of poverty, and the pathologizing of African American families in the 1960s. Monteith, "Never-Ending Cycle of Poverty"; Margalit Fox, "Sarah E. Wright, Novelist of Black Experience, Dies at 80," *New York Times*, October 2, 2009.
17. J. Bryant, *Victims and Heroes*, 190–91.
18. In appreciation of Fuller's influence on a black aesthetic, Houston Baker dispensed with "universal, objective, and standard causal models that mark a normal practice of literary criticism in the United States." Baker, *Afro-American Poetics*, 173. Carolyn Rodgers expressed frustration with "objectivity" and "racism in the criticism of literature." Rodgers, "Feelings of Sense," 5.
19. Schraufnagel, *From Apology to Protest*, 184–85. The reader gains little from description of the novel because Schraufnagel includes mistakes: police do not instigate a riot;

members of the white elite do—and shoot at black people in the streets; there is a single civil rights organization based on SNCC, rather than two with the second led by local militant Raz X.

20. Else, *True South*, 185.

21. Hill, *Deacons for Defense*, 188; Dittmer, *Local People*, 36. Natchez was the subject of Allison Davis, Burleigh B. Gardner, and Mary R. Gardner's social anthropological study *Deep South* (Chicago: University of Chicago Press, 1941). Jack Davis tested his sense of scholarly objectivity while researching *Race against Time*, which explicates Natchez's reputation as a "history laboratory." Jack Davis, *Race against Time*, 20.

22. This contradicts Lynd's later description of Lowndes as SNCC's "only major initiative after 1964," *Accompanying*, 54.

23. Davis, *Race against Time*, 46. White southern novelist Ellen Douglas recounted a northern visitor observing, "[Natchez] isn't a real town is it?" The implication was that "Faulkner might have invented it." Ellen Douglas, *Truth: Four Stories I Am Finally Old Enough to Tell* (1998; repr., New York: Plume, 1999), 33–34.

24. SNCC, "Background Report on Natchez (October 1963–August 1965)," n.d., 1–2, box 38, folder 9, JF.

25. "Klan Beats Miss. Negro," *Student Voice*, February 18, 1964, 1; Carver Neblett, field report, n.d., Natchez subject file 1964–1956, box 38, folder 9, JF.

26. R. Hall, *Long George Alley*, 113, 114.

27. Dick Gregory quoted in "Act of Savagery," *Time*, March 10, 1967, 25.

28. Stephen Bingham, "Mississippi Letter," February 15, 1965, 2, 3, 4, series 4, reel 7, 110, SNCC.

29. *Natchez Democrat*, August 11, 1965; Jack Davis, *Race against Time*, 177.

30. "A Conversation with Richard Hall," in R. Hall, *Long George Alley*, back matter.

31. Zinn, *SNCC*, 55–56; Forman, *Making of Black Revolutionaries*, 273.

32. McLaurin's talk recounted in Sugarman, *Stranger at the Gates*, 95.

33. Mahoney, "Risking Life and Liberty"; Freedom School mimeo materials, 1963–64, folder 1, M85-013, Pamela P. Allen Papers, Wisconsin Historical Society, Madison.

34. Carson, *In Struggle*, 104–5. At the "Meeting on Washington Unemployment Demonstration," December 23, 1963, Mahoney presided, with plans for activities around evictees, slum landlords, a clothing warehouse for the unemployed, and visits to Washington (to the United Mine Workers, Kentucky congressmen and the president) by forty unemployed Kentucky miners. Mahoney, "The Job Problem," 1963, box 8, folder 20, Ella Baker Papers, Schomburg Center for Research in Black Culture, New York Public Library. For Mahoney liaising between organizers and unions, see Minutes of SNCC Executive Committee, September 6–9, Atlanta, 4, SNCC.

35. Thelwell, "Professor and the Activists," 622; on National Negro Congress in Washington, D.C., see Gellman, *Death Blow to Jim Crow*. Joseph points out that this led to SNCC opening the Washington office in the first place and notes Mahoney's contribution to the Nonviolent Action Group. Joseph, *Stokely*, 65–66. Essays examining SNCC's engagement with labor activists include Araiza, "Complicating the Beloved Community," which brings Mike Miller, Marshall Ganz, and Dickie Flowers into focus, along with support of Cesar Chavez.

36. "Rent Strike Organized" and "Children Picket the White House," *Student Voice* 5, no. 3 (January 27 1964), 3; "Tenants Start First 'Rent Strike' in District," *Washington Post*, January 25, 1964.

37. Carmichael, *Ready for Revolution*, 160. David Braswell, "A Freedom Rider at Rest: Bill Mahoney of Atlanta," February 12, 2016, https://homemadegospel.org/?p=2026, was

written after Braswell noted a Black History Month display about Mahoney in the lobby of the building where he resides. It makes no mention of Mahoney's activism after the 1961 Freedom Ride.

38. Derby notes Mahoney's involvement in preparation for the March on Washington, "Sometimes in the Ground Troops," in Holsaert et al., *Hands on the Freedom Plow*, 441.

39. Fay Bellamy, "Report on Lowndes County Tent City," December 30, 1965, http://www.crmvet.org/lets/651230_sncc_lowndes_bellamy.pdf.

40. Bond, "Letter to the Editor," microfilm 44, reel 3, segment 48, Lucile Montgomery Papers, Wisconsin Historical Society, Madison.

41. Aitken, *Cotton Plantation South since the Civil War*, 226.

42. Robert and Vicki Gabriner, "Fayette County–Seven Years After," *Movement* (SNCC of California), October 1967, 8–9; Jon Nordheimer, "Fayette Protest An Anachronism," *New York Times*, October 12, 1969.

43. SNCC press release by Jack Minnis, "Lowndes County Voters Seek to Invalidate Elections," December 31, 1965, 2, http://www.crmvet.org/docs/651231_sncc_lowndes-election.pdf.

44. Mahoney, "Travels in the South," *Black Fire*, 144. Subsequent references are in parentheses.

45. The white man wielding the snake as a weapon was future county commissioner Deans Barber Jr., and the African American man charged with disturbing the peace instead of Barber was Johnny Creer. The incident was reported as "Ala. White Tries Stuffing Snake in Negro's Mouth," *Jet*, October 3, 1963, 55. See also J. Mills Thornton, *Dividing Lines: Municipal Politics and the Struggle for Civil Rights in Montgomery, Birmingham and Selma* (Tuscaloosa: University of Alabama Press, 2002), 456.

46. Edward M. Rudd, "Freedom City, Alabama: Lowndes Families Start Tent Village," *Southern Courier* (Montgomery), January 8–9, 1966; Jerry DeMuth, "Black Belt, Alabama," *Commonweal*, August 7, 1964, http://crmvet.org/info/6408_blackbelt_demuth.pdf.

47. David Colston Sr.'s death: "Protests Erupt after White Alabama Farmer Kills Negro," *Jet*, February 10, 1966, 8–9.

48. Mahoney wrote that he was "miseducated" in the New Jersey system "until 1959, when Howard University took over the job." "My education ended," he wrote, "when I was expelled from Howard University (they say I was not expelled but was suspended; a tricky legal point) for refusing to take my final ROTC course." "Miseducated" would become a popular self-descriptor for writers associated with the Black Arts Movement, riffing on Carter Woodson's thesis in *The Mis-education of the Negro* (Washington, D.C.: Associated Publishers, 1933). Mahoney was not afraid of making waves, publishing "Howard University: Neither Red nor Black, Just Servile," *Liberator*, June 1965, 18, and "The Statue of Liberty Conspiracy Trial: No Hiding Place in Foley Square," *Liberator*, July 1965, 18–19.

49. Mahoney uses "U.S. 59," but the route described in the novel corresponds to today's I-59 in Alabama, not U.S. 59 traveling south through Arkansas and Texas.

50. Mahoney incorporates a plantation tragedy as a story within the story: the 1929 lynching of Aubrey Blue, Jacob's father, hidden by his mother. Aubrey is lynched because of what he sees: Bernard Nicholson's father killing a black man with whose wife he is having an affair. The story is hidden in the family Bible at Genesis 22 (118–24). Jacob is unaware that he has a brother, a plantation worker and petty criminal, whose life chances are reduced when his mother selects Jacob as the son whose education will be supported financially by her husband's murderer. Once he knows, Jacob facilitates his brother's family's removal to Memphis, the day before his own life is ended by a sniper's bullet, having effected the briefest of reconciliations. In 1969, Sarah E. Wright in *This Child's Gonna Live*

and Mahoney each reworked the motif Twain explored in *Pudd'nhead Wilson* (1894). Like Jacob of biblical narrative, in each novel a character called Jacob has an estranged brother who grows up with a different class background.

51. James Forman's "Sad Day For Elizabeth," part 1, closes on her ambition; part 2 emphasizes how unhappy she is at Howard University (she is reading Turgenev's "An Unhappy Girl"). Box 171, folder 1, JF. The clearest description of her conflicted feelings appears in the excerpt published in Forman, *High Tide of Black Resistance*, 67–72.

52. Ralph Ellison, *Invisible Man* (1952; repr., New York: Penguin, 1972), 72.

53. Demby, *The Catacombs* (1965; Boston: Northeastern University Press, 1991), 6.

54. Dittmer, *Good Doctors*, 5, 7, 45; Holland, *From the Mississippi Delta*, 241–42. When Dittmer mapped the hidden history of the Medical Committee for Human Rights in 2009, he described it as an act of atonement—previously unaware of how significantly the organization had impacted the segregated and civil rights South, he had overlooked it in his earlier studies. Dittmer, *The Good Doctors*, ix–x. See also Cobb, *The Most Southern Place on Earth*, 262–266.

55. Samuel Block, "A Day in a Mississippi Court," box 67, folder 3, FST.

56. Heilman, *Tragedy and Melodrama*, 93–94.

57. "Fannie Lou Hamer interviewed by Robert Wright," August 9, 1968, Oral History Collection, Civil Rights Documentation project, Moorland-Spingarn Research Center, Howard University; "Let the Circle Be Unbroken," Program Files and Sound Recordings 1.3, box 8, folder 6, Southern Regional Conference Papers, Georgia State University Library, Special Collections, Atlanta; Guyot in Raines, *My Soul Is Rested*, 268. Carmichael describes the excruciating pain of being clamped and twisted in wrist breakers in *Ready for the Revolution*, 207–8.

58. Dittmer, *Local People*, 404; "Violence Breaks Out with Mass Negro Registration," *Student Voice*, April 30, 1965, 1, 4.

59. Bond, "Movement We Helped to Make," 18.

60. Larry Still, "Candidates Making Serious: How 2 Negroes Campaign in Mississippi for Congress," *Jet*, January 25, 1962, 18–23; "King Gets 9,000 in S.W. GA. Election," *Student Voice*, September 23, 1964, 1, 4.

61. "FDP SAYS.... HINDS COUNTY MUST TURN OUT.... 25,000 VOTES FOR EVERS!" *FDP [Freedom Democratic Party] News*, February 26, 1968, 1, box 2, folder 4, EK. See Crosby, "Charles Evers's Own Little Empire," in *A Little Taste of Freedom*, 207–23, for detailed analysis of his Mississippi campaign, including his relationship with the Mississippi Sovereignty Commission. In 1968, Dr. Gilbert R. Mason, a black doctor on the Gulf Coast, was an elected delegate to the Democratic National Convention for the Fifth Congressional District, which Mason writes about in *Beaches, Blood, and Ballots*. Robert G. Clark of Holmes County was elected to the state legislature in 1968.

62. Gwen Patton, "No Clouds in the Sky: Lowndes County," which together with Janet Dewart, "Caging the Panther," and "Let the Facts Decide," SNCC press release, November 29, 1966, comprise the "Lowndes County Story" in "The Black Power Controversy," special issue of *New South Student* (Southern Student Organizing Committee), December 1966, 3–6. A longer version of Patton's piece was published in SNCC's *Aframerican News for You*, January 12, 1967, 20–26, box 25, Richardson Papers, David M. Rubenstein Library, Duke University Libraries, North Carolina.

63. Visser-Maessen, *Robert Parris Moses*, 184.

64. "Natchez Mississippi Project: Report by Carver Neblett," n.d., 2–3, "Natchez, 1964–65," box 39, folder 9, JF.

65. Worth Long, "Dealer," *Movement* (SNCC of California), July 1965, 1.

66. Bill Mahoney manuscript (untitled), box 4, folder 2, DD.
67. Saul, *Freedom Is, Freedom Ain't*, 17.
68. Gen. 32:24–32.
69. Mahoney sat with others outside the prayer circle in SNCC meetings. Carson, *In Struggle*, 38, 105; Branch, *Parting the Waters*, 484. Bond discusses his own lack of religious faith in *Julian Bond: Reflections from the Frontlines of the Civil Rights Movement*, directed by Eduardo Montes-Bradley (Alexandria, Va.: Filmmakers Library, 2012).
70. R. H. King, *Civil Rights and the Idea of Freedom*, 52–53.
71. Benjamin, *Illuminations*, 249.
72. Benjamin, *Illuminations*, 249; Bond, "Movement We Helped to Make," 18.
73. Bond, "Movement We Helped to Make,"19.
74. Benjamin, *Illuminations*, 249.
75. Lewis's first paintings in this vein are *Metropolitan Crowd* (1946), *Ritual* (1950), and *Congregation* (1950). E. Fine, "Mainstream, Blackstream and the Black Art Movement," 374–75; F. Coleman, "Changing Same, "147–57; Browne, "Norman Lewis." Abstract paintings and installations by Jack Whitten and Sam Gilliam may also have influenced Mahoney's thinking.
76. Thelwell, "Fish Are Jumping," 75.
77. Rancière, *Politics of Aesthetics*, 25.
78. Letters from Mahoney to Jesse Morris via Doris Derby, n.d. and November 29, 1968, box 4, DD.
79. SNCC, "Background Report on Natchez (October 1963–August 1965)," n.d., 2, box 38, folder 9, JF; *Student Voice*, August 19, 1964, 2; Holt, *Summer That Didn't End*, 238.
80. Weil, *In a Madhouse's Din*, 147.
81. Von Hoffman, *Mississippi Notebook*, 58.
82. "Natchez Mississippi Project: Report by Carver Neblett," n.d., 1, "Natchez, 1964–65," box 39, folder 9, JF.
83. For example, Charles Gordon, "City Fire Bomb Story Folds Up, Rumor Spread by COFO," McComb *Enterprise-Journal*, August 21, 1964.
84. "New Blasts Rock 2 Mississippi Sites: Violence Erupts in Vicinity of Freedom Houses," *New York Times*, August 16, 1964.
85. Curtis Hayes's affidavit about the bombing of the McComb Freedom House: Misseduc Foundation, *Mississippi Black Paper*, 76.
86. Samstein and King quoted in Carpenter, "From Heroism to Madness," 26, 25.
87. Carmichael and Thelwell, *Ready for the Revolution*, 320. Greene describes a car forcing his off the road, its white occupants shooting, and how, at 105 mph, he succeeded in losing them. Misseduc Foundation, *Mississippi Black Paper*, 38–39. The SNCC Legacy Project records the incident on its "In Memoriam" page (under "George L. Greene"): https://www.sncclegacyproject.org/about/in-memoriam. Night drivers skilled in evading hostile pursuers were legendary internally, as Thelwell indicates in "Fish Are Jumpin' an' the Cotton Is High" and as Hall reimagines in *Long George Alley*.
88. Von Hoffman, *Mississippi Notebook*, 58, 25; "A Reporter's Look at the Heat and Hate of a State in Turmoil: Mississippi Notebook," *Chicago Daily News*, August 1, 1964; Robert Coles, "Natchez, Lovely Natchez," *New Republic*, February 18, 1967, 31.
89. Stembridge in Gitlin, *Campfires of the Resistance*, 32.
90. *Panola*, directed by Ed Pincus and David Neuman (1970), Ed Pincus collection, 1965–1967, Amistad Research Center, Tulane University, New Orleans; Hill, *Deacons for Defense*, 28–29.

91. Chico Neblett, letter to Tina, November 19, 1964, box 38, folder 9, JF. After putting down $500 for a $5,000 house and paying $50 monthly, insurance was impossible to secure.

92. "Negro Testifies Later Arrested," *Student Voice*, December 16, 1963, 1, 4; Sutherland, "Cat and Mouse Game." Sutherland's article was reprinted by SNCC and used as a campaign poster. Box 2, folder 6, EK. Among many incidents, African American Johnny Davis reported to COFO in August 1964 being offered $200 by local chief of police to "get rid of" the three strongest Mississippi Student Union leaders. *Freedom Flame* (newsletter), August 23–29, 1964, box 3, folder 13, 1, Michael J. Miller Civil Rights Collection, McCain Library and Archives, University of Southern Mississippi.

93. "Natchez Boycott Success," *Movement* (SNCC of California), December 1965, 1.

94. For James Jackson's contribution to the Natchez campaign, see Hill, *Deacons for Defense*, 189–95.

95. Matt Heron's photographs captured the officer in action: Long, *We'll Never Turn Back*, 44.

96. Dittmer, *Good Doctors*, 103–7.

97. Varela in Gitlin, *Campfires of the Resistance*, 39.

98. A Mr. Peavine supported SNCC activists in Fayette and Natchez, as Janet Jemmot Moses recalls, but Hall does not create biographical studies. J. J. Moses, "If We Must Die," in Holsaert et al., *Hands on the Freedom Plow*, 267–68.

99. Jim [Kates], "Letter from Natchez," July 29, 1965, box 33, folder 4, JF. A white Wesleyan student, Jim Kates volunteered for Freedom Summer in 1964 and again in 1965, and he assessed his experience in 2014 in Wesconnect, "the Wesleyan Alumni App," accessed June 18, 2019, http://wesconnect.wesleyan.edu/ (page discontinued).

100. Newfield, "Question of SNCC," 38.

101. Sutherland, "Mississippi: Summer of Discontent," 202, 213, 215.

102. Jim [Kates], "Letter from Natchez."

103. Hogan, *Many Minds, One Heart*, 238. For staffing, see Natchez Project Report by Annie Pearl Avery, n.d. [1964] and Field Report by Eugene Rouse, December 8, 1964. At this point there were only four or five staff. Rouse and Janet Jemmott requested support. Box 38, folder 9, JF.

104. M. M. Bakhtin, *Problems of Dostoevsky's Poetics*, translated by R. W. Rotsel (Ann Arbor, Mich.: Ardis, 1973), 72.

105. David Karp, "Black Jacob," *New York Times*, March 9, 1969.

106. For example, the description of Mahoney in the Civil Rights Digital Library at http://crdl.usg.edu/people/m/mahoney_william_1941; Toni Cade Bambara, review of *Black Jacob*, *Liberator* 10 (1970), 20.

107. Claude Brown's blurb, back cover of Mahoney, *Black Jacob*.

108. Sutherland letter to Forman, June 1967, box 1, folder 5, ESM.

109. A. Morris, "Retrospective on the Civil Rights Movement," 535.

110. Polletta, "Contending Stories," 428, "Plotting Protest," 35.

111. It was not easy to capture the frenzy, even on film. As Haxwell Wexler discovered when shooting the fallout at the Democratic National Convention in Chicago in 1968 for *Medium Cool* (1968), he needed a fictional protagonist to lead viewers through the maze. Monteith, *American Culture in the 1960s*, 97–98.

112. Thelwell, "Organizer," 4, 8–9, 14.

113. Mahoney, *Black Jacob*, 69–70, 233.

114. Karen Pate, collating Vicksburg reports for Ruby Doris Smith Robinson, noted Dennis Sweeney's attempts in McComb to repair a station wagon that did not run. January 21, 1965, series 4, reel 7, p. 241, SNCC.

115. Nicholas, *Freshwater Road*, 216, 217.

Chapter 9. The Walking Wounded

Epigraphs are from Lester in Nicholas Von Hoffman, "'The Movement' at Ebb Tide," *Washington Post*, February 5, 1969; Carson in Greenberg, *Circle of Trust*, 199; Joyce Ladner in Miss Dorie Ann Ladner and Dr. Joyce Ann Ladner interview by Joseph Mosnier, September 20, 2011, Civil Rights History Project, Library of Congress, 61, https://www.loc.gov/item/afc2010039_crhp0054.

1. Alberto Manguel, *Reading Pictures: A History of Love and Hate* (London: Random House, 2000), 28.

2. Charles McDew, opening plenary, April 15, 2010, "SNCC Legacy project," *SNCC 50th Anniversary Conference*, vol. 1 (San Francisco: California Newsreel, 2011).

3. Dittmer, "Battle Fatigue," chap. 14 in *Local People*. Payne sets it against the media tendency to frame the movement through "what Joyce Ladner calls the 'Big Events'" (393) and details tension throughout *I've Got the Light of Freedom*.

4. Charles Sherrod quoted by Benj DeMott, "Part 1: That Floating Bridge," in *That Floating Bridge*, First of the Year 5 (London: Routledge, 2013), 4.

5. For black characters disempowered in white-authored texts, see Sharon Monteith, "Between Girls: Friendship as a Monologic Formulation," in *Advancing Sisterhood?*, 50–73.

6. Martin Luther King Jr. acknowledged his place in history but worried about it, beginning in sermons including "Conquering Self-Centeredness," "Problems of Personality Integration," "Factors That Determine Character," "Overcoming an Inferiority Complex," and "The Mastery of Fear." See M. L. King, *Papers of Martin Luther King, Jr.*, vol. 4, 255, 248.

7. Crosby cites Hollis Watkins intervening in a panel discussion in Port Gibson, Mississippi, in 2003 to make the point that we are not yet "where we should be." Crosby, *Little Taste of Freedom*, 279.

8. Thelwell in Greenberg, *Circle of Trust*, 202; Harding, *Other American Revolution*, 185.

9. King quoted by Coles, *Call of Service*, 141.

10. Coles, "A Black Civil Rights Worker" (1971), in *Farewell to the South*, 331. Coles delivered this as a lecture, "Psychological Sanctity and Social Protest," December 16, 1970.

11. Belfrage, *Freedom Summer*, 55, 195.

12. Block interviewed by Sinsheimer, December 12, 1986, 33, 77, 79, 52–3, 77, JAS. When such feelings are shared it may involve naming others who may not choose to be interpreted by or for others, as when Block described Willie Peacock escaping into alcohol in the aftermath of a beating. See also Sinsheimer, "Never Turn Back."

13. Mike Miller, "Renewing the Beloved Community (AKA 'Walking Wounded' Project)" http://www.crmvet.org/wwp/wwphome.htm.

14. Eighteen years after being accepted for but not serving in Freedom Summer, Mary Aickin Rothschild published the first scholarly appraisal of northern volunteers, *Case of Black and White*.

15. Hall, *Long George Alley*, 214.

16. Carson, *In Struggle*, 48–49; Dittmer, *Local People*, 109–10.

17. Crosby, introduction to *Civil Rights History from the Ground Up*, 23; Moses and Cobb, *Radical Equations*, 50; Newfield, *Prophetic Minority*, 49–50.

18. Layhmond Robinson, "Robert Kennedy Consults Negroes Here about North," *New York Times*, May 25, 1963. This quotation expresses a chasm between the Kennedy administration and organizers on the ground. See also Branch, *Parting the Waters*, 809–11; Bryant, *Bystander*, 402–26.

19. Sugarman, *Strangers at the Gates*, 9.

20. See, for example, description of individuals on civil rights front lines as "a fleshly reminder of the paradoxical nature of an American citizenry built around the ideology of difference" in Carol E. Henderson, *Scarring the Black Body: Race and Representation in African American Lit*erature (Columbia: University of Missouri Press, 2002), 3. George Yancy theorizes "the Black body's efforts at engaging existential claims to freedom" and how "it is torn asunder through the internalization of the white gaze," in his *Black Bodies, White Gazes: The Continuing Significance of Race* (Lanham, Md.: Rowman and Littlefield, 2008), xxiii. Leigh Raiford and Heike Raphael-Hernandez describe "the interplay between black bodies as objects and subjects; as visual specters and spectacles and visual spectators; as objects of visual culture and as visual producers in a transnational context" in their *Migrating the Black Body: The African Diaspora and Visual Culture* (Seattle: University of Washington Press, 2017), 5. These indicate the many theoretical abstractions persisting where art and literary works are primary texts.

21. Lester, "Beyond Ideology."

22. Lafayette and Johnson, *In Peace and Freedom*, 23.

23. Moses quoted in "Samuel Block, 60, Civil Rights Battler, Dies," *New York Times*, April 22, 2000.

24. The story of Shiloh: Gen. 49:10–12.

25. Lester, *Falling Pieces of the Broken Sky*, 97, 98.

26. Zinn, "Commentary," in *We Shall Overcome: Martin Luther King, Jr. and the Black Freedom Struggle*, eds. Peter J. Alpert and Ronald Hoffman (New York: Da Capo Press, 1993), 81, 79.

27. Forman, *Making of Black Revolutionaries*, 99.

28. Judith Rollins, *Between Women: Domestics and their Employers* (Philadelphia: Temple University Press, 1985), 227.

29. Suzanne Jones posits that Lester's novel "probes not the civil rights movement so much as the consequences that occurred when the Black Power movement and black nationalism overwhelmed Marshall's/King's model of passive resistance and integration." Jones, *Race Mixing: Southern Fiction since the Sixties* (Baltimore: Johns Hopkins University Press, 2004), 170. "Lester's view" of the movement is voiced through John Calvin Marshall's narration for Charles Pete Banner-Hayley in *From Du Bois to Obama: African American Intellectuals in the Public Forum* (Carbondale: Southern Illinois University Press, 2010), 89. Another critic focusing on "the depiction of interracial sexual liaisons between a white woman and a black cultural hero," Opal Moore, in her critique of Lester's 1995 novel *Othello*, asks whether Lester intended to write "anticivil rights agitprop." Opal Moore, "Othello, Othello, Where Art Thou?," *Lion and the Unicorn* 25, no. 3 (September 2001): 375–90, quotation from 377.

30. Tewkesbury, "Sex, Violence, and Suffering," 129–30, 134. He argues convincingly against Trudier Harris's "The Power of Martyrdom: The Incorporation of Martin Luther King Jr. and His Philosophy into African American Literature," in *Media, Culture and the Modern African American Freedom Struggle*, ed. Brian Ward (Gainesville: University Press of Florida, 2001), 273–91.

31. Tewkesbury, Sex, Violence, and Suffering," 136.

32. Carson, "Paradoxes of King Historiography"; Branch, *Parting the Waters*, 276, 466–68.

33. Jimmy Garrett, "Marching through Selma," *Movement* (SNCC of California), April 1965, 6. Tensions between SNCC and the SCLC and NAACP are evident across staff meetings where the need for civil rights organizations not to disagree publicly was reiterated.

See, for example, SNCC Executive Committee Minutes, November 24–29, 1965, 8–9, SNCC. The assumption that SNCC was led by King has persisted. Even veteran reporter Al Kuettner misrepresented the story of SNCC's beginnings: Kuettner, "Would You Believe? Few Remember That Dr. King Founded SNCC," *Chicago Daily Defender*, September 14, 1966. The notion that young people could not organize themselves also involves some other mistakes of fact, as when Debbie Harwell states, "Young people in the SCLC formed the Student Nonviolent Coordinating Committee (SNCC, 1960) to engage in nonviolent direct action under their own leadership, but they soon found that escalating activity in the South required better organization. To address this need, the leaders of SNCC, CORE, and the NAACP formed the Council of Federated Organizations (COFO, 1962) as an umbrella organization to oversee the expansion of voter education and registration drives in Mississippi. None of these groups, however, initiated civil rights projects reaching out to women." Debbie Z. Harwell, *Wednesdays in Mississippi: Proper Ladies Working for Radical Change, Freedom Summer 1964* (Jackson: University Press of Mississippi, 2014), 5.

34. King interviewed by John Freeman, BBC *Face to Face*, 1961, YouTube.com; Lester, *All Is Well*, 225–26.

35. It is unclear if this was the speech King delivered in Fisk Memorial Chapel on April 25, 1957. It is more likely the speech in the university gymnasium on April 20, 1960: M. L. King, *The Papers of Martin Luther King Jr.*, vol. 4, 43.

36. Lester, *Look Out, Whitey!* 106; Lester, "Martin Luther King I Remember," 16. Tewkesbury mentions the version of the essay published in Lester's *All Is Well*.

37. Monteith, "Where Do We Go From Here?," 224.

38. Monteith, "Where Do We Go From Here?," 228–29; Lester, *Search for the New Land*, 151–52.

39. Lester, "The Angry Children of Malcolm X," *Sing Out!* 16 (October/November 1966): 22–25. It was reprinted in SNCC's *Aframerican* News for You 3 (January 12, 1967), box 25, Richardson Papers.

40. Alvin Poussaint, "A Negro Psychiatrist Explores the Negro Psyche," *New York Times Magazine*, August 20, 1967, 55.

41. Lester, *Lovesong: On Becoming a Jew* (New York: Holt, 1988), 43. For an analysis of Lester's changing political views through the lens of religious conversion, see Cole, "Blue Lester," and for analysis of the wider context, see Dillard, *Guess Who's Coming to Dinner Now?* Dillard demonstrates how Lester mounted a searching critique of the conservative illusion of "color-blindness" in attacks on black radical ideas (178–80).

42. Lester, *Falling Pieces of a Broken Sky*, 125.

43. Caruth, *Unclaimed Experience*, 4.

44. Hamer, *To Praise My Bridges*, 14.

45. "Fannie Lou Hamer interviewed by Robert Wright," August 9, 1968, Oral History Collection, Civil Rights Documentation project, Moorland-Spingarn Research Center, Howard University; "Let the Circle Be Unbroken," Program Files and Sound Recordings 1.3, box 8, folder 6, Southern Regional Conference Papers. Only in 1971, for example, did she speak publicly in detail about the man who hauled her dress over her head and groped her while other men watched. The sexualized details of abuse suffered by June Johnson, Euvester Simpson, and Annell Ponder when arrested with Mrs. Hamer were equally horrific, and Guyot was stripped so nine assailants could beat him and take sharp sticks to his genitals over four hours. Federal charges were made and denied—officers stated that Guyot had been in a car accident—and some prisoners were forced to recant statements that they had been coerced or beaten in jail. Guyot, *My Soul Is Rested*, 268–70; "Law Officers Deny Negroes Were Beaten," *Jackson Daily News*, December 5, 1963. These experiences were

not unusual. In Clarksdale on February 6, 1962, a young woman was stripped naked and beaten about her legs and across her breasts in a jail cell, as Minnis recorded in *Chronology of Violence and Intimidation*, 6. Foucault explored the anger of prisoners "exposed . . . to suffering, which the law has neither ordered nor envisaged," in *Discipline and Punish: The Birth of the Prison*, translated by Alan Sheridan (New York: Vintage, 1977), 266.

46. Watters, *Down to Now*, 131; Zinn, *SNCC*, 216.

47. Kenneth B. Clark, "Behind the Harlem Riots—Two Views," the *New York Herald Tribune*, July 29, 1964, 7.

48. Caruth, *Unclaimed Experience*, 7–8, 115n5.

49. King, "Letter from Birmingham Jail," https://kinginstitute.stanford.edu/king-papers/documents/letter-birmingham-jail; House, foreword to *Negroes with Guns*, ix.

50. Joyce Ladner interview by Joseph Mosnier, September 20, 2011, Civil Rights History Project, Library of Congress, 61, https://www.loc.gov/item/afc2010039_crhp0054.

51. Thelwell, *Duties, Pleasures, and Conflicts*, 191; Moses and Cobb, *Radical Equations*, 83.

52. Hogan in Crosby, *Civil Rights History from the Ground Up*, 186.

53. Mary King, *Freedom Song*, 532, 530–31.

54. Interview with Ekwueme Michael Thelwell by Emilye Crosby, August 23, 2013, Civil Rights History project, Library of Congress, https://www.loc.gov/item/afc2010039_crhp0104.

55. House, foreword to *Negroes with Guns*, ix.

56. Lester, *Falling Pieces of the Broken Sky*, 78.

57. Lester, *Falling Pieces of the Broken Sky*, 79.

58. Hogan, *Many Minds, One Heart*, 167.

59. R. H. King, "Politics and Fictional Representation," 163; John Berger and Jean Mohr, *Another Way of Telling* (1982; repr., New York: Vintage, 1995), 105.

Epilogue

1. Payne, *I've Got the Light of Freedom*, 420; McDew, "Participatory Democracy," 69.

2. Watters and Cleghorn, *Climbing Jacob's Ladder*, 288.

3. Carson, *In Struggle*, 5; endorsement on the cover of Forman, *Making of Black Revolutionaries*.

4. Forman, *Making of Black Revolutionaries*, 102. On race and rights as his primary subject, see Forman, letter to Kenneth McCormick, November 3, 1958, box 144, bolder 8, 1–2, JF. Forman's interviews with Frantz Fanon's mother in 1969 (in French) are in box 131, folder 1, JF.

5. Jeffries, "Remaking History," 271. This extends Jeffries's research in *Bloody Lowndes* and "SNCC, Black Power, and Independent Political Party Organizing in Alabama, 1964–1966." See also Theoharis and Woodard, *Groundwork*. Particularized studies include Tyson, *Radio Free Dixie*, and Wendt, *Spirit and the Shotgun*.

6. Chambers, *Migrancy, Culture, Identity*, 121.

7. Nasaw, introduction to "AHR Roundtable: Historians and Biography," *American Historical Review* 114, no. 3 (June 2009): 575.

8. Novick, *That Noble Dream*, 386.

9. Monteith, "I Second That Emotion"; Felski, *Limits of Critique*, 188, 150.

10. "Stokely Carmichael Visits and Speaks at St. Louis Rally," *St. Louis Argus*, September 6, 1968; "Liberators, SNCC Form an Alliance," *St. Louis Post Dispatch*, November 9, 1968; "SNCC Forms Ties to Black Liberators," *New York Times*, November 28, 1968. See

also Sellers, *River of No Return*, 240–52; Sherrod, *Courage to Hope*, and Forman's diaries of 1967–69, saved by Elizabeth Sutherland and Cheryl Greene, which address this feeling.

11. Reagon, "Coalition Politics," 356–68. The essay is a transcript of a workshop she led in 1981. Becky Johnson cites Reagon's "coalition politics" as a theoretical guidepost for multiracial feminism in *No Permanent Waves*, 39–60.

12. Reuben, "Politics of Literature," 325; R. H. King, "Politics and Fictional Representation," 163.

13. Olson, *Freedom's Daughters*, 377.

14. K. Collins, *Whatever Happened to Interracial Love?*, 41–42; Kathleen Conwell [Collins], field report, August 1962, and letter to sister Frannie, August 3, 1962, in K. Collins, *Notes from a Black Woman's Diary*, 59–60.

Peggy Dammond's reports are equally detailed and more analytical. A July 1962 report for Forman reads: "It is important we feel, as you all well know, that communities take on responsibilities and concern for the adverse as well as the providence .. of action taken. This must be handled carefully so that no hostilities are created, but rather a deeper understanding of what we are about and what can be done as a result of such joint and unified action." Series 4, reel 215, p. 2, SNCC.

15. Avery is noted in Cobb, *This Nonviolent Stuff'll Get you Killed*, 161, and Fleming, *Soon We Will Not Cry*, 125–26, for example.

16. "Making a Difference: Natchez Civil Rights Workers," November 5, 2015, WLBT (Jackson, Miss.), https://www.wlbt.com/story/30449895/making-a-difference-natchez-civil-rights-workers.

17. Nicholas, *Freshwater Road*, 96.

18. Sonia Sanchez, "Untitled, a poem by Sonia Sanchez for Gloria House, July 2017," in N. Christian, *Life Speaks*, 87.

19. The panel was "Art and Democracy in the King Years and Beyond: Scholarly Assessments," in Let Freedom Ring: Art and Democracy in the King Years, 1954–1968, Lannan Center for Poetics and Social Practice, Georgetown University, Washington, D.C., April 2008, a symposium organized by Maurice Jackson and Angelyn Mitchell.

20. SNCC Fiftieth Anniversary "Meet the Author" program, http://www.sncc50thanniversary.org/authors.html; *SNCC and the Black Arts Movement: "We Had to Change the Conversation,"* SNCC Legacy Video, 25 (San Francisco: California Newsreel, 2011).

21. Casey Hayden, "Movement," 247.

22. Thelwell in Greenberg, *Circle of Trust*, 204.

23. Kates quoted in Benjamin Hedin, "Do The Right Thing," *Oxford American*, Fall 2014, https://www.oxfordamerican.org/magazine/item/553-do-the-right-thing.

24. Angeline Butler's "Voices of a Sit-In" had Septima Clark as featured speaker after each performance. Endesha Mae Holland transformed her play into a memoir that includes her time in SNCC, *From the Mississippi Delta*. The draft of the play is listed as being in her papers at the University of Minnesota but was not present among them. My thanks to archivist Cecily Marcus for pursuing this source for me; it is yet to be found.

25. Carson, *In Struggle*, 76, 73; Phillip Sparer, "Harvard Guy Shares His Jim Crow Schooling," *Regis Highlander* (Denver), February 21, 2006; "3-Judge Federal Panel Set to Hear Perdew's Suit Charging 'Conspiracy,'" *Harvard Crimson*, October 17, 1963. Perdew was held with Don Harris, Ralph Allen, and Zev Aelony. Perdew, *Education of a Harvard Guy*.

26. Pratt, "Arts of the Contact Zone," 586.

27. "Junebug Productions," in *Mississippi American Festival Project* (Whitesburg, Ky.: Appalshop, 1991), 6. O'Neal founded the Mississippi American Festival Project in 1982.

28. Lorde, "Poetry Is Not a Luxury," in *Sister Outsider: Essays and Speeches* (New York: Crossing Press, 1984), 37.
29. Umoja, "1964," 201.
30. Lorde, "Poetry Is Not a Luxury."
31. G. Fine, "Storied Group," 240; Polletta, "Plotting Protest," 48.
32. Chude Pam Allen, "To Be Twenty Again," http://www.crmvet.org/poetry/pchude.htm.
33. Lester, "The Duty of a Revolutionary Is . . . ," *Movement*, December 1967.
34. Ellen Willis, "Arts and Leisure," *New York Times*, August 20, 2000.
35. Mary King, *Freedom Song*, 532.
36. Gertrude Wilson, "A New Army," *New York Amsterdam News*, December 28, 1963. Justine Smadbeck (Tyrell Priestley) reported from the civil rights South and was a columnist under the name of "Gertrude Wilson." She sent Donaldson her column, saying that "500 words is not much space to tell a story" but thanking him for "how much you are doing for all of us, which we cannot do ourselves." Justine Smadbeck to Ivanhoe Donaldson, December 28, 1963, box 1, DD.
37. In 2016, Moses reiterated one of the reasons behind his Algebra Project: "We still run a sharecropper education, aimed at preparing people of color for lifetimes of menial jobs." Bob Moses in discussion with Janet Moses and Topper Carew in Daniel L. Chandler, "Pick an Issue and Dive In! Veterans of Civil Rights Movement Urge Students to Join Ongoing Battle against Injustice," *MIT News*, December 15, 2016, http://news.mit.edu/2016/mlk-luncheon-civil-rights-1215.
38. Tim Hall, "A Plea" (for John Love, project director, Selma SNCC, 1964), in Gitlin, *Campfires of the Resistance*, 47.
39. Cobb, *In the Furrows of the World*, 32–33.
40. Cobb, *In The Furrows of the World*, 21.
41. Wade Gayles, *Anointed to Fly*, 129–31.
42. Wade Gayles, *Anointed to Fly*, 79.
43. Baldwin, introduction to Thelwell, *Duties, Pleasures, and Conflicts*, xviii–xix.
44. Stembridge, *I Play Flute* (1966), 89.
45. Forman, *Making of Black Revolutionaries*, 223; Nicholas, epigraph to Dent, Schechner, and Moses, *Free Southern Theater*, n.p.; Lester, *And All Our Wounds Forgiven*, 190.
46. Bond, "Review of Clayborne Carson, *In Struggle*," *Journal of Higher Education* 54, no. 4 (July–August, 1983): 471.
47. Mary King quoted in Carpenter, "From Heroism to Madness"; Cannon, "Literature of Protest," 7. A compilation of Bond's own writings is forthcoming in *Race Man: Selected Works, 1960–2015*, edited by Michael G. Long (San Francisco: City Lights Books, 2020).

Selected Bibliography

Archival Sources (and Abbreviations)

Amistad Research Center, Tulane University, New Orleans

Free Southern Theater Papers (FST)
John O'Neal Papers (JO'N)
Tom Dent Papers

David M. Rubenstein Library, Duke University Libraries, North Carolina

SNCC Critical and Oral Histories, Center for Documentary Studies, Duke (CDSD)
Constance Curry Papers
Faith Holsaert Papers
Judy Richardson Papers
Cleveland Sellers Papers
Joseph A. Sinsheimer Papers (JAS)

Georgia State University Library, Special Collections, Atlanta

Southern Conference Educational Fund Papers
Southern Regional Conference Papers
Pat Watters Papers

Hargrett Rare Book and Manuscript Library, University of Georgia Libraries, Athens

Lillian Smith Papers

J. D. Williams Library, University of Mississippi, Archives and Special Collections, Oxford

Ed King Papers (EK)
Fannie Lou Hamer Collection
Inventory of Race Relations Collection

Library of Congress, Washington, D.C.

James Forman Papers (JF)
SNCC Papers (SNCC)
NAACP Papers

Manuscript, Archives, and Rare Books Library, Emory University, Atlanta

Constance Curry Papers (CC2)
Robert Churchwell Papers
Doris Derby Papers (DD)
Elizabeth Sutherland-Martínez Papers (ESM)
Sarah E. Wright Papers

Robert W. Woodruff Library, Archives Research Center, Atlanta University Center, Atlanta
Atlanta Student Movement Collection
Hoyt W. Fuller Papers

Schlesinger Library, Radcliffe Institute, Harvard University
Elaine DeLott Baker Papers

Schomburg Center for Research in Black Culture, New York Public Library
Ella Baker Papers

Valdosta State University Archives, Georgia
Margaret Long Papers

Washington University Libraries, Special Collections, St. Louis
Eyes on the Prize: America's Civil Rights Years (1954-1965), Henry Hampton Collection

Wisconsin Historical Society, Madison
Sally Belfrage Papers
Lucile Montgomery Papers
Pamela P. Allen Papers
Howard Zinn Papers

Selected Works by SNCC Organizers and Volunteers

Adickes, Sandra. *Legends of Good Women*. Long Lake, Minn.: Castalgia Bookmakers, 1992.
Allen, Pamela. *Free Space: A Perspective on the Small Group in Women's Liberation*. New York: Times Change Press, 1970.
Anderson, S. E. "Revolutionary Black Nationalism Is Pan-Africanism." *Black Scholar* 2, no. 7 (1971): 16-22.
Beal, Frances. "Double Jeopardy: To Be Black and Female." In *Sisterhood Is Powerful: An Anthology of Writings from the Women's Liberation Movement*, edited by Robin Morgan, 382-96. New York: Vintage, 1970.
———. "Slave of a Slave No More: Black Women in Struggle." *Black Scholar* 6, no. 6 (March 1975): 2-10.
Beal, Frances, and Loretta J. Ross. "Excerpts from the Voices of Feminism Oral History Project: Interview with Frances Beal." *Meridians: Feminism, Race, Transnationalism* 8, no. 2 (2008): 126-65.
Belfrage, Sally. *Freedom Summer*. 1965; Charlottesville: University Press of Virginia, 1999.
Bellamy, Fay. "Being Me Is a Gas." *Southern Exposure* 3, no. 1 (1975): 38-41.
Bond, Julian. "Culture in the Cause of Negro Freedom." *Freedomways* 2, no. 2 (1962): 117-18.
———. Foreword to *Making of Black Revolutionaries*, by James Forman, xi-xiii. Seattle: University of Washington Press, 1997.
———. Foreword to *This Little Light of Ours: Activist Photography of the Civil Rights Movement*, edited by Leslie G. Kelen, 13-17. Jackson: University Press of Mississippi / Center for Documentary Arts, 2012.
———. Foreword to *The Wrong Side of Murder Creek: A White Southerner in the Freedom Movement*, by Bob Zellner with Constance Curry, 9-14. Montgomery, Ala.: NewSouth Books, 2008.

———. "The Media and the Movement: Looking Back from the Southern Front." In *Media, Culture and the Modern African Freedom Struggle*, edited by Brian Ward, 16–40. Gainesville: University Press of Florida, 2001.
———. "The Movement We Helped to Make." In *Long Time Gone: Sixties America Then and Now*, edited by Alexander Bloom, 11–22. New York: Oxford University Press, 2001.
———. "Nonviolence: An Interpretation." *Freedomways* 3, no. 2 (1963): 159–62.
———. "SNCC: What We Did." *Monthly Review* 52, no. 5 (2000), https://monthlyreview.org/2000/10/01/sncc-what-we-did.
———. "The Southern Youth Movement." *Freedomways* 2, no. 3 (Summer 1962): 308–10.
———. *A Time to Speak, a Time to Act: The Movement in Politics*. New York: Simon and Schuster, 1972.
Bond, Julian, and Andrew Lewis, eds. *Gonna Sit at the Welcome Table*. Mason, Ohio: Thomson Learning, 2002.
Brown, H. Rap. *Die, Nigger, Die*. London: Allison and Busby, 1970. First published 1969.
Browning, Joan C. "Invisible Revolutionaries: White Women in Civil Rights Historiography." *Journal of Women's History* 8, no. 3 (Fall 1996): 186–204.
Cannon, Terry. "The Literature of Protest: Tell It Like It Is." *Movement* (SNCC), July 1965, 7.
Carmichael, Stokely. "Black Power." In *To Free a Generation: The Dialectics of Liberation*, edited by David Cooper, 150–74. New York: Collier Books, 1969. First published 1968.
———. "Pan-Africanism—Land and Power." *Black Scholar* 1, no. 1 (1969): 36–43.
———. *Stokely Speaks: Black Power Back to Pan-Africanism*. New York: Random House, 1971.
———. "We Are Going to Use the Term 'Black Power' and We Are Going to Define It Because Black Power Speaks to Us" (speech delivered June 28, 1966). In *Black Nationalism in America*, edited by John H. Bracey Jr., August Meier, and Elliott Rudwick, 470–76. Indianapolis: Bobbs-Merrill, 1970.
———. "Who Is Qualified?" In Hayden, *Thoughts of the Young Radicals*, 26–34.
Carmichael, Stokely, with Ekwueme Michael Thelwell. *Ready for the Revolution: The Life and Struggles of Stokely Carmichael*. New York: Scribner, 2003.
Carson, Clayborne, ed. *The Student Voice, 1960–1965: Periodical of the SNCC*. Westport, Conn.: Mecker, 1990.
Christian, Nichole, ed. *A Life Speaks: Gloria House: 2019 Kresge Eminent Artist*. Troy, Mich.: Kresge Foundation, 2019.
Cieciorka, Bobbi, and Frank Cieciorka. *Negroes in American History: A Freedom Primer*. Atlanta: Student Voice, 1965.
Cobb, Charles. "African Notebook: Views on Returning Home." *Black World*, May 1972, 22–37.
———. "Empowering Communities: The Gift of the Civil Rights Movement." In *United We Serve: National Service and the Future of Citizenship*, edited by E. J. Dionne, Kayla Meltzer Drogosz, and Robert E. Litan, 146–54. Washington, D.C.: Brookings Institution Press, 2003.
———. *Everywhere Is Yours*. Chicago: Third World Press, 1971.
———. *In the Furrows of the World*. Tougaloo, Miss.: Flute Publications, 1967.
———. *On the Road to Freedom: A Guided Tour of the Civil Rights Trail*. Chapel Hill, N.C.: Algonquin Books, 2008.
———. "Over My Head I See Freedom in the Air: A Foreword." In *Don't Start Me to Talking . . . Plays of Struggle and Liberation: The Selected Plays of John O'Neal*, edited by Theresa Ripley Holden, xi–xv. New York: Theatre Communication Group, 2016.
———. *This Nonviolent Stuff'll Get You Killed: How Guns Made the Civil Rights Movement Possible*. 2014; Durham, N.C.: Duke University Press, 2016.

Collins, Kathleen. *Notes from a Black Woman's Diary: Selected Works of Kathleen Collins.* Edited by Nina Lorez Collins. New York: HarperCollins, 2019.

———. *Whatever Happened to Interracial Love?* London: Granta, 2017. First published 2016.

Cowan, Paul. *The Making of an Un-American: A Dialogue with Experience.* New York: Delta, 1970.

Curry, Constance, Joan C. Browning, Dorothy Dawson Burlage, Penny Patch, Theresa Del Pozzo, Sue Thrasher, Elaine DeLott Baker, Emmie Schrader Adams, Casey Hayden. *Deep in Our Hearts: Nine White Women in the Freedom Movement.* Athens: University of Georgia Press, 2000.

De Lissovoy, Peter. *Angels of Zimbabwe.* Lancaster, N.H.: YouArePerfect Press, 2012.

———. "The Failure in Albany Georgia." *Harvard Crimson,* October 22, 1963.

———. "Failure in Albany II: The White Minority." *Harvard Crimson,* November 12, 1963.

———. *Feelgood: A Trip in Time and Out.* New York: Houghton Mifflin, 1971. First published 1970.

———. "Gambler's Choice in Georgia: C. B. King for Congress, June 1964." *Nation,* June 22, 1964, 618–21.

———, ed. *The Great Pool Jump and Other Stories from the Civil Rights Movement in Southwest Georgia.* Lancaster, N.H.: YouArePerfectPress, 2010.

———. "Moments in a Southern Town: 'This Little Light...'" *Nation,* December 21, 1964, 486–90.

Dent, Tom. "Portrait of Three Heroes." *Freedomways* 5 (Spring 1965): 250–62.

———. *Southern Journey: A Return to the Civil Rights Movement.* New York: William Morrow, 1997.

Dent, Tom, Richard Schechner, and Gilbert Moses, eds. *The Free Southern Theater by the Free Southern Theater.* Indianapolis: Bobbs-Merrill, 1969.

Donaldson, Ivanhoe. "Notes from Southern Diaries: Ivanhoe Donaldson, SNCC Field Worker." *Freedomways* 4, no. 1 (Winter 1964): 139–42.

Else, Jon. *True South.* New York: Viking, 2017.

Forman, James. "Control, Conflict and Change." In *Black Manifesto: Religion, Racism and Reparations,* edited by Robert S. Lecky and H. Elliott Wright, 34–51. New York: Sheed and Ward, 1969.

———. "'Corrupt Black Preachers' and 'God Is Dead': A Question of Power." In *By These Hands: A Documentary History of African American Humanism* edited by Anthony B. Pinn, 261–85. New York: New York University Press, 2001.

———. *High Tide of Black Resistance and Other Political and Literary Writings.* Seattle: Open Hand Publishing, 1994.

———. *Liberation Viendra d'une Chose Noir.* Paris: Masterro, 1968.

———. *Liberation Will Come from a Black Thing.* Chicago: SDS, 1968.

———. *The Making of Black Revolutionaries.* Seattle: University of Washington Press, 1997. First published 1972.

———. *1967, High Tide of Black Resistance.* SNCC International Affairs Commission, 1967.

———. *The Political Thought of James Forman.* Detroit: Black Star Press, 1970.

———. *Sammy Younge Jr.: The First College Student to Die in the Black Liberation Movement.* Washington, D.C.: Open Hand Publishing, 1986. First published 1968.

———. *Self-Determination: An Examination of the Question and Its Application to the African-American People.* Washington, D.C.: Open Hand Publishing, 1984.

———. "Some Random Notes from the Leflore County Jail." In *Black Protest,* edited by Joanne Grant, 329–35. New York: Fawcett, 1968.

Freeman, Roland. *A Tribute to Worth Long: Still on the Case: A Pioneer's Continuing*

Commitment. Washington, D.C.: Smithsonian Center for Folklife and Cultural Heritage and the Group for Cultural Documentation, 2006.

Garrett, Jimmy. *We Own the Night: A Play of Blackness*. In Baraka and Neal, *Black Fire*, 527-40.

Grant, Joanne. *Black Protest: History, Documents, and Analysis*. New York: Fawcett, 1968.

———. *Ella Baker: Freedom Bound*. New York: John Wiley and Sons, 1998.

———. "Mississippi and 'The Establishment.'" *Freedomways* 5 (1965): 294-300.

———. "Mississippi Politics: A Day in the Life of Ella J. Baker." In Cade, *Black Woman*, 65-73.

———. "The Negro Movement–New Heights." *Freedomways* 3, no. 2 (1963): 163-68.

———. "The Time Is Always Now." *Freedomways* 2, no. 2 (1962): 150-54.

———. "Way of Life in Mississippi." *National Guardian*, February 13, 1964.

Guyot, Lawrence. "Foreword: Reflections on the Local Movement." In *Thunder of Freedom: Black Leadership and the Transformation of 1960s Mississippi*, edited by Sue [Lorenzi] Sojourner with Cheryl Reitan, xv-xvi. Lexington: University Press of Kentucky, 2013.

Guyot, Lawrence, and Mike Thelwell. "The Politics of Survival and Necessity in Mississippi." *Freedomways* 6, no. 2 (1966): 120-32.

Hall, Richard. *Long George Alley*. New York: Washington Square Press, 2000. First published 1972.

Hamer, Fannie Lou. *To Praise My Bridges: An Autobiography of Mrs. Fannie Lou Hamer*. Recorded and edited by Julius Lester and Maria Varela of SNCC. Jackson, Miss.: KIPCO, 1967.

Hayden, Casey. "The Movement." In *The Sixties*, edited by Peter Stine, 244-48. Detroit: Wayne State University Press, 1995.

Hayden, Casey, et al. "Old Hands, Young Blood." *Southern Exposure* 16, no. 2 (Summer 1988): 47-58.

Hayden, Tom. *Revolution in Mississippi: Special Report*. Chicago: SDS, 1962.

———. *Thoughts of the Young Radicals, and Four Critical Comments on Their Views of America: A Collection of Essays from "The New Republic."* New York: Pitman, 1968. First published 1966.

Henry, Aaron, with Constance Curry. *Aaron Henry: The Fire Ever Burning*. Jackson: University Press of Mississippi, 2000.

Holland, Endesha Mae. *From the Mississippi Delta: A Memoir*. Chicago: Lawrence Hill, 1997.

Holsaert, Faith S., Martha Prescod, Norman Noonan, Judy Richardson, Betty Garman Robinson, Jean Smith Young, and Dorothy M. Zellner. *Hands on the Freedom Plow: Personal Accounts by Women in SNCC*. Urbana: University of Illinois Press, 2010.

Holt, Len. *An Act of Conscience*. Boston: Beacon, 1965.

———. *The Summer That Didn't End: The Story of the Mississippi Civil Rights Project of 1964*. New York: Da Capo Press, 1992. First published 1965.

Holt, Len, and Bill Mahoney. "Make Harlem Black–Therefore Beautiful." *Liberator*, September 1964, 10-11.

House, Gloria (Aneb Kgositsile). *Blood River: Poems 1964-1983*. Detroit, Mich.: Broadside Press, 1983.

———. Foreword to *Negroes with Guns*, by Robert F. Williams, vii-xiv. Detroit: Wayne State University Press, 1998.

———. "The Road to Internationalism: A SNCC Movement Worker Reflects." *Against the Current*, January-February 2013, 14-17.

Jackson, Mae. *Can I Poet with You*. Detroit: Broadside, 1969.

Jones, Junebug Jabbo [John O'Neal]. "America's Blackest Child." *Southern Exposure*, Fall/Winter 1997, 63–65.
———. "The Brass Balls of Handsome Bailey." *Southern Exposure*, Fall 1996, 44–46.
———. "Elmer Fudge's Fingers." *Southern Exposure*, Winter 1994, 56–57.
———. "Mama Dolly's Tale." *Southern Exposure*, Fall 1993, 57–58.
———. "Preacher in the Cornfield." *Southern Exposure*, Spring 1994, 52–53.
———. "Silence Is Golden." *Southern Exposure*, Spring/Summer 1997, 46–47.
———. "So That's Where Junebug Came From." *Southern Exposure*, Fall/Winter 1995, 54–55.
———. See also O'Neal, John.
Kahn, Si. *Creative Community Organizing: A Guide for Rabble-Rousers, Activists, and Quiet Lovers of Justice*. San Francisco: Berrett-Koehler, 2010.
———. *Organizing: A Guide for Grassroots Leaders*. Revised ed. Silver Spring, Md.: National Association of Social Workers Press, 1991.
Kgositsile, Aneb. See House, Gloria (Aneb Kgositsile).
King, Mary. *Freedom Song: A Personal Story of the 1960s Civil Rights Movement*. New York: William Morrow, 1987.
Ladner, Joyce. *The Death of White Sociology*. Baltimore: Black Classic Press, 1998. First published 1973.
———. *Tomorrow's Tomorrow: The Black Woman*. New York: Doubleday, 1972. First published 1971.
———. "What 'Black Power' Means to Negroes in Mississippi." *Trans-action* 5 (November 1967): 7–15.
Lafayette, Bernard. "The Freedom Rider." In *Generation on Fire: Voices of Protest from the 1960s*, edited by Jeff Kisseloff, 6–23. Lexington: University of Kentucky Press, 2007.
Lafayette, Bernard, and Kathryn Lee Johnson. *In Peace and Freedom: My Journey in Selma*. Lexington: University Press of Kentucky, 2013.
Lauter, Paul. "Race and Gender in the Shaping of the American Literary Canon." *Feminist Studies* 9 (1983): 435–63.
Lester, Julius. *All Is Well: An Autobiography*. New York: William Morrow, 1976.
———. *And All Our Wounds Forgiven*. New York: Harcourt, Brace, 1994.
———. "Beyond Ideology." *Tikkun* 3, no. 1 (1988): 53–56.
———. *Black Folktales*. New York: Grove Press, 1969.
———. "The Black Writer and the New Censorship." *Evergreen Review*, April 1970, 19–21, 73–75.
———. *Falling Pieces of the Broken Sky*. New York: Little, Brown, 1990.
———. "Four Faces from SNCC." *Massachusetts Review* 44, nos. 1–2 (Spring–Summer 2003): 88–91.
———. *Look Out, Whitey! Black Power's Gon' Get Your Mama!* New York: Dial, 1968.
———. "The Martin Luther King I Remember." *Evergreen Review*, January 1970, 16–21, 70.
———. *Revolutionary Notes*. New York: Grove, 1969.
———. *Search for the New Land: History as Subjective Experience*. London: Allison and Busby, 1971. First published 1969.
———. "To Recapture the Dream." *Liberation*, August–September 1969, 26–30.
———. "You Can't Go Home Again." *Dissent*, Winter 1985, 21–25.
Lewis, John, with Michael D'Orso. *Walking with the Wind: A Memoir of the Movement*. New York: Simon and Schuster, 1998.
Llorens, David. "Ameer (LeRoi Jones) Baraka." *Ebony*, August 1969: 73–78, 80–83.
———. "Julian Bond: 'Down by the Lake, Shootin' Fish.'" *Ebony*, May 1969, 58–62, 64, 66–68, 70.

———. "Writers Converge at Fisk University." *Negro Digest*, June 1966, 54–68.
Long, Worth. *We'll Never Turn Back: A Photographic Exhibit Created by Worth Long*. Washington, D.C.: Smithsonian, 1980.
Louis, Debbie. *We Are Not Saved*. New York: Doubleday, 1970.
Mahoney, William. *Black Jacob*. New York: Macmillan, 1969.
———. "Risking Life and Liberty: In Pursuit of Freedom." *Liberation*, September 1961, 7–11.
———. "Travels in the South: A Cold Night in Alabama." In Baraka and Neal, *Black Fire*, 144–48. Originally published in the *Village Voice*, March 10, 1966.
McDew, Charles. "Participatory Democracy Is Putting Your Body on the Line." In *Inspiring Participatory Democracy: Student Movements from Port Huron to Today*, edited by Tom Hayden, 67–71. New York: Routledge, 2012.
———. "Spiritual and Moral Aspects of the Student Nonviolent Struggle in the South." In *The New Student Left*, edited by Mitchell Cohen and Dennis Hale, 51–57. Boston: Beacon, 1967.
Miller, Dorothy. *Danville, Virginia*. Atlanta: Student Nonviolent Coordinating Committee, 1963.
Minnis, Jack. *The Care and Feeding of the Power Structures Revisited*. Louisville: Southern Conference Educational Fund, 1967. https://www.crmvet.org/docs/67_scef_minnis_cfpsr-r.pdf.
———. *A Chronology of Violence in Mississippi since 1961*. Atlanta: SNCC Publications, 1964.
Morton, Eric. "Tremor in the Iceberg." *Freedomways* 5 (1965): 318–23.
Moses, Bob. "Letter from Magnolia Jail." *Liberator*, November 12, 1961, 5; *Harvard Crimson*, January 22, 1962.
———. "Mississippi: 1961–1962." *Liberation*, January 1970, 6–17.
Moses, Bob, and Charles Cobb. *Radical Equations: Civil Rights from Mississippi to the Algebra Project*. Boston: Beacon Press, 2001.
Nash, Diane. "Inside the Sit-Ins and Freedom Rides: Testimony of a Southern Student." In *The New Negro*, edited by Matthew A. Ahmann, 43–62. Notre Dame, Ind.: Fides, 1961.
Nicholas, Denise. *Freshwater Road*. Chicago: Agate, 2005.
O'Neal, John. "As a Weapon Is to Warfare." *Callaloo*, no. 11/13 (1981): 65–70.
———. *Don't Start Me to Talking . . . Plays of Struggle and Liberation: The Selected Plays of John O'Neal*. Edited by Theresa Ripley Holden. New York: Theatre Communication Group, 2016.
———. "Freedom Takes the Stage." *American Dialog* 1, no. 2 (October–November 1964): 27–29.
———. "A Freedom Theater in the South." *American Dialog* 1, no. 1 (July–August 1964): 27–29.
———. "The Free Southern Theater: Living in the Danger Zone." *Black Scholar* 10, no. 10 (July–August 1979): 11–13.
———. "'Motion in the Ocean': Some Political Dimensions of the Free Southern Theatre." *Drama Review* 12, no. 4 (Summer 1968): 70–77.
———. "A Road through the Wilderness" (1998). In *A Sourcebook on African-American Performance: Plays, People, Movements*, edited by Annemarie Bean, 97–101. New York: Taylor and Francis, 1999.
———. "Yours in Struggle." *Southern Exposure* 27, no. 1 (Spring 1999): 31–32.
———. *See also* Jones, Junebug Jabbo [John O'Neal].
O'Neal, John, Cheryl Yuen, and Theresa Holden. "Junebug Productions Color Line Project." *Animating Democracy*, 2003, 1–16.

Patton, Gwendolyn. "Black People and the Victorian Ethos." In Cade, *Black Woman*, 143–48.
———. "Black People and War." *Liberator*, February 1967, 11.
Payne, Bruce. "SNCC: An Overview Two Years Later." In *The New Student Left*, edited by Mitchell Cohen and Dennis Hale, 86–103. Boston: Beacon Press, 1967.
Perdew, John. "Difficult to Organize the Poorest and the Wealthiest among Negroes." *I. F. Stone's Bi-Weekly*, December 9, 1963, 3, 6.
———. *Education of a Harvard Guy: Footsoldier in the Civil Rights Movement*. Jonesboro, Ark.: GrantHouse Publishers, 2010.
Poussaint, Alvin, and Joyce Ladner. "'Black Power': A Failure for Racial Integration—Within the Civil Rights Movement." *Archives of General Psychiatry* 18, no. 4 (1968): 385–91.
Reagon, Bernice Johnson. "Coalition Politics: Turning the Century." In *Home Girls: A Black Feminist Anthology*, edited by Barbara Smith, 356–68. New York: Kitchen Table Women of Color Press, 1983.
———. Introduction to *We'll Never Turn Back: A Photographic Exhibition*, by Worth Long, 8–11. Washington, D.C.: Smithsonian Performing Arts, 1980.
Reagon, Bernice Johnson, and Sweet Honey in the Rock. *We Who Believe in Freedom: Sweet Honey in the Rock . . . Still on the Journey*. New York: Anchor, 1993.
Richards, Dona. "With Our Minds Set on Freedom." *Freedomways* 5, no. 2 (1965): 324–42.
Richardson, Judy. "Womanpower and SNCC." *Massachusetts Review* 52, no. 2 (2011): 179–88.
Samstein, Mendy. "The Murder of a Community." *Student Voice*, September 23, 1964, 2–3.
Savio, Mario. "An End to History." *Humanity*, December 1964, 18–24.
Sellers, Cleveland, with Robert Terrell. *The River of No Return: The Autobiography of a Black Militant and the Life and Death of SNCC*. Jackson: University Press of Mississippi, 1990. First published 1973.
Sherrod, Shirley, with Catherine Whitney. *The Courage to Hope: How I Stood Up to the Politics of Fear*. New York: Atria, 2012.
Simmons, Gwendolyn Zoharah. "Martin Luther King Jr. Revisited: A Black Power Feminist Pays Homage to the King." *Journal of Feminist Studies in Religion* 24, no. 2 (Fall 2008): 189–213.
Smith, Jean Wheeler. "Frankie Mae." In *Black-Eyed Susans/Midnight Birds*, edited by Mary Helen Washington, 21–34. New York: Doubleday, 1990.
———. "Frankie Mae." *Negro Digest*, June 1968, 42–48, 84–89.
———. "How to Help the Ones at the Bottom." In Hayden, *Thoughts of the Young Radicals*, 57–62.
———. "I Learned to Feel Black." In *The Black Power Revolt: A Collection of Essays*, edited by Floyd B. Barbour, 209–17. New York: Collier Books, 1968.
———. "I Learned to Feel Black." *Redbook*, August 1967, 15–18.
———. "Let Us All Be Black Together." *Negro Digest*, January 1964, 19–21.
———. "The Machine: A Short Story." *Negro Digest*, November 1967, 60–74.
———. "O. C.'s Heart." *Negro Digest*, April 1970, 56–76.
———. "That She Would Dance No More." *Negro Digest*, January 1967, 59–68.
Smith, Jean Wheeler. *See also* Wheeler, Jean.
SNCC and Lorraine Hansberry. *The Movement: Documentary of a Struggle for Equality*. New York: Simon and Schuster, 1964.
Stembridge, Jane. *I Play Flute*. Tougaloo, Miss.: Flute Publications, 1966.
———. *I Play Flute and Other Poems*. New York: Seabury Press, 1968.
Stoller, Nancy (Shaw). "Lessons from SNCC–Arkansas 1965." In Wallace and Kirk, *Arsnick*, 132–38.

Student Nonviolent Coordinating Committee Papers, 1959–1972. Sanford, N.C.: Microfilming Corporation of America, 1982.
Sugarman, Tracy. *Drawing Conclusions: An Artist Discovers His America*. Syracuse, N.Y.: Syracuse University Press, 2008.
———. *Strangers at the Gates: A Summer in Mississippi*. New York: Hill and Wang, 1967. First published 1966.
———. *We Had Sneakers, They Had Guns: The Kids Who Fought for Civil Rights in Mississippi*. Syracuse, N.Y.: Syracuse University Press, 2009.
Sutherland, Elizabeth. "The Cat and Mouse Game." *Nation*, September 14, 1964, 105–8.
———. *Letters from Mississippi*. Brookline, Mass.: Zephyr Press, 2007. First published 1966.
———. "Mississippi: Summer of Disconnect." *Nation*, October 11, 1965, 212–15.
———. "SNCC Takes Stock: Mandate from History." *Nation*, January 6, 1964, 30–33.
Thelwell, Michael. "*Another Country*: Baldwin's New York Novel." In *The Black American Writer*, vol. 1, *Fiction*, edited by C. W. E. Bigsby, 47–53. Deland, Fla.: Everett/Edwards.
———. "The August 28th March on Washington: The Castrated Giant." *Presence Africaine* 21, no. 49 (1964): 145–62.
———. "Back with the Wind: Mr. Styron and the Reverend Turner." In *William Styron's Nat Turner: Ten Black Writers Respond*, edited by John Henrik Clarke, 79–91. Boston: Beacon Press, 1968.
———. "Black Studies: A Political Perspective." *Massachusetts Review* 10 (Autumn 1969): 701–12.
———. "Community of Victims." In *The Stone Soldier: Prize College Stories 1964*, edited by Whit and Hallie Burnett, 205–16. New York: Fleet, 1964.
———. "Direct Action." In *Prize College Stories 1963: The Story Magazine Contest*, edited by Hallie and Whit Burnett, 213–24. New York: Random House, 1963.
———. *Duties, Pleasures, and Conflicts: Essays in Struggle*. Amherst: University of Massachusetts Press, 1987.
———. "Fish Are Jumping an' the Cotton Is High: Notes from the Mississippi Delta." In *Black and White in American Culture*, edited by Jules Chametzky and Sidney Kaplan, 37–50. New York: Viking, 1971.
———. "*The Harder They Come*: From Film to Novel." *Grand Street* 10, no. 1 (1991): 134–65.
———. "Mr. Styron and the Reverend Turner." *Massachusetts Review* 9 (Winter 1968): 7–29.
———. "The Organizer." In *Duties, Pleasures, and Conflicts: Essays in Struggle*, 3–27. Amherst: University of Massachusetts Press, 1987.
———. "The Professor and the Activists." *Massachusetts Review* 40, no. 4 (1999–2000): 617–38.
———. "Publishing the Black Experience." *Ramparts*, October 1969, 60, 62–63.
———. "What Is to Be Done? Review of Harold Cruse, *The Crisis of the Negro Intellectual*." *Partisan Review* 35, no. 4 (Fall 1968): 619–23.
Thelwell, Michael, and Nathan Hare. "From San Francisco State and Cornell: Two Black Radicals Report on Their Campus Struggles." *Ramparts*, July 1969, 47–59.
Varela, Maria. "Crumpled Notes (Found in a Raincoat) in Selma." In Gitlin, *Campfires of the Resistance*, 36–39.
———. "The Night Willie Peacock Preached Us." In Gitlin, *Campfires of the Resistance*, 35–36.
Wade Gayles, Gloria. *Anointed to Fly*. New York: Harlem River Press, 1991.
———. *Pushed Back to Strength: A Black Woman's Journey Home*. Boston: Beacon, 1993.
Watkins, Hollis, with C. Liegh McInnis. *Brother Hollis: The Sankofa of a Movement Man*. Clinton, Miss.: Sankofa Southern Publishing, 2015.

Wheeler, Jean. "Let Us All Be Black Together: A College Coed's Please to the Middle Class." *Negro Digest*, January 1964, 19–21.
Wheeler, Jean. *See also* Smith, Jean Wheeler.
Zellner, Bob. "The Traitor." In *Generation on Fire: Voices of Protest from the 1960s*, edited by Jeff Kisseloff, 26–50. Lexington: University of Kentucky Press, 2007.
Zellner, Bob, with Constance Curry. *The Wrong Side of Murder Creek: A White Southerner in the Freedom Movement*. Montgomery, Ala.: NewSouth Books, 2008.
Zimmerman, Mitchell. "Journal Entry, 6 December 1965." In Wallace and Kirk, *Arsnick*, 228–31.
———. *Mississippi Reckoning*. Palo Alto, Calif.: Hunts Point Press, 2019.

Other Works

Abel, Elizabeth. *Signs of the Times: The Visual Politics of Jim Crow*. Berkeley: University of California Press, 2010.
Abrams, Kathryn. "Emotions in the Mobilization of Rights." *Harvard Civil Rights-Civil Liberties Law Review* 46 (2011): 551–89.
Ahmann, Mathew H., ed. *The New Negro*. Notre Dame, Ind.: Fides, 1961.
Aitken, Charles S. *The Cotton Plantation South since the Civil War*. Baltimore: Johns Hopkins University Press, 2003.
Albert, Judith C., and Stewart E. Albert. *The Sixties Papers: Documents of a Rebellious Decade*. New York: Praeger, 1984.
Alexander, Michelle. *The New Jim Crow: Mass Incarceration in the Age of Colorblindness*. New York: New Press, 2012. First published 2010.
Anderson-Bricker, Kristin. "'Triple Jeopardy': Black Women and the Growth of Feminist Consciousness in SNCC." In *Still Lifting, Still Climbing: African American Women's Contemporary Activism*, edited by Kimberly Springer, 49–69. New York: New York University Press, 1999.
Araiza, Lauren. "Complicating the Beloved Community: SNCC and the National Farm Workers Association." In *The Struggle in Black and Brown: African American and Mexican American Relations during the Civil Rights Era*, edited by Brian D. Behnken, 78–103. Lincoln: University of Nebraska Press, 2011.
Armstrong, Julie Buckner, ed. *The Cambridge Companion to American Civil Rights Literature*. New York: Cambridge University Press, 2015.
Armstrong, Julie Buckner, and Amy Schmidt, eds. *The Civil Rights Reader: American Literature from Jim Crow to Reconciliation*. Athens: University of Georgia Press, 2009.
Austin, David, ed. *Moving against the System: The 1968 Congress of Black Writers and the Making of Global Consciousness*. Toronto: Between the Lines, 2018.
Babson, Steve, Dave Riddle, and David Elsila. *The Color of Law: Ernie Goodman, Detroit, and the Struggle for Labor and Civil Rights*. Detroit: Wayne State University Press, 2010.
Baker, Houston A., Jr. *Afro-American Poetics: Revisions of Harlem and the Black Aesthetic*. Madison: University of Wisconsin Press, 1988.
———. *Betrayal: How Black Intellectuals Have Abandoned the Ideals of the Civil Rights Era*. New York: Columbia University Press, 2008.
———. *Long Black Song: Essays in Black American Literature and Culture*. Charlottesville: University Press of Virginia, 1990.
———. *Turning South Again: Re-thinking Modernism/Re-Reading Booker T*. Durham, N.C.: Duke University Press, 2001.

Bakhtin, M. M. *The Dialogic Imagination.* Translated by Caryl Emerson and Michael Holquist. Austin: University of Texas Press, 1981.
Baldwin, James. "Fifth Avenue Uptown." *Esquire*, July 1960, 72–73, 76.
———. *The Fire Next Time.* London: Penguin, 1964. First published 1963.
———. Introduction to Thelwell, *Duties, Pleasures, and Conflicts*, xvii–xxii.
———. "A Letter to Americans." *Freedomways* 8 (1968): 112–16.
———. "The Uses of the Blues." *Playboy*, January 1964, 131–32, 240–41.
Baldwin, James, and Nikki Giovanni. *A Dialogue.* New York: J. B. Lippincott, 1973.
Baraka, Amiri. *The Autobiography of LeRoi Jones.* Chicago: Lawrence Hill, 1997.
———. *Selected Poetry of Amiri Baraka / LeRoi Jones.* New York: Morrow, 1979.
———. See also Jones, LeRoi.
Baraka, Amiri, and Larry Neal, eds. *Black Fire: An Anthology of Afro-American Writing.* New York: Morrow, 1968.
Barratt, Russell H. *Integration at Ole Miss.* Chicago: Quadrangle Books, 1965.
Bass, Jack, and Jack Nelson. *The Orangeburg Massacre.* Macon, Ga.: Mercer University Press, 1996. First published 1984.
Bean, Annemarie, ed. *A Sourcebook on African-American Performance: Plays, People, Movements.* New York: Taylor and Francis, 1999.
Beardslee, William R. *The Way Out Must Lead In: Life Histories in the Civil Rights Movement.* Westport, Conn.: Lawrence Hill, 1983. First published 1977.
Bedford, Robert D., and David A. Snow. "Framing Processes and Social Movements: An Overview and Assessment." *Annual Review of Sociology* 26 (2000): 611–39.
Bell, Daniel. *The Cultural Contradictions of Capitalism.* New York: Basic Books, 1975.
Benjamin, Walter. *Illuminations.* Edited by Hannah Arendt. Translated by Harry Kohn. New York: Schocken, 1968. First published 1955.
Bennett, Lerone. "The King Plan for Freedom." *Ebony*, July 1956, 63–68.
———. *The Negro Mood and Other Essays.* New York: Ballantine, 1965.
———. "SNCC: Rebels with a Cause." *Ebony*, July 1965, 146–53.
Berger, Dan. *Captive Nation: Black Prison Organizing in the Civil Rights Era.* Chapel Hill: University of North Carolina Press, 2014.
Berrey, Stephen A. *The Jim Crow Routine: Everyday Performances of Race, Civil Rights, and Segregation in Mississippi.* Chapel Hill: University of North Carolina Press, 2015.
Blair, Sara. *Harlem Crossroads: Black Writers and the Photograph in the Twentieth Century.* Princeton, N.J.: Princeton University Press, 2007.
Blake, John. *Children of the Movement.* Chicago: Lawrence Hill, 2004.
Bloom, Alexander, and Wini Breines, eds. *Takin' It to the Streets: A Sixties Reader.* New York: Oxford University Press, 1995.
Brace, John H., Sonia Sanchez, and James Smethurst, eds. *SOS—Calling All Black People: A Black Arts Movement Reader.* Amherst: University of Massachusetts Press, 2014.
Branch, Taylor. *At Canaan's Edge: America in the King Years, 1965-68.* New York: Simon and Schuster, 2006.
———. *Parting the Waters: America in the King Years, 1954-63.* New York: Simon and Schuster, 1988.
Breaux, Quo Vadis Gex. "Tom Dent's Role in the Organizational Mentoring of African American Southern Writers: A Memoir." *African American Review*, 40, no. 2 (Summer 2006): 339–44.
Breines, Wini. "Review of *Deep in Our Hearts: Nine White Women in the Freedom Movement* and *Going South: Jewish Women in the Civil Rights Movement* by Debra L. Schultz." *Signs* 30, no. 2 (Winter 2005): 1670–73.

Bromberg, Walter, and Franck Simon. "The 'Protest' Psychosis: A Special Type of Reactive Psychosis." *Archives of General Psychiatry* 19, no. 2 (August 1968): 155–60.
Brown, Sterling. "A Century of Negro Portraiture." In *Black and White in American Culture*, edited by Jules Chametzky and Sidney Kaplan, 333–59. New York: Viking, 1971.
———. *The Collected Poems of Sterling Brown*. Edited by Michael Harper. Evanston, Ill.: Northwestern University Press, 2000. First published 1996.
———. "Negro Folk Expression." *Phylon* 11 (Fall 1950): 318–27.
Browne, Vivian. "Norman Lewis: Interview, August 29, 1974." *Artist and Influence* 18 (1999): 70–79.
Brown-Nagin, Tomiko. *Courage to Dissent: Atlanta and the Long History of the Civil Rights Movement*. New York: Oxford University Press, 2011.
Bryant, Jerry H. *Victims and Heroes: Racial Violence in the African American Novel*. Amherst: University of Massachusetts Press, 1997.
Bryant, Nick. *The Bystander: John F. Kennedy and the Struggle for Black Equality*. New York: Basic Books, 2006.
Bullins, Ed. *New Plays From the Black Theater: An Anthology*. New York: Bantam, 1969.
Burner, Eric. R. *And Gently He Shall Lead Them: Robert Parris Moses and Civil Rights in Mississippi*. New York: New York University Press, 1994.
Butler, Judith. *Precarious Life: The Powers of Mourning and Violence*. London: Verso, 2004.
Byrum, Thomas L. *NACCP Youth and the Fight for Black Freedom, 1936–1965*. Knoxville: University of Tennessee Press, 2013.
Cade, Toni, ed. *The Black Woman*. New York: New American Library, 1970.
Camp, Jordan T. *Incarcerating the Crisis: Freedom Struggles and the Rise of the Neoliberal State*. Oakland: University of California Press, 2016.
Camus, Albert. *Neither Victims nor Executioners: An Ethic Superior to Murder*. 2nd ed. Translated by Dwight McDonald. Eugene, Ore: Wipf and Stock, 2007.
Carawan, Guy, and Candie Carawan, eds. *Freedom Is a Constant Struggle: Songs of the Freedom Movement*. New York: Oak Publications, 1968.
———. *Sing for Freedom: The Story of the Civil Rights Movement through Its Songs*. New York: Sing Out, 1990.
Carpenter, Teresa. "From Heroism to Madness: The Odyssey of the Man Who Shot Al Lowenstein." *Village Voice*, May 12, 1980.
Carson, Clayborne. "Charismatic Leadership in the Mass Struggle." *Journal of American History* 74 (1987): 448–54.
———. *In Struggle: SNCC and the Black Awakening of the 1960s*. Cambridge, Mass.: Harvard University Press, 1995. First published 1981.
———. *Martin's Dream: My Journey and the Legacy of Martin Luther King Jr.* New York: Palgrave Macmillan, 2013.
———. "The Paradoxes of King Historiography." *OAH Magazine of History*, January 2005, 7–10.
———. "A Scholar in Struggle." *Souls* 4, no. 2 (2002): 28–37.
Carter, Hodding. *Where Main Street Meets the River*. New York: Rinehart, 1953.
Caruth, Cathy. *Trauma: Exploration in Memory*. Baltimore: Johns Hopkins University Press, 1995.
———. *Unclaimed Experience: Trauma, Narrative, and History*. Baltimore: Johns Hopkins University Press, 1996.
Cash, W. J. *The Mind of the South*. London: Thames and Hudson, 1971. First published in 1941.

Chafe, William H. *Civilities and Civil Rights: Greensboro, North Carolina, and the Black Struggle for Freedom*. New York: Oxford University Press, 1981.
Chambers, Iain. *Migrancy, Culture, Identity*. London: Routledge, 1994.
Chametzky, Jules, and Sidney Kaplan, eds. *Black and White in American Culture*. New York: Viking, 1971.
Chappell, Marisa, Jenny Hutchinson and Brian Ward. "'Dress Modestly, Neatly... as If You Were Going to Church': Respectability, Class, and Gender in the Montgomery Bus Boycott and the Early Civil Rights Movement." In Ling and Monteith, *Gender and the Civil Rights Movement*, 69–98.
Christian, Barbara. "The Race for Theory." *Cultural Critique* 6 (Spring 1987): 51–63.
Clarke, Cheryl. *After Mecca: Women Poets in the Black Arts Movement*. New Brunswick, N.J.: Rutgers University Press, 2005.
Cobb, James C. *The Most Southern Place on Earth: The Mississippi Delta and the Roots of Regional Identity*. New York: Oxford University Press, 1992.
Cohen, Robert. *Freedom's Orator: Mario Savio and the Radical Legacy of the 1960s*. New York: Oxford University Press, 2009.
Cohen-Cruz, Jan. *Local Acts: Community-Based Performance in the United States*. New Brunswick, N.J.: Rutgers University Press, 2005.
Cole, Alyson M. "Blue Lester: Two Faces of Victimhood." In *The Cult of True Victimhood: From the War on Welfare to the War on Terror*, 79–107. Stanford, Calif.: Stanford University Press, 2007.
Coleman, Floyd. "The Changing Same: Spiral, the Sixties, and African-American Art." In *A Shared Heritage: Art by Four African Americans*, edited by William Taylor and Harriet G. Werkel, 147–17. Bloomington: Indiana University Press/Indiana Museum of Art, 1996.
Coleman, Jeffrey Lamar, ed. *Words of Protest, Words of Freedom: Poetry of the American Civil Rights Movement and Era*. Durham, N.C.: Duke University Press, 2012.
Coles, Robert, and Joseph Brenner. "American Youth in a Social Struggle: The Mississippi Summer Project." *American Journal of Orthopsychiatry* 35, no. 5 (October 1965): 909–27.
Coles, Robert. *The Call of Service: A Witness to Idealism*. Boston: Houghton Mifflin, 1993.
———. *The Call of Stories: Teaching and the Moral Imagination*. Boston: Houghton Mifflin, 1989.
———. *Children of Crisis: A Study of Courage and Fear*. Boston: Little, Brown and Company, 1967.
———. *Doing Documentary Work*. New York: Oxford University Press, 1997.
———. *Farewell to the South*. New York: Little, Brown, 1972.
———. "A Fashionable Type of Slander." *Atlantic Monthly*, November 1970, 53–55.
———. *A Festering of Sweetness: Poems of American People*. Pittsburgh: University of Pittsburgh Press, 1978.
———. *Rumors of Separate Worlds*. Iowa City: University of Iowa Press, 1989.
———. "Serpents and Doves: Non-Violent Youth in the South." In *Youth: Change and Challenge*, edited by Erik H. Erickson, 188–216. New York: Basic Books, 1963.
———. "Social Struggle Weariness." *Psychiatry* 27 (November 1964): 305–15.
———. "The South That Is Man's Destiny," *Massachusetts Review* 6, no. 2 (Winter–Spring 1965): 257–69.
———. "A Young Psychiatrist Looks at His Profession." In *Psychiatry in American Life*, edited by Charles Rolo, 102–13. Boston: Little, Brown, 1963.

Colley, Zoe. *Ain't Scared of Your Jail: Arrest, Imprisonment and the Civil Rights Movement.* Gainesville: University of Florida Press, 2012.
Collins, Lisa Gail, and Margo Natalie Crawford, eds. *New Thoughts on the Black Arts Movement.* New Brunswick, N.J.: Rutgers University Press, 2006.
Connerton, Paul. *How Societies Remember.* Cambridge, UK: Cambridge University Press, 1989.
Cooper, David, ed. *To Free a Generation: The Dialectics of Liberation.* New York: Collier Books, 1969. First published 1968.
Cosby, Camille O., and Renee Poussaint, eds. *A Wealth of Wisdom: Legendary African American Elders Speak.* New York: Washington Square Press, 2004.
Cox, Julian, ed. *Danny Lyon: Message to the Future.* New Haven, Conn.: Yale University Press, 2016.
Cox, Karen L. *Dreaming of Dixie: How the South Was Created in American Popular Culture.* Chapel Hill: University of North Carolina Press, 2011.
Crawford, Margo Natalie. *Black Post-Blackness: The Black Arts Movement and Twenty-First-Century Aesthetics.* Urbana: University of Illinois Press, 2017.
Crosby, Emilye, ed. *Civil Rights History from the Ground Up: Local Struggles, a National Movement.* Athens: University of Georgia Press, 2011.
———. *A Little Taste of Freedom: The Black Freedom Struggle in Claiborne County, Mississippi.* Chapel Hill: University of North Carolina Press, 2005.
Cruse, Harold. *The Crisis of the Negro Intellectual: A Historical Analysis of the Failure of Black Leadership.* New York: New York Review of Books, 2005. First published 1967.
Dabbs, James McBride. *Civil Rights and Recent Southern Fiction.* Atlanta: Southern Regional Council, 1969.
———. *Who Speaks for the South?* New York: Funk and Wagnalls, 1967. First published 1964.
Daniel, Pete. *Dispossession: Discrimination against African American Farmers in the Age of Civil Rights.* Chapel Hill: University of North Carolina Press, 2013.
———. *Lost Revolutions: The South in the 1950s.* Chapel Hill: University of North Carolina Press, 2000.
———. *The Shadow of Slavery: Peonage in the South, 1901–1969.* Rev. ed. Urbana: University of Illinois Press, 1990.
Davis, Jack E. *Race against Time: Culture and Separation in Natchez since 1930.* Baton Rouge: Louisiana University Press, 2001.
Davis, Joseph E., ed. *Stories of Change: Narrative and Social Movements.* Albany: State University of New York Press. 2002.
Dawley, Edward A. "Kinoy contra Dixie." *Guild Practitioner* 47 (1990): 42–44.
Derrida, Jacques, and Hélène Cixous. "From the Word to Life: A Dialogue between Jacques Derrida and Hélène Cixous." *New Literary History* 37, no. 1 (Winter 2006): 1–13.
De Schweinitz, Rebecca. *If We Could Change the World: Young People and America's Struggle for Racial Equality.* Chapel Hill: University of North Carolina Press, 2009.
Dicker/sun, Glenda. *African-American Theater: A Cultural Companion.* Cambridge, UK: Polity Press, 2008.
Dillard, Angela. *Guess Who's Coming to Dinner Now? Multicultural Conservatism in America.* New York: New York University Press, 2001.
Dittmer, John. *The Good Doctors: The Medical Committee for Human Rights and the Struggle for Social Justice in Health Care.* New York: Bloomsbury, 2009.
———. *Local People: The Struggle for Civil Rights in Mississippi.* Urbana: University of Illinois Press, 1994.
Dollard, John. *Caste and Class in a Southern Town.* Madison: University of Wisconsin Press, 1988. First published 1937.

Douglas, Mary, ed. *The Collective Memory*. New York: Harper Colophon, 1980.
Dowling, John H., ed. *The Encyclopedia of Social Movement Media*. London: Sage, 2011.
Draper, Hal. *Berkeley: The New Student Revolt*. New York: Grove Press, 1965.
Du Bois, W. E. B. *Dusk of Dawn*. In *Writings*, edited by Nathan Huggins, 550–802. New York: Library of America, 1986.
Dunbar, Leslie W. "The Changing Mind of the South: The Exposed Nerve." In *The American South in the 1960s*, edited by Alexander Heard, 3–21. New York: Frederick A. Praeger, 1965. First published 1964.
Eagles, Charles W. "Toward New Histories of the Civil Rights Era." *Journal of Southern History* 66, no. 4 (2000): 815–48.
Eakin, Paul John. *Touching the World: Reference in Autobiography*. Princeton, N.J.: Princeton University Press, 1992.
Edmonds, Michael, ed. *Risking Everything: A Freedom Summer Reader*. Madison: Wisconsin Historical Society Press, 2014.
Ellison, Ralph. *Going to the Territory*. New York: Vintage, 1986.
———. *Shadow and Act*. New York: Random House, 1994. First published 1964.
Elton, Geoffrey. *The Practice of History*. London: Methuen, 1967.
Erikson, Erik H. *Youth: Change and Challenge*. New York: Basic Books, 1963.
Euben, J. Peter. "The Politics of Literature." In *Radical Future Pasts: Untimely Political Theory*, edited by Romand Coles, Mark Reinhardt, and George Shulman, 321–31. Lexington: University Press of Kentucky, 2014.
Evans, Mari. "Contemporary Black Literature: A Statement." *Black World*, June 1970: 4, 93–94.
Fabre, Geneviève. "The Free Southern Theatre, 1963–1979." *Black American Literature Forum* 17, no. 2 (1983): 55–59.
Fairclough, Adam. *To Redeem the Soul of America: The Southern Christian Leadership Conference and Martin Luther King, Jr.* Athens: University of Georgia Press, 1987.
Farber, Jerry. *The Student as Nigger: Essays and Stories*. Hollywood, Calif.: Contact Books, 1969.
Felman, Shoshana, and Dori Laub. *Testimony: Crises of Witnessing in Literature, Psychoanalysis, and History*. New York: Routledge, 1991.
Felski, Rita. *The Limits of Critique*. Chicago: University of Chicago Press, 2015.
Fenderson, Jonathan. *Building the Black Arts Movement: Hoyt Fuller and the Cultural Politics of the 1960s*. Urbana: University of Illinois Press, 2019.
Feuer, Lewis S. *The Conflict of Generations: The Character and Significance of Student Movements*. New York: Basic Books, 1969.
Fiedler, Leslie. "The New Mutants." *Partisan Review* 32, no. 4 (1965): 505–25.
———. "The War against the Academy." *Wisconsin Studies in Contemporary Literature* 5, no. 1 (1964): 5–17.
Fields, Arthur C. *War without Heroes*. New York: McGraw-Hill, 1950.
Fine, Elsa Honig. "Mainstream, Blackstream and the Black Art Movement." *Art Journal* 30, no. 4 (1971): 374–75.
Fine, Gary Alan. "The Storied Group: Social Movements as 'Bundles of Narratives.'" In *Stories of Change: Narratives and Social Movements*, edited by Joseph E. Davis. New York: State University of New York Press, 2002, 229–45.
Fleming, Cynthia Griggs. *In the Shadow of Selma: The Continuing Struggle for Civil Rights in the Rural South*. Langham, Md.: Rowman and Littlefield, 2004.
———. *Soon We Will Not Cry: The Liberation of Ruby Doris Smith Robinson*. Lanham, Md.: Rowman and Littlefield, 1998.

Fleming, Karl. *Son of the Rough South: An Uncivil Memoir*. New York: PublicAffairs, 2005.
Foley, Barbara. "Generic and Doctrinal Politics in the Proletarian Bildungsroman." In *Understanding Narrative*, edited by James Phelan and Peter J. Rabinowitz, 43–64. Columbus: Ohio State University Press, 1994.
——. "History, Fiction, and the Ground Between: The Uses of the Documentary Mode in Black Literature." *PMLA* 95, no. 3 (1980): 389–403.
Foner, Eric. *The Story of American Freedom*. New York: Norton, 1998.
Foucault, Michel. "Nietzsche, Genealogy, History." In *Language, Counter-Memory, Practice: Selected Essays*, edited by Donald F. Bouchard, 139–63. Ithaca, N.Y.: Cornell University Press, 1977.
Franklin, V. P. "Hidden in Plain View: African American Women, Radical Feminism, and the Origins of Women's Studies Programs, 1967–1974." *Journal of African American History* 87 (2002): 433–45.
Friedman, Leon, ed. *Southern Justice*. New York: Random House, 1965.
Frazier, E. Franklin. *The Black Bourgeoisie: The Rise of a New Middle Class*. New York: Collier, 1962. First published 1957.
Fuller, Hoyt W. "Towards a Black Aesthetic." In *The Black Aesthetic*, edited by Addison Gayle, 3–15. New York: Doubleday, 1971.
Gabbin, Joanne V. *Sterling A. Brown: Building the Black Aesthetic Tradition*. Charlottesville: University Press of Virginia, 1994. First published 1985.
Garrow, David. *Bearing the Cross: Martin Luther King, Jr., and the Southern Christian Leadership Conference*. New York: Vintage, 1988.
Gayle, Addison, ed. *The Black Aesthetic*. New York: Doubleday, 1971.
Geary, Daniel. "Feminism and the Nuclear Family Norm." In *Beyond Civil Rights: The Moynihan Report and Its Legacy*, 139–70. Philadelphia: University of Pennsylvania Press, 2015.
Gellman, Erik S. *Death Blow to Jim Crow: The National Negro Congress and the Rise of Militant Civil Rights*. Chapel Hill: University of North Carolina Press, 2012.
Gitlin, Todd, ed. *Campfires of the Resistance: Poetry from the Movement*. Indianapolis: Bobbs-Merrill, 1971.
Giovanni, Nikki. *Black Feeling, Black Talk, Black Judgement*. New York: Morrow Quill, 1979. First published 1970.
——. *Gemini: An Extended Autobiographical Statement on My First Twenty-Five Years of Being a Black Poet*. New York: Viking, 1971.
Glass, Loren. *Rebel Publisher: Grove Press and the Revolution of the Word*. New York: Seven Stories Press, 2018. First published 2013.
Good, Paul. *The Trouble I've Seen: White Journalist, Black Movement*. Washington, D.C.: Howard University Press, 1975.
Goodwin, Jeff, James M. Jasper, and Francesca Polletta, eds. *Passionate Politics: Emotions and Social Movements*. Chicago: University of Chicago Press, 2001.
Gorrell, Nancy. "Let Found Poetry Help Your Students Find Poetry." *English Journal* 78, no. 2 (1989): 30–34.
Gosse, Van. *Where the Boys Are: Cuba, Cold War America, and the Making of a New Left*. London: Verso, 1993.
Grady-Willis, Winston A. *Challenging U.S. Apartheid, 1960–1977*. Durham, N.C.: Duke University Press, 2006.
Graham, Allison. "The South in Popular Culture." In *A Companion to the Literature and Culture of the American South*, edited by Richard Gray and Owen Robinson, 335–51. Oxford: Blackwell, 2007.

Graham, Allison, and Sharon Monteith, eds. *The New Encyclopedia of Southern Culture: Media.* Chapel Hill: University of North Carolina Press, 2011.
Graves, Roy Neil. "Julian Bond's 'Habana.'" *Explicator* 76, no. 1 (2008): 4–7.
Greenberg, Cheryl Lynn, ed. *A Circle of Trust: Remembering SNCC.* New Brunswick, N.J.: Rutgers University Press, 1998.
Gregory, Dick, with Robert Lipsyte. *Nigger.* New York: Washington Square Books, 1964.
Gregory, Dick, with Sheila P. Moses. *Callus on My Soul: A Memoir.* Atlanta: Longstreet, 2000.
Griffin, John Howard. *Prison of Culture: Beyond Black Like Me.* San Antonio: Wings Press, 2011.
Hadley, Elizabeth Amelia. "Leontyne Price: Prima Donna Assoluta." In *Black Women and Music: More Than the Blues,* edited by Eileen M. Hayes and Linda Williams, 197–209. Chicago: University of Illinois Press, 2007.
Halberstam, David. *The Children.* New York: Fawcett, 1998.
———. "The Education of a Journalist." *Columbia Journalism Review* 33, no. 4 (1994): 29.
———. "The Kids Take Over." *Reporter* (New York), June 22, 1961, 22–23.
Halbwachs, Maurice. *On Collective Memory.* Translated by Lewis A. Coser, 1992.
Hale, Grace Elizabeth. *A Nation of Outsiders: How the White Middle Class Fell in Love with Rebellion in Postwar America.* New York: Oxford University Press, 2011.
Hale, John N. *The Freedom Schools: Student Activists in the Mississippi Civil Rights Movement.* New York: Columbia University Press, 2016.
Hall, Jacqueline Dowd. "Reflections." In *Jumpin' Jim Crow: Southern Politics from Civil War to Civil Rights,* edited by Jane Dailey, Glenda Elizabeth Gilmore, and Bryant Simon, 304–7. Princeton, N.J.: Princeton University Press, 2000.
Hall, James C. *Mercy, Mercy Me: African American Culture and the American Sixties.* New York: Oxford University Press, 2001.
———. "On Sale at Your Favorite Newsstand: *Negro Digest/Black World* and the 1960s." In *The Black Press: New Literary and Historical Essays,* edited by Todd Vogel, 188–206. New Brunswick, N.J.: Rutgers University Press, 2001.
Hall, Simon. *Peace and Freedom: The Civil Rights and Antiwar Movements in the 1960s.* Philadelphia: University of Pennsylvania Press, 2005.
———. "The Response of the Moderate Wing of the Civil Rights Movement to the Vietnam War." *Historical Journal* 46, no. 3 (September 2003): 669–701.
Harding, Vincent. "Black Students and the Impossible Revolution." *Journal of Black Studies* 1, no. 1 (September, 1970): 75–100.
———. *Hope and History: Why We Must Share the Story of the Movement.* New York: Orbis, 2009. First published 1990.
———. *The Other American Revolution.* Atlanta: Institute of the Black World, 1980.
———. *There Is a River: The Black Struggle for Freedom in America.* New York: Harcourt Brace and Jovanovich, 1981.
Hampton, Henry, and Steve Fayer, eds. *Voices of Freedom.* New York: Vintage, 1995.
Hansberry, Lorraine. "Genet, Mailer, and the New Paternalism." *Village Voice,* June 1, 1961.
———. *To Be Young Gifted and Black: An Informal Autobiography of Lorraine Hansberry.* Adapted by Robert Nemiroff. New York: Signet, 2011. First published 1969.
Harper, Michael S., and Robert B. Stepto, eds. *Chant of Saints: A Gathering of Afro-American Literature, Art, and Scholarship.* Urbana: University of Illinois Press, 1979.

Harrington, Michael. "The Mystical Militants." *New Republic*, February 17, 1966, 20–22.
Hayden, Robert. *Kaleidoscope: Poems by American Negro Poets*. New York: Harcourt, Brace & World, 1967.
Heilman, Robert. *Tragedy and Melodrama: Versions of Experience*. Seattle: University of Washington Press, 1968.
Hellerstein, David, and Robert Coles. "On Medicine and Literature: An Interview with Robert Coles." *North American Review* 265, no. 2 (June 1980): 6–14.
Hendrickson, Paul. *Sons of Mississippi: A Story of Race and Its Legacy*. New York: Knopf, 2003.
Hernton, Calvin. "Umbra: A Personal Recounting." *African American Review* 27 (Winter 1993): 579–83.
Herschberger, Mary. *Traveling to Vietnam: American Peace Activists and the War*. Syracuse, N.Y.: Syracuse University Press, 1998.
Hill, Lance. *The Deacons for Defense: Armed Resistance and the Civil Rights Movement*. Chapel Hill: University of North Carolina Press, 2004.
Hirschkop, Ken. "Is Dialogism for Real?" *Social Text* 30 (1992): 102–13.
Hitchcock, Peter. *Dialogics of the Oppressed*. Minneapolis: University of Minnesota Press, 1993.
Hobsbawm, Eric. *Bandits*. Rev. ed. New York: Pantheon, 1981.
Hobson, Fred. *But Now I See: The White Southern Racial Conversion Narrative*. Baton Rouge: Louisiana State University Press, 1999.
Hoffman, Nicholas Von. *Mississippi Notebook*. New York: David White, 1964.
Hogan, Wesley. *Many Minds, One Heart: SNCC's Dream for a New America*. Chapel Hill: University of North Carolina Press, 2007.
Honigsberg, Peter Jan. *Crossing Border Street: A Civil Rights Memoir*. Berkeley: University of California Press, 2002.
Hooper, Lita. *Art of Work: The Art and Life of Haki R. Madhubuti*. Chicago: Third World Press, 2007.
Horton, John, and Andrea T. Baumeister, eds. *Literature and the Political Imagination*. London: Routledge, 1996.
Houck, David W., and David E. Dixon, eds. *Rhetoric, Religion and the Civil Rights Movement 1954–1965*. Waco, Tex.: Baylor University Press, 2006.
Houston, Benjamin. *The Nashville Way: Racial Etiquette and the Struggle for Social Justice in a Southern City*. Athens: University of Georgia Press, 2012.
Hudson, Theodore R. "Activism and Criticism during the Black Arts Movement." In *Connections: Essays on Black Literature*, edited by Emanuel S. Nelson, 89–99. Canberra, Australia: Aboriginal Studies Press, 1988.
Ismaili-Abu-Bakr, Rashidah. "Slightly Autobiographical: The 1960s on the Lower East Side." *African American Review* 27 (Winter 1993): 585–89.
Jackson, Esther Cooper, and Constance Pohl, eds. *The Freedomways Reader: Prophets in Their Own County*. Boulder, Colo.: Westview Press, 2000.
Jackson, Lawrence P. *The Indignant Generation: A Narrative History of African American Writers and Critics, 1934–1960*. Princeton, N.J.: Princeton University Press, 2011.
Jackson, Luther P., Jr. "The Story of Danville: Len P. Holt's *An Act of Conscience*." *Freedomways* 5, no. 4 (1965): 430–32.
Jacobs, Saul, and Paul Landau. *The New Radicals*. New York: Vintage, 1966.
Jameson, Fredric. *The Political Unconscious: Narrative as a Socially Symbolic Act*. London: Methuen, 1981.

JanMohamed, Abdul. *The Death-Bound Subject: Richard Wright's Archaeology of Death.* Durham, N.C.: Duke University Press, 2005.
JanMohamed, Abdul, and David Lloyd, eds. *The Nature and Context of Minority Discourse.* New York: Oxford University Press, 1990.
Jasper, James. *The Art of Moral Protest: Culture, Biography, and Creativity in Social Movements.* Chicago: University of Chicago Press, 1997.
Jasper, James, and Jane D. Poulsen, "Recruiting Strangers and Friends: Moral Shocks and Social Networks in Animal Rights and Anti-Nuclear Protests." *Social Problems* 42 (1995): 493–512.
Jeffries, Hasan Kwame. *Bloody Lowndes: Civil Rights and Black Power in Alabama's Black Belt.* New York: New York University Press, 2009.
——. "Remaking History: Barack Obama, Political Cartoons, and the Civil Rights Movement." In Crosby, *Civil Rights History from the Ground Up*, 259–77.
——. "SNCC, Black Power, and Independent Political Party Organizing in Alabama, 1964–1966." *Journal of African American History* 91, no. 2 (Spring 2006): 171–93.
Jensen, Meg, and Jane Jordan, eds. *Life Writing: The Spirit of the Age and the State of the Art.* Newcastle upon Tyne: Cambridge Scholars Press, 2009.
Johnson, Abby Arthur, and Ronald Mayberry Johnson. *Propaganda and Aesthetics: The Literary Politics of African-American Magazines in the Twentieth Century.* Amherst: University of Massachusetts Press, 1991. First published 1979.
Johnson, Becky. *No Permanent Waves: Recasting Histories of United States Feminism.* New Brunswick, N.J.: Rutgers University Press, 2010.
Johnson, Charles. *Being and Race: Black Writing since 1970.* London: Serpent's Tail, 1988.
Johnson, John H., with Lerone Bennett Jr. *Succeeding against the Odds.* New York: Warner Books, 1989.
Jones, Gareth Stedman. "The Meaning of the Student Revolt." In *Student Power: Problems, Diagnosis, Action,* edited by Alexander Cockburn and Robin Blackburn, 25–56. Harmondsworth, UK: Penguin, 1969.
Jones, LeRoi. *The Dead Lecturer: Poems.* New York: Grove, 1964.
——. *Dutchman and The Slave.* London: Faber, 1964.
——. "The Need for a Cultural Base to Civil Rites and Bpower Moovments." In *The Black Power Revolt,* edited by Floyd B. Barbour, 136–44. New York: Collier Books, 1968.
——. *See also* Baraka, Amiri.
Jones, Suzanne, ed. *Crossing the Color Line: Readings in Black and White.* Columbia: University of South Carolina Press, 2000.
Jordan, June. "White English/Black English: The Politics of Translation." In *Moving towards Home: Political Essays,* 29–40. London: Virago, 1989.
Joseph, Peniel. *Stokely: A Life.* New York: Basic Books, 2014.
——. *Waiting 'til the Midnight Hour: A Narrative History of Black Power in America.* New York: Henry Holt, 2006.
Juncker, Howard. "Free University: Academy for Mavericks." *Nation,* August 16, 1965: 78–80.
Kelley, Robin D. G. *Freedom Dreams: The Black Radical Imagination.* Boston: Beacon, 2002.
——. *Hammer and Hoe: Alabama Communists during the Great Depression.* Chapel Hill: University of North Carolina Press, 1990.
King, Martin Luther, Jr. *The Papers of Martin Luther King, Jr.,* vol. 4: *Symbol of the Movement.* Edited by Clayborne Carson, Susan Carson, Adrienne Clay, Virginia Shadron, and Kieran Taylor. Berkeley: University of California Press, 2000.

King, Richard H. "Citizenship and Self-Respect: The Experience of Politics in the Civil Rights Movement." *Journal of American Studies* 22 (1988): 7–24.
——. *Civil Rights and the Idea of Freedom.* New York: Oxford University Press, 1992.
——. "The Civil Rights Debate." In *A Companion to the Literature and Culture of the American South*, edited by Richard Gray and Owen Robinson, 221–37. Oxford: Blackwell, 2007.
——. "The Discipline of Fact / The Freedom of Fiction?" *Journal of American Studies* 25, no. 2 (August 1991): 171–88.
——. "Politics and Fictional Representation: The Case of the Civil Rights Movement." In *The Making of Martin Luther King and the Civil Rights Movement*, edited by Brian Ward and Tony Badger, 162–78. London: Palgrave McMillan, 1996.
——. "The Role of Intellectual History in the Histories of the Civil Rights Movement." In *Race and Class in the American South since 1890*, edited by Melvyn Stokes and Rick Halpern, 159–80. Providence, R.I.: Berg, 1994.
Kisseloff, Jeff, ed. *Generation on Fire: Voices of Protest from the 1960s.* Lexington: University of Kentucky Press, 2007.
Kodish, Debora. "Imagining Public Folklore." In *A Companion to Folklore*, edited by Regina F. Bendix and Galit Hasan-Rokem, 579–97. Oxford: Wiley-Blackwell, 2012.
Kopkind, Andrew. Prologue to *The Thirty Years' Wars: Dispatches and Diversions of a Radical Journalist, 1965–1994*, edited by JoAnn Wypijewski, xix–xxvi. London: Verso, 1995.
Kunstler, William M. *Deep in My Heart.* New York: William Morrow, 1966.
LaCapra, Dominick. *History and Its Limits: Human, Animal, Violence.* Ithaca, N.Y.: Cornell University Press, 2009.
Lake, Alice. "Last Summer in Mississippi." *Redbook*, November 1964, 63–64, 111–17.
Larocco, Christina. "'COFO Is Not Godot': The Free Southern Theatre, the Black Freedom Movement, and the Search for a Usable Aesthetic." *Cultural and Social History* 12, no. 4 (2015): 509–26.
Lasch, Christopher. *The Agony of the American Left.* New York: Vintage, 1969.
Lash, John S. "Dimension in Racial Experience: A Critical Summary of Literature by and about Negroes in 1958." *Phylon Quarterly* 20, no. 2 (1959): 115–31.
Lathan, Rhea Estelle. *Freedom Writing: African American Civil Rights Literacy Activism, 1955–1967.* Urbana, Ill.: National Council of Teachers of English, 2015.
Lawson, Steven. *Black Ballots: Voting Rights in the South, 1944–1969.* New York: Columbia University Press, 1976.
——. "Long Origins of the Short Civil Rights Movement, 1954–1968." In *Freedom Rights: New Perspectives on the Civil Rights Movement*, edited by Danielle McGuire and John Dittmer, 9–37. Lexington: University Press of Kentucky, 2011.
Lee, Chana Kai. *For Freedom's Sake: The Life of Fannie Lou Hamer.* Urbana: University of Illinois Press, 1999.
Lee, Don L. *Black Pride.* Detroit: Broadside Press, 1968.
Lefever, Harry G. *Undaunted by the Fight: Spelman College and the Civil Rights Movement, 1957–1967.* Macon, Ga.: Mercer University Press, 2005.
Leffler, Phyllis. *Black Leaders on Leadership: Conversations with Julian Bond.* New York: Palgrave Macmillan, 2014.
Lehman, Christopher P. *Power, Politics and the Decline of the Civil Rights Movement.* Santa Barbara, Calif.: Praeger, 2014.
Lemann, Nicholas. *The Promised Land: The Great Migration and How It Changed America.* London: Macmillan, 1991.

Lewis, Andrew B. *The Shadows of Youth: The Remarkable Journey of the Civil Rights Generation*. New York: Hill and Wang, 2009.
Lewis, David Levering. *King: A Biography*. Chicago: University of Illinois Press, 2013. First published 1970.
Ling, Peter. "Social Capital, Resource Mobilization, and Origins of the Civil Rights Movement." *Journal of Historical Sociology* 19, no. 2 (June 2006): 202–14.
———. "SNCCs: Not One Committee, but Several." *From Sit-Ins to SNCC: The Student Civil Rights Movement in the 1960s*. Edited by Iwan Morgan and Philip Davies, 81–96. Gainesville: University Press of Florida, 2012.
Ling, Peter, and Sharon Monteith, eds. *Gender and the Civil Rights Movement*. New York: Garland, 1999.
Lipsitz, George. *The Possessive Investment in Whiteness: How White People Profit from Identity Politics*. Philadelphia: Temple University Press, 1998.
Lischer, Richard. *The Preacher King: Martin Luther King, Jr. and the Word That Moved America*. New York: Oxford University Press, 1995.
Littlejohn, Jeffrey L., and Charles H. Ford. *Elusive Equality: Desegregation and Resegregation in Norfolk's Public Schools*. Charlottesville: University of Virginia Press, 2012.
Long, Margaret. "All God's Chillun." *Progressive*, January 1963, 9–13.
———. "Black Power in the Black Belt." *Progressive*, October 1966, 20–24.
———. "Let Freedom Sing." *Progressive*, November 1965, 27–31.
Lowenfels, Walter, ed. *In a Time of Revolution: Poems from Our Third World*. New York: Random House, 1969.
———, ed. *The Writing on the Wall*. New York: Doubleday, 1969.
Lynd, Alice, and Staughton Lynd. *Stepping Stones: A Memoir of Life Together*. Lanham, Md.: Lexington Books, 2009.
Lynd, Staughton. *Accompanying: Pathways to Social Change*. Oakland, Calif.: PM Press, 2012.
———. "The Freedom Schools: Concept and Organization." *Freedomways* 4, no. 2 (1965): 302–9.
———. "Remembering SNCC" (2003). In *From Here to There: The Staughton Lynd Reader*, edited by Andrej Grubacic, 68–73. Oakland, Calif.: PM Press, 2010.
Marsh, Charles. *God's Long Summer: Stories of Faith and Civil Rights*. Princeton, N.J.: Princeton University Press, 1997.
Marshall, James P. *Student Activism and Civil Rights in Mississippi*. Baton Rouge: Louisiana State University Press, 2013.
Martin, Christopher R. *Framed! Labor and the Corporate Media*. Ithaca, N.Y.: ILR Press, 2004.
Martin, Waldo B. *No Coward Soldiers: Black Cultural Politics in Postwar America*. Cambridge, Mass.: Harvard University Press, 2005.
Mason, Gilbert R., with James Patterson Smith. *Beaches, Blood, and Ballots: A Black Doctor's Civil Rights Struggles*. Jackson: University Press of Mississippi, 2000.
Matlin, Daniel. *On the Corner: African American Intellectuals and the Urban Crisis*. Cambridge, Mass.: Harvard University Press, 2013.
Maxwell, William J. F. B. *Eyes: How J. Edgar Hoover's Ghostreaders Framed African American Literature*. Princeton, N.J.: Princeton University Press, 2015.
Mayfield, Julian. "And Then Came Baldwin." *Freedomways* 3, no. 2 (Spring 1963): 143–55.
Maynes, Mary Jo, Jennifer L. Pierce, and Barbara Laslett. *Telling Stories: The Use of Personal Narratives in the Social Sciences and History*. Ithaca, N.Y.: Cornell University Press, 2008.

McAdam, Doug. *Freedom Summer.* New York: Oxford University Press, 1988.
McClymer, John F. *Mississippi Freedom Summer.* Belmont, Calif.: Thomson Wadsworth, 2004.
McCord, William. *Mississippi: The Long, Hot Summer.* New York: W. W. Norton, 1965.
McGehee, Molly. "'You Do Not Own What You Cannot Control': An Interview with Activist and Folklorist Worth Long." *Mississippi Folklife* 31, no. 1 (Fall 1998): 12–20.
McGurl, Mark. *The Program Era: Post-War Fiction and the Rise of Creative Writing.* Cambridge, Mass.: Harvard University Press, 2009.
McMillian, John. *Smoking Typewriters: The Sixties Underground Press and the Rise of Alternative Media in America.* New York: Oxford University Press, 2011.
Meier, August, and Elliott Rudwick, eds. *Black Protest and the Sixties.* Chicago: Quadrangle Books, 1970.
Metress, Christopher. "Making Civil Rights Harder: Literature, Memory, and the Black Freedom Struggle." *Southern Literary Journal* 40, no. 2 (Spring 2008): 138–50.
Michna, Catherine. "Performance and Cross-Racial Storytelling in Post-Katrina New Orleans: Interviews with John O'Neal, Carol Bebelle, and Nicholas Slie." *Drama Review* 57 (2013): 48–69.
Miller, Timothy. *The Hippies and American Values.* Knoxville: University of Tennessee Press, 1991.
Mills, Laura, and Lynn Y. Weiner. *Roosevelt University.* Charleston, S.C.: Arcadia, 2014.
Minchin, Timothy J., and John A. Salmond. "'The Saddest Story of the Whole Movement': The Clyde Kennard Case and the Search for Racial Reconciliation in Mississippi, 1955–2007." *Journal of Mississippi History,* Fall 2009, 191–234.
Misseduc Foundation. *Mississippi Black Paper.* New York: Random House, 1965.
Mitchell, Loften. *Black Drama: The Story of the American Negro in the Theatre.* New York: Hawthorn Books, 1967.
Monteith, Sharon. *Advancing Sisterhood? Interracial Friendships in Contemporary Southern Fiction.* Athens: University of Georgia Press, 2000.
———. *American Culture in the 1960s.* Edinburgh: Edinburgh University Press, 2008.
———. "The Bridge from Mississippi's Freedom Summer to Canada: Pearl Cleage's *Bourbon at the Border.*" In *Cultural Circulation: Canadian Writers and Authors from the American South—A Dialogue,* edited by Waldemar Zacharasiewicz, 155–75. Vienna: Austrian Academy of Sciences, 2013.
———. "Civil Rights Fiction." In *The Cambridge Companion to the Literature of the American South,* 159–73. New York: Cambridge University Press, 2013.
———. "Exploiting Civil Rights: Pulp Movies in the 1960s." In *American Cinema and the Southern Imaginary,* edited by Kathryn McKee and Deborah Barker, 194–217. Athens: University of Georgia Press, 2011.
———. "'I Second That Emotion': A Case for Using Imaginative Sources in Writing Civil Rights History." *Patterns of Prejudice* 49, no. 5 (2015): 440–65.
———. "The Never-ending Cycle of Poverty: Sarah E. Wright's *This Child's Gonna Live.*" In *Poverty and Progress in the U.S. South after 1920,* edited by Suzanne Jones and Mark Newman, 81–93. Amsterdam: VU University Press, 2006.
———. "SNCC's Stories at the Barricades." In *From Sit-Ins to SNCC: Student Civil Rights Protest in the 1960s,* edited by Philip Davies and Iwan Morgan, 97–115. Gainesville: University of Florida Press, 2012.
———. "'Where Do We Go from Here?': Revisiting the 1960s in Contemporary Fiction." In Ling and Monteith, *Gender and the Civil Rights Movement,* 215–38.

———. "'Who Was William Faulkner to Them?': Racial Liberals and Civil Rights Workers in the Civil Rights Era." In *Fifty Years after Faulkner*, edited by Jay Watson and Ann J. Abadie, 222–35. Jackson: University Press of Mississippi, 2016.
Morgan, Iwan, and Philip Davies, eds. *From Sit-Ins to SNCC: The Student Civil Rights Movement in the 1960s*. Gainesville: University Press of Florida, 2012.
Morgan, Robin, ed. *Sisterhood Is Powerful: An Anthology of Writings from the Women's Liberation Movement*. New York: Random House, 1970.
Morris, Aldon D. *The Origins of the Civil Rights Movement: Black Communities Organizing in Anger*. New York: Free Press, 1984.
———. "A Retrospective on the Civil Rights Movement: Political and Intellectual Landmarks." *Annual Review of Sociology* 25 (1999): 517–39.
Morris, Tiyi M. *Womanpower Unlimited and the Black Freedom Struggle in Mississippi*. Athens: University of Georgia Press, 2015.
Moye, J. Todd. "Focusing Our Eyes on the Prize: How Community Studies Are Rewriting and Reframing the History of the Civil Rights Movement." In Crosby, *Civil Rights History from the Ground Up*, 147–70.
———. *Let the People Decide: Black Freedom and White Resistance Movements in Sunflower County, Mississippi, 1945–1986*. Chapel Hill: University of North Carolina Press, 2004.
Munslow, Alun. "A Reply to Richard King, 'The Discipline of Fact / The Freedom of Fiction?'" *Journal of American Studies* 26, no. 1 (April 1992): 90–93.
Murphree, Vanessa. *The Selling of Civil Rights: The Student Nonviolent Coordinating Committee and the Use of Public Relations*. New York: Routledge, 2006.
Nasaw, David. "Introduction, AHR Roundtable: Historians and Biography." *American Historical Review* 114, no. 3 (June 2009): 573–78.
Neal, Larry. "Any Day Now: Black Art and Black Liberation." In *Black Poets and Prophets: A Bold, Uncompromisingly Clear Blueprint for Black Liberation*, edited by Woodie King and Earl Anthony, 148–65. New York: Signet, 1972.
———. "The Black Contribution to American Letters: Part II: The Writer as Activist—1960 and After." In *The Black American Reference Book*, edited by Mabel Smythe, 767–89. Englewood Cliffs, N.J.: Prentice Hall, 1976.
Neary, John. "A Hero at Large: Julian Bond, a Militant inside the System." *Life*, November 8, 1968: 43–46.
———. *Julian Bond: Black Rebel*. New York: William Morrow, 1971.
Nelson, Alondra. "A Black Mass as Black Gothic: Myth and Bioscience in Black Cultural Nationalism." In *New Thoughts on the Black Arts Movement*, edited by Lisa Gail Collins and Margo Natalie Crawford, 137–53. New Brunswick, N.J.: Rutgers University Press, 2006.
Nelson, Jack. *Scoop: The Evolution of a Southern Reporter*. Jackson: University Press of Mississippi, 2013.
Newfield, Jack. *A Prophetic Minority: A Probing Study of the Origins and Development of the New Left*. New York: Signet, 1967. First published 1966.
———. "The Question of SNCC." *Nation*, July 19, 1965, 38–40.
———. "The Student Left: Revolt without Dogma." *Nation*, May 10, 1965, 491–95.
Nicholson, David. "A Commitment to Writing: A Conversation with Kathleen Collins Prettyman." *Black Film Review* 5, no. 1 (Winter 1988–1989): 6–15.
Norrell, Robert J. *Reaping the Whirlwind: The Civil Rights Movement in Tuskegee*. Chapel Hill: University of North Carolina Press, 1985.
Novick, Peter. *That Noble Dream: The "Objectivity Question" and the American Historical Profession*. New York: Cambridge University Press, 1989. First published in 1988.

Nussbaum, Martha C. *Love's Knowledge: Essays on Philosophy and Literature.* New York: Oxford University Press, 1990.

O'Brien, James P. "The New Left's Early Years." *Radical America* 2, no. 3 (May–June 1968): 1–25.

O'Dell, Jack. "Foundations of Racism in American Life." *Freedomways* 4, no. 4 (1964): 518–35.

———. "Life in Mississippi: An Interview with Mrs. Fannie Lou Hamer." *Freedomways* 5, no. 2 (1965): 231–42.

Olson, Lynne. *Freedom's Daughters: The Unsung Heroines of the Civil Rights Movement from 1830 to 1970.* New York: Simon and Schuster, 2001.

O'Malley, Seamus. *Making History New: Modernism and Historical Narrative.* Oxford, UK: Oxford University Press, 2015.

Payne, Charles. *I've Got the Light of Freedom: The Organizing Tradition and the Mississippi Freedom Struggle.* Berkeley: University of California Press, 1995.

Polletta, Francesca. "Contending Stories: Narrative in Social Movements." *Qualitative Sociology* 2, no. 4 (1998): 419–46.

———. *Freedom Is an Endless Meeting: Democracy in American Social Movements.* Chicago: University of Chicago Press, 2002.

———. "'It Was Like a Fever...': Narrative and Identity in Social Protest." *Social Problems* 45, no. 2 (May 1998): 137–59.

———. *It Was Like a Fever: Storytelling in Protest and Politics.* Chicago: University of Chicago Press, 2006.

———. "Plotting Protest: Mobilizing Stories in the 1960 Student Sit-Ins." In *Stories of Change: Narrative and Social Movements,* 31–51. New York: State University of New York Press, 2002.

———. "Strategy and Democracy in the New Left." In *The New Left Revisited,* edited by John McMillian and Paul Buhle, 156–77. Philadelphia: Temple University Press, 2003.

———. "The Structural Context of Civil Rights Claims: Southern Civil Rights Organizing, 1961–1966." *Law and Society Review* 34 (2000): 367–406.

Polsgrove, Carol. *Divided Minds: Intellectuals and the Civil Rights Movement.* New York: W. W. Norton, 2001.

Pratt, Mary Louise. "Arts of the Contact Zone." In *Ways of Reading,* edited by David Bartholomae and Anthony Petroksky, 528–42. New York: St. Martin's, 1999.

Priestley, Justine Tyrell. *By Gertrude Wilson: Dispatches of the 1960s from a White Writer in a Black World.* Edgartown, Mass.: Vineyard Stories, 2005.

Rabinowitz, Victor. *Unrepentant Leftist: A Lawyer's Memoir.* Urbana: University of Illinois Press, 1996.

Rahv, Philip. "The Cult of Experience in American Writing." *Partisan Review* 7 (November–December 1940): 412–24.

Raiford, Leigh. *Imprisoned in a Luminous Glare: Photography and the African American Freedom Struggle.* Chapel Hill: University of North Carolina Press, 2011.

Raines, Howell, ed. *My Soul Is Rested: The Story of the Civil Rights Movement in the Deep South.* New York: Penguin, 1983. First published 1977.

Rancière, Jacques. *The Politics of Aesthetics.* Translated by Gabriel Rockhill. New York: Continuum, 2004. First published 2000.

Reuben, J. Peter. "The Politics of Literature." in *Radical Future Pasts: Untimely Political Theory,* edited by Romand Coles, Mark Reinhardt, and George Shulman, 321–32. Lexington: University Press of Kentucky, 2014.

Riffel, Brent. "In the Storm: William Hansen and the Student Nonviolent Coordinating Committee in Arkansas, 1962–1967." In Wallace and Kirk, *Arsnick*, 23–24.
Riva, Sarah. "Desegregating Downtown Little Rock: The Field Reports of SNCC's Bill Hansen, October 23 to December 3, 1962." *Arkansas Historical Quarterly* 71 (Autumn 2012): 264–82.
Robbins, Tom. *Wild Ducks Flying Backwards*. New York: Bantam, 2005.
Roberts, Gene, and Hank Klibanoff. *The Race Beat: The Press, the Civil Rights Struggle, and the Awakening of a Nation*. New York: Vintage, 2006.
Robnett, Belinda. "African-American Women in the Civil Rights Movement, 1954–1965: Gender, Leadership, and Micromobilization." *American Journal of Sociology* 101, no. 6 (May 1996): 1661–93.
———. *How Long? How Long? African-American Women in the Struggle for Civil Rights*. New York: Oxford University Press, 1997.
———. "Women in SNCC: Ideology, Organizational Structure, and Leadership." In Ling and Monteith, *Gender and the Civil Rights Movement*, 131–68.
Rodgers, Carolyn. "Feelings of Sense." *Black World*, June 1970, 4–11.
Rogers, Kim Lacy. *Life and Death in the Delta: African American Narratives of Violence, Resilience, and Social Change*. New York: Palgrave Macmillan, 2006
———. *Righteous Lives: Narratives of the New Orleans Civil Rights Movement*. New York: New York University Press, 1993.
Rolo, Charles, ed. *Psychiatry in American Life*. Boston: Little, Brown, 1963.
Rothschild, Mary Aickin. *A Case of Black and White: Northern Volunteers and the Southern Freedom Summers, 1964–1965*. Westport, Conn.: Greenwood, 1982.
Rowell, Charles. "With Bloodstains to Testify": An Interview with Keorapetse Kgositsile." *Callaloo* 2 (February 1978): 23–42.
Rustin, Bayard. "The Meaning of the March on Washington." *Liberation* 8, no. 8 (October 1963): 11–13.
———. "The New Radicalism: Round III." *Partisan Review* 32, no. 4 (Fall 1965): 526–42.
Sacks, Karen Brodkin. *Caring by the Hour: Women, Work, and Organizing at Duke Medical Center*. Urbana: University of Illinois Press, 1988.
Salm, Nell. "The New Abolitionists." *Monthly Review* 16, no. 8 (January 1965): 562–66.
Sanders, Katrina M. *Intelligent and Effective Direction: The Fisk University Race Relations Institute and the Struggle for Civil Rights, 1944–1969*. New York: Peter Lang, 2005.
Saul, Scott. *Freedom Is, Freedom Ain't: Jazz and the Making of the Sixties*. Cambridge, Mass.: Harvard University Press, 2005.
Schraufnagel, Noel. *From Apology to Protest: The Black American Novel*. Deland, Fla.: Everett/Edwards, 1973.
Scott, James C. *Domination and the Arts of Resistance: Hidden Transcripts*. New Haven, Conn.: Yale University Press, 1990.
Sinsheimer, Joseph. "Never Turn Back: An Interview with Sam Block." *Southern Exposure* 25, no. 2 (Summer 1987): 42–43.
Smethurst, James. *The Black Arts Movement: Literary Nationalism in the 1960s and 1970s*. Chapel Hill: University of North Carolina Press, 2005.
———. "The Black Arts Movement and Historically Black Colleges and Universities." In *New Thoughts on the Black Arts Movement*, edited by Lisa Gail Collins and Margo Natalie Crawford, 75–91. New Brunswick, N.J.: Rutgers University Press, 2006.
Smethurst, James, and Howard Ramsby II. "Reform and Revolution, 1965–1976: The Black Aesthetic at Work." In *The Cambridge History of African American Literature*,

edited by Maryemma Graham and Jerry W. Ward Jr., 405-50. New York: Cambridge University Press, 2011.

Smith, David Lionel. "The Black Arts Movement and Its Critics." *American Literary History* 3, no. 1 (Spring 1991): 93-111.

———. "Chicago Poets, OBAC, and the Black Arts Movement." In *The Black Columbiad: Defining Moments in African American Literature and Culture*, edited by Werner Sollors and Maria Diedrich, 253-64. Cambridge, Mass.: Harvard University Press, 1994.

Smith, Lillian. *Killers of the Dream*. New York: W. W. Norton, 1949.

———. *The Winner Names the Age: A Collection of Writings*. Edited by Michelle Cliff. New York: W. W. Norton, 1978.

Shawn, Michelle Smith. *Photography on the Color Line: W. E. B. Du Bois, Race and Visual Culture*. Durham, N.C.: Duke University Press, 2004.

Spears, Deanne Milan. *Modern College Reading: Techniques with Exercises*. New York: Scribner, 1971.

Spencer, Robyn C., and Wesley Hogan. "Telling Freedom Stories from the Inside Out: Internal Politics and Movement Cultures in SNCC and the Black Panther Party." In Crosby, *Civil Rights History from the Ground Up*, 330-64.

Spigelman, Candace. *Personally Speaking: Experience as Evidence in Academic Discourse*. Carbondale: Southern Illinois University Press, 2004.

Steedman, Carolyn. "Something She Called a Fever: Michelet, Derrida and Dust." *American Historical Review* 106, no. 4 (2001): 1159-80.

Showalter, Elaine. *Faculty Towers: The Academic Novel and its Discontents*. Philadelphia: University of Pennsylvania Press, 2005.

Smiley, Tavis. *The Covenant in Action*. Los Angeles: Smiley Group, 2006.

Spearman, Walter, and Sylvan Meyer. *Racial Crisis and the Press*. Atlanta: Southern Regional Council, 1960.

Spears, Deanne Milan, ed. *Modern College Reading: Techniques with Exercises*. New York: Scribner, 1971.

Spellman, A. B. *Things I Must Have Known*. Minneapolis: Coffee House Press, 2008.

Stearns, Peter N. "Historical Analysis in the Study of Emotion." *Motivation and Emotion* 10, no. 2 (1986): 185-93.

Sterling, Dorothy. "What's Black and White and Read All Over?" *English Journal* 58, no. 6 (September 1969): 817-32.

Stoper, Emily. *The Student Nonviolent Coordinating Committee: The Growth of Radicalism in a Civil Rights Organization*. New York: Carlson, 1989.

Street, Joe. *The Culture War in the Civil Rights Movement*. Gainesville: University Press of Florida, 2007.

———. "From Beloved Community to Imagined Community." In *From Sit-Ins to SNCC: The Student Civil Rights Movement in the 1960s*, edited by Iwan Morgan and Philip Davies, 116-34. Gainesville: University Press of Florida, 2012.

Sturkey, William, and John N. Hale, eds. *To Write in the Light of Freedom: The Newspapers of the 1964 Mississippi Freedom Schools*. Jackson: University Press of Mississippi, 2016.

Styron, William. *The Confessions of Nat Turner*. New York: Random House, 1967.

———. "This Quiet Dust." *Harper's Magazine*, April 1965, 134-46.

Swaim, Lawrence. "Hippies: the Love Thing." *North American Review* 252, no. 5 (September 1967): 16-18.

Taylor, Clyde. *Vietnam and Black America: An Anthology of Protest and Resistance*. New York: Anchor, 1973.

Tewkesbury, Paul. "Sex, Violence, and Suffering: Rethinking Martin Luther King, Jr., in Julius Lester's *And All Our Wounds Forgiven.*" MELUS (Multi-Ethnic Literature of the U.S.) 40, no. 4 (2015): 129–49.
Theoharis, Jeanne F., and Komozi Woodard, eds. *Groundwork: Local Black Freedom Movements in America.* New York: New York University Press, 2005.
———. *Want to Start a Revolution? Radical Women in the Black Freedom Struggle.* New York: New York University Press, 2009.
Thomas, Lorenzo. "The Need to Speak: Tom Dent and the Shaping of a Black Aesthetic." *African American Review* 40, no. 2 (2006): 325–38.
Tidwell, John Edgar and Steven C. Tracy, eds. *After Winter: The Art and Life of Sterling A. Brown.* Oxford: Oxford University Press, 2009.
Tisdale, John R. "Different Assignments, Different Perspectives: How Reporters Reconstruct the Emmett Till Civil Rights Murder Trial." *Oral History Review* 29, no. 1 (Winter–Spring 2002): 39–58.
Tuck, Stephen G. N. *Beyond Atlanta: The Struggle for Racial Equality in Georgia, 1940–1980.* Athens: University of Georgia Press, 2001.
Tyson, Timothy B. *Blood Done Sign My Name: A True Story.* New York: Crown, 2004.
———. *Radio Free Dixie: Robert F. Williams and the Roots of Black Power.* Chapel Hill: University of North Carolina Press, 1999.
Umoja, Akinyele O. "1964: The Beginning of the End of Nonviolence in the Mississippi Freedom Movement." *Radical History Review* 85 (Winter 2003): 201–26.
Van Deburg, William L. *New Day in Babylon: The Black Power Movement and American Culture, 1965–1975.* Chicago: University of Chicago Press, 1992.
Visser-Maessen, Laura. *Robert Parris Moses: A Life in Civil Rights and Leadership at the Grassroots.* Chapel Hill: University of North Carolina Press, 2016.
Walker, Margaret. *This Is My Century: New and Collected Poems.* Athens: University of Georgia Press, 1989.
Wallach, Jennifer Jensen. *Closer to the Truth than Any Fact: Memoir, Memory, Jim Crow.* Athens: University of Georgia Press, 2008.
Wallach, Jennifer Jensen, and John A. Kirk, eds. *Arsnick: The Student Nonviolent Coordinating Committee in Arkansas.* Fayetteville: University of Arkansas Press, 2011.
Walmsley, Mark Joseph. "Tell It Like It Isn't: SNCC and the Media." *Journal of American Studies* 48, no. 1 (2014): 291–308.
Walter, E. V. *Terror and Resistance: A Study of Political Violence.* New York: Oxford University Press, 1969.
Walzer, Michael. "A Cup of Coffee and a Seat." *Dissent,* Spring 1960, 111–20.
Ward, Brian. *Just My Soul Responding: Rhythm and Blues, Black Consciousness and Race Relations since 1945.* London: Routledge, 1998.
Ward, Stephen M., ed. *Pages from a Black Radical's Notebook: A James Boggs Reader.* Detroit: Wayne State University Press, 2011.
———. "The Third World Women's Alliance: Black Feminist Radicalism and Black Power Politics." In *The Black Power Movement: Rethinking the Civil Rights-Black Power Era,* edited by Peniel Joseph, 119–43. New York: Routledge, 2006.
Warren, Robert Penn. "Two for SNCC." *Commentary,* April 1965, 38–48.
———. *Who Speaks for the Negro?* New York: Vintage, 1966. First published 1965.
Washington, Harriet A. *The Dark History of Medical Experimentation on Black Americans from Colonial Times to the Present.* New York: Doubleday, 2007.
Washington, Mary Helen. *Black-Eyed Susans: Classic Stories by and about Black Women.* New York: Anchor, 1975.

———. "Jean Wheeler Smith." In *Black-Eyed Susans/Midnight Birds: Stories by and about Black Women*, 18–20. 1988; New York: Anchor, 1990.

Watkins, Mel. *On The Real Side: A History of African American Comedy*. Chicago: Chicago Review Press, 1999. First published 1994.

Watson, Bruce. *Freedom Summer: The Savage Season That Made Mississippi Burn and Made America a Democracy*. New York: Viking, 2010.

Watters, Pat. *The Angry Middle-Aged Man*. New York: Grossman, 1976.

———. *Down to Now: Reflections on the Southern Civil Rights Movement*. Athens: University of Georgia Press, 1993. First published 1971.

———. *Encounter with the Future*. Atlanta: Southern Regional Council, 1965.

———. "The South and the Nation." *New South* 24, no. 4 (Fall 1969): 2–29.

Watters, Pat, and Reese Cleghorn. *Climbing Jacob's Ladder: The Arrival of Negroes in Southern Politics*. New York: Harcourt, Brace and World, 1967.

Weil, Susan. *In a Madhouse's Din: Civil Rights Coverage by Mississippi's Daily Press*. Westport, Conn.: Praeger, 2002.

Wendt, Simon. *The Spirit and the Shotgun: Armed Resistance and the Struggle for Civil Rights*. Gainesville: University Press of Florida, 2007.

Whitt, Margaret Early, ed. *Short Stories of the Civil Rights Movement: An Anthology*. Athens: University of Georgia Press, 2006.

Wiegand, Wayne A., and Shirley A. Weigand. *The Desegregation of Public Libraries in the Jim Crow South: Civil Rights and Local Activism*. Baton Rouge: Louisiana State University Press, 2018.

Wilkins, Fanon Che. "The Making of Black Internationalists: SNCC and Africa before the Launching of Black Power, 1960–1965." *Journal of African American History* 92, no. 4 (2007): 467–90.

Williams, Juan, ed. *My Soul Looks Back in Wonder: Voices of the Civil Rights Experience*. New York: Sterling Publishing, 2004.

Williams, Sherley Anne. *Give Birth to Brightness*. New York: Dial, 1968.

Woodruff, Nan. *American Congo: The African American Freedom Struggle in the Delta*. Chapel Hill: University of North Carolina Press, 2012. First published 2003.

Wright, Richard. *12 Million Black Voices*. New York: Thunder's Mouth Press, 1988. First published 1941.

Zinn, Howard. *Albany: A Study in National Responsibility*. Atlanta: Southern Regional Council, 1962.

———. "Changing People: Negro Civil Rights and the Colleges." *Massachusetts Review* 5, no. 4 (Summer 1964): 60–70.

———. "Finishing School for Pickets." *Nation*, August 6, 1960, 71–73.

———. "Kennedy: The Reluctant Emancipator." *Nation*, December 1, 1962, 373–75.

———. "The Limits of Nonviolence" *Freedomways* 4, no. 1 (1964): 143–48.

———. "SNCC: The Battle-Scarred Youngsters." *Nation*, October 5, 1963: 193–96.

———. *SNCC: The New Abolitionists*. Cambridge, Mass.: South End Press, 2002. First published 1964.

———. *The Southern Mystique*. New York: Simon and Schuster, 1964.

———. *You Can't Be Neutral on a Moving Train: A Personal History of Our Times*. Boston: Beacon, 2002. First published 1994.

Žižek, Slavoj. *The Fragile Absolute*. New York: Verso, 2000.

———. "The Lesson of Rancière." Afterword to *The Politics of Aesthetics*, by Jacques Rancière, 65–75. New York: Continuum, 2004.

Index

Abel, Elizabeth, 44
Abernathy, Ralph, 297n68
Abernethy, Thomas, 205
Act of Conscience, An (L. Holt), 119–20, 121–24, 194
Adams, Victoria Gray, 27
Adickes, Sandra, 15, 152
African American studies. *See* black studies
Africa tours, 190, 302n75
Afro-American Poetics (Baker), 303n18
Agee, James, 128–29
Albany, Ga., xvii, 5, 52, 54, 83, 84–85, 89, 104–5; Abernathy on, 297n68; Barrett, 244; De Lissovoy, 36, 47–48, 83; federal government and, 117; in fiction, 50–51, 52–53, 196; Fleming, 106; *Freedom in the Air*, 279n53; Bernice Johnson Reagon, 118; Watters, 110, 112; Zinn, 117
Algebra Project, 102, 283n144, 314n37
Allen, Chude Pamela Parker, 110, 247, 262n159
Allen, Ivan, 262n154
Allen, Louis, 11, 227, 228
Allen, Ralph, 27
American Congo (Woodruff), 20
American Negro Slave Revolts (Aptheker), 300n34
Americus, Georgia, 35, 134, 246
Amite County, Miss., 77; in fiction, 227–30
Amos 'n' Andy, 60
And All Our Wounds Forgiven (Lester), 7, 24, 31, 71, 124, 221, 223–35, 237–38, 240, 250; stream of consciousness in, 213; Tewkesbury on, 234, 310n30
Anderson, S. E., 74, 174, 176, 184
Anderson, William G., 8
Angelou, Maya, 172
Ani, Marimba (Dona Richards), 10, 19, 159
Anointed to Fly (Wade Gayles), 15, 243
Appadurai, Arjun 42

Aptheker, Herbert, 179; *American Negro Slave Revolts*, 300n34
Arkansas, 3, 5, 12, 83; Little Rock, 37, 279n58; Pine Bluff, 95
Arsnick (Wallach and Kirk), 12, 83
Ashmore, Harry, 105
As I Lay Dying (Faulkner), 214, 217
Atlanta, 21, 218, 262n154; Atlanta–Albany Freedom Ride (1961), 107; Commission on Interracial Cooperation, 277n30; Gwen Robinson, 244; SNCC conference (1960), 91–92, 114; SNCC headquarters, 62, 75, 76, 272n23; tent city, 199; Askia Touré, 175; Vine City, 187, 302n69; Michael Wright, 156
Atlanta Inquirer, 86
Atlanta Journal, 81, 110, 112
Auerbach, Erich, 12
Autobiography of Miss Jane Pittman, The (Gaines), 140–41
Avery, Annie Pearl, 122, 182, 244, 300n46

Baker, Elaine DeLott. *See* DeLott, Elayne
Baker, Ella, xvi, 115, 116, 143, 253n2; as *fundi*, 136; storytelling paradigm, 191
Baker, Houston, 14, 180; *Afro-American Poetics*, 303n18
Baldwin, James, 97, 142, 195, 250
Ballantine Books, 84–85
Bambara, Toni Cade, 194, 219
"band of brothers and sisters" (SNCC phrase), 22, 69
Baraka, Amiri (LeRoi Jones), 123–24, 157, 172, 173–74, 176, 177, 193; *Black Fire* (with Neal), 174, 187, 211; *Dutchman*, 177, 178–79; echoed by Forman, 192; SNCC anniversary conference, 245
Barbour, Floyd B., 162
Barbour, Hayley, 290n37
Barnett, Ross, 138
Barrett, Joyce, 244

343

Barry, Marion, 70, 76, 256n39
Battle, Randy, 50, 95, 181
battle fatigue. *See* burnout and posttraumatic stress
Beacon Press, 115–16
Beal, Frances, 43, 167, 182
Bearden, Romare, 176
Beardslee, William R., 23
Beckett, Samuel, 79
Belfrage, Sally, 115, 152, 225, 291n53
Bell, Daniel, 49
Bell, Jeanie, 83
Bellamy-Powell, Fay, 16, 100, 200, 220, 244
Benjamin, Walter, 93, 209–10, 211
Bennett, Lerone, 36, 159–60
Berrey, Stephen, 47
Bess, George, 16
Bevel, James, xvi, 268n73
Bingham, Stephen, 197
Birmingham, Ala., 79, 182, 196, 199; Avery, 122, 182; Gregory, 289n18; Holt on, 115, 122; MLK, 238; Sixteenth Street Baptist Church, 186, 298n73; Watters, 79, 111
Bishop, Gloria. *See* Wade Gayles, Gloria
Black and White in American Culture (Chametzky and Kaplan), 298n77
Black Arts Convention, Detroit: first (1966), 174; second (1967), 156
Black Arts Movement (BAM), 15, 30, 156, 157, 160, 171–82, 242; *Freedomways*, 158; in SNCC anniversary conference, 245; SNCC occlusion and, xv, 82; urban focus, 167
Black-Eyed Susans/Midnight Birds (M. H. Washington), 165, 166
Black Fire (Baraka and Neal), 174, 187, 211
Black Folktales (Lester), 58
black informants (police informers), 216, 217
Black Jacob (Mahoney), 24, 192–96, 198–212, 219, 220, 222, 229, 305–6n50; Derby and, xviii, 199, 209
Black Natchez (Pincus and Neuman), 216
Black Panther Party, 5, 17–18, 182, 184, 243
Black Power, 4, 15, 70, 156, 160, 162, 171, 172, 176, 242; *Black Fire*, 187; Sterling Brown, 14; Carmichael, 27, 70, 115, 156, 157, 160, 162, 174; Cobb, 185, 186; in *Ebony*, 159–60; Forman, 162, 184, 191–92; Holt, 121, 180–82; House on, 173, 176; Joyce Ladner on, 70; Lester, 25, 58, 186, 36; Mahoney on, 207; MFDP and, 3; Patton, 186; Poussaint on, 236; slogan, 19, 113, 187, 210; Jean Wheeler Smith, 161–62; SNCC positions, 5, 175, 276n22; symbolic fist, 16, 156–57, 187; Wade Gayles, 187
Black Power Revolt (Barbour), 162
Black Protest (Grant), 20, 114–15
Blackside, Inc., 8, 196
black studies, 130, 158, 177, 298n3
Blackwell, Unita, 70, 135
Black Women's Liberation Committee, 167
Black World, 160, 295n29
Blair, Sara, 89
BLKARTSOUTH, 15
Block, Sam, 63–64, 214, 224, 225, 228; "Day in a Mississippi Court," 97–99, 204; in fiction, 144; in poetry, 22
Blood River (House), 7, 188–89, 243
Bloody Lowndes (Jeffries), 9, 132
Bond, Julian, xv–xvi, 1–2, 64, 86, 105–6, 250–51; advice to journalists, 289n7; Black Power, 160; college major, 94; as communications director, 75, 76–77, 87, 105–6, 244; on electoral campaigns, 205; eulogies for Louis Allen, 11; *Eyes on the Prize*, 8; on field-workers as "protective barrier," 143; on Forman and office sweeping, 61; on Forman and record keeping, 77; on *Freedomways*, 158; on "frustrated novelists," 83; Georgia legislature, 89, 218–19, 244, 279n58, 302n69; *Gonna Sit at the Welcome Table* (with Lewis), 102; on Grant biography of Baker, 115; on Holt, 120; "I Too Hear America Singing," 25, 187; Kennard and, 137; on local people, 133; Long advice to, 81–83; Lowndes County, Ala., 199; poetry, 25, 86–87, 124, 187, 279n63; Rabinowitz and, 279n58; *Southern Exposure*, 73; Southern Poverty Law Center, 246; view of Bradens, 80; view of journalists, 99; Zinn and, 279n63
boycotts, 45–46, 111, 205; in fiction, 41
Braden, Anne, 80, 85–86, 97, 106
Braden, Carl, 80, 97
Branch, Taylor, 97, 137, 234
Branch, William, 155
Breazeale, C. E. 137
Breines, Wini, 23
"bridge leaders" and "centerwomen," 142, 149–50, 154, 293n87

Bridges, Ruby, 126
Broadside Press, 7, 26, 190
Brooks, Gwendolyn, 245
Brooks, Paul, 234, 266n42
Brown, Claude, 219
Brown, Ed, 5, 18, 57, 67, 72, 145
Brown, H. Rap, 58, 67, 68, 156–57, 180; *Die, Nigger, Die*, 193
Brown, Joyce, 13
Brown, Luvaughn, 63, 90
Brown, Rosellen, 13
Brown, Sterling, 14, 72, 123, 124, 141–42, 145
Browning, Joan, 35, 75–76, 263n171
Brown-Nagin, Tomiko, 121, 124
Brown v. Board of Education, 108, 119, 125
Bryant, C. C., xvi, 135
Bryant, Jerry H., 7, 195–96
Bryant, Ora, 135
Buffington, John, 102
Bullins, Ed, 172; *Electronic Nigger*, 177–78
Burlage, Dorothy Dawson, 6
Burlage, Rob, 6
burnout and posttraumatic stress, 24, 31, 125, 126, 204, 220–40
Butler, Angeline, 144, 245, 313n24
Butler, Judith, 134
But Now I See (Hobson), 111–12

Campbell, Cull, 117
Camus, Albert, 178, 185, 229, 299n29
Cannon, Terry, 24, 29, 47, 91, 94
Carew, Jan, 195, 303n14
Carmichael, Stokely (Kwame Ture), 14, 92, 100, 156; Baker on, 180; Black Power, 70, 156, 160, 162; on Sterling Brown, 142; in fiction, 249; in "Four Faces from SNCC," 27; on Freedom Rides, 198; on Holt, 120; international conferences, 157; Lowndes County (Ala.) tent city, 200; on Mahoney, 199; *New Republic* forum, 162; "paradoxes of King historiography," 234; in poetry, 249; *Ready for the Revolution* (with Thelwell), 7, 66, 73, 239; SNCC chair election, 237; "Starmichael," 26; on Turnbow, 135; on "unlearning," 281n97; view of local people, 133, 135, 141–42; "What We Want," 174
Carolina Israelite, 47
Carson, Clayborne, 8, 17, 82, 106, 152, 189, 241, 246; on Bond poem, 25; on countercultural values, 56; on King historiography, 234; *In Struggle*, 2, 3, 4, 16, 254n8, 256n50; on Moses as model, 259n93; on myth, 222; on organizers, 17, 102; *Student Voice* and *Movement* anthologies 9; on writing as activism, 256n50
Carter, John, 123
Carter, Mae Bertha, 115
Caruth, Cathy, 236, 238
Caston, Billy Jack, 64
casualties. *See* burnout and posttraumatic stress
Catacombs, The (Demby), 203
Centaur, The (Updike), 54
Césaire, Aimé, 189
Chafe, William, 85, 132
Chambers, Iain, 242
Chametzky, Jules, 294n13; *Black and White in American Culture* (with Kaplan), 298n77
Chaney, James, 12, 52, 98, 143, 148, 171, 189, 246; Cobb and, 292n80; memorial service, 151
Chase, Lendell, 122
Chatfield, Jack, 22, 33, 83, 86, 92, 94, 105
Chicago, 39, 40, 41, 77, 138, 140, 160, 161
Chicago Defender, 28, 37, 77, 140
Children, The (Halberstam), 108–10
Children of Crisis (Coles), 126–29, 139–40, 223
Childress, Alice, 155
Christian, Barbara, 175
Churchwell, Robert, 108
Cieciorka, Bobbi, 89
Cieciorka, Frank, 89, 157
"circle of trust" (SNCC phrase), 22, 181, 220, 231, 240
Circle of Trust, A (Greenberg), 22
Civil Rights Act of 1964, 46, 232, 286n63
Civil Rights and the Idea of Freedom (R. H. King), 6, 17, 209
Clark, Jim, 83, 133
Clark, Kenneth B., 125, 176, 287n89
Clark, Septima, 46, 268n75, 313n24
Clarke, John Henrik, 155; *William Styron's Nat Turner*, 179–80
Clarksdale, Mississippi, 47, 269n99, 312n45
Clayton, Claude F., 205
Cleghorn, Reese, 83, 102, 111, 241
Climbing Jacob's Ladder (Watters and Cleghorn), 83, 102, 111

Closer to the Truth than Any Fact (Wallach), 11–12, 257n64
Cobb, Charles, 1, 7–8, 9–10, 14, 61, 90–91, 185–91, 244–45; Africa tours, 190; ancestors, 69; in *Black Fire*, 174; "Black Power for Black People," 113; in *Black Protest* (Grant), 115; "Charlie's Poem" ("I Want to Say"), 173, 183–84; college major, 94; commemoration of "crazy" blacks, 68; on communications team, 87, 199; conferences, 157; Cultural Program Committee, 10; *Don't Start Me to Talking* foreword, 74; eulogy for Forman, 13–14; *Everywhere Is Yours*, 190–91; feelings about historical tourism, 292n80; on field reports, 80; Flute Publications, 19; Freedom Schools, 148; haiku, 185; *In the Furrows of the World*, 91, 185, 186, 187, 302n66; "In the Furrows of the World" ("Nation") 26, 186; letter to James Eastland, 296n59; "Lowndes County Staff Sketches," 249; on "middle-class . . . control," 170; "Most People," 249–50; "movement is . . . organizing," 103; on *Negro Digest*, 160; *New Republic* forum, 142; northern roots, 133; O'Neal on, 245; *On the Road to Freedom*, 12, 27, 35, 102; *Radical Equations* (with Moses), 27, 102; search for Jesse Harris, 239; SNCC Legacy Project, xix; "Story of Charlie Cobb," 43; storytelling skills, 18; *Student Voice*, 102; in Tanzania, 190; *This Nonviolent Stuff'll Get You Killed*, 53, 182, 202; TV show idea, 59; Vietnam War, 33, 184, 185, 186; "Word You Want?," 174–75; writing as space, 247
COFO. *See* Council of Federated Organizations
Cohen, Miriam, 53
Coleman, J. P., 139
Coles, Robert, 6, 14, 52, 86, 106, 125–29, 149, 284n13; catalog of emotional overload, 223; *Children of Crisis*, 126–29, 139–40, 223; Clark on, 287n89; on *Climbing Jacob's Ladder*, 111; confidentiality concerns, 132; on emotional truths, 225; on Greene, 214; on MLK's view of burnout, 225; Sweeney and, 214; sweeping assignment, 61–62; William Carlos Williams and, 127, 287–88n97

Collins, Kathleen, 37, 54, 56, 73; "Whatever Happened to Interracial Love?," 40, 54–55, 73, 243–44; *Whatever Happened to Interracial Love?*, 54, 248–49
Collins, Nina Lorez, 54
Colston, David, Sr., 201
Columbus, Miss., 97, 155
Commission on Interracial Cooperation, 277
Confessions of Nat Turner (Styron), 68, 179–80, 298n77
Congress of Racial Equality (CORE), 2, 81, 272n38; Cobb, 43; Dennis, xvi; Garrett, 177; Louis, 18; McKissick, 155–56; Raymond, 96; Charles Sherrod view, 105; Jerome Smith, 144, 146, 227, 272n38
Conrad, Joseph, 216
Cooper, Annie Lee, 133
CORE. *See* Congress of Racial Equality
Cortez, Jayne, 175
Cothran, John Ed, 97–98
Council of Federated Organizations (COFO), xvi, 18, 27, 96, 143; Coles, 127, 129; demise, 218; Greenwood, Miss., 291n53, 301n49; Holt, 119; Lowenstein, 8; McComb, Miss., 13; McCord, 118; Nash, 114; Oxford, Ohio, 127; Ponder, 159; Jerome Smith, 146; Sutherland, 87
Courage to Dissent (Brown-Nagin), 121, 124
Cowan, Paul, 169–70; *The Making of an Un-American*, 149, 265n22
Cox, Courtland, 14, 33, 157; Africa tours, 190; Drum and Spear Bookstore, 190; Junebug, 58; Mahoney and, 198; in poetry, 249; SNCC Legacy Project, xix; Supersnick, 57; Vietnam War, 182–83; Washington, D.C., 190, 198
Cox, Harold, 205
"crazy Negroes" (mischaracterization), 68–69, 139–40, 216
Crisis, 9, 194, 196
Crisis of the Negro Intellectual, The (Cruse), 171, 194
Crmvet.org, xix, 23, 74
Crosby, Emilye, 2, 17, 132, 227, 239
Cruse, Harold, 174; *Crisis of the Negro Intellectual*, 171, 194
Culture War in the Civil Rights Movement, The (Street), 15, 258n81
Cummings, Pete, 86
Curry, Connie, 115, 116, 253n7, 256n36, 276n20

Curry, George, 102, 283n142
Curtis, Archie, 197

Dabbs, James McBride, 24, 111
Dada, Mukasa. *See* Ricks, Willie
Dahmer, Vernon, 139
Dammond, Margaret (Peggy), 54, 167, 243, 244, 313n14
Daniel, James, 50
Daniel, Pete, 91, 167, 280n91
Daniels, Carolyn, 135
Danner, Margaret, 15
Danville, Va., 45, 47, 79–80, 89, 122–24
Davis, Jack E., 197, 304n21
Davis, Thulani, 179
Dawley, Edward A., 121–22, 124, 287n76
Deacons for Defense, 147, 151
Death of White Sociology (Ladner), 130
Deep in My Heart (Kunstler), 27, 124–25
Deep in Our Hearts (Curry et al.), 28
Deep South Says Never (J. B. Martin), 84, 85
De La Beckwith, Byron, 225
De Lissovoy, Peter, 28, 36, 83, 268n82, 269n84; *Feelgood*, 36–37, 47–53, 55, 84, 151, 280n75; *Great Pool Jump and Other Stories*, 48, 254n1
DeLott, Elayne (Elaine DeLott Baker), 18, 28, 62, 78; jail writings, 95–97, 99
Demby, William, 203
Democratic National Convention: Atlantic City (1964), 33, 66; Chicago (1956), 39
Dennis, Dave, xvi
Dent, Tom, 4, 15, 138, 174, 175, 177
Derby, Doris, 10, 14, 147; on Mahoney, xviii, 199, 209, 212, 305n38
Derrida, Jacques, 13
Devine, Annie, 27, 135
Diamond, Dion, 18
Dicker/sun, Glenda, 177
Die, Nigger, Die (H. Rap Brown), 193
Diop, Alioune, 190
"Direct Action" (Thelwell), 36, 42–47, 49, 53, 72, 193, 220
Dittmer, John, 2, 26, 120, 139, 149, 152, 193, 203; *Good Doctors*, 306n54; *Local People*, 31, 36, 222
Dixon, David, 77
Doar, John, 35, 64
Dollard, John, 72, 145
Donaldson, Ivanhoe, 90–91, 122, 155, 190, 248–49, 280n85, 314n36

Don't Start Me to Talking (J. O'Neal), 66, 67, 72; Cobb foreword, 74
Douglas, Ellen, 304n23
Down to Now (Watters), 110–14
Drake, St. Clair, 38
Dreamer (C. Johnson), 233
Drummond, Dock, 205
Duberman, Martin, 148
Du Bois, W. E. B., 68, 77, 114, 123, 162, 195
Dutchman (Jones), 177, 178–79
Duties, Pleasures, and Conflicts (Thelwell), 142; "Fish Are Jumping an' the Cotton Is High," 72, 92–94, 142. *See also* "Organizer, The"

Eagles, Charles, 261n137
Eastland, James, 205, 296n59
Ebony, 159–60, 193
Edmonds (Spellman), Karen, xi, 175, 190
Education of a Harvard Guy (Perdew), 269n84
Education of a Harvard Guy (C. L. Williams), 246
Electronic Nigger (Bullins), 177–78
Eliot, T. S., 91
Ellison, Ralph, 29, 35, 72; *Invisible Man*, 203
Else, Jon, 8, 196
Elton, Geoffrey, 118–19
Emerson, Ralph Waldo, 270
Epstein, Joseph, 287n89
Ethridge, Tom, 107
Euben, J. Peter, 103, 243
eulogies, 11, 13–14, 26, 278n43
Evans, Mari, 193, 194
Evans, Walker, 128
Evers, Charles, 68, 205–6
Evers, James, 68
Evers, Medgar, xvi, 68, 137, 138, 139, 195, 225
Everywhere Is Yours (Cobb), 190–91
Eyes on the Prize, 8, 9, 196, 256n43, 260n127
Eyes on the Prize II, 8–9

Fabio, Sarah Webster, 155, 156
Fairclough, Adam, 104
Falling Pieces of a Broken Sky (Lester), 231
Farber, Jerry, 33
Farnum, Eric, 200–201
Faulkner, William, 94, 127, 215, 218, 304n23; *As I Lay Dying*, 214, 217
Fayette County, Tenn., 140, 141, 200

FBI, 5, 8, 63, 64, 156, 228, 272n38
Featherstone, Ralph, 157, 190
Feelgood (De Lissovoy), 36–37, 47–53, 55, 84, 151, 280n75
Feifer, George, 125
Felski, Rita, 242
feminism: evolving in SNCC, 166–67, 182, 185, 243, 296n58, 297n61; misunderstanding about SNCC and, 166–67, 297n62, 310–11n33
Ferdinand, Val (Kalamu ya Salaam), 15
Fiedler, Leslie, 35, 48, 268–69n82
field reports, 75–103; Bingham's, 197; in *Black Protest*, 114; Kates's, 218; Nicholas poetry in, 278n47; O'Neal's, 70; Payne on, 29; in *SNCC* (Zinn), 131; Watters and Cleghorn on, 241
Fields, Arthur C., 37–38, 265n33; *World without Heroes*, 38
films: Ella Baker documentary, 115; *Black Natchez*, 216; Julian Bond documentary, 307n69; Dorie Ladner documentary, 244; movement exploitation genre, 51, 269n98; novelizations, 180; *Panola*, 216
Fine, Gary Alan, 247
Fire in the Flint, The (White), 203
"Fish Are Jumping an' the Cotton Is High" (Thelwell), 72, 92–94, 142
Fisk University, 109, 110, 175; black writers' conferences, 155, 172; Lester, 223, 235, 260n121
Fleming, Cynthia Griggs, 16, 167, 298n73
Fleming, Karl, 106–7, 129
Flute Publications, 19, 58, 186
Foley, Barbara, 13, 112
Foner, Eric, 19
Foote, Shelby, 13
Forman, James, 1, 11, 15–16, 26, 63, 104–5, 156, 216; anger, 175; Ballantine book proposal, 84–85; black doctor short story, 203; Black Power book idea, 162; Anne Braden on, 85–86; Cobb eulogy for, 13–14; college major, 94; Cortez and, 175; Danville, Va., 122; in fiction, 143; field reports and documentation, 29, 75, 76, 77–78; Fisk writers' conference (1966), 155; in "Four Faces from SNCC," 27; *Freedomways* piece on nonviolence, 89; *High Tide of Black Resistance*, 141, 192, 302–3n85; Holt and, 121; on Holt, 104; internationalism, 157, 190; "janitorial research," 61, 62; Leflore County (Miss.) jail, 62, 114; "Liberation Will Come from a Black Thing," 16; Lyon on, 287n78; on Mahoney, 198; *The Making of Black Revolutionaries*, 26–27, 37, 40, 89–90, 141, 241–42; "Mother Africa," 191–92; "One Man, One Vote," 19; on "our little histories," 22; PASOA, 6; poetry, 191–92; reparations demand, 302–3n85; "river of no return," 4; "Rock Bottom" and *Rock Bottom*, 100–102, 142; *Sammy Younge Jr.*, 54, 193; "Somewhere in Glory," 140; "Song Festival," 15; Sutherland view, 261n135; "Thin White Line," xviii, 28–29, 36, 37–42, 49, 53–54, 55, 182, 220; "thin white line" (metaphor), 164; Vietnam War, 184–85; view of journalists, 99; "we are all a book," 250; writing as action, 177, 241
Foss, Daniel, 122
Foucault, Michael, 312n45
Framed! (C. R. Martin), 113
Franz, Marge, 142
Frazier, E. Franklin, 32, 54
Freedom Now Brick Company, 162
Freedom Rides, 18, 81, 85, 107, 120; Garrett, 177; Jesse Harris, 239; Mahoney, 198; McLaurin, 198; MLK, 234–35
Freedom Schools, 15, 37, 148, 159; Cobb on, 185; Kennard as subject, 138; Mahoney and, 198; McComb, Miss., 13; workshops, 135
Freedom Singers, 19, 119, 258n83
freedom songs. *See* songs and singing
Free Southern Theater (FST), 10, 14–15, 66, 90, 147; Derby ethos, 14; "Frankie Mae" (Smith), 167–68; Holly Springs, Miss., 258n83; Holt support of, 121; *In White America* (Duberman), 148; logo, 174; McComb, 70; Nicholas, 7, 90, 146–47; O'Neal ethos, 59–60, 66–67; *Waiting for Godot* (Beckett), 79
Freedom Summer, xvi, 2, 100, 148, 159; Coles, 127; in *Freshwater Road*, 146–53, 154; Ganz, 77; Lester, 223, 240; Lowenstein, 8; McCord account, 96; volunteers' hometown media, 87; Weaver, 57
Freedomways, 2, 10, 89, 90, 105–6, 138, 139, 158–59, 294–95n15
Freeman, Rosemary, 205

Index   349

Freshwater Road (Nicholas), 7, 15, 19, 94, 146–53, 154, 221, 226, 244
Friedman, Leon, 125
Friends of SNCC, 23, 25, 114, 175
From Apology to Protest (Schraufnagel), 196, 204
FST. *See* Free Southern Theater
Fuller, Hoyt, 24, 155, 156, 159–61, 163, 164, 172, 245; on critical blind spot, 193, 195
"fundi" (Swahili word) 136, 241

Gaines, Ernest, 140–41
Ganz, Marshall, 77, 276n13, 289n14
Garman, Betty, 87
Garrett, Jimmy, 135, 157, 170, 172, 176, 177, 190; in *Black Fire*, 174; on leaders and the press, 235; San Francisco State, 177; *We Own the Night*, 177, 182, 187
Garrow, David, 22, 104
Gayles, Gloria Wade. *See* Wade Gayles, Gloria
Gelfand, David, 261–62n150
Genovese, Eugene, 118, 179–80
Giovanni, Nikki, 156, 163, 175, 256n36
Gober, Bertha, 18
Golden, Harry, 47, 268n78
Gonna Sit at the Welcome Table (Bond and Lewis), 102
Good, Paul, 106
Good Doctors (Dittmer), 306n54
Goodman, Andrew, 12, 52, 98, 143, 148, 171, 189, 246
Gorton, D., 106
Graham, Donald E., 286n61
Grant, Joanne, 19, 114–15, 130, 159, 279n58; *Black Protest*, 20, 114–15
Gray, Hunter, 65
Gray, Victoria, 135
Great Pool Jump and Other Stories, The (De Lissovoy), 48, 254n1
Greenberg, Cheryl Lynn, 22–23; *A Circle of Trust*, 22
Green Book, The, 46
Greene, George, 214, 307n87
Greenhaw, Wayne, 121
Greensboro, N.C., 85, 95, 132
Greenwood, Miss., 63, 70, 97–98, 117, 144, 214, 225; COFO office, 291n53, 301n49; Mary Lane, 244; tent cities, 200
Gregory, Dick, 45, 77, 276n15, 289n18; on jail, 95; Kennard support, 138; on Natchez, Miss., 197; *Nigger*, 45

Griffin, John Howard, 138
griots, 67, 69
Guyot, Lawrence, 62, 63, 78–79, 153, 159; as campaign manager, 206; in fiction, 144; jailing and torture of, 95, 205, 311n45; in *Making of Black Revolutionaries*, 90; papers, 276n11

Halberstam, David, 6, 264n2, 284n24, 301n49; *The Children*, 108–10
Halbwachs, Maurice, 22
Hale, John N., 15
Hall, Prathia, 132, 160, 161, 166, 244
Hall, Richard, 198, 214, 303n14; *Long George Alley*, 30, 192, 195, 196, 197–98, 212–21, 226, 303n14
Hall, Tim, 249
Hamer, Fannie Lou, 27, 71, 135, 141, 145, 205, 274n78; Carmichael reference to, 133; challenge to Whitten, 71, 205; Cortez elegy for, 175; echoed in fiction, 145; epitaph, 292n66; in *Eyes on the Prize*, 8; FST and, 147; jail beating and sexual abuse, 95, 205, 217, 236, 311n45; mother, 68; O'Dell interview, 68–69, 159; Joe Pullum as inspiration, 68–69, 139; sharecropping roots, 70; *To Praise Our Bridges*, 236; Wade Gayles's ode to, 15; on *Waiting for Godot*, 79; Wilkins disrespect, 259–60n114
Hamilton, Charles V., 100
Hampton, Henry, 8
Hands on the Freedom Plow (Holsaert et al.), 22–23, 27–28, 167, 182
Hansberry, Lorraine, 19, 38, 61; *The Movement* (with SNCC), 19, 20, 87–89, 259n106
Hansen, Bill, 3, 27, 46, 70, 95, 117, 266n45, 278n45; field reports, 83; Xavier University, 39, 266n45
Harder They Come, The (Thelwell), 180
Harding, Vincent, 14, 33, 147, 162, 172; on burnout and walking wounded, 224–25; *There Is a River*, 29; in *William Styron's Nat Turner*, 179–80
Hardwick, Elizabeth, 51
Hardy, John, 27
Harris, Don, 53
Harris, Jesse, 90, 133, 144, 196, 239
Harris, Rutha, 246
Harris, Scott, 71

Harris, Tina, 180
Harris, Trudier, 167, 297n62
Hartford, Bruce, 295n22
Harvard University, 48, 52, 57, 246; Coles, 126, 287n97; De Lissovoy, 36, 48, 50; in fiction, 49; Ganz, 77; Perdew, 35, 48; Weaver, 48, 57
Hattiesburg, Miss., 133, 137, 138, 139, 152
Hayden, Casey, 6, 24-25, 39, 59, 245; in *Campfires of the Resistance*, 91; communications work, 87, 102; education program advocacy, 100; *New Republic* forum, 142
Hayden, Robert, 109, 185
Hayden, Tom, 6, 33, 114, 277n35; *Revolution in Mississippi*, 81, 114, 115
Hayes, Curtis (Curtis Muhammad), 190, 214, 273n49
Heart Is a Lonely Hunter, The (McCullers), 203
Heilman, Robert, 204
Helfrich, Bob, 290n37
Henry, Aaron, xvi, 45, 115, 135; in *Eyes on the Prize*, 8
Herbers, John, 52
Hernton, Calvin, 156
Highlander Folk School, 28
High Tide of Black Resistance (Forman), 141, 192, 302-3n85
Hobsbawm, Eric, 60
Hobson, Fred, 111-12
Hoffman, Abbie, 48
Hogan, Wesley, 17-18, 55-56, 102, 121, 127, 219; on buried feelings, 240; on "economic inequities," 171; on internal culture, 57, 240; on journalists and academics, 129; Legacy Project, xix; *Many Minds, One Heart*, 6-7, 18, 121; "memories of white brutality," 239; on Moses, 136; on Nashville workshops, 110; on recruits, 106
Hogue, W. Lawrence, 167, 297n62
Holland, Endesha Ida Mae, 203, 245-46, 313n24
Hollander, Ron, 137, 138, 139, 140
Hollowell, William I., 144
Holmes, Joe, 139-40
Holt, Buford, 80
Holt, Len, 27, 104, 115, 119-25, 130, 244; *An Act of Conscience*, 119-20, 121-24, 194; advice to Forman, 27; "Defendant or Decedent?," 180-82, 244, 247; "Harlem," 176; *Liberator* and, 121, 175; as *Movement* contributor, 102; as "Snake Doctor," 120, 210; *Student Voice*, 102, 180-82; *The Summer That Didn't End*, 119-20
Honigsberg, Peter Jan, 148
Hose, Sam, 123
Houck, David, 77
House, Gloria (Aneb Kgositsile), 7, 173, 175, 176, 201, 244; Broadside Press, 190; *Blood River*, 188-89, 243; on casualties, 238; on "menace of unmitigated violence," 240; on Ruby Doris Smith Robinson, 16-17; Vietnam War, 184
Houston, James M., 196
Howard, T. R. M., xvi, 45
Howard University, 43, 121, 142; Nonviolent Action Group, 14, 198, 199
Hudson, Winson, 115
Hughes, Langston, 25, 37, 46, 123
humor, 45, 72, 93, 124, 145, 202, 292n68; in "Direct Action" (Thelwell), 44-47; Junebug, 66, 72; Supersnick, 57-65; Weaver, 64, 65
Hunter, Floyd, 21
Hurst, E. H., 227, 228
Hurston, Zora Neale, 58, 68
Hutchings, Phil, 157

Indianola, Miss., 71, 93, 144
informants, black, 216, 217
In Struggle (C. Carson), 2, 16, 256n50
internationalism, 21, 172, 176, 180, 189-91, 302n75; Pan African Students Organization in the Americas, 6, 46. *See also* Vietnam War
International War Crimes Tribunal (1966), 33, 185
In the Furrows of the World (Cobb), 26, 91, 185, 186, 187
Invisible Man (Ellison), 203
In White America (Duberman), 148
I Play Flute (Stembridge), 24, 59, 92, 99-100, 134-35

Jackson, Aaron G., 203
Jackson, Esther Cooper, 2, 158
Jackson, James (Natchez barber), 217
Jackson, Jesse, 65-66, 273n49
Jackson, Jimmy Lee (Marion, Ala., activist), 173, 301n50

Jackson, Luther P., Jr., 124
Jackson, Mae, 176
Jackson, Miss.: courthouse mural, 212; Ethridge, 107; FBI, 64; in fiction, 148, 149; FST, 70, 147; Kennard, 138; sit-ins, 65; Thelwell reunion with Jesse Harris, 239; Tillinghast, 244; Brenda Travis, 114
Jacobs, Saul, 255–56n34
jail texts, 20, 88–89, 94–99, 238
James, C. L. R., 190
James, Melody, 102
janitors and cleaning, 57, 60–62, 271n22, 272n30
Jasper, James M., 220
Jeffries, Hasan Kwame, 2, 68, 242; *Bloody Lowndes*, 9, 132
Jenkins, Tim, 6
Jet, 123, 138, 159, 166, 205
Jim Crow Routine, The (Berrey), 47
Joans, Ted, 156, 172
Johnson, Charles, 295n29; *Dreamer*, 233
Johnson, John H., 159
Johnson, June, 205, 311n45
Johnson, Lyndon B., 65, 97, 232, 234
Johnson, Paul, Jr., 213
Johnson, Warren, 95
Johnson Publishing Company, 89, 159
Jones, Charles, 35, 54, 84–85, 103, 144; in fiction, 248–49
Jones, Gareth Stedman, 32
Jones, James, 97, 198
Jones, LeRoi. *See* Baraka, Amiri
Jones, Matthew, 80, 122
Jordan, Joseph A., 121–22, 287n76
Joseph, Peniel, 182, 189
journalists and journalism, 104–15, 129–30, 132–33, 260n127, 284n24; black journalists' association, 191; Bond advice, 289n7; Cobb, 7–8, 191; De Lissovoy, 50; in fiction, 143–46, 206, 208; Halberstam, 6, 108–10, 264n2, 284n24, 301n49; Herbers, 52; I. F. Stone, 34–35; Kennard story and, 137–39; Newfield, 6; Searles, 283n3; *Southern Exposure*, 73; student press, 156; *Texas Observer*, 75; Fred Travis, 141. *See also* Watters, Pat
Juncker, Howard, 32
Junebug Jabbo Jones (imaginary character), 29, 34, 56, 57–60, 65–74, 140, 246
Junebug/Jack (J. O'Neal), 273n56

Kahn, Si, 15, 141, 262n160
Kaplan, Sidney, 298n77
Karenga, Ron, 157, 173, 193
Kates, Jim, 218, 245, 308n99
Kennard, Clyde, 137–39, 140, 290n37
Kennedy, Robert F., 64, 207, 227
Kennedy, Stetson, 73
Kgositsile, Aneb. *See* House, Gloria
Kgositsile, Keorapetse, 156–57, 175, 190
Khaalis, Abdul Aziz (Jan Leighton Triggs), 25, 198
Killens, John O., 100, 155, 303n14
King, C. B., 117, 135, 198, 205
King, Edward, Jr., 75
King, Marion, 117
King, Martin Luther, Jr., xvi, 95, 104, 105, 119, 133, 209, 234–35; acknowledgment of "hidden and unsung," 224; Branch on, 234; on burnout, 225, 230; Civil Rights Act of 1964, 232; Danville, Va., 122–23; Forman and, 268n73; Lester on, 235; "Letter from Birmingham Jail," 238; literary language, 20; mirrored in fiction, 195, 233–34; Moses view, 231; satirizing of, 64; Shirley Sherrod view, 283n3; Vietnam War, 184; Watters and, 111; worry about place in history, 309n6
King, Mary, 21, 78, 79, 87, 91, 92, 123, 214; on Bond, 87; on Jesse Harris and walking wounded, 239; on *The Movement* (SNCC and Hansberry), 87; on Supersnick, 57
King, Richard H., 11, 13, 35, 95, 209, 243; *Civil Rights and the Idea of Freedom*, 6, 17
King, Slater, 117, 135
Kingston Springs, Tenn., May 1966 retreat, 4, 100
Kirk, John, 12, 83
Knox, Roosevelt, 217
Koli, Stephen E., 46
Kopkind, Andrew, 130
Ku Klux Klan, 35, 143, 171; in fiction, 94, 203; Gelfand and, 261–62n150; Natchez, Miss., 197, 213
Kunstler, William, 120; *Deep in My Heart*, 27, 124–25

Ladner, Dorie, 133, 244, 270n2; ballad, 22; Kennard and, 137, 138, 139, 140; Natchez, 142, 213, 214, 244
Ladner, Joyce, 133, 167, 238–39; *Death of White Sociology*, 130; Kennard and,

Ladner, Joyce (*continued*) 137–39, 140; Jean Wheeler Smith and, 166, 167; *Tomorrow's Tomorrow*, 166; "What 'Black Power Means," 70
Lafayette, Bernard, xvi, 77, 79, 95, 229
Lafayette, Colia, 77
Lake, Alice, 132
Lake, Ellen, 52
Landau, Paul, 255–56n34
Lane, Mary, 244
Larocco, Christina, 15
Larry, Gloria. *See* House, Gloria
Laue, Jim, 45
Laurel, Miss., 151, 239, 240, 244, 262n150
Laursen, Per, 107–8
Lauter, Paul, 82
Lawson, Bob, 102
Lawson, James, 110, 284n32
Lawson, Jennifer, xix, 100
LCFO. *See* Lowndes County Freedom Organization
Leaks, Sylvester, 155
Lee, Bernard, 253n4
Lee, Don L. (Haki Madhubuti), 26, 68, 172, 175
Lee, Herbert, 11, 81, 135, 153, 227
Lee County, Ga., 70, 84, 132
Leflore County, Miss., 62, 164, 134–35. *See also* Greenwood, Miss.
Lemann, Nicholas, 14
Leonard, Margaret "Sissy," 81
Lester, Julius, 6, 32, 63, 67, 100–101, 103, 152, 185, 222; *And All Our Wounds Forgiven*, 7, 24, 31, 71, 124, 213, 221, 223–35, 237–38, 240, 250, 310n29; in *Black Fire*, 174; *Black Folktales (Our Folktales)*, 58; Black Power, 25, 236; on communications team, 199; Cultural Program Committee, 10; "Dressed Like Freedom," 263n172; *Falling Pieces of a Broken Sky*, 231; Flute Publications, 19; on Forman, 85; in "Four Faces from SNCC," 27; haiku, 185; Hamer and, 236; Junebug, 58, 67; *Look Out, Whitey!*, 193–94, 235, 236; on *Massachusetts Review*, 158; "memory is my subject," 240; "one needs a lyric poet," 25; *Othello*, 310n29; "put your bodies / upon the gears," 169; "revolutionary notes" (1967), 247–48; *Revolutionary Notes*, 186; on Thelwell, 298n77; *To Be a Slave*, 193; Vietnam War, 33, 185–86; view of Jesse Jackson candidacy, 65–66; on whites, 260n121; on why he writes, 28; on witnessing, 231
"Letter from Birmingham Jail" (M. L. King), 238
"Letter from Magnolia Jail" (B. Moses), 20, 88–89
Letters from Mississippi (Sutherland), 87, 218, 226
Let the People Decide (Moye), 2, 6, 71, 274n78
Let Us Now Praise Famous Men (Agee), 128–29
Lewis, Andrew, 102
Lewis, John, 20, 63, 90, 149–50; Africa tour, 190; Carmichael election over, 237; Christianity, 15; in *Eyes on the Prize*, 8; *Gonna Sit at the Welcome Table* (with Bond), 102; on "good trouble," 32; Halberstam on, 109; on Halberstam, 108; on local women, 293n87; March on Washington (1963), 19, 115; on Nation of Islam, 88; on *On the Road to Freedom* (Cobb), 27; on reporters, 104, 108; sharecropping roots, 70; view of Laurie Pritchett, 52; *Walking with the Wind*, 12, 293n87
Lewis, Norman, 211
Liberator, 20, 121, 175, 194
Liberty, Miss., 227, 228
Limits of Critique, The (Felski), 242–43
Ling, Peter, 6, 15
Lischer, Richard, 113
Llorens, David, 56, 155, 160, 173–74, 175, 298n3
Local People (Dittmer), 36, 222
Long, Margaret, 18, 80–81, 82–83, 87, 106, 277n34; Grant and, 114; influence on Coles, 127; support for SNCC antiwar stand, 185
Long, Worth, 19, 102, 119, 139, 140, 278n42; "Arson and Cold Grace," 157, Birmingham church bombing and, 298n73; "Dealer," 170–71, 208, 297–98n72; folklorist career, 286n65, Margaret Long on, 82–83
Long George Alley (R. Hall), 30, 192, 195, 196, 197–98, 212–21, 226, 303n14
Look Out, Whitey! (Lester), 193–94, 235, 236
Lord, Walter, 138
Lorde, Audre, 247
Los Angeles, 175, 188

Louis, Debbie, 18
Love, John, 249
Lowen, Marilyn, 91
Lowenfels, Walter, 186
Lowenstein, Allard, 8, 169–70
Lowndes County, Ala.: *Black Jacob* (Mahoney), 196; Black Panthers, 181; Bond, 199; Cobb, 249; elections, 206; *Eyes on the Prize II*, 9; House, 187–88; tent cities, 200, 201; "Travels in the South" (Mahoney), 200
Lowndes County Freedom Organization (LCFO), 5, 77, 181, 195, 199
Lucy, Autherine, 41
Lynd, Staughton, 86, 115, 118, 120, 159, 266–67n47
Lyon, Danny, 88, 89, 287n78

Mack, McKinley, 70, 71
Madhubuti, Haki. *See* Lee, Don L.
Magnolia, Miss., 20, 89
Mahoney, Bill, 7, 14, 64, 198–99; in *Black Fire*, 174; *Black Jacob*, xviii, 24, 192–96, 198–212, 219, 220, 222, 229, 305–6n50; as butt of joke, 83; college major, 94; on communications team, 87; "Harlem," 176; Holt and, 121, 175; *Liberator*, 175; minister characters, 15; "miseducation" of, 305n48; *Student Voice*, 102; "Travels in the South," 200–201, 247
Mailer, Norman, 61
Making of an Un-American, The (Cowan), 149
Making of Black Revolutionaries, The (Forman), 26–27, 37, 40, 89–90, 141, 241–42
Malcolm X, 162, 180, 195, 302n75
Mants, Bob, 18, 72, 102, 133–34, 249
Many Minds, One Heart (Hogan), 6–7, 18, 121
March on Washington (1963), 19, 20, 33, 115, 117, 165–66
Marsh, Charles, 220
Marshall, Thurgood, 137
Martin, Christopher R., 113
Martin, John Bartlow, 84, 85
Martínez, Elizabeth Sutherland, 87–88, 218, 219, 279n70, 301n48, 308n92; Forman and, 26–27, 261n35; *Letters from Mississippi*, 87, 218, 226; *Movement* (SNCC and Hansberry), 87–88; Younge murder and, 26

Marvell, W. T., 278n42
Matlin, Daniel, 176
Matthews, Z. T., 98
Matusow, Alan, 22
Maxwell, William J., 156
Mays, Benjamin, 133
McAdam, Doug, 81
McCain, William D., 138–39
McClymer, John F., 83
McComb, Miss., 4, 8, 35, 64, 86, 89, 196, 272n38, 277n35; bombings, 13, 107, 142–43, 213–14; in fiction, 198; Freedom House, 13, 58, 70, 107, 213–14; FST, 70; Tom Hayden, 81; Samstein on, 144, 146; Brenda Travis, 114; Jimmie Travis, 144; Bob Zellner, 63
McCord, William, 96, 128; *Mississippi*, 118, 132
McCullers, Carson, 203
McDew, Chuck, 18, 32, 63, 81–82, 137, 153, 222, 241
McFarland, Henry, 16
McFerrin, John, 141
McGhee, Hildreth, 80
McGill, Ralph, 119, 286n63
McGurl, Mark, xviii
McKay, Claude, 123, 124
McKinney, Lester, 244
McKissick, Floyd, 155, 156
McKnight, Leo, 228
McLaurin, Charles, 6, 33, 97, 144, 149–50, 198; in *Black Protest* (Grant), 115; jail letters, 95; storytelling skills, 18
McNeill, Joseph, 36
media. *See* journalists and journalism
Meely, Fred, 1; "Organizer's Handbook," 61, 72, 144
Meredith, James, 12, 60, 117, 137, 261n137
MFDP. *See* Mississippi Freedom Democratic Party
Michaels, Sheila, 26
Miller, Dorothy. *See* Zellner, Dorothy Miller
Miller, Mike, 26, 100, 101, 226
Miller, Timothy, 270n112
Mills, C. Wright, 21
Minchin, Timothy J., 137
Minnis, Jack, 21, 63, 75, 100, 159, 197, 260n127, 275n8, 312n45
Mississippi (McCord), 118, 132
Mississippi Freedom Democratic Party (MFDP), 3, 5, 33, 66, 82, 134, 159, 195

Mississippi Freedom Summer (McClymer), 83
Mississippi Freedom Summer (1964). *See* Freedom Summer
Mississippi Notebook (Von Hoffman), 107
Mississippi Reckoning (Zimmerman), 21, 170, 246
Mississippi Southern College, 137, 138–39
Mississippi State Penitentiary, Parchman, 137, 168, 297n64, 299n29
Mitchell, Loften, 155
Mitchie, Thomas, 123, 287n81
Montgomery, Ala., 46, 232; bus boycott, 41, 111
Moore, Amzie, xvi, 45, 135
Moore, Bob, 102, 283n142
Morehouse College, 86, 98, 133–34
Morris, Aldon, 85, 174, 219–20
Morris, Jesse, 18, 162, 212
Morris, Willie, 111, 257n64
Morton, Eric, 159
Moses, Bob, xvi, xvii, 1, 18, 23–24, 63, 153, 245; on activist-community cohesion, 194; Algebra Project, 249, 283n144; attack by Caston, 64; on Ella Baker, 136; Bond and, 83; as campaign manager, 205; Coles and, 61; college major, 94; education program advocacy, 100, 282n135; in *Eyes on the Prize*, 8; on fear, 146; in fiction, 144, 168, 249; as *fundi*, 136; on historical gaps, 239; on hunger, 79; Kennard and, 137; letter from Magnolia jail, 20, 89; on local people, 170; Lynd transcription, 86; in *Making of Black Revolutionaries*, 89–90; on McDew, 21; on Amzie Moore, 135; on movement as ocean and MLK as wave, 231; on murder of Herbert Lee, 227; on "One Man, One Vote," 19, 20; on Willie Peacock, 144; in poetry, 22, 59; *Radical Equations* (with Cobb), 27, 102; reading of Camus, 299n29; RFK and, 207; role model for Carson, 259n93; Sutherland view, 261n135; sweeping, 62; Tanzania, 190, 249; Washington, D.C., SNCC conference (1963), 63; "we are on a boat," 4
Moses, Gilbert, 10, 148, 245
Movement, 9, 25, 102, 157, 177
Movement, The (SNCC and Hansberry), 19, 20, 87–89; British edition, 259n106
Moye, J. Todd, 118; *Let the People Decide*, 2, 6, 71, 274n78

Moynihan, Daniel Patrick, 16
Muhammad, Curtis (Hayes), 190, 214, 273n49
Muhammad Speaks, 88, 280n75
Mulholland, Joan Trumpauer, 26, 45, 97
murals. *See* paintings and murals
Murphree, Vanessa, 15, 247
Murphy, Alice Gardner, 75

NAACP. *See* National Association for the Advancement of Colored People
Nasaw, David, 242
Nash, Diane, xvi, 10, 44, 100, 109, 144, 234; education program advocacy, 282n135; in *Eyes on the Prize*, 8; Vietnam War, 185
Nashville, 95, 108, 110; in fiction, 223–24, 227, 233. *See also* Fisk University
Nashville Tennessean, 108, 284
Natchez, Miss., 142, 192, 195, 196–97, 205, 212–21, 298, 304n23
Natchez Democrat, 197, 213
Nation, 87, 114, 117, 130, 179, 279n70
National Association for the Advancement of Colored People (NAACP), xv, xvi, 20, 60, 116, 137; Kenneth Clark and, 125; *Crisis*, 9, 194, 196; in fiction, 197, 206; Holt view, 122; Roy Wilkins, 184, 253n4
National Guardian, 114, 121
National Lawyers Guild, 121, 286n71
National Negro Congress, 2, 199
National Student Association (NSA), 248, 276n20, 277n35
Nation of Islam, 88, 280n75
Neal, Larry, 174, 193; *Black Fire* (with Baraka), 174, 187, 211
Neary, John, 64–65
Neblett, Carver (Chico), 70, 208, 213, 214, 216
Negro Digest, 124, 155, 156, 158, 159–61, 163–65, 172, 174, 295n29
Negroes in American History (Cieciorka and Cieciorka), 89, 157
Negro Motorist Green Book, The, 46
Nelson, Jack, 105
Nesbit, Lynn, 107–8
Neshoba County, Miss., historical tourism, 292n80
Neuman, David, 216
New Action Army, The, 65
Newfield, Jack, 6, 33, 82, 99–100, 117–18
New Freedom, 86

New Journalism, 12, 257n67
New Left, 21, 23, 41, 56, 81–82. *See also* Students for a Democratic Society
New Orleans, 70, 73, 147
New Republic, 117, 130, 162
New South, 81, 82–83, 277n32, 278n43
Newsweek, 107
Newton, Huey P., 180, 194
New York City office, 198, 261n135
Nicholas, Denise, 90, 133, 250, 278n47; Black Arts Convention (1966), 174; college major, 94; *Freshwater Road*, 7, 15, 19, 94, 146–53, 154, 221, 226, 244; *Student Voice*, 102
Nigger (Gregory), 45
Nonviolent Action Group, 14, 198, 199
Novick, Peter, 119, 242
NSA (National Student Association), 248, 276n20, 277n35

O'Connor, Flannery, xviii, xix, 127
O'Dell, Jack, 68, 158, 159
Olsen, Tillie, 165
Olson, Lynne, 243
O'Neal, John, 10, 29, 30, 77, 83, 271n14, 271n18, 313n27; on Bond, 64; college major, 94; *Don't Start Me to Talking*, 66, 67, 72, 74; FST, 147, 148; Holt advice to, 121; Junebug columns in *Southern Exposure*, 73; *Junebug/Jack*, 273n56; on Junebug source, 271n14; Junebug storytelling plays, 29, 57–58, 59, 66–74, 140, 246; papers, xviii, poem celebrating local people, 154; SNCC anniversary conference, 245; story circles, xviii, 59–60, 110, 181; *Trying to Find My Way Back Home*, 73; on useable past, xix–xx, 10; on "yours in struggle," 16
O'Neal, William, 59, 73–74
"One Man, One Vote" (slogan), 19–20
On the Road to Freedom (Cobb), 12
Orangeburg (S.C.) Massacre, 1968, 272n38
"Organizer, The" (Thelwell), 24, 72, 93–94, 99, 136, 142–46, 153, 200, 202, 247
Oshinsky, David, 110
Our Folktales (Lester), 58
Oxford, Miss., 117
Oxford, Ohio, 127

paintings and murals, 212; in fiction, 41, 205, 211–12

Pan-African Cultural Festival (PACF), Algiers, 1969, 157, 172
pan-Africanism, 158, 171, 190
Pan African Students Organization in the Americas (PASOA), 6, 46
Panola (Pincus), 216
Panola County, Miss., 71, 93, 274n79
Parchman Penitentiary. *See* Mississippi State Penitentiary, Parchman
Patch, Penny, 3, 254n10
Patton, Gwen, 167, 184, 186, 206
Payne, Charles, 1, 2, 222, 241, 282n122; on community stories, 30; on field reports, 29; on Lee's murder, 153; on *On the Road to Freedom* (Cobb), 27
Peacock, Willie (Wazir), 20–21, 22, 90, 97, 144
Perdew, John, 35, 48, 246; *Education of a Harvard Guy*, 269n84
Pincus, Ed, 216
plantation system, 67–69, 70–71, 78–79, 141, 274n79, 296n59; in fiction, 164–65, 202, 205, 206, 207, 212
poetic forms: ballad, 22, 58, 60, 157; elegy, 9, 16–17, 175, 189; haiku, 185; lyric, 16, 24–26, 92, 263n172; ode, 15, 185; prose poem, 187
police informers, 216, 217
Pollack, Merrill, 38
Polletta, Francesca, 36, 46–47, 82, 153, 172, 220, 247
Polsgrove, Carol, 118
Ponder, Annell, 20, 159, 205, 295n22, 311n45
Porter, William, 89
Port Huron Statement, 33, 81
posttraumatic stress. *See* burnout and posttraumatic stress
Potter, Paul, 33, 277n35
Poussaint, Alvin, 162, 236
Powell, Fay Bellamy. *See* Bellamy-Powell, Fay
Prescod, Martha, 6, 33, 79, 132, 135, 147, 154
Price, Leontyne, 151, 293n90
Price, Reynolds, 293n90
Priestley, Justine Tyrrell Smadbeck ("Gertrude Wilson"), 248, 314n36
Pritchett, Laurie, 52, 85
PTSD. *See* burnout and posttraumatic stress
Pullum, Joe, 68–69, 139
Pushed Back to Strength (Wade Gayles), 133, 152

Quinn, Alyene, 135, 142–43, 154, 218; in fiction, 144–45
Quinn, Anthony, 218

Rabinowitz, Joanne Grant. *See* Grant, Joanne
Rabinowitz, Joni, 121, 275n8
Rabinowitz, Victor, 85, 121, 279n58
Rabinowitz Foundation, 159
Radical Equations (Moses and Cobb), 27, 102
Rahv, Philip, 37
Raiford, Leigh, 15
Raines, Annie "Mama Dollie," 132, 135, 136; fictional counterpart, 243–44
Randall, Dudley, 7, 26, 155, 156, 190
Randolph, A. Philip, 9, 115, 116
Ransby, Barbara, 28
Rauh, Joe, 33
Raymond, George, 96, 97, 281n10
Ready for the Revolution (Carmichael and Thelwell), 7, 66, 73, 239
Reagon, Bernice Johnson, 14, 15, 77, 104, 119, 128, 243, 245; "Songs My Mother Wrote Me," 139; storytelling skills, 18; on Zinn, 119; on Zinn's *SNCC*, 118
Reagon, Cordell, 84–85, 144
Redbook, 161, 163
Reddick, L. D., 32, 34
Reeves, Jim, 201
Reform, Ala., 139–40
Regional Council of Negro Leadership (RCNL), xvi, 20, 45, 115, 135
reparations, 192, 302–3n85
restroom segregation, 43–47, 148
Reuther, Walter, 33
Revolutionary Action Movement (RAM), 5, 181, 255n18
Revolutionary Notes (Lester), 186
Revolution in Mississippi (T. Hayden), 81, 114, 115
Rexroth, Kenneth, 34
Richards, Dona (Marimba Ani), 10, 19, 159
Richardson, Judy, 8–9, 21, 57, 62, 190; *Eyes on the Prize*, 260n127; on sexism, 297n61; SNCC Legacy Project, xix
Ricks, Willie (Mukasa Dada), 6, 16, 70, 84; in fiction, 181–82
Rinzler, Alan, 88, 89
Riva, Sarah, 83
Robinson, Gwendolyn (Zoharah Simmons), xvi, 180, 244
Robinson, Reggie, 62

Robinson, Ruby Doris Smith, 9, 16–17, 89, 100, 144, 243; in "Four Faces from SNCC," 27; Margaret Long on, 82; poems for, 9, 189, 191, 256n43
Robnett, Belinda, 142
Rock Bottom (Forman), 100–102, 142
Rock Hill, S.C., 95, 248
Rodgers, Carolyn, 163, 303n18
Rollins, Avon, 114, 122
Romaine, Howard, 73
Rothschild, Mary Aickin, 34, 226
Rowan, Carl, 4
Ruffin, Suzie, 141–42
Ruleville, Miss., 147, 198, 214, 263n173
Russell, Sandra Gail, 134
Russell Tribunal (International War Crimes Tribunal, 1966), 33, 185
Rustin, Bayard, 116, 264n12

Sacks, Karen, 142
Salm, Nell, 131
Salmond, John A., 137
Salter, John (Gray), 65
Sammy Younge Jr. (Forman), 54, 193
Samstein, Mendy, 19, 143, 144, 146, 214
Sanchez, Sonia, 177, 244
Sartre, Jean-Paul, 128
Saul, Scott, 209
Savio, Mario, 33, 41, 55, 64, 169
SCEF. *See* Southern Conference Educational Fund
Schott, Webster, 51
Schraufnagel, Noel, 196, 204
Schwerner, Mickey, 12, 52, 98, 143, 148, 171, 189, 246; Cobb and, 292n80
SCLC. *See* Southern Christian Leadership Conference
Scott, James C., 10–11
SDS. *See* Students for a Democratic Society
Searles, A. C., 283n3
Secret Agent (Conrad), 216
segregated restrooms, 43–47, 148
Segrest, Marvin, 46
Sellers, Cleveland, 4, 5, 45, 100, 155
Selma, Ala., 77, 83, 105, 130, 133, 200–201, 278n42, 302n75; in poetry, 183, 189, 218
sexism, 297n61
sharecroppers, 70, 71, 133, 134–35, 162, 167; in fiction, 163, 164, 201, 229
Shaw, Nancy (Stoller), 4

Sherrod, Charles, 2–3, 51, 54, 84–85, 99, 102, 244; Chatfield initiation, 105; Christianity, 15; in fiction, 144; on local women, 154; in *Making of Black Revolutionaries*, 90; namesake park in Albany, Ga., 5; papers, 276n11; on PTSD, 222–23; Raines quotation, 132, 136; storytelling skills, 18
Sherrod, Shirley, xvii, 102, 104, 283n3
Shockley, Skip, 17–18
Showalter, Elaine, 36
Simmons, Zoharah (Gwendolyn Robinson), xvi, 180, 244
Simon and Schuster, 87–88
Simpson, Euvester, 205, 311n45
Sinsheimer, Joseph, 225–26
sit-ins, xv, 32, 43–44, 45, 47, 53; in fiction, 36, 43–44, 46, 248; Grant, 114; Greensboro, N.C., 36, 95; Halberstam and, 109, 110; Jackson, Miss., 65; "jail no bail" and 95; Nash, 10; Nashville, 44, 109, 110; in plays, 245; Sissy Leonard, 81; training for, 110
Sitton, Claude, 98, 105
Skidmore College, 54, 248
slave rebellions, 68, 179, 300n34
slavery, legacy of, 69, 71, 105, 165, 198
Smethurst, James, 173
Smith, Anna Deavere, 271n18
Smith, Ben, 120
Smith, David Lionel, 173, 174
Smith, Frank, 84, 90, 97, 161, 162; in fiction, 98, 144
Smith, Jean Wheeler, 3, 23, 113, 155, 160–72; Black Arts Convention (1966), 174; in *Black Fire*, 174; "Frankie Mae," 71, 164–68, 297n62; "Machine," 168–69, 170, 202
Smith, Jerome, 146, 227, 272n38
Smith, Kelly Miller, 110
Smith, Lillian, 35, 40, 91–92, 111, 156
Smith, R. L. T., 205
Smith, Ruby Doris. *See* Robinson, Ruby Doris Smith
Smith, Shawn Michelle, 77
Smith, Wilbur Wardine, 97
SNCC (Zinn), 24, 86, 115–19, 121, 131, 248, 286n61
SNCC Legacy Project, xix, 23, 254n15
Snellings, Roland (Askia Touré), 21, 175
songs and singing, 6, 15, 80, 97, 121, 223, 246

So Red the Rose (Young), 196
Southern Christian Leadership Conference (SCLC), xvi, 2, 20, 46, 104, 106, 116; Abernathy, 297n68; Freedom Rides and, 234; Holt view, 122, 123; O'Dell, 158; Ponder, 159, 295n22; Charles Sherrod view, 105
Southern Conference Educational Fund (SCEF), 80, 98, 106, 277n30
Southern Conference for Human Welfare, 277n30
Southern Echo, 5
Southern Exposure, 73, 80, 168, 244
Southern Justice (Friedman), 125
Southern Mystique (Zinn), 85
Southern Negro Youth Congress (SNYC), 2, 198
Southern Patriot, 80
Southern Regional Council (SRC), 43, 80, 85, 97, 106, 276n20, 277n30; funding of Coles and, 125; funding of physicians' tour, 94; Long, 80, 82; Minnis, 76, 275n8; Watters, 112, 285n37; Zinn, 117
Southern Student Organizing Committee (SSOC), 4, 6, 73
Spellman, A. B., 175–76, 245, 299n17
Spellman, Karen Edmonds, xi, 175, 190
Spelman College, 14, 32, 116, 271–72n23
Spencer, Robyn C., 17–18, 127
Spiral (artist group), 211
SSOC (Southern Student Organizing Committee), 4, 6, 73
Stagolee (mythical character), 58
Stahlman, James G., 108
Stearns, Peter, 10
Steedman, Carolyn, xvii
Stembridge, Jane, xv, 78, 79, 91–92, 113, 144, 165; college major, 94; Fuller view, 163; *I Play Flute*, 24, 59, 99–100, 134–35; Jacobs and Landau on, 255–56n34; "Mississippi Field," 25; "one corner at a time," 250; poem for "those who froze," 134; Lillian Smith and, 91–92, 280n91; SNCC records, 75; *Student Voice*, 87; writing to explore feelings, 246–47
Steptoe, E. W., 133, 135, 141, 289n14
Sterling, Dorothy, 193
Stern Family Fund, 19
Stewart, Nick, 60
Still, Larry, 138
Stoller, Nancy, 4

Stone, I. F., 34–35, 185
Stoper, Emily, 119
story circles, xviii, 59–60, 69, 110, 181, 271n19
storytelling paradigms: "nitty gritty," 187, 207, 302n69; "tell it like it is," 23–26, 112–13, 145, 154, 180, 278n43, 302n69
Street, Joe, 15, 258n81
Stuckey, Sterling, 14
Student Press Association, 156
Students for a Democratic Society (SDS), 6, 43, 81–82; Port Huron Statement, 33, 81
Student Voice, 9, 25, 76, 86–87, 102; commended by Danish journalist, 107; commended in *Freedomways*, 159; Holt and, 121, 180–81; Reddick letter, 34; *Southern Patriot* as model for, 80
Sturkey, William, 15
Styron, William, 300n34; *Confessions of Nat Turner*, 68, 179–80, 298n77; "This Quiet Dust," 179
Sugarman, Tracy, 18, 52, 65, 94, 228, 263n173
Summer That Didn't End, The (L. Holt), 119–20
Sunflower County, Miss., 6, 71, 269n104, 296n59; Indianola, 71, 93, 144. *See also* Ruleville, Miss.
Supersnick (imaginary character), 29, 44, 56, 57, 58–65, 73, 246
Supreme Court, U.S. *See* U.S. Supreme Court
Sutherland, Elizabeth. *See* Martínez, Elizabeth Sutherland
Swaim, Lawrence, 55
Sweeney, Dennis, 8, 214, 308n114

Tabori, George, 90
Talmadge, Herman, 262n154
Tanzania, 190, 249
television: *Amos 'n' Andy*, 60; civil rights movement documentaries, 8, 9, 196, 256n43; Cobb show idea, 59; reporting on McComb, Miss., 146
Tennessean, Nashville, 108, 284
tent cities, 140, 141, 199–200; in fiction, 199–202, 210
Terrell County, Ga., 84, 98
Tewkesbury, Paul, 234
Thelwell, Ekwueme Michael, xviii, 9, 14, 92, 113, 133, 171–72, 245; Baldwin on, 250; on burnout and walking wounded,

224; college major, 94; "Community of Victims," 177–78, 179, 256n36; "Direct Action," 36, 42–47, 49, 53, 72, 193, 220; *Duties, Pleasures, and Conflicts*, 142; "Fish Are Jumping an' the Cotton Is High," 72, 92–94, 142; on "fuzzy-minded" sentimentality, 136; *The Harder They Come*, 180; on Jesse Harris, 239; on historical gaps, 239; on Holt, 120; Junebug, 29, 73; on justice and peace, 123; *Long George Alley* (Hall) and, 195; on March on Washington, 166; *Massachusetts Review*, 158; MFDP article, 159; minister characters, 15; "The Organizer," 24, 72, 93–94, 99, 136, 142–46, 153, 200, 202, 247; *Ready for the Revolution* (with Carmichael), 7, 66, 73, 239; on rebellion of enslaved people, 300n34; reunion with Jesse Harris, 239; on "scholarly objectivity," 130; on sixties short stories, 10; Supersnick, 59; view of Jesse Jackson campaign, 65–66; view of local people, 141–42; on waiting, 78–79; Washington, D.C., SNCC office, 198; in *William Styron's Nat Turner*, 179–80
There Is a River (Harding), 29
"Thin White Line" (Forman), xviii, 28–29, 36, 37–42, 49, 53–54, 55, 182, 220
Third World Press, 26
This Child's Gonna Live (S. E. Wright), 195, 303n16, 305–6n50
This Nonviolent Stuff'll Get You Killed (Cobb), 53, 182, 202
Till, Emmett, 12, 39, 163
Tillinghast, Muriel, 26, 244
Tillman, John P., 100
Tisdale, John, 23
To Be a Slave (Lester), 193
Tomorrow's Tomorrow (J. Ladner), 166
Toomer, Jean: *Cane*, 195
To Praise Our Bridges (Hamer), 236
torture, 204, 228, 229, 236, 311n45
Tougaloo College, 65, 244, 272n45
Touré, Askia (Roland Snellings), 21, 175
Townsend, Lou Ella, 68
Trammell, Theodore, 205
Travis, Brenda, 114
Travis, Fred, 141
Travis, Jimmie, 144
Triggs, Jan Leighton (Abdul Aziz Khaalis), 25, 198

Trumpauer (Mulholland), Joan, 26, 45, 97
Trying to Find My Way Back Home (J. O'Neal), 73
Tuck, Stephen, 52
Ture, Kwame. *See* Carmichael, Stokely (Kwame Ture)
Turnbow, Hartman, 135, 141
Turner, Georgia Mae, 140, 141
Turner, Nat, 68, 88, 162, 179, 180, 298n77
Tuskegee Institute, 26, 85, 156
Tyson, Tim, 18

Umoja, Akinyele, 247
Uncle Tom's Children (R. Wright), 68
United Nations, 5, 33
University of Mississippi, 60, 117, 137
University of Southern Mississippi, 137, 139
Updike, John, 54
U.S. 49 (highway), 88, 92
U.S. House of Representatives, 70–71, 205; Judiciary Committee, 76
U.S. Supreme Court, 25, 137; *Brown v. Board of Education*, 108, 119, 125

Varela, Maria, 6, 20–21, 134, 135, 165, 301n48; in *Campfires of the Resistance*, 91; "Crumpled Notes," 218; Flute Publications, 19, 58, 186; Hamer and, 236
verbatim theatre, 59, 271n18
Vicksburg, Miss., 165, 196, 308n114
Vietnam War, 4, 25, 33, 58, 65, 82, 182–86, 234; RAM and, 255n18
Von Hoffman, Nicholas, 213, 214; *Mississippi Notebook*, 107
Voter Education Project slogan, 19

Wade Gayles, Gloria, 7, 133, 152, 187, 250; *Anointed to Fly*, 15, 243; *Pushed Back to Strength*, 133, 152
Waiting for Godot (Beckett), 79
Walcott, Derek, 67
Walker, Alice, 11, 13, 163, 164
Walking with the Wind (J. Lewis), 12, 293n87
"walking wounded." *See* burnout and posttraumatic stress
Wallace, Mike, 146, 227–28
Wallach, Jennifer Jensen, 11–12, 17, 83
Walmsley, Mark Joseph, 1
Walter, E. V., 99
Ward, Brookes, 86

Ward, Douglas Turner, 79
Ward, Jerry, 14
Ware, Bill, 5, 46
Ware, Charles, 95
Ware, George, 156
Warren, Robert Penn, 12–13, 62, 153, 301n49; *Who Speaks for the Negro?*, 37
Washington, Cynthia, 87, 198, 244
Washington, D.C.: Barry, 256n39; Center for Black Education, 177, 190; Drum and Spear Bookstore, 190; Mahoney, 198, 199; SNCC conference (1963), 63, 65; SNCC office, 87, 198, 199. *See also* Howard University
Washington, Mary Helen, 165, 166
Waskow, Arthur, 87
Watkins, Hollis, 5, 8, 55, 70, 102, 273n49
Watters, Pat, 22, 23, 30–31, 53, 83, 106, 108, 241; "beyond ordinary limits," 153; *Climbing Jacob's Ladder* (with Cleghorne), 83, 102, 111; *Down to Now*, 110–14; epiphany, 129; influence on Coles, 127; on jail experience, 95; on SNCC as metaphor, 136; on SNCC demise, 237; view of Black Power, 156
Watts, Los Angeles, riots, 1965, 187–88
Waveland, Miss.: November 1964 retreat, 3–4, 22, 187; Work-Study Institute (1965), 135
Way Out Must Lead In, The (Beardslee), 23
Weaver, Claude, 29, 48, 57, 60–65
Wechsler, James, 63–64
We Own the Night (Garrett), 177, 182, 187
West, James, 205
"Whatever Happened to Interracial Love?" (K. Collins), 40, 54–55, 73, 243–44
Whatever Happened to Interracial Love? (K. Collins), 54, 248–49
Wheeler, Jean. *See* Smith, Jean Wheeler
White, Walter, 203
"white power structure" (term), 21
Whitley, Clifton R., Jr., 205
Whitten, Jamie L., 70–71, 205, 274n76
Who Speaks for the Negro? (Warren), 37
Wilder, Douglas, 287n76
Wiley, Jean, 26, 33, 39, 244
Wilkins, Fanon Che, 176
Wilkins, Roy, 184, 253n4, 259–60n114
Williams, Curtis L., 246
Williams, John A., 58, 159
Williams, Robert F., 88, 162, 265n30

Williams, William Carlos, 127, 287-88n97
William Styron's Nat Turner (Clarke), 179-80
Willis, Ellen, 248
Wilson, Gertrude (Justine Tyrrell Smadbeck Priestley), 248, 314n36
Wilson, Johnny, 100
Wilson, Sondra Kathryn, 9
Winona, Miss., 95, 205, 236
Winter, William, 290n37
Wisconsin Historical Society, 275-76n11
Wise, Stanley, 16
Wood, Rob, 135-36
Woodruff, James, 155
Woodruff, Nan, 20
World without Heroes (Fields), 38
Wright, Michael (Oshoosi), 102, 156
Wright, Richard, 41, 71, 69, 71, 127; *Uncle Tom's Children*, 68
Wright, Sarah E., 155, 156, 195; *This Child's Gonna Live*, 195, 303n16, 305-6n50

Young, Stark, 196
Youngblood, Doug, 41-42
Younge, Sammy, Jr., 26, 46, 85, 184, 185, 201; Forman's biography, 54, 193

Zellner, Bob, 4, 61, 63, 75, 107-8, 115, 122
Zellner, Dorothy Miller, 9, 16, 79-80, 87, 100, 122, 138, 256n43
Zimmerman, Mitchell, 4, 98, 148; *Mississippi Reckoning*, 21, 170, 246
Zinn, Howard, xvi, 10, 32-33, 34, 35, 47, 48, 108, 189; Albany, Ga., 85, 117; in *Black Protest*, 115; Bond poetry and, 279n63; Coles compared, 125, 128; Mahoney, 198; as mentor, 130; on movement as ocean and MLK as wave, 231; SNCC, 24, 86, 115-19, 121, 131, 248, 286n61; *Southern Mystique*, 85; view of De Lissovoy, 48, 269n87; view of Holt, 123; on young people's discovery of evil, 237
Žižek, Slavoj, 58

CPSIA information can be obtained
at www.ICGtesting.com
Printed in the USA
LVHW042208150820
663286LV00002B/94